The Price of Vision

The Diary of
Henry A. Wallace

1942-1946

Also by John Morton Blum

JOE TUMULTY AND THE WILSON ERA

THE REPUBLICAN ROOSEVELT

WOODROW WILSON AND THE POLITICS OF MORALITY

YESTERDAY'S CHILDREN (*Editor*)

THE NATIONAL EXPERIENCE (*Editor*)

THE PROMISE OF AMERICA

FROM THE MORGENTHAU DIARIES

I. *Years of Crisis, 1928–1938*

II. *Years of Urgency, 1938–1941*

III. *Years of War, 1941–1945*

ROOSEVELT AND MORGENTHAU

The Price of Vision

The Diary of

Henry A. Wallace

1942-1946

EDITED

AND WITH AN INTRODUCTION BY

JOHN MORTON BLUM

Boston

Houghton Mifflin Company

1973

First Printing w

Library of Congress Cataloging in Publication Data

Wallace, Henry Agard, 1888–1965.
  The price of vision.

  1. Wallace, Henry Agard, 1888–1965. 2. United
States—Politics and government—1933–1945. 3. United
States—Politics and government—1945–1953. 4. United
States—Foreign relations—1933–1945. 5. United States
—Foreign relations—1945–1953. I. Blum, John Morton,
1921–   ed. II. Title.
E748.W23A36 1973   973.917′092′4 [B]   72–6806
ISBN 0–395–17121–0

Printed in the United States of America

To the Century of the Common Man

Foreword

To THOSE who do not remember Henry A. Wallace or American history during World War II, the significance of the contents of his diary may not be immediately apparent. The editing of this book is intended to help those readers to understand him and the men and issues he discussed. The biographical sketch of Wallace assays to explain his background, his beliefs, his early years, and his years in public office as they relate to questions of policy about which he wrote from 1942 through 1946. The headnotes to each section of the book attempt to accomplish a similar purpose much more briefly and with reference only to the parts of the diary that follow each of them. The still briefer footnotes to the diary entries provide identifications immediately relevant to his ongoing remarks. In different depth and different contexts, the introduction, headnotes, and footnotes, which can be read independently of each other, cover some of the same developments.

There follows a discussion of the nature of the diary as a document and the processes adopted for its editing.

A NOTE ON METHOD AND MATERIALS

The diary of Henry A. Wallace, as readers of this edited edition will quickly surmise, consists primarily of daily entries that Wallace ordinarily dictated for typing. Since he did not dictate spelling or punctuation, I have corrected and standardized spelling and punctuation but retained his paragraph structure. I have also, as the note to the text indicates at the appropriate place, made other editorial changes for the period of Wallace's trip to Siberia and China. In order to conserve space, I have eliminated the daily calendar of appointments that usually preceded Wallace's diary entries. Indeed on almost all days in which he kept no diary, his secretary kept the calendar. Notes to the text mark periods of any considerable length, for example, February, March, and most of April 1945, when Wallace made no diary entries. Ordinarily he dictated six or seven days a week, but I have not selected material from every day. For the days from which I have used material, ellipses (. . .) indicate my omissions from the full text.

Two short spurts of diary, one in 1935 during the controversy within the Department of Agriculture, one in 1939–40 preceding, during, and following Wallace's nomination for Vice President, predate the start of the almost consecutive diary that runs, as this edition indicates, from early 1942 through September 20, 1946. (As Wallace once observed, he had more time to play tennis after he became Vice President than he had ever had before; he also had more time to keep a diary, which he never resumed after leaving public office.) Because the material for the fragments of diary of 1935 and 1940 bears no direct relationship to the material for the period beginning in 1942, I have, according to my understanding with the Wallace family, included none of the earlier entries in this edition.

As the notes to the text show, I have selected for publication here some of the letters to the Presidents and others that Wallace attached to his diary. I have referred to and used in the notes other such letters, as well as texts of speeches and clippings from newspapers and magazines which Wallace also occasionally attached to or interpolated within his record.

Of the actual diary entries for the period 1942–46, this edition includes what I consider a representative sample of Wallace's comments about all significant issues to which he adverted, and a much fuller selection of his remarks about Presidents Roosevelt and Truman, and about questions deeply important to him. Those questions involved the Board of Economic Warfare and its sundry activities, American occupation policy during the war, the development of American trade, the problem of postwar full employment, the control of atomic energy, and American relations with China, the United Kingdom, and the Soviet Union. Overall the selections total about twenty-five percent of the full text. I made the selections with the intention of providing a sufficient record for laymen or historians interested in the period. Of course a biographer of Wallace will want to go to the full, original text, but the diary as here published should satisfy the ordinary needs of a scholar working on the problems that interested Wallace, and should reveal the nature of Wallace's ideas and policies as well as his modes of thought and operation.

As his temperament dictated, Wallace was a frank but never an intimate diarist. Because he recorded no intimacies, and because, again in keeping with his character, his frankness never assumed mean or brutal forms, I have had no occasion to omit passages which might be embarrassing, libelous, or slanderous. Still, by previous, friendly agreement, I did ask the Wallace family to review my selections. Mrs. Wallace suggested only a few deletions, none of them of historical significance and all of them involving only a brief phrase not of her late husband's but of an acquaintance talking to him about still a third person.

For the notes to the text and for the introduction, the responsibility is solely mine. The notes are intended economically to identify the people and the issues Wallace mentioned. They are not designed to provide a period history, though now and then I have had to write a paragraph or two in order to place a development within a context which the diary does not adequately provide. Especially in those longer passages, as also in the introduction, I have profited from memoirs, biographies, and historical studies that I have cited at relevant points. I have also gained much understanding and received much hospitable encouragement from the Wallace family, from Henry A. Wallace's sons, Henry B. Wallace and Robert B. Wallace; from his daughter, Mrs. Leslie Douglas; from his sister, Madame Charles Bruggmann; and especially from his widow, Mrs. Henry A. Wallace, who is a great lady. I met Mrs. Wallace and undertook this venture at the suggestion of Paul Brooks of Houghton Mifflin Company whose comments have improved the final product. This project, like others, my wife has suffered gladly in spite of the unavoidable burdens it has occasionally placed upon her family and her professional life.

The diary of Henry A. Wallace will be closed until November 1975, as his will stipulates. The original text, along with a rich collection of other Wallace manuscripts and records, is in the Special Collections Department of the University of Iowa Libraries, Iowa City, Iowa. Wallace's correspondence as Vice President, which consists primarily of incoming letters, is in the Franklin D. Roosevelt Library at Hyde Park, New York, while further Wallace materials are at the Library of Congress in Washington, D.C. An ongoing indexing and microfilming project should soon make all the Wallace Papers available in all three places. At the request of the Wallace family, the Special Collections Department at the University of Iowa made the diary itself available to me on microfilm. Also at the request of the family, I was permitted to see parts of the voluminous oral memoir of Henry A. Wallace, which is at the Oral History Office of Columbia University in New York. That memoir, like the diary, will be closed until November 1975. I used it sparingly, only where the notes to the text specifically refer to it.

Concerned as I have been with editing the diary for the war years, I have not consulted the extensive manuscript materials (except the diary) for the periods before 1942 or after 1946. The years this edition covers constitute, I believe, a special and significant part of Wallace's career, as well as of American history, for public policy during World War II moved without sharp interruptions into the early months of the Cold War. That development in turn assumed a more intractable quality precisely because Wallace was forced to leave public office. The portrait of Wallace, while focusing on the period of 1942–46, attempts, albeit briefly, to relate his spirit, ideas, and policies in that time both to his earlier and to his later life. That relationship, however, alike in content and spirit, emerges most clearly and forcefully in the pages of the diary itself.

JOHN MORTON BLUM

New Haven, Connecticut

Contents

Portrait
of the Diarist

Henry Agard Wallace wanted to be Vice President of the United States, mounted no campaign to secure or retain that office, disliked many of its duties and limitations, and yet desired renomination and resented those who prevented it. Those attitudes reflected predictable responses by the kind of man Wallace was to the nature of the vice-presidency, especially under the conditions that Franklin D. Roosevelt imposed upon the conduct of business during his administrations. The President could prescribe political snake oil even to so practical an intelligence as Wallace's. At his ebullient best, Roosevelt could engage Wallace's transcendental faith in progress and brotherhood. Within the privacy of his person, as his diary disclosed, Wallace recognized with bemused skepticism his own accepting vulnerability to the combination of guile and greatness that characterized his chief. In that privacy he also conceded nothing, though officially he had continually to yield, to those decisions of Roosevelt's that bore adversely on policies to which Wallace attached some personal and larger public importance.

During the portentous years of World War II, the relationship of the President and the Vice President of the United States, their common objectives and their intermittent disagreements, deeply affected their party, their country, even the world. In considerable measure those relationships also forecast the more bitter and ominous conflicts that were later, at a critical time, to force Wallace out of public life and deprive American government of his humane sensibilities.

*   *   *

Wallace's path into and out of the vice-presidency began in the Middle Border, in the Iowa of the late nineteenth century, where the determining roots of his being grew out of his family, the soil it nurtured, and the culture it both shaped and absorbed. Always a man of that west, Wallace brought to Washington the perspectives and commitments that his western experience fostered continuously from his childhood to his middle life.

He was the third Henry Wallace, the son of Henry Cantwell Wallace and grandson of the first Henry Wallace, "Uncle Henry," who had grown up on the farm of his Ulster-Scot father near West Newton, Pennsylvania. The first Henry Wallace began his westering in search of a seminary that offered a liberal Calvinist training. After ordination of improved health and of a seminary that offered a liberal Calvinist training. After ordination he continued west to Iowa to find a parish comfortable with his own reformist views. Soon he had to escape the tensions of his over-conscientious pastorate by turning to work the good ground of Winterset, Iowa, where he taught his neighbors about the scientific farming he practiced. Believing, as did thousands of Americans—all spiritual heirs of Thomas Jefferson—that farmers were the special agents of the Lord on earth, Wallace believed, too, that they had a duty to preserve the bounty of the earth. Christian faith, agrarian pride, and a conservationist practicality provided the foundations for the secular sermons that Uncle Henry contributed to his local newspaper during the 1880s. Those doctrines made him, too, a devoted Granger whose editorials attacked industry and the railroads —"the trusts"—that seemed to arrogate hard-won earnings of Iowa husbandmen to monopolistic profits of remote eastern capitalists.

Those messages were the texts also of the ablest farm leaders of his generation, Wallace's friends Seaman Knapp of Iowa State College and James Wilson ("Tama Jim"), another Iowan who was in time to serve the longest term (1897–1913) as Secretary of Agriculture in American history. Together, in sundry ways, they promoted scientific agriculture, sound farm management, and government policies favorable to their constituents. Uncle Henry counseled his constituents primarily through the newspaper he edited, *Wallaces' Farmer*, a farm weekly purchased in 1895 by his eldest son and published first in Cedar Rapids and later in Des Moines. He and his two friends, with others of similar mind, took their texts to the entire nation in their "Report of the Commission on Country Life," prepared in 1908–09 at the instigation of President Theodore Roosevelt. A persuasive summation of the program of agrarian progressives, the report called for redressing the grievances of rural America so as to preserve a "scientifically and economically sound country life." For Uncle Henry, that objective would ensure the future of the nation. "Good farming," he believed, "is simply obedience to natural law, just as good living is obedience to moral law." In 1916 his last will and testament encapsulated his creed: "Religion is not a philosophy but a life."[1]

No one influenced Henry A. Wallace more than did Uncle Henry.

[1] Quoted in Edward L. and Frederick H. Schapsmeier, *Henry A. Wallace of Iowa: The Agrarian Years, 1910–1940* (Ames, 1968), p. 15. For the period it covers, the

Born in 1888, Wallace as a small child lived in Ames, where his father was teaching at the state agricultural college. In 1895 the family moved to Des Moines where the boy began to spend hours almost daily with his devoted grandfather. From Uncle Henry, who delighted in his grandson's quick mind and serious manner, young Henry learned about his family, about pioneering, about the land and plants and beasts. He learned, too, to recognize God in nature and man, and to serve him through work—work at the chores that sustained the land and its tillers, and work at the services that profited mankind. "Be sure," his mother often told her sons, "that you have clean hands. And remember that you are a Wallace and a gentleman."

Those lessons reached young Wallace from every point of his boyhood compass. His mother, a dedicated gardener, showed him the satisfactions of cultivating flowers, which he always loved. "Become gardeners," he recommended to his associates many years later. "Then you will never die, because you have to live to see what happens next year."[2] His father guided him through the laboratories at the college and introduced him to a student he had befriended, a lonely, young black genius, George Washington Carver. The boy, habitually a solitary individual, eschewed his contemporaries to follow Carver, always an encouraging tutor, on botanical excursions. Carver "made so much of it," Wallace recalled, ". . . that, out of the goodness of his heart, he greatly exaggerated my botanical ability. But his faith aroused my natural instinct to excel . . . [and] deepened my appreciation of plants in a way I can never forget."[3] And like Uncle Henry, Carver saw a divine force in all living things.

The boy's father encouraged his son's emerging interests. Henry C. Wallace, "H.C." or Harry to his friends, eldest of Uncle Henry's children, had a professional competence in breeding livestock and improving grains. From one of his friends, his teen-age son received some seed corn to test for productivity. With the seed, in 1904, Henry A. Wallace proved that the contours of an ear of corn did not correlate with its propensity to yield. The shape of the ear did not matter; what did was the genetic quality of the kernel.

At sixteen Wallace had discovered that the symmetry of a plant in

Schapsmeiers' thorough work has been continually an important source for this introduction. Also useful for that period were Russell Lord, *The Wallaces of Iowa* (Boston, 1947) and Mordecai Ezekiel, "Henry A. Wallace, Agricultural Economist," *Journal of Farm Economics*, Vol. 48, No. 4, Part I, November 1966, pp. 789–802.

2 Henry A. Wallace, "The Department as I Have Known It," Ms., Wallace Papers in the possession of his family.

3 Quoted in Schapsmeier and Schapsmeier, *Wallace: Agrarian Years*, p. 19.

no way assured its utility; indeed that in all life appearances could deceive. His characteristically tousled hair and rumpled clothes attested to his own indifference to appearance, as did his vigorous but conspicuously inelegant tennis. More important, he had learned from Carver as well as from genetics the lesson that he was later to label "genetic democracy," a doctrine by no means prevalent in the Middle Border or elsewhere in the United States in 1904.

His other lessons, some yet fully to be absorbed, had similar vectors. The experience of westering, for Uncle Henry and through him for his grandson, was an experience of cooperation, of a mingling of strangers in a common land where essential collective efforts gave individuality a chance to thrive and permitted groups of individuals to bargain with aggregates of distant economic power. The brotherhood of man, an article of Christian faith, was a palpable necessity as a means for surviving the rigors of the receding frontier and for controlling the threatening circumstances of contemporary life. So, too, the application of intelligence to environment, the employment of science to improve the products of nature, the utilization of economic data to manage the otherwise uncertain fluctuations of the market—those acts of mind and will guaranteed an abundance ample for the comfort of all men, truly a land of milk and honey, a new Jerusalem.

At Iowa State College and then on the family newspaper, Wallace refined his understanding of those conclusions. Sober, diligent, ascetic, he made few friends, studied hard, and conducted his experiments with genetics and with techniques for hybridizing corn. His Bachelor's essay demonstrated the importance of soil-building, one form of conservation, for raising livestock. Problems of land utilization were to interest him for the rest of his life. Though uninvolved in politics, he was, like his father and grandfather, an enthusiastic supporter of Theodore Roosevelt and the Progressive Party in 1912. The regulatory state that Roosevelt advocated, Wallace believed, would ultimately prevail even though the Bull Moose failed. Indeed for the sake of a prosperous agriculture, it had to prevail.

Wallace's studies in economics and mathematics convinced him of that. After college he undertook to educate himself in those subjects, as well as to exploit the other resources of the Des Moines Public Library. His children remember him arriving home at night always with a stack of books in his arms. Soon an expert on statistical correlations, Wallace used that method to derive accurate indices of the cost of production of hogs. He began publishing those indices in the family newspaper in 1915. On the basis of other data, he suggested in 1919 that productivity cycles in livestock had a seven-year pattern—higher productivity followed rising prices until the saturation of the market led to falling prices that induced lower productivity. Further study, now of census figures, persuaded Wallace that with industrialization and urbanization, the average size of families diminished. With the domestic market consequently curtailed, farmers would need larger markets abroad for their crops. His book summarizing his work, *Agricultural Prices* (1920), was, in the judgment of one leading economist, "perhaps the first realistic econometric study ever published."[4] Later Wallace mastered even newer techniques for computing multiple correlations and regressions. With a mathematician as his collaborator, in 1925 he published *Correlation and Machine Calculation*, an early venture in the creative march toward computer technology. Statistics, mathematics, genetics, scientific husbandry, economics, demography, all those skills impinged upon the future of his Iowa neighbors, the men and women throughout the state who lived on the farms they worked.

* * *

Those men and women could control some of the variables that affected them. Wallace proved as much by putting into commercial use his knowledge about hybridization. With some business associates, he founded in 1926 the Hi-Bred Corn Company (later the Pioneer Hi-Bred Corn Company) to produce and sell hybrid corn. Characteristically, he also realized that the establishment of two competing concerns would help to supply the market, which would need all they could furnish. That act of faith in science, abundance, and competitive capitalism reflected no lack of business acumen. Wallace intended his company to make a legitimate profit. More, he intended his customers to profit from the use of his superior product, and in profiting to improve the quality and reduce the price of corn, to the advantage of all who purchased it. During years of agricultural depression the company shrewdly built the market for its seed by offering it to customers without demanding payment in cash on the condition that they plant half their acreage in hybrid, half in ordinary corn, and then repay a portion of the value of the higher yield on the acres growing the hybrid variety. By 1966, the higher yield from hybrid seed accounted for one quarter of the total national corn crop.

That innovative method for selling seed drew upon the example of Wallace's grandfather's friend, Seaman Knapp, who had devised the

[4] Ezekiel, "Wallace."

system of demonstration farming to persuade cotton growers to improve their methods of cultivation. Wallace's readiness to promote hybrid corn by inducing others also to enter the business revealed in some measure his intellectual debt to Thorstein Veblen, the powerful critic of American capitalism whose books Wallace read with enthusiastic reward. Veblen provided a systematic analysis to support the suspicions of monopoly that Wallace had absorbed from his family and their adherence to the old Granger program. In industries dominated by a few large firms, Veblen argued, management could adjust production to demand in order to sustain prices and profits. That process, administered pricing in the vocabulary of a later generation, held production below capacity. In Veblen's words, it involved the sabotage by managers of the abundance which engineers were capable of creating. It inhibited productive potentialities which, if realized, would assure plenty for all Americans. Veblen imagined a solution in a revolution that would transfer industrial authority to a soviet of technicians, men committed to maximum production and equitable distribution.

Wallace, educated also by other economists, was moving toward a less dramatic formulation, but one from which he expected similar results. Like other western progressives, he advocated a vigorous application of the antitrust laws and other federal controls to limit the size and power of industrial concentrations, and to prevent them from restricting production or retarding technological advances that increased productivity. Like Veblen, he envisaged a technologically dynamic society dedicated to the efficient making and sharing of industrial and agricultural commodities, a society that would need scientists and managers to fashion an abundant life for the common man. In its agricultural sector, that society—capitalistic but not beholden to laissez-faire doctrines—would function according to the model he had created for marketing hybrid corn. Through management, science and technology would overcome poverty and hunger, "Science," Wallace later wrote, ". . . cannot be overproduced. It does not come under the law of diminishing utility . . . It is perishable and must be constantly renewed."[5] It was for him the continuing frontier, the limitless source of new plenty and leaping hope.

The selfishness of industrial practices, in Wallace's view, had its political equivalent in the selfishness of economic nationalism, of protective tariffs and other artificial restraints on international trade. That trade, he believed, if unfettered, would provide the avenue to sharing

[5] Wallace, "The Department as I Have Known It."

abundance throughout the world. Wallace had grown up with the "Iowa Idea," a plan that called for removing or reducing the protection afforded products manufactured by larger corporations, including many products farmers bought, like barbed wire and harvesters. Confronted by European competition, American manufacturers would have to reduce their prices or lose some of their market. In either case, farmers would benefit. Just as important, as Europeans gained access to the American market, they would earn dollars which they could then spend to purchase American agricultural commodities.

Reduction of tariffs, as Wallace saw it, also related to the preservation of peace. In the absence of restraints on trade, nations would become more dependent upon each other and therefore less able to embark upon war. To that issue Veblen also spoke. Imperial Germany, he believed, constituted the greatest threat to peace, for the Prussian autocracy and the military elite formed a combination of purpose and power committed to domination and conquest. For Wallace, that grim potentiality could mark the United States if an industrial plutocracy and an ambitious military combined to direct national policy.

Accordingly Wallace anguished over the future of his country when he observed during the years of World War II that Standard Oil of New Jersey, part of a cartel controlled by I. G. Farben, had manipulated patents to prevent the American development of synthetic rubber; that oil companies in general came to foster that development but to oppose increasing natural sources of rubber in Latin America, sources on which the United States would be partially dependent; that industry and the military combined to dampen, almost to eliminate, federal prosecution of firms violating the antitrust laws; that the American cornucopia, sufficient to feed a devastated world, was to be confined, according to the preferences of the same men of money and of arms, to helping only those peoples, whatever their need, whose politics followed American prescriptions; and that the findings of American science were to be similarly contained. Those developments made profits and even plenty the handmaidens of politics. Yet for Wallace politics was only a necessary means for setting policies that would put both profits and plenty within the reach of every man.

*   *   *

Wallace disliked politics in all its aspects. Never gregarious, he was uncomfortable alike in smoke-filled rooms and noisy halls. Shy but candid and sometimes blunt, he lacked small talk. He detested both the manipulation of men and the prolonged conniving it demanded. He learned to campaign, but his speeches, while often effective, made only clumsy concessions to the harmless blarney that ordinarily punctuated political oratory. "Farmer Wallace," he was called by Alice Long-worth, Theodore Roosevelt's daughter and Washington's social doyenne. She did not mean it as a compliment, but as usual her description had some substance. In her salon, in her world of genial conspiracies, Wallace was never wholly at ease.

Yet Wallace entered politics, first as an editor supporting compatible candidates, later as a holder of high office, ultimately as a candidate himself, because he had no alternative except to abandon the public policies he urged upon the nation. Like his Iowa neighbors, as a private citizen he could control only some of the variables affecting his life and theirs. The others fell to the control or misdirection or indifference of the government.

Both major political parties continually disappointed the Wallaces. The Republicans during the Taft years did nothing to help agriculture. The Democrats under Woodrow Wilson proved to be rather stingy benefactors. Congress did reduce the tariff and ease conditions for agricultural credit. Further, the Food Administration under Herbert Hoover during World War I stimulated the production of corn and hogs. But, as Wallace's father continually demonstrated, Hoover —Iowa-born but otherwise bred—paid Iowans meanly for their efforts.

In 1921 Henry C. Wallace accepted appointment as President Warren G. Harding's Secretary of Agriculture. His son, now editor of the newspaper, had also a close view of the operations of his father's department. H.C. recruited a staff of experts who brought unprecedented technical talents to their tasks. He was able, too, with Harding's support, to persuade Congress to enact legislation to assist agricultural marketing and to curb speculation in commodities. But the senior Wallace failed in his program to reach markets overseas. His successful antagonist was again Herbert Hoover, now Secretary of Commerce, whose relentless opposition to promoting agriculture contrasted with his vigorous efforts in behalf of industry. Hoover, so Henry A. Wallace believed, contributed inadvertently to the frustration and fatigue that taxed his father's strength and reduced his resistance to the operation from which he was unable to recover in 1924.

Before his death, H. C. Wallace had endorsed a plan for agriculture for which his son helped thereafter to organize increasing support. Incorporated in a succession of bills sponsored by Senator Charles L. McNary of Oregon and Representative Gilbert N. Haugen of Iowa, that plan proposed a two-price system for commodities. Government purchases were to sustain the domestic price at the level of "parity"—

the ratio between agricultural and industrial prices that had prevailed during the years 1910–14, good years for farmers. The government would sell its purchases abroad at a lower price while taxing farmer-beneficiaries to cover any losses. There were shortcomings to the plan. European tariffs, rising to compete with American protection, would impede the necessary sales. Europeans were in any case short of dollars because of the drain of repaying the United States for debts incurred during the war. More important, the McNary-Haugen plan placed no limits on production, which would increase to unmanageable proportions if the government guaranteed farmers a high price on all their crops. President Calvin Coolidge and Herbert Hoover both opposed the plan, which Congress twice passed and Coolidge twice vetoed, primarily on other grounds. They contended that it would destroy individualism, establish artificial prices, and create a dangerous federal bureaucracy to administer it. Those objections ignored the artificial prices, large bureaucracies, and collective rather than individualistic nature of American corporate enterprise.

A registered Republican, Wallace condemned the GOP for its callousness toward the farmer, whose share of national income was steadily falling, and for its acceptance of the business creed. He urged his readers in 1924 to vote for Robert M. La Follette and his new Progressive Party, and in 1928 to vote for Alfred E. Smith, the Democratic nominee who had endorsed the latest McNary-Haugen bill. Yet so unpolitical was Wallace that he neglected to change his party registration until 1936.

From 1924 forward, he consulted continually with some of the economists his father had employed in the Department of Agriculture, in particular Henry C. Taylor , at one time chief of the Bureau of Agricultural Economics, and two younger men, Mordecai Ezekiel and Louis H. Bean, who were to continue fruitfully to advise the department and its head throughout the 1930s and 1940s. He also came to know the two leading academic experts on agricultural economics, John D. Black of the University of Minnesota and later Harvard, and M. L. Wilson of the University of Montana. After the onset of the Great Depression, with its devastating consequences for markets at home and abroad, Black and Wilson worked out the Domestic Allotment Plan, the program that Wallace and like-minded farm leaders endorsed in 1932 as a preferred substitute for the defeated McNary-Haugen proposals. The new plan, the basis for the Agricultural Adjustment Administration of the New Deal, looked to the federal government to pay farmers to withdraw acreage from cultivation and thus curtail their production of crops. The withdrawal of marginal land and the rotation of cultivation of fertile soil applied the principles of conservation. More immediately, reduction in supply to the domestic market would lift commodity prices, while government payments would enlarge farm income, with parity in purchasing power again the goal.

Especially after the crash of 1929, farmers had other crushing problems. Land values had fallen during the 1920s and now shrank further, while the interest payments on mortgage debts incurred during the prosperous war years remained cruelly high. The deflation in commodity prices made the weight of debt intolerable, led to more and more foreclosures, and embittered the countryside. Wallace came to advocate federal action for mortgage relief and controlled inflation. Influenced by Irving Fisher, the foremost American economist of his generation, Wallace served as vice president of Fisher's Stable Money League. It demanded a commodity dollar, a dollar valued not on a fixed ratio to gold but by a constant relationship to purchasing power, in itself elastic. *Wallaces' Farmer* educated its readers in those ideas, while Wallace became a familiar figure at conferences concerned with preserving a healthy rural America.

Like his father and grandfather, Wallace became a reformer without becoming a radical. He saw the need for strong federal action and for a large federal establishment to protect the existence of the independent farmer. Price supports, mortgage relief, and managed money were adventurous departures from past policy. As their advocate, Wallace contemplated major institutional change. But he did not approve farmer strikes to withhold crops from market, or the sudden liquidation of mortgages, or an undisciplined recourse to printing paper or coining silver money. Those more radical measures had their many champions by 1932, for an angry impatience naturally flowed from the desperation of American farmers. But Franklin D. Roosevelt, the successful aspirant for the Democratic nomination that year, by temperament a moderate, found the reforms with which Wallace was identified compatible with his own sense of proper remedy. Wallace, one of the experts whose advice Roosevelt solicited, supported him both before and after his nomination. Once elected, Roosevelt decided, after reviewing several other possibilities, that Wallace had the confidence of the farm leaders and the qualities of mind and purpose that he wanted in his Secretary of Agriculture. Wallace accepted the position. Now, in spite of himself, his commitment to agricultural reform had drawn him into politics, both the politics of decision-making within the federal government and the politics of competition between the parties.

*   *   *

There was a part of Henry Wallace that Franklin Roosevelt recognized but never criticized. Some of his less sympathetic associates worried about what they considered Wallace's mysticism, a quality they considered disturbing and unpredictable in its consequences. Yet Wallace was not a mystic, unless that description, as he once said, applied to any man of Christian faith. What made him seem a mystic to those who called him one was primarily his indomitable curiosity, a curiosity that led him to explore everything that caught his interest, religion not the least.[6]

Essentially Wallace's religion was the Christianity common in the Middle Border. It had its foundation in faith rather than theology. Like Uncle Henry, Wallace concluded that the rigid tenets of orthodox Calvinism clashed with his generous belief in the pervasive goodness of God. Those tenets were at variance, too, with his sense of the presence of God in nature and life. He did not use the vocabulary of transcendentalism, but he shared the convictions of that creed about the immanence of God in man. Still he also tried continually to find God, not palpably but spiritually, whether in the beauty of growing things, in the symmetry of genetic patterns, or in the evocations of religious rituals. Consequently he experimented with religion, just as he experimented with corn, seeking the most satisfying yield.

Wallace tested his responses to various churches. He was conscious of the spiritual excitement that Methodism could stir but too private a man to find continuing fulfillment in collective rhapsody. The gorgeous rituals of Catholicism also moved him, but Catholic dogma and hierarchy put him off. He tried to feel what the saints had felt by practicing one kind of asceticism or another, but for him deprivation of the flesh or spiritual removal from the world divorced religion too much from life, which he was resolved to serve. He was at times fascinated by the occult and he studied oriental faiths, but they, too, failed to answer his needs, though his reading led him to a concept of Confucius, a "constantly normal granary," a phrase he adapted for his own use. He settled in the end for membership in the Episcopal church, which he attended regularly during his years in Washington. Here, particularly in the communion service, he received as much as formal religion could offer him. He interpreted the Lord's Supper his own way. "It is the function of the church," Wallace said at one communion breakfast, "to emphasize the ties which draw men together no matter how much finite differences may appear to separate them

6 For a somewhat contrary but informed and incisive view of the questions covered in this section of the introduction, see Arthur M. Schlesinger, Jr., *The Coming of the New Deal* (Boston, 1959), pp. 28–34.

. . . Weak as is the church . . . it is a synthesizing, centripetal force . . . on behalf of the sacredness of the individual and the unity of humanity."[7] It was the symbol and the agency of the brotherhood of man.

That brotherhood had a special psychological importance for Wallace. Just as he was not a hail-fellow, so, outside of his immediate family, he was not an intimate man. His aloneness in life fostered his need for brotherhood in spirit, a need he recognized in other men, particularly those who lived on the soil. He put it best, perhaps, in discussing the people of Soviet Asia: "All of them . . . were people of plain living and robust minds, not unlike our farming people in the United States. Much that is interpreted . . . as 'Russian distrust' can be written off as the natural cautiousness of farm-bred people . . . Beneath the . . . new urban culture, one catches glimpses of the sound, wary, rural mind."[8] Those wary men and women Wallace discovered everywhere he went, in Siberia, China, throughout Latin America, as well as in the countryside of the United States and beneath the skins of Americans in labor unions or military regalia or governmental suites. Not their spiritual comfort only, but also, in the shadows of an awful war, the prospects for a genuine peace depended upon a centripetal force that would assure the sacredness of every one of them and the unity of mankind.

Essential though it was, the church was not enough. Always a Calvinist in part, Wallace had a sense of duty, even of mission, to accomplish the work of the Lord. His continual recourse to biblical metaphor was more than the rhetorical habit of a minister's grandson. He was an austere moralist, impatient less with impiety than with sloth, deceit, selfishness, and materialism. More, he cast himself often as prophet or witness, now in the role of Joseph husbanding his people's resources, now as Micah beating swords into ploughshares, now as Gideon attacking a wicked citadel. That last role he assumed in 1948, in his predictably futile campaign for the Presidency as the candidate of a disorganized new party, against the advice of his family and his loyal friends, indeed against his better judgment. He had, he felt, to bear witness against the policies he had attacked and for the beliefs he had broadcast.

Yet the compulsions of mission that inhered in Wallace's religion were balanced by a contemplative gentleness. It was not just that he loved his family, which he did, deeply though undemonstratively. It

[7] Wallace Diary, February 22, 1940.
[8] Henry A. Wallace, *Soviet Asia Mission* (New York, 1945), p. 21.

was also that when he crossbred corn or strawberries, he had more at stake than productivity. He loved the plants, just as he loved grasses—grasses, as he described them, growing quietly taller, silently dropping their seeds onto the earth and into the winds, full fields of grasses bending with the prevailing breeze, full fields observed from the air in huge patterns of contrasting greens and browns. He loved the soil, the way it felt between the fingers, its pungent darkness. Without direct contact with growing things, he lost touch with the universe and its creator. His Washington victory garden, planted in his sister's yard, provided a useful crop, but more important, gave him when he worked in it a serenity he could capture no other way. In the soil he found his ultimate communion. His was strongly a Social Gospel, but he tempered that gospel with a tenderness that displayed his natural charity. Joseph he could emulate, or Gideon, but at the core he was more akin to Paul.

To the secular mind, Wallace's faith seemed outmoded, his witnessing quaint, his spirituality incomprehensible. To the urban mind, his affinity with nature appeared irrelevant and distracting. As for his inquiries into the occult, secular and urban Americans took them for an eccentricity. Washington was filled with the polished, the urbane, and the fashionable, so in Washington Farmer Wallace, spiritually as well as culturally uncomfortable, felt often bored and out of place. As Roosevelt realized, that did not matter. He needed Wallace to manage the Department of Agriculture and its programs, and for that task, Wallace, practical scientist and progressive reformer, was admirably equipped.

* * *

During his eight years as Secretary of Agriculture, Henry A. Wallace accomplished more than did any one else who has ever held that office. Each of the many programs the department initiated, as one of its officers later attested, "had Wallace's close attention and support."[9] Each profited, too, from the support Wallace solicited from the President and from the skills of the administrators, lawyers, economists, and agronomists to whom the Secretary delegated responsibilities for the detailed supervision and the technical research without which the department could not have functioned. They were impressive men, several of whom became Wallace's lifelong friends. Among the most effective were Rexford G. Tugwell, Wallace's first Under Secretary, one of Roosevelt's original brain-trusters, who, like Wallace, had

9 Ezekiel, "Wallace."

studied Veblen; Mordecai Ezekiel, senior economic adviser, and his
talented associate, Louis Bean; Paul Appleby, chief administrative officer, and Milo Perkins who ran various special programs like the Food
Stamp Plan for the distribution of surplus commodities to impoverished
Americans; Chester Davis, who for some years managed the Agricultural Adjustment Administration; and, for a brief period, Jerome N.
Frank, a brilliant young New York lawyer.[10]

The Agricultural Act of 1933, a keystone in Roosevelt's recovery
program, made national policy of the various proposals with which
Wallace had been identified before the election. Among the provisions
of the act, one founded the Agricultural Adjustment Administration
within the Department of Agriculture to manage the Domestic Allotment Plan. In developing policy under that plan, Wallace confronted
two major crises which he resolved with a practical opportunism that
revealed both a disciplined toughness and a political sensitivity surprising to his critics.

The earlier episode arose because the Domestic Allotment program
was established too late to affect planting or husbandry in the spring of
1933. Farmers in the south had already started their cotton, farmers in
the west had already bred their hogs, before the Agricultural Adjustment Administration could begin to make payments for the withdrawal
of acreage or the limitation of production. Yet cotton and hogs, glut-
ting the market, were selling at historically low prices. To remove the
glut, to prevent it from carrying over to 1934, to raise prices and to
increase farm income, Wallace deliberately violated his own profound
belief in abundance and its distribution. He mobilized the Extension
Service of the department to enlist cotton farmers, in return for boun-
tiful payments ($100 million in all), to plough up a quarter of their
crop. Less drastic measures assisted grain farmers. As for hogs, on the
advice of local committees throughout the west and of the Farm Bureau Federation, the department purchased and slaughtered six million
little pigs. Much of the baby pork was given to the hungry on relief,
but Wallace deeply regretted the conditions that had forced his hand.
"The plowing under . . . of cotton . . . and the slaughter of . . .
pigs," he said, "were not acts of idealism in any sane society. They
were emergency acts made necessary by the almost insane lack of world
statesmanship . . . from 1920 to 1932." He had to play, he explained,

[10] The best account of the agricultural policies of the early New Deal, an account
on which I have relied heavily, is in Schlesinger, *Coming of the New Deal,*
Ch. 1. Also helpful and sometimes of a contrasting interpretation were the
works of the Schapsmeiers and of Ezekiel, cited above.

the cards that were dealt him; industry had limited production artificially for many years, and "agriculture cannot survive in a capitalistic society as a philanthropic enterprise."[11]

The unavoidable destruction of crops in 1933 prepared the stage for the successful operation of AAA and in later years for new directions of policy, but a second crisis intruded before Wallace could embark on those new directions. Recourse to the Extension Service, as Wallace knew, reinforced the position within the department of one of its most conservative sections, for the Service had long fostered the interests of the Farm Bureau Federation, an organization dominated by large commercial farmers, whose needs often conflicted with those of small, independent farmers, tenants, and farm laborers. Further, Wallace had had temporarily to accept as head of the AAA George N. Peek, a father of the McNary-Haugen scheme, who remained committed to dumping surpluses abroad rather than controlling production at home. Soon able to get rid of Peek, Wallace replaced him with Chester Davis who, like his predecessor, had the confidence of the Farm Bureau Federation. Wallace felt he needed that group's large influence in Congress, but the price proved high. In 1935 Davis and Jerome Frank clashed over AAA contracts which Frank and his young associates had written to protect farm tenants and sharecroppers in the South. Either he or Frank, Davis told Wallace, would have to go.

Wallace regretfully fired Frank and most of his group in the General Counsel's office. Frank was shocked, as was Rex Tugwell, for they believed they had been following the Secretary's wishes. Years later, others believed Wallace had acted to purge the department of communists, of whom a few were in Frank's office. The latter issue simply did not occur to Wallace. The former pained him, for, as with the little pigs, he realized that he had departed from principle in order to preserve his ability to move ahead, albeit with reduced speed, toward larger goals. He had already concluded that the habit of dissent, typical in his experience of the western Democrats who had jointed La Follette in 1924, obstructed a practical approach to solving urgent problems. "It seems," Wallace wrote in 1935, "as though . . . Progressives are splendid critics but very poor builders."[12]

The episode of the purge, perhaps especially Tugwell's angry disappointment with the Secretary's expediency, had a double impact on Wallace. It persuaded him, under the tutelage of Will Alexander of his staff, more thoroughly to examine the wretched circumstances of

11 Quoted in Schlesinger, *Coming of the New Deal*, p. 63.
12 Wallace Diary, January 26, 1935.

southern croppers, white and black, and of the displaced and miserable migrant farm laborers of the west. He proceeded then more aggressively to seek effective remedies for their problems. He added his own support to the efforts to create the Resettlement Administration (under Tugwell and later Alexander) and the Farm Security Administration (under Alexander, Milo Perkins, and C. B. Baldwin). Those agencies began, though belatedly, to help the downtrodden in American agriculture. Wallace had earlier sponsored the Rural Electrification Administration that carried inexpensive electricity to farm homes, an objective first defined by the Country Life Commission. As Ezekiel wrote, REA "revolutionized the face of rural America." Further, Wallace's growing concern for eradicating rural poverty and his growing suspicions of the Farm Bureau Federation sensitized him to the problems of urban poverty and of American blacks, and rekindled his apprehensions about big business and its privileges. By the time of World War II, he had become the champion of the common man alike on the streets and on the land. He had become, too, an opponent of the demands not only of arrogant industrialists but also of the equally arrogant Farm Bureau.

The episode of the purge had also a more personal effect on Wallace. Because he had to decide between Davis and Frank, he had no escape from the politics of allocating power. Because he accepted a short-run loss in order to try to win long-run gains, he had to bend principle to expediency. In so doing, he had to wound an able and trusting subordinate. Later, during World War II, Wallace may have recalled the pains of 1935 when Roosevelt in effect fired him first from the chairmanship of the Board of Economic Warfare and later from the vice-presidency. In both cases the President sacrificed some principle to more expediency; in both he sacrificed a valued colleague to his own assessment of political exigencies. In both instances, Wallace, though gravely wounded, remained loyal to Roosevelt, whom he still preferred to any other chief. The problem, Wallace realized even in 1935, grew out of the New Deal's style of administration. "In this administration," he wrote, "the objectives are experimental and not clearly stated; therefore, there is certain to be, from the White House down, a certain amount of what seems to be intrigue. I do not think this situation will be remedied until the President abandons . . . his experimental and somewhat concealed approach. There are . . . many advantages to this approach but it does not lead to the happiest personal relationships and the best administration."[13] Roosevelt never abandoned his ap-

[13] Wallace Diary, February 3, 1935.

proach. In the politics of the New Deal, as Wallace discovered, one had on occasion to dish it out, and on other occasions to take it.

The game was worth the anguish if the stakes were high enough. For Wallace they were, for during the middle 1930s he succeeded in advancing his most cherished objectives. The Supreme Court's invalidation of the Agricultural Adjustment Act of 1933 forced the department to devise a constitutionally acceptable alternative. The Soil Conservation and Domestic Allotment Act of 1936 and the Agricultural Adjustment Act of 1938 preserved the practice of managing production. Those measures also put a new emphasis on conservation, on withdrawing acreage not only to reduce crops but also to follow a rational system of land utilization. From 1936 forward, as Wallace said, "the Department launched a positive attack on the dual problem of soil destruction and unbalanced cropping."[14]

The dreadful dust storms of the years immediately preceding had attested to the indispensability of protecting the "voiceless land." Those disasters also reminded Americans of the vulnerability of agriculture to nature and of the possibility of shortages in food stuffs. The act of 1938 gave Wallace the opportunity he had long sought to create an "ever-normal granary," to employ government purchases, storage, and sales so as to assure adequate supplies without future gluts or shortages. The resulting program provided food for Americans and their allies during the extraordinary years of World War II and the early postwar period. As Wallace admitted, he had not foreseen the war when he formulated his program, but his success led him to hope, as he wrote in 1942, for the establishment of an ever normal granary on a worldwide scale. That concept underlay the plans recommended in 1946 by Sir John Boyd Orr, Director-General of the Food and Agricultural Organization of the United Nations, plans Wallace energetically endorsed. He had earlier adopted comparable policies to build up American strategic reserves through the Board of Economic Warfare.

Just as the accumulation of reserves depended upon sources abroad, so, as Wallace saw it, did the efficient functioning of the American economy. Contending during the 1930s, as he long had, that "America must choose," he related the choice to national prosperity. The option lay between domestic self-sufficiency, which would inhibit and distort economic growth, and open international trade, which would encourage the United States to produce and export what it did best and to import goods produced more efficiently elsewhere. Wallace took the side of maximum growth, for it would provide employment for men

14 Wallace, "The Department as I Have Known It."

and capital and permit the elimination of want. The New Deal's reciprocal trade treaties took a limited step toward freer trade, but Wallace envisaged much more dramatic changes that would open all markets and all shipping and air routes. The war spurred him to urge even more insistently interrelated policies to promote free trade, economic growth, and full employment.

*   *   *

Wallace's objectives, accomplishments, and expanding sympathies marked him by 1940 as one of the country's outstanding statesmen. He had demonstrated the personal loyalty to the President that John N. Garner, Vice President since 1933, so stubbornly withheld. Wallace had, too, the liberal credentials that Roosevelt wanted for his running mate in 1940. And during the first six months of that year Wallace had taken a position on the war in Europe that answered Roosevelt's political needs.

The President, in the view of his isolationist critics, was leading the nation too close to the conflict abroad. In the view of those, still a minority, who wanted at once to join the endangered British cause, the President had delayed too long in taking steps to supply Great Britain and to develop American armed forces for employment overseas. Privately Roosevelt may have shared the latter assessment but politically, he believed, he could not afford either to increase his pace or to give the isolationists further cause for complaint. Wallace stood about where the majority of Americans did after the Germans had overrun most of western Europe. He detested Nazism, which he continually attacked, as he always had. He saw potential danger to the Americas in Germany's advance. He therefore preached hemispheric solidarity and national preparedness—the mobilization of the economy and of a strong and balanced military force. "We must," he told Roosevelt, "be in a position to command fear and respect."[15] Yet Wallace also opposed American entry into the war and resisted the thought that it was inevitable. Further, he believed that mobilization need not entail a surrender of policy to generals and financiers, and that a good neighbor should sponsor democratization along with friendship in Latin America. Indeed with the spread of fascism in Europe, the new world more than ever before had to provide a persuasive example of effective democracy.

Wallace, as Roosevelt insisted, suited his needs, but few of the President's counselors or of the party leaders agreed. Wallace had

15 Wallace Diary, May 22, 1940; see also January 2, 1940, on hemispheric policy.

always ignored the powerful captains of the great Democratic city machines. He disliked and distrusted, perhaps even despised, men like Kelly of Chicago and Hague of Jersey City, who felt the same way about him. His increasing zeal for civil rights for black Americans and for relieving the poverty of the sharecroppers of the South, many of them black, offended most of the influential senior southern Democrats in the Senate. Like many of their northern colleagues, they considered his ideas radical, his religion puzzling, and his manner remote.

Wallace also lacked the confidence of Roosevelt's circle of immediate advisers, particularly those whom Felix Frankfurter had recruited. They knew he was learned, but he was not one of them, and by their standards he had none of the polish the White House required. For his part, Wallace did not quite trust them. He called them "connivers" and considered them preoccupied with power, though he knew they had made significant contributions to reform. Even Ben Cohen, perhaps the gentlest and ablest man in the group, operated too guardedly for Wallace's taste. Cohen, along with some others, feared for a time in 1939 that Paul McNutt, a handsome but vacuous Indiana Democrat, might be Roosevelt's choice for the vice-presidency. Against that chance, Wallace observed that "the New Dealers"—he used the phrase pejoratively—resisted taking a "position of too great an opposition against McNutt . . . The New Dealers . . . don't like the McNutt possibility but feel they must prepare for it as a contingency." Wallace did not feel that way, nor did he have any enthusiasm for a Vice President selected from the inner circle of the White House or from its outer fringe, perhaps Harry Hopkins, the President's éminence grise, or William O. Douglas. They were little to be preferred, he felt, to Secretary of State Cordell Hull, a favorite of conservative Southerners, or National Chairman James A. Farley, whom the city bosses liked.

Farley, an active candidate, felt that Roosevelt was blocking his ambitions. Always on pleasant terms with Wallace, Farley early in 1940 complained to him about the President. "Farley was incorrect," Wallace judged, "in calling the President a sadist although there is a certain amount of that element in his nature. The predominant element, however, is the desire to be the dominating figure, to demonstrate on all occasions his superiority. He changes his standards of superiority many times during the day. But having set for himself a particular standard for the moment, he then glories in being the dominating figure along that particular line. In that way he fills out his artistic sense of the fitness of things."[16]

16 Wallace Diary, January 18, 1940.

In spite of that insight, in spite of the opposition he knew he provoked, Wallace was a completely receptive, though never an active,
candidate for nomination. He organized no movement on his own
behalf because, as he told a cabinet colleague, "I did not look on myself
as very much of a politician."[17] He did not think that nomination as
Vice President would lead to the Presidency, for unlike Farley, he
expected Roosevelt to live out a third term. "The President," Wallace
observed, "is more likely to maintain his vitality by being President than
by retiring."[18] Nor did he expect Roosevelt to retire. One of Wallace's Iowa friends asked him if he "was interested in having my name
presented to the national convention in case the President did not run.
I told him that it was scarcely worth thinking about because I was so
certain the President was going to run. I said, of course, if the President did not run, I would be interested." As for the vice-presidency,
"I said that would depend altogether on what the powers that might
be might think would best insure victory."[19]

Roosevelt was the power that was. To a reluctant convention he
dictated the choice of Wallace as his running mate. He even contemplated withdrawing himself if the convention should reject his selection.
It almost did, but Roosevelt's adamancy, the energetic politicking of
Harry Hopkins, the President's emissary on the floor, and the timely
appearance of Eleanor Roosevelt as her husband's special ambassador
for Wallace brought the unhappy delegates around.

Roosevelt made Wallace Vice President in 1940. Four years later,
when Wallace had far more support within the party, Roosevelt
dumped him. He announced his personal preference for Wallace but
he also expressed his satisfaction with several other possible candidates
and then let the party leaders move the convention to a decision he
had previously approved. That change in Roosevelt's tactics, as Wallace realized, constituted a complete reversal. The President again had
been the dominating figure, filling out, now to Wallace's disadvan-
tage, "his artistic sense of the fitness of things."

*   *   *

Receptive though he had been to nomination as Vice President,
Wallace discovered little satisfaction in that office when he entered
it in January 1941. Usefully busy almost every day for the eight preceding years, he now had almost nothing to do. Presiding over the

17 Wallace Diary, May 24, 1940.
18 Ibid.
19 Wallace Diary, June 27, 1940.

Senate's meandering debates bored him. Often he appeared to doze in the chair. More often he turned the chair over to a colleague. The Democratic Majority Leader, Alben Barkley, an engaging Kentuckian, ran the business of the Senate. Most of the members of that body respected Wallace but few welcomed him to the informal gatherings, the Senate's club, which by temperament he had no desire to join.

He had, Wallace said, more time for tennis than ever before in his life, but seldom had the nation faced more urgent issues. For their resolution Roosevelt intended to harness Wallace's talents, but he was slow in finding an appropriate role for him, for he was slow in establishing offices properly geared first for mobilization and then for war. While the President procrastinated, Wallace educated himself in the problems of national defense and of the defense economy by discussing them regularly with experts on the staffs of the White House, the departments, and the defense agencies. At Roosevelt's initiative, he was among the few originally to learn about S–1, the then infant project to develop an atomic bomb. In July 1941 the President gave him a first assignment as chairman of the Economic Defense Board, established at that time as a "policy and advisory agency" to deal with "international economic activities" including exports, imports, preclusive buying, shipping, foreign exchange, and similar matters.[20]

That mandate, as it turned out, was as broad as the agency's actual authority was narrow. Power over its supposed functions remained dispersed among the executive departments, and decisions, when they were made, remained the prerogative of the White House. So, too, with the Supply Priorities and Allocations Board that the President created in August 1941 with Wallace as chairman. In characteristically Rooseveltian fashion, it was superimposed upon the Office of Production Management, which had been crippled by friction within its staff and by its rivalry with the War and Navy departments. SPAB was to serve as the coordinating center for defense mobilization. It failed for the reasons that had vitiated the Economic Defense Board and OPM.

Even before the Japanese attack on Pearl Harbor, those responsible for mobilization chafed at Roosevelt's reluctance to delegate and centralize authority. The advent of war forced the President to act. At least in theory, real authority over the domestic economy was granted in January 1942 to the new War Production Board under Donald Nelson, a former vice president of Sears, Roebuck who had been executive director of SPAB. Wallace was to sit as chairman, along

[20] Edward L. and Frederick H. Schapsmeier, *Prophet in Politics: Henry A. Wallace and the War Years, 1940–65* (Ames, 1970), p. 9.

with various Cabinet officers as members, of WPB's governing committee. He liked and admired Nelson, but he did not, as one friend observed, "find it congenial to work with the big businessmen who dominated that organization, nor with the admirals and generals who were their military counterparts."[21]

Far more satisfying to the Vice President, Roosevelt had also made him chairman of another new agency, established by executive order on December 17, 1941, the Board of Economic Warfare. It was to assume the responsibilities of the Economic Defense Board but with strengthened authority—as it turned out, less than enough—to deal directly with foreign governments in the procurement of strategic materials and related functions. Wallace now had a mandate, one he believed he could use both to abet the war effort and to influence postwar policy.

As he had in the Department of Agriculture, Wallace in the Board of Economic Warfare devoted himself to questions of policy and delegated responsibility for daily administrative and technical decisions. The major weight of that responsibility he assigned to his executive director, Milo Perkins, an old friend and associate and an energetic promoter of Wallace's own purposes. Under Perkins were the three sections of BEW: the Office of Imports, charged with procuring strategic materials and with preclusive buying all over the world, but especially in Latin America where neither the Germans nor the Japanese had become a military threat; the Office of Exports, which was to use its licensing authority to prevent goods from reaching Axis nations; and the Office of Warfare Analysis, which selected targets of economic importance for strategic bombing. The first of those sections commanded most of Perkins's and Wallace's attention, and its operations were the bases for the controversies that were to mark the history of the agency.

About two months after the establishment of BEW, with those controversies in their first stages, Wallace resumed keeping a diary. Twice before he had initiated and abandoned that practice, on both occasions initiating it when political events in Washington especially involved him. He had kept a diary briefly during the Davis-Frank episode, and he had again for the months preceding his nomination for Vice President. Now he began once more, with few lapses until he left public office. The content of the diary revealed his continual engagement in political developments within government and in the policies that politics affected. More than an outlet for reflection, it

21 Ezekiel, "Wallace."

served, as its author intended, as a record of his activities. Such was also the case with the diaries of so many of Roosevelt's Cabinet, Henry Stimson, Henry Morgenthau, Jr., Harold Ickes, and James Forrestal in particular. With varying degrees of self-consciousness, they recorded an account of what they had said and heard and done, an account to which they could refer should some colleague challenge their consistency or veracity. Such challenges emerged from the personal frictions engendered by Roosevelt's style of administration. As Morgenthau, speaking from experience, warned Wallace, relationships with Jesse H. Jones especially imposed on a prudential man the self-protective task of keeping a full record. Like the diaries of his colleagues, Wallace's diary, while incidentally convenient for history, had a more contemporary and expedient use.

While he kept the diary for himself, Wallace in 1942 also took his thoughts to the American people with greater frequency and moment than ever before. No member of the administration except the President made more public speeches or attracted more continual attention. Roosevelt probably planned it that way. In the interests of national unity and of harmony within the Grand Alliance, the President during the war years moved with more than his customary caution. But Roosevelt typically was less cautious privately than he appeared to be in public. By no means averse to examining bold policies for adoption once the war had been won, he needed a scout to test the responses of both national and international audiences, a semiofficial spokesman whose proposals he could embrace if they were well received or repudiate if they were not.

The President did not have to cast Wallace in that role, for the Vice President without prompting seized every occasion he could to publicize his hopes for the postwar world. Indeed Wallace was restless with the failure of the American government to set forth in clear detail a plan for the future that would lift the spirits and galvanize the wills of men everywhere. He fretted not the least because the relative silence from the White House permitted other voices to seem louder and more persuasive than in his opinion they should have. So, for one example, though he shared many of the sentiments of Wendell Willkie's *One World*, he distrusted Willkie's instincts in domestic policy. So, for another, he detested the confident chauvinism of Henry Luce's "American Century." Like Archibald MacLeish, the eminent poet who served for a short and unhappy season as the head of the Office of Facts and Figures, Wallace believed that Roosevelt was forgoing a commanding opportunity to define the war as a vehicle for practical

idealism. The President, preoccupied with military problems and the
conflicts among the nation's major allies, emphasized victory above all
other considerations. After victory, he told MacLeish, he would speak
more concretely about the nature of the peace. Wallace, for his part,
while always committed to the eradication of Nazism as a first priority,
was determined, too, to stir the blood of democrats everywhere, to
prophesy, as he did, the coming century of the common man.

His rhetoric in that cause gave a testamental cast to the sundry objectives that engrossed him. As his diary disclosed, his activities on the
Board of Economic Warfare aroused the quick opposition of two of
the most powerful conservatives within the administration, both noted
for their influence on the Hill, Secretary of State Cordell Hull and
Secretary of Commerce Jesse Jones, who was also head of the federal
lending agencies. Both men had a long record of defending any apparent invasion of what they jealously considered their personal domains. Now Hull resented any independence from State Department
supervision of BEW representatives negotiating with foreign governments. Jones was even more indignant over Milo Perkins' efforts to
arrange loans for the development abroad of sources of strategic materials without proceeding through the dilatory, sometimes obstructionist, lending agencies. Enlisted by Perkins, Wallace tried to persuade
Roosevelt to grant BEW independence from Hull and Jones, but the
President, under pressure also from Wallace's antagonists, gave BEW
more the semblance than the sinew of what it sought.

The bureaucratic struggle merely clothed fundamental disagreements
about policy, particularly in Latin America. There Wallace and Perkins had two large goals. "International trade," Wallace had earlier
written, "has always been closer to economic warfare than the American people have been trained to think."[22] Through international trade
he endeavored in Latin America to develop sources for essential materials of war—rubber and quinine for two—which the United States had
previously obtained from areas the Japanese had conquered. Preclusive
buying also denied those and other materials to the Germans. The
procurement of adequate supplies, Wallace believed, depended upon
increasing the productivity of Latin American workers, whose physical
strength and morale suffered from malnutrition, disease, miserable sanitation and housing, and skimpy wages. Efficiency demanded social
reform, as did the first step toward a decent future for the laborers.
BEW tried to take that step by writing into procurement contracts
obligations on the part of Latin American governments or entrepreneurs

[22] Wallace Diary, June 6, 1940.

"to furnish adequate shelter, water, safety appliances, etc.," to consult with BEW "as to whether the wage scale is such as to maximize production," and to cooperate "in a plan to improve conditions of health and sanitation," a plan for which the United States would pay half the costs.[23]

Hull attacked that policy indirectly. The State Department endorsed some of BEW's conditions for contracts, but it also complained that the conditions as a whole constituted interference in the domestic affairs of a foreign nation, a course the department claimed to eschew. Noninterference, as practiced by the State Department, had special connotations. The doctrine served for several years as Hull's excuse for protecting the pro-Nazi but officially neutral government of Argentina from the disciplinary measures of economic warfare recommended continually by Army Intelligence and the Treasury Department. Too, the State Department helped to arrange shipments of Lend-Lease arms to Latin American governments, non-fighting allies against the Axis, that were openly repressive toward workers and peasants. Hull knew that Wallace welcomed social change in Latin America. Indeed Wallace had identified that change with peaceful revolution. The Board of Economic Warfare did not demand that Latin American states alter their laws; it attempted only to write contracts to help Latin American workers. But that was too much revolution for Hull, and therefore by his standards too much interference.

Like Wallace, Hull was a dogged proponent of freeing international trade from artificial restraints. Like Wallace, he was eager to enlarge American markets abroad in the postwar period, temporarily by advancing generous credits. But the Secretary of State and most of his colleagues equated that objective with the spread of American institutions, political and economic. They expected their trading partners to be or to become capitalistic republics in the model of the United States. When the war ended, they attached political conditions to commercial negotiations. Wallace did not. He sought postwar trade with any nation, whatever its system of government or pattern of property ownership. And, during the war, he wanted American credits, trade, and contracts to turn the calendar toward the century of the common man. He lost.

As much as Hull, Jesse Jones contributed to that defeat. The delays and the parsimony of Jones' lending agencies retarded procurement, as Wallace and others demonstrated and Jones self-righteously denied. Wallace found just as aggravating the political objections to BEW con-

23 Quoted in Schapsmeier and Schapsmeier, *Prophet in Politics,* p. 45.

tracts, which Jones claimed were needlessly costly. Preoccupied with prices and interest rates, Jones never grasped the greater importance, during the crisis of war, of productivity, one of Wallace's goals. He did understand and reject Wallace's long-range social concerns, which he scoffed at as an international WPA. He scoffed, too, at Wallace's worries about the postwar implications of American policy on synthetic rubber. Wallace feared that federal assistance for the synthetic rubber industry, which he knew was essential for wartime supply, would lead to postwar tariff protection for that industry, and consequently inhibit postwar natural rubber developments which BEW was nurturing in Brazil and elsewhere. As ever, Wallace argued that without a market in the United States, those natural rubber producers would be unable to survive, and unable, too, to purchase American products. Jones fixed his interest on the postwar profits of the domestic rubber industry.

Jones had the sympathy and support of like-minded senators, including senior southern Democrats like Kenneth McKellar and Harry Byrd, who chaired powerful committees. They gave him a platform from which to attack BEW, its policies, and the concessions to it that Roosevelt had made. Where Hull ordinarily expressed his negative opinions in colorful but private invective, Jones habitually broadcast his vitriol. He both offended and infuriated Milo Perkins, who regrettably struck back in kind. Provoked largely by Perkins, so did Wallace, with little more circumspection. After several public skirmishes, the open warfare between two of his subordinates, a circumstance Roosevelt would not tolerate, led to the President's decision in June 1943 to abolish BEW. He transferred its functions to a new superagency, the Office of Economic Warfare, and appointed to the chairmanship of the body Leo Crowley, whose ability to flatter the President and to placate Congress considerably exceeded his taste for reform or his personal probity. Perkins left the government. Wallace remained, his authority and status severely diminished, his spirit undeterred.

* * *

Wallace's "Century of the Common Man," a major address he delivered in May 1942, set forth themes which he repeated and elaborated for the next several years. They grew out of his previous ideas, some partially formed even in his youth, and they foreshadowed the disagreements between him and others in government during his last year in office. Yet his speeches, book, and articles said less about his precise objectives than did his diary, and his written words communicated his purpose only in the context of the actual issues to which he adverted daily. Each theme he associated with the century of the common man had hard correlatives in the questions that occupied wartime Washington.

Peace, the essential first condition for the future of mankind, meant different things to different Americans during World War II. For Wallace, the establishment and preservation of peace demanded a true internationalism, a world community of nations and peoples linked economically and politically through the agency of a United Nations. His vision included his familiar convictions about trade and economics, and his expectations for the economic development of underdeveloped areas along the lines that BEW drew. As he saw it, with the end of the war the United Nations would assume the bulk of that task. It would first have to concentrate on the restoration of areas devastated by war, a function which devolved before the end of hostilities to the United Nations Relief and Rehabilitation Administration. An enthusiast for that agency, Wallace recognized that it had to rely in its early work primarily on American resources, for the United States alone of the great nations was emerging from the war with an ebullient economy. But Wallace believed that American wealth should not give the United States a proportionate influence either in UNRRA or within the United Nations. Those agencies, in his opinion, had to bend to multilateral direction and to serve multinational interests.

The internationalizing of responsibility for providing nourishment, relief, and development throughout the world depended upon political internationalism, which Wallace stressed. It could eventuate only with the end of European imperialism and with the abandonment of balance-of-power politics. On that account, he was especially critical of the British, particularly Winston Churchill. Continued British domination over India, in Wallace's understanding, violated the whole purpose of the war, as did Churchill's impulse for empire, his unabashed belief in Anglo-Saxon superiority, his disdain for China and distrust of Russia, his preference for secret negotiations, and his manifest intention to hold the reins of world leadership, whatever the semblance of world government, in British, American, and, unavoidably, Soviet hands.

Roosevelt, too, expected the great powers to dominate the UN and enjoyed and exploited his secret conferences either alone with Churchill or in the larger company that included Stalin. But the President seemed to Wallace to share his anti-imperialism and even some of his other doubts about the British. So also, Roosevelt was determined to get along with the Russians. Further he was as emphatic as was Wallace in calling for the withdrawal of British and European, as well as

Japanese, political influence in East and Southeast Asia. They looked forward there not to American encroachments but to the independence, in most instances after a period of transition, of the various Asian peoples. In the case of China, as they both realized, Chiang Kai-shek could expect to rule only if he cleared out the corruption of the Kuomintang, embarked upon major social reform including distribution of land to the peasantry, and reached a modus operandi with his communist opponents, whose growing strength fed on the discontent his policies fostered.

Still, Roosevelt's concern for victory first and victory as fast as possible resulted in wartime decisions that struck Wallace as ominous for the future. The United States, Wallace believed, had to align itself unequivocally with the forces of democracy everywhere. On the ground of military expediency, Roosevelt did not. He authorized the negotiations and arrangements in North Africa and Italy that made notorious fascists the approved local agents of Anglo-American occupation. The State and War Departments nurtured those policies which Wallace came privately to oppose.

Wallace also parted with the President, though without public or private acrimony, over the question of the peace-keeping role of the United Nations. Roosevelt talked in general terms about a postwar international police force to prevent aggression, but while the fighting continued, he deliberately postponed serious consideration of the nature and structure of such a force. Indeed he seemed often to regard it as a convenient substitute for the positioning of American units abroad. Further, he was too busy with grand strategy to give time to detailed postwar planning. More important, he did not want predictable British, American, and Russian disagreements about postwar policies to impede the functioning of the wartime alliance. He sensed, too, that the Congress and the American people were loath to approve much more than the principles of international organization, and he dreaded a divisive domestic debate that might generate the kind of opposition to a United Nations that had defeated Woodrow Wilson's League of Nations. Roosevelt had not wholly decided about his course. He did expect after victory rapidly to withdraw American forces from Europe and Asia. He had no apparent sympathy for postwar American military adventures overseas. Yet his announced descriptions of postwar world organization, at best opaque, appeared to presume a political stability founded on a balance of influence among the strong.

Wallace for his part advocated wartime planning for a United Nations that would exercise responsibility for peace and for disarmament.

Like Undersecretary of State Sumner Welles, he saw regional agreements as a necessary foundation for the larger mandate of the UN. Regionalism, as he later admitted, could provide a cloak for spheres of influence—of the United States in the Americas, of the Soviet Union in eastern Europe, and of the British, French, and Chinese in areas of their traditional concern. But he counted on the United Nations to prevent regionalism from becoming colonialism. Further, to estop aggression of any sort he advocated endowing the United Nations with its own army and air force, and with authority to impose economic sanctions.

He contemplated a degree of surrender of national sovereignty to an international body larger by far than was acceptable to any but an insignificant few in high offices in any of the governments of the major partners in the war against the Axis. Indeed few Americans who understood Wallace's purpose fully supported it. The senior members of the State Department especially looked upon his proposals as fanciful. So did the senior Democrats in the Senate, while the Republican leadership was even more chary of international commitments. For those critics, as for most of their constituents, peace, in whatever international garment, implied primarily "freedom from fear"—from threats to the security of the United States. That security was to be assured essentially by American power alone or in willing alliance with demonstrably trustworthy friends. As Wallace realized, from that position the step was short to unilateral American adventurism undertaken in the name of peace.

* * *

As in international, so in domestic policies, Wallace by 1944 had advanced well beyond the consensus of the American people and their congressional representatives.[24] That gap reflected their conservatism, for Wallace, by no means alone in the forward sector, had not departed from the traditional objectives of American reform movements or the growing body of economic doctrine of the time.

The bases for the political democracy that Wallace associated with his century of the common man were so conventionally American that he did not need to spell them out. The nuances of his speeches and the thrusts of his activities indicated that he meant by political dem-

[24] Compare the Wallace Diary with the analysis of public opinion in Jerome S. Bruner, *Mandate from the People* (New York, 1944) and the analysis of congressional roll calls in Roland Young, *Congressional Politics in the Second World War* (New York, 1956); see also Richard Polenberg, *War and Society: The United States 1948–1945* (Philadelphia, 1972).

ocracy representative government, universal suffrage, and the civil liberties guaranteed by the Constitution of the United States. Those conditions did not wholly obtain during the years of World War II. He worried particularly about the distortions of representation that resulted from the disfranchisement of blacks in the South, from the power of Democratic machines in the North (Chicago especially bothered him), and from the influence that wealthy individuals and corporations exerted on Congress and on some executive agencies. He also despised the redbaiting techniques of the Dies Committee in the House and the McKellar Committee in the Senate. Obsessed with fears about radicals, those committees, reckless in their accusations, bullied the witnesses they disliked. Again and again in his diary Wallace expressed his own reservations about "Communists" or "reds," but in his distress about the tactics of the witch-hunters in Congress and the FBI, he constantly also expressed a discriminating opposition to professional anticommunists.

Only men with the truncated mentality of Dies or McKellar could discover, as they did, sinister and radical tendencies in Wallace's ideas about economic democracy. Wallace simply incorporated his understanding of wartime developments into his long-standing proposals for promoting and distributing an economy of abundance. The experience of the war provided a telling verification of the theories of John Maynard Keynes and his American interpreters and disciples. The enormous federal deficits of the war years spurred private investment and employment, and achieved at last the full recovery that had eluded the New Deal. To Wallace, as to the Keynesians he regularly saw, it was patent that properly managed federal fiscal policy could sustain prosperity in the postwar years. Accordingly he believed, with Roosevelt, in the ability of the government to establish and preserve the conditions that would provide sixty million jobs, a figure that seemed outrageously high in 1944 to the adherents of conventional economics. In order to achieve that goal, as Wallace understood, the government had systematically to employ experts to study the economy and its performance, and to make continual recommendations about federal fiscal and monetary policies to sustain maximum employment. To that end he supported each of the series of bills introduced by Senator Murray of which the last was passed, after revisions, as the Employment Act of 1946.

The long years of depression had whetted the interest of all Americans, however much they disagreed about means, in achieving an economy of plenty. Americans, however, disagreed profoundly about how and to whom to allocate shares of prosperity. Debates about the particular aspects of that general question proceeded through the war years. After the Democratic reverses in the elections of 1942, a coalition of Republicans and southern Democrats controlled congressional decisions. While that coalition tried, with considerable success, to roll back the New Deal, the President accepted most of the defeats his policies suffered without more than token protest. Eager for the support of the conservative coalition for his military and foreign policies, he deferred battle over domestic issues. "Dr. New Deal," Roosevelt told the press, had been succeeded by "Dr. Win-the-War." Depressed by the resulting situation, Henry Morgenthau commented that he could put all the remaining New Dealers in his own bathtub. He exaggerated. There was in Washington a group of young liberal Keynesians who were eagerly planning a new postwar New Deal. They had the significant cooperation of the leadership of the CIO and the Farmers' Union. In the Senate they had influential friends like Claude Pepper of Florida and Robert Wagner of New York. And they had visible champions in high office, of whom Wallace was the most senior in rank and most articulate in speech. His program for economic democracy reflected their thinking, as well as his own.

As he had for so long, Wallace during the war combated the power of big business. In the continuing struggle for control of the War Production Board, he sided with Donald Nelson, a protector of small industry, against Ferdinand Eberstadt, the ingenious investment banker who represented the preferences of the armed services and their corporate allies.[25] Increasingly in 1943 and thereafter, Wallace also consulted the lawyers in the antitrust division of the Justice Department, serious young attorneys who were frustrated by the President's suspension of antitrust proceedings at a time when bigness was growing rapidly. With them, Wallace attacked American corporate giants that had been (and would again be) associated with international cartels, and, like them, he searched for ways to revise the patent laws so as to prevent monopolies based on patent rights, especially patents developed at large cost to the federal government. He was not anti-business but anti-bigness; he was not an opponent of capitalism but a proponent of competition.

So, too, Wallace allied himself with the workers against their employers. He had earlier applauded the success of the CIO in using collective bargaining to increase the share of labor in corporate profits.

[25] See Bruce Catton, *The War Lords of Washington* (New York, 1948), chap. 10 ff.

Unions, he believed, would have to function to that end after the war. Though he deplored wartime strikes that retarded production, he recognized the validity of many of the demands of the strikers and he opposed congressional efforts to punish union labor and its leadership. Supporting Roosevelt, Wallace also advocated holding down wartime agricultural prices so as to prevent inflation from eroding the gains in income that labor had achieved. To his satisfaction, the strength of the unions, the impact of wage and price controls, and the incidence of wartime taxes resulted during the war years in a significant redistribution of income favorable to working men and women.

Wallace stood behind other programs to assist industrial and agricultural workers. He advocated federal support for education, especially in technical and scientific subjects, so as to make learning available to qualified candidates who could not otherwise afford it. He praised the proposals of the National Resources Planning Board (an agency which congressional conservatives dissolved out of spite) and of the Social Security Administration for postwar increases in old age and unemployment benefits, and for postwar extension of coverage to millions of Americans then still outside of the social security system. Eager to improve the delivery of health care within the United States, he commended the program Henry Kaiser had devised for the collective care of workers employed by his firms. Wallace applauded, too, the less adventurous but still controversial plan of the Social Security Administration to include medical insurance within its province. "Socialized medicine," as the American Medical Association called it with characteristic imprecision, stirred up so much opposition that Roosevelt would not attach his prestige to a Treasury measure sponsoring it. He could not, the President argued, take on the AMA in the middle of a great war. Wallace could and did, as did Bob Wagner and the other authors of the unsuccessful Wagner-Murray-Dingell bill for revising social security to encompass medical insurance.

For Wallace, then, economic democracy directly affected the common man. It would increase national income by utilizing fiscal policy to encourage economic growth and antitrust policy to discourage monopolistic restraints on production. It would increase the share of the common man in national income. It would also provide him with protection against the trials of unemployment, old age, and illness. Taken together, those purposes constituted what Roosevelt meant by "freedom from want." Taken together, they also constituted what Wallace's critics called either communism or socialism or the welfare state. They were anathema to the still formidable number of businessmen and their lawyers, accountants, and clerks who believed, in spite of all that had happened since 1929, in something they called "the American system," by which they meant the political economy of the Harding-Coolidge-Hoover years.

Wallace disturbed an equally large constituency by his advocacy of "genetic democracy," another major facet of his century of the common man. The phrase was peculiarly his own. His experiments in hybridizing corn had led him to an adjective for which most other men substituted "racial." He meant that and more. He urged equal opportunities for black Americans in voting, employment, and education, but he sought the same objectives for women of whatever color. Further, he envisaged in the not distant future equal political and economic opportunities for Asians and Latins, not only for American citizens. In the case of the Jews, he came before 1944 to agree with the Zionists that a prosperous and dignified future for European Jews, particularly after the ghastly experience of Nazi persecution, could materialize only in an independent Jewish state in the area of Palestine, then British-controlled. His were politically dangerous convictions. Even during a war against Nazism, most white Americans remained openly prejudiced against men and women of darker skins, most were uneasy about directly assisting European Jews, most were indifferent about the rights of women. Indeed Roosevelt disagreed with Wallace. The President had doubts about Zionism, little patience with militant women, and little respect for most women in public life. Further, he had condoned the incarceration of the Japanese-Americans, and he had erected a bureaucratic barrier of personal aides to spare him from having to listen to the legitimate demands of American blacks. Wallace's genetic democracy put him in a lonesome salient far out ahead of the army of American voters and of their elected commander.

He had a related vision still further from the American consensus. It was a prospect incomprehensible except to those few who shared Wallace's belief in the brotherhood of man, his faith in the experience of westering as an avenue to that brotherhood, and his conviction that commerce brought and held societies together. When first he met Molotov, he described to him, as he later did in print for American readers, a huge stretch of highways and airports reaching northward from the west coast of South America to Alaska and across the Bering Sea westward through Siberia to European Russia. Along that line he saw potentialities for a vibrant commerce. When he reflected about strategy in the Pacific, Wallace gave Alaska a high priority for defense, for he viewed Alaska as the last American frontier. But the larger frontier, the one he postulated for settlement and development in the late twentieth century, made Alaska only one part of a vast area that also included Soviet Asia and Mongolia. There he believed a commingling of peoples from America, Siberia, China, and Mongolia could build a new center of civilization, a center founded on agriculture, the commerce to sustain it, and the industry that would follow population and employ the extraordinary resources of the northern Pacific triangle. That prospect beguiled him before his visit to Soviet Asia and China. The observations he made on that trip, recorded in his diary and in his *Soviet Asia Mission*, confirmed his sense of the possibilities for realizing the prospect. The rivalries of international politics made it only a dream in 1944, but it was precisely those rivalries which Wallace believed had to be tempered and contained so that the century of the common man could begin in the northern Pacific as in all lands.

Wallace's beliefs provoked the opposition to his renomination that was virtually universal among Roosevelt's advisers and the Democratic party leadership. He knew they did not want him. He knew, too, that thousands of rank and file Democrats shared his kind of aspiration and supported his candidacy. But in 1944, as in 1940, he did not campaign. By default rather than by direction, he left his chances to a few friends who were almost as clumsy and uninfluential as they were ardent and dedicated. At Roosevelt's request, Wallace even left Washington for Asia during the critical weeks before the national convention. Again, as in 1940, he knew his presence or his activity made little difference. The decision about the nomination was the President's to make. And Roosevelt dropped him. The President's disingenuous remarks during their discussion of the nomination wounded Wallace at least as much as did the President's decision. Once he became aware of it, Wallace fought, too late and with too few allies, to hold his office, but he accepted defeat in good grace and campaigned hard for the ticket. That earned Roosevelt's gratitude and Wallace's nomination as Secretary of Commerce.

The episode confirmed Wallace's sense of the President's style. Eager to dominate yet reluctant to offend, Roosevelt hated to tell a loyal friend the simple truth when that truth was bound to hurt. Instead he fenced, he turned to humor, evasion, and half-truths. He would have been kinder in 1944 to tell Wallace the truth, for Wallace had the character to accept it. The truth was that the renomination of Wallace would probably have hurt the ticket. Wallace admitted as much in 1951 in conversation with an interviewer who asked him what would have happened if he had been renominated and then succeeded to the presidency after Roosevelt's death. "Anyone with my views," Wallace answered, "would have run into the most extraordinary difficulties . . . It would have been a terrific battle for control of public opinion . . . It's quite possible that I would not have been able to get the support of Congress."[26]

Indeed, it was quite probable, for the Senate, with the Democrats bitterly divided, in 1945 barely approved Wallace's appointment as Secretary of Commerce, and then only after stripping that office of the lending authority Jesse Jones had exercised. As for public opinion, in 1944, as Wallace realized, it was running against him. In his own retrospective assessment, the American people were "prosperous, fully employed, complacent." They were weary of controls, weary of shortages, eager for victory and for postwar security and personal comfort. They were not seeking new obligations, new causes, or strange adventures.[27] Accordingly they were uncomfortable with the implications of Wallace's century of the common man. In Wisconsin the voters had eliminated Wendell Willkie, Wallace's closest Republican counterpart, from the race for his party's nomination. Roosevelt, accepting the counsel of his advisers and of his own instincts, removed Wallace, who had taken positions the President was willing to have tested but, in the President's judgment, had failed the test. Wallace had said in 1940 that the question of his nomination was subordinate to the best interest of the party. In 1944 he had not changed his mind. Though he and his friends thought that his renomination would strengthen the ticket, he had to defer to Roosevelt's contrary conclusion. He would have found it more palatable if the President had been more candid.

* * *

After Roosevelt's death, Wallace remained in the Cabinet because he expected, as Secretary of Commerce, to initiate programs to expand both the American and the world economy, and because he hoped to exert a liberalizing influence within the government. As he confided in his diary, he did not trust the new President. Harry Truman, though his own record was clean, had ties to the corrupt Pendergast machine in Kansas City. His sponsors included men like Robert Hannegan and Edwin Pauley whose motives and methods Wallace sus-

26 Oral History, Henry A. Wallace, pp. 4566–4570, Oral History Project, Columbia University.
27 Ibid. and Bruner, *Mandate from the People.*

pected. Further, in Wallace's view Truman had followed a devious
course in winning the vice-presidential nomination. In time, Wallace
was to consider his suspicions confirmed. Where Roosevelt had been
engagingly disingenuous, Truman, in dealing with Wallace, became
transparently dishonest. But at first, though he did not much like
Wallace, the President was disarming. His apparent openness, his
earthiness, his self-effacing eagerness to master his new office and its
problems persuaded Wallace that they might be able to work together
productively.

They remained within reach of each other on domestic policies.
Truman approved Wallace's plans for reorganization of the Commerce
Department, though he kept Wallace off the governing board of the
Export-Import Bank. After some hesitation, the President gave his
full support to the employment bill. With less commitment than
Wallace, he also supported the continuation of the Office of Price
Administration and its efforts to retard inflation. He recommended
continuing wartime policies designed to provide equal employment
opportunities for blacks. He opposed Republican measures to cripple
labor unions, but he had limited sympathy for the postwar militancy
of the CIO, and he recommended punitive action against the railroad
brotherhoods when they walked out on strike. Recognizing his own
political weakness in labor circles, Truman, as he later disclosed, kept
Wallace in the Cabinet primarily to placate the unions. He listened to
Wallace's advice about labor issues and on occasion used him as an
emissary to CIO leaders. That role pleased Wallace, who also knew
that Truman as a senator had voted consistently for New Deal
measures. As President, he now urged Congress to expand social security, to provide for national medical insurance, and to increase
minimum wages. No more than Roosevelt could he be faulted for the
conservative coalition in Congress or for the yearning for "normalcy,"
so like the mood of the early 1920s, that infected so many Americans,
war veterans not the least.

To Wallace's growing disillusionment, however, the President acted
in a manner at variance with his rhetoric. It was not the conservatives
in Congress but Truman himself who altered the profile of the Cabinet.
Like any President, he naturally wanted his own men around him—
men loyal to him, not to the memory of FDR. But most of those he
chose struck Wallace, as they did others, as less able than their
predecessors, less liberal, and often meaner in personal and public
spirit. Wallace had never found James F. Byrnes, the new Secretary
of State, a sympathetic colleague. He had liked Henry Morgenthau
and valued his spontaneous enthusiasm for myriad good causes, but

after Morgenthau resigned, Fred Vinson and John Snyder, both personal friends of Truman, brought to the Treasury department a narrow view of both domestic and international issues. Wallace had had his problems with Harold Ickes, but he cheered Ickes' opposition to the nomination of Edwin Pauley, another Truman crony, as Assistant Secretary of the Navy. The Senate blocked that appointment, for Pauley's associations with the oil industry made the prospect of his control over Navy oil reserves ominous. Still, Ickes resigned, dubious as was Wallace about Truman's concern for the conservation policies Roosevelt had nurtured. Even more disheartening had been the President's earlier selection of Howard McGrath to replace Francis Biddle as Attorney General. A political hack from Rhode Island, McGrath filled the Justice Department with nonentities who vitiated the antitrust division that Biddle's men had energized. The incompetence as well as the permissiveness of many of the newcomers to the Justice and Treasury Departments led to the series of episodes of petty corruption that later gave Truman's cronies a deservedly shoddy reputation, one that hurt the President, too. Wallace, who saw government gradually losing its indispensable integrity before those scandals occurred, lamented equally the concurrent loss of constructive social purpose. The President's selection of associates, in Wallace's opinion, cost him much of his credibility.

The last of the New Dealers to remain in the cabinet, Wallace held on primarily because of his overriding concern about military and foreign policy. Truman let him stay in order to appease the restless liberal intellectuals and labor leaders. Wallace symbolized their hopes, and as long as he was there, though they might grumble about Truman, they were unlikely to desert him. Only slowly did Wallace learn that he was just a symbol, that he had no influence, that Truman from the outset had had no intention of taking his advice. The President let him talk, but he made him an outsider. As they moved apart from each other, Truman contributed to the ultimate separation by dissembling in what he told Wallace. Though Wallace would probably have dissented anyway, he could not be expected to understand, much less to approve, policies about which he was at least partially misinformed.[28]

28 The entire discussion in this section of the introduction rests primarily upon Wallace's Diary and Harry S. Truman, *Year of Decisions* (Garden City, 1955). On questions of military and foreign policies, I found particularly stimulating Walter La Feber, *America, Russia, and the Cold War, 1945–1966* (New York, 1967). Also useful was Thomas G. Patterson, ed., *Cold War Critics* (Chicago, 1971). For another informed but doctrinaire interpretation, see Norman D. Markowitz, *The Rise and Fall of the People's Century: Henry A. Wallace and American Liberalism, 1941–1948* (New York, 1973).

Still, the failure of communication between Truman and Wallace counted far less than did their fundamental disagreement about the role of the United States in world affairs. They started with different assumptions. The President and his closest advisers believed that national security depended upon military strength and position, on a large and poised strategic air force that could retaliate in the event of an attack, on the availability of safe bases from which both bombers and naval aircraft could operate, and on a large reserve army ready for quick mobilization. They were, in a sense, preparing for the war that had just ended, for defense against another blitzkrieg or another attack upon Pearl Harbor. They were fashioning a system of deterrence (before that word had become the vogue), a system to which the American monopoly of the atomic bomb gave unparalleled power. But there was no point in building that system of defense in the absence of an enemy. They identified the Soviet Union as that potential enemy. That identification rested on several premises. Those who made it considered Russian policy in Poland and in the eastern zone of Germany evidence of an expansionist purpose at least as extensive as were historic Russian ambitions in the Black and the Mediterranean seas. They tended to forget or to ignore the natural concern for their own security that the Russians felt, especially about Poland through which the Germans had attacked twice within one generation. They tended, too, to overlook the Russian need for reparations to replace capital equipment destroyed by war and unavailable from the United States in the absence of a credit which the State Department would not approve. Too, suspicions of the Soviet Union fed on American fears about communism as a doctrine and about Stalin as a dictator, as a mad and evil genius who quickly replaced Hitler in American demonology. The Soviet Union did intend to protect its interests as it defined them, but Truman's counselors exaggerated the dangers to the United States inherent in that intention. Truman's own tough talk to Molotov early in his presidency expressed his real opinion of the Soviet Union better than did his more placatory public pronouncements. And more and more the President accepted as fact the presumptions about a Soviet menace that were advanced with rising emphasis by Secretary of State Byrnes, Ambassador Averell Harriman, and their staffs.

Wallace proceeded from a different set of assumptions. National security, in his view, depended not on American arms but on a strong United Nations, on the abatement of international hostilities rather than the deployment of American forces, on comity, not deterrence. A large reserve army, a powerful strategic air force and navy, the bomb, and a global ring of American bases, he argued, served only to alarm the Soviet Union, obviously the only potential target for American strength. So alarmed, the Russians in their turn were bound to be hostile. It was not some demoniacal quality in Stalin or in communism, as Wallace saw it, but ancient Russian fears that accounted for their policies in eastern Europe. New anxieties about American encirclement would provoke them to an arms race that no nation could afford and the peace of the world might not survive.

As before, like some others in Washington, Wallace accepted the existence of spheres of influence as at least a temporary circumstance of the postwar period.[29] He did not expect the Soviet Union to intrude in Latin America, and he did not expect the United States to intrude in eastern Europe. Probably he underestimated the repression that accompanied Soviet domination; certainly he did so in 1947 and 1948. But at no time, his critics to the contrary, did Wallace condone repression by any nation. Rather, he believed that the elimination of international tension would, over time, lead both to a softening of Soviet foreign policy and a relaxation of police methods within areas of Soviet control. To encourage that relaxation he advocated more patience in diplomacy than Byrnes or Truman ordinarily displayed. He urged, too, energetic cultivation of Soviet-American commerce, first of all by the extension of a credit to Russia, exactly the policy Harriman and the State Department blocked. The establishment of a basis for trade, Wallace predicted, would serve the economic advantage of both nations and help gradually to convert suspicious hostility to tolerant rivalry between two different political and economic systems. He wholly expected the American system to prove its greater worth.

Truman's stance toward the Soviet Union was the most continual but by no means the only source of distress to Wallace. He worried, too, about relations with Great Britain, with Latin America, and with China, as well as about decisions affecting the control of the atomic bomb. With respect to China, he had no quarrel with Truman's attempt, unsuccessful though it was, to work out an accommodation between Chiang Kai-shek and the communists. In contrast to Truman, however, Wallace held that the presence and deployment of Soviet troops in Manchuria, which militated to the advantage of the Chinese communists, accorded with agreements between Roosevelt and Stalin. Still, Wallace and Truman agreed that the United States had done and was doing all it could for the Generalissimo; if he fell, the fault would be his.

They came close to agreement, too, about domestic control of

---

29 On that attitude in the early postwar period, see H. Stuart Hughes, "The Second Year of the Cold War," *Commentary*, August 1969, pp. 27–32.

atomic energy, though not about related international policy. Wallace, who had known from the beginning about the project to develop the atomic bomb, turned for advice about its control to the nuclear scientists who had created it. Informed by those physicists, whom he trusted as the experts in their field, he concluded that atomic weapons were far too destructive to be left to the control of the military. Too, the development of atomic science was far too important to be removed from control of the physicists. Wallace realized there was no secret about atomic energy. European scientists had played indispensable roles in the American project; the Germans and Japanese had built cyclotrons during the war; the Soviet Union, whose scientists were first-rate, had an atomic bomb within its reach if it was prepared to defray the enormous costs of making one. But the prospect of a nuclear arms race appalled Wallace. He envisaged instead the utilization of atomic energy as a source of power and a field of research, in both thrusts as a boon instead of a threat to mankind.

Those considerations accounted for his opposition to the May-Johnson bill which would have left the military with authority over American atomic development. With many of the nuclear scientists, with the essential assistance of Director of the Budget Harold Smith, and against the devious opposition of General Leslie Groves, Wallace encouraged the drafting and enactment of the McMahon bill. It provided, he felt, even after unfortunate amendments designed to mollify congressional saber-rattlers, acceptable assurances of civilian control over the domestic atomic energy program.

The McMahon Act could not guarantee that civilian authorities, the President included, would not yield to military counsel. In Wallace's opinion, many of them already had. Vannevar Bush had supported the May-Johnson bill, as for a time had other scientists and administrators of organized science including James B. Conant. Even Robert Oppenheimer had not enlisted against it, and until Harold Smith and others persuaded him to reconsider, Truman had gone along with Bush and thus with General Groves. In the end the President did exert his influence for the McMahon measure, but he accepted, with far more equanimity than did Wallace, the amendments to the bill that gave the military a stronger voice than most of the veterans of Los Alamos deemed safe or wise.

With too few exceptions to matter, congressmen felt a kind of panic at the thought of sharing the supposed secret of the bomb with any nation, especially with the Soviet Union. Yet science recognized no national borders. Passionately, therefore, Wallace advocated a policy of openness about American scientific information, as his communications to Truman and others disclosed. That policy would ease apprehensions about American intentions, a politically desirable eventuality. It would also avail people everywhere of knowledge with which they could harness atomic energy to build an abundant society. That view, close to the opinion of Secretary Stimson and a few others in the Cabinet, was neither radical nor irresponsible. The sharing of basic scientific information did not imply the disclosure of technical details about the production of fissionable materials or the triggering mechanism for an implosion weapon. But the sharing of basic scientific information seemed to the timid and the ignorant equivalent to the loss of a precious secret on which national security depended. So thought Secretary of the Navy James Forrestal. So thought enough congressmen and ultimately, with less intensity, the President himself, to limit American flexibility in approaching the issue.

Privately Truman concluded that Wallace's opinions about atomic policy were unsafe. He also took pains not to venture beyond what Congress would approve. He could not obtain that approval without Republican support, so in atomic, as in all foreign policy, he paid the high price of bipartisanship. At the least that price involved continual concessions to the outsized vanity of Senator Arthur Vandenberg, senior Republican on the Foreign Relations Committee. On that and other accounts, Truman found it necessary often to employ anticommunist rhetoric, which he seemed not to consider distasteful. Further, he drew back without any prodding from offering the Soviet Union anything, even basic scientific information that he could not long keep secret, without receiving in return something he felt he had been denied. In the case of atomic energy, he moved to circumvent the Soviet position on the use of the veto in the Security Council of the United Nations. The proposals that he had Bernard Baruch put forward in the UN were less liberal than the preliminary recommendations drafted by David Lilienthal and Dean Acheson, who was by no means soft in his view of Moscow. As Wallace complained, the Baruch plan, unlike Acheson's, eliminated the veto as it applied to questions of atomic energy while it also guaranteed for a decade American monopoly of atomic weapons, and offered the Soviet Union information only on the installment plan, with each installment conditional upon Soviet good behavior during the previous period. A proud and powerful nation, capable of mounting an atomic energy program on its own, was bound to reject the Baruch proposals. A more generous offer, Wallace believed, would have won Soviet trust and acceptance.

As he saw it, men like General Groves, Secretary Forrestal, and Baruch had infected American opinion and warped American policy. As for Truman, who had seemed to wobble for months, he struck Wallace, as he did Eleanor Roosevelt, as a weak and vacillating man.

By Wallace's standards, the President also appeared cynical. Truman looked upon Latin America as a counter in the game of world politics. To hold the nations to the south to a hemispheric coalition dominated by the United States, the President through his spokesmen at San Francisco arranged the admission of Argentina, then manifestly a fascist country, to the UN. That maneuver aroused the suspicions of the Soviet Union, which had been no less cynical in its role in the politics of the conference. It also presaged the meretricious manner of the State Department in Latin American relations—the appointment of ambassadors content to cooperate with the conservative forces of the military, the church, and the large landholders; the arming of those governing coalitions which used the weapons they received to stifle opposition; the abandonment of the objectives the Board of Economic Warfare had advanced. Wallace had seen Latin America as the first beneficiary of the policies he advocated for the common man. Now he watched the President and State Department revert to the neocolonialism of the 1920s, to a policy pitched to the alleged needs of national defense and the palpable advantage of American investors, a policy impervious to the woeful conditions of daily life which he believed the United States had an obligation to mitigate.

Wallace also interpreted as cynical Truman's early approach to the Palestine question. Disinclined to alienate Great Britain, the President yielded to London's anxieties about placating the Arabs and protecting British control in the Middle East. The definition of Palestine's borders and the limits on Jewish immigration on which British and American negotiators first agreed left Palestine too small and weak for economic development or military security, and left thousands of displaced European Jews without access to a permanent home. Wallace, who urged Truman to demand a solution more favorable to the Jews, played on the President's political sensitivities. British convenience and prospects for American oil investments in the Middle East came gradually to count less with Truman than did the Jewish vote. But Wallace had meanwhile concluded that the President had little more humane concern for the Jews of Europe than for the impoverished in Latin America. He also considered the President's original position on Palestine as typifying an unfortunate course of American relations with Great Britain.

That issue disturbed Wallace as much as did any other. He admired the heroic role of the British common people in their resistance to the Nazis. But like so many Middle Western democrats, he despised the British upper classes for their haughty manner and their arrogance about race, national origin, and social position. Further, he blamed them for British imperialism, which he wished to eradicate. On that account he distrusted Churchill, alike for his aristocratic ways and his imperialistic sentiments, so freely expressed whenever the Prime Minister visited Washington. Even after the election of a Labor government, Wallace feared that Great Britain would remain Churchillian in purpose, would continue to hold the uncritical affection of Anglophiles in the Department of State, and would induce the United States to assume a partnership in world politics. He had trusted Roosevelt to resist that role, but Truman was more vulnerable to British influence, partly because he shared Churchill's fear of Russia, partly because among his closest advisers were men like Dean Acheson, who characteristically associated American with British interests.

From April 1945, when Roosevelt died, through the remainder of the year, Wallace grew more and more restive with the international policies of the administration. Increasingly he realized that Truman in private conversations gave him assurances that the President's public actions contradicted. Still Wallace allowed himself to hope that Truman might change. During 1946 he lost that hope. The Baruch plan alarmed him. So did the hard line toward the Soviet Union that Averell Harriman advanced upon his return from Moscow to Washington, the tough policy that Secretary of State Byrnes pursued in his negotiations with the Russians, the tough talk of State Department Russian specialists like Charles Bohlen and George Kennan. They read Stalin's monitory address of February 9, 1946, as a trumpet of hostility, of communist militancy and Russian expansionism. Wallace read it as a regrettably inimical response to threats that Stalin perceived in his exaggerated interpretation of American policy. According to that reading, there was still room for reciprocal understanding. But then at Fulton, Missouri, with Truman on the platform, Churchill delivered his celebrated "iron curtain" speech, that called for a fraternal alliance of the English-speaking people. It was precisely the alliance Wallace most opposed. Involving, as it did, the fading grandeur of the British empire and the implicit threat of the atomic bomb, it was addressed aggressively against the Soviet Union. It portended the rejection of spheres of influence in Europe that had been defined by the deployment of troops at the end of the war. It invited Anglo-American penetration of the

Soviet sphere. Speaking at Stuttgart, Germany, in September, Secretary of State Byrnes sounded the first notes of that new policy which would gradually make the United States the catalyst, initially in the economic and later in the military reconstruction of West Germany as a part of a larger anti-Soviet bloc.

There were provocations, as Wallace knew, for Byrnes' address. The Soviet Union had permitted no democracy in the areas it ruled; it had seized German industrial equipment and commandeered German labor in its eastern zone; it had broken promises made at Yalta and at Potsdam; it had disregarded human rights in Poland and elsewhere in eastern Europe; it had been intransigent in preventing a common policy for occupied Germany as a whole. But the United States had been intransigent, too, in its unilateral control over occupied Japan, in its deployment of strategic air power, in its manipulations in Latin America. American occupation authorities in Japan had wantonly destroyed the Japanese cyclotron. Washington officials, while denying a credit to Russia, had arranged one for Great Britain, possibly on harder terms to the Labor government than they would have extended to the Tories.

Politically and ideologically, the world had begun to polarize by September 1946. Wallace's hopes were evaporating for the kind of world he had associated with a century of the common man. At Madison Square Garden on September 12, he tried again to put his message across, to warn against Churchill's proposals and to urge another approach to the Soviet Union. He criticized alike British imperial and Russian political practices, and the communists in the audience booed him, for he was pleading not for Russia but for peace. Truman, who had read and approved the speech, disavowed it after Wallace's opponents opened fire and Byrnes and Vandenberg insisted that the speech impeded their diplomacy at the ongoing conference of foreign ministers. On Truman's order, Wallace promised to speak no more until that conference was over. But that tenuous arrangement only postponed the obvious solution. Byrnes, dissatisfied, demanded that Truman fire Wallace, and Truman did. The President had, after all, issued the directions Byrnes was following. As Wallace and Truman both knew, there could be at any one time only one American foreign policy. Once the issue was openly joined, Wallace had to go.

* * *

Though Truman's administrative decision was incontestably correct, his foreign policy was not. Like his critics at the time, so critics since have questioned both his presumptions and his tactics. Wallace was only one of the first to do so. In the absence of access to the Soviet archives, there can be no sure assessment of Wallace's case. American provocations may only have confirmed fixed Soviet decisions about postwar policy. But provocations there certainly were, as Wallace argued. At least until the time of Fulton, the possibility existed of a practical accommodation between the United States and the Soviet Union, of a temporary coexistence of mutually suspicious spheres of influence, of a gradual lessening of hostility and a gradual movement, as Wallace recommended, first toward commercial and scientific and then toward political cooperation, all within the framework of the United Nations. Even after the Fulton speech, the United States could have assisted the countries of the Southern Hemisphere more on an altruistic and less on a political basis. American records, easy of access, disclose that Truman never expected a rapprochement with the Soviet Union. Wallace had reason to disagree. He had the prescience to realize that the hard line abroad would generate hysterical reactions to dissent at home, lead to the postponement of urgent domestic reforms, and encourage military adventures costly alike of men and morale. He had the foresight to propose alternatives to which the United States government turned only after a quarter century of terrible waste had made accommodation more attractive to most of the American people.

Yet in the months immediately following his departure from public office, Wallace's insights were cloudy. As his fears about Truman's policies grew, so did his vulnerability to those who were urging him to run for the presidency on a third party ticket.[30] He was tempted to embark on that unhappy course on several counts. Out of government, he was removed from the councils of state to which he had often contributed and from which he had often also learned. He was removed, too, from easy access to the kinds of experts who had given him such influential assistance in earlier years, for one example in the making of agricultural policies. He had to rely instead more on his intuitions and hopes than on hard data and salient technical knowledge. Further, those who now advised him lacked the experience and judgment of his former counselors. Many of the men in the group around him were naive; some were eager to use him to advance their own interests; none had much political insight. Yet their pressure moved

[30] Wallace kept no diary after he left office. Further, there is no wholly satisfactory study of his role during the years 1946–48 or of the Progressive Party, for his papers for that period have not been available. One useful brief account and another compendious one are respectively Karl M. Schmidt, *Henry A. Wallace: Quixotic Crusade 1948* (Syracuse, 1960) and Curtis D. MacDougall, *Gideon's Army*, 3 vols. (New York, 1965). The sympathies of the latter imbue Markowitz, *The Rise and Fall of the People's Century*.

Wallace less than did his own temperament. Believing that Truman was leading the country and the world toward war, committed to a contrary view of the new century, Wallace disregarded the warnings of his family and old friends and followed his own compulsion to stand political witness to his faith.

In his eagerness to find a rapprochement with the Soviet Union, he blinded himself to the mounting evidence of Russian tyranny in eastern Europe. In his determination to resist redbaiting, he became indifferent to the debilitating tactics of communists within his Progressive Party of 1948. For several years, his passion overcame his practicality.

Even so, he remained perceptive. Long an advocate of American assistance in the rebuilding of the European economy, he urged employing international agencies to administer aid programs and granting aid exclusively on social and economic rather than political bases. Those considerations led him to underestimate the responsibility of the Soviet Union for keeping eastern Europe out of the Marshall Plan. Earlier, however, he had protested against the Truman Doctrine and its applications in Greece and Turkey. As Wallace then said, that doctrine ignored and weakened the United Nations, substituted unilateral for multilateral aid, and gave military assistance unfortunate priority over economic assistance. Worse, the anticommunist rhetoric of the doctrine expressed a universal commitment to antirevolutionary interventions. As Wallace foresaw, both the precedent and the rhetoric had ominous portents.

Indeed Wallace's fundamental trepidations about American policy, all of them prominent before he left office, had become by the early 1970s common criticisms of the history of the interceding years. The collusion of the military with those industrial interests that depended upon defense expenditures had resulted in enormous waste and bureaucratic inefficiency. The military-industrial establishment against which Dwight D. Eisenhower warned his countrymen in 1961 had worried Wallace two decades earlier. Indeed the military, as Americans learned by 1970, had proved unable to maintain the standards of financial probity and disciplined warfare on which professional soldiers liked to pride themselves. Unilateral military intervention, as Wallace had feared, had become something of a national habit, with the war in Vietnam only the most recent and most dreadful example of the corrupting dangers of American adventurism. Too, war and preparation for war, deterrence and its cost, balance-of-power politics with their related expenditures—even bribes—for the purchase of allies, had debilitated the UN and absorbed national income needed for domestic social programs, the very programs Wallace had urged for relief of poverty, conservation of the land and its resources, education of the young, the delivery of health care, and the protection of the aged. The inversion of national priorities, attacked in 1968 by Eugene McCarthy and Robert Kennedy and in 1972 by George McGovern, had drawn Wallace's criticisms in 1942.

In other ways also Wallace proved prescient, a man far ahead of his times, as he had so often been. After the revolution in Cuba, Washington recognized Latin America again as a continent full of people, not just a reservation for private investment and seductive military aid. The Alliance for Progress that John F. Kennedy launched in 1961 had as its social targets precisely those of the Board of Economic Warfare. Even Richard Nixon discovered what Wallace had always maintained, that communist ideology did not constitute an insuperable hurdle to communication. In 1971 Nixon went to China, which he had condemned as demoniacal for more than two decades, and in 1972 to Moscow, there to suggest that the encouragement of commerce between the Soviet Union and the United States would benefit both nations and ease their political relationship. For saying such things Wallace had been called a red or at least a pink from 1946 through 1948, as were others of his opinion, with Nixon one of their most fervent accusers.

The irony of history should have restored Wallace's reputation, but in the early 1970s he was still remembered more for his occasional fallibility than for his extraordinary foresight. Three decades earlier he had imagined a splendid century which still had yet convincingly to begin. He would have welcomed a century of the common man, as he welcomed the New Deal, whenever it began. He would have lost none of his verve for administering the agencies to promote it, shed none of his worries about the persisting impediments to it, surrendered none of his zeal for opposing the enemies of it. While he found armor for his missions in his faith, while he preached his best hopes, Henry A. Wallace sought their fulfillment less in his message than in the hard labor of learning and doing. By his works, he believed, practical Christian that he was, men would know him.

In his works they would find a good man.

I
The Board of
Economic Warfare

February 1942 — July 1943

1

The Board of
Economic Warfare

February 1942 – July 1943

THIS SECTION of the diary of Henry A. Wallace begins, as it ends, on the continual controversy over the Board of Economic Warfare, of which he was chairman. That controversy involved him in a struggle for authority with both Jesse H. Jones, the Secretary of Commerce and head of the major federal lending agencies, and Cordell Hull, the Secretary of State. At one level the struggle was a bureaucratic contest, characteristic of Washington during Roosevelt's administrations. Wallace, an experienced infighter, had been through similar battles before, for example with Harold Ickes over control of the Forest Service. Now again he had to defend his authority, which was exercised primarily by Milo Perkins, director of the BEW, from Jones' deliberate foot-dragging in making loans for the procurement of vital commodities abroad, and from Hull's insistence on State Department supervision over American nonmilitary activities in foreign nations. Jones and Hull, for their part, viewed Wallace and his associates as intruders in their domains.

At another level, the Board of Economic Warfare operated as Wallace's particular instrument for the vigorous prosecution of the war. He would not have fought for authority as he did had he not believed that the BEW was providing essential services to the country, particularly in arranging to procure scarce commodities, but also in other activities relating to export controls and to the identification of industrial targets for aerial bombardment. Jones' dilatory and parsimonious habits, annoying in themselves, became significant for the nation, as Wallace saw it, because they delayed the essential stockpiling that the BEW was understaking. So, too, the State Department's constraints on overseas personnel had similar effects.

Even more important, Wallace disagreed with his antagonists about the desirable nature of the postwar world. Their behavior, he felt, interfered with his efforts to construct a thriving and equitable postwar international economy. He and his agency, in contrast to the Departments of State and Commerce, were eager to use the contracts they negotiated, especially in Latin America, to raise the standards of working and living of agricultural and other laborers. The increased costs paid off immediately in increased efficiency and permanently in a more democratic social order.

Economic democracy, democracy among the races, and political democracy—all to be shared by all men everywhere—constituted the goals Wallace defined in his speech of March 8, 1942, on the century of the common man (see Appendices). He repeated and rephrased those goals in several important speeches thereafter, including his address in Detroit in July 1943 at the time this section ends. The pursuit of those goals and their corollary policies, such as freedom for all nations in the use of the air, occupied Wallace's attention during the entire period of the fight over the BEW. That pursuit led him, too, to the conclusions he drew during the same period about the dangers of British imperialism, the need for postwar cooperation with the Soviet Union, the failures of American policy in North Africa, and the drift toward conservatism in American domestic politics.

For Wallace, all those issues were related, all bore upon the conduct of the war and the nature of the peace. All, for him, including the control of the Board of Economic Warfare and the extent of its authority, were essentially matters not of bureaucratic politics but of fundamental principle. The significance of the stakes, as he defined them, pervaded the episodes of the struggle.

HENRY A. WALLACE TO FRANKLIN D. ROOSEVELT

Dear Mr. President: [1]

. . . We have a few competent people in the Board of Economic Warfare working on postwar problems and recently we have gotten the help of Alvin Hansen and Winfield Riefler[2] on an international ever-normal granary program. We have very little faith, however, in how effective it will be to present ideas of this sort to a peace conference.

Our feeling is that we are writing the postwar world as we go along and that we need some of the RFC powers now to do a good job of it. Those powers can be used to get in raw materials from abroad more aggressively than they have been used in the past. The administrative machinery thus set up to help win the war will be the most effective economic means through which we can win the peace later on. Without labeling it as such, we can thereby get an international ever-normal granary functioning long before we ever come to an armistice.

[1] Wallace occasionally included among the papers of his diary letters which he considered particularly important. This letter and the several that follow it were of that kind. They made the case, which he also pressed in conversations with the President, for administrative changes intended to increase the authority and independence of the Board of Economic Warfare.

As the letters reveal, Wallace was eager to become his own banker so as to escape the slow and often obdurate responses of Jesse Jones to BEW requests for loans for stockpiling. Further, Wallace wanted his subordinates in the field freed from the need to report to American ambassadors or ministers who tended to reflect the characteristic inflexibilities of the State Department. Those changes, Wallace believed, would significantly enhance his ability to create and regularly replenish stockpiles of critical war materials. He had in mind as a model the "ever-normal granary" which he had built up from domestic production in the prewar years and which in 1942 was proving to be an indispensable source of food supplies for the United States and its allies.

[2] Alvin H. Hansen and Winfield Riefler, able economists, served continually as advisers to various federal agencies during the New Deal and the Second World War. Hansen was in his time probably the most influential American advocate of Keynesian principles, and Riefler was perhaps the most distinguished economist of those who worked at any time for the Board of Economic Warfare.

I have given a great deal of thought to this matter following our recent luncheon and have come to the conclusion that we had better not ask you at this time for an outright transfer of the Export-Import Bank together with certain foreign purchase functions of the Federal Loan Agency. Rather, I think it would be less difficult if we set up a new International Supplies and Development Corporation to be administered by the Board of Economic Warfare. An executive order to accomplish this has been drawn and has been cleared by the Department of Justice as to its legality. If you approve this, the Federal Loan Agency could then concentrate on domestic rather than foreign activities . . .

MARCH 4, 1942

HENRY A. WALLACE TO FRANKLIN D. ROOSEVELT

Dear Mr. President:

The Board of Economic Warfare was set up to manage the flow of goods from this country to other nations and from other nations to us. Unfortunately, there is a great deal of administrative confusion in getting the job done, particularly on the import side. A summary follows: . . .

The Old Federal Loan Agency

There is a basic conflict of principles between their banker-minded approach and our goods-minded approach to getting in more raw materials from abroad. It takes weeks to get action that should be gotten in a day or two. (e.g.—quinine, opium, and Portuguese tungsten.) We feel that we are ineffective without a checkbook and that even at this late date we can do more than is now being done. Public indignation over raw material shortages will be at white heat by fall; our government cannot escape some of the blame for our small stockpiles but a bold administrative change now might ward off some of the blows later on. On the other hand, such a move might make it more difficult to withstand criticism. You alone can decide.

The State Department

Our relations with them blow hot and cold but are better on the whole than they were last fall. State plans a balance-of-power game with other agencies and our difficulties with them in connection with raw materials problems have been mostly jurisdictional ones without any reference to principles.

War Production Board

Our relations are excellent. Don Nelson and Bill Batt[1] have repeatedly indicated that they want us to be responsible for increasing production of raw materials abroad. Don Nelson favors our running an International Supplies and Development Corporation to achieve this, if you agree.

Straight Economic Warfare

The Army and Navy are making increased use of our facilities for the mapping of bombing objectives[2] and those for the analysis of the enemy war potential as well as that of the United Nations. We have close day-to-day relations with the British Ministry of Economic Warfare and in conjunction with State Department have just sent two men to London to coordinate their navicert system with our export control system as it applies to trade with European neutrals. We are also sending small groups, which include engineers, to help nations like India step up industrial production within their own countries with a minimum investment of capital goods from this country.

Recommendations

Administrative responsibility for handling exports and imports and all their related problems of economic warfare should be placed in one accepted spot. We think the Board of Economic Warfare is staffed to do an aggressive job. It would make for efficiency if the Lend-Lease Administration were placed under its jurisdiction. The same reasoning applies to the foreign lending and purchase functions of the old Federal Loan Agency, although a more tactful approach might be to authorize us to run an International Supplies and Development Corporation. Centralized authority on the foreign front is as necessary as that which you have brought about under Don Nelson on the domestic front . . .

MARCH 20, 1942

HENRY A. WALLACE TO FRANKLIN D. ROOSEVELT

Dear Mr. President:

The proposed order which Harold Smith [3] and I discussed with you

[1] Donald M. Nelson and William L. Batt, respectively chairman and vice chairman of the War Production Board.

[2] Within the BEW, the Office of Economic Warfare Analysis under William T. Stone had the responsibility for selecting enemy industrial targets for aerial attacks.

[3] Budget Director Harold D. Smith, sympathetic to Wallace's plans for BEW, was because of the duties of his office and the qualities of his mind one of the

Tuesday affects our relations with the State Department in three respects. Here is a summary for your use when you see Mr. Welles:[1]

1. *Negotiation of Lend-Lease agreements.* The new draft will be
revised so as to eliminate the provision for "joint" negotiation of Lend-
Lease agreements. Instead, the order will provide that such agreements
will be negotiated by the State Department upon the advice and recommendation of the new agency.

2. *Taking State Department out of economic work on raw materials.*
The State Department now has a unit working on preclusive purchases,
raw materials procurement, expanded production abroad, and shipping.
Tom Finletter[2] heads this work and has been doing an excellent job
considering the limitations under which he has been working. If the
order is signed, we shall try to persuade Finletter and his group to join
our staff. There would seem to be no necessity for absorbing the unit
in the order itself, however, in view of the way in which you plan to
handle the matter.

3. *Sending development personnel abroad.* This will be the very
heart of our new functions. We need engineers and technicians out in
the field. They must be aggressive operators who will wake up every
morning with action ideas on how to step up production.

They must do their day-to-day work away from the bankers and
the diplomats in foreign capitals. They belong out in the country
where the raw materials are being produced. We can clear such personnel with State before they leave the country and have them check
in at the embassies on arrival, but they must be *administratively responsible* to us. This seems utterly obvious, but State may object and thereby
hamper this work as they have hampered it in the past. If we can bring
State around on this point, it will strengthen our war effort enormously . . .

MARCH 25, 1942
HENRY A. WALLACE TO FRANKLIN D. ROOSEVELT

Dear Mr. President:

Supplementing the letter which I gave you following cabinet meeting last Friday, March 20, I am suggesting that as background to be
emphasized with Undersecretary Welles in connection with the specific
points, you stress the following general point of view:

---

foremost of Washington officials in his understanding and mastery of federal
administration.

[1] Undersecretary of State Sumner Welles, a close adviser to Roosevelt and a
continuing object of the hostility and jealousy of Secretary of State Hull.

[2] Thomas K. Finletter, then special adviser to the Secretary of State.

The need for extreme speed in getting strategic raw materials for which Don Nelson is holding the Board of Economic Warfare responsible is such that the BEW must act with the greatest speed possible. The State Department should be informed at all times of action taken by the BEW but should not be in position of giving its specific approval before action can be taken.

From the standpoint of the State Department itself, it is better both from the viewpoint of the personnel in the field and in Washington that it move on a higher level than that which is involved in the economic melée. Let the State Department negotiate the master agreements with the advice of the BEW but let the State Department be in position to say that the responsibility for the economic action rests with the BEW. The State Department can act much more effectively in its own true field if it passes the buck on questions of annoying details to those who are charged with handling the details.

The chief of our embassy or legation in a foreign country where we must get for Donald Nelson with all possible speed the maximum supply of critical raw materials, can be of inestimable help in furnishing political guidance to our engineering and business personnel. This engineering and business personnel should, however, be responsible to BEW rather than to our ambassador or minister in order for our chief of mission best to conserve his usefulness for your service in the political field.

Let the personnel of BEW both in the field and in Washington keep the State Department fully informed and use the good offices of the State Department as much as possible.

Time is short. The all-out drive is coming this summer. Let's go! ...

MARCH 26, 1942
HENRY A. WALLACE TO FRANKLIN D. ROOSEVELT

Dear Mr. President:

Mr. Jones' report of March 21, which you sent me for comment is that of an agency which is on the defensive. Since it has moved forward timidly on the fiscal front, it is naturally trying to protect a vulnerable position. Congress may not have foreseen Pearl Harbor and Singapore specifically, but it must have foreseen trouble somewhere or it would not have appropriated vast amounts of money for stockpiles. The Department of Agriculture used its share of the money to build up a full ever-normal granary, whereas the Federal Loan Agency did not build up adequate government stockpiles in the industrial field.

The observation that the Federal Loan Agency works on directives from other agencies and does not make policy itself, is rather astonishing. The unkind truth is that it does what it wants to do when it wants to do it, and when it doesn't want to act it keeps documented records so that the responsibility for inaction can be placed elsewhere.

The report seeks to create the impression that tremendous sums of money have been used freely in a wide variety of fields. The language is carefully drawn to refer to "authorizations" and "commitments" and not to money actually spent. A very different story would be told by a detailed statement indicating:

1. The date each project was proposed and by whom
2. How much time was consumed in subsequent negotiations
3. What objections were raised by the Federal Loan Agency
4. A list of the projects rejected
5. When funds for authorized projects were committed
6. When contracts were actually let
7. The amounts actually spent to date
8. The percentage of raw materials actually put in government stockpiles and the percentage turned over to industry.

The report refers to an act of Congress of September 26, 1940, allowing a revolving fund of up to $500 million "to assist in the development of the resources, the stabilization of the economies, and the orderly marketing of the products of the countries of the Western Hemisphere." It further states that out of this $500 million, "loan authorizations" of $496 million have been made for Latin America.

Fully detailed figures are not published by the Export-Import Bank, but as nearly as we can determine from an analysis of the reports available to us, only $3,527,000 was outstanding as of December 31, 1941, on loans to Latin America made since the passage of this legislation. Some very helpful and rather sizable currency stabilization loans were made but the money was not needed for long. Relatively little was lent from these funds for direct development of the raw material resources of Latin American countries. As you know, the Federal Loan Agency was not in sympathy with this aspect of the legislation when it was pending before the Congress immediately following the Havana Conference.

The report contains an impressive list of "commitments" made regarding a list of strategic and critical materials. It is difficult to get actual figures from the various parts of the Federal Loan Agency, but in many cases these amounts indicate nothing more than paper commitments to buy goods if private industry does not take all that is available in its usual course of business. It is certain that a total of what has actually been purchased with federal money would be far under these figures. Many of the foreign raw materials presumably bought for stockpiles during the last 18 months have not been put in government stockpiles at all, but have been turned over to industry on arrival. This is a very important omission of fact in the March 21 statement.

The report creates an impression that after Pearl Harbor everything possible was done to buy quinine. This hardly gears in with the facts . . .

The March 21 report refers to a contract to produce abaca in Central America. United Fruit Company tried in vain to make such a deal with the Federal Loan Agency at various times during the last two years. It was finally made in early '42 on terms far less favorable to the government than the early United Fruit proposals. The Federal Loan Agency was unwilling to act until we actually lost our supply of hemp in the Philippines.

When Germany goes in for preclusive buying, she sends a flood of men into foreign countries to do the job. Our government has been laboring for months to get a preclusive buying program started in Spain and Portugal. The Federal Loan Agency has finally sent one man there to survey the situation . . . Wherever relatively small losses have been involved in preclusive buying, he [Jones] has gone along willingly. The Germans have been paying over $300 per unit for tungsten in Portugal that is selling for $21.00 per unit elsewhere . . .

MARCH 31, 1942

. . . Sam said[1] the people were very much alarmed about the fact that we had not been able to defeat the Japanese in six weeks . . . The President then went on to say that it would take a while for us to get into shape but eventually our superior economic power would tell . . .

. . . Bullitt[2] is a vivid kind of person whose heart seems definitely

---

[1] Speaker of the House Sam Rayburn of Texas was talking with Roosevelt, Wallace, and several other congressmen that morning at the White House.

[2] William C. Bullitt had served in various offices during both the Wilson and the Roosevelt administrations. Wilson's envoy to Lenin during the Paris Peace conference, Bullitt had also been appointed by Roosevelt as the first American ambassador to the Soviet Union (1933–36). Later ambassador to France (1936–41), Bullitt at this time was "ambassador at large," a post without real responsibility. Later for a time in a similar position within the Navy Department, Bullitt during the war years spent his energies primarily in contriving unsuccessfully to obtain high office in the State Department and in gossiping with calculated malice about those whom he would like to have replaced. Wallace, who saw Bullitt at irregular intervals, seemed sometimes entertained, sometimes appalled by that gossip, which he never took seriously.

in the right place but I would judge from looking at him that he probably has been drinking a little too much in recent years and that he never in his life has done enough work with his hands or lived enough with the rank and file of the people to understand the world as it is . . .

APRIL 1, 1942

. . . Bill Herridge[1] brought me a message from Cripps,[2] saying how anxious Cripps was to have me come to London and how important it was for me to make the visit. Herridge thinks Cripps made a great mistake in going to India and told him so. Herridge said he was with Cripps a few days before he went into the Churchill government and that Cripps knew that Churchill had to have him in the government. Herridge thinks Churchill is done for, that he is nothing but a cavalry man of the Blenheim School and a rhetorician. Herridge thinks the common man in England is O.K. but the Tories are pretty awful. He is very anxious for me to see Winant[3] and told me that Winant ranked very high in England. He said he is going to go over to see Harry Hopkins and urge on Harry the desirability of my going to England . . .

APRIL 2, 1942

. . . Before cabinet took up, I talked to Sumner Welles about Vichy,[4] saying that I was convinced that the moment Hitler felt it was safe

1 William B. Herridge, Canadian minister to the United States (1931–35), founder in 1939 of the Canadian New Democracy "to unite all progressives behind the front for total use of our resources," shared many of Wallace's hopes for the postwar world. In the United States continually during the war years, Herridge put forward his own ideas in *Which Kind of Revolution?* (Boston, 1943). During 1942 and 1943 Wallace saw him frequently, usually at Herridge's initiative, as in this instance when Herridge was seeking a sympathetic ear.

2 Sir Stafford Cripps, socialist Labourite, member of the British War Cabinet, and friend of Jawaharlal Nehru, had just returned from India after a special mission for Churchill to solicit more vigorous Indian engagement in the war. Cripps had found the Indian government unwilling to operate in a position as subservient to the British as Churchill demanded, and unwilling, too, to accept wartime arrangements that might deflect the program of the Congress Party for the postwar independence of India as a single nation.

3 John G. Winant, United States ambassador to the Court of St. James's, onetime Republican governor of New Hampshire (1925–26, 31–34), and chairman of the Social Security Board (1935–37), always a sentimental liberal whose good hopes and Lincolnesque profile compensated in part at least for his administrative inefficiencies.

4 In this familiar usage, the government, located at Vichy, of the part of France unoccupied by Germany but scarcely independent on that account.

and so desired, he would get the full support of Vichy and it was highly important, therefore, for everyone to watch every possible move of Vichy with the utmost care. Welles agreed. I said I thought the all-important point was to know when the Vichy government was going to let its fleet be used by the Germans. He said there were some disturbing elements along that front recently.

Landis said Henderson[1] was going to fix prices on the broad front in the near future and asked if the President should not go on the air in supporting him. I said it seemed to me the President should tackle the whole problem of inflation, wages, agricultural prices, taxation, etc., in the broadest possible way, thus outflanking both agriculture and labor, that I was sure the rank and file of both agriculture and labor would be with the President on any move which would prevent skyrocketing. I would judge the President will move in about three weeks . . .

APRIL 3, 1942

I asked Ambassador Winant about Bill Herridge. He said Bill had plenty of energy but definitely underestimated Churchill. With regard to Cripps, Winant was rather critical saying that Cripps was the product of accidental combination of circumstances. The story is that in Russia,[2] Stalin was definitely bored with Cripps and did not care to see him, saying that Cripps always wanted to talk to him about communism. Evidently Stalin long since has found doctrinaire communists from foreign countries definitely sickening to have around. Winant strongly hopes there will be some type of League of Nations of the United Nations Association after the war is over and that it will be located in Geneva. Above everything else he would like to be located there himself. I told him there were some who felt very strongly that in case anything happened to Secretary Hull's health they wished he, Winant, would be Secretary of State. He made no comment on this but it was obvious to me that he was much flattered by the suggestion . . .

[1] James M. Landis, then head of the Office of Civilian Defense, and Leon Henderson, then head of the Office of Price Administration.
[2] Where Cripps had gone earlier on a wartime mission.

APRIL 8, 1942
HENRY A. WALLACE TO FRANKLIN D. ROOSEVELT

Dear Mr. President:

On Wednesday, March 18, I handed you a letter which asked for action to end the confusion in the foreign economic field.[1] That confusion is worse today than it was then. Your letter of April 3[2] indicates you do not think it advisable at the present time to take the kind of action provided for in the executive order that Harold Smith and I presented to you.[3]

In order to strengthen our raw materials program, may I respectfully suggest two possible solutions:

1. That you delete from our Executive Order No. 8839 certain powers over the import of raw materials which we are unable to discharge effectively. In that order we are specifically authorized to "coordinate the policies and actions of the several departments and agencies" and "develop integrated economic defense plans and programs with respect to all international economic activities," among which there is specific mention of:

   (a) The acquisition and disposition of materials and commodities from foreign countries, including preclusive buying

   (b) International investments and extensions of credit

---

[1] Actually a memorandum incorporating in general the points made in Wallace's letters to the President and emphasizing the "frustration and confusion" inherent in existing administrative arrangements.

[2] In his letter of April 3, 1942, Roosevelt had written:

I have been giving a great deal of thought to our several conversations about the BEW's having a corporation of its own to purchase raw materials throughout the world.

I have come to the conclusion that it would be best to leave the actual financing the way it is but to have the BEW determine the policy which should govern our foreign purchases. This, of course, is only one phase of the BEW's work and I do hope that our original conception of the board itself, made up as it is of the heads of the several interested departments, would meet frequently and make the determinations which must necessarily be implemented by the several departments.

I have finally come to the belief that concentration of administrative authority in the BEW would complicate rather than simplify our necessities in the field of economic warfare . . .

I have considered the problem of the field personnel of the BEW and am of the opinion that at this time we should not have additional personnel in various countries acting independently of the ambassador or minister. It seems to me it would be quite possible to work out a complete understanding with the State Department as to the duties of any staff which the BEW should send abroad.

[3] Then still in draft form.

May I urge that you repose these powers in one spot, preferably in the War Production Board, and that the power given it in this field be at least as great as that in the executive order which Harold Smith and I submitted to you in connection with the Board of Economic Warfare. If you decide to give these functions to Donald Nelson, may I also urge that you call in the affected agencies, particularly Commerce and State, and make it clear to them that you will stand behind Don in his work in the foreign field and not listen to complaints about him unless he is also present. You have given him this backing on the domestic front, but as you know the obstacles within government are greater on the foreign front which is my reason for being bold enough to bring this openly to your attention.

2. Another approach might be to leave BEW about as is which you suggest in your letter of April 3, but with a certain tightening of its present executive order which Harold Smith can suggest to you . . . I can then hold regular board meetings during which every effort will be made to establish as much harmony and unity of purpose as is possible. After a few of these meetings, the entire board can meet with you and you can make it clear as to just what kind of cooperation you intend to give Milo[1] in doing an exceedingly difficult job. A verbal "laying down of the law" by you is worth ten executive orders. In case you go this route, may I again respectfully suggest that if other agencies run to you with complaints about BEW or ask for you direct decisions on matters within its field, that you not listen to them unless either Milo or I is present.

Under the executive order of July 30,[2] there is a specific clause indicating that where necessary my decisions shall be final. This power is worthless to me unless the other affected departments know that you

[1] Milo R. Perkins, the executive director of the BEW, had been in the bag business in Houston, Texas, when Wallace in 1935 called him to the Department of Agriculture as his assistant. During the following years Perkins had executive responsibilities in the Farm Security Administration, the Agricultural Adjustment Administration, and the Federal Surplus Commodities Corporation. In those roles he became one of Wallace's most trusted associates. He was Wallace's first choice for the post in BEW. There Perkins brought to his duties energy, purpose, and a scrappy administrative toughness. He initiated the proposals for reorganization that Wallace had put forward, and Wallace expected him, if the President expanded the authority of the BEW, to discharge the enlarged mandate with the precision and vigor that had characterized his work. For his part, Perkins knew that he owed both his job and his influence to Wallace, for whom he had both admiration and affection.

[2] Under which the BEW was operating.

are wholeheartedly behind me. I succeeded with my work in the Department of Agriculture because I had:

1. The power to act
2. The power commensurate with my responsibilities
3. You behind me at all times like a rock

The present situation on foreign raw materials is in a terrible mess because no one has power commensurate with his responsibilities, and no one feels he can do what ought to be done with the certainty that you are backing him up.

If it were possible for you to meet with the board once a week that would be ideal. As you may not have time for that, however, it seems to me that you must delegate unreserved authority to someone to act and make day-to-day decisions in the foreign economic field as Don now does in the field of domestic production.

In my letter of March 18 to you, we did not ask for any increased powers for BEW. I am not asking for them now. What I am asking for is unmistakable decision on your part as to who is responsible for getting in raw materials from abroad which are so necessary to the winning of this war. If that authority is not defined clearly now, there will be a major explosion before fall. This is my last effort to make this as clear to you as I possibly can before that explosion is upon us . . .[1]

[1] Characteristically, Roosevelt split the differences between Wallace and Jones, and between Wallace and Hull. The President, eager to conciliate his associates, also, as always, resisted centralizing authority under any one man. He preferred, as Arthur Schlesinger, Jr., has best explained, a division of authority that forced his subordinates to compete with each other. That condition led them also in some instances to be inventive, in some to be conniving, and almost invariably to feel insecure. As they competed, the power of ultimate decision rested, of course, in the President's own hands.

Yet the executive order of April 13, 1942, satisfied Wallace and Perkins at the time. It authorized the BEW to "coordinate the policies and actions of the several departments and agencies" and to "develop integrated defense plans and programs" with respect to all international economic activities, among them "the acquisition and distribution of materials . . . from foreign countries, including preclusive buying." Grinning, Wallace told newspapermen off the record that he now expected to get from Jones and the State Department "enthusiastic cooperation, not dignified acquiescence." Also off the record, Perkins regretted "the sort of dirty, under-the-table fighting we have had to contend with" and said he now had "the authority to stop it." But Hull, a persistent and sometimes devious antagonist, had not yet surrendered, and Jones retained his long-standing power of the purse.

APRIL 21, 1942

Secy. Hull looked much better than when he went away. He started in on a very lengthy discussion of the events which led to his nervous collapse in the early winter. He spoke of the long hours which he had given to negotiating with the Japs in an effort to build up the political strength of the peace party in Japan. He felt very deeply the criticism which had been directed against him in many quarters in the late summer and fall. Apparently newspaper criticism is harder for him to take than it is for most people.

I congratulated him on having had the wisdom to have seen from the first the alliance of the Germans, Italians, and the Japs but said in view of that alliance I did not see how we could have any assurance whatever that his delaying policy with Japan could possibly have any other value except delay.

Shortly it appeared that his discussion of his own nervous state and his sensitivity concerning criticism . . . was part of the buildup toward a discussion of . . . the rules and regulations which I had put out on April 20.[1] The thing which most disturbed him was that part of the rules . . . which permitted Milo on occasion to delegate his authority to an assistant. I learned later that Secretary Hull had asked Dean Acheson who this man was and when Hull found it was Morris Rosenthal[2] he went straight up in the air at the thought of the Department of State being dictated to by a Jew . . .

I told Secretary Hull that I had no confidence in Sumner Welles because of the way in which Welles had acted since he came back from Rio. I reminded Hull of how I had come first to him and then to Welles after the Rio conference and had spoken to them of my deep interest in Latin American affairs and said I would be glad to take a trip to Latin America if such a trip would have the whole-hearted, enthusiastic cooperation of the State Department. I told Secy.

[1] The executive order had also authorized the BEW to "represent the United States government in dealing with the economic warfare agencies" of Allied nations, and to send abroad such technical, engineering, and economic representatives as it deemed necessary. Those provisions, as Dean G. Acheson, then Assistant Secretary of State, later recalled in his memoirs, trenched upon traditional State Department prerogatives in the conduct of negotiations with foreign nations and the control of American representatives abroad. As Acheson put it, the order was "a painful, bitter, and humiliating defeat" for Hull. At the time Acheson resisted the new authority of the BEW, though in his memoirs he noted his respect for Milo Perkins; see Dean G. Acheson, *Present at the Creation* (New York, 1969), pp. 41–42.
[2] Morris S. Rosenthal, vice president of Steinhall and Company of New York City, was assistant director of the BEW in charge of the office of imports.

Hull how I had wanted to get certain results in Latin America in co-operation with Secretary Welles and that Secretary Welles seemed to be quite completely in harmony with me—and then all of a sudden without talking to me he went absolutely in the opposite direction. I told him that this experience had called to my mind certain statements made by Secretary Welles on the train coming back from Senator Bankhead's funeral in 1940. On this occasion I mentioned that I had gone into the diner late to eat and had found Welles and John Carmody[1] sitting together drinking. When I finished eating they came over and sat at my table or vice versa, and Sumner Welles continued to drink one whiskey after another, discussing his recent trip to Europe, and mentioning among other things his very high esteem for Mussolini and the Pope. I told Secy. Hull that while I looked on the present Pope as a very excellent man, I could not help wondering what Welles' high esteem for the Pope and Mussolini meant with the Latin American situation as it is today. I told Secy. Hull that the combination of Welles' deep-seated admiration for Mussolini with his actions since Rio had caused me to have a profound distrust of him. I said I had not had any unkind words with Welles but that I did not care to work with him on matters having to do with the Board of Economic Warfare.

I said furthermore that I was greatly concerned about Fifth Column activities in Latin America and that what conversations and inter-changes of correspondence I had had with Welles regarding Latin America made me feel that he was not sufficiently aware of the danger in Latin America, possibly by reason of an inherent bias. I urged Secy. Hull to check independently on the Latin American situation. He seemed to be most appreciative of the suggestion and the atmosphere of the visit was on the whole very cordial . . .

APRIL 23, 1942

At the meeting with the President at noon . . .

The President made it clear that all disputes of a technical nature were to be left to Harold Smith . . . The President made it clear that merely setting the price was not enough to get rubber in Latin America.[2] It was necessary also to organize to get the rubber . . .

---

1 John M. Carmody, an industrial executive, during the New Deal held a series of federal positions relating both to labor relations and work relief. In 1942 he was a member of the Maritime Commission.

2 Wallace and Perkins, eager to develop natural rubber supplies in Brazil and elsewhere in Latin America, recognized that workers in the Amazon region needed higher wages, better food, and much improved medicine and conditions

At one stage in the proceedings, I made it very clear that I was tired of having State and Commerce go around my back to the President without my having an opportunity to be there at the same time. Jesse Jones immediately said he did not like to have an executive order formulated and signed without his knowing anything about it. The President said he understood from Harold Smith and me that the order had been cleared with State and Commerce. I told him this was not true, that I had known at all times that it would be impossible to get the agreement of State and Commerce . . . that I had told him that he and he only could get the assent of Commerce and State. The President then passed the buck to Harold and Harold had to take it . . .

Jesse Jones . . . suggested that the State Department have in every embassy and legation a man to whom all our operating people could go in the field. I said this would be fine provided the man was mutually acceptable to Jesse, the State Department, to Nelson Rockefeller, and to Milo. I said it might be possible to find such men but that they should be men who are thinking in terms of getting the most stuff in the shortest possible time.

Nelson Rockefeller[1] was exceedingly complimentary of the way in which I had handled the meeting. Apparently he admired my utter frankness.

Henry Morgenthau[2] took Milo and me off to one side and said, "I am sorry, Henry, that you are licked. I knew it from the moment I found Jesse sitting with the President at the moment when you came in." Milo told Henry Morgenthau that he did not agree at all, that he thought the meeting had come out fine. Henry Morgenthau said, "You don't know what a terrible staller Jesse is. He will wear you out with conference after conference and not get anything done." I was amazed at the depth of feeling which Morgenthau has against Jesse Jones. Morgenthau indicated he would be ready to go with me at any time to the President in cases where there were disputed points in the board. I appreciated his spirit but I doubt if it is a wise thing to do.

---

of hygiene if they were to produce efficiently. The BEW was trying to write into contracts those and other necessities. Jones considered that policy both too expensive and too radical. The State Department agreed with Jones and argued further that the BEW policy constituted interference in the internal affairs of a foreign country.

[1] Then Co-ordinator of Inter-American Affairs.

[2] Secretary of the Treasury Henry Morgenthau, Jr., had frequently fought with Wallace about agricultural policy during the early years of the New Deal. During the war, the two men, while never intimates, were often allied in their common support of progressive domestic and foreign policies.

Morgenthau urged on Milo that he keep a time check on all projects routed through Jesse. He said, "Wait until you start initiating contracts of your own. You will find that week after week will go by without your being able to get anything done. You will get along all right as long as you are clearing up Jesse Jones's own contracts but not when you start initiating new ones." Milo and I insisted on taking the rosy view of things, saying we felt the importance of the times were such that Jesse simply could not stall.

APRIL 24, 1942

. . . At the close of cabinet meeting, I suggested to Don Nelson that he and I both stay behind to talk with the President about my resignation from the WPB.[1] I told the President that I wanted to resign. Don said that he thought I should not resign, that my presence on the WPB was valuable, that I had the more unbiased judgment than the other members on the board, that he felt I was of a great service to him. The President agreed completely with Don, saying that no one could tell at what time some unbalanced person might take a potshot at him and that I should know as much as possible about the various aspects of government and that I should by all means keep my WPB contact. He felt that my constitutional duties as Vice President made it inadvisable for me to get into the hurly-burly of actual administrative details and that I should work as much as possible on the high policy level . . .

APRIL 26, 1942

At the Eugene Meyers',[2] Mrs. Meyer sat on my left and Ambassador Litvinov across from me. On Litvinov's left was Alice Longworth. Some mention was made of Henry Morgenthau's hope of selling 12 billion dollars' worth of bonds in his volunteer bond drive effort. I questioned whether it would be quite enough. Alice Longworth said,

[1] Wallace had contemplated resigning so as to concentrate on the affairs of the BEW.
[2] Eugene Meyer, editor and publisher of the Washington *Post,* had been an effective public servant, especially in dealing with financial problems, during every administration from Wilson's through Hoover's. Luncheons at the Meyers' regularly included both the socially and the politically prominent in Washington. Among those at the occasion here described were Soviet Ambassador to the United States Maxim Litvinov; Theodore Roosevelt's older daughter, Alice Longworth, a caustic critic of her distant cousin Franklin; and Supreme Court Justice Felix Frankfurter, FDR's old friend and influential counselor.

"So says Farmer Wallace." I then commented in view of the vast amount of money being paid out in the war effort that it would be essential for the people either to be taxed very heavily or to invest very heavily in bonds or some of both. Alice Longworth then made a statement to the effect that it was all very simple, just like taking in each other's washing. I said, "Yes," that was true until the point where we began to run short of labor and materials. She said she did not like my approach to the problem and Mrs. Meyer joined in. I said they would either have to take that approach or the communistic approach, that there was no alternative if they were to get the job done. Both Mrs. Meyer and A. Longworth said they would prefer to go communistic. Litvinov called on the others to witness that he engaged in no propaganda himself.

After lunch Felix Frankfurter again spoke most highly of the help I had been to Weizmann[1] in enabling him to see the different people on his program of utilizing agricultural products as a source of rubber. I told Felix that he could be of service to me with Dean Acheson, that the State Department was not cooperating enthusiastically in our Economic Warfare program, that I was not sure whether Dean Acheson or Cordell Hull was the greater source of the difficulty. Felix began to hem and haw, and I realized from the few remarks which he dropped that Acheson had been talking to him about the problem and that he had probably been counseling Acheson about what to do. I realized at once that Felix Frankfurter could be of no help. Acheson is Felix's candidate for Secretary of State if anything should happen to Cordell.

APRIL 29, 1942

. . . I talked at some length with William Shirer.[2] He was great impressed by the fact that FBI seemed to think we were fighting the Russians instead of the Nazis. He said every week the FBI called him

[1] Dr. Chaim Weizmann, the Zionist leader, was an informed advocate of the use of grain alcohol as a basis for the manufacture of synthetic rubber. The severe shortage of natural rubber (a result of Japanese conquests in Indonesia and the East Indies) and the backwardness of American technology in synthetic rubber (a result partially of I. G. Farben agreements with Standard Oil of New Jersey) made essential the quick establishment of a national synthetic rubber program. Weizmann's arguments encouraged agricultural interests in the United States but they were less influential by far than were the sponsors of petroleum as the preferred source for synthetic rubber. The case for petroleum also ultimately won the support of most scientists.

[2] William L. Shirer, in 1942 already an eminent foreign correspondent and author of the then best-seller, *Berlin Diary* (1941).

up half a dozen times or so asking whether or not such a man had ever made such and such a statement which was supposed to be favorable to the Russians. One FBI man had called on him to investigate a complaint with regard to a man who was reported to have been overheard to say, prior to December 6, 1941, that he hoped the Germans would not be able to take Moscow. Shirer thought it was pretty terrible when the government of the United States would be running down people who were supposed to have made statements of this sort. Shirer said he asked this particular boy who had come from Iowa and who was no intellectual heavyweight why he did not spend his time running down people who were supposed to be members of the Bund, the America First Committee[1] or some similar organizations. The boy duly consulted his list of subversive organizations and said very bravely, "None of the organizations which you mention are on my list." I called up the Attorney General's office and made an appointment for Shirer with the Atty. Gen. at 4:30. Shirer said he did not know whether Biddle[2] would be glad to see him because he had an article in the *Atlantic Monthly* which was rather critical. He said he thought Biddle was a good man but rather soft, and asked why he (Biddle) did not proceed against Hearst, Joe Patterson, and McCormick as well as against the little fellows. Shirer then proceeded to answer his own question and said, "I will tell you why it is. It is because he is afraid of the newspapers. He thinks they would pan hell out of him. He would be right too." Shirer agreed with me that if the Germans did not give a knockout blow this summer they would be so short of material and of men that the mounting power of the United Nations would begin to count in a very decisive way . . .

APRIL 30, 1942

. . . Admiral King[3] at the WPB meeting presented the viewpoint that we should have about twice as big a Navy program as we now have in order that we might have a full-fledged two-ocean Navy. It seems to me that what Admiral King was up to was to present the Navy point of view for the record. It was not a realistic presentation in view of our materiel supplies. It appears to me that the Army and Navy people have become so accustomed to making presentations be-

[1] An isolationist but not a subversive organization.
[2] Francis Biddle, Attorney General of the United States (1941–45).
[3] Admiral Ernest J. King, Commander-in-Chief, United States Fleet, and Chief of Naval Operations (1942–45).

fore congressional appropriation committees that they do not know how to make a statesmanlike presentation in view of our economic resources.

MAY 1, 1942

. . . At the close of cabinet meeting, I stopped to talk to the President about another matter and found him in the very best of spirits. He asked me if I had heard about his press conference.[1] I told him I knew very little about it. He then went ahead to explain and his explanation was totally different from that which appears in the attached clipping. In talking to me he apparently took the slant that BEW was an operating agency. After he has been with Jesse Jones, he usually takes the slant that BEW is a policy-forming body. It all depends on who he has been talking to last.

He told me that A. A. Berle[2] had been in to see him and that Berle told him the State Department was wrong, that BEW was right, and that many of the State Department methods were seriously out of date. I told the President it would be a fine thing if he could get Secy. Hull to call on Harold Smith for some help in bringing the State Department methods up to date so that a cable coming in from one of our men in the field would not have to stay around in the State Department for five days before getting to us. I told him that our relationships with the people in the State Department down the line were of the best and that everything was working out very nicely. The trouble came, I said, from the way in which Dean Acheson and Welles

[1] Cordell Hull had persuaded Roosevelt to modify the executive order of April 13 in a way that again attributed to the State Department the prerogatives that Hull and Acheson had considered threatened. The Secretary argued that since he had been away from Washington when the order was drafted, he had not had a proper chance to present his views to the President. With Hull at his side, Roosevelt told the press he would never have signed the order if he had known about Hull's objections. "There is no question," the President said, "that the State Department is in complete charge of the nation's foreign relations despite the recent executive order giving the BEW control of imports of vital war materials . . . Negotiations with our sister republics ought to go through our State Department, and after the negotiations . . . the process of actual procurement will be carried out by the BEW . . ." Further clarification would be forthcoming in an amendment to the original order. Roosevelt's statement to the press and the ensuing amendment had the effect of restoring conditions to substantially what they had been before April 13, which, as the press reported at the time, constituted something of a victory for the State Department.

[2] Adolf A. Berle, Jr., Assistant Secretary of State, one of the original New Dealers, was still now and then an influence at the White House.

needled Cordell Hull. I told the President the all-important thing was to get the imports as rapidly as possible, that I did not care how far the State Department went in saving its face, provided it did not interfere with getting the job done. I spoke of Brazilian rubber, how I had written Sumner Welles and how Sumner Welles had written me a face-saving document back. I said this kind of thing was all right so far as I was concerned but that after S. Welles had sent the face-saving documents, they should immediately have gotten busy to reform their procedure so as to get better results. I repeated that I did not care how many face-saving documents they produced, provided results were produced. I said I was going to continue to needle the State Department, if it was necessary, to get results. The President said, "By all means, continue to do so" . . .

I had a very interesting meeting with Ralph Ingersoll[1] of *PM*. He has a background of wealth and breeding in New York City but he has broken with his class because he has seen so clearly and vigorously the trend of the times. He thinks Francis Biddle of Justice is exceedingly weak, thinks he should move in strongly against the hard-headed leaders of the Fifth Column movement instead of operating only against the small fry. Ingersoll feels very strongly that there are a number of wealthy hard-headed men in Chicago, Detroit, and New York City who at the present time are not working especially closely together but who will be drawn together by the political situation as it develops this summer and fall. He thinks this group is exceedingly dangerous and that it should be smoked out into the open. Ingersoll now has a circulation of *PM* of about 180,000 and he only needs about 30,000 or 40,000 more to make the paper self-sustaining. He says when the regular newspapers are forced to go on the basis of only one edition night and morning his paper will come into its own. He is very optimistic about the financial success of his paper but a little pessimistic about the slowness of the people of the United States to wake up to the peril which confronts them. I am convinced I must start reading *PM* much more carefully than I have hitherto.

MAY 2, 1942

I spent some time with Harold Smith and Milo getting the slant on the conference which had taken place between the President, Secy.

---

[1] Ralph A. Ingersoll, who had a high regard for Wallace, had resigned from Time, Inc. in 1939 to organize and publish *PM*, an aggressively liberal New York evening newspaper. In July 1942 Ingersoll enlisted in the Army.

Hull, and Harold Smith. Harold felt that the President's press conference on Secy. Hull and BEW was very unfortunate. He said at the conference with Hull and the President, the President had suggested that there be certain clarifications of the executive order, and that acting on that Hull had immediately through Dean Acheson brought up with Smith the idea of a change in the executive order. I told Smith frankly that if there was going to be any change, I would see that BEW got entirely out of the foreign procurement field and that I would tell the public just exactly why we got out. This is the same thing that I had previously told Acheson. Smith then presented to me a memorandum of understanding which had been prepared by Acheson and Hackworth[1] of the State Department. For the most part, it was well phrased and along the lines of our understanding of the executive order in the first place. However, there were one or two points which were definitely bad and which would make it possible for certain foreign ministers and ambassadors in the field to slow up or make impossible effective work. Milo and I suggested alternative wordings. I suggested that in view of the fact that this memo would be sent out to all the foreign ambassadors and ministers, it would be well to include mention that the spirit of this agreement was to make sure that everyone operated in conformity with the seriousness of the times and that there should be no holding back or delays . . .

de Lozada[2] . . . told me that . . . he had it from Escalante, the Venezuelan Minister, that Secy. Hull had told him, Escalante, that the people of South America did not need to worry about the Russians because even if the Russians did lick the Germans, the United States would be in position to neutralize the Russian influence. This word of Secy. Hull had become at once widespread among the Latin American embassies and legations. de Lozada is sure that it has reached Litvinov and that there is bound to be trouble arising between Russia and the United States because of it. It is even conceivable, de Lozada thinks, that statements of this sort might cause Russia to make a separate peace or even to throw in with Germany.

[1] Green H. Hackworth, since 1931 legal adviser to the State Department.
[2] Enrique de Lozada of the Office of the Co-ordinator of Inter-American Affairs frequently called on Wallace, ordinarily to discuss the labor movement in Latin America or to complain about State Department conservatism in that region. Wallace found de Lozada a useful but excitable and sometimes unreliable source of information.

MAY 5, 1942

At the White House meeting, there was some discussion of cost of living figures and wages. Alben Barkley[1] was greatly shocked when the President suggested he could have Lubin[2] doctor up the cost of living figures by leaving out some item so as to make it appear that the cost of living was not really rising so much as it really is. I spoke up at once, saying that the President should not do this. Alben said he would have spoken if I had not . . .

In talking with Don Nelson before the WPB meeting, I found that he believed very vigorously that after the war was over, we would be getting our rubber exclusively from synthetic sources. I told him I did not agree with him at all, that I believed rubber could be produced more cheaply from vegetable sources. There is a great fight brewing between the oil and alcohol people with regard to production of synthetic rubber . . .

MAY 10, 1942

. . . When I was leaving to go to the luncheon at the Berles' Sunday noon for the President of Peru,[3] it occurred to me that my speech on Friday night[4] might have scared Berle and I began to be so sure that

[1] Senator Alben W. Barkley of Kentucky, Democratic Majority leader.

[2] Isador Lubin, New Deal economist, at this time held several positions including that of statistical adviser to the White House.

[3] Manuel Prado Ugarteche.

[4] On May 8, 1942, Wallace had delivered an address to the Free World Association. That speech "The Price of Free World Victory," soon known as "The Century of the Common Man," appears in the appendices to this volume. It expressed his most ardent and controversial beliefs about the purpose of the war and the desirable nature of the postwar world. At first little noticed, the address gained attention after *PM* had published it twice and A. N. Spanel, president of the International Latex Corporation, had bought space to print it in the Washington *Post* and *Women's Wear Daily*. Those publications received thousands of requests for copies. L. B. Fisher Company on May 28 printed the speech and various interpretations of it in a pamphlet that sold some 20,000 copies during the next six weeks. By that time the Office of Facts and Figures and other federal agencies had distributed hundreds of thousands of copies of the speech, which had become a subject of continual debate between its conservative critics and its liberal supporters. The text in the appendices is that which Wallace endorsed for Russell Lord, who edited Henry A. Wallace, *Democracy Reborn* (New York, 1944), a selection of speeches from the years 1936–1943. Wherever possible elsewhere in this volume the texts in that book have been considered reliable because of Wallace's own involvement in it. Lord's editorial comments, however, in Wallace's judgment tended rather often to the imaginative.

this was the case that I visioned a conversation in which I would say to Mrs. Berle, "I am so sorry that Adolf did not like my speech on Friday night."

When we arrived at the Berles' place, we found about eight policemen on the street outside, four or five in the front yard, and two or three in the backyard. Berle said in his heavy choppy way, "I suppose there are so many policemen here because of your talk about revolutions." There was not a single kind word from either of the Berles about my speech so I am convinced that they disapproved of it.

Berle spoke to me at considerable length about what a great man the President of Peru was and how he had handled the situation in Peru with considerably less violence than the other Presidents. He said he did not have nearly as many of the Apristas in jail. I asked Berle about the background of the President. He told me that he was a big landowner, a banker, and a lawyer. I found the President to be an agreeable, rather quiet man, obviously with a financial type of mind. He was very proud of the Prado Museum which his family owns in Lima. Berle, in analyzing the Peruvian and the typical Latin American situation, indicated that in Peru, as elsewhere, the ruling class was a combination of the military, the landlords, and the church; that the rank and file of the people did not know how to read and write. Under the circumstances, he thought the only thing to do was to work through the ruling class. He felt the ruling class should be looked on with much favor, provided it ruled the rank and file of the common people without too much violence. In other words, he felt that Prado was a good dictator.

At the Rockefellers' in the evening, I met R. Henry Norweb, our ambassador to Peru, who had been boosted by the career men of Mexico City in December of 1940 as the best possible person to succeed Daniels when he did resign. Norweb's wife is a heavy stockholder in the Cleveland *Plain Dealer*. Norweb himself is a good illustration of the type of career diplomat who either has money himself or who has a wife who has money. He was all atwitter about the significance of Prado's visit to the United States, what an enormous success he was, etc., etc. He felt that Prado was an unusually fine man and had done remarkable things for his country. Norweb himself impressed me as being a very weak sister. It seemed to me incredible that a man of his type should rank high at the State Department. The fact that he does rank high makes me believe that the State Department is probably the weakest department in our entire government. Sooner or later this department will inevitably manifest its weakness to the entire American public. There have been a great many fine devoted servants in the

State Department but the percentage of career diplomats with little to commend them aside from a wealthy background is altogether too high. Secy. Hull, while he belongs utterly to the Manchester School of Economics, and, therefore, lives the spirit of the 19th century, is far above 99 percent of the State Department people . . .

MAY 12, 1942

. . . Milo brought to me a memorandum of understanding[1] which would be signed by Hull, the President, and myself. This memo had been worked out by Harold Smith in cooperation with Dean Acheson. Harold said that the State Department wanted to get the memo published in the Official Register in order that the public might understand that the President had given the BEW another spanking. Milo and I agreed that if it made the President's load any easier to carry, this was perfectly all right but that we did not want any phraseology in the memo that would later interfere with the war effort. We made a few minor modifications.

Milo said that the letter from the President directing us to set up a corporation to take over the Axis communications system in Latin America was meeting with resistance from Jesse Jones. Milo said he was disposed to let Jesse Jones run this thing, that we had plenty to do without it. However, he had told J. Jones frankly when the matter was brought up at BEW meeting that he (J. J.) should have spoken up. Milo doesn't think we will get anywhere if every time someone doesn't like a directive from the President, that person kicks and then a different approach is taken. It is pretty bad business when a government gets into a situation in which those who do the most kicking have their own way. This kind of a situation leads to a curious type of intriguing ruthlessness which makes for uncertainty and eventually to the employment of dictatorial methods.

MAY 13, 1942

. . . At the close of the Biddle-Crowley[2] conference, I talked for a little while with Biddle. He said that S. Welles was pushing very hard to have the executive order of BEW changed. I told Biddle how much

---

[1] Incorporating the President's clarification of the roles respectively of the BEW and the State Department.
[2] Leo T. Crowley, Wisconsin Democrat, chairman of the Federal Deposit Insurance Corporation (1934–39), in 1942 Alien Property Custodian, always an adroit manipulator of some patronage and less influence in party affairs.

I had done for State Department over the years, of the way in which I had fought for the reciprocal trade agreements, pointed out that at no time while I was Secy. of Agriculture did State have any complaint against any of our men working in the foreign field, that I had always cleared my speeches with the State Department, that after I became Vice President I had continued to clear my speeches with State Department until the last one of May 8 which I cleared direct with the President, that the State Department had no kicks against the men in Milo's office who operated in the foreign field, that they had made no specific complaints to me whatsover. I pointed out that I could continue to be of the utmost service to the State Department and if it would do the President any good for the State Department to give the BEW another public whipping, it was all right with me, but if at any time any move by the State Department gave any indication of interfering with the war effort, I was going to fight them like hell. Biddle said that he was on my side and that I could count on him. I told him that the people down the line in the State Department in Washington were good people but they were somewhat handicapped by the 19th century methods and in many cases they were woefully understaffed. I pointed out that they had only about one-fifth as many people working on the problem of non-American activities in the American Republics as should be there. I told Biddle I was seriously alarmed about Axis activity in Latin America and the inability of people at the top in State Department to comprehend just how serious this activity is.

MAY 14, 1942

. . . At the White House luncheon I sat between Mrs. Roosevelt and Mrs. Henry Morgenthau. They were both exceedingly complimentary about my May 8 speech. Mrs. Morgenthau said she thought it was the best speech that had been made during the last two years. Mrs. Roosevelt and I talked about political democracy, economic democracy, and genetic democracy. She seemed to like the phrase "genetic democracy" . . .

MAY 15, 1942

. . . At cabinet meeting the President started out by telling a story which he has told many times before of how Cordell Hull when he was captain of a company in the Spanish-American War won all the money away from the other members at poker. Hull said with a certain shy pride that the story was only partially true. The President then went on to tell how Cordell Hull had played his cards with the French on the question of Martinique and the disarming of the battleships there.[1] It was obvious that the President throughout the entire cabinet meeting was going out of his way continually to sweeten up Hull.

During the course of the cabinet meeting, Morgenthau passed over to me a note which said, "I have the President's approval to continue our study in Argentina."[2] A few days before Henry Morgenthau had told me that the President had called him up giving him instructions to discontinue the study of Argentina. The President said that Cordell Hull had objected to the study. Morgenthau said, "Mr. President, you don't know what it is you are asking to be discontinued. You must admit that we don't get our story to you through Arthur Krock." Henry said that the President laughed and laughed at this indirect slap at the methods used by the State Department . . .

After the Senators left, Henry Morgenthau and I stayed a little while. I brought up the matter of freezing the Argentine funds, saying that Milo's man Coe[3] had received instructions from Dean Acheson that the study of Argentine funds was to stop on the basis of what the President had told Cordell Hull on Thursday. Then I said that on Friday the word came from Henry Morgenthau that the President wants the study to continue, that I had not had any direct word from the President himself and I would like to know just where he stood. The President then told me he thought this study should continue. Afterward Henry Morgenthau rode home with me and said he was about ready to drop through the floor when I opened up the question, that it came out remarkably well, and apparently the President was in very good humor. Henry, like everyone else, is baffled by the sudden shifts.

[1] Hull had negotiated an agreement with the Vichy government's senior representative in Martinique to preserve the status quo in that French island in the Caribbean.

[2] A Treasury study of the complicity of the government of Argentina in German espionage, propaganda, and financial transactions. The Treasury, opposed by the State Department, wanted to freeze Argentine funds within the United States so as to prevent their use for purposes helpful to the Germans.

[3] Frank Coe, a technical specialist in international monetary and economic policy, was then in the BEW and later in the Treasury. Accused after the war of being a communist, Coe may have been, but in no office he held did he exert telling influence on American policies.

MAY 18, 1942

At the White House conference on Monday, May 16, the topics of conversation were oil and rubber. Both Rayburn and Barkley were tremendously concerned that the rationing scheme of oil would be spread to the entire country. They felt the effect on the petroleum producers would be terrible. The President made the point that the need for spreading the rationing of gas over the entire country was based on the need for conserving rubber . . .

When I came in Monday with Rayburn, Barkley, and McCormack the President started out by telling me what a swell speech I had delivered on May 8, how many good reports he had had on it and how well Mrs. Roosevelt liked it.

MAY 19, 1942

. . . Milo called me on the telephone about the modifications in the executive order which Secretary Hull wants. He said Bernard Baruch[1] had talked with Secretary Hull in an effort to smooth things out between Milo and the Secretary. Baruch advised Milo that it might be a good thing to appease the old man by giving him the modifications in the executive order he wanted. Milo recommended letting Secretary Hull have the modifications in the executive order instead of putting out a memorandum of agreement signed by Hull, the President, and myself. Apparently all Hull is after is to get something which is published in the Federal Register so that the newspapers can take it up and point out the supremacy of the State Department . . .[2]

MAY 26, 1942

. . . It will be noted from the last paragraph of the President's statement that the one sentence which I insisted be in his statement, "The spirit animating this memorandum is to promote the widespread realization of the importance of the present emergency and the need for everyone to act with the utmost speed without delay or the holding

---

[1] Bernard M. Baruch, wealthy, celebrated, at all times self-appointed éminence grise of the President and cabinet, at this time also head of Roosevelt's fact-finding committee on synthetic rubber.

[2] Roosevelt issued an 800-word executive order on May 21, 1942. It reasserted the authority of the State Department over foreign policy and relations with other nations, and it bestowed on the BEW primary responsibility for importing war materials. The order emphasized Roosevelt's expectation that each agency grant the other "mutual consultation and mutual confidence." It designated the President as the court of last resort in any unresolved controversy.

back of important matters," was changed to read, "Both the Department of State and the Board of Economic Warfare and their officers
recognize in the present emergency the need for speed in action and
the importance of avoiding all delay in the decision of important matters."

It seems that Cordell Hull insisted that the spirit animating the memorandum was not as is stated in my words. This made it clear that he felt
the spirit of the memorandum was to slap the BEW. His changed wording, however, was altogether satisfactory to me.

At the WPB meeting when rubber was discussed, Jesse Jones ventured the statement that after the war, the various synthetic plants
would be operating in a big way. I told him they could not do it without the benefit of a tariff, that I was convinced that plantation rubber
in Latin America could be produced for less than 10 cents a pound.
I said he had better talk with the technicians. He said he did not care
what the technicians said, he knew they were wrong. Jesse said he
realized the President wanted the government to take over the synthetic
plants after the war was over but he thought that Congress would have
something to say about the matter. I told him that if we expected to
sell anything to the rest of the world after the war, we would have to
figure out what we could accept from the rest of the world, and rubber
was one of those things. I said that while we should have some synthetic rubber in this country, we should not allow rubber to develop
into the same situation as sugar, at the expense of the automobile user,
and we should definitely plan on receiving some rubber from both
Latin America and the East Indies. Jesse said . . . that Congress was
going to insist on rubber coming from alcohol.

We had it hot and heavy and finally Jesse retreated. It is obvious
to me that oil and alcohol people between them, with agricultural
support sucked in from the alcohol end, are going to form a block to
gouge the American consumer on the plea that in order for us to be
safe in time of war, we will have to produce all the rubber we consume in the United States right here in the United States. This kind
of plea will result in our adopting the same policy as after World War
No. 1, which will mean we will try to export but not import, and thus
throw the economy of the world into such a mess as to make another
war inevitable. Jesse's plea is that of the isolationists and his slant is
purely political. Don Nelson told me he agreed with me. I think James
Forrestal did also because he interjected, "Your contention is the same
as that you made in *America Must Choose.*"[1]

---

[1] James Forrestal, then Undersecretary of the Navy, Secretary after the death of
Frank Knox in May 1944, was referring to Wallace's pamphlet of 1934, which

MAY 28, 1942

. . . At the White House the President made it rather clear that he wanted us to engage in postwar planning but not to do enough of it so that we would get caught by the State Department. I told the President the story of Jesse Jones and the rubber tariff and pointed out the significance of this situation for the postwar period. I told the President I thought Jesse's significance in this was merely as a reflector of what other people were up to. The President said he wanted to talk to Jones about this matter. I said I did not think it was necessary, that I thought I had jumped on Jones sufficiently . . .

MAY 29, 1942

Wall Doxey told how Eastland, who is in the senatorial race along with Ross Collins running against Doxey, is introducing the racial issue.[1] I told him that the President would absolutely have to keep hands off the primaries. It seems an effort is being made to indicate that Doxey should be defeated because he has been for Farm Security Administration and that FSA should be knocked out because it has been too friendly to the Negro tenants. Doxey gave me a letter from Bledsoe, one of the Delta planters, who is supporting Eastland. This letter was so amazing in its frankness that I decided to pass it on to the President . . .

JUNE 1, 1942

. . . Sir Frederick Phillips[2] wanted to talk about postwar economic problems. I told him I thought it was too soon to discuss details along this line. I said I thought England and the United States together by their mishandling of the situation in the decade of the '20s had brought

stressed the need for lowering tariffs in order to encourage imports so that foreign nations could earn the dollars they needed to purchase American exports, agricultural surpluses in particular.

1 Wall Doxey, Democratic senator from Mississippi, was running to retain his seat for the balance of the unexpired term of Pat Harrison, who had died in 1941. James O. Eastland, who won the primary and the ensuing election, brought to the Senate the flamboyant oratory, obdurate conservatism, and malicious racism that were to characterize his performance for three decades. Doxey received some small solace in his appointment as sergeant at arms of the Senate. Ross A. Collins, also a contestant for the seat, had served twenty years in the House of Representatives.

2 Sir Frederick Phillips, ranking permanent civil servant in the British Treasury, who then, as often during the war, was in Washington to negotiate about questions of supply and finance.

about so much hardship to so many countries of the world as to produce the present conflict. I told him I thought it was important that England and the United States, Russia and China meet the economic situation following the present war in a much broader gauged spirit; otherwise there was certain to be more revolution and more war. I said I thought it was necessary that the leading nations of the world keep in mind the problems of the producers of raw materials that move in world trade. He asked if I was referring to the International Wheat Agreement. I said, "Yes." I said I thought the price of such raw materials should be neither too high nor too low. I told him I thought if we properly organized it would be possible to make sure that all the people of the world had enough to eat . . .

Ray Clapper[1] told me he was going to appear on the "Forum of the Air" Sunday night on the subject of my speech. He hopes to elaborate on the following paragraph:

> *The march of freedom of the past 150 years has been a long-drawn-out people's revolution. In this Great Revolution of the people, there were the American Revolution of 1775, The French Revolution of 1792, the Latin American revolutions of the Bolivarian era, the German Revolution of 1848, and the Russian Revolution of 1918. Each spoke for the common man in terms of blood on the battlefield. Some went to excess. But the significant thing is that the people groped their way to the light. More of them learned to think and work together.*

Clapper wanted to ask my opinion whether it would not be better to use the word "evolution" rather than "revolution." I told him it did not make any difference, that if adjustments were made continuously and smoothly, it was evolution but if the adjustments were not made, there would be inevitable revolution. The spirit of evolution and revolution are the same. Revolution is merely dammed up evolution . . .

[1] Raymond Clapper, the noted political analyst for the Scripps-Howard newspapers, was a native Kansan who had become a friend and admirer of Wallace. Clapper likened "The Century of the Common Man" to Lincoln's Gettysburg Address.

JUNE 3, 1942

. . . Caldwell King, President of Johnson and Johnson in Brazil and Argentina, told the most fascinating story of a trip up the Amazon to Manaus, then to Río Branco, through the state of Acre in extreme western Brazil close to the Peruvian-Bolivian border. It seems that the greatest supply of wild rubber trees is found in the state of Acre and the adjoining part of the state of Mato Grosso, back a little bit from the river at an altitude of about 200 feet higher than the rivers. The health conditions in these areas are deplorable with about one third of the rubber workers dying within the year, another one third sick and less than one third in sufficiently good health to work hard. The trouble comes from malaria, malnutrition, venereal disease, and bad water. Caldwell King said he kept in good health throughout his trip by letting a chlorine tablet stand in his water for half an hour before he drank, by taking atabrine every day and vitamin tablets. He thinks it will require about 40,000 workers or including the families about 200,000 people to take out 20,000 tons of rubber annually. He says that at the present time there has been so much diversion of labor from customary farming occupations in the Amazon area that there is a great shortage of food. At Manaus the American Consul has been trying for several weeks to buy a chicken without any success. The markets open at 3 A.M. and everything is sold by 4 A.M.

King . . . felt that a satisfactory rubber job simply could not be done until some of our head people had spent some time on the field. King is a graduate of West Point and has had a lot of South American experience in the Rio plant of Johnson and Johnson. He has been paying three times the going rate of wages and in addition furnishing a substantial noon meal. As a result, his workers have turned out five times as much per person as workers doing similar work elsewhere in Rio.

At the USSR embassy I sat beside Molotov,[1] who, I found, was exceedingly interested in postwar problems. He is very deeply interested in an enduring peace and realizes that Russia cannot have the enduring peace which she requires to develop her territory unless there is economic justice elsewhere in the world (as well as complete and enduring disarmament of Germany). I told him I thought one of the great problems of the postwar world was to bring about a rapid industrialization and improvement in nutrition in India, China, Siberia,

[1] Vyacheslav Molotov, Soviet Foreign Minister, one of Stalin's closest associates, was at this time on a special mission to the United States.

and Latin America. He agreed completely and felt that there was a 50- or a 100-year job in developing these areas and that the job should be done by the United Nations together. No one nation could do it by itself.

We talked about a highway with an airplane route more or less paralleling it from Buenos Aires through Canada to Alaska and across Siberia and Russia to Europe with branches into China and India. He said he believed in our lifetime we would see such a route. He was very enthusiastic about the way in which the United Nations could cooperate to develop the so-called backward areas of the world which have not yet been industrialized . . .

At the British embassy were present only Sir Oliver Lyttleton,[1] Secretary Knox, Lord Halifax, an attaché by the name of Brown, and another attaché. The object of the meeting seemed to be to create an atmosphere that we Anglo-Saxons implicitly had very little use for the Russians. Lyttleton made the statement that the present regime in Russia had more than 16 million Russians in concentration camps. The figure seemed to be quite fantastic and Lyttleton's motives seemed to be so obvious that I did not question his statement.

Frank Knox[2] made certain statements indicating that he felt the Latin Americans to be a very inferior order of being. He obviously felt they were born that way and there was nothing that could be done to change them either via food or training. I disputed his views very vigorously as did also one of the Britishers who said he had spent considerable time in Spain and he felt that by heredity they were very vigorous fine people.

Oliver Lyttleton told a lot about his experiences in North Africa and Syria. He said Rommel[3] was not a great general, that he was a stubborn man who had made a number of tactical mistakes.

It was obvious that none of the Britishers had any use for Lord Beaverbrook. Halifax,[4] on the whole, seemed to me to be the sweetest,

---

[1] Sir Oliver Lyttleton was then in Washington to set up the Combined Production and Resources Board, established June 9, 1942, of which he became joint head with Donald Nelson as his American counterpart. Lyttleton deplored the discord between the American Joint Chiefs of Staff and Nelson's War Production Board, which the new Combined Board failed to remedy.

[2] Frank Knox, publisher of the Chicago *Daily News*, Republican vice-presidential candidate in 1936, appointed Secretary of the Navy in 1940.

[3] General Erwin Rommel, then commander of the German forces in North Africa which during April and May had driven the British back to the Egyptian frontier.

[4] Lord Beaverbrook, successively Churchill's Minister of Air Production, for a brief period Minister of Production until Lyttleton succeeded him, then Minister

least Torylike of the lot. Lyttleton seemed to be a very hard kind of person. Brown seemed to have considerable economic comprehension of the kind of world we would be facing after the war was over, quoting Keynes at some length.

Lyttleton then told a story that in 1970 there was a meeting of the United Nations to consider the problem of unemployment. There were 16 million unemployed in Europe. The Prime Minister of Norway proposed that the only way out of the difficulty was to declare war. They decided, therefore, that they would declare war against the Atlantic Ocean which they proceeded to do, making vast quantities of ships and ammunition, thus ending the unemployment problem. Then one of the Ministers of Finance appeared on the scene and said all the nations of the world would go bankrupt unless there was some assurance that the war was a permanent thing. They made the war permanent and everybody lived happily ever afterward.

JUNE 5, 1942

At cabinet meeting the first subject of conversation was the attack on the Aleutian Islands.[1] The attack was still continuing at the time cabinet was meeting. It seems that some of the planes had spotted the Jap aircraft carrier and then all of a sudden a fog had descended and the carrier had been lost again. Apparently both in the Aleutian Islands and in Midway Island, we have done considerable damage to the Jap ships; nevertheless our forces seem to be inadequate in this area. The Secretary of War made the observation that we did not have enough planes in Alaska. This admission interested me in view of the fact I had tried on various occasions to induce the Army to send more

---

of Supply, had offended old-line Tories, as he frequently did, most recently by his cooperative attitude toward the Soviet Union. Beaverbrook revealed that quality during his joint mission to Moscow with Averell Harriman to facilitate Anglo-American support to Russia. Outspoken and unconventional though he was by the standards of his critics, Beaverbrook throughout the war was one of Great Britain's most effective negotiators with Americans about issues of military supply. Halifax was British ambassador to the United States.

[1] Japanese forces had invaded Attu in the Aleutian Islands and were about to take Kiska. The Japanese were also attacking Midway Island, June 4-7, 1942, but there the naval and air forces of the United States, while dispersing the enemy, inflicted such heavy losses that the battle proved the turning point in the struggle for domination of the central Pacific. Wallace could not have known on June 5 what would be the outcome and significance of the engagements then underway. He did express his special concern about Alaska, which he considered essential both geopolitically and as America's next frontier.

planes to Alaska. Also I had urged Governor Gruening[1] to go the absolute limit to see that he got planes. Gruening reported back to me that the Army just could not spare more planes for Alaska.

Ickes[2] criticized Milton Eisenhower[3] for doing a bad job in relocating the Japs on the Indian reservations. When it was suggested, however, that Eisenhower be returned to Agriculture and the whole matter be put into the hands of Interior, he backed rapidly away from the problem. The Attorney General and various others spoke most highly of Eisenhower's capacity . . .

JUNE 9, 1942

. . . I called up the President . . . and he immediately started telling me how important it was for me to associate with royalty[4] in New York on June 13, that I was to have a Navy or military aide, that I was to dress in regular business clothes, that it was illegal to wear striped pants during the war, etc., etc. I told him it seemed to me the Axis plans had gone seriously askew, that their timetable was out of order, that I was confident that a unit of effort put forth in June and July of 1942 would be more important in defeating the Axis than two units of effort put forth in June and July of 1943. He said he agreed wholeheartedly and he had undertaken to sell this thought to Molotov. I also urged that it was exceedingly important to hold on to Alaska so that it could serve as a base for operations against Japan a little later on. He said that it might be possible for Japanese to take momentarily some of the islands in the Aleutian group but that we could take these back again just as easily. Frankly I am still concerned that we have not paid as much attention as we ought to Alaska.

[1] Governor Ernest Gruening of Alaska.
[2] Secretary of the Interior Harold L. Ickes, forceful, ambitious, valuable, and volatile, had been dedicated for many years to sundry liberal causes, as he was dedicated to the unstinting prosecution of the war. His passion and determination sometimes warped his judgment. Wallace, who respected Ickes' ability, distrusted his political motives and those of some of his advisers.
[3] Milton S. Eisenhower, younger brother of General Dwight D. Eisenhower, had served as director of information and then as land use co-ordinator in the Department of Agriculture (1928–42). He was director of the War Relocation Authority from March through June 1942. In that post he exercised an intelligent restraint in the difficult task of evacuating Japanese-Americans from their homes on the West Coast to internment camps in the interior. Not Eisenhower, but the War Department, with the approval of the President, had initiated the policy of internment, a national disgrace. In June 1942 Eisenhower became for a year associate director of the Office of War Information, which felt his judicious but cautious influence.
[4] King George II of Greece and his entourage.

JUNE II, 1942

. . . Henry Beyster, engineering member of the commission we sent to India, had an exceedingly interesting story. He said he had made a number of talks to Chambers of Commerce of Hindu and Mohammedan men who had money to invest and who wanted to build up India but men who have no confidence whatever in England. These men think that England by unfavorable legislation would cut their throats at the earliest possible moment. They pointed out that England had prevented the building of roads in India because she wanted to keep the railroad bonds good so that they would return 5 percent annually to the investors. He said the whole psychology of the British in India is still business as usual. He says furthermore most of the Hindus would rather have the Japs in India than the English but that they have confidence in the United States. He believes that India is an ideal base to use against Japan and that the war effort in India can be enormously strengthened provided an American who has the confidence of the armed forces of the United States in the Far East can head up the all-out industrial effort. So far it really seems as though the English and the United States have made a mess of it in India . . .

JUNE 12, 1942

. . . Jean Monnet[1] reminded me of the time I had lunch with him and General Westervelt[2] last fall. He said he thought I had been largely responsible for the great speedup which had come to pass in our productive effort, that he felt my . . . speeches had had enormous effect and that he was very greatly interested in postwar planning. He felt that Welles' formula was impractical, that Welles was the Clemenceau[3] of this coming era and that something ought to be done to avoid Clemenceau's mistakes. I asked him to make me a memorandum and send it to me at the hotel. I told him we ought to figure which things ought to be acted on before the Armistice, which at the Armistice, and which 6 months later and which 5 years later . . .

[1] Jean Monnet, who had been chief of the French procurement mission in the United States before the fall of France, continued thereafter to work in Washington, with the British Supply Council, for a liberated and independent France, and for a postwar Europe free of its prewar political and economic parochialisms.
[2] Brigadier General William I. Westervelt (retired), one-time director of processing and marketing for the Agricultural Adjustment Administration.
[3] Georges Clemenceau, French Premier during the Paris Conference of 1919, a fierce advocate of French interests and of punitive treatment of Germany.

JUNE 15, 1942

. . . I gave to the President a memorandum on India prepared by
Henry Beyster, a member of the commission which BEW and the
State Department sent jointly to India. I told the President that Mr.
Beyster was not the chairman of the Indian Mission and that the report
was an informal one submitted to me personally. I said I hoped he
would read it and either throw it into the wastebasket or pass it on
to Harry Hopkins. He was very much interested in the report and
seemed to have definitely the feeling that the British had made a botch
of things in India. I told the President that Grady had told me about
Louis Johnson, how he seemed to be persona non grata in India.[1] The
President said that Churchill had personally requested him to see that
L. Johnson did not come back. This interested me greatly in view of
the fact that I had taken a very strong stand against L. Johnson going
to India as a member of the India Mission. After my protest against
Johnson had become well known at the State Department, Welles
came out the following day announcing Johnson as head of the Mission
and a few days later as our Minister to India. This was a direct and
deliberate slap at me over a very firm protest which I had registered
through Milo. I told the President nothing about the stand which I had
taken against Louis Johnson before he ever went to India.

The President was feeling in a very critical mood with regard to the
State Department, saying that on the preceding day when Mexico and
the Philippine Islands were to sign the United Nations Agreement,
nobody could find the agreement. The State Department boys fussed
and fussed around but still no agreement; a hasty telephone call but
still no agreement. It was finally discovered that the agreement was
in a safe in the State Department and the man who had the combination
to the safe lived 10 miles out in the country. Thereupon the President
took a sheet of paper and reached for a pen to write out an addendum
to the agreement which Ambassador Najera and President Quezon
could sign.[2] No ink in the pen. The President reaches for another pen.
No ink! The President said he was so mad he was on the point of

[1] Louis A. Johnson, Assistant Secretary of War (1937–40), had been a curious
choice to head the President's ill-defined mission to India. A West Virginia
politician and one-time commander of the American Legion, Johnson had been
a quarrelsome administrator. He knew little about India or its problems, though
he was informed about questions of military supply. His energetic efforts in
India to break the deadlock between Churchill and Nehru failed partly because
of his bumptiousness and insensitivity, largely because of Churchill's obduracy.

[2] Mexican Ambassador Francisco Castillo Najera and Philippine President Manuel
Quezon.

saying, "Jeesus Christ." Thereupon Ambassador Najera produced a fountain pen.

The President told me that the one thing which he had determined to do back in 1932 was to clean up the State Department. He said Cordell Hull had not done a thing. He said he had tried to provide for career service but the career service was not much good. I told the President my story of the letter from the Mexican Secretary of Agriculture to me that had been delivered on May 6 to the State Department but still had not arrived five weeks later. I told him I did not know whether it was the attitude or inefficiency. The President said it was inefficiency. There is no question but that the President has it in for the State Department and at the right time will move in on them.

It begins to appear more and more that in the month of June 1942 the following points stand out in the President's ideas concerning foreign policies:

1. It is highly essential that the United States and Russia understand each other better. This means there must be better understanding among United States citizens concerning Russia and among Russian citizens concerning the United States. It means that we must get more goods to Russia more promptly. It means we must cooperate with Russia in the postwar period.

2. The President has a very profound concern about India and a definite belief that England has not handled India properly.

3. The President believes that the United States and Russia are young powers and that England is an old tired power, that England must be in second place behind the United States, Russia, and China.

4. The President says that the nations leading the world are the United States, Australia, New Zealand, China, Russia, the Scandinavian countries, and possibly Holland. This concept is definitely different from what the State Department has in mind. Of course, I would include Latin America in it as well and it may be necessary to give England a larger place than he visualizes . . .

Milo told me that he had a very frank talk with Dean Acheson of State. He told Acheson that he was utterly and completely disgusted with some of the stories that had been planted in the press as to how BEW was imperiling good relations with Argentina and other countries by taking certain action. Milo told Acheson that he, Acheson, knew that BEW was completely following the State Department directives, said he was sick and tired of it and wanted Acheson to put out word along the line that he wanted the State Department to stop putting out stories of his sort to the press. Since then stories of this kind have stopped (for the time being).

JUNE 16, 1942

. . . Vannevar Bush reported on the progress of a certain matter in which he, I, and the Secretary of War have all been intensely interested for at least a year . . .[1]

JUNE 30, 1942

The most interesting thing at the WPB meeting was the report by Newhall[2] that butyl rubber was now giving great promise. This is exceptionally interesting in view of the fact that I had pushed butyl rubber at the board for a good many months and Newhall himself several months ago claimed that butyl rubber was no good. He based his claim several months ago on a report by one of the rubber companies which had done some experimenting with butyl rubber. This report was to the effect that inner tubes made from butyl would run for only about 50 miles and that the rubber was no good at all for

[1] This elliptical statement characterized all but one of Wallace's references in his diary to the construction of the first atomic bombs. The exception, an entry of June 29, 1940, reported his first conversation about Uranium 235 with Vannevar Bush, director of the Office of Scientific Research and Development:

> The Germans . . . began in September of 1939 by putting practically all of the facilities of the Kaiser Wilhelm Institute to work on the problem. It seems that if two or three pounds of Uranium 235 are assembled together . . . a chain reaction would be set in motion and nobody knows what would happen. The result might be an explosion as great as that when the meteor hit Arizona many thousands of years ago. Or the result might be merely continuous heat.
>   It seems that the President turned over to the Research group the job of working on Uranium 235 and Bush says that it is his greatest headache. In view of the German activity, he absolutely must work on it but at the same time it is one of the most dangerous jobs he has ever tackled.

Bush, who played a central role in wartime atomic developments, was eager to keep Wallace informed, for the Vice President, alone within high administration councils, had some knowledge of science. Roosevelt, who agreed, instructed Bush and his colleague, James B. Conant, initially to restrict discussions of policy to Wallace, Stimson, and General George C. Marshall. Budget Director Smith was soon also included. Wallace had a key part only in calling one meeting late in 1941 to review the whole situation. Those who attended agreed to expedite the work on the fundamental physics and engineering. Thereafter Bush occasionally brought Wallace up to date but the Vice President by his own choice received no information about practical military aspects of the venture. In his words, he "never got into details," though during the war he did oppose sharing technical information with any nation.

[2] Arthur B. Newhall, an executive in the rubber business, was co-ordinator of rubber for the War Production Board.

casings. He now says butyl rubber casings have recently been made which will run about 8000 miles. This is better than the regular rubber used to do 20 years ago. He says the present contracts for plants which will produce 60,000 tons of butyl rubber a year will really result in about 120,000 tons of butyl. He says there is enough material as a by-product from the production of 100-octane gas to produce 300,000 tons a year. It seems to me that the slowness of working out butyl is a reflection both on the Standard Oil Company of New Jersey[1] and the tire companies. I asked if they were now going to plan on 320,000 tons of butyl a year. They said no, there was no advantage at this date of substituting butyl for Buna S . . .

I asked Newhall exactly how many tons of Buna S had been contracted for. He said 700,000 tons. I asked how many of this would be from alcohol. He said 200,000 tons.

Don Nelson and Leon Henderson were extremely angry with Ickes. Seems as though Ickes by himself, without consulting with Don and Leon, had announced extension of the rubber collection program to July 10. They felt that this extension delayed coming to grips with the problem of nationwide gas rationing. Ickes, Nelson, and Leon are supposed to be members of a committee to work on this problem. Then Ickes had acted without saying a word to them. Leon said he recently had a "hate Ickes afternoon."

Bob Patterson[2] felt that it was absolutely vital that something be done at once to prevent unnecessary automobile driving. Leon said he would bring in plans at the next meeting.

JULY 2, 1942

. . . Alvin Hansen is still concerned about the possibilities of inflation and wonders just when it will be desirable to talk with the President about a fresh approach to the overall program. I told him I thought it would come sometime during the next month or two.

At the evening meeting, the discussion was on how to take care of the business unemployment situation during the first few months after the armistice. William Batt is going to circulate an informal proposal to the various folks who were at this meeting and we shall probably have another meeting later on.

---

[1] During the immediate prewar years, Jersey Standard, as a condition of its arrangements in a cartel dominated by I. G. Farben, had retarded the development in the United States of processes under its patents for the production of butyl.

[2] Undersecretary of War Robert P. Patterson.

JULY 6, 1942

At the WPB meeting there was an interesting conflict between Don Nelson and General Somervell[1] as to who was to run the civilian economy of the United States. I don't think the fight was completely settled but it would seem as though the disputed points are going to be brought up at WPB . . .

JULY 8, 1942

. . . After dinner I started jumping on Frank Knox again about getting the Japs out of the Aleutians. He said that we could get them out any time we wanted to but it was not a matter of sufficient importance to warrant the trouble right now. I said half jokingly that I did not have much money but if he would get them out next week, I would be glad to give him $500. Bullitt said he would too. Then Bullitt said we had better be careful, that we should be in the position of bribing a cabinet officer. Knox claimed it was impossible for the Japs to put in an airfield. I asked if this were true, why it was he thought the Japs took these islands. He made the incredible comment that the Japs took them so that they would know something about the weather that was going to be coming to Kamchatka. I immediately replied this could not be true because the weather movement was from northwest to southeast and not from northeast to southwest as Knox seemed to think. Bill Bullitt chimed in and said I was right. I gained the impression that Knox is incredibly ignorant but on the whole a very goodhearted fellow. Knox said there were 500 Japs in Kiska and 500 in Attu. It appears that the Navy is working on some other plan which makes it impossible to move against Attu and Kiska. I would assume this plan is in the South Pacific and that the bulk of the Japanese fleet is in the Kuriles. This suggests to me that when the weather clears in September, there will be great Japanese activity in the North Pacific—and there is grave danger that our Navy will be caught asleep at the switch. I did everything I could to wake up Knox but without any effect whatever because he is resting peacefully in the arms of his admirals.

[1] Brehon B. Somervell, Commanding General of the Army Service Forces and in that role the chief procurement officer for the Army, had become one of the most powerful men in Washington. He was already visibly restive, as were the civilian authorities in the War Department, with what they considered to be the inadequate supply targets of the War Production Board, and with the resulting degree of industrial mobilization.

Loy Henderson's[1] wife was born in Latvia. He has very strong feelings against the Bolshevik regime. Henderson spoke very vigorously on behalf of the State Department career men, claiming that the great bulk of them were very progressive in their attitudes. No one agreed or disagreed with him. Henderson then went on to say that the difficulty with the State Department might be higher up. Bill Bullitt then said that the State Department could not do an effective job as long as it had four different chiefs, some of which were criminals. Again nobody agreed or disagreed . . .

I found Henderson, who handles Russian affairs in the State Department, very much concerned about what would happen in Europe if Germany and France were unarmed whereas Russia would be armed.

JULY 9, 1942

. . . After the cabinet meeting, Dean Acheson, Harry Hawkins,[2] Milo, and I met in Secretary Hull's office. Secretary Hull seemed to have a slant very similar to Milo's. Acheson, however, was pushing for a very vigorous action agency formed at once to do business on the problem of distributing food in Europe. He said the Norwegians and the Dutch were very eager to buy food to be stored in Latin America, Canada, and the United States so that it could be shipped to their starving peoples the moment the war was over. He said he had stopped them from making these purchases, saying that a plan would be worked out. Acheson had already worked out a United Nations Food Procurement and Distribution organization setup. It was finally agreed that Milo should take the paper description which had been worked out by Acheson and submit an alternative . . .

Riefler described at length the situation in London, indicating how much better fed the poor people are in England under the war situation. He conveyed a message from Sir Stafford Cripps urging me to come to England and from there to pass on to Egypt and India. Both Riefler and Jack Fischer[3] think of lot of Cripps.

Going back to the close of cabinet meeting today—the President in

---

[1] Loy W. Henderson, a veteran foreign service officer, assistant chief of the State Department's Division of European Affairs (1938–44), was also in 1942 inspector of diplomatic missions and consular affairs, and briefly counselor of the embassy and chargé d'affaires in Moscow.

[2] Harry C. Hawkins, chief of the State Department's Division of Commercial Policy and Agreements.

[3] John Fischer, then with the BEW, after the war distinguished editor of *Harper's*, that night a guest at a dinner for Riefler at the Swiss legation.

the presence of Cordell Hull asked me to have a special meeting with President-elect López[1] of Columbia. Later on, after Cordell had left, I asked the President just what he meant. He said he wanted me to impress López that I was the one man in the United States whom he could look to for help in case of need.

JULY 10, 1942

At the meeting with López, we went into the economic situation in Colombia in some detail. It appeared that López had been an investment banker and had served in the '20s as an agent of New York banking houses in the placing of loans in Colombia. He is very much interested in having a large flow of American capital to Colombia when the war comes to an end. He would like to see the agriculture of Colombia improved and industry greatly expanded. He wants to make his administration an administration which really accomplishes something. López has made about 35 different trips to the United States and he has lived here for extended periods of time. He impresses one as a typical American businessman. He thinks Colombia has the resources to make her one of the best rounded of all the Latin American nations . . .

Henry Morgenthau is out to get Leo Crowley's scalp. He says Leo is now getting a salary of $50,000 a year from Standard Gas and Electric and that as long as he is getting this salary he should not be serving as head of Federal Deposit Insurance Corporation nor as Alien Property Custodian. He drew a chart of the power of a certain Victor Emanuel, a young Jew of about forty-five in New York City, who is really paying Crowley his $50,000. Victor Emanuel is chairman of the parent organization of Standard Gas and Electric and also of a half dozen organizations which have contracts with the federal government for building ships, etc., totaling several billion dollars. Morgenthau pointed out the way in which Crowley determines who is to go on the board of different German organizations, mentioned particularly the recent appointment of Colonel Louis Johnson as president of General Dyestuff Corporation . . .

Henry has told the President about Crowley but the President has not done anything. Henry says Crowley was used by the President among influential Catholics to put the skids under Father Coughlin. Henry thinks that the newspapers may get hold of the story and that the President ought to act. I asked Henry pointblank if he had told

[1] Alfonso López.

the President that Crowley was already getting $50,000 from Victor Emanuel and he said he had not emphasized that part of it . . .

JULY 13, 1942

Aldrich[1] said that he was vice president of the International Chamber of Commerce and was especially interested, with Thomas Watson [2] of International Business Machines (who is said to have paid the second biggest income tax in the country last year), in a committee of the International Chamber which is working on postwar problems. He told me what serious mistakes had been made after World War No. 1 in our management of the flow of capital in international affairs. He felt that the British empire was a thing of the past and that it would be necessary after this war for the United States to furnish worldwide leadership. I told him that I agreed with those who said, "The loan without the lender is bare." He did not quite get the significance of it and I asked him if he remembered Lowell's poem in which he used the phrase, "The gift without the giver is bare." He said he did not. I then referred to the "Vision of Sir Launfal" and he began to remember. I made the point very strongly that in international banking it would be necessary to approach the problem much differently from domestic banking, that the government would of necessity be very much interested in the overall problem and that it was important to see that the loans were made for the right purposes, and that they resulted in productivity. Aldrich said he was going to London in a short time and would like to stop in to see me when he came back . . .

JULY 15, 1942

. . . At the White House the President indicated his strong interest in very simple legislation which would give him power to prevent inflation from originating on the farm and labor fronts. Leon Henderson was asked to prepare the proposed legislation and congressional message after conferences with Jimmy Byrnes.[3] The President asked

1 Winthrop W. Aldrich, chairman of the board of directors of the Chase National Bank of New York.
2 Thomas J. Watson, president of IBM, a dedicated patron of the arts, friend of Latin America, and supporter of Franklin D. Roosevelt.
3 Associate Justice James F. Byrnes, formerly for twelve years Democratic senator from South Carolina, was to resign from the Supreme Court in October 1942 to become Director of Economic Stabilization and in 1943 Director of War Mobilization, offices Roosevelt created as he moved to centralize authority over the domestic economy. In those posts Byrnes served, not least in his own interpretation, as a kind of assistant President for domestic affairs.

that the word not be spread that Jimmy Byrnes was sitting in on matters of this sort . . .

JULY 17, 1942

. . . At the cabinet meeting, the President was in very good humor, continually cracking jokes. Landis had proposed that prizes be given to victory households which were doing a good job in buying bonds, observing defense measures, etc. Madame Secretary[1] was violent in her opposition, saying that the households should not be pried into. The President spoke up saying, "Yes, grandpa might be upstairs drunk." Madame Secretary brightly responded, "Yes, and one of the cousins might be in the attic who is feeble-minded." The President said that in his family there was a great-aunt who is feeble-minded, whose mentality never got beyond that of five years and that at the age of fifty she was being kept in the attic playing with dolls. Nothing of real importance came up at cabinet meeting.

After cabinet Leon Henderson, Secretary Perkins, Don Nelson, Paul Appleby,[2] and I got together to go over Henderson's proposed legislation and the President's message with regard to labor and farm price control to prevent inflation.[3] In the main we agreed and the material will now go to the President . . .

[1] Secretary of Labor Frances Perkins.
[2] Paul H. Appleby, an Iowa newspaperman, served as Wallace's executive assistant in the Department of Agriculture (1933–40) and as Undersecretary of Agriculture (1940–44). A friend and frequent adviser to Wallace, Appleby was also in 1942 chairman of the International Wheat Council, special adviser to the Lend-Lease Administration, and in 1943 an American delegate to the United Nations Conference on Food and Agriculture.
[3] Wallace and Henderson had continually favored strong controls to temper inflation which was spurting during the summer of 1942. That July, while commodity and food prices were rising, the National War Labor Board, facing a possible steel strike, adopted the "Little Steel" formula for substantially all workers. It approved a 15 percent increase in wages to cover rises in the cost of living during the period January 1941–May 1942. More stringent controls awaited Roosevelt's September 7, 1942, message to Congress which called for quick action to impose higher taxes and for "overall stabilization of prices, salaries, wages, and profits," including the prices of farm commodities. If Congress failed to act, the President warned, he would act himself. Congress passed a partially satisfactory stabilization bill on October 2.

JULY 23, 1942

. . . Warren Thompson,[1] who is a real population expert, came in to say he would like to do some work with BEW on the problem of population in China and India, looking to the postwar situation. I told him that some months ago I had asked Milo to work out an index of pressure of population, the idea being to discover a common denominator by which to express productive power of soil, coal, petroleum, iron, etc., an index expressing a relationship between natural resources and population in the various countries of the world. Thompson said he would like to work on such a problem and I arranged for him to get in touch with Milo . . .

JULY 27, 1942

. . . Nelson Rockefeller wanted to talk about the desirability of making the Office of Export Control in Milo's outfit less military. He thought there ought to be some men in the office who had more experience in the exporting business. Milo pointed out that the outfit we had inherited from General Maxwell[2] was almost exclusively military and that it had been a real slow job to make it over. Milo then said confidentially that Bob Patterson had indicated to him that the Army would want to take over from the Office of Export Control practically all of its military men by the first of the year. Milo said that Colonel Lord[3] had just returned from Latin America with observations on the weaknesses of the present method of export control. Milo thought that in view of the shortage of shipping, it would be necessary to do more of the work of determining priorities for export on the ground in Latin America. This would mean decentralizing the Office of Export Control. Milo had found on working with this problem that there were difficulties with State Department especially with

1 Warren Thompson of the Scripps Population Foundation had been introduced to Wallace, along with D. Kenneth Rose, national director of the Planned Parenthood Federation, by Morris Ernst, a liberal New York lawyer, civil liberties champion, and author who often called upon the Vice President.
2 Major General Russell L. Maxwell, an ordinance expert, administrator of export controls (1941–42), recently appointed to command American forces in the Middle East.
3 Royal B. Lord, a professional army officer, then assistant director of the BEW, had also been chief of operations for the board and earlier coordinator of the Resettlement Administration and chief engineer and coordinator of the Farm Security Administration.

Collado.[1] It appears Welles has told some of the South American ambassadors that in his opinion the BEW is on its way out. This means the State Department is continuing to fight instead of to cooperate.

JULY 28, 1942

At the luncheon with the President I spoke at some length with him about the Aleutians, telling him that I thought it was sound both psychologically and tactically to get the Japs out of the Aleutians at the earliest possible moment. He said he agreed with me that it was something which should be done from a psychological point of view, that the effect would be fine on our own people. He said the Navy felt very strongly that it was not a sound thing to do tactically. He then pointed out our far-flung battle line—

     the 100,000 soldiers we had in Australia
     the   25,000 we had in New Caledonia
     the   10,000 we had in New Zealand
     the   15,000 we had in the Fiji Isles
     the   50,000 we had in the North of Ireland
     the   20,000?? we had in Iceland
     the   3,000 in Greenland,
     etc., etc.

He said we had nearly 500,000 soldiers abroad and that the problem was one of shipping and that it was of vital importance to keep the line to Australia open. In other words, it seems that the Navy had such a job on its hands that it could not keep all the lines open and at the same time chase the Japs out of the Aleutians.

I asked the President if the British were keeping us fully informed at all times as to their weaknesses. He said he thought they were now. He said the British were beginning to develop an inferiority complex, to feel that their generals were not as good as the German generals, that their men were not as good fighters.

I told the President that from the standpoint of world politics and world psychology, it was important that we find some objective that was within our strength and strike hard at the earliest possible moment. He said he had been working on this for some time, that Harry Stimson did not want to strike until 1943. I said I thought one unit of

[1] Emilio G. "Pete" Collado, a professional economist, assistant chief of the State Department's Division of American Republics (1940), special assistant to Sumner Welles (1941–43), and executive secretary of the Board of Economic Operations (1941–43).

effort put forth this summer and fall would be worth three units of effort put forth a year hence. The President said that in spite of opposition from some of the British, it now looked as though we would be launching forth somewhere. I told him I did not care to know where the second front effort would be . . .

JULY 30, 1942

At the BEW meeting, the chief topic of consideration was whether or not to give the Sydney Ross Company their license for exporting their product—Mejoral—which is a combination of aspirin and caffein and which competes with the German product—Cafiaspirina. It was obvious that the State Department was very keen about the Sydney Ross Company going ahead. So also was Nelson Rockefeller's office. It was pointed out that they had wide channels of publicity including sound trucks, radio announcements, newspaper advertising, etc., etc. It appears that the average consumption of aspirin tablets is about three or four times as great in Latin America as in the United States. Whether this is due to salesmanship or faulty nutrition or bad health, no one seemed to know. Milo Perkins said the first thing his people wanted was a clean bill of health from Treasury with regard to the Ross Company products so as to be sure there was absolutely no trace of any German connection such as they had enjoyed before the war . . . Army and Navy were finally satisfied that giving the Ross Company the license for exportation would not interfere with the needs of Army and Navy for necessary drugs. It was an interesting concept that a part of the economic warfare should be a battle between a United States concern and a German concern as to who could distribute the most aspirin and along with it the most propaganda . . .

Condliffe came in with Bean[1] to tell me about his close relationship with the International Chamber of Commerce and his presence at the meeting of the British and American members of the International Chamber in New York on July 23–25. In view of Winthrop Aldrich's interest in the International Chamber, I was interested in getting the opinion of Condliffe, who is now employed by Bean. I asked Condliffe to send me a report of his observations at the meeting . . . The highlight of it is the belief on the part of British and American businessmen that after the war there is needed a period of decontrolling

---

[1] John B. Condliffe, Australian-born and English-trained economist, and Louis H. Bean, economist, statistician, valued counselor to the Department of Agriculture and other federal agencies, long-time friend and admirer of Wallace.

control. Also I was interested in noting that they seem to believe in
the necessity for international action to raise the living standards and
prevent recurrences of future wars. Apparently the International
Chamber of Commerce has really become New Deal although no doubt
they would hate to hear themselves so designated.

AUGUST 6, 1942

. . . McDougall[1] talked very much like Herridge of Canada. He
thinks the time has come for the President to speak out clearly with
regard to how the United Nations are going to make the world ability
to produce abundantly work in terms of a higher standard of living
for all the people. He thinks if something of this sort is said very
clearly and very strongly it will have a decisive effect on the people
of Germany . . .

. . . Dr. Townsend[2] now wants to change his program and make it a
security, accident, and disability program. Apparently he feels the
need for getting wider support than he could get from the old people
alone. He wants to finance his program in the same way as the old
program . . . He wanted to know how to start such a program . . .
It is evident that Dr. Townsend is guided by his heart rather than by
his mind and that he knows very little about the process of legislation . . .

At the Netherlands Embassy I sat next to the queen.[3] Her English
is pronounced exceedingly well but it is obvious that she understands
English only rather slowly. She is a solid, slow, nice kind of person.
Justice Black,[4] who sat on the other side of her, found it rather difficult to talk with her because she apparently had no enthusiasm about
anything. She has solid determination to beat the Germans but there is
no evidence whatever of fire in her manner. Her people have most
extraordinary loyalty toward her and I judge she has done a more
unusual job of governing than any of the other crowned heads of
Europe. She is an admirable person but most dispiriting to talk to . . .

[1] F. L. McDougall, special representative on agricultural matters of the High
Commissioner of Australia.
[2] Dr. Francis E. Townsend, originator of the Townsend National Recovery Plan,
a celebrated panacea of the middle 1930's, which envisaged large monthly pen-
sions for those over sixty to be financed by a 3 percent gross income tax.
[3] Queen Wilhelmina.
[4] Associate Justice Hugo L. Black.

AUGUST 7, 1942

At the cabinet meeting the President started out by saying how much he enjoyed the sweet corn I sent him last night. This grew out of a conversation with Mrs. Roosevelt at a dinner for the queen on Wednesday night. The President said he ate three ears and had no bad after effects.

The President started out at once talking about India, Gandhi, and Churchill.[1] He refreshed our memories about the plan he had suggested to Churchill at the time Cripps went to India, then went on to say that Chiang Kai-shek had recently been in touch with him wanting China and the United States both to intervene at the present time. The President had taken this matter up with Churchill, who said that he did not want any intervention, that Gandhi did not represent the India people. The President said Gandhi might be all right in his way but he did not have any governmental experience, that he was like a man who might take a watch apart and might understand every part of the watch but could not put the watch together again and make it tick . . .

[Wendell Willkie[2] had . . .] very little use for Churchill, saying that he was altogether too self-assured, that a self-assured man made a poor planner. He said Churchill was gifted with the ability to speak like a Demosthenes and write like an angel, that he came from the most aristocratic bloodlines from Britain, that he had been subject to flattery from early youth, that the women had always adored him, and that in personal conversation he was scintillating, that he was an excellent raconteur of stories, couched in the most correct English language. He felt that Churchill was just the man to lead the British during the period after Dunkirk. He had no one to suggest as Churchill's substitute; nevertheless it was obvious that he has no confidence in Churchill . . .

[1] Gandhi, depressed by the failure of the Cripps mission, was urging civil disobedience in behalf of Indian independence. In a letter to Roosevelt, he had suggested the Allies keep troops in India at their own expense, but use them not to buttress British rule but only to prevent Japanese expansion and to defend China. For its part, India was to become free. Chiang Kai-shek, who had advised Roosevelt and Churchill to solve India's political problems before a collapse of morale damaged necessary military operations based there, in August supported Gandhi's plea for independence. The President nevertheless followed the British line. For a brief, sensible, informed discussion of this, as of so many issues of the Second World War, see James M. Burns, *Roosevelt: Soldier of Freedom* (New York, 1970).

[2] Wendell Willkie, Republican presidential candidate in 1940 and aspirant for 1944, was about to depart upon his famous global mission for Roosevelt. On the basis of that experience Willkie wrote his best-selling *One World* (1943), a passionate, liberal prescription for postwar internationalism.

Harlan Miller[1] told me, after Wendell Willkie had left, that when Willkie was pointing out the many weak spots in Churchill . . . Willkie had in mind Roosevelt just as much or perhaps even more than Churchill. Curiously enough, when Willkie finished his discourse on Churchill I mentioned that I had received the day previous from the New York Genealogical Society a genealogical table indicating that in the eighth generation Churchill and Roosevelt had three pairs of ancestors in common. I had pointed this out without having in mind at all what . . . was in Willkie's mind.

It seemed to me that Willkie went out of his way to be unusually pleasant, talking only about the need for defeating the common enemy. Willkie maintained that as nearly as he could get at it, we had only about 100,000 soldiers in England and Ireland. He thought there were 400,000 Germans in France. He said the British with all their observations of the Germans had been unable to locate 30 German divisions. I mentioned that there was a considerable part of the German air force which had not been spotted. We both agreed that there was a considerable supply of German strength being held in reserve. Willkie spoke quite bitterly about Senator Danaher[2] of Connecticut, claiming that his isolationism was totally at variance with the sentiment of the people of Connecticut. He pointed out that Danaher was governed to a considerable extent by the church of which he is a member . . .

I suggested that the best information indicated the Germans themselves did not expect to destroy the Russian army this year but they did expect to make sufficient progress so they would be able to put on a strong peace offensive directed at England. Willkie said he thought there was much more likelihood of a peace offensive taking hold in the United States than in England and mentioned the probability of Ham Fish's[3] reelection as an indication of the thoughtlessness of even the most intelligent American people. Willkie said he presumed that the district represented by Fish was one of the most highly educated in the United States . . .

AUGUST 11, 1942

. . . Colonel Lord told me that he thought Don Nelson was on his way out, that he probably would not last more than two months

---

[1] Harlan Miller, Iowa journalist, since 1940 a columnist for the Washington *Post*, had just been ordered, as a captain in the Air Corps reserve, to active duty as a War Department liaison officer.

[2] John A. Danaher, Republican senator from Connecticut (1939–45).

[3] Hamilton Fish, articulate Republican conservative and isolationist, United States representative from the 26th New York district (1919–45).

longer, that the battle fundamentally was between Army and civilian control over procurements, the difficulty was that Army had the money. Lord felt it would be unfortunate for the Army to come out on top because he thought the war effort could be put across in a more balanced, complete, and rapid way under civilian control.

I called up David Niles, who has just taken on the job of being one of the President's assistants, and found that he shared some of Colonel Lord's views, said that he and Lubin had been talking about the matter. I suggested that Niles get in touch with Colonel Lord.

The Brazilian party was a barbecue with the meat cooked out of doors over an open fire according to the system which is used in Rio Grande do Sul . . . Leon Henderson proclaimed that he was really good at things which were vulgar and required plenty of energy. He said that Milo was the kind of guy who started fires but I was the kind of guy who put fires out and he was the kind of fellow who enjoyed fires. Leon danced for about two hours continuously and seemed to be fresh as a daisy at the finish . . .

AUGUST 12, 1942

I had an exceedingly interesting conversation with McDougall of Australia about postwar planning, especially with regard to food. McDougall has the idea that one of the ways of keeping peace would be to require that Europe grow not more than 75 percent of all wheat which she consumes, which is the proportion that she used to grow prior to 1930, and that she be required to have not more than certain stocks on hand. In return for this, the United States, Argentina, Canada, and Australia would agree to have certain quantities of wheat stored up, and hold it in world ports available at reasonable prices. The idea is that if none of the western European countries had any large quantities of wheat stored up, it would be impossible for them to start a war . . .

AUGUST 13, 1942

. . . General George and Colonel Smith[1] are handling air transport for the Army. Most of the men in this work came from the commercial airlines. Colonel Smith, e.g., was president of the American Airlines. They are very much interested in our getting suitable air bases in various spots over the world when the war comes to an end. The

[1] Major General Harold L. George, commanding general of the Air Transport Command, Army Air Forces, and Colonel Cyrus R. Smith, who had resigned as president of American Airlines, Inc. to become George's deputy.

Army has these bases today, but the question is, will we be traded out
of them when the peace comes? In some ways this is one of the most
important of all the peace problems. I sketched to them my idea of the
importance of the highway and air route from Argentina to Siberia
with feeders coming in from India and China. I believe this idea, which
I have tried out on many people, will eventually take hold . . .

Espada[1] wanted to tell me how disappointed he had been in his contacts with the Export-Import Bank, etc. He had not been able to borrow the money which he thought was necessary to build some highly
important roads and irrigation systems.

de Lozada thought the BEW ought to pass out directives to the State
Department and to Jesse Jones which would give Espada what he
wanted. I told him we are not in position to do that but nevertheless
made an appointment for Espada with Milo Perkins.

At the Ezekiel[2] party, Kaiser[3] seemed to be more interested in housing for defense workers than anything else . . .

There was considerable discussion about the division of authority in
Washington, the failure to get things promptly decided, the failure to
maintain proper supervision over inventories, etc., etc. Kaiser was very
keen about getting a prompt expansion in steel production, claiming that
he could start today and have a steel mill running in 10 months. The
view he presented was directly at variance with the views presented by
Robert Patterson in November of 1941 when Bob was trying to prevent steel expansion that I was trying to bring to pass. Bob was very
sincere and very fine but is always battling for the needs of the immediate present.

AUGUST 20, 1942

. . . Fowler Hamilton[4] is hard at work on the problem of determining just which industries in the enemy countries best deserve bombing.
He told how he had worked with various businessmen who had been in
Japan to determine just what were the industrial potentialities of Japan
for the making of airplanes. He claims that the Army has been too low

---

[1] Joaquin Espada, Bolivian Minister of Finance.
[2] Mordecai J. Ezekiel, economic adviser to the Secretary of Agriculture (1933–
  44), a liberal Keynesian whose advice, like that of Louis Bean, often influenced
  Wallace.
[3] Henry J. Kaiser, industrialist extraordinary of the Second World War, then
  about to turn his remarkable entrepreneurial energies to steel production, the
  object of his constructive ambitions on that evening.
[4] Fowler Hamilton of the BEW's Office of Economic Warfare Analysis.

in their estimates of Japanese potentialities. The Army thought the Japs could make only 6500 airplanes a year. Hamilton finally got them up to about 10,000. He really thinks they have potentialities for making between 15,000 and 20,000 planes a year . . .

The President was very much interested in a new type of colonial administration. He told of a conversation with Churchill in which he told Churchill he did not think there should be mandating after the war was over. Roosevelt thought there were certain areas of the world that should be run by trustees representing several nations—one from Latin America perhaps, one from the United States and Canada perhaps, and one other.

The President indicated very clearly that he was not going to get into the Texas situation. It was evident that he had considerable disgust with the Texas congressmen and senators for letting O'Daniel[1] get into a position of so much power. He had no question but that O'Daniel would win, and spoke contemptuously of Jesse H. Jones, who had not done anything to hold the line in Texas . . .

The President has received information from someone whose information has hitherto been correct about Japanese moves that the Japanese have now decided not to attack Siberia this fall. The President said he had passed this information on to Stalin and he thought Stalin had withdrawn some men from Siberia on the strength of this report to strengthen his line in the West against the Germans. I told the President I thought it was still in the cards for the Japs to attack Siberia. The President did not think so, however, because he said only two months of good weather were now left and that the Japs would hardly dare to strike with winter closing down so soon . . .

The President entered into a rather lengthy discourse about a conversation he had had with Churchill. Before he ended up the discourse, he had forgotten that it was with Churchill he had been talking to and the other man had become Willkie . . .

The President, speaking to Milo and me about an international system of public works, said that he had always had the idea it was all right to construct public works with a special kind of money, provided this special kind of money were retired over a number of years by the receipts from the public works. He spoke of a conversation which he had many years ago with Adolph Miller[2] and other members

---

[1] W. Lee "Pappy" O'Daniel, anti-New Deal Texas Democrat, victor over Lyndon B. Johnson (whom FDR supported) in a special election in 1941 for the United States Senate, successful candidate for re-election in 1942.

[2] Adolph C. Miller, economist, member of the Federal Reserve Board (1914-36).

of the Federal Reserve Board with regard to this idea. I recognized it as the idea known as the Guernsey Market House Idea. Miller, according to the President, said the plan was perfectly sound provided that there did not eventually come to pass public works of such poor quality that they could not produce the income necessary to retire the capital structure. While I did not say so to the President, my own fear would be that under some conditions such a large volume of public works might be started that inflation might result. This could happen, however, only if there were full employment or employment at wages unduly high. If inflation is prevented and the quality of the public works is income-producing, it would seem that the President's idea has in it much of merit.

While Milo and I were talking with the President, I mentioned incidentally the pride which the American people had in the fact that at last we were able to take the offensive even if only for a short time in the Pacific. The President did not seem to be completely happy about it all and said with regard to MacArthur[1] as though he found him a problem child, "Some boy" . . .

AUGUST 21, 1942

Jerry Green[2] came in for the specific purpose of finding out whether I did not think the President was going to run for a fourth term. He said the *Time* people were convinced that that was the case. I said so was Joe Patterson,[3] that he had been running editorials along this line for at least six weeks. I said I was sure the President himself was not thinking about this but that it was quite possible there might be a fourth term in case the war were still going on in May of 1944 and it were apparent that he was vital to keeping the country united in vigorous prosecution of the war effort. I told Jerry that that was the way I had read the situation last time, that I was quite convinced the President himself did not finally make up his mind until along in May of 1940 . . .

At cabinet meeting the President seemed to have especially on his mind the problem of preventing inflation. Apparently he has decided to use his powers as Commander-in-Chief to prevent agricultural prices from getting out of line and simultaneously take action also on the

[1] General Douglas MacArthur, Supreme Commander of Allied Forces in the Southwest Pacific, had ordered the attack of August 7, 1942, by United States Marines, on Tulagi and Guadalcanal in the Solomon Islands.
[2] Jerry Green, *Time* reporter.
[3] Joseph M. Patterson, editor of the New York *Daily News*.

labor front, not throwing the matter into Congress but taking executive action.

He also mentioned that 40 or 50 ships could be saved in moving meat if Great Britain bought her meat in the United States instead of in Argentina. He estimated that this might reduce meat available to the people of the United States by about 15 percent, and to make the remaining meat go around, it would probably be necessary to have meatless days. I told the President I thought the American people would rise to the need for saving shipping in a very splendid way but that there would be a political repercussion when the price of cattle went down because the farmers would then blame the government for having destroyed the appetite of the American public for meat and would say that it was because of that that the price of meat went down.

At the close of cabinet meeting, I told the President about President López' desire to have me visit Colombia sometime this fall, indicating that the Colombian ambassador, Turbay, would probably be approaching me on the subject sometime during September. I also mentioned the fact that Prado, the President of Peru, had written me a letter wanting me to come down. The President was quite enthusiastic about my going down but I said I did not want to go unless the State Department really wanted me to. I said it would be impossible for me to find out how the State Department really felt. The President said he would find out and would call Sumner Welles . . .

I told the President I thought the offensives of the past 10 days had had a splendid effect on American psychology. He said they were not really as significant as the public believed. I said it seemed to me nevertheless they served a very important function.

I pointed out to the President that in certain Latin American circles the story is going the rounds that the United States looks on Russia as pretty well finished and does not take her so very seriously. I said I realized that this attitude was not true but as long as certain Latin Americans were spreading this idea, it had to be kept in mind because it would through certain left-wing sources reach the Russians. Probably this is the reason for Litvinov's rather red-headed attitude vis-à-vis the State Department, I said. I told the President I thought this situation ought to be taken into account in our handling of Litvinov. I did not mention to the President the way in which our Army officers had tried to bring pressure to bear on the Mexican embassy to prevent the Russian Military Mission from getting a visa to Mexico. Undoubtedly Quintanilla must have gotten this word over to Litvinov or his people.

AUGUST 23, 1942

I met Adolf Berle Sunday evening and he began talking at once about the importance of working on our access to commercial as well as military airports in various countries after the war is over.[1] It was evident to me that the talk Milo and I had had with the President had been passed on to Berle. Berle thought this question of having air bases was exceedingly important. I told him it did not necessarily mean that we should have exclusive rights to these air bases but that some mechanism should be worked out whereby these airports could be used in such a way as to increase the commercial traffic of the world, saying that anything that helps the world in a big way is going to help the United States. Berle agreed wholeheartedly. He thinks we ought to work on a series of mechanisms for handling problems like internationalization of airports, public works, relief, etc., etc. Berle at times has a considerable amount of imagination. He is the only member of the original brain trust left around the capital and I suspect that on certain kinds of jobs he is still being used extensively by the President.

AUGUST 26, 1942

. . . Nelson Rockefeller wanted to know what he should tell the Brazilians with regard to our future demand for rubber in the United States. I told him to tell them that improvements were being made in the breeding of natural rubber just as they were being made in synthetic rubber and let them draw their own conclusions. I described for him—as I have for a good many others in recent months—the problem of the billion people located in Latin America, eastern Asia, three fourths of which live on the land and three fourths of which cannot read or write. I said these billion people were a great challenge from an altruistic point of view but from the strictly selfish point of view of safety and security of the United States in the future, they were just as much of a challenge. If we did not help them to read and write and improve their agriculture and become mechanically literate, there would inevitably be a considerable amount of chaos among these billion people or the Germans and Japs would organize them. I said we had absolutely no choice, whether we approached the problem

[1] Berle was in charge of American negotiations about postwar commercial aviation.

from an altruistic point of view or a selfish one. I described this as a new "missionarism" which would appeal both to the church people and to businessmen. Nelson seemed to respond . . .

AUGUST 27, 1942

. . . . Lauchlin Currie,[1] who has just returned from China and India, said the Chinese people are very much interested in the Indian question, not so much, he thinks, from the military point of view as from the point of view of the racial situation, said confidentially that Chiang Kai-shek thinks it important for the United States to make a pass at intervening even though it is rejected. He thinks it very important for the United States to maintain her position with regard to races like the Indians and Chinese and not get sucked into taking the British position. The British, because of their censorship control over India, are printing only the newspaper reports from the United States which indicate that the United States is favorable to the British position. This is rapidly alienating the Indian sympathy from the United States. I asked Currie if he had passed on this point of view to the President. He said he had . . .

AUGUST 29, 1942

When I called on Jim Farley after the Democratic Convention in Chicago in July of 1940, the one thing which he dwelt on was that he still would have control of the New York State party machinery. It was obvious to me then that he felt very deeply and was planning for the future.[2]

I was always very fond of the unspoiled Jim Farley in the early days of the New Deal and have felt in recent years that he has perhaps been used too much by others, that he has responded to their needling . . .

[1] Lauchlin Currie, economist, since 1939 an administrative assistant to Roosevelt, head of the President's economic mission to China in 1941–42.

[2] James A. Farley had just won a personal victory over the President by arranging the Democratic nomination for governor of New York for John Bennett, the state's incumbent attorney general. Roosevelt and his friends in New York had preferred Senator James Mead.

AUGUST 31, 1942

Owen Lattimore[1] came in to tell me he was going on the payroll of Chiang Kai-shek for a couple of months or so and he was leaving soon for China. He wondered if there was any information I had that he ought to have. I told him he ought to see Milo, that there was a possibility there would be a Chinese Mission set up on the opposite number basis with a Chinese expert to match each American expert. He told me that the Chinese experts in road and construction engineering were unusually good, said there were certain fields of chemistry where the world had made great progress in which the Chinese had not kept up; the Chinese knew that they could not keep up because it had been impossible for them to send their men out of the country.

I asked Lattimore if the Chinese by heredity did not have just as good minds as we. He said he was sure they did and that as a matter of fact all races were about the same as far as heredity was concerned. He said training had resulted in some rather marked differences, said the Chinese were good at remembering things but were perhaps not as good on initiative. He said the Mongols were on the other hand good on initiative. He said he thought this was a result of their nomadic life. He said the Mongols were extraordinarily ingenious with machinery and made the world's best mechanics . . .

SEPTEMBER 1, 1942

At the WPB meeting the chief thing up for discussion was Thurman Arnold.[2] Don Nelson felt very deeply that Arnold was interfering

[1] Owen Lattimore, professor at the Johns Hopkins University, an outstanding American authority on China, was in 1941–42 political adviser to Chiang Kai-shek and in 1942–44 deputy director of Pacific Operations of the Office of War Information. Increasingly critical of Chiang's corruption and inefficiency, Lattimore became one advocate of a détente among the United States, Chiang, and the Chinese communists. He often advised Wallace about Asian affairs. A controversial figure during the period of postwar hysteria about alleged communist influences on American Chinese policy, Lattimore was falsely accused of subversion.

[2] Thurman Arnold, then head of the antitrust division of the Justice Department, in his few years in that office initiated more prosecutions for violations of the antitrust laws than had his predecessors during the fifty preceding years. He believed that "the function of the Antitrust Division was just as important during the war as it was prior to the war," especially since wartime procurement "created a great opportunity for conspiratorial agreements . . . with respect to prices, bidding, consolidations, and mergers"; see Thurman Arnold, *Fair Fights and Foul* (New York, 1965). Further, Arnold had helped the Truman Committee to reveal many connections between large American

with the war effort by some of the prosecutions which he was starting. Bob Patterson of War feels the same way. Lubin took up the cudgels for Arnold . . .

Richard Law[1] asked me pointblank if I did not think that it was the duty of the United States and England to cooperate to solve the postwar situation. I told him in reply that a great deal depended on how England handled the India situation, that the people of the United States did not believe in imperialism and it would seem to me that England and the United States could hardly go it alone, that it seemed to me necessary to take into account China, Russia, and perhaps Latin America. I gave my customary talk on the importance of the 800 million people in eastern Asia and the necessity of a great public works program in Asia. I mentioned McDougall's great interest in food and especially his plan to set up ever-normal granaries in the United States, Canada, Australia, Argentina, and possibly England but not allowing Europe to have more than three months' supply of food on hand in any country. This had to do particularly with wheat and fats. The idea would be to make wheat and fats available at very reasonable prices but not to allow any of the European nations an opportunity to accumulate supplies enough to allow them to start another war. Law took up the cudgels very vigorously on behalf of Europe. I told him it seemed to me England was much more definitely faced toward Europe than she was toward the rest of the world. He then announced it was England's game to play part of the time with Europe and part of the time with the rest of the world. Evidently the new balance-of-power tactics of England are going to be on this theory; by playing off Europe against the United States, Latin America, and Asia. Apparently my anti-imperialistic remarks irritated Law because he said, "How about America's dollar diplomacy?" . . .

---

firms and German cartels. In wartime, as Arnold saw it, the antitrust laws, if they were enforced, would exercise a symbolic deterrence greater even than their actual legal effect. But the War and Navy Departments and the WPB feared that recourse to antitrust prosecutions against major suppliers would at the least tie up business executives in work unrelated to procurement, and at the worst cripple and alienate indispensable firms. That cautious attitude, to which Roosevelt also subscribed, prevailed. Yielding to the greater influence of the Army and Navy, the Justice Department on March 20, 1942, had agreed, except in instances when the President specifically ruled otherwise, to suspend for the duration of the war prosecutions to which the War or Navy Department objected. That policy was later to strike Wallace as providing an unwarranted shield for big business.
[1] Richard Law, Undersecretary of the British Foreign Office, was in charge for Great Britain of plans for the reconstruction of liberated and conquered areas.

SEPTEMBER 2, 1942

. . . At the luncheon with the President, I found the President in complete accord with Cordell Hull and myself that the United Nations Rehabilitation Commission as tentatively worked out should not be announced at the present time, but that the memorandum adopted by the BEW and as modified by the Army and Navy should be used as a basis for further discussion.

The President spoke about how at the end of the war all the fleets of the world should be put together in one pot and then divided on the basis of the prewar percentages—for example, if the Dutch had 8 percent of the shipping in 1939, they might perhaps have 7 percent when the war ended, etc.

I gave the President a copy of the McDougall memorandum . . . and urged that now was the time to strike with single-mindedness on all fronts including the psychological front as suggested by Mc-Dougall . . .

I told the President about Mrs. Friant and Mrs. Cunningham[1] coming over on behalf of wanting the President to have a lady as one of his six anonymous advisers. He said, "My God, no." He said the question would come up at once as to who should have the job. I judge his experience with Mrs. Roosevelt has left its mark . . .[2]

. . . Cordell Hull quoted at some length from a report made to him by Murphy,[3] one of his observers in northern Africa, in which both Hull and the President have a great deal of confidence. Murphy, according to Hull, says that the oil and food we are sending into northern Africa are tremendously appreciated by the population. It appeared that Cordell wished to get from the President a blessing for continuing the State Department policy with respect to Vichy France, and that the President was quite willing to give the blessing . . .

[1] Mrs. Bertha Friant and Mrs. Minnie Fisher Cunningham, both information specialists in the Agricultural Adjustment Administration, had called on the Vice President on August 28, 1942.

[2] Wallace, who always held Mrs. Roosevelt in high regard, intended no slur in his remark. He was referring to the difficulties that had attended her earlier, abbreviated role in the Office of Civilian Defense; see Joseph P. Lash, *Eleanor and Franklin* (New York, 1971), Ch. 51.

[3] Robert D. Murphy, a foreign service officer, had as Roosevelt's personal representative investigated conditions in French North Africa. There in 1941 he concluded an economic agreement with Vichy forces. In 1942 he was engaged in making preparations, later the subject of major controversy, to facilitate the Allied landings in North Africa in November.

While the President was talking so vigorously about not having any woman among his six helpers, he made reference to Miss Harriet Elliott[1] whom he had appointed on the first national defense board and there she had an excellent opportunity to do things. He said she was an excellent educator but she just did not know how to measure up to the job . . .

SEPTEMBER 3, 1942

. . . I spoke to Admiral Leahy[2] . . . found that Leahy knew very little about Alaska . . . I thought the best point from which to proceed against Japan would eventually prove to be the Aleutians and Leahy said that our submarines were executing great havoc among the Japanese merchant marine. He felt we could lick Japan and that we should go ahead and destroy her utterly. He felt Japan was our Carthage and that we ought to take advantage of this opportunity to make it certain that she never could again be a world power. It was either us or Japan, according to Leahy . . .[3]

OCTOBER 1, 1942

. . . Gallarza[4] wanted to let me know that his friend Jim Carey[5] who is secretary of the CIO is being kicked around in the CIO by the communist group, including Lee Pressman,[6] who is still very strong. Gallarza said that the CIO leaders wanted to know whether they should put money into the political campaign this fall like they did in the fall of 1940 through the Labor Non-Partisan League. He said Phil

1 Harriet W. Elliott, professor and later dean at the Women's College of the University of North Carolina, an active Democrat who held various advisory positions during the New Deal, had been consumer member on the Advisory Committee to the Council of National Defense.

2 Admiral William D. Leahy, ambassador to Vichy France (1940–42), now back in Washington as Roosevelt's Chief of Staff.

3 Wallace kept only a record of appointments, not a diary, for the period September 8–29, 1942. He was away from Washington September 12–22, primarily on vacation but also for an address in Los Angeles on September 16 to mark Mexican Independence Day.

4 Ernesto Gallarza of the Pan-American Union.

5 James B. Carey, formerly president of the United Electrical Workers, since 1938 national secretary and in 1942 also secretary treasurer of the Congress of Industrial Organization.

6 Lee Pressman, assistant general counsel for the Agricultural Adjustment Administration (1933–35), general counsel for the Works Progress Administration (1935–36), in 1942 general counsel for the CIO.

Murray[1] wanted to know that but that Murray had not talked to him direct. I suggested it might be better if Murray would get in touch with the President direct, that obviously this was a decision that could be made only by the President . . .

OCTOBER 2, 1942

. . . At cabinet the President was in the very highest spirits. He told about his trip in some detail. He said that Henry Ford still was not producing any bombers at Willow Run but he probably would be in three or four weeks. He felt Ford had not done an especially good job. He thought on the whole the best job was being done on the Pacific Coast. He mentioned visiting Jack Garner in Texas and said that Garner had told him there was no trouble in getting labor to run the cattle business. I said the situation in the dairy regions was different, that a survey of dairy farmers who had lost one man indicated that they had reduced the number of cows about 43 percent whereas those who had not lost any men had increased their number of cows . . . The President said the farmers of the Middle West were not using any ingenuity, that they were adopting a defeatist attitude, that they had no imagination about cooperating with the town people about getting the necessary labor. I told him I was convinced the problem of manpower on the farms of the country was ten times more important in farmers' minds than the price squabble which had been going on the last two weeks. He went into specific instances which he had run into in Hyde Park and on the West Coast indicating that if the farmers would only use a little ingenuity they would have plenty of manpower to get by.

The President continued to take what to me seemed to be a rather strong anti-farmer attitude, saying that they were not working like they used to work 20 or 30 years ago. I replied that I thought the farmers were coming closer to working like they did 30 years ago than any other group of our people. McNutt[2] rather supported the President's view and Don Nelson and Forrestal supported me. Nelson said he had been before the Senate Agricultural Committee on the question of manpower for the farmers and he had found the committee up in arms because word had gone out that an army of 13 million

[1] Philip Murray, since 1940 president of the CIO.
[2] Paul V. McNutt, Indiana Democrat, onetime national commander of the American Legion, a handsome, undistinguished, and inordinately ambitious conservative whom Roosevelt appointed to various positions, including the chairmanship of the War Manpower Commission, which he held at this time.

men was to be raised. McNutt confessed that General Hershey[1] had made such a statement. I then interpolated it was this 13 million statement which had somewhat stirred up the farmers of the Middle West, if the present army of only 2 million had created such a tightness. The President said that the total Army force by the end of 1943 would not be more than 6,400,000. I asked if there would be any objection to making figures of this sort public. He said, yes, there would.

There was considerable discussion of the lack of uniformity in methods used by the draft boards. McNutt said there would have to be better appeal machinery worked out.

Biddle then began to talk about the way in which the Army had taken men in the various departments. He said Justice had lost 24 percent and some of the other departments had lost a higher percentage. Henry Morgenthau took rather sharp issue with Biddle saying that the government in Washington should lose its men just as much as people out in the open country. The President finally appointed a committee composed of Biddle, Morgenthau, McNutt, and Army and Navy representatives to go into the question of policy relative to the drafting of men in government.

I pled with the President on the necessity for having an overall look at the manpower picture from the standpoint of how the total war effort of the country could best be served. It was obvious that this proposal greatly disturbed McNutt. The President ducked. Don Nelson thinks that probably the war effort could better be served by having armed forces of 5 or 6 million men fully equipped with a civilian economy in shape fully to support them than by having a large Army.

McNutt said he had testified to the Senate Agricultural Committee that the maximum should not be in excess of 10½ million.

At the conclusion of the cabinet meeting, I gave to the President a little bust of himself in the nature of a caricature made in Cuba . . . The President was tickled to death with it and is going to put it in his museum at Hyde Park. I gave him the wording of the homage as passed by the Cuban Congress and told about the idea of putting a statue of him at the Panama Canal. He said what he really wanted was a University of the Americas established north of the Panama Canal at an altitude of 3000 feet close to the Costa Rican border.

I gave the President the BEW report on Japan shipping in which he was very greatly interested and also the report which BEW had prepared for me on the weakness of the German transportation lines

[1] General Lewis B. Hershey, since 1941 director of the Selective Service System.

back of Stalingrad and Rostov on the Don. I was greatly pleased to find that he had been thinking about this problem himself and had been working with the British, the Russians, and our own high command to have the maximum of bombing to come up to these points. I told him I thought the heart of the problem this winter was to keep up an everlasting bombing attack against the German transportation systems in Russia, against Germany herself, and against the Japanese shipping. He said with great glee that our submarines had been doing a great execution in sinking Jap ships. He mentioned a number of very encouraging specific instances which I had not read about in the press. It would seem that the Japanese from now on will surely bleed to death pretty fast.

The President started out by saying that one of the things that that impressed him most on his trip was the large number of women working in the factories. He said that in the factories in the near future, 40 percent of the workers would be women. He was not referring to women in white collar jobs but women actually doing things with their hands. He said morale was highest on the West Coast, second highest in the Middle West and South, third in the East, and that in Washington morale would rank down about 15th, that in fact the morale in Washington was the worst of any place in the country.

OCTOBER 5, 1942

. . . Lauchlin Currie told me that the present ambassador to China[1] was not getting along at all well and that a new one was going to be appointed in his place. He said that he would like to be ambassador to China. He said that the Chinese sense it when there is a feeling of superiority. He said he himself had no feeling of superiority and thought he got along very well with the Chinese.

Currie says that the present Chinese regime is very conservative including Chiang Kai-shek, the Soongs, et al. He said that T. V. Soong has had his wings clipped, that his brother-in-law Kung had taken away most of Soong's bank perquisites. Kung's wife is Soong's sister but Mrs. Kung doesn't think much of T.V. according to Currie . . .[2]

[1] Clarence E. Gauss, United States ambassador to China (1941–44), an informed, impatient, and often impious critic of Chiang Kai-shek.

[2] T. V. Soong, chairman of the Bank of China, and H. H. Kung, Chinese Finance Minister, were respectively brother and brother-in-law of Madame Chiang Kai-shek. For many years both men had influenced Chinese financial and economic policy, and engaged, with shifting success, in the rivalries and intrigues that marked the regime of the Generalissimo and his wife.

OCTOBER 6, 1942

. . . At the WPB meeting Nathan[1] outlined the total productive resources of the nation and the percentage that could go to the war effort without too much disruption. He seemed to doubt, in case we went to $50 billion this year in the war effort, that we could do very much beyond it or $60 billion next year without bringing about such a reduction in the civilian life as to make the situation dangerous. General Somervell took very violent exception. Then he (Somervell) and Henderson got into a very picturesque verbal fight. Somervell proclaimed that if the armed forces only had 60 billion dollars' worth of help for the year 1943, that was just like giving them only 50 cents. This made Leon Henderson thoroughly angry and he started calling the general very picturesque names. I could not figure out what Somervell's motives were in saying things which were obviously unbalanced and untrue. Perhaps he was trying to make Henderson blow up . . .

OCTOBER 12, 1942

. . . T. V. Soong told me that he would like to carry word to the Generalissimo of my very great interest in the improvement in the efficiency of Chinese agriculture. I again told Soong that I believed the first step in raising the Chinese standard of living was increasing the efficiency of agriculture, and ventured the belief that an improvement of 30 percent could be made in ten years. T. V. Soong said he thought an even greater improvement could be made and spoke of a number of projects which had to do with irrigation and flood control.

Kingsley Martin[2] was seriously disturbed about Henry Luce's letter to the British in the October 12 issue of *Life*. He felt the Indian situation was causing a serious difference of opinion between the Americans and the British. I told him I did not think the Indian situation was so very much on the American people's mind but that when it was called to their attention the great bulk of the people were against the British, believing that the situation in India was a little bit like that of the American colonies in 1765. He asked what I would suggest. I told him I did not care to suggest anything . . . Martin professed great alarm about the proposal to build a 10-million-man army in the United States. He felt that an army of such size would interfere seriously with the total war effort. I told him I agreed . . .

[1] Robert R. Nathan, liberal economist, chairman of the Planning Commission of the War Production Board (1942–43), and acting director of the Anglo-American Combined Production and Resources Board (1942–43).
[2] Kingsley Martin, editor of the English *New Statesman and Nation*.

OCTOBER 13, 1942

. . . At the WPB meeting both Leon Henderson and Somervell had
cooled off. Leon had the figures to back up his position, figures indicating that the consumers of the United States would only be getting
in the year 1943 less than one-fifth as much of the consumer durable
goods as they had gotten in 1942. Nelson called attention to the fact
that the President had issued a number of "must programs" such as
Russian requirements, 30 million additional airplanes, etc., etc., that
these "must" programs which had come in were of such magnitude
that it would be impossible to accomplish the rest of the program
set for the year 1943 until sometime in the fall of 1944. We all agreed
that there should be a fresh overall examination of the situation by
the Joint Chiefs of Staff in cooperation with Don Nelson and finally
by the President. I said I thought the key figure in this matter of
harmonizing the different programs was the number of men which
we expected to have overseas at certain specific dates. Somervell said
that we expected to have over two million men overseas by December
of 1943 and four million by December of 1944.

Somervell also said it took about 9 tons of material for each man in
the first instance and after that about one ton a month. He said in
the case of airmen, it took 14 tons of material in the first instance.
I asked Somervell if we would have enough shipping by December
1943 to transport supplies to two millions.

I hastily calculated that the transportation of 3,400,000 tons a month
(or perhaps 500 or 600 ships) together with the necessary protection
would be required to supply our overseas forces from December 1943
onward. I asked Somervell if we would have enough shipping to do
the job. He said yes.

Admiral Robinson[1] started to say something and then kept quiet. I
judge he is not quite so certain.

Somervell said the British were carrying on a regular propaganda
campaign all over town against a large army in the United States.

Nathan of the WPB had told me earlier that Somervell was exceedingly anxious to have a big army so that the United States could
have more influence at the peace table. Nathan felt that Somervell
would be glad to see the war continue a year or so longer if thereby
the United States Army could have a chance to show its power. I
said to Somervell, why should we not be happy to have the British and

[1] Admiral Samuel M. Robinson, formerly chief of the Bureau of Ships, in 1942
chief of the Office of Procurement and Material.

Russians do the fighting for us while it needed to be done, with our furnishing the materials laid down at the battle front instead of using them in the United States to create an exceedingly big army. Somervell said it was all right provided the British would really fight.

It appeared to me there has been a lamentable lack of overall planning. I would say the fault is with the Joint Chiefs of Staff and Don Nelson. Somervell has rushed in to grab everything he can without any sense of balance or understanding of the program as a whole. I made the point to Don Nelson that it was high time he presented the whole problem to the President . . .

Cox[1] with his interest in Lend-Lease took a very strong sta..d on the side of a moderately sized American army. Lend-Lease wants to continue to be able to furnish the British, Russians, et al., with substantial quantities of materials and they don't like the Army program for such an excessively big army. I made Somervell's point about the British carrying on propaganda for the Americans having a small army so that the British would have more influence at the peace table. Cox claimed that the British were not carrying on any propaganda of this kind, that it was just a commonsense expression by the British based on their own experience.

The final success of the war effort will depend in very considerable measure on the President's skill in determining just how many American soldiers should be abroad at certain definite times, how many men altogether should be in the American Army at certain definite times and how much material should be allotted at different times to the American, British, Russian, and other armies. This whole problem from now on will jell very rapidly.

OCTOBER 14, 1942

. . . I asked Milo to get for me what information he could on the food situation in Russia. I told him I was going to speak on November 8 on behalf of American-Soviet Friendship and that I was doing everything in my power to make sure that the Russians did not make a separate peace.[2]

[1] Oscar S. Cox, a creative lawyer with a seasoned skill in maneuvering through the labyrinth of official Washington, was general counsel of the Lend-Lease Administration and of the Office of Emergency Management (1941–43). He became general counsel of the Foreign Economic Administration when it was established in 1943.

[2] Wallace had begun to draft his address scheduled for November 8, 1942, before the Congress of American-Soviet Friendship at Madison Square Garden. In

It is becoming increasingly clear to me that sometime within the next 60 days there will be a second front started in northwest Africa. This is the front I suggested to the President within two or three weeks after the Japanese attack on Pearl Harbor. I can't help thinking that the Germans know all about our plans, and hope they don't beat us to the punch.

When I talked to the President about my November 8 speech, I told him I had no desire to take on a speaking engagement and that the only reason I was considering it was because of the possibility of a separate peace by the Russians. The President said he thought I ought to make the talk and said I might well bring out the extent to which Russian and American ideals were coming together, that the Russians had gone perhaps 40 percent of the way toward making their system into a democracy and that the United States had gone perhaps 40 percent of the way in making our capitalistic structure more social, that now we are perhaps only 20 percent apart. I asked the President how it would be if I mentioned my conversation with Molotov about combining American high-airway across the American hemisphere into Siberia with feeders coming in from China and India. He said it would be all right.

OCTOBER 15, 1942

. . . In the discussion with the President with regard to the attitude of Henry Luce toward the British empire, someone ventured to say that Mrs. Luce [1] was probably responsible for Henry's slant. The President spoke up brightly saying, "Oh, you mean that loose woman."

---

general, the speech followed the lines of "The Century of the Common Man." At the suggestion of Roosevelt, Wallace, in looking forward to the triumph everywhere after the war of the democracy of the common man, called for a balance between the economic democracy of the Soviet Union and the political democracy of the United States. He also commended Russia for its "educational democracy" and for its equality of opportunity for women and for all races and minority groups. He referred, as Roosevelt had agreed he might, to his conversation with Molotov about highway and air transport, and he associated that conversation with the importance of a United Nations charter that would include an international bill of rights and economic guarantees of international peace. Stripped of imperialism, a free world of the future, Wallace concluded, would depend upon the continuing cooperation of all nations.

[1] Clare Boothe (Mrs. Henry) Luce, author, playwright, elected that November Republican congresswoman from Fairfield County, Connecticut, a handsome lady with an acid tongue that did not spare Wallace, whom she characterized as an advocate of "globaloney."

OCTOBER 21, 1942

W. Beatty[1] told of the extraordinarily low state of Indian education in . . . Bolivia, Peru, and Ecuador . . . He quoted the President of Bolivia as saying to Allan Dawson[2] of the State Department that it was communistic to educate the Indians. When Dawson pressed him, he said, after the Indians were educated, they wouldn't work for nothing. Beatty hopes that the United States can cooperate with the Indian countries on the West Coast of Latin America to set up a number of schools for training teachers to give the right kind of education to the Indians. I suggested that he get in touch with E. de Lozada . . .

Milo and I had a nice visit with King and Marshall. I pressed in the most tactful way for the desirability of bombing the mainland of Japan and watching any possible drive of the Germans toward Dakar. Marshall took the slant that the Russians had not killed nearly as many Germans as is popularly assumed. He felt that too much emphasis had been placed on the Aleutian Islands and that the Army had been forced by political pressure to send too much strength up there. Of course, I disagreed with him on this but I did not say so . . .

Knox started out the conversation[3] brightly by saying he thought all the Junkers ought to be sterilized, both men, women, and children. He insists that by heredity they are a different type of humanity, and that the world cannot have peace until this blood strain is eliminated. Halifax asked for a vote on the subject of whether or not the Junkers ought to be sterilized. Halifax and Knox voted vigorously on the affirmative. I insisted vigorously that from the standpoint of pure heredity there is no difference between Prussian Junkers and anyone else. Felix Frankfurter quoted somebody that ever since the Napoleonic war, the whole system of education in Germany had been directed toward war. I agreed enthusiastically with Felix and said that the Prussian indoctrination had in effect gone back many, many centuries. I said the all-important thing was to take control of the German educational system for a generation. Halifax and Knox concurred, saying it would be too difficult a job.

It was very apparent that the British are exceedingly sensitive with regard to India . . . I was inclined to question this but I said nothing because of the exceedingly real sensitivity of the British Tories on the

---

1 Willard W. Beatty, since 1936 director of education in the Office of Indian Affairs.
2 Allan Dawson, foreign service officer, in 1942 on assignment to the Division of American Republics in the Department of State.
3 At dinner at the British embassy.

Indian problem. I assumed that the British did not want the United States to butt in on India any more than we would like to have England butt in on Puerto Rico. The situation, however, has an importance from the standpoint of the United Nations even aside from its democratic human importance, which can't help giving us in the United States the greatest concern even though out of deference to the British we do not express it at the moment . . .

OCTOBER 24, 1942

. . . Mike Cowles[1] gave a very complete and interesting account of his trip with Willkie around the world. Mike was exceedingly impressed with the Russians and said that Willkie was even more impressed. He said Stalin has the greatest pride in the fact that he changed Russia from a country that was 90 percent illiterate to a country that was 10 percent literate in 22 years. Stalin, Mike says, has a very deep feeling against the British. It seems that he and Churchill did not get along well and that both of them have made very biting comments about the other to various people since.

At the big party in the Kremlin, there were many courses of food and many courses of Vodka. It is supposed to be a matter of courtesy to do "bottoms up" every round of drinks. Finally they finished with champagne. Everyone had a terrible hangover the next morning when they flew for about three or four hours.

Mike was tremendously impressed with the fact that half of the people working in the Russian factories were women . . . The managers of the factories were getting paid about ten times as much as the average worker.

Mike told of some personal experiences in Baghdad. He and Willkie had been getting sort of bored with all the dinners and luncheons. When the governor general, a severe Britisher, called on Mike to make arrangements for the evening banquet, Mike suggested a little entertainment. Somebody had told him about the girls of Baghdad so he suggested they be invited. At the evening luncheon, Mike was seated next to the wife of the governor general who was the only woman

[1] Gardner Cowles, Jr., publisher of the Des Moines *Register and Tribune*, briefly in 1942–43 domestic director of the Office of War Information, resigned from that position to accompany Wendell Willkie on his trip around the world. A Willkie supporter, Cowles was also an old friend of the Wallace family. He rendered his account of the trip at dinner at the home of Wallace's younger sister Mary, Madame Charles Bruggmann, whose husband was Swiss minister to the United States.

present. She was quite a plain woman of the typical angular British type and spoke at length about archaeology. The governor general arose and said, "At the request of Gardner Cowles, we shall now be entertained by the girls of Baghdad." The wife of the governor general then put her elbow out on the table to shut off Mike's view and said, "We are not interested in this, are we, Mr. Cowles?" It seems that the girls of Baghdad run the houses of prostitution and appeared on the scene with the minimum of clothing. Willkie was greatly delighted and kept shouting to Mike but Mike was operating under difficulties with the archaeologist absorbing all his attention.

Mike indicated on a map the various airfields and said that at no time were they delayed by as much as 10 minutes because of plane difficulties, weather, or shortage of gas. He spoke at some little length about the town of Yakutsk in Siberia, north of the Gobi Desert, not far from the Arctic Circle. This is a town on the Lena River of about 55,000 people. They have an opera house and put on an opera which would have done credit to a town of 200,000 people in the United States. The library had 500,000 volumes as compared with about 300,000 volumes in Des Moines. When they visited this library, they found it very actively in use. Mike reached the conclusion that the Russians are a very fine people with an up-and-coming spirit very similar to that which the United States people had in 1910.

In China Mike found Chiang Kai-shek had exactly the same strong feeling against the British as Stalin had. Chiang Kai-shek thought it would be quite possible to throw the Japs out of Burma and open up the Burma Road provided the British would cooperate. Chiang Kai-shek believes that the British want the Japs in possession of Burma when the war comes to an end so that they can be sure to get Burma back. He believes that the British would hate to see a combination of Chinese-American-Hindu and British troops capture Burma because that would throw a cloud on the British right to the territory.

Mike spoke out vigorously against the American ambassador in China, Mr. Gauss, who has lived in China more than 20 years and has not learned to speak Chinese and seems to glory in his ignorance. He seems to antagonize the Chinese. This is exactly the same story which Lauchlin Currie had previously brought me. This man did a good job in Shanghai but is apparently totally unadapted to Chungking. I judge the State Department knows the man is not fitted for this particular post and will replace him shortly.

Mike was impressed by the extent to which the various Siberian airports have been developed and provision made for snowplows.

OCTOBER 28, 1942

. . . At the lunch with Generals Strong and Deane[1] . . . I told
Strong that Mike Cowles had talked to Chennault in Chungking and
Chennault had told him that if he could only have 60 DC-s, 80 medium-
sized bombers, and 100 pursuit planes, he could lick the Japs by himself.
Strong said, "By God, I believe he could too." I then went on to say
that I understood from Cowles that in order to have sufficient gas to
operate this number of planes, it would be necessary to chase the Japs
out of Burma so that we could reopen the Burma road. Strong indicated that the Chinese could operate more planes than they now have.
Strong was very much of the opinion that more of our supplies ought
to be going to Russia and China. However, we agreed that the best
second front and the place to keep well supplied at all costs was North
Africa. Strong agreed with me that bombing the homeland of Japan
would have a very strong psychological effect. I quoted . . . Craigie,[2]
the British ambassador to Japan, to the effect that the bombing of
Tokyo had caused great consternation among the civilian population . . .

OCTOBER 29, 1942

. . . At cabinet, the President started out by indicating that the
Admirals had done a poor job in handling the publicity with regard to
Guadalcanal. He said the battle there was not a decisive battle, no
matter whether we won or lost. He said the Guadalcanal operations
had gained us precious time to fortify New Caledonia and a number
of other isles.

The chief subject of discussion had to do with the desirability of
appointing a Food Administrator for handling the reoccupied countries
in Europe the same way as Hoover did in 1919 and 1920. The President had the impression that Hoover did an unusually good job at
that time. Stimson spoke up to say that he had seen Hoover a couple
of weeks ago for the first time in several years and that Hoover was
in a very patriotic frame of mind and would like to serve.

The President and the Atty. General indicated that they were quite
skeptical of the school at Charlottesville being conducted by General

---

[1] General George V. Strong, head of Military Intelligence, was also attached to
the Joint Chiefs of Staff, as was General John R. Deane, who was American
secretary to the Combined Chiefs of Staff.
[2] Sir Robert Craigie.

Guillion and General Wickersham.[1] I said that Louis Brownlow [2] had told me that the school was getting along better than he had anticipated it would, that there were a number of good men in the school. The President told Stimson that he had just sent him a memorandum with regard to the Charlottesville school that would make his hair curl.

Cordell Hull spoke of the work done by Leith-Ross[3] and Dean Acheson. Claude Wickard mentioned that Paul Appleby had been doing a lot of work along this line in cooperation with Dean Acheson. It was evident that the President wanted to think particularly about the type of organization that would handle the food and clothing problem of the occupied territories after the Army left. The final decision was to appoint a committee of myself, Cordell Hull, Claude Wickard, and Don Nelson to make a recommendation to him with regard to a skeleton group which might take over from the Army the food and clothing problem in the occupied countries.

After cabinet meeting, I stopped to give to the President the accompanying memorandum which I had received from Barnes[4] . . . I told him the Willkie ballerina story and the Mike Cowles Baghdad story both of which he greatly enjoyed. He said that Willkie when he came in to see him had obviously been drinking considerably and on checking with the newspaper boys later, they said he had not been drinking excessively, that he had had only four or five drinks in the

[1] The War Department had established a school for military government at Charlottesville, Virginia, to train army officers for managing civil affairs in areas conquered by American forces. Acting under instructions from Secretary Stimson, Provost Marshal General Allen W. Gullion had founded the school, which was under the immediate command of Brigadier General Cornelius W. Wickersham, in civilian life a partner in the New York law firm of Cadwalader, Wickersham and Taft. The school, in the view of its critics, emphasized the military role in civil affairs in occupied territories to the detriment of civilian authorities. Wickersham, in that view, symbolized the Wall Street influences which many New Dealers considered endemic in the War Department. Among those critics, whom Stimson disdainfully dismissed as "the cherubs," Harold Ickes had urged Roosevelt on October 27 to act quickly "to displace the huge organization which the Provost Marshal General is building." Roosevelt, as Wallace here reported, scolded Stimson, but to no effectual end.

[2] Louis Brownlow, journalist and specialist in public administration, in 1942 president of the American Society for Public Administration, then and later an occasional visitor at Wallace's office.

[3] Sir Frederick Leith-Ross, Director General of the British Ministry of Economic Warfare, then in Washington to work out with Dean Acheson plans for providing relief to liberated areas, as well for general postwar relief.

[4] Joseph Barnes, foreign news editor of the New York *Herald Tribune* (1940–42), deputy director of the overseas branch of the Office of War Information (1941–44), had accompanied Willkie on his trip. His memo related to that journey.

45 minutes before he went in to see the President. The President wanted to know if Barnes or Cowles said anything about Willkie drinking too much. I said they did not. The President said he told Cowles before he left on the trip to see that Willkie did not say anything that would antagonize the Allied nations. The President feels that Willkie had his chance and has muffed it.

When I told the President about Chiang Kai-shek's slant vis-à-vis the British in Burma, the President seemed to think it was true. He started to talk about the Atlantic Charter, saying that it had been his idea all along that it was a charter which applied to the Pacific as well as the Atlantic and that Churchill was responsible in the first instance for calling it the "Atlantic Charter." He said, however, that Churchill thought it applied to a wider area until he got mixed up in the Indian trouble. Then Churchill began to take the slant that it would not apply to the East. The President said, "I hope Chiang Kai-shek does not know this."

OCTOBER 30, 1942

Bill Hutcheson[1] indicated his exceeding friendliness. He breathed fire and brimstone against the CIO and claimed they were a bunch of communists. He proclaimed AFL had never allowed any communists to belong to any of the AFL unions. He was very proud of the fact that he had worked closely with employers. He said he had been trying to straighten out the Petrillo situation[2] and that he would like to be of service in any way possible to the President in the war effort. One or two things he let drop lead me to believe he is fairly close to John L. Lewis.[3] On the whole, he seems like a conservative well-meaning fellow who is not fully aware of the signs of the times . . .

NOVEMBER 2, 1942

. . . I read over the closing part of my November 8 speech to Bill Herridge. He liked it very much. He thinks it is important that both the President and myself come out strongly with regard to an interna-

[1] William L. Hutcheson, president of the United Brotherhood of Carpenters and Joiners, vice-president of the American Federation of Labor, a steady Republican in his politics and a conservative in his views about labor organization.
[2] James C. Petrillo, president of the American Federation of Musicians, who were then conducting a prolonged strike.
[3] John L. Lewis, stormy president of the United Mine Workers, a founder and the first president of the CIO, and in those roles a bitter enemy of Hutcheson, had since moved his union into an unaffiliated status and in 1940 moved himself into opposition to Roosevelt.

tional New Deal, saying that the United States has gone as far as she could with our domestic New Deal and that in order to make the New Deal really effective it is necessary also to have an international New Deal. Russia has her New Deal and it will help China to build hers. The prosperity of America cannot stand up against the poverty of the world.

Bill still thinks we are losing the war because we do not have a fighting spirit, that we do not have a fighting spirit because we do not know what we are fighting for. He says the people of the world really want an international New Deal. He said he was going to be down again about November 15 and wanted to see me at that time. I said O.K. I told him when I took in my Russian speech over for the President's O.K., I would discuss with him the need for taking the offensive with regard to an international New Deal; also with regard to a food offensive directed toward Europe ...

NOVEMBER 4, 1942

At the meeting with Hull, Wickard, and Nelson, the discussion naturally turned to the election.[1] Hull seemed to think the country was going in exactly the same steps it followed in 1918. He thought it was utterly important to keep the sequence of events from following the 1918–1921 pattern because he felt if we went into isolationism this time, the world was lost forever. There is something very noble but exceedingly dispiriting about Hull's approach to things. He was very sore at Willkie and was inclined to blame Willkie's performance on Joe Barnes, who he said was half communist, who, Hull said, associated with Oumansky in Moscow. Hull said Oumansky was a great enemy of the United States . . .

[1] Tuesday, November 3, 1942, the Republicans had won 44 additional seats in the House of Representatives and 9 in the Senate. They had also turned Democratic governors out of office in New York, Michigan, and California. Among the losers were some of the ablest liberal congressmen, Senator George Norris of Nebraska for one, and among the victors were many Republicans like Hamilton Fish with intractable conservative and isolationist records. Most contemporary interpretations of the returns stressed the degree to which a light turnout, especially among young defense workers and soldiers who were unable to vote, hurt the Democrats, as also did ethnic issues, not the least, Italian-American hostility against the administration's policy, only recently reversed, toward enemy aliens. The Democrats suffered, too, from intraparty divisions, as in New York, and from public dissatisfaction over both inflation and consumer-rationing programs. Further, the war news since Pearl Harbor had been regularly depressing, and the invasion of North Africa had yet to occur. In the new Congress, coalitions of Republicans and conservative, mostly southern, Democrats would dominate both houses.

Secretary Wickard bumbled along with some miscellaneous unintelligible comments, which caused Cordell to say, "I agree with what you are thinking but I can't understand what you are saying."

The purpose of the meeting was to make a recommendation to the President as to what should be done about a skeleton organization to take over the job of feeding and clothing the hungry peoples of Europe when the Army went out of the picture. Hull began talking in an abused tone of voice to the effect that the State Department had had a committee working with the help of the other departments under the leadership of Dean Acheson on the so-called Leith-Ross Plan. He said this plan had been approved by the various departments and the BEW, that he and I had taken it to the President, and the President had approved it as eventually the right thing to do. Wickard asked if China and Russia had approved the plan. Hull said they had been kept informed. I put forward the idea that the best man to run a show of this kind was F. L. McDougall of Australia, that he was genuinely progressive, that he knew the lines both in England and the United States and that he had a positive passion for the food problem. Hull said that the British had suggested the man to handle the show ought to be an American and that the United States would get a great deal of prestige out of doing the job. I asked if the State Department people had examined the McDougall plan. He did not know but said that the State Department people thought very highly of McDougall. I suggested that the Dean Acheson committee meet again and examine the McDougall plan and see whether or not it should not be incorporated. I asked if Hull, Wickard, and Nelson had a better man to suggest than McDougall. The only man put forward was that by Nelson. He thought that Governor Lehman[1] would be excellent for the job. We all agreed . . .

NOVEMBER 5, 1942

. . . At the White House the President read my proposed Russian speech and suggested the addition of the clause making it apparent we would furnish Russia supplies to the limit of our shipping. He also did not like my reference to Anglo-Saxon snobbishness and wanted me to

[1] Herbert H. Lehman, governor of New York (1932–42) had declined to run again that year. An old friend of Roosevelt, Lehman in December 1942 was appointed director of foreign relief and rehabilitation operations within the State Department. He later became director general of the United Nations Relief and Rehabilitation Administration. Roosevelt's plans to the contrary notwithstanding, Lehman in 1943 played a role subordinate to the Army's in relief in occupied areas.

make it clear in the speech that I was supporting economic equality and not social equality. Apparently the President is very sensitive as to what the southern senators feel. I made the changes and the President seemed quite well satisfied with the speech with the suggested changes added . . .

NOVEMBER 6, 1942

. . . Smathers[1] wanted to let me know how Leon Henderson and various other New Dealers' activities contributed to his defeat in New Jersey. He claims that if he had run on a platform opposed to the President, he would have won. He said Senator Johnson's[2] ability to win in Colorado was because of having been in opposition to the President. I told Bill about Lincoln's situation in 1862 and 1864 and told him I thought he was thinking a little too much about small things and not enough about the big trend . . .

NOVEMBER 7, 1942

. . . A typical American communist is the contentious sort of individual that would probably be shot in Russia without any ceremony . . .

NOVEMBER 10, 1942

At the Big Four[3] meeting, the President started out by giving the details on the planning necessary for the North African invasion.[4] He mentioned how it had been talked over with Churchill when he was here last June. I said it was my recollection he had had it in his mind as early as December of 1941 in a theoretical way. He said, yes, that was true (I remembered that I had sent him as a Christmas present, in December of 1941, a book on the Mediterranean, calling his attention to certain chapters and recommending to him the N.W. African at-

---

[1] William H. Smathers, Democratic senator from New Jersey (1937–43).
[2] Edwin C. Johnson, since 1936 Democratic senator from Colorado.
[3] The Big Four: the Vice President, the Speaker of the House, and the majority leaders of both houses—respectively Wallace, Rayburn, Barkley, and Representative John McCormack of Massachusetts.
[4] On November 8, 1942, American forces, commanded by General Eisenhower, invaded French Morocco and Algeria in the largest amphibian operation ever ventured to that date. They quickly defeated, though not without substantial casualties, French garrisons at Casablanca, Oran, and Algiers. On November 11 in Algiers French Admiral Jean-François Darlan signed an armistice.

tack). The President said the matter began to take more definite form in July of 1942 when Hopkins visited London but it did not really take definite form until along in August. Then the question came up as to just when the attack should be. They thought it should be at a time when there was a minimum of moonlight at night. This meant that it should be along about the tenth of October or the seventh of November (darkest moon at this time). It was impossible to do it in October; therefore, it had to be delayed until November.

The President referred in a very grieved tone of voice to the Joe Patterson editorial on the threat of the Japs to the United States because of their occupation of Kiska. The President claimed that Patterson was utterly wrong, that the Japs' occupation of Kiska was an advantage to the United States because it gave us an opportunity to sink a number of their ships . . . I objected mildly, "But surely you would occupy Kiska if the Japs should leave it, wouldn't you?" . . .

NOVEMBER 12, 1942

Just before the BEW meeting took up, Harry White[1] of Treasury congratulated me most strongly on my New York speech, saying that it was very rare when a person could make one outstanding speech in a year but I had made two . . .

A little later in the day, Milo called me to say that Dean Acheson had tried to get him to release oil for shipment to Sweden, thus violating the agreement which was made that morning at BEW meeting. To do so would rightfully have made Bob Patterson and Harry White intensely angry. I told Milo to push the Joint Chiefs of Staff for their opinion at the earliest possible moment, that I thought we should accommodate Dean Acheson as soon as possible but obviously we could not agree to do contrary to the action of the Board just because State Department was pushing.

Aguirre[2] told me of visiting the priests, bishops, et al., in the Latin American countries. He claimed about 10 percent of the American clergy in all of Latin America are of fascist origin and that they are friends of the Allied cause. He spoke to the various Catholic meetings

---

[1] Harry Dexter White, Assistant Secretary of the Treasury, architect of that department's policies in international finance, a contentious but learned and effective administrator, was accused after the war of communist affiliations, which he denied under oath.

[2] José Aguirre, formerly president of the Basque government which had enjoyed a short period of home rule before the victory of General Franco in the Spanish Civil War.

about the need of charity in the Catholic church. He asked why the Catholics could claim to be charitable when Franco had at least 300,000 or perhaps 500,000 people in concentration camps in Spain.

At cabinet the President again told the North African story. C. Hull said there was a problem of how to handle the civilian government behind the military lines in N. Africa. The President then spoke up and told of the good work done by Consuls Murphy and Matthews[1] during the past year. (Henry Morgenthau had told me the preceding evening of the gold money which had been passed out by Murphy, et al., to various key figures among the French in N. Africa). The President apparently thinks that Murphy and Matthews know so much about the political life (˙ N. Africa that their suggestions should be supreme. At the moment their suggestions are that the French authorities be left in control of civilian life. The President's statement was of considerable interest because the preceding day Milo Perkins had received from General Deane of the Joint Chiefs of Staff a letter directing BEW to handle the civilian problem in N.W. Africa. The President's statement meant that Deane's letter would be withdrawn. I knew Milo would be somewhat disappointed but it seemed to me that the President had probably taken a wise stand and that Milo need not be concerned about this particular stand being a precedent for running the postwar world.

I stopped just a moment after cabinet to let the President know that I was beginning the study of Russian. He seemed to be delighted and said he understood that their alphabet made it quite difficult.

NOVEMBER 16, 1942

Harold Smith and I discussed postwar problems at some length. He has a feeling that the National Planning Board is at sixes and sevens and that it is not doing the planning on the domestic front that it should. He says Frederic Delano has now become very forgetful and that there is great difference of opinion between the different members of the board.[2]

1 Robert Murphy and H. Freeman Matthews, who had succeeded Murphy as minister in Vichy and in 1942 had become acting chief of civil affairs on Eisenhower's staff.
2 The National Resources Planning Board under its aging chairman, Frederic A. Delano, was actually developing, albeit slowly, postwar domestic programs, including, among others, plans for national medical insurance and federally financed urban renewal. The liberal, Keynesian attitudes of the board and its advisers irritated the conservative majority in Congress which in 1943 cut off the board's appropriations and ordered it to wind up its affairs.

Harold Smith said that he had been a strong League of Nations man and that he was very eager to do everything he could to insure the winning of the peace. He thought it was important to utilize the institutions of higher learning in building up public sentiment. I agreed with him wholeheartedly—and we agreed that when we ate dinner with Biddle Friday night, we would turn the conversation in that direction . . .

Senator Truman[1] came in to say that they had lost five congressmen from Missouri and he thought the farmers in the Middle West had gone Republican partly because of the way in which Leon Henderson had administered livestock prices and partly because of the shortage of manpower on the farms. I told him part of the situation could be handled by putting food administrators over in the Department of Agriculture and part could be handled by manpower legislation. I told him that if Claude Wickard was not big enough to handle the food administrators, there should be a new Secretary of Agriculture but I thought it was possible Claude might handle the job if the organization situation was straightened out. We talked about the type of legislation that would handle the farm labor problem. His observations were exactly the same as my own based on my contact with Iowa farm folks in September . . .

NOVEMBER 18, 1942

. . . The President spoke about his press conference concerning Darlan, referring to a Serbian proverb about how it was permissible crossing a stream to ride on the back of the devil until you got to safety. I said to the President that it appeared that Robert Murphy had done an exceedingly good job in North Africa. The President then went on to say he had been responsible for Murphy's rise, that he had brought him into the embassy in Paris when the consular service was looked on owlishly by the embassy.[2]

[1] Senator Harry S. Truman.
[2] Many American liberals, in government and out, were protesting against Murphy's preinvasion agreements with Admiral Darlan, who deemed himself the North African spokesman for the Vichy government, a claim that government repudiated after the invasion. Roosevelt, like the State and War Departments, had considered the arrangements with Darlan essential to minimize French resistance, which the President believed they had, even though each side suffered about 3000 casualties and considerable naval and air losses. Continuing Anglo-American collaboration with Darlan resulted in December in his retention by the Allies as chief of state in North Africa, a position he held until he was assassinated on Christmas eve. Darlan's dominance seriously offended General Charles de Gaulle, the leader of the Fighting French and head of the

I told the President I noted that Clark Eichelberger[1] was on his appointment list recently and asked him if he did not think it was about time to give Eichelberger's organization and similar organizations the green light to go ahead. The President said he had suggested to Eichelberger that he use "United Nations" instead of "League of Nations." The President mentioned that the others had not paid any attention to the statement he had given out with regard to the Philippine Islands last Sunday, November 15. He himself looked on it as a very significant statement, holding up the P. Isles as a pattern which might well be followed by other nations with regard to colonies, like Java, Sumatra, Borneo, etc., etc. He mentioned a conversation with Chiang Kai-shek in which Chiang said he thought Java would be ready for complete independence in 15 or 20 years, Sumatra ready in 40 or 50 years, and Borneo not for 100 years . . .

NOVEMBER 20, 1942

The President, after having had Cordell Hull in for lunch, opened up with the most vigorous statement which I have ever known him to make in cabinet. He said there had been altogether too much power-grabbing and backbiting, and that everybody around the table had been guilty of it except the Postmaster General.[2] The President was making a statement relative to North Africa. He paid a strong tribute to the splendid work done by Robert Murphy there and said that the job of running the civilian life in North Africa, as far as the United States was concerned, should be done through the State Department. He said that any monetary work which might be done by Mr. Bernstein[3] of Treasury should clear through State Department, and if Mr. Bernstein

Free French government-in-exile. De Gaulle blamed the Americans for the development of Allied policy in North Africa. "It is a strategic error," he told the British, "to place oneself in a situation contradictory to the moral character of the war"; see *The War Memoirs of Charles de Gaulle* (New York, 1959), Ch. 2.

1 Clark M. Eichelberger, national director of the League of Nations Association, consultant to the State Department (1942–43), later a consultant to the American delegation to the San Francisco Conference that established the United Nations.

2 Frank C. Walker held that office (1940–45) and was also chairman of the Democratic National Committee (1943–44).

3 Bernard Bernstein, lawyer and monetary expert, held various posts within the Treasury during the New Deal. In 1942 a lieutenant colonel, Bernstein was financial adviser to the Allied Forces and to the North African Economic Board. Later he performed similar services in Sicily, Italy, and Germany. In those roles, ordinarily for good reason, he frequently criticized policies the Army adopted and regularly communicated his views to Secretary Morgenthau and others in the Treasury Department.

wanted to get in touch with Henry Morgenthau he should do so through State Department.

After cabinet meeting was over, I stopped to see the President a moment about Josh Lee's desire for a job, and then ventured to say that when the Joint Chiefs of Staff wrote Milo asking him to do this work, that Milo had had nothing to do with getting them to write him, and that when Cordell Hull had stepped into the picture and Milo called me about it, I had told Milo about the Murphy matter. Biddle then spoke up and said that the President was putting on a show for Ickes' special benefit. The President said Ickes was power-hungry. I told the President I regretted that he had not given the State Department a spanking too; that they had held up our telegrams and had changed some of them in transmission and that I felt his statement would cause the State Department to become harder than ever to get along with. The President said that was a different problem; that Cordell was absolutely helpless as an administrator and that he claimed he didn't have any control over his own department. The President said Sumner Welles was hungry for publicity, was a bureaucrat, and that Berle was bitten by the same bug. I told the President that much of our trouble was due to Collado, who was working under Welles' instructions. The whole affair was an interesting demonstration of the way in which the President will respond to suggestion . . .

Dean Acheson took violent exception to Harold Smith's suggestion.[1] Francis Biddle proclaimed that the President didn't want anything going on that was in the nature of postwar planning. I told Biddle I thought he was wrong; that the President didn't want the government to be hooked up with postwar planning at the present time but he was anxious for other people to start public education, especially with regard to a United Nations setup.

It was rather obvious that most of those present were chiefly concerned with some method of keeping the Army from taking charge of everything.

Reference was made to the high percentage of reactionaries in the Army. I raised the question as to whether there were more reactionaries in one department than another. Jessup[2] said there was a strong element in the Army who felt we should start strengthening France

---

[1] Smith had proposed a civilian-dominated Occupation Authority independent of the Army and of all cabinet departments.

[2] Philip C. Jessup, distinguished authority on international law, was soon to become chairman of the Office of Foreign Relief in the State Department and later assistant general secretary of UNRRA.

and Germany so as to avoid Russia having things too much her way. I replied I thought there were just as many people of this kind in the State Department. I further said that while it was perfectly clear that the channel in running civilian affairs in North Africa should be the State Department, I nevertheless felt that the State Department's experience and personnel were not such as to make them ideal for doing the occupied job in other places. I strongly favored Harold Smith's proposal of an Occupation Authority. Dean Acheson said he thought it was very dangerous . . .

NOVEMBER 26, 1942

. . . At the close of the Thanksgiving Service, the President motioned to me to sit down beside him and after the crowd left, I said I would like to approach him in the spirit of Queen Esther approaching King Ahasuerus, only I was going to speak on behalf of the liberals rather than the Jews. I told him I thought the liberals were finding themselves in an increasingly difficult position. Many officials were putting out the story, for example, that men in uniform were going to run the country for the next 10 years. Businessmen in Commerce and their kindred souls in State Department were increasingly getting the idea that big corporations were going to run the country. The President indicated he was gravely concerned about the situation in the Army. I said that Milo's difficulties were becoming increasingly severe, that I understood there was an executive order in process which would be taken by Milo's liberals as indicating that BEW was on its way out. I told the President that logically BEW should be split and given to State and Commerce but I felt with the situation in State and Commerce as it was, this would be increasingly unfortunate from the liberal point of view. The President said he agreed entirely. I said the executive order granting the food administrator food export control powers in the Department of Agriculture would take away certain export controls from BEW. The President said I need not be concerned about that, that he was hoping to get Marvin Jones[1] to run the food administration in Agriculture. I said to him "Mr. President, . . . it might be better to give the power exclusively to Claude or to put Marvin Jones in as Secretary of Agriculture." The President

---

[1] Marvin Jones, Democratic congressman from Texas (1917–40), chairman of the House Committee on Agriculture (1931–40), appointed judge of the United States Court of Claims in 1940 and in June 1943 United States Food Administrator.

said that he just could not replace Claude . . . This meant to me that
he was going to make some other cabinet change . . .

    I told the President that hitherto . . . he had rather wanted me to
stay out of executive work but that now with the attack against the
liberals going on so actively in the government, I felt I should get into
administration work in BEW, get more intimately acquainted with
the personnel and their problems. Much to my surprise, the President
said, "Fine. Go ahead" . . .

NOVEMBER 27, 1942

    . . . I told Milo about my conversation with the President and that
I wanted to spend a lot of time getting acquainted with his personnel
and their problems. I told him I would be in the following day. I
think I shall give an hour a day to this until I meet at least the top 10
men in Milo's shop . . .

NOVEMBER 30, 1942

    At the White House the President raised the question as to whether
the time wasn't ripe now to speak out on behalf of how the United
Nations would use their power to keep the peace. He said he did not
think the United States would have to have an army of more than
200,000 men provided there were proper organization to prevent Germany and Japan from rearming. He felt there ought to be inspectors
from countries like Latin America and Scandinavia to go over all the
places where Germany and Japan might make parts for airplanes, tanks,
etc. If any evidence of activity along this line became apparent, the
United Nations would at once tell the offending country that if she
didn't stop by next Monday, for instance, a quarantine would promptly
be imposed so that neither goods nor people could go in or out. If
the offending country still persisted, then the statement would be made
that at such and such a date Cologne would be bombed, the next day
Frankfurt, the next day Düsseldorf, etc, etc. Sam Rayburn spoke up
and said he didn't think the time was ripe yet for such a statement.
McCormack took the other side. So did I. Barkley was neutral. I
urged the President to make the parallel column presentation showing
to the American people the relative costs of isolation and a big army
as compared with the United Nations collective security approach.

    Sam Rayburn mentioned that he had been in conference with Mrs.
Luce. The President and all the rest of us began to kid him and Sam

turned pink. Sam said Mrs. Luce was a great friend of Madame Chiang Kai-shek and had talked to Sam to urge him to tell the President that Madame Chiang Kai-shek would be attending some meeting as soon as she got out of the hospital, at which she would say just what she thought of the British. Sam thought the President should see Madame Chiang Kai-shek before she spilled the beans.

Charlie Marsh told me that he had positive information that Tom Corcoran[1] . . . was working very closely with Sam Rayburn and the Luces. He said that Corcoran had recently taken Mrs. Luce around to see Sam Rayburn. According to Marsh, Corcoran is also working very closely with Jim Rowe,[2] Francis Biddle, Justice Douglas, Lyndon Johnson, and perhaps his old friend, Felix Frankfurter. According to Charlie, Corcoran arranges for Douglas to meet a great variety of people. Between them they arranged for Lyndon Johnson to go out to speak in Oregon at the Navy Day launching the first week in December. Johnson showed the speech to Charlie Marsh and said that it had been approved by Douglas. The speech, according to Charlie, kicks the New Deal into a cocked hat. Apparently, the Corcoran line is that the public is now tired of the New Deal; that they must be given something new. After the New Dealers and all that they stand for have been kicked around, Tommy will bring out Douglas as a breath of fresh air from the Far West. Douglas will have taken an attitude sufficiently to the right of the New Deal so that he will be acceptable to Baruch et al. . . .

DECEMBER 1, 1942

. . . At the WPB meeting Somervell introduced General Clay,[3] who made a very fine presentation to the modification of the Army program. It appears now that the Army is going to reduce its sights to a more practical basis. On the whole, I thought the Army did a good

---

[1] Thomas G. Corcoran, Democratic lawyer and political manipulator, had been an effective assistant to the Attorney General (1932–35) and to congressional committees drafting the Securities Act of 1933, the Securities and Exchange Act of 1934, and the Public Utility Holding Company Act of 1935. During the early years of the war, Corcoran, while a paid lobbyist for Chiang Kai-shek, was busier promoting the candidacy of his old friend William O. Douglas, Associate Justice of the Supreme Court, for the Democratic nomination as Vice President.

[2] James H. Rowe, Jr., like Corcoran at one time a clerk for Associate Justice Oliver Wendell Holmes, and an accomplished New Dealer, was in 1942 an assistant to the Attorney General.

[3] General Lucius D. Clay was at this time assistant chief of staff for Material Service of Supply. Appointed deputy director for war programs in December 1944, he became deputy to General Eisenhower the following year.

job in presenting the program thus far completed and prospects for production in 1943.

The young liberals like Bob Nathan and Ezekiel in their hammering on the Army have done both the Army and the country a real service.

DECEMBER 2, 1942

. . . Gene Casey[1] claimed that there was a cabal between Somervell, Forrestall and Eberstadt[2] with Harry Hopkins in the background manipulating it. He said that these men felt that the Democratic Party needed to be given a completely new line. They felt that the Army should be brought into the Democratic Party in a big way and also certain big business interests. Their program, according to Casey, was to build up Bob Patterson to run for them in 1944. Casey said that Patterson had recently changed his affiliation from Republican to Democratic and that he was the only one from the Republican side who had attended the party at the Democratic Committee headquarters election night. I told Casey that I had known that Eberstadt was boosting Patterson for 1944 but that I did not think there was anything in the nature of a cabal, and that I didn't agree with him that these men believed in a fascist, military dictatorship for the United States. Apparently Casey is very unhappy in his White House job . . .

DECEMBER 3, 1942

At Secretary Hull's office, in introducing Lazo, I said I hoped the Secretary had no objection to shaking hands with men who had been accused of murder. The Secretary did not understand me and began talking at great length justifying all that he had done in North Africa, and especially dealing with Darlan. I then told him that as a result of the statement of one of the five top men in the State Department to about thirty people, including some Britishers, I had found it necessary to get more actively into BEW administration. I said in the first instance the President had indicated he wanted me to stay out of active administration, but that when one of the top men in the State Department had stated that BEW was responsible for the murder

[1] Eugene B. Casey, an executive assistant to the President.
[2] Ferdinand Eberstadt, New York investment banker, was in 1942–43 vice chairman of the War Production Board, an office in which he ordinarily sided with the Army in its continual disagreements with his administrative senior, Donald Nelson. Though Nelson ultimately discharged him, Eberstadt remained a force in Washington, particularly within the Navy and War Departments.

of American men in North Africa, I felt that I, having the administrative responsibility for BEW, should get more actively into administration; that therefore, I had spoken to the President on Thanksgiving Day and the President had given me the green light to get into active administration. I said that I had been visiting with BEW administrators in their own offices, not merely the men at the top but also second, third, and fourth string men. I stated that I had found some things that were not good and other things that were excellent. Among other things I had found that there seemed to be some misunderstanding between our Office of Export Control and the State Department. I said we had brought in Hector Lazo about two months ago; that he was the son of the former Minister from Guatemala; that he was enthusiastically in favor of Secretary Hull's Good Neighbor Policy; that he had had much business experience and that he wanted to do a practical, efficient job. Secretary Hull indicated that he had never before heard of Berle's statement and said that if we wanted to discuss technical details he would like to have in one of his men. He sent for Acheson and I told Acheson about the same story that I had told Secretary Hull. Acheson stated that Berle was completely in the wrong. Hull started to indicate that he had no control over Berle but then thought better of it and didn't complete his statement. I told him that I was not interested in the past; that all I was thinking about was the future; that I was relating this incident only to account for why I had suddenly gotten into the executive side of BEW. Lazo gave Secretary Hull and Dean Acheson a copy of the points of difficulty between the State Department and BEW. Both Acheson and Hull agreed that the points were reasonable. Acheson said he had been guilty of putting out the statement to the Chiefs of Mission in the Foreign Field with regard to export control, but said he had been informed by his people that BEW had approved it. He said he never would have done it if he had known that we had not approved. Secretary Hull was most amicable and told how his desire was always to bring about the finest relations possible. We discussed the situation in Mexico at some little length and I think some progress was made . . .[1]

---

[1] Ambassador George S. Messersmith instructed BEW personnel in Mexico to report to Washington through him. In their view, he used his authority to delay the execution of their procurement programs and attending agreements about working conditions for Mexican laborers.

DECEMBER 5, 1942

. . . In Barkley's office I met with both Barkley and Brown[1] and we went over the Jesse Jones' testimony. I told the Senators that I felt that BEW had a right to be heard before they took any action on the Danaher amendment, which would, in effect, transfer BEW power to RFC. I found both Barkley and Brown laboring under a number of perfectly natural misconceptions growing out of Jones' testimony. About all I did was to impress on them the desirability of Milo, and perhaps myself, being heard.

I told Clyde Herring[2] that Barkley and Brown had agreed that Perkins would be heard before any action should be taken on the Danaher Amendment to Jesse Jones' 5 billion dollar additional funds bill. Clyde agreed and said he would be present at the Committee meeting . . .[3]

DECEMBER 11, 1942

. . . After cabinet meeting which was the shortest we ever had, I showed the President my December 28 speech.[4] He liked it but said

[1] Prentiss M. Brown, Democratic senator from Michigan (1936–43), defeated for re-election in 1942, appointed in January 1943 to succeed Leon Henderson as head of the Office of Price Administration, a position from which he resigned the following October.

[2] Clyde L. Herring, Democratic senator from Iowa (1937–43), defeated for re-election in 1942, from March to November 1943 senior assistant administrator for OPA.

[3] Wallace and Perkins testified on December 8, 1942, before the Senate Committee on Banking and Currency. They contradicted each of the major points Jesse Jones had made on December 2. Jones had asserted that he was powerless to prevent expensive, inefficient, and socially undesirable procurement contracts that the BEW negotiated abroad. The proposal that Senator Danaher was contemplating, one Jones denied inspiring but did approve, would have given Jones' Reconstruction Finance Committee veto power over BEW projects. The committee tabled that proposal, but Jones' guileless attack provoked Wallace to retaliate at the end of the month by asking Roosevelt again to transfer to the BEW the borrowing authority necessary to make the agency self-financing. Again the President declined to do so.

[4] Wallace spoke over the radio on December 28, 1942, the 86th anniversary of the birthday of Woodrow Wilson. The first job, he said, was to win "this world-wide people's war," but the country was justified in looking forward to the general principles of the peace to come. "Obviously," Wallace continued, "the United Nations must first have machinery which can disarm and keep disarmed those parts of the world which would break the peace. Also there must be machinery for preventing economic warfare and enhancing economic peace among nations." If Americans expected guarantees from aggression, they would have to give reciprocal guarantees. So, too, they would have to adjust their

that in view of the fact that I was giving it over the air, he thought it would be wise to reduce the amount of philosophic discussion dealing with the nature of liberty and equality.

He outlined to me at some length his own ideas about his congressional message the first week in January. He intends to emphasize, in talking about the postwar world, the necessity of young people who come out of the Army feeling that they have won a war in which there is more freedom from want and more freedom from fear. By freedom from fear, he meant freedom from fear of war. When he talked about freedom from want, he brought up the question of the Beveridge report.[1] I told him I thought the Beveridge report was a good approach for England and while I thought it might be used to some extent in the United States, I thought that in a dynamic country like the United States, it was more important to lay emphasis on the right of labor to full employment, that labor was just as much entitled to full employment as agriculture was to parity.

I told the President that inasmuch as Congress was going to adjourn about December 15 that I wondered whether or not he had talked with Cordell about the advisability of my making a Latin American trip such as the President had outlined the last time I was with him. He said he had talked with Hull about it but that his (Hull's) answer was sort of funny. It was in very broad philosophical terms, that it was a good thing for all of us to cultivate the best of relations with Latin America at all times. So I promptly said to the President, "I don't believe I care to go to Latin America at the present time unless the State Department is more enthusiastic than that."

I told the President it was common gossip in Wall Street that the President had gotten over his foolishness now, that he had settled down, and that we were now headed toward the kind of world in which Wall Street felt comfortably at home. Furthermore I said the Tories in England are now feeling very much more comfortable. This is evidenced by moving Cripps out of the picture. I said that it was probable the conservatives in both England and in the United States are working together and that their objective will be to create a situation which will eventually lead to war with Russia. I told the President . . . that apparently there was in the State Department a

---

tariffs to meet the responsibilities of a creditor nation. Their ultimate aims, he concluded, should be "to preserve . . . liberty in a political sense, equality of opportunity in international trade, security against war and business depression . . . and unity of purpose in promoting the general welfare of the world."
[1] On "cradle to the grave" security for the British people after the war.

strong group that felt that Russia was the real enemy. I suggested that if we were to avoid a situation that would lead to World War No. 3, it was very important for the President and Stalin to meet. The President said that he had already talked to Stalin about this and that the proposal was that he meet Stalin either at Iceland, or in Nome, Alaska. Stalin, however, could not get away with the winter campaign just coming on. It would seem from the President's attitude that the meeting will take place in the not too distant future.

I told the President about Berle's efforts to destroy Michael Straight's Free World crowd. I said I thought Berle was animated by profound religious convictions but that his soul was a tortured one . . . The President indicated that Berle and others who were trying to control the peace need not worry too much, that if every department of this government were represented at the peace and other governments had each department represented, there would be at least 40,000 people at the peace conference . . . The President said there were just going to be three folks making the peace conference . . .

DECEMBER 14, 1942

At the Big Four meeting, Senator Lister Hill[1] was present instead of Alben Barkley. The President started out by saying that Joe Kennedy[2] had called him. The President said something about how he always liked Joe Kennedy but how he especially liked Mrs. Kennedy. John McCormack agreed that Mrs. Kennedy was very fine. The President said Kennedy had told him he had not recognized the Catholics in recent appointments. The President told Joe that he had. Out of 20 recent appointments in Massachusetts, 19 were Catholics. John McCormack said what a fine thing it would be if Joe Kennedy could be appointed to something. The President rejoined that unfortunately Joe Kennedy told everything he knew to Arthur Krock and Frank Kent.[3] I observed drily that there were others in executive positions who leaked to Krock and Kent. Senator Hill suggested that Kennedy be put on the job of small business problems. John McCormack said that it was especially important to give Joe Kennedy a job be-

[1] Democratic senator from Alabama since 1938.
[2] Joseph P. Kennedy had had no federal office since resigning, largely in protest against Roosevelt's foreign policy, as Ambassador to the Court of St. James's.
[3] Columnists Arthur Krock of the New York *Times* and Frank R. Kent of the Baltimore *Sun*, both widely syndicated, both constantly privileged recipients of gossip and information that the State Department wanted to plant.

cause that would solve the problem with regard to a certain clique (Catholic clique) in the East. I asked who were in the clique but John did not specify . . .

. . . Milo told me that he had lunch that day with Oscar Cox, Harry Hopkins, and Leon Henderson. Milo gained the impression that Harry was much disturbed for fear the President was losing liberal support. Harry said the purpose of the meeting was to find out just how to launch the President's candidacy in 1944. Oscar Cox and Harry suggested to Milo that he ought to try to strengthen the State Department by getting liberal people into the State Department. They also advocated that Milo work harmoniously with Jesse Jones and the State Department. Milo answered them very forthrightly and vigorously with regard to both Jones and State. Leon was inclined to support Milo.

It is apparent that Harry Hopkins and Oscar Cox want to soft-soap everybody as a part of launching the 1944 candidacy. Milo's slant is —what is the use of winning an election if you lose in advance the things you are fighting for—I am inclined to think Milo is right.

At the W. House this morning:

The President spoke very vigorously about Claude Pepper[1] and the poll tax legislation and said that Pepper ought to be paddled for bringing up the poll tax legislation at this time.

DECEMBER 16, 1942

. . . At the White House . . . I sat next to Mrs. Roosevelt, who said she was glad to see me fighting Jesse Jones. She mentioned how exceedingly cold it was staying in the castle with the mother of King George. She has very little use for Churchill and told Mrs. Wallace about a dinner at which she had spoken out quite strongly against Franco, and Churchill had talked on the other side. Mrs. Churchill said to Mrs. Roosevelt that she agreed with Mrs. Roosevelt. Then Churchill got a little angry and said he had been the way he was for 58 years and was not going to change now.

I spoke across the table to the President saying I understood there had been a meeting of the Institute of Pacific Relations up in Canada over the weekend and that some very high class Britishers were there. The President asked if the Britishers took their typical slant. I said

[1] Claude D. Pepper, outspoken Southern liberal, Democratic senator from Florida (1936–45).

"yes." The President then said when there were four people sitting in at a poker game and three of them were against the fourth, it is a little hard on the fourth. This I took to mean that he, Stalin, and Chiang Kai-shek would be playing the game together . . .

At the showing of the movies, there were a number of additional folks in who were not in for dinner. William Green [1] of the AFL was there. I said to him that I had come to the conclusion that the leadership of labor would have to go into a new field and go beyond the urging of higher wages, shorter hours, and better conditions of labor —that the most important field of all is taking an active interest in producing full employment. I said to him that undoubtedly housing was one of the best ways of bringing about full employment. Green said that he agreed and that he was going to have talks with his people about getting into this broader field.

The President asked Palmer,[2] Fred Delano, and me into his study. Palmer urged that the President empower me to head up all the housing activities of the government. I ducked and ran as fast as I could and was glad to see that the President agreed with me. I told the President that Nelson Rockefeller's definition of a coordinator is a man who can keep all the balls in the air without losing his own. Palmer then said that the people of England were very anxious to have me come over to visit them. The President said that neither he nor I should go to England now, that it would be politically fatal to either one of us and he did not want to see my reputation destroyed in this way. He was really serious when he said this.

The President talked again about his message to Congress and I urged very strongly that he play up the need of full employment and especially employment for the soldier boys when they return . . .

DECEMBER 17, 1942

At the BEW meeting after brief discussion of fiber and the bringing in of strategic materials by transport planes, the time was fully taken up by the discussion of the need for a committee to define governmental policy with regard to Lend-Lease exportation (both reimbursable and nonreimbursable) vs. the using of private exporters in various areas. It seems that the exporters are beginning to gang up a little bit on Lend-Lease, claiming that government goods are being

[1] William Green, since 1924 president of the American Federation of Labor.
[2] Charles F. Palmer, Atlanta realtor, defense housing coordinator (1940–42), Roosevelt's representative and head of a special housing mission to Great Britain, March–December 1942.

given away free in certain areas where they have the dollars to buy the goods through regular private channels. It seems that some little time ago when the British dollar balance sunk as low as 200 million dollars, they gave Britain assurances that when their balances were built up to 600 million dollars, they would not need Lend-Lease except when their dollar balances fell below 600 million dollars. It seems that we pay dollars for bauxite in British Guinea and then give the British the resulting aluminum on Lend-Lease. This, combined with the way we are handling the gold situation in South Africa, has resulted in building up the British dollar balances to $1100 million dollars. One of the problems has to do with whether the British Empire should be considered as a whole or broken into its parts. Apparently the British so far have preferred to play it one way part of the time and the other way part of the time so as to have it on a "heads I win, tails you lose" basis. It was obvious that Dean Acheson[1] was rather restless about having BEW get into this problem. I told him I would be glad to talk to Secy. Hull about the matter at any time but it seemed to me that the State Department for its own sake should decide what its policy really was in this field . . .

At the close of cabinet meeting, Henry Morgenthau let me know that any time I needed him in BEW meeting to offset Jesse Jones, just to let him know. He said he was glad to see that we had kept a record on Jesse in the way which he (Henry) had suggested last April and he noticed we had used that record to good effect . . .

DECEMBER 18, 1942

. . . At Frankfurter's were present: Henry Morgenthau, Ambassador Halifax, Justice Byrnes, Harry Hopkins, Secretary Stimson, General Marshall, V. P. Wallace. Immediately after dinner the purpose of the meeting became apparent. Felix cited a number of statements by different individuals indicating that all was not well between the British and the United States. He thought it was exceedingly important that the two great English-speaking nations be pulling together at the peace table. It is evident that Felix has very profound reverence with regard to British institutions. He was so choked with emotion that he did not speak very clearly. After Felix concluded his strong appeal for Anglo-American harmony at the peace, I said that I had understood from Gardner Cowles that Willkie found at both Moscow

---

[1] Acheson, eager to permit British balances to rise, was already fighting with the Treasury, which wanted to hold them to one billion dollars.

and Chungking very strong feeling, first, against the British and, second, against the United States. Hopkins then spoke up to say that too much importance should not to be attached to what was said to Willkie by either Stalin or the Chiang Kai-sheks. He said flatly that Stalin knew all about the North Africa offensive whereas no one on the Willkie trip knew anything about it. He said Stalin for purposes of his own had taken Willkie for a ride, that both Stalin and Chiang Kai-shek used words not to portray their thoughts or to tell the truth but merely to get the desired effect. He paid great tribute to the Chiang Kai-sheks as supreme artists in diplomatic propaganda in sucking folks in and deceiving them. Harry claimed that Willkie was playing pure politics and that he was really friendly enough to the British empire but for political purposes had criticized the empire and come out strongly for a second front. It is apparent that Harry has no faith in anyone and believes that everybody moves in response to self-interest.

With regard to our relations to China and Russia, he thinks the only thing that counts is what the eventual mutual self-interest may be.

Harry said flatly that Joe Barnes had been a member of the Communist Party, that he was a close friend of Oumansky,[1] that Oumansky was not a friend of the United States, that Barnes and Oumansky together filled Willkie up with the Russian point of view, that they were exceedingly unjust to Admiral Standley.[2]

Harry said that Churchill would be Premier only for the war period, and after that undoubtedly the British people would select somebody else. He did not see why people were so much disturbed about peace at the present time. He claimed that if we had real faith in democracy, we would not be disturbed, that the people could be trusted to find the right answer when the time came. He said that for his part he had faith in democracy.

I said I too had great faith in democracy but I felt that democracy without education as to the changing nature of the situation could bring about a situation such as existed after the last war. I said the world made a bally ass out of itself after the last war and that it was right that we should be concerned at the present time about the peace.

[1] Constantine A. Oumansky, in Hull's phrase "a walking insult," had returned to Moscow in 1942 after serving as Soviet Ambassador to the United States. Maxim Litvinov had succeeded him in that post.

[2] Admiral William H. Standley, United States Ambassador to the Soviet Union (1942–43), tended to bridle whenever Roosevelt sent a special emissary to Moscow. Standley was particularly upset by Willkie, who went his own way, which included a private meeting with Stalin, without consideration for the ambassador's delicate sense of his own prerogatives.

Felix said that the nature of the peace was being determined by every action we took at the present time and that we should be very deeply concerned.

Halifax mentioned how rapidly the whole atmosphere changed the moment the war came to an end. Secretary Stimson gave a talk on how the world at the present time was in somewhat the same state as the North American colonies from 1782 to 1787. I said the United Nations charter was in the nature of a preamble to a world constitution, and the problem was what was the minimum of power which the United Nations should have in order to assure peace. Stimson said that he had been at variance with the Republican party with regard to free trade. He said he was very strongly behind Secretary Hull in his efforts to bring about lower tariffs. I said that unless the United States acted as a creditor nation had to act with regard to tariffs, there would be grave danger of the United States causing World War No. 3. Stimson indicated he agreed with me but he thought it would be politically impossible to do anything with regard to giving the United Nations control over tariffs. I did not argue the point because I recognized the political truth of his contention. Justice Byrnes made an impassioned talk, saying that the one thing which everyone was agreed on was the need for power to enforce the peace. I said that, in brief, the absolute minimum of power for the United Nations would be a series of international airports and a strong international air force. Before Byrnes spoke, Hopkins had gone home. All the rest seemed to be agreed that this was the absolute minimum.

I said the important thing which the United States might be able to give to the general welfare of the United Nations, in addition, would be an assurance that she would act as a creditor nation must act with regard to her trade and tariff policies, and that the one thing which the British Empire should give, above everything else, was an assurance that she would act toward the people of India and China in conformity with the principles of the United Nations charter. Halifax did not seem to think it would be too hard for the British to do the last part. Knowing about the British part in the discussion at the Institute of Pacific Relations a week previous in Canada, I had my fingers crossed.

Morgenthau rode home with me and observed that Hopkins was a funny fellow and he could not understand him. He wondered why Harry had emphasized so strongly that Churchill would be through when the peace came.

DECEMBER 19, 1942

Henry Morgenthau told how back in 1937 or 1938 the President had put him in charge of the job of helping the British and the French get war materials here in the United States, and how when Lend-Lease was set up, this function was transferred from him over to Harry Hopkins . . .

Henry again expressed surprise that Harry Hopkins, the preceding evening, should have referred to the possibility of the British people throwing Churchill out when the peace came. Henry said that England herself now had a gold and dollar balance amounting to 1 billion dollars. The rest of the British empire had about 1 billion dollars in gold and dollar exchange, of which the greater part is in South Africa. The whole matter probably has such an exceeding touchiness because of the fact that from 1933 onward, the United States had financed the British empire every year to the extent of several hundred million dollars by buying gold at a high price from South Africa—gold for which the United States had no use except for the purpose of giving dollar exchange to the British empire. In other words, our gold policy was a method whereby we gave away several hundred dollars' worth of goods each year to the British empire. The British vitally needed this help to keep going. They will need it even more after this war; therefore, those in the State Department who are particularly interested in the British will be gravely concerned that anyone should even think of looking into this delicate situation except those who have the proper degree of friendliness to the British.

I suspect that Cordell Hull doesn't know a thing about the ultimate implications of the situation. As far as BEW is concerned, all we are interested in at the moment is that the various governmental departments should know of the extent to which the British empire has piled up dollar exchange and gold and that some point should be set beyond which we should stop giving goods away to the British under Lend-Lease. Also the British cannot indefinitely look on the empire as a unit on the one hand and as being composed of separate parts on the other, and thus endeavor to get an answer forever of "heads I win, tails you lose."

At Justice Byrnes' office, I discussed the same thing I had with Morgenthau. I told him I thought the matter might perhaps be getting hot in Congress and that we ought to arrive at some kind of policy, that in view of the personalities involved, I felt a little hesitant. I told Byrnes about how vigorously Oscar Cox had pushed the matter in

Morgenthau's meeting on behalf of Lend-Lease being responsible only to the President and it being nobody else's business to get into the picture. Jimmie said he thought Harry Hopkins did not know anything about Cox's action, that when I called him (Byrnes) on the telephone yesterday, Harry had been sitting in his office, that he told Harry about my call and that Harry expressed complete ignorance . . .

De Lozada expressed the . . . view that in Latin America the trend of public opinion since the elections and since the North African successes had been very bad. He says this feeling is especially emphasized because of the State Department policy of cooperating only with the conservative elements in Latin America. In brief, the signs of the times and the State Department both have caused the liberals in Latin America to have a profound distrust of the United States. The Good Neighbor policy is at a lower ebb than it has been for some time . . .

Enrique de Lozada told me about the strike in the tin mines in Bolivia. It seems that legislation has passed the Bolivian Congress providing for a social security program. Enrique said we had in BEW copies of cables sent in by Boal,[1] our ambassador to Bolivia, telling about the situation. It seems that Boal has made representations to the government there that the United States was against this legislation. In other words, Boal has intervened in the internal affairs of Bolivia, a thing which the State Department says it never does. I told Enrique I would get hold of the cablegrams and try to find out from Milo whether or not the situation was likely to affect our tin supply adversely . . .

Enrique believes that the fundamental line in the State Department at the present time is cooperation with the Vatican. He thinks the State Department will cooperate with the Vatican to bring about a negotiated peace, that the Vatican is interested in the corporative forms of governmental organization, in other words, modified fascism. He

---

[1] Pierre de L. Boal, United States ambassador to Brazil, had no sympathy for Wallace's aspirations for social reform in Latin America or for the Vice President himself. Boal had written Wallace on October 21, 1942, about rumors reported by the Bolivian foreign minister accusing Wallace of encouraging the "Leftist Opposition" to the incumbent (and characteristically undemocratic) government. On November 11, 1942, Wallace replied, denying the charge. Now Boal supported the Bolivian government for declaring a state of siege as part of an effort to stop the strike in the mines. He had also told the Bolivian president that the modest social security legislation recently enacted would prove costly to major producers of tin and copper, and force them to seek a higher price from the United States for their products. He had, too, interpreted the strike more as a political than an economic development. Further, though Boal understood that inflation in Bolivia had aggravated the poverty of the workers, he considered their strike for higher wages unjust and anti-American.

thinks both the Vatican and the State Department want to see the war end in such a way that there will be semi-fascist governments in the United States and most of the other countries of the world. The Vatican wants to be in position to deal with such governments on a diplomatic basis as a temporal power. The State Department line relative to South America, Franco and the Vatican seems to be definitely Catholic . . .

DECEMBER 21, 1942

. . . Vannevar Bush came in with a report to be transmitted to the President about the matter which has the most profound significance not only for the war but for the peace as well. This is a matter which I have been following with Bush for more than a year and which I hope to have the privilege of continuing to follow. It is a matter in which the British are trying to play their customary role of getting more than they are entitled to.[1]

DECEMBER 22, 1942

The Prime Minister,[2] who speaks no English, told what a remarkable

[1] That was also Bush's opinion, for the United States was doing 90 percent of the work on the production of the atomic bomb and neither Bush nor his senior associates were prepared to accede to British requests for a bilateral agreement about the sharing of information and the control of the prospective weapon. The exchange of information, Bush had concluded, was justified only when it advanced the war effort, and a joint production effort would cost time in the race against Germany for the bomb. Though the United States had profited from British scientific information about both atomic energy and various weapons, Roosevelt in December decided to confine further exchange of atomic information to the limits acceptable to his advisers, a rather ungenerous decision. Wallace supported it at the time, but he was not then wholly informed about the extent to which the British had reason to expect better treatment, nor did he know that the President decided as he did partly to head off Ambassador Winant's proposal for exchanging information with the Russians. After the bomb had been dropped, Wallace came to advocate much more freedom of information than he contemplated in 1942. On this and all questions relating to atomic energy and to Wallace's ideas about it and his role within government debates about it, see the indispensable work: Richard G. Hewlett and Oscar E. Anderson, Jr., *The New World, 1939–1946* (University Park, Pa., 1962).

[2] General Wladyslaw Sikorski, Prime Minister of the Polish government-in-exile in London, had called on Wallace with that government's ambassador to the United States, Jan Ciechanowski. Stalin had already refused to consider restoring Poland's prewar eastern border, though he contemplated compensating Poland by extending her border in the west. In April 1943, shortly before Sikorski was killed in an airplane accident, the Soviet Union broke off relations with the government-in-exile and moved to form a rival government which would accede to Soviet policies.

job the Poles were doing and what horrible sufferings they were undergoing. He indicated that there were 40 divisions in Poland organized to carry out commands, that they had wrecked 897 locomotives and had broken up 3 bridges recently. He told about how they had given the Russians very valuable information as to just where the Germans were going to strike, that the Russians thought that the Germans this past summer would strike at Moscow, that the Poles had told them the blow would come at Stalingrad and, therefore, the Russians were prepared . . . He says Stalin is a dictator in a far greater sense than anyone here in the United States can possibly understand, that Molotov who is second in command is as small as a particle of dust. Sikorksi said when he was with Stalin in September of 1941 he was able to arrive at certain understandings with regard to Polish and Russian matters. But since then matters have been going better with Russia and he is not sure that Russia will be disposed to feel as kindly toward Poland. However, he thinks Russia is still grateful to Poland for what she has done. He said he had had a talk with the President, that he was now going to Mexico and when he came back, he would see the President again.

When Sikorski left the office, Callendar[1] of the New York *Times* came in and said he had met the Polish Ambassador but never the Prime Minister. He said there was considerable distrust of Sikorski, that he was very busy working with some of the dissatisfied Catholic elements in the country spreading distrust of Russia and that his trip to Mexico was for the purpose of meeting with the good Catholics down there, the whole aim being to build up as much support as possible for Poland as a buttress against Russia in the peace to come. This did not altogether jibe with what Sikorski said about Stalin. Sikorski said that thus far Stalin in his dealings with the people of Europe and the United States had never spoken frankly and had always dealt double but the reason for it was that the people of the Western world had always dealt double with him. Sikorski thought it was possible to deal frankly with Stalin but only in case we were prepared to go straight down the line. The first time Stalin caught us dealing double, he would immediately go back to his old tricks.

Sikorski claimed that great emphasis had been laid on Stalin's realism. He said, as a matter of fact, Stalin was 50 percent realist and 50 percent egotist. Sikorski said he knew as early as 1934 that the Russians had a stronger military machine than the world appreciated . . .

[1] Harold Callendar.

DECEMBER 23, 1942

Secretary Morgenthau called about ten this morning, saying that Stettinius [1] had been in to see him yesterday and wanted to have a meeting with him and Hull on the problem of how large the British gold and dollar balances should be before we stopped giving them Lend-Lease goods. Henry said that Stettinius was playing very closely with the State Department and he was obviously trying to cut me out of the conference. Henry insisted that I should be included and suggested that I hold a meeting at 11 a.m. I said OK ...

Stettinius presented the general nature of the problem, how the United Kingdom had about one billion dollars in gold and dollar balances and the rest of the Empire nearly a billion dollars more. He indicated how problems of this sort had always been handled with Treasury and State. Hull indicated that this was a State and Treasury problem. I then pointed out that because BEW had the function of dealing with exports, the matter had come up to us and it was because of a particular letter written by an exporter who wanted to do business with South Africa that I had brought the problem up in BEW meeting last week. I said this particular exporter had written Ed Stettinius but had sent copies of his letter to a list which he named, including Drew Pearson. I said it looked to me like a move on the part of the exporters to set up a drive against New Deal bureaucracy when Congress met. Stettinius said he thought the exporter had a lot of justification on his side. He said the thing he wanted particularly was to have a policy decided by high officials so that he would know how to conduct himself on January 11 when he appeared before the House Appropriations Committee. I finally appointed a Committee with Harry White as chairman, Frank Coe, a member from BEW, Dean Acheson from State, Ed Stettinius, and a man added from the War Department. Morgenthau, Hull, myself, Stettinius and the technical people will meet again at 11 a.m. on December 30 ...

DECEMBER 24, 1942

... Mike[2] mentioned that the FBI had asked OWI to fire Joe Barnes because of his communistic sympathies. Without mentioning Hull's or Hopkins' name, I said certain highly placed people in the administration

---

[1] Edward R. Stettinius, Jr., at that time Lend-Lease Administrator, later Undersecretary of State (September 1943–November 1944) and then Secretary of State until June 1945.
[2] Gardner Cowles.

thought Barnes was a communist on the basis of the Russian trip. Mike then said, "If Barnes is a communist, I am one. We were in the same room together all through the trip around the world." Remembering that both Secretary Hull and Hopkins had laid great emphasis on Barnes' being close to Oumansky, I asked Mike what his impressions were of Oumansky. He said on the occasion of the big dinner at the Kremlin, that Oumansky was drinking a lot of vodka, was very tight, spoke very freely of his dislike for the United States. I told Mike I thought that Joe Barnes' troubles traced to Admiral Standley's hurt feelings. Mike said that he was sure that was true, that on one occasion in Moscow Standley had taken Mike by both coat lapels and shaken him, saying, "What are you doing here? Are you trying to get my job?"

Mike also mentioned about our Army men being exceedingly anxious to get the airplanes backed up at Nome across to Russia where they could do some good. Willkie called up Standley on the telephone and asked how it would be if he would talk to Stalin when he met him the next day about this problem. Standley stood on his dignity and said he was ambassador and it was his business to do this kind of thing and Willkie should not butt in. Mike thinks it is a very bad thing for the interests of the United States and Russia that Standley is going back . . .

DECEMBER 28, 1942

. . . I told the President that when he gave me the green light to get into the administrative work of BEW last Thanksgiving, I had spent quite a bit of time talking with the people down the line in Milo's outfit. I said I had asked these people about their opposite numbers in RFC and in State Department. I had found that there was a very good relationship between Milo's rubber people and the people down the line in RFC, that the real trouble came with Will Clayton[1] and Jesse Jones. I said the trouble there was that they liked to haggle indefinitely, and that the needs required a production type of mind rather than the banker controlled type of mind. I gave the President the boiled-down summary of the testimony before the Senate Banking and Currency Committee . . . I spoke at some little length about the labor clauses, saying that Jesse Jones in his testimony had left the situation such that the senators had tackled me on the grounds of being impractical and

1 William L. Clayton, Houston cotton broker, friend of Jesse Jones, Assistant Secretary of Commerce (1942–45).

idealistic. I said that we had handled the labor clause matter from the standpoint of how to get the maximum of production.

The President then went into a lengthy discussion of how King Leopold of the Belgians had operated personally in the Belgian Congo about 40 years ago and how a great scandal had developed. It was obvious the President thought that it was our duty to push the labor contracts a little harder if anything.

He mentioned the Bolivian tin situation and Pierre Boal, our ambassador there. I told the President that BEW had not had a man in Bolivia but that we now had one on the way. He inquired about the background of the Bolivian situation. I told him about the Bolivian inflation and the failure of wages to keep pace with the degree of inflation. I mentioned that we had an excellent working arrangement with the Commodity Credit Corporation, that we bought in the field and about all the CCC did was to clear the checks.

I told the President I was convinced that the attitude of the Luces was not friendly either toward him or me. I thought this was particularly true of Mrs. Luce. I told him I was sure that anything which they put out that appeared to be friendly toward me was designed not for friendliness but for other purposes. I said there was a friendly relationship between the Luces, Sam Rayburn, and Tommy Corcoran. He was much interested in the Corcoran hookup and would like to know more about it.

I said there was one group of people in the United States at the present time definitely moving toward producing a postwar situation which would eventually bring us into war with Russia; and another group moving into a situation that would eventually bring us into war with England. I said the time had come when we must begin to organize skillfully and aggressively for peace. He said he was going to go a long way in his speech to Congress on the 7th, that he was going to appeal particularly to the soldier boys, saying that he knew what kind of world they were fighting for; they were fighting for a world in which there would be no more war and in which they as individuals could be sure of a job. He said he was going to put in his speech that he had been advised that it was bad politics to say what he had said, but he felt it was the thing to do anyway. He said obviously he could not get into the details of the peace at this time.

I told the President that I thought there were certain bigoted Catholics and certain reactionaries who were trying to get control of the Democratic Party and that he should step in aggressively to save the party from these people who are enemies of what the President stands for. I said Frank Walker was fine but the question was whether he had the time and energy to do the job which needed to be done. I said it required some one with the tireless energy of a Tommy Corcoran but who also had the broad concept of the general welfare. The President said he agreed that Tommy had no broad philosophy. He then began to say, "I wish I had Tommy back. He has not called on me for a long time. Why doesn't he call? I suppose Tommy is too busy making money. They say he is making it hand over fist." I suggested to the President before he had Tommy in that he make a checkup on his relationship with the Time-Fortune-Life crowd . . .

DECEMBER 29, 1942

. . . In presenting the Collier award, I said that in the future freedom of the air would be as important to peace as freedom of the seas had been in the past. Dr. George W. Lewis of the National Advisory Committee for Aeronautics was deeply impressed with this part of my talk. He wants me to go with him to see some of the experimental work which the National Advisory Committee is doing with the money which has been appropriated to it by the government.

Litvinov was very much disturbed about the fact that the British were not going ahead faster in N. Africa.[1] He spoke of the need for going ahead now with talks dealing with the postwar situation. He said Russia was very much interested in the Baltic area, in Esthonia, Latvia, Lithuania, the eastern Russian-speaking part of Poland and Bessarabia. I asked if Russia were interested in the Dardanelles and he said, no. He said he feared there would be difficulties with the United States concerning Russia's need for this territory because of the ideological questions that would be raised. Certain of the reactionary groups in different areas had representatives in the United States who would shriek to high heaven about the Red menace.

I asked Litvinov if he had presented this point of view to the President. He said no, that he had not been authorized to do so. I said I thought it was important for the President and Stalin to get together. He said just between us that Stalin was a very suspicious man, that he had to have everything in his own hands, that he could not delegate authority and, therefore, he found it very difficult to get away. I con-

[1] In October the British Eighth Army under General Montgomery had defeated the Germans at El Alamein. In November they pushed the Germans out of Egypt. Pressing on, they reached Tripoli on January 23, 1943. Their difficult task had been eased in some measure by the transfer of German units from North Africa to the Russian front.

gratulated the ambassador on the remarkable progress made by the Russian armies.[1] He said the progress was much better than he had anticipated, that he did not see how the Russians could possibly be doing it, that they had very serious shortages. He said, however, that the progress was not as significant as it seemed, that the German plan was to hold on to the fortified centers and let the Russians break through in between, that the Germans had learned from the Russians the trick of defending themselves in occupied cities and for this kind of defense the Germans were able to get in the necessary supplies by plane.

I suggested to Litvinov that public sentiment in the United States might be greatly improved if Stalin would make a clear-cut statement indicating that neither he nor the Russian government were behind the American communists. Litvinov said Stalin had made such a statement. I asked him to send it to me. He then went on to indicate, however, that Comintern was separate from the Russian government and that various nations belonged to the Comintern . . .

DECEMBER 31, 1942

At the BEW meeting there was extended discussion on the Bolivian tin situation. I presented the general background of the case and then Duggan of the State Department promptly spoke up and said the Bolivian ambassador had been in and had suggested the appointment of a committee. I was glad to learn that he had made formally the suggestion which he had made informally to me.

Henry Morgenthau and Harry White both entered into the discussion very vigorously on behalf of the Bolivian tin miners. Jesse Jones thought we ought to have the FBI look into the cause of the strike in Bolivia. Nelson Rockefeller had indicated that the strike might have been started for political purposes . . .

I pointed out that last June when we raised the price of tin 14 cents a pound retroactive to January 1, less than 2 cents of the rise went to the workers. I said I did not know how much of the remainder went to the operators' net profit. Will Clayton spoke up to say that he had no doubt that the profits of the big tin companies had been greatly increased.

---

[1] In November and December the Russians had stepped up their successful pincer attack against German forces in Stalingrad while also initiating drives toward Rzhev and Kharkov. In January Soviet forces relieved the long siege at Leningrad and forced the Germans remaining at Stalingrad to surrender. Though severely damaged, the Germans launched a new offensive in March.

There was considerable discussion about the need for an increase in the price of tin going to the workers in the form of food. I made it clear repeatedly that the request of the Bolivian ambassador for a committee would make it possible for us to make recommendations which otherwise would be looked on as an invasion of the Bolivian sovereignty . . .

Jones took quite a reactionary attitude, saying that we ought to avoid any action that would make people think we were engaging in social reform of any kind. Harry White made the point, however, that if the United States was getting the reputation of supporting the owners of the mines in the exploitation of labor, that we would lose the sympathy of the people. Treasury point of view and Jesse Jones' point of view were at opposite poles. I suppose the handling of this matter in the future will depend on just who is appointed on the committee. I suggested that inasmuch as the mine owners' point would undoubtedly be fully represented, we ought to have someone representing labor on the committee.

When we discussed the matter of British Empire dollar and gold balances, the statement was made that one aspect of the situation was being cleared by the cabinet committee report to the President. Attention was called to the Wayne Coy committee to consider the commercial aspects of day-by-day handling of Lend-Lease. Rockefeller said that Coy had told him that the President had asked him to form such a committee. Dean Acheson was rather seriously alarmed and wanted to talk to Secretary Hull about it. I suggested that the committee meet and if any of the departments represented on the committee felt that Coy was stepping out too far to let me know. My guess is that Frank Coe, our man, wanted to get off the hot spot on the committee and that Budget was anxious to get in on the committee so as to familiarize itself with what was going on in this rather delicate Lend-Lease field . . .

At cabinet meeting, Hull started out by giving an indignant tirade against the British for the propaganda they had been putting out on behalf of de Gaulle and against the United States. He said he had the second man in the British Embassy in and had given him a very vigorous lecture about the propaganda being conducted by the British against the United States in London. The President said it was the "old school tie crowd" that was doing this . . .

After cabinet meeting, I told the President about my conversation with Litvinov. He said so far as Latvia, Lithuania, Esthonia, Eastern Poland, and Bessarabia were concerned, he felt that the thing to do after the war would be for them to be in close economic relationship with Russia but separate politically until four or five years after the war, at which time a plebiscite might be held. He said he knew that Russia would claim that a plebiscite had recently been held, but he, the President, felt that the plebiscite had not been held under fair conditions. He said that he had stepped in and prevented the British and Russians from arriving at an accord that would give the Russians this area. The President said he had had Litvinov and his wife in secretly to dinner, that he had kidded Litvinov in his pessimism by saying, "Well, how is the hole in the doughnut today?" Neither Litvinov nor his wife understood the idiom and then the President proceeded to explain it. Madame Litvinov enjoyed it immensely. Litvinov, of course, had been exceedingly pessimistic. It was only at the last meeting that I found him to show any sign of optimism . . .

JANUARY 1, 1943

. . . Francis P. Miller, who heads one of the divisions dealing with espionage in the Office of Strategic Services, came in to express the deepest concern about the way in which the situation in North Africa was going. He submitted . . . information about one of the members of the French Military Mission now in this country and said this man[1] was very close to Robert Murphy . . . Miller felt the methods we were using in North Africa would lose us the peace. He also stated the following:

> "I am reliably informed that the youth who shot Darlan told the priest that he acted only because he hated the Vichy regime, and for the honor of France."

Miller said that if we continued to shoot our friends, it would be very difficult to have an uprising in France. He said people in France and in other occupied countries would ask why we didn't cooperate with Hitler in the first place.

Miller said terrific things against the State Department. He mentioned one case in which they (OSS) were sending one of their espionage agents into France. The State Department knew about it, tipped off the Vichy ambassador in Washington and as a result the man was met at the border by a Gestapo agent and was continually shadowed by this agent all the time he was in France. This meant, of course, that he endangered the lives of everyone he came in touch with while he was in France. Miller thinks a good bit of this is due to what might

[1] Lemaigre Dubreuil, whom Miller considered a collaborationist.

be called the Catholic line in the State Department . . . However, he thinks the whole situation goes very much deeper and is really what might be called the underlying State Department conservatism.

I told Miller a little bit about what Hull said at cabinet the previous day and Miller said the old man was gaga, that the vengeful instincts of the mountaineer had been aroused when the Free French took the French isles at the mouth of the St. Lawrence.[1] The Free French had told Cordell in advance but Cordell did not know it and ever since then he has had it in for the Free French. Miller doesn't have the best judgment in the world and it may be that Donovan's[2] outfit is completely wrong. The disturbing thing, of course, is that one government could have such completely opposing ideas . . .

I saw Milton Eisenhower at the suggestion of Henry Morgenthau. He told me there was a very strong fight on between Office of Strategic Services and OWI. I asked him what kind of men Donovan's outfit had in N. Africa and he said they were very poor. He told about a conference he himself had had with Darlan. He feels that Murphy has given his brother, General Eisenhower, poor advice, that Murphy had suggested calling in for an adviser a man from the French Embassy in Argentina and that the man had been flown in an American bomber as far as Brazil.[3] In the meantime an inquiry had been made in the State Department at Milton's suggestion, and it was found that the fears of Milton's boys were warranted so he was shipped back to Argentina again. Milton feels very strongly that his brother should not be called on to do both military and political work but he also feels that his brother ought to have sound political advice.

He was inclined to attribute Murphy's bad advice to his being short-handed and not having the right kind of help.

Milton said that contrary to the general impression a very poor po-

[1] In December 1940, the Free French had taken St. Pierre and Miquelon, small islands off the Newfoundland coast, from Vichy representatives stationed there.
[2] William J. Donovan, director of the Office of Strategic Services.
[3] Marcel B. Peyrouton at Darlan's suggestion was to become Governor General of Algeria. Peyrouton had been Minister of the Interior at Vichy and in that post in charge of the French police. While he held that office, the Vichy government promulgated its first decrees against the Jews. In Peyrouton's behalf, Cordell Hull argued that he had assisted Pétain in the temporary removal of Pierre Laval from the Vichy cabinet because Laval advocated collaboration with the Germans. Further, Peyrouton had once been Resident General in Tunis. Murphy later regretted supporting Peyrouton's appointment in Algeria "without adequate information." See Cordell Hull, *Memoirs*, 2 vols. (New York, 1948), Vol. 2, pp. 156–160 and Robert Murphy, *Diplomat Among Warriors* (Garden City, 1964), pp. 156–160. In June 1943, Peyrouton, accepting a commission as a captain in the Free French army, resigned his position in Algeria. De Gaulle put one of his followers in the vacated office.

litical job was done in advance of the Army coming in. As a matter of fact, nearly everything had gone wrong on the political front. Milton thinks that Murphy is bad either because of lack of ability or short-handedness whereas Francis Miller thinks he is bad because of wrong motive. It is interesting to note how entirely different the slants of Eisenhower and Miller are as compared with the slant of Bullitt on Murphy.

Milton said there were only about 40,000 Americans on the front in Tunis, that their airplane fields were a sea of mud about two feet deep, that the only place to land was on the hard strips and they were very incomplete. The Germans on the other hand had airplane fields which were far better and also they had the advantage of good airplane fields in Sicily. Our fields were so bad it was necessary to do our fighting 600 or 700 miles away to the east and west where the climate was drier.

Milton mentioned that his boys in N. Africa were away over to the left . . . He said some of these boys slipped information out in a way which was pretty close to treasonable. He also mentioned that his boys were working pretty closely with a man by the name of Ed Taylor with Donovan's outfit and whom Eisenhower looks on as a very good man. Altogether, he says, there are about 200,000 American troops in N. Africa and by next February there should be 500,000.

Eisenhower talked to the President about the Murphy situation relative to his brother and got permission to talk to General Marshall. Marshall was going to talk to Hull to see that General Eisenhower got more adequate political support.

At the Welles' New Year's affair, I told Welles I appreciated the kind words he had written me about my speech[1] and said I thought there was going to be great difficulty in Congress in renewing the trade agreements program. Welles was his usual very cold self and had very little to say, except to suggest that on the Republican side it might be possible to work with Austin and Gurney.[2]

JANUARY 5, 1942

. . . At WPB meeting I went to bat repeatedly for doing everything possible to construct two types of destroyers, one weighing 2200 tons and the other 1350 tons. Apparently the construction of these destroyers which are so important in fighting the submarines was held

---

[1] The speech of December 28, 1942.
[2] Republican Senators Warren R. Austin of Vermont and Chandler Gurney of South Dakota.

up for several months because of the emphasis placed last summer on building land craft for invasion of Europe. When the switchover to N. Africa was decided, this land craft became useless and is now clogging our harbors. For first place in construction, there is great competition between synthetic rubber, 100-octane airplane, and the building of vessels to combat the submarine. It was finally decided to give them all an equal and a coordinated rating. This is probably sound. I felt, however, that it was exceedingly important to point out the growing submarine menace so I hammered on that repeatedly. Knox was there and I told him I thought he ought to talk with the President himself about the growing menace. He said he had but would do so again. I also indicated I thought the Joint Chiefs of Staff should reexamine the whole situation from the standpoint of the growing submarine menace.

JANUARY 7, 1943

Congressman Celler[1] is seriously disturbed about the way in which the Jews are being killed off by Hitler and wanted to know if I thought there was anything Congress could do about it. I said I thought the best thing to do was to consult with the liberal-minded Republicans and suggested he talk with Senator Austin on the Senate side . . .

JANUARY 8, 1943

I had an excellent meeting with the exporters, at which I sketched in some of the background of the problem of overlicensing. I told how we were getting out of the negative phase in which export control had been handled and now we were hoping to get into the positive end, how we hoped to serve the needs of the various importing countries and the exporters within the framework of the overall necessities. I said I was very glad to see that there was general agreement as to the methods needed to reduce paperwork and expedite action. I put in a strong word for trade agreements and pointed out that a large volume of exports was dependent on a large volume of imports, especially so in the case of a creditor nation. It was a good crowd and I think we have established a friendly relationship with them . . .

At cabinet meeting it was obvious that the President, Hull, and Stimson were all quite confused as to what was the path out with regard to the political situation in North Africa. On the whole, I think

[1] Emanuel Celler, Democratic congressman from Brooklyn, New York since 1923.

the feeling on the part of the President and Hull seemed to be very strong against de Gaulle and the British backing of de Gaulle. There is no question about de Gaulle's personal characteristics. Yet somehow I feel that the President has received a very incomplete picture and that both his and Hull's judgment is based on partial evidence.

At the close of cabinet meeting, the President told Frank Knox and me very confidentially his plans for the next three weeks, plans which I shall write up later.[1] I told the President in Knox's presence that we had discussed the escort vessel situation in WPB meeting and I felt that Knox might need his backing to be sure this program was pushed with sufficient speed. Knox thanked me for backing him, and the President said if Jeffers[2] gets in the way of the program and Don Nelson couldn't handle him, "Tell Don to have Jeffers come to you." The President made it clear that he was thinking of Jeffers breaking loose in public print.

When I was talking with the President by himself, I told him I thought that the future peace and security of the world depended on the Democratic Party winning in 1944. Looking toward that winning, I felt it was highly important to consolidate the progressive, forward-looking elements in labor, agriculture, and youth. I mentioned that Jim Patton[3] and Phil Murray had both talked to me about their program and that Phil had said to me that morning over the phone that a word from the President would result in bringing in the American Federation of Labor in this new organization which they are trying to form with Norris[4] at the head. I told the President that Phil thought the Railroad Brotherhoods would line up with the CIO and the Farmers Union. The President seemed to think it was a good idea to have one organization considerably to the left of where he and I stood. His phraseology sounded as though he took it for granted that he and I were going to run again in 1944. When he spoke of the organization to the left of himself and myself, he seemed to think that it would be a fine thing to have this organization continually criticizing because we were not going far enough left and then at the last minute come out in support. He mentioned that he thought it would be a fine thing if we could have an organization strong enough so if the Republicans get out on a limb, say with respect to social security, it would be possible for

---

[1] Plans for the Casablanca Conference.
[2] William M. Jeffers, president of the Union Pacific Railroad, United States Rubber Director (1942–43), a tough, blunt, sometimes insensitive administrator.
[3] James G. Patton, since 1940 president of the National Farmers Union.
[4] George W. Norris.

this organization to start enough activity so as to give the Republicans a really good licking.

I mentioned to the President that Jim Farley was cultivatitng certain people in Latin America as well as good Catholics in the United States and that probably he would control one third of the delegates at the next convention. The President said he thought that estimate was about right. I said to the President, "Do you think it would be a good thing for me to see Jim Farley?" and told him how I had been half minded to call up Jim prior to the last election and urge him to come out for the President's international policies as a method of helping Bennett. I told him I had not seen Farley, however, and was glad I had not. The President thought that I should not ask Farley to call on me. Then he began to speculate as to how I might make accidental contact with him. I suggested Basil O'Connor.[1] He said no, that would not do at all. I suggested Archbishop Spellman.[2] The President said, "No, Jim doesn't like Spellman." The President said Jim did not like Frank Walker either. When I mentioned to the President that I had always had a friendly basis with him, he said he had never had an unkind word with him. We both agreed that the difficulty with Jim was the continual nagging coming from his wife. He said it was the same difficulty which Al Smith had . . .

JANUARY 14, 1943

At BEW I brought up the problem which I discovered three days previously while going through the export section in . . . Division of Transportation in the Brazilian files. It seemed to me that an unusually tight spot was certain to develop with respect to Brazil and that the increasing quantities of scarce shipping tonnage devoted to the Amazon rubber program might have repercussions with regard to the rest of the economy of Brazil. We discussed the problem at some little length and I appointed a committee with Dean Acheson as chairman. We then discussed with considerable heat the extent of the problem of furnishing gold machinery to Nicaragua and Colombia. It appears that President Somoza[3] of Nicaragua gets about 15 percent of the 7 million dollars of gold which Nicaragua produces. The United States does not need the gold but we are being called on to send 10,000 tons of material

[1] Basil O'Connor, Roosevelt's one-time law partner and constant, though never intimate, supporter.
[2] Archbishop (later Cardinal) Francis Joseph Spellman of New York.
[3] President (and dictator) Anastasio Somoza.

down to keep the gold mines going. The State Department recommends that we send 3000 tons but we question whether we should send any. It is true that on April 7, 1942, the President made a commitment, but in view of the shortage of shipping and the need of shipping by the Brazilian rubber program, the whole matter ought to be re-examined to find if there is not some way in which the 7000 workers mining gold in Nicaragua can find equally good employment which will not require so much material from the United States. Collado of the State Department claimed this all had been adequately examined. I appointed a committee with Hector Lazo as chairman . . .

JANUARY 16, 1943

Milo wanted to let me know he was sending up to me on Monday an order transferring Metals Reserve functions to us. Under our executive order we have just as mucn power and just as much reason for doing this as Jeffers and Jesse Jones had for similar action with regard to rubber—taking powers away from us and giving them to Jesse Jones' Rubber Reserve Corporation. I told Milo after he sent the order up, I might hold the thing over for a day or two but I was very much inclined to go along[1] . . .

At the dinner at home . . . the most interesting discussion had to do with international airports as related to Lend-Lease. Tydings[2] is on the Appropriations Committee which will have to do with Lend-Lease. He made it very clear that it was high time, before more money was given to Britain, for Britain to indicate that she was willing to internationalize the airport facilities which we had developed on her land especially on the bases which we had gotten in exchange for our destroyers in August of 1940. Senator Burton[3] mentioned that Canada had not come through very well with regard to the air rights in connection with the Alcan Highway. Both Burton and Tydings were feel-

---

[1] Wallace published the order in the *Federal Register* on January 20, 1943. It stipulated that, effective February 25, "the negotiation, preparation, supervision, and administration both in the United States and abroad of all . . . imported materials contracts," but not the financing, should "be carried on by the Office of Imports of the Board of Economic Warfare." Wallace wrote Jesse Jones on January 19 that he intended the order to clarify responsibilities of the procurement and the financing agencies. Jones interpreted the order as an attack on his authority, just as Wallace and Perkins had considered the earlier order about rubber as an invasion by Jones and Jeffers of authority previously exercised by the BEW.

[2] Millard E. Tydings, since 1927 Democratic senator from Maryland.

[3] Harold H. Burton, since 1941 Republican senator from Ohio.

ing very critical with regard to the way in which the British were trying to sew up the postwar air traffic.

With respect to international air force after the war, Tydings felt this should be done on a regional basis. The United States would probably be the dominant factor in the New World, Russia and China the dominant factor in the Far East, and England and France together the dominant factor in Western Europe. He would have certain problems handled by a combination of regional and international air force. This idea is very rough and would have to be shaped up considerably but I am convinced there is some ingenious way of making the various countries feel safe by means of the proper combination of regional and international air force. I indicated we would have to do considerable thinking about the proper representation of Latin America and hemispheric air force; also about the proper rotation of civilians into and out of the various air forces so that there would be no danger of developing a military caste that felt it had the power to take over in a civilian sense.

Cowles[1] was keen about Tydings' idea. Burton was also in complete accord. Tydings stated flatly that the Democratic Party had no chance of success in 1944 unless it took prompt and vigorous action to see that we were getting a square deal on international airports in exchange for our Lend-Lease help.

JANUARY 20, 1943

. . . I called up Milton Eisenhower about the Peyrouton matter[2] and found him much disturbed about it. However, he figured it might be part of something bigger. Apparently the pressure for Peyrouton came from Giraud[3] and was from the second highest military authority in the United States (on talking with Milton later, I found he was referring to Admiral Leahy when he referred to the second highest military authority).

Yesterday Secretary Hull stated that Murphy knew exactly what he was doing in taking on Peyrouton. Then last night Eric Sevareid[4] raked the State Department over the coals for bringing Peyrouton to

---

[1] John Cowles, older brother of Gardner Cowles, Jr., president of the Minneapolis Star Journal and Tribune Company.

[2] The official announcement of Peyrouton's appointment as governor general was released on January 19 while Roosevelt was in Casablanca.

[3] General Henri H. Giraud had succeeded Darlan.

[4] Eric Sevareid, at that time already a celebrated radio correspondent, had covered France for the Columbia Broadcasting System.

N. Africa. This morning Berle retreats and states that the State Department had nothing to do with bringing Peyrouton to N. Africa, that the matter was solely engineered by the military. According to Berle, the State Department tried to stop Peyrouton from going from Argentina to N. Africa. This checks with what Milton Eisenhower had told me two weeks ago. Admiral Leahy, whom General Giraud says is responsible for Peyrouton being in N. Africa, was very close to Murphy when he (Leahy) was ambassador to France. Leahy, of course, is very close to the President and it may be that the President knows exactly what he is doing. The public impression among all liberals is, of course, very bad.

Eisenhower reports that he thinks the planted stories with *Time* and New York *Herald Tribune* probably came from Free French sources. The Free French are now beginning to take their story direct to the papers . . .

JANUARY 22, 1943

. . . At the enemy branch of the BEW meeting, the outstanding presentation to my mind was the fact that the vital strength of the Japanese economy is in Japan, Manchuria, Korea, and the adjoining parts of China. As far as 1943 and 1944 are concerned, the East India islands do not add as much to Japanese strength as is customarily assumed. The whole presentation indicated the supreme importance of a successful drive against Burma at the earliest possible moment so as to make it possible to get supplies into China to back up a strong air offensive against the heartland of Japan. Attrition against Japanese shipping in the East India islands is all right but the really important thing is continuous airplane attack against Japan from the mainland of China.

JANUARY 23, 1943

At BEW I went into detail with different groups regarding the different kinds of products which we hope to get in increased quantities out of Mexico. I dealt particularly with fats and oils, mahogany, fibers, and minerals. It is clearly evident that our embassy in Mexico is not cooperating as it should and it also was evident that some of our men had not fully understood how to go about the job of working in a foreign country. It was clearly apparent too that George Messersmith has been thinking much more about bureaucratic rights than he has of getting the job done. Even Bateman,[1] the minerals man, who knows his subject exceedingly well, who has been many times in Mexico and who knows all the ropes and is a very conservative operator, complained to some extent about Messersmith. On the whole, it seems that Bateman got along better with Messersmith than anyone else [did] and this is probably due to the fact that he is a more skilled judge of human nature . . .

At Mrs. Roosevelt's dinner were present a number of population experts . . .

If the world increases in population at the rate of 18 million a year, it is probable that more than half of the increase will be in Russia, India, and China. Some of the population experts . . . were alarmed that there might be a lot of immigration into the United States after the war. I told them they did not need to worry about that, that the attitude of the senators was such as to make certain that there would be no letting down of the immigration bars. In view of the current admiration for China, there was a possibility that they might let Chinese in under the nominal quota, which would mean about 100 Chinese in a year.

Everyone was agreed that it was important to get industrialization spread over the so-called backward parts of the world where the population growth is fastest so that the higher standard of living, which goes with industrialization, would result in damping down the birthrate.

I pointed out that it is appropriate for a debtor nation and a pioneer nation to have a definite tariff policy which would encourage infant industries by means of a relatively high tariff. But that a creditor nation like the United States should definitely not have a high tariff.

JANUARY 27, 1943

. . . Eric Johnston, the president of the U.S. Chamber of Commerce, is an exceedingly likable young fellow who has been making a great many speeches over the country to local Chambers of Commerce, spreading the word of what is necessary for the postwar period. He is chairman of the U.S. branch of the Inter-American Committee and Sumner Welles is chairman of the Committee of the Twenty-one Republics. Johnston is leaving shortly on a trip to South America and will meet with the business groups in the different countries of South

[1] Alan M. Bateman, professor of geology at Yale, in 1942 head of a special BEW mission to Mexico, later director of Metals and Minerals for the Foreign Economic Administration.

America, assuring them that the business of the United States is friendly
to Latin America. Johnston claims that in his personal talks over the
country that our businessmen respond very well to the idea of greater
hemispheric consciousness. The greatest trouble, he says, comes from
agriculture. Johnston thinks the agricultural leadership of the United
States, especially Ed O'Neal[1] of the American Farm Bureau Federation,
and Albert Goss[2] of the Grange, is exceedingly benighted, narrow,
and selfish, much worse than either business or labor.

He says that O'Neal went up to see William Witherow, chairman
of the Board of Directors of the National Association of American
Manufacturers, and sold him on the idea of agriculture and business
ganging up against labor. Witherow said, "Fine." Johnston, who was
at the meeting, was asked for his opinion. He said he did not believe
in any two of the three groups ganging up against the third. And so
the thing fell to the ground.

I told Johnston that it had taken many years for agriculture to get
a square deal and that now she had gotten a square deal but that she
was overplaying her hand, and I very much feared that when trouble
came, agriculture would not have friends when she most needed them.
Johnston believes that agriculture has a much stronger prejudice
against labor than the average businessman. I told him this was not
true of the average farmer but only of some of the wealthier farmers
and farm leaders.

Walter Lippmann[3] had a splendid idea—that the President should
send up to Congress messages asking for peacetime authorizations.
These peacetime authorizations should be very large sums of money
and the purpose of the authorizations should be to handle the postwar
readjustment. Lippmann thinks it is not only good economics but also
very good politics. I agreed with him and asked him to write me a
letter which I could show to the President.

I had a very satisfactory conference with Messersmith. I told him
how much we appreciated the fine cooperation he had given Lazo and
he spoke in the highest terms about Lazo. I said we wanted to get
into a similar close cooperation with regard to increasing imports,
that Mexico was going to have a greater importance in the import
picture, because of the shipping shortage. I said I had conferred with
a number of people in BEW about the prospect of increasing imports
from Mexico . . .

[1] Edward A. O'Neal, since 1931 president of the American Farm Bureau Federation, the politically powerful organization of agribusiness.
[2] Albert S. Goss, master of the National Grange.
[3] Walter Lippmann, the pre-eminent American columnist and influential author,
was an old and good friend of the Wallace family.

JANUARY 28, 1943

. . . First and foremost on Bill Bullitt's mind was the need for the President coming to an understanding with Stalin. Bill feared that Russia would dominate the whole world if the President did not come to such an understanding in the very near future. I asked Bill for some back history about how Eden happened to agree that Russia should have the Baltic States. Bill said that England had promised to send Russia some troops by way of Archangel at a time when she desperately needed troops. When England found that she could not deliver the troops, Eden was sent to tell Russia that England was not in position to come through. To soften the blow, Eden hit on the idea of tentatively offering to Russia the Baltic States at the close of the war. When the proposal was sent over to the State Department, Hull drafted a strong memorandum to the President, saying that this would muddy up the peace, that there ought to be no agreements of this sort in advance of the peace. The President accepted Cordell's viewpoint. I told Bill the President had the idea that the Baltic States should be in Russia's economic sphere and that five years after the war a plebiscite should be held. Bill said this was an utterly cockeyed idea. Bill said when Molotov was here, the President told him the only nations with an army after the war was over should be the United States, England, and Russia, and that France should have no army. Word of this conversation got back to de Gaulle which made de Gaulle utterly furious and a hater of Roosevelt. Since that time de Gaulle has worked with the Russians.

Bill tells me that Peyrouton is everything that has been told me by the Argentineans and the Uruguayans. In other words, a gourmet, a wine bibber, a hunter, a sportsman, a woman chaser, and a very competent executive. Bill thinks he will do a first class job in North Africa although he believes in many other respects that the N. African job has been handled badly. Bill believes that Germany and Italy should be completely disarmed but that there should be an army on the continent of Europe officered by the Swiss general staff. He thinks it will take this army, combined with the power of the United States and England, to keep Russia from overrunning Europe. Bill thinks we ought to make a definite offer to Stalin on the basis of the boundaries as they existed in 1939 except that Russia would be given Bessarabia. We would also agree to give Russia certain help with regard to technical and other assistance, and the western democracies would guarantee to order their economic systems so as to prevent unemployment and to promote full use of natural resources. There should be provision for international air bases inside Siberia. The trade should be worked out now while Russia needs us. Bill thinks it will be impossible to work out anything with either England or Russia the moment they do not need us.

Bill would like to see Sumner Welles, Adolf Berle, and Dean Acheson fired, and Cordell Hull given carte blanche. He reminded me that some years ago he had been given a letter from the President, and exactly the same letter signed by Hull, giving him (Bullitt) the privilege of giving the State Department a complete overhauling. Bullitt decided, however, that he would rather go to Europe as ambassador. Bullitt thinks the President is now traveling down exactly the same path as Woodrow Wilson in 1918 and that the result is going to be a tragedy unless he uses his power more effectively in the near future in international affairs with both England and Russia.

Bill seemed to think the Germans had definitely reached the end of their expansion, that their birthrate was tending downward, and that the vitality of the race had fully expressed itself. On the contrary, he felt that the Russians were just beginning their expansion, that there would be an enormous growth in population there during the next two generations. He felt the Russian people were extraordinarily gifted. He said Lenin was the most gifted man he had ever met anywhere in the world, barring none. The most gifted people of all, he said, were the Ukrainians. But the Russians were superior in one respect to the Ukrainians—they had larger families. According to Bill, the Russian women are amazing creatures. In doing the hard physical work on the Moscow subway, they averaged 20 percent more work than the men. Bill's tribute to the Russian people was to some extent part of a buildup to indicate why it was necessary for the Western Hemisphere and Europe to prevent Russian domination of the world. In the Bullitt scheme of things, he would eventually have Germany and Italy as part of the European-American alliance vs. Russia.

Bill said Stalin was the most capable, hard-boiled realist in the world. From some points of view, he thinks he is much more capable than either Roosevelt or Churchill. He makes the customary point that Stalin is thinking primarily about Russian nationalism rather than communistic ideology. He says he has no evidence, however, that Stalin has changed his ideas of the western democracies . . .

Bill said that for a long time he had believed it was advisable to have some one in the President's office working on the coordination of peace plans. He had now reached the conclusion that the only place to have this work done was in the State Department but that with the State Department as now constructed, the job was impossible. He said there were four State Departments; one under Hull, one under Welles, one under Berle, and one under Acheson. The State Department as now constructed could not do the job and no one else can do the job because the minute anyone else tries, the State Department undercuts his efforts. The State Department can do nothing itself but it is very good at preventing anybody else from doing anything. Bill said he had reached the conclusion that the job could not be done in the President's office when he suddenly realized that the President was relying on Harry Hopkins as a foreign affairs man. With Harry as the President's man, it is obvious that nobody else could be put into this job without incurring Harry's ill will. Bill said Harry knew absolutely nothing about foreign affairs, that his first visit abroad was during the war, that he was a babe in the woods in this field. He said Hull was also a babe in the woods in the foreign political field when he became Secretary of State but that he had learned a lot since he had become Secretary. Bullitt is a great admirer of Hull but he described Berle as a shifty, smart, little person. Clever little Adolf! . . .

Bullitt mentioned at some little length the way in which the Russians get a favorable plebiscite in a country like Latvia. First, they get rid of the leading citizens that do not have communistic ideas. Next, they put Communists in charge of the various offices. Next, they put up for vote just one ticket or proposition to be voted on. By using this technique, which is the Hitler technique, they get 97 percent "yes" votes. It is for this reason that Bill thinks the President is crazy when he talks about a plebiscite in the Baltic States 5 years after the war is over . . .

Roy Howard[1] started out by saying he wanted to see the guy who had so sold himself to a man like Raymond Clapper. He just could not believe that I was as good as Clapper said I was and wanted to see me in my office. He said he liked my December 28 speech but did not like my May 8 speech. Clapper said he liked both of them. He said he had always been strong for the Hull trade agreements, had always been against high tariffs. I told him that the trade agreements were not enough, that they would not suffice to bring about imports of one billion dollars' worth of goods in excess of our exports—that we had taken care of our creditor position in the '20s by loaning money abroad and in the '30s by buying gold and silver. He wondered

[1] Roy W. Howard, president since 1936 of the Scripps-Howard newspapers, editor and president of the New York *World-Telegram*, long-time critic of the New Deal.

how much longer we were going to go ahead buying gold and silver. I said with the political situation as it was in the United States that I did not think even the Democrats would permit enough imports of goods in excess of exports to meet our creditor position, and that if we were to avoid such international irritation as to produce another war, it would probably be necessary for the next 10 years to continue buying gold and silver.

I told Howard at some little length about international airports and that I felt item No. 1 in world peace was a satisfactory understanding between Russia and the United States. He took the slant that the imporant thing was for England and the United States to gang up against Russia. I told him I thought it was a mistake for any two of the big three to gang up against the third, just as it was a mistake for agriculture and labor to gang up against capital, or for agriculture and capital to gang up against labor. When he left he gave me a very urgent invitation to spend several hours with him the next time I was in New York City.

Howard told me he thought I had grandiose ideas about all the nations of the world getting together to settle the world picture. When I told him I thought in the first instance the important thing was England, Russia, China, and the United States getting together settling certain fundamentals before calling in the others, he seemed to think I was talking sense . . .

JANUARY 29, 1943

. . . Lubin has just returned from England and North Africa. He thinks the North African thing is still a mess and is afraid the President was so isolated in N. Africa that he did not see the right people. He does not have much faith in Murphy, says he is a nice fellow but not too strong, that he arrives at judgments based on insufficient evidence. He said he had spent some time with Churchill while he was in England. Churchill said to him, "I hope you are not one of these men who think we are going to have a better world after the war. It is going to be pretty bad." Then went on to say that he did not expect to have anything to do with the postwar world, that his opportunity was to do what he could while the war was on. Lubin said that Churchill had a modification of a pinball game, operated by hand, which intrigued him so much that he spent all his spare time this way on Sunday afternoons. Then he expected a physics professor from Oxford,[1] who

1 Professor Frederick Lindemann, later Lord Cherwell, Churchill's frequent companion and personal adviser.

has the statistical job corresponding to Lubin's, to add up his score for him . . .

The real reason that Paul Appleby quit the State Department,[1] according to Milo, is that there is too much confusion. It seems that there are 51 offices and bureaus that report directly to Hull. There are 60 individuals in the State Department who can send out cables to foreign governments signing Hull's name. There are 18 in N. Africa on work who have this right. Appleby, who presumably had been asked by the President to be No. 2 man in Lend-Lease to represent Lend-Lease in the State Department, responsible directly to Hull, found that when he tried to get a policy set with some of them, that did not mean he had it cleared with all of them. Thus it came about that cables would be sent out within a few days of each other, carrying opposite instructions. According to Captain Bernstein, political prisoners in N. Africa are not yet released. The Spanish Republicans are still in concentration camps. Some of the men who helped us in our landing are still in prison because of their help to us . . .

JANUARY 31, 1943

. . . Butler[2] . . . said. . . . undoubtedly there were continuous peace discussions going on between the Russians and the Germans. I ventured that the more military successes Stalin had, the more a certain group of people in the United States and England would be tempted also to have peace discussions with the Germans. I said furthermore that if the British and the Americans should find it easy to land in Greece and Bulgaria and proceed from there to Berlin, it would indicate that such a discussion had been held, and that an agreement had been arrived at between the German army chiefs and the British to the effect that the British should occupy Berlin in advance of the Russians so as to prevent the Russians from wreaking their vengeance on the Germans. I also ventured the statement that those English and Americans who played with the Germans on this kind of proposal were doing a most dangerous thing and laying the groundwork for World War No. 3, that the Russians would look on a move of this sort as a double-cross.

Butler said that he agreed with me wholeheartedly and completely, that the only way to handle the Russians was to gain their confidence and be worthy of it, to cultivate them and be close to them. I was glad to find that all of the British do not have the Cazalet slant.

[1] The press had attributed Appleby's resignation to his opposition to the appointment of Peyrouton.

[2] Nevile Butler, second in command at the British embassy in Washington.

John Cowles mentioned that through his conversations with the Washington taxicab drivers he had found extraordinary prejudice in Washington against the Negroes. Mention was made that when McNutt talked to the streetcar and bus people about Negro workers on the street cars, after McNutt left, one of the streetcar men got up and said he would be perfectly happy to have a Negro work along side of him in the street car. He was promptly set upon by the union workers present and beaten up. This story had been told Cowles by at least three taxicab drivers.

Butler mentioned that some years ago when he was in South Africa, a union had been established among the Negro workers. Butler was attending one of the white union meetings and asked them what they thought about the Negro union's demand for having their wages raised. One of the white workers got up and said, "The demand is unconscionable and cannot be tolerated. Do you realize that three-fourths of the men work in the homes of the white workers here in South Africa?" Apparently democracy in practice still has a long way to go. The common man still doesn't like the man who is more common than himself.

FEBRUARY I, 1943

. . . We then got started talking about Russia. It was very much on Luce's mind.[1] I told him that on the immediate front I thought control of the submarine menace was No. 1, and the furnishing of adequate military supplies to China so we could attack Japan via China was No. 2. "But," said I, "in the long-range situation, I feel an understanding with Russia is the most important thing before us." On the whole, Luce seemed rather to favor the idea of learning to live with Russia as a completely isolated power. He seem to think that Russia would prefer to be completely isolated. I told him about my conversation with Molotov with regard to the American-Asiatic combined highway and airway, that Molotov had said, "No one nation can do it by itself." I said, of course, Molotov cannot speak for Stalin but it is my opinion that it is possible to have Russia as a member of the family of nations and it is much safer for the peace of the world if Russia is a member of the family of nations. Luce said, of course, it would be necessary if we brought Russia into the family to give

[1] Henry R. Luce, founder of *Time, Life,* and *Fortune,* author of the then renowned editorial, "The American Century," which had set forth, with its sequels, a vision of a peaceful world dominated by American power and American missionary Christianity.

Russia reason for having confidence in us. I pointed out that if we have unemployment and underutilization of our natural resources, there will inevitably be fifth column and communistic activities.

I told Luce that the best basis for an understanding with the Russians would be, first, a demonstration that we can keep everyone fully employed, and second, that we are willing to cooperate with the Russians in fully developing the resources of Siberia and the rest of eastern Asia. I told him I thought it was very important for the Latin American countries to have direct contact with Russia and that there should be a three-way understanding between the Anglo-Saxon soul of the United States, the Latin American soul of Latin America, and the Russian soul of Asia. I told him about the farewell parties for Quintanilla[1] and told him I looked on Quintanilla's going as ambassador from Mexico to Russia as a significant thing. He said that he would have representatives of *Life* present at these parties.

At the White House the President started out by saying that he had celebrated his birthday 8000 feet above Haiti and that they had a nice cake for him on the plane. He told how he had gone down to Brazil and hopped across from Brazil to Bathurst, a British colony just south of Dakar. He said the British had had Bathurst ever since 1620 but that they had done nothing with it. The natives went around half clothed and obvious seriously undernourished. He paid a tribute to our troops in the tropical areas, saying that they lived under difficult climatic and disease conditions, and that they deserved credit just as much as the boys who were on the active fighting fronts. He mentioned that the civilian population in the various tropical countries was from 70 to 100 percent infected with venereal disease, and that a good many of our boys had become infected. Some of them had been infected twice. He said he believed it is going to be necessary when our boys come back from the tropics to station them for several months somewhere in the north before mustering them out so as to get them free from the various tropical diseases so they will not infect the civilian population.

The President said the Germans had about 175,000 troops in N. Africa. We and the English would have within a few months a total of 500,000, of which 375,000 would be Americans and 125,000 would be British. He said the French were very much better colonizers than the British. He said the possibility of Spanish invasion was keeping large numbers of our men immobilized on the Moroccan border.

He spoke of the deep mud in Tunisia. He said that sometimes the dry weather began in late February and sometimes not until April.

[1] Luis Quintanilla, Mexican diplomat for whom Wallace had a high regard.

Senator Barkley started to talk about Peyrouton, saying that he had been told about Peyrouton by the Uruguayan Ambassador. The President did not allow Barkley to finish his statement but immediately became very indignant. He mentioned that when Peyrouton was Minister of Interior in the Petain cabinet he had given instructions to put Laval in jail and had put Laval in jail but was reversed by the cabinet. Thereupon Peyrouton had resigned. It is obvious that the President has been fed solely the Murphy point of view. There are so many other aspects to Peyrouton's history than those mentioned by the President, and these other aspects are so well known to people in Uruguay and Argentina, as well as the French people in the United States, that I very much fear that this Peyrouton incident will ultimately have a more damaging effect on the President's reputation in world history than anything he has done.

No doubt the President was right about de Gaulle, about his inability to muster any support in N. Africa. From a completely practical point of view, the President may be right and yet the appeasement aspects of the whole situation are such as to have intangible repercussions which will cause the people of the whole world to begin to think "The United States preaches democracy but it doesn't practice it."

The President mentioned about Turkey's desire to be on the winning side, saying that Turkey had now reached the conclusion that the Allies were going to win, that there were one million very well trained soldiers in Turkey but that for them to be an effective fighting force, they would require tanks, aircraft, antitank guns, and antiaircraft guns, together with Americans to man these different types of modern war machines. He thought these one million Turks might be very useful in the final cleanup.

Some one brought up the subject of China and the Chinese military mission. The President said the head of the Chinese military mission could not speak English, that when anyone asked him a question about China, he never answered, that he was the most unsatisfactory man to deal with that had ever been sent to the United States.

The President recognized it was very important to get more supplies into China so there could be bombing of Japan from the mainland of China. Joe Martin[1] asked if it was true that the Chinese had only received 5 or 6 planes from us. The President said no, they had re-

[1] Joseph W. Martin, Jr., since 1925 Republican congressman from Massachusetts, chairman of the Republican National Committee (1940–42), in 1943 Minority Leader of the House of Representatives.

ceived about 50. There were then some questions about Japan. The President said that Japan had about 6000 airplanes when the war began, that we had destroyed about 1000 and that they had not been able to replace them.

He also said that when the war began, they had 6 million tons of shipping. We have destroyed 1,400,000 tons and they have been able to rebuild only 400,000 tons; therefore, they now have only 5 million tons of shipping. He said attrition was getting the Japs. He says when they have only 4 million tons of shipping, they will have to shorten their lines very greatly.

When the President used the 6000 figure on Japanese planes, I remembered that that was the figure which the War Department first had. Our economic analysis indicated that Japan had more nearly 11,000 planes. I think the President definitely is over optimistic as to the small number of planes which the Japs have. However, I made no attempt to correct his figures, because it was so obvious to me that he was in the glow of his return from a most successful trip and he wanted to tell other people, and did not want other people to tell him.

The President returned via Liberia and visited with President Barkley who, the President said, was a Kentucky Negro of a pretty poor type. He said there were about 200,000 Negroes who had come from the United States and who had been descended from those who lived in the United States. The total population, he said, was about 3 million, but the only ones who voted were the 200,000 who came from the United States . . .

FEBRUARY 3, 1943

. . . M. Rosenthal told me the story of N. Africa. So did Colonel Bernstein, who has been over there for the Treasury. Murphy is a very likable fellow who preaches continually that just because a Frenchman has been a collaborationist in the past and has hated the British does not mean that he doesn't hate the Germans. If we are to practice democracy as well as preach it, apparently there must be a real military occupation in N. Africa or there must be greater pressure put on those Frenchmen who have been put in charge in North Africa to relax their laws against Jews, Spanish Loyalists, and those who have been put in jail because they helped the Americans to land.[1] Rosenthal

[1] Moved partly by British and American influence, Giraud on March 14, 1943, restored sequestered properties and civil rights, and removed other, lesser discriminations imposed during the period of Vichy rule in North Africa. Neither

says that anyone who knows how to speak French and talks with the
civilian French population soon finds out that we made an awful mess
of things, and that the French cannot understand why we have handled
the situation as we have. Murphy and the State Department are to
blame for most of it. Rosenthal claims, however, that Welles has taken
a different slant from most of the other State Department people. He
thinks Dean Acheson will take another slant when he gets the information which Donald Hiss[1] will bring back. Don Hiss has been over
in North Africa for the State Department and came to exactly the
same conclusions as Rosenthal. Rosenthal speaks very highly of General Gale,[2] who is operating for the British. He says Gale is far superior
to any of our generals in his understanding of economic and political
matters. When the North African thing finally blows up, the State
Department will put the blame on Eisenhower who is really guilt-
less . . .

One of the Latin American members of the Coordinator's Office
(not de Lozada) gave me a copy of the minutes of the meeting of the
Coordinator's Committee for Cuba held in the American Club in
Havana on December 21, 1942. Those attending the meeting were
Americans Kenneth D. Campbell, the secretary, and Robert McBride,
the third secretary of our embassy. The object of this committee
meeting was to consider whether or not the Spanish translation of my
May 8 speech entitled "La Marcha Hacia La Libertad" should be distributed. Campbell told the committee members that a letter had
already been sent to the Co-ordinator's office on November 19, expressing the committee's disapproval that material of this sort should
be sent to local labor organizations without consulting the committee.
The minutes of the December 21 meeting showed that . . . it disapproves of certain parts of the new pamphlet and feels that in general
it will not contribute to creating good will between the United States
and Cuba, and might result in additional unrest among labor factions
in this country. The committee is particularly alarmed at illustrations
in the pamphlet showing labor unrest and strikes in the United States,
and drawings of scenes of the French and American revolutions. It is
felt that in these days when the political situation of France is so
variable, as little emphasis as possible should be placed upon this

---

he nor de Gaulle later reinstituted the Crémieux law of 1870, abolished by
Vichy, which had given Algerian Jews the special privilege of French citizenship at birth.
[1] Donald Hiss, an assistant to Dean Acheson (1941–44).
[2] The reference is probably to General Sir Humfrey Gale, see Dwight D.
Eisenhower, *Crusade in Europe* (Garden City, 1952 ed.), pp. 158–159.

country. It is further felt that no particular purpose is served at this time by recalling the American Revolution, since we are now engaged in a life-and-death struggle with Great Britain as our ally. The Committee therefore disapproves of the distribution of this pamphlet in Cuba, and the Secretary is instructed not to distribute the 500 copies which have been received.

The members of the Co-ordinator's Committee in the various Latin American countries are Americans who were 90 percent against Roosevelt in the 1940 election. They are more conservative by far than the average American living in the United States. There is no doubt but that similar action will be taken by other Co-ordinator's Committees . . .

FEBRUARY 5, 1943

. . . I gave him the following two letters suggesting that he ask Congress for the authorization for what might be called a Lend-Lease program on the domestic front.

FEBRUARY 5, 1943

HENRY A. WALLACE TO FRANKLIN D. ROOSEVELT

Dear Mr. President:

Following your speech to Congress, OWI conducted a poll asking, "Do you think that one of our aims should be to see that everyone in this country has a chance to get a job after the war?" Ninety-nine percent said, "Yes." Of those who said, "Yes," 68 percent said they thought this could actually be done.

Of the 99 percent who said it would be our objective to get a job for everyone after the war, 72 percent said we should start in right now to make plans for this. Twenty-three percent said we should wait until later. Only 4 percent said they didn't know.

I am citing these figures to back up my contention that it is good politics now to ask in the near future for what might be called "lend-lease authorizations on the domestic front." There is opportunity, perhaps, for several more idealistic speeches of a general nature, but it is my impression that the people are now ready and eager for definite action looking toward the assurance of postwar jobs. The problem of demobilizing the army, relocating the war workers, and reconverting the war industries is one of tremendous magnitude and one which cannot be faced by private industry alone. I agree with you that because of shortages of goods there will be a certain amount of hangover prosperity for the first year or two. But both the immediate and ultimate objectives are of such magnitude that we have no time to lose in starting our planning . . .

FEBRUARY 5, 1943
HENRY A. WALLACE TO FRANKLIN D. ROOSEVELT

Dear Mr. President:

Most schemes for postwar organizations of the United Nations take in so much territory that it is difficult to see how they will work.

I want to make this suggestion for your thinking:

A United Nations Organization could be set up *now* to consider two specific things:

1. Internationalization of worldwide airports for use by the United Nations.
2. Formulation of worldwide policies regarding international cartels, so as to prevent these "private governments" from thwarting the true peace aims of the common peoples of the world.

There would be a wide popular support for a United Nations approach to these two problems. If they were handled satisfactorily, new functions could be assigned to the international group which had dealt successfully with them. In this way, international administration of international problems could grow and develop naturally . . .

. . . After he read my letters he changed his mind somewhat, although he still thinks there will be a "hangover" of prosperity for two years after the war. I admitted that he might be right about this, but said I felt that, nevertheless, the planning should start at once. He said he didn't think either he or I should take the lead in asking for the authorization and suggested that I get somebody like Senator Truman, Senator Maybank,[1] or Senator Hatch[2] to work on the problem . . .

During cabinet meeting the President called attention to the fact that we had set the rate of exchange between the French franc and the American dollar at 75 francs to the dollar, and the British had set the rate at 43 francs to the dollar, so he intervened and used his "rule of thumb" method on behalf of easy calculation, and made it 50 francs to the dollar. In other words, he made the franc worth 2 cents, or as

[1] Burnet R. Maybank, elected Democratic senator from South Carolina in 1942.
[2] Carl A. Hatch, since 1933 Democratic senator from New Mexico.

someone put it, he put in his 2 cents' worth. He had lots of fun kidding both the State Department and Treasury on how he had done it. Danny Bell,[1] who was there for Henry Morgenthau (who is still down in Cuba) grinned and said, "That's your story, Mr. President." Apparently there is a black market in North Africa, where the rate has been around 120 francs to the dollar. The Treasury has felt that the true rate of exchange should be around 100 francs to the dollar. The British, on the basis of 43 or 44 francs to the dollar, were deliberately overvaluing the franc, so our Treasury people thought. Danny Bell really believes that the franc is probably only worth a cent, and that the President, in valuing it at 2 cents, may later have to back up. The Treasury is happy, however, that it won't have prolonged discussions with the British as to where the true rate should be. The Treasury believes that most of the fussing that has appeared in the press about North Africa really traces back to this warfare on the rate of exchange between Britain and the United States. Morris Rosenthal reports that when he was at Dakar, the British were pointing to the very favorable effect their rate of exchange was having on the African French economy and the very unfavorable effect our rate of exchange was having on the African French economy. According to Danny Bell, everyone in North Africa was satisfied with our rate of exchange except the French officials. As usual in money matters of this sort, there is room for a great variety of opinion.

Cordell Hull brought up the Chinese problem, how Madame Chiang Kai-shek and Mrs. Wellington Koo[2] were both spreading the story of how little we had given China, etc., etc. The President then proceeded to say that he had been insisting, against strong opposition, that the Chinese be given more transport planes. It was rather obvious that the President is rather strongly pro-Chinese but that the military people and the British have not been so strong for the Chinese.

The President called on Frank Knox for a report on his trip to Guadalcanal. Frank said the boys down there were eager to fight the Japs and confident that they could lick the Japs. He said flatly that malaria was just as dangerous to our boys down there as the Japs.

At cabinet meeting the President told one story which he told again at dinner that night of how when he was riding along in a jeep in N. Africa reviewing some of the troops, when he passed by the first two companies, the officer said, "Eyes right" (and the President

---

[1] Daniel W. Bell, long-time Treasury official, since 1940 Undersecretary of the Treasury.
[2] Mrs. Wellington Koo, wife of the Chinese diplomat who was then ambassador to Great Britain.

said this in the characteristic officer tone of voice). The men looked at the President in the jeep and their jaws dropped. Apparently they were completely dumb with astonishment. When they reached the third company, the situation was the same except that from about the middle of the back row the President heard very distinctly the voice of one astonished private say, "Jesus!" He gave this in the characteristic tone of voice used by certain irreverent young men . . .

At the White House dinner party were present the President and Mrs. Roosevelt, Henry Roosevelt (a nephew of Mrs. Roosevelt), the wife of Elliott Roosevelt, who is running a Hereford ranch near Fort Worth, Texas, several other young people, and the following refugee Germans: Paul Tillich of the Union Theological Seminary, Frederick Polak of Columbia University, Adolph Lowe and Hans Standinger of the New School of Social Research. Lowe and Polak are Jews and have had excellent training in statistical economics. All four of them have been connected with the movement which had some influence in Germany some twenty years ago, known as "Christian Socialism." Tillich, a theologian, is a good friend of both Reinhold and Richard Niebuhr. At the request of Mrs. Roosevelt, they outlined at the dinner table the possible directions for Europe to go in the postwar world:

1. The so-called Metternich, reactionary, or modern Holy Alliance solution. This, they thought, could be imposed on Europe only by the authority of the United States troops. They felt that if and when the United States troops were removed that Europe would then go either communistic or fascist.

2. The authoritarian, power-drive approach based on the dominant influence of certain powerful economic groups, such as steel, aluminum, etc.

3. True democracy, based on serving the welfare of the people, with the people well educated, community by community, for supporting it. It is obvious that the professors were all very strongly against the Metternich solution. They felt, however, that the impulse of both the American Army people and the State Department people would be to play with those elements in the European population which would lead to the Metternich solution.

FEBRUARY 8, 1943

. . . Milo gave me full documenation commodity by commodity on Jesse Jones' failures to build up a stockpile prior to April 13, 1943 (the time when our second Executive Order was signed).

Harold Young[1] brought in Father Massey,[2] the Jesuit priest who is editing the magazine *America*. It was the first time I had known that the magazine was a Jesuit publication. Massey is a very intelligent man, well trained in economics and history, and professes great liberalism in his thought. He said very frankly he wanted to be in my corner and hoped I would not make it too hard for him. He indicated that in practically every speech I made there were a few sentences or possibly a paragraph which because of his clientele made it hard for him to support my point of view. I told him very frankly that I thought it was very important for the future peace of the world that there be an understanding between the western democracies and Russia, and I felt the true formula was full production and full employment on the part of the western democracies. Curiously enough, Massey said nothing whatever against Russia but he did come out flatly against what he called "popular front" government. He says the magazine *America*, while it has no official standing in Catholic circles, does circulate in a fairly extensive way among members of the hierarchy and he felt that it had a lot of influence in forming Catholic opinion. What he really was saying was that there were more votes among the Catholics than among the crackpot liberals; also he made it clear that the Catholic church was the real friend of the common man. I asked him pointblank what percentage of the hierarchy above the rank of priests had read and had understood the papal encyclical *Quadragesimo Anno*. We then had an extended discussion on the social movement in the Catholic church, beginning with Leo XIII. Massey said that the Catholic church had had no social vision until some Catholics in Germany started thinking along those lines in the late seventies and eighties. This resulted in Leo's encyclical *Rerum Novarum*.

Massey admitted that in some places in Latin America the hierarchy was pretty reactionary (I then remembered that Messersmith had told me that Franco had brought pressure to bear on the Vatican to appoint bishops to Latin America who had been approved by Franco. I had also had this confirmed from other sources). As Jesuits go, I would say that Massey is an unusually liberal, likable, social-minded person. For reasons of his own and partly because he really believes very much as I do and partly because he believes in it as policy, I suspect he will follow my line for the most part although he will probably be shocked by many things I say . . .

---

[1] Harold Young, assistant to the Vice President and his office manager, as well as the member of his staff who was informally and unofficially the most active in working for Wallace's renomination in 1944.
[2] Father Benjamin J. Massey, S.J.

FEBRUARY 10, 1943

. . . Morgenthau had a splendid time in Cuba for about three weeks at a spot on the north coast about 100 miles east of Havana not far from Cardenas. He and Mrs. Morgenthau had a cabin on the beach and it cost them only $42 a week for each of them for room and board. He visited a number of the health centers in Cuba and found them marvelous. Only working people can belong to these centers. They pay only $2 or $2.50 a month. They have hospitals that are equal to the best in New York City; also the doctors and nurses are the very best.

I told Henry about Paul de Kruif's[1] opinion of the plan worked out by Dr. Garfield for one of the Kaiser shipyards where the workers pay 7 cents a day for check-over insurance, hospitalization, etc. I told him that Kaiser had borrowed the money from the banks to start this program and how payment by the workers was liquidating it. Moreover the payment by the workers was amortizing a capital investment in hospital buildings on a basis which would result in a complete payoff within three years. Morgenthau said he would be willing to go with me and Paul de Kruif to see the President . . .

Jimmie Byrnes telephoned about Jesse Jones having written a letter to the President wanting to see the President. [2] I sent down to see Jimmie. He followed his usual compromising technique, saying he was a friend of both Jesse and myself, that he was anxious that whatever Jesse did would not hurt either the President or myself. It seems that Jesse in his letter to the President asked that the effective date of Executive Order No. 5, which I put out on January 19, be postponed for 60 days until the President could go over the matter with Jesse. The President had given Jimmie the letter, saying he did not have time to go into it and asked Jimmie to go into it with Jesse. Jimmie had talked with Jesse and Jesse complained bitterly about the BEW and Milo, saying that

---

[1] Paul de Kruif, bacteriologist and author, was a frequent contributor to the *Reader's Digest* and a popularizer of medical developments in books such as *Microbe Hunters* (1926) and *Kaiser Wakes the Doctors* (1943). The latter provided a glowing description of Henry Kaiser's innovative and successful program to provide broad, inexpensive delivery of group health care to his workers.

[2] Jones held that Wallace's order about the Metal Reserves Corporation placed a strained, illegal construction upon the President's earlier Executive Orders relating to the BEW. Jones' senior representatives in Brazil, loath to operate under BEW direction, were resigning their positions. Jones therefore argued further that Wallace's order would prove unworkable and impractical, and would lead to the substitution in the field of a new and inexperienced staff. He made those points directly in a letter to Wallace of February 25, 1943.

Milo had planted stuff in the newspapers against Jesse personally. I told Jimmie Byrnes that I had never cared to bother the President with matters of this sort, that when Jesse ganged up with Jeffers to take rubber away from BEW immediately after the President left town, I did not undertake to get the effective date of Jeffers' rubber order postponed by appealing to the President. I said I hoped the President would keep hands off but I thought the order ought to stick, that so far as I was concerned, the more publicity about it the better because Milo had done a good job and could stand publicity.

Jimmie did not think publicity was a good thing, saying the Democratic Party was split in many directions, and that publicity would give the Republicans opportunity to shoot at us some more. I told him there was only one alternative so far as I was concerned and that was to return to the situation that existed prior to last December, and give us back the rubber, and have assurance from Jesse Jones that there would be full cooperation and not the frozen situation which existed since the fight before the Senate Banking and Currency Committee, a fight which had been started by Jesse Jones himself by the way in which he answered questions before the Committee . . .

FEBRUARY 11, 1943

. . . Roy Roberts and Henry Haskell[1] both claimed that the sentiment toward Russia was marvelous in the Midwest, they said that people out that way thought Russia had saved the United States. Apparently the fewer the Catholics in the locality, the greater the enthusiasm for Russia. They said the Chinese were even more popular than the Russians. They said the people of the Midwest were going to continue to raise hell about gasoline rationing and farm labor shortage. Roberts predicted that food shortage would be the most important problem before the American people next fall. He felt the administration had been awfully slow in waking up to the manpower problem. He said he had seen it last September. I said I had too . . .

It appears that the Egyptians are scared of both Russia and Germany, and hate England. They profess great admiration for the United States. They have great resentment against the British because the British ran their tanks into the palace courtyard of the king on February 5 and forced the king to continue with a British minister whom he thoroughly detested. The Egyptian minister and his wife both pro-

[1] Roy A. Roberts, publisher, and Henry J. Haskell, editor of the Kansas City *Star* were, like Wallace, guests at the Egyptian legation.

fessed great admiration for my speech of May 8 and said they hoped the United States would not continue to allow England to oppress small nations. They have no use for Churchill. At the same time they declare that they are very strongly anti-Nazi . . .

FEBRUARY 12, 1943

Atherton Lee, who is in the employ of Jeffers, came in to say that he realized that he was going across administration lines but he was so seriously disturbed about the war effort that he wanted me to know that Jeffers was doing a very bad job; that there was very little real interest in natural rubber. As a matter of fact, there seems to be an actual prejudice against natural rubber; that they are actually failing to get 37,000 tons of natural rubber from Ceylon which they could get if they tried. He thinks the chemists in the organization are so interested in setting up a tariff-protected rubber industry in the United States that they want to have all the rubber we can possibly consume produced synthetically. Lee claims that Jeffers has been given more of a priority over escort vessels, planes, and 100-octane gas than should have been given—that the true figures do not bear out the contentions which they have made. Lee says Jeffers is a bull in a china shop and is much more interested in interorganizational politics than he is in getting a job done. Lee prepared a letter for Jeffers to sign to Nelson Rockefeller arranging for Rockefeller to help on the health program in Brazil. Jeffers refused to sign it, saying, "First, I want to find out just which team Rockefeller is playing on."

Chaim Weizmann came in to talk to me about Zionism and said he was going to be seeing President Roosevelt. After he sees President Roosevelt he says he wants to come back to see me again. I told him I would be glad to see him. He thinks that Trans-Jordania can be developed by irrigation so that it could support at least a million Jews without taking away any of the livelihood of the 350,000 Arabs who are living there now. I asked Weizmann how the rubber program was getting on and he said the only part of it that was coming along well was the part conducted by the Union Carbide Company. He says most of our program is not yet out of the experimental stage; that they still don't know how to make the Buna S rubber serve satisfactorily in the making of tires, and that there is need for a special soft kind of rubber between the tread and the fabric. He said much of the butadiene produced is very impure and they have not yet worked out satisfactory methods of purifying butadiene. He said the Baruch Committee did a very poor job; that Baruch was a man of immense vanity; that Conant,[1] while he was a competent chemist, had no courage because he was afraid of the oil industry. He, Weizmann, said that he had been threatened by one of the members of the oil industry, in the words, "You can't buck a thirty billion dollar industry." I asked Weizmann how long the production of rubber had been delayed by reason of spending so much time on the oil route instead of going the alcohol route. Weizmann said, "At least six months and probably more." It is evident that the oil people, interested in building up an industry which will be profitable to them, have sacrificed the national welfare to their own cupidity or ignorance . . .

Ed Flynn[2] was interested in working out an organization which would work for the peace. He wants to stay in the background himself, but thinks we ought to have a precinct-by-precinct organization. He said there should be no Jews in it but that there should be a lot of Catholics. I told him I didn't think he should have too many Catholics in the Middle West. He wants to be sure there are no communists and he wants respectable people. He said he talked over this general idea with the President; that the President liked it and suggested that he talk to me about it. I told Flynn I thought Dan Roper[3] was interested in much the same kind of thing and that I thought it would be a fine thing if he and Dan Roper would work together. Flynn thinks it would be a fine thing to get together about the same crowd of people who used to work on the old Committee to Defend America. Flynn thinks the membership ought to be about half Republican and about half Democratic. He would like to concern himself with the organization and stay utterly in the background. Flynn is very much prejudiced against the Jews and urged me to read a book by Hilaire Belloc about the Jews. He bemoaned the fact that the Jews had control of all phases of the amusement business, movies, radio, song writers, theater, etc. He said the trouble with their having control is that in this way they con-

---

[1] James B. Conant, distinguished chemist and educator, on leave as president of Harvard, had been a member of the Baruch committee on rubber and was chairman of the National Defense Research Committee. He had worked from the outset with Vannevar Bush on the atomic energy program and other projects of the Office of Scientific Research and Development. In the matter of rubber, Conant may have been wrong, but it would have been wholly out of character for him to have been intimidated.

[2] Edward J. Flynn, Bronx Democratic boss, long-time supporter of Roosevelt, chairman of the Democratic National Committee (1940 to January 1943), had resigned that post when the President appointed him ambassador to Australia, an appointment the Senate would not confirm.

[3] Daniel C. Roper, active in Democratic politics since the Wilson years, had been Roosevelt's first Secretary of Commerce.

sciously or unconsciously impose on all the people in the United States their own ideals of what culture really is. I said I hadn't noticed this in the movies. He said he could name a hundred movies portraying the sufferings of the downtrodden Jews. I challenged him to name one and he couldn't. Ed likes to pose as a man of very great culture. He says he has an LL.D. from Fordham; told how he had written a letter to Turner Catledge[1] of the Chicago *Sun* with regard to an editorial in which Catledge criticized Ed for being unfitted for appointment as ambassador to Australia. Ed in his letter told about how he had studied logic at college. Ed says that the Bronx is 60 percent Jewish but every time a Jew sticks up his head in the Bronx he knocks it down. He says that is the reason he has gotten along so well there. He said Jim Farley wanted to be elected National Committeeman after Ed resigned; he said, however, that he was stronger in New York State than Jim and that he was able to get the place back again. He said he has always been a good friend of Jim Farley and has never said anything against him. He said Jim now, however, was beginning to believe his own publicity . . .

I had a most interesting visit with John Winant. He told me the real lowdown on the British agreement with Russia involving the Baltic provinces and Bessarabia.[2] It seems that the agreement did not take place, as Bill Bullitt suggested, when Eden visited Russia but that a special Russian commission visited London and held a series of conversations with Eden. Winant tried repeatedly to see the commission but they ducked him. Eden kept Winant informed. When Winant found that things were drifting toward a settlement, he finally in desperation got in touch with Ivan Maisky, the Soviet ambassador, and said he had to see him. Maisky tried to put him off until after the agreement was signed. Winant insisted that he must see him that very night and he did. Winant told Maisky that the situation in the United States was much different than it was in England. In England the people were much more friendly toward Russia than the administration, whereas in the United States the administration was much more friendly to Russia than the people. Winant wanted Maisky to know that if an agreement of this sort which had been worked out with the British went through, it would put the administration in the United States in a very difficult position. Winant made his point stick. Later the President told him

---

[1] William Turner Catledge, journalist, editor-in-chief of the Chicago *Sun* (1942–43) left that post to become national correspondent for the New York *Times*.
[2] Winant was referring to discussions about the Baltic states that took place after the Eden negotiations that Bullitt had described to Wallace; see William L. Langer and S. Everett Gleason, *The Undeclared War* (New York, 1953) pp. 122 ff, 553.

that he (the President) was very glad of what he had done. It appears then that both Welles and Bullitt are wrong when they say that the President himself stopped the Russian-British deal . . .

FEBRUARY 16, 1943

. . . Milo Perkins brought in a letter from Will Clayton and a proposed draft of a reply to Jesse Jones with regard to the personnel involved in the transfer under my Executive Order of January 19. Milo is very anxious for me to have lunch with Elmer Davis [1] on Thursday. Elmer is very much depressed by State Department policy and has been eager to resign. Milo has urged him not to do so, saying that he thinks all of the progressive people should stay on their jobs and saw wood as long as they possibly can. It seems that quite a left wing boy by the name of David Karr in OWI who has been serving on the liaison committee between OWI and Berle of the State Department brought back word that Berle was preparing for setting up a postwar government in Hungary under Horthy.[2] This aroused Davis and he went over to see Hull to protest. Hull blew up. He said, "The State Department, the Army, and the Navy are interested in winning the war. You and Milo Perkins and the Vice President are interested in winning the war but even more than that, you are interested in producing worldwide social revolution even at the danger of producing revolution in the United States." I asked Milo just when this conversation between Hull and Davis took place. Milo said within the last four or five days. This interested me because Winant had told me last Friday that Hull had recently told him, "You know we in the State Department now think that Henry is a fine fellow." So apparently Hull has one story when talking to a progressive man whom he knows is sympathetic with my ideas and another story when he is annoyed or irritated . . .

At the WPB meeting after routine business was disposed of, Don Nelson asked that only members of the Board remain . . .

Don opened up by saying that he had asked for Eberstadt's resignation that morning. He said that the situation between him and Wilson [3] had become impossible, that he had tried to live with it for a long time but would be unable to do so any longer. Jim Forrestal spoke up quite

[1] Elmer Davis, celebrated radio newscaster, head of the Office of War Information, a troubled agency throughout the war.

[2] Admiral Nikolaus Horthy, prewar regent in Hungary, an opponent of communism and of the Soviet Union.

[3] Charles Edward Wilson, president of the General Electric Company, vice chairman of the War Production Board (1942–44).

sharply, saying that he thought a serious mistake was being made. Patterson reiterated the same idea by most bitterly claiming that there were many men in WPB who are thinking first, last and all the time about how to undermine the armed services. Forrestal joined in. I asked them for a specific citation, and they indicated that WPB was trying to get into matters that were solely the concern of the War Department, such as the size of the Army. I took this as a slap at Nathan and said I thought Nathan had performed a great service for the Army and Navy themselves in bringing out the figures which he had presented to the board several months previously. Forrestal said he did not think anyone could really appreciate the gravity of the situation who did not have a son in the armed services. I took this again as an indirect slap at Nathan and said I thought the Army and Navy themselves were both being protected by having another point of view brought to their attention. Patterson said many of these men were afflicted with the same disease that Hoover was afflicted with. He said that on October 27, 1917, Hoover had written a letter to Colonel House. He had a copy of the letter. In this letter Hoover had stated that he thought it was the function of the United States to send food and munitions to Europe but not men. Patterson made the point that if Hoover's advice in the war of 1917 had been followed, the result would have been victory for the Germans in 1918. He said it was the large number of men we placed in France in the summer of 1918 which made it possible to defeat the Germans that fall. In the summer of 1918 Ludendorf had 30 or 40 divisions in reserve and the Allies had none. In the fall we had 50 divisions in reserve and the Germans had none. Many of these men were green but the volume of our supplies had turned the tide. I told Bob that I myself felt that if the United States and England put forth an effort during the next 7 or 8 months corresponding to that which the Russians had put forth, it was quite conceivable the war could end in the year 1943. By conversation of this type, I blunted the hardness of the feeling between Forrestal and Patterson on the one side and Nelson on the other.

Forrestal doesn't question Wilson's ability but says that his training has been along the line of assembling materials and not along the line of producing and allocating the necessary raw materials. Don said that Wilson was very acceptable to industry with the possible exception of the iron and steel branch.

After the meeting was over, I went around to talk to Don alone and told him I thought it would be helpful if Wilson would have a heart-to-heart talk with Nathan and Ezekiel and urge them not to make themselves too conspicuous for a time. I told Don I had seen very little of Ezekiel but from what I knew of his temperament I would assume that he would be doing quite a bit of propagandizing of a sort which would be quite obnoxious to the Army and Navy. Don said that the Army and Navy folks had been planting a lot of propaganda, said their game was to get him out and get Eberstadt in control and, in effect, have Barney Baruch running the WPB. Eberstadt is, of course, Baruch's man. Don said many of the men in WPB had no confidence in Eberstadt, that he was slippery. He said Wilson was a deeply religious man. He said the purpose of the Army and Navy was to get Eberstadt in control, which would mean Eberstadt would be running WPB under Baruch's guidance . . .

FEBRUARY 18, 1943

. . . Rabbi Berlin[1] asked pointblank for a message which he could take to the Jews in Palestine concerning what I would do for them after the war. I told him with equal frankness that I would not give them any such message. I said I had the greatest sympathy with the Jewish people but that there was a difference of opinion among the Jews themselves, that while I personally was very friendly toward the fine efforts the Jews had put forth in Palestine, I was not in position to say anything that could be interpreted as an official commitment. He was very much disappointed. I must confess there are certain types of religious leaders who have a very poor sense of time and place . . .

Bill Herridge had a very bad cold. He said he had had a few minutes with the President and the President invited him to come back on Monday for lunch. Bill and I find ourselves in more nearly complete accord on world affairs and economic matters than any other two people. Bill wants to save our democratic capitalism but he knows it has got to make a lot of changes if it is to be worth saving. He thinks Churchill is absolutely no good for the postwar period.

At the lunch for Madame Chiang Kai-shek I sat next to Congressman Bloom[2] who told me that Rabbi Wise[3] was a racketeer and that the

[1] Rabbi Meyer Berlin, head of the World Mizrachi, a Zionist organization.

[2] Sol Bloom, Democratic congressman from New York since 1923 and long-time chairman of the House Committee on Foreign Affairs, continually displayed a controlled patience with State Department delays in assisting the rescue of European Jews, whom the Nazis were systematically slaughtering. His attitude contrasted with that of Emanuel Celler; see Henry L. Feingold, *The Politics of Rescue* (New Brunswick, 1970).

[3] Rabbi Stephen S. Wise of New York, a leading American Zionist, member of the executive committee of the World Zionist Organization, president of both the American Jewish Congress and the World Jewish Congress, had asked Wallace to see Rabbi Berlin.

Zionists were troublemakers; if I had any more trouble with fellows like Rabbi Berlin to send them over to him.

FEBRUARY 19, 1943

. . . Elmer Davis is rather discouraged about the State Department. I told him about Sumner Welles' new slant on Russia. He says the reason is that Litvinov has recently been very cold to the State Department and to the United Nations meetings, and has refused to attend some meetings which he could have attended just as easily as not. Davis has been trying to get about 15 of his men abroad. The Army is anxious to have them but the State Department holds up their passports.[1] Davis apparently has had even more trouble with State Department passports than Milo.

At cabinet meeting, Ickes brought up the problem of manpower on the farms, indicating the kind of trouble he was having. There was much animated discussion of the sort which I had predicted when the subject was first brought up in cabinet meeting last September. The President was still sensitive on the subject but he is beginning to see the light and is willing to do something about it. He thinks now the way out is to have what might be called a universal manpower bill and directed McNutt to submit such a bill to him within the next few days.

After cabinet meeting, Jesse Jones submitted a variety of monetary allocations to the President to sign. The President came to one about money to set up a natural rubber corporation and asked if this was O.K. with BEW. I was sitting across the table awaiting my turn and said, "You know, Mr. President, BEW doesn't have anything to do with natural rubber anymore." Jesse also mentioned about Alcoa making 79 million dollars this year, and he, Jesse Jones, being in a dilemma as to whether to recapture this money for the government or to cut the price of aluminum.

I stopped to talk with the President about the formal invitation to visit Chile which had been delivered by the Chilean ambassador.[2] I

---

[1] In one recent major case, Hull had refused a passport to Edgar A. Mowrer, deputy director of the OWI, whom Davis wanted to send to North Africa. A distinguished correspondent, Mowrer had been of the Chicago *Daily News* bureau in France and before Pearl Harbor a strong advocate of American intervention in the war, as Secretary of War Stimson knew from personal observation. Hull, however, resented Mowrer's unabashed sympathies for the Free French, as he also ordinarily resented the operations of the OWI.

[2] On behalf of President Juan Antonio Ríos, Chilean Ambassador Michels had issued that invitation. Earlier Costa Rican Minister of Foreign Affairs Alberto Echandi had asked Wallace to visit his country, and the Vice President had

asked the President when he thought I ought to go. He said it was altogether up to me. I asked him what countries I ought to visit. He said he thought Costa Rica, Panama, Colombia, Ecuador, Peru, and Chile. Then he said there was just one thing he was concerned about and that was that Russia so strongly wanted someone of cabinet rank to visit Russia. He thought I ought to visit Russia sometime in the summer. I told him I would very much like to visit Russia but I thought it was important to visit Latin America before going to Russia. He said if I went to Russia the important thing was to be thoroughly familiar with the military situation so as to let Stalin know why it was that we could not do some of the things he wanted us to do. Let him know about the shipping problem, about how it takes 10 tons of shipping a month to support an American boy overseas and in the case of an American boy in the air force, it may take 20 tons of shipping a month. The President outlined quite a sales talk along this line to give to Stalin. It was all in the direction of why Stalin should not expect too much from us.

On leaving, I told the President that immediately after he left on his recent trip to N. Africa, Jeffers and Jesse had taken rubber away from BEW and that there had been some other troubles since, although I did not think it was necessary to bother him about them. He said, "Fine," that he guessed Jeffers was happy now . . .

FEBRUARY 20, 1943

At the luncheon with Pogue, Warner, and Lee,[1] we had considerable discussion about the feasibility of an international air authority. Warner and Pogue were inclined to look at the problem in a small, slow, and cautious way. Lee was inclined to look at it in a big way but without too much information. Warner and Pogue tend to magnify the difficulties in the way of setting up an international air authority. Pogue says that the thing which Juan Trippe[2] is really afraid of is that other American airlines will get into the business of competing with them. Pogue says that Trippe is really pretty selfish, that when he

received other invitations from Bolivia, Colombia, Ecuador, Panama, and Peru. On February 23, 1943, he announced his plans to visit those nations on a trip to begin in mid-March. He intended while en route to open the Tropical Institute of Agriculture in Costa Rica, study production elsewhere of rubber, quinine, abaca, and other tropical commodities, and examine the development in Chile of agriculture in a temperate zone.

1 Joshua B. Lee, Edward Warner, and L. Welch Pogue, all of the Civil Aeronautics Authority.

2 Juan T. Trippe, president of Pan American Airlines.

spoke of turning his business over to the government what he really meant was give the government preferred stock in return for money but to maintain control himself. Pogue was raised on a farm near Grant in Montgomery County, Iowa.

I had a talk with Frank Walker in his apartment Saturday night . . . Walker said that Jim Farley had talked to him and admitted he was out organizing the 1944 convention against the President.

I told Frank I thought it was possible to get clean money to finance the Democratic Party. Walker said all the time he was treasurer of the Democratic Party the money was clean and he proposed to keep it clean now.

I told Frank I thought the President at the right time should come out on behalf of incentive taxation after the war, taxation of a sort that would make it possible for the small businessman to build up. I said I had talked to both Henry Morgenthau and the President on behalf of incentive taxation at the time of the depression in 1937. Frank said he also had been in favor of incentive taxation, that it had a lot to recommend it both from the standpoint of small business and from the standpoint of full employment. I told Frank that the President and Morgenthau had been against incentive taxation on moral grounds. I told them frankly I thought they were wrong. It was all right during times of war profits to have very heavy taxation on excess profits but in the case of small and growing businesses which are building plant extensions, buying new machinery, it seems to me that taxation should be such as to make it possible for the growing business to invest in new machinery without heavy excess profit taxes. I said to Frank that if we cannot do something of this sort, I suspect we may be forced to go socialistic after the war is over.

FEBRUARY 25, 1943

. . . Madame Chiang told me how deeply interested she was in agriculture, that she had been told by the President that part of our agricultural program was based on Chinese philosophy. I then told her the story of how I had gotten the phrase "Ever-Normal Granary" out of a book, *Economic Principles of Confucius*. She called my attention to the fact that her niece, Miss Kung, was the 76th lineal descendant of Confucius. She said she was very eager to have me come to China to study Chinese agriculture. I described to her some of the methods we use in our agricultural colleges, the extension services, etc., saying that these methods were not popular with the farmers during the first decade of the century but after that they became increasingly popular as they more and more demonstrated themselves to be useful. I told her that the last 40 years we had improved our efficiency at least 40 percent in the United States and I was sure that the same thing could be done in China, that we are not interested in doing anything for the Chinese unless the Chinese want us to.

She said that while the Chinese are very conservative, they changed very rapidly as soon as they thought something was practical and that they are very eager to learn from the United States. I said I felt that the improvement of agriculture and the increase in industrialization of China was vital to the future peace of the world. She agreed . . .

FEBRUARY 26, 1943

. . . At the dinner at Herbert Feis' [1] there were present Mr. and Mrs. Burden,[2] Assistant Secretary of Commerce; Mr. and Mrs. Bowes-Lyon (he is the brother of the Queen of England). Burden is a great grandson of Commodore Vanderbilt and was brought into government by Nelson Rockefeller.

The conversation turned to air. I said bluntly that Joe Martin's statement about American supremacy of the air as made on January 5 was very disturbing to me and I feared it meant a race for air supremacy between England, Russia, and the United States, and that it had in it the seeds of another World War. I came out strongly for an international air authority running all the planes. I found that Mr. Burden was very much disturbed about having an international air authority running all the planes. He wants to preserve private initiative. I pointed out that an international air authority could license individual companies. Burden thought that private companies could best carry on the invention which was necessary to further improvement in airplanes. I said to Burden, "Doesn't it seem probable now that airplanes will stabilize around a carrying capacity of fifty to one hundred tons and a cruising speed of one hundred fifty to two hundred miles?" He said that there were some very promising inventions going forward which would use the propulsion power of gas jets instead of propellers. Also he said there were inventions going forward looking toward change in the shape of the wings, that the present type of wings re-

1 Herbert Feis, at that time, as he had been since 1937, adviser on international economic affairs in the Department of State.
2 William A. M. Burden, aviation expert, special aviation assistant to the Secretary of Commerce (1942–43), then Assistant Secretary of Commerce.

sulted in jerky passage of the air when high speeds were attained, that when the proper shape of wing was discovered and the gas jet was put into effect, he thought it was possible to attain 700 miles an hour. He did not think this was coming to pass at any time within the next 5 or 10 years but it would come to pass ultimately.

I told Burden that generally speaking I was in favor of invention unlimited but that definitely I was not in favor of taking any move that would jeopardize an enduring peace. I thought we could by means of an international air authority license the various private companies and insure peace while at the same time we retained the benefits of private initiative in certain areas.

. . . The one thing which Pan American is interested in is a continuation of its monopolistic position over large areas of the earth. It seems that there are certain Americans who would welcome a fight for supremacy of the air, believing that we in the United States have the resources and the ingenuity to win the fight. I said flatly it seemed to me that such a fight had in it the germs of the next World War and I was absolutely against anyone who had such ideas, no matter who he or she might be.

Herbert Feis proclaimed that he saw a new American imperialism forming, that he noted that imperialism was rearing its ugly head even in BEW. He thought that BEW was interfering in the internal affairs of Latin America countries in trying to bring about an increased production by asking for certain clauses in labor contracts. I went to bat very vigorously on this with Feis and he retreated. I told Feis I had no interest whatever in exploitation of Latin America but we did want to get as rapidly as possible the necessary products for winning the war and I regretted it whenever the State Department slowed up the process . . .

MARCH 4, 1943

. . . After cabinet I showed to the President the latter part of my proposed March 8 speech[1] to the farmers, calling his attention particu-

---

[1] Wallace spoke in Columbus, Ohio, on March 8, 1943, on the tenth anniversary of the National Farm Program. He began with a tribute to the ever-normal granary and the prewar stock of surpluses that had helped to provide necessary food during the war. He went on to warn against a new isolationism: "I am convinced that we cannot have national security if we follow as isolationist or excessively nationalist policy." Instead the United States had to use its influence to prevent another war. Too, Americans had to "help other countries to develop their agriculture and industries . . . raise their own standards of produc-

larly to that dealing with international air. It all seemed to be satisfactory to him. The only suggestions he made were in the nature of sharpening and making it more controversial. The President would like to see me interject short choppy sentences, designed to wake up the audience even though the sentences may be rather unfair in their context.

I told the President I thought the Republicans were using vigorous, vicious methods against us among the farmers and that the administration at the present time stood lower with the farmers than at any time during the past 10 years. I told the President I thought his leadership was so exceedingly important to the world that something ought to be done to solidify and strengthen the Democratic Party. He asked if I had talked with Frank Walker about the President's visit with Walker and the National Committee. He said it was a good visit. I gained the impression that the President is still unwilling to step out and furnish active leadership on the international front but that he is thinking about strengthening the internal political situation . . .

MARCH 5, 1943

I talked with Senator George about his committee for postwar planning which will undoubtedly be authorized next week. He told me he had made no commitments whatever with regard to men who should be on the committee. I told George I thought this committee would be one of the most important ever set up in Congress and . . . gave him the letter which I had received from Walter Lippmann and urged on him that he get enough of an appropriation so that he could set up a staff to receive postwar plans that might be sent in by the people of the United States. I told him such a staff should really study the plans, classify them, and let the people who wrote in know that their ideas were receiving adequate consideration. Senator George does not yet have in mind what technical staff he will have . . .

Walter Nash of New Zealand, whom I look on as being the most progressive of any of the diplomats, brought in Fred Jones,[1] and we talked about New Zealand's war effort which in some ways is the most amazing of any country. New Zealand is probably the most progressive

---

tion and consumption." To that end, the United States would have to establish fair international trade relations rather than reverting to protectionism, and have to share air facilities at home and abroad with other countries rather than engaging in an imperialistic struggle for supremacy of the air.

[1] Walter Nash, New Zealand minister to the United States, and Fred Jones, New Zealand minister of Agriculture.

democratic country in the world. They were the first to have old age insurance, woman suffrage, etc., etc. Nash said that the United States was about 40 years behind New Zealand in her social outlook . . .

MARCH 9, 1943

Gifford Pinchot[1] thinks the President ought to get busy as fast as possible on leading public sentiment with regard to the peace. He thinks we have already delayed too long . . .

James Reston, who is now special assistant to Arthur Sulzberger, wanted to know if I was now getting along all right with Sumner Welles. I told him about a month ago I had found that Sumner shared my fears about discord between the United States and Russia, and that we had been cooperating. Reston was exceedingly friendly and I would judge his attitude reflects to some extent growing friendliness on the part of Sulzberger. This is probably also due to the sudden desire of the State Department to start appeasing me . . .

MARCH 10, 1943

. . . Bob Patterson was not at the Forrestal luncheon. Instead there was the Secretary of the Navy, James Forrestal, and a couple of Navy assistants. They all seemed to be afraid of Russia and to have a strongly American imperialistic idea. Knox was especially interested in having an arrangement with Great Britain at once to get the Japanese mandated isles for us after the war came to an end. They all claimed everyone came out of Russia feeling like they had been released from prison.

At the White House reception, which was purely social, the President spoke a few words which were very informal and of no political consequence. Mrs. Luce was there but I avoided meeting her.

Fulbright[2] of Arkansas who has been fighting Mrs. Luce on the floor of the House was with her part of the time. It was apparent that Mrs.

---

[1] Gifford Pinchot, indefatigable conservationist and dauntless progressive, White Knight of the American woodlands since the turn of the century, had been Theodore Roosevelt's chief of the Bureau of Forestry. Pinchot had commended Wallace's successful effort to keep that bureau within the Department of Agriculture in spite of Ickes' continual efforts to move it to the Interior Department.

[2] J. William Fulbright, Arkansas Democrat, was then serving his first term in the House of Representatives. In 1944 he was elected to the Senate. Though not yet forty years old in 1943, Fulbright had already held office in the antitrust division of the Justice Department and as president of the University of Arkansas.

Luce is cultivating an atmosphere which causes the boys to enjoy fluttering around her. I walked home with Senator Ball and Congressman
Judd,[1] both from Minnesota. While both are Republicans, they both
have a disdain for Mrs. Luce . . .

Senator Ball was very frank in telling about the Chicago *Tribune*
money and the Ohio gang money that had been sent into Minnesota to
defeat him for the Senate and also Mr. Judd for Congress. Ball thinks
that the old party labels are passé. Judd, who voted Democratic in
1929, has cooperated with Fulbright, the Democrat from Arkansas, on
an informal bloc of new members, which is composed of about 50
congressmen, 25 of which are Democrats and 25 Republicans. The idea
of these 50 congressmen is to see if they can't be the balance of power
in the House.[2]

MAY 22, 1943

. . . Churchill[3] started out by talking about the postwar organization. He said he thought there ought to be three regional organizations
and one supreme. He visioned the U.S., British Empire, and Russia
really running the supreme show. There would be an American region in which the U.S. would have membership and a Pacific region
in which the U.S. would have membership. The British would have
membership in all three regions. The U.S. might or might not have
membership in the European. He went into quite some detail with re-

1 Senator Joseph H. Ball and Representative Walter H. Judd, both identified with
  the more liberal and internationalist wing of the Republican Party.
2 Wallace, who left Washington on March 16, kept no diary, only a calendar of
  appointments, March 13–May 21, 1942, even though he returned from Latin
  America on April 26. The trip was a success. Accompanied by Lawrence
  Duggan of the State Department and Hector Lazo of the BEW, Wallace
  followed a strenuous itinerary in each of the seven nations he visited. Everywhere he went he spoke Spanish, both to officers of state and to cheering
  crowds. On successive occasions he said he was "not a politician," that he
  believed in making loans to Latin America "in every manner possible," and that
  Pan-Americanism was "the vertical column" for any new world organization.
  Addressing the parliament of Chile, where a progressive government ruled, he
  said: "The people continue their thousand-year march, a revolutionary march
  in the purest sense, whose aim is to affirm, here on earth, the dignity of the
  human spirit." Before hundreds of coal miners at Lota, Chile, he said: ". . . we
  are entering the Century of the Common Man . . . There is no place in that
  century for any nation which under any pretext considers itself rightfully able
  to dominate or exploit any other nation." Wallace's language of humanity and
  sincerity and his open personal manner helped in Chile and elsewhere to alle-
  viate growing Latin American skepticism about United States foreign policy.
  He was accepted, as he had hoped to be, as a genuine good neighbor.
3 At luncheon at the British embassy.

gard to the European. Described a Danubian confederation with Bavaria as a part of it. Prussia would stand by herself with 40 million people. France would be made strong even though she did not deserve it. The Scandinavian countries would be a bloc. He had no ideas about handling Switzerland or the Low Countries. He visioned Holland in as a part of the Pacific. Disputes would be arbitrated first by the regional council and then validated by the supreme council before the troops started to move. He visioned each nation continuing to have its own armed forces but each nation would also put troops at the disposal of the supreme power. He seemed to vision, but was not very specific, an air power at the immediate disposal of the supreme council. When I pressed him about airports he was pretty vague. Connally[1] and Welles expressed themselves as in complete agreement. Stimson said it was very important to have the new setup grow out of the war setup —otherwise the U.S. would slump into isolationism. Churchill ended on the note of the U.S. and England having special, nonwritten understandings amongs themselves. He said he wanted to see the U.S. have the seat in the Pacific to make her safe also in the Atlantic. He said the U.S. and England could pull out of any mess together. Senator Connally told Churchill with only myself listening that the U.S. and England could run the world by themselves . . .

Churchill spoke very contemptuously of the vanity, pettiness, and discourtesy of de Gaulle, saying he had raised him from a pup but that he still barked and bit.

The object of the whole meeting as far as Churchill and Halifax were concerned was to do everything possible to establish a working relationship with the U.S. The bait was attractive and most of the Americans present swallowed it. It was better bait than I anticipated but Churchill really was not as definite as he sounded.

Tom Connally said that 8 members of the Foreign Affairs Committee, some of whom have the reputation of being isolationists, are sitting as a subcommittee and they have come surprisingly far in their thinking with regard to postwar world organization. Everyone is getting more honest and sincere on this point. The world massacre must not happen again.

Churchill on the whole was quite complimentary to Stalin but nevertheless was all the time . . . building an atmosphere of "we Anglo-Saxons are the ones who really know how to run the show."

---

[1] Tom Connally, Democratic senator from Texas since 1929, in 1943 chairman of the Senate Foreign Relations Committee, to which he brought the string-tie style, inflated ego, and opaque intelligence that characterized all his ventures.

JUNE 4, 1943

At the White House, while [I was] discussing my speech for Sunday with the President and with Secretary Hull, Hull spoke very strongly against putting in any reference to an international police force, claiming that the sentiment among the rank and file of the people was such and that the Republican tactics were such that it would be dangerous politically to do so.

I was very much interested to note that the Gallup poll in the Washington *Post* the following morning indicated that 74 percent of the people of the United States and 74 percent of the people of England were in favor of an international police force . . .

I was also interested in noting [that] in the New York *Times*, [in] a report on the same Gallup poll, June 4, the statement was made: "Furthermore, nearly two-thirds questioned in another recent poll thought the government should take steps now to set up with our Allies a world organization to maintain the future peace of the world."

On June 2 I phoned Cordell Hull and read to him the following from my proposed June 6 speech:

"Maintaining a peace is like keeping a garden in good order. You have to work at it day in and day out, otherwise the rains wash away the soil, and the weeds get so deeply rooted that it is impossible to pull them out without destroying many good plants as well.

"If we are not to break faith with the boys who have died, we must invent better machinery for weeding the world garden. First, and above everything else, we must have an intense desire to make this machinery succeed. We can then work out the details of the world council and the regional councils that will be needed. We can find ways to arrive at just decisions and to enforce those decisions. We can determine which powers the nations ought to reserve to themselves, which powers will need to be delegated to regional councils, which powers ought to be held jointly by the regional councils and the world council, and which will have to be delegated to the world council alone if the peace of the world is to be preserved. The airplane, which has brought so many thousands of boys to their death, can also enforce peace. It should not be hard to work out that phase of the problem if we really want to do it."

Hull obviously didn't like and so I sent it over to him. His letter came back as follows:

June 2, 1943

Dear Henry:

I herewith return page from your proposed speech with the

suggestion that if consistent you say that these are your individual views.

The opposition is moving with great care and precision to formulate the language of the issues they propose to raise on postwar questions. I prefer not to get into a discussion among the friends of the policy which this government is expected to offer, with reference to the verbiage or subject matter in some respects, until further and fuller conference with the President and others relative to the exact phraseology we may decide to adopt in given instances . . .

I also sent a copy of my speech to President Roosevelt with the following letter:

> Dear Mr. President:
>
> I am breaking over a rule of some years' standing of never making commencement day addresses because of the fact that my daughter, Jean, is graduating from Connecticut College for Women next Sunday.
>
> The boy referred to in the early part of the talk is Milo Perkins' son.[1]
>
> The particular part of the address to which I would call your attention, however, is on page 6. If you have any objections to the phraseology as I have put it on that page, I would be pleased to have your suggestions in the not too distant future. I shall be glad to stay after cabinet meeting on Friday to get your feeling about this matter.

The President sent it to Hull and so we both saw the President about the speech after cabinet on June 4. I pointed out that what I

[1] George Perkins, an aviator in the Marine Corps, had been killed in a training flight. A thoughtful, sensitive young man, he had been opposed in principle to war but enlisted after Pearl Harbor. Shortly before he died he had written his father that he and his contemporaries were "depending on you older men not to let this thing happen again. What we're fighting for now must not die in an armistice." George's symbolic death, Wallace said in his speech, forced him to "a more complete appreciation of the meaning of the death of Christ to his disciples." For Milo Perkins, too, the death of George (his other son had been killed earlier in an accident) had a symbolic and a traumatic influence. In his dedication to his duties in the BEW, Perkins had seen himself as executing an equivalent task to that George had undertaken in the Marines. Now success in that task became even more vital to Perkins. Accordingly he responded with increasing acerbity to what he interpreted as the deliberate dallying of Jesse Jones. In a time of crisis between the BEW and the lending agencies, Perkins' personal tensions mounted beyond the ordinary boundaries of bureaucratic exasperation and moved him to volatile outbursts uncharacteristic of his normal manner.

was saying was essentially the same as what Sumner Welles said last Sunday, May 30, in North Carolina. Both Hull and the President disowned Welles, saying he had not cleared with them. Hull said if other people didn't stop making speeches on foreign policy he would resign—that important people who ought to come to see him no longer came to see him because they thought he didn't have anything to do with foreign policy.

The President thought I ought to eliminate from my speech reference to regional councils. He said Churchill had laid great emphasis on the United States and Britain both being members of the three regional councils but he (the President) had pointed out that the Senate and the people of the United States would never stand for us joining a European regional council. I replied that apparently his argument had impressed Churchill because I had heard him arguing only for the United States as a member of the American and Asiatic councils.

Hull then thought I should not mention a supreme council and the President seemed to agree. I replied, "What can we tell the young folks we are fighting for?"

Hull said, "Because we had to, to avoid being slaves."

The President said the same thing and then when I pressed him by saying such an answer would not satisfy the young folks, listed the following as our objectives:

1. To disarm the aggressor
2. To prevent exploitation of small, weak nations
3. To develop some form of united action to nip aggression in the bud in the future.

Cordell thought Item No. 3 was dangerous to mention . . .

JUNE 10, 1943
HENRY A. WALLACE TO FRANKLIN D. ROOSEVELT

Dear Mr. President:

General Watson[1] called me today and indicated that you would be ready to see Jesse and me sometime next week with regard to the transfer of the U.S. Commercial Company to the Board of Economic Warfare. We have asked RFC to make us a written proposal including details as to interim financing for USCC under BEW management prior to the time we go before Congressional committees to ask that additional program funds be made available to carry out our work,

[1] Major General Edwin M. Watson, "Pa" Watson in Roosevelt's affectionate form of address, was in charge of the President's appointments schedule.

and we have also asked for a detailed compilation of the records, funds, credits, personnel, equipment, office space, et cetera, which would be transferred from the other subsidiaries of RFC to USCC as part of the transfer of functions.

Our interest here is to be sure that work now being done by the various RFC subsidiaries which might henceforth be done by USCC can be continued without interruption to the war effort.

It is essential that we get the business side of this worked out completely before we ask to see you. Personally, I should doubt that RFC can complete this task short of two or three weeks but we shall be ready whenever they are.

Unfortunately, Jesse's appearance before the Byrd Committee last week raised the same kinds of questions with regard to BEW authority over imports that were raised last December when he made a similar appearance before the Senate Banking and Currency Committee. His recent appearance before the Byrd Committee resulted in a speech on the floor of the Senate by Senator McKellar on June 4 in which he made several untrue statements about BEW and its work. As a result of all this, Milo has been summoned before the Byrd Committee Friday morning and will do the best he can. Incidentally, he received a fine reception by Mr. Cannon and other members of the House Appropriations Committee a week ago when he was up there for two days . . .

[P.S.] McKellar and Byrd[1] are lined up with Jesse and determined to get BEW.

JUNE 16, 1943

Crawford[2] spoke about the need for a renewal of private initiative in the period after the war. I told him I agreed with him. I said I believed in incentive taxation, that I had worked for it in 1938. I said, of course, while the war was on the corporations profiting out of the war should lose a greater part of their excess profits due to the war. But I said it seemed to me that when the war period was over, it was vital, if we were to prevent unemployment, to encourage maximum

[1] They were dangerous enemies, both of whom viewed BEW policies abroad as radical and wasteful. Both also wielded large power in the Senate where Kenneth D. McKellar of Tennessee, a man of inordinate vanity and quick temper, was acting chairman of the Committee on Appropriations and Harry F. Byrd of Virginia chaired a special committee on economy in government, his personal weapon for attacking New Deal programs. McKellar was openly attempting to abolish the BEW.

[2] Frederick C. Crawford, president of the National Association of Manufacturers.

initiative especially on the part of small and growing concerns by revising our taxation system. He said that everybody in the country now was in favor of a federal policy that would bring about full employment. The only dispute was in the method that would bring about this full employment. He thought it would be a great help to relax the restrictions of the Securities and Exchange Commission. He said there ought to be a Fifth Freedom—freedom to invest your money the way you wanted to. I told him I was not sufficiently posted on the Securities and Exchange Commission to offer an opinion but that I was sure an incentive should be placed on young and growing concerns and on concerns which wanted to use new methods.

I also said that insofar as private initiative failed, it might be necessary to use government funds to bring about full employment. I said there were certain fields having to do with handling of forests, building of roads, airports, etc., where the adequate use of government funds might even increase the field for private initiative rather than reduce it. I rather liked Crawford but I am not at all sure that he really agrees with me as much as he said he did . . .

MAY 22, 1943

Churchill luncheon[1]

Churchill stated that Willkie disapproved of his speech before Congress as interfering too much in the internal affairs of the United States. I said, "It appears that Willkie does not like you, Mr. Prime Minister." The Prime Minister said that Willkie reminded him of a Newfoundland dog, rushing into the water and coming out again, shaking himself, jumping up on the ladies and putting his paws on their shoulders, wagging his tail and sweeping all the dishes off the table at the same time. He said, of course, it might be all right to have a Newfoundland dog around to save a child that might fall into a lake occasionally.

The President quoted Madame Chiang Kai-shek as saying that he (Willkie) was a perpetual adolescent. Churchill indicated the various smart things he could have said over the radio to squelch Willkie from time to time but said he was glad he had been able to resist the temptation.

According to Churchill, Stalin saw through Willkie at once.

Churchill expressed great dislike of Lady Astor because of the un-

[1] At the White House.

warrantedly harsh things she said about people. The President and Churchill joined in their feeling about Clare Luce.

After the lunch was over, Churchill began talking on his favorite theme, joint citizenship for certain purposes for the citizens of the British Empire and the United States—freedom to travel in any part of the United States or the British Empire for citizens of both countries, provided the travel did not run counter to the local laws in any particular region. He made it more clear than he had at the luncheon on Saturday that he expected England and the United States to run the world and he expected the staff organizations which had been set up for winning the war to continue when the peace came, that these staff organizations would by mutual understanding really run the world even though there was a supreme council and three regional councils.

I said bluntly that I thought the notion of Anglo-Saxon superiority, inherent in Churchill's approach, would be offensive to many of the nations of the world as well as to a number of people in the United States. Churchill had had quite a bit of whiskey, which, however, did not affect the clarity of his thinking process but did perhaps increase his frankness. He said why be apologetic about Anglo-Saxon superiority, that we were superior, that we had the common heritage which had been worked out over the centuries in England and had been perfected by our constitution. He himself was half American, he felt that he was called on as a result to serve the function of uniting the two great Anglo-Saxon civilizations in order to confer the benefit of freedom on the rest of the world.

I suggested it might be a good plan to bring in the Latin American nations so that the citizens of the New World and the British Empire could all travel freely without passports. Churchill did not like this. He said if we took all the colors on the painter's palette and mix them up together, we get just a smudgy grayish brown. I interjected, "And so you believe in the pure Anglo-Saxon race or Anglo-Saxondom ueber Alles." He said his concept was not a race concept but a concept of common ideals and common history.

I said in an aside to Harry Hopkins, "What do you think should be the relative percentage of 'air and land' in the attack on Europe?" Harry said in effect that he was convinced there ought to be a lot of land. "Before we finish this thing," he continued, "we have got to have two million men in Europe." Lord Cherwell took the air side very strongly. He was keen on air doing it all, said that the British had it over the Germans in the air but on land the Germans were better than the British.

(Later on in the day I called up Harry to congratulate him on pushing Cherwell with regard to the necessity for more land, telling him that I felt that more "land" at the present stage of the game in the right spots, carefully picked, would greatly shorten the war. Harry agreed completely and indicated that time and again it seemed as though everything was all set for us and the British to go in at some particular spot and then they kicked over the traces. I urged him to keep trying.

Harry then volunteered comment with regard to the Drew Pearson column, in which Drew had said in effect that Harry Hopkins was working for the President for a fourth term but was against me for a second term. Harry said he wanted me to know that there was no truth in it. I replied that I knew that, that Drew's percentage of accuracy was rather low.)

Churchill was happy as a lark with the report on submarine sinkings. He said the first 25 days in May we had sunk a total of 26 subs. Churchill felt that after two months of this the German crews would refuse to go out. There is a new device which is very effective which I will not describe here. Apparently this device has only been in use during the past two or three weeks. In April there were 15 subs sunk. Probably the German loss is greater than this because these sinkings are only those which are known of a certainty and do not include those which have run into mines or have been lost in other ways unknown to the allies. We shall be greatly increasing our escort vessels, the result of which should be to help us further in meeting the submarine menace.

The President told how in World War No. 1 the first sign of German break was in September when the submarine crews refused to go out, then [they] mutinied in October 1918.

All through the luncheon Churchill came back with the greatest joy to the submarine situation. The motto is "A submarine a day keeps the famine away."

Apparently the British have been planning on importing only 26 million tons of certain materials as compared with 60 million tons in normal prewar years. For an island people, depending on imports, they certainly have been doing a most extraordinary job in the way of hard work and self-denial. Churchill claims that the last hope of the Germans is its subs and that that hope is now wrecked. I said that their next to the last hope was the submarines but that their last hope was the possibility of working out a separate peace with Russia. Churchill then replied that their really last hope was that they could prolong the war long enough that we all would get tired (that is the reason why a second front well chosen now is so exceedingly important; also from the standpoint of making sure that Russia is absolutely solid, a second front is exceedingly important).

Churchill and Cherwell still think that the job can be done from the air and the sea without the help of the land.

Various reports were made of faking by German airplane officers, who claimed that they had reached certain objectives when they really had turned around 10 miles away. Also recently a German airplane with a crew of four had landed in England with everything intact. Churchill said at a Dutch movie house recently there was shown a picture of Hitler on the steps leading into a plane. Someone in the audience called out in the dark "Give my regards to Hess." Everybody in the audience roared and the Germans were furious.

The President told Churchill how hard he found it to get Molotov to talk when he was here. But finally by a combination of a cocktail, a brandy, and some champagne, he finally loosened him up some. It developed that the Soviet plane had to be repaired and Molotov had to stay two days longer. Molotov said to the President, "Mr. President, I want to go up to New York for a couple of days. I wish you would take these secret service men off my trail." Molotov and the President finally compromised by Molotov taking with him just one secret service man. Churchill said the sequel of it was when he was in Russia talking with Stalin and Molotov. He said to Stalin, "Did you ever hear what Molotov did those two days when he was in New York?" Molotov started to hem and haw about having the plane fixed up. But before he got very far, Stalin interjected and said, "The only surprise to me is that he did not go to Chicago where he could have gotten in with the other gangsters." Churchill repeated several times that these were the exact words of Stalin.

The President started to talk about Isaiah Bowman's[1] plan for the Jews. He said that Bowman started more than three years ago on the problem of working out the best way to settle the Jewish question. Bowman's plan essentially is to spread the Jews thin all over the world. The President said he had tried this out in Marietta County, Georgia,

[1] Isaiah Bowman, president of Johns Hopkins University, geographer, territorial specialist in the American delegation to the Paris Conference of 1919, chairman of the territorial committee of the State Department (1942–43), then vice chairman of that department's postwar advisory council (1943–44).

and at Hyde Park on the basis of adding four or five Jewish families at each place. He claimed that the local population would have no objection if there were no more than that. The President said that in Palestine the Jews produced only about 80 million dollars' worth of stuff a year and that the worldwide Jewry sent in about 50 million dollars' worth a year.

Churchill cussed out the various Arabian leaders and pointed especially at their failure to come through with substantial help of any kind. It seemed that Churchill was rather for the development of Trans-Jordania for the Jews. The President, however, seems to have in mind a really solid Arab block around the southern and eastern shores of the Mediterranean Sea. Churchill remarked that there were more Jews than Arab votes in the Anglo-Saxon countries and we could not afford to ignore such practical considerations. I suggested that perhaps half of the Jews might agree with the President about the slow amalgamation of the Jews with the Gentiles but that the other half of them would be very vehemently in favor of Zionism. I mentioned also that the density of population in Trans-Jordania relative to the natural resources was exceedingly thin and that the construction of an irrigation dam would make it possible to support a lot of people there. At the present time there are only about 300,000 people in Trans-Jordania and the area is greater than that of Palestine with its one and a half million people.

The President asked Churchill if the Belgian refugees in England were behaving any better this time than they did in World War I. Churchill said yes. He said in War No. 1 unfortunately there were a large number of "tarts" from Ostend. He spoke of a very Victorian lady friend of his who had taken in a couple of these tarts as her patriotic duty. They proceeded to stay in bed until along about ten o'clock in the morning and did no work about the house. The lady suggested that they might make themselves useful, which they proceeded to do by bringing in some gentlemen friends, quite horrifying the Victorian lady. Churchill then broke into some rather ribald verse beginning with "Put on your bustle and get out and hustle."

Churchill likes short quotations to characterize a man he does not think much of. For example, referring to Josiah Wedgwood, he gave a Burns quotation to the effect that "he had a head of feathers and a heart of gold." Referring to Willkie, Churchill said he was sure he would not have to deal with a German at the head of the United States nation after we got rid of Hitler in Germany.

All the time Churchill was snuffling just very faintly in the same way he did the last time he was here. Apparently it was the burbling of the brandy in his sinuses. He was quite disdainful of Lord Cherwell's failure to drink. He mentioned the last time he was with Stalin he had to drink 34 different toasts. He said for the most part he just touched his lips to the glass and that Stalin himself drank practically nothing. The story about having to drink "bottoms up" all the time which Mike Cowles and Willkie had told about Stalin apparently is not true.

MAY 25, 1943

At Charley Marsh's Major Eliot[1] was present. He said his good friend Sir John Dill,[2] Chief of Staff for the British, is a very splendid fellow, who thinks that the thing to do is to put on a second front. Churchill, however, believes the other way. Apparently the ruling class in England is very anxious not to sacrifice too many British men. They lost so many men in World War I that they feel they cannot afford to lose more in World War II. They want to wait until the American armies have been sufficiently trained so that the losses will be at least fifty-fifty. Dill does not belong to this school of thought (so I called up Harry Hopkins and suggested he arrange a meeting at which would be present the President, Harry Hopkins, Admiral Leahy, and Dill. I suggested that Harry ask Dill in front of the President, "What would you do if you were in complete charge of the whole show?" Harry liked the idea and said he would see if he could not arrange it).

Charley Marsh told me that it had just come to him during the last few days that the British had their fingers crossed so far as I was concerned. Apparently my frank talking with Churchill at the Saturday and Monday luncheons has caused the British to reach the conclusion that I am not playing their game of arranging matters so that the Anglo-Saxons will rule the world. Frankly I am glad to know where they stand and that they know where I stand. I am sure that the 200 million Anglo-Saxons in the United States, England, Canada,

---

[1] George Fielding Eliot, educated in Australia, military analyst for the New York *Herald Tribune* and the Columbia Broadcasting System, major in the Military Intelligence Reserve of the United States Army (1922–30), in 1943 president of the Association of Radio News Analysts.

[2] Field Marshal Sir John G. Dill, Chief of the Imperial General Staff, had, in Churchill's words, "come to be regarded by the Americans as an indispensable link between the United States and British Chiefs of Staff on military policy," see Winston S. Churchill, *The Hinge of Fate* (Boston, 1950), p. 684.

Australia, New Zealand, and South Africa are not enough to run the world and that if they try it in the spirit which seems to be animating Churchill, there will be serious trouble ahead. I am quite sure, in spite of all his protestations to the contrary, that Churchill is capable of working with Russia to double-cross the United States, and with the United States to double-cross Russia. Perhaps the United States and Russia are equally willing to shop around within the triangle. It seems to me important, however, that there should be a really honest accord and a complete understanding. It is important not to forget the Chinese, the small nations, or the Latin Americans.

MAY 31, 1943

Justice Murphy was full of gossip about the quality of the men around the President. He especially had it in for Felix Frankfurter and Harry Hopkins. He says Felix gets great joy out of being the power behind the throne, out of writing speeches for the Secretary of War, and suggesting to the President that he should set up a War Labor Relations Board. He says he contacts the representatives from foreign countries and then talks in a large way about the situation being very grave in China, says Felix is completely sycophant so far as the English are concerned . . .

Murphy thinks that if the President runs for a fourth term, he can win but he will have to do it without New York State. I said I thought the President could win New York State. Murphy said, "Let's put it away in our memories and see which is right."

According to Murphy, Felix and Hopkins are behind the strong build-up for Jimmie Byrnes. He says that Jimmie was very happy on the Court but that he was undoubtedly promised something to get him to step down off the Court. Murphy spoke of Byrnes having been a Catholic, born in Washington, D.C., but that later he went to South Carolina with his brother-in-law and changed his religion on account of politics. I told Murphy this had been up for discussion in 1940 (Harry indicated they had turned Byrnes down on that account at that time but I doubt if it was adequate). Murphy said that the Catholics were very unforgiving about a matter of this kind.

Murphy indicated that Joe Kennedy was strong for Bill Douglas for Vice President. Joe brought Douglas into the Security Exchange Commission in the first place, Murphy said, and also said Kennedy had no use whatsoever for Felix . . .

JUNE 1, 1943
HENRY A. WALLACE TO FRANKLIN D. ROOSEVELT

Dear Mr. President[1]:

Mr. Jones and I have agreed that, if you approve, the U.S. Commercial Company be turned over to the Board of Economic Warfare for the purpose of handling, with certain exceptions, the development and procurement of all strategic and critical materials abroad as well as for the preclusive buying in which it is now engaged.

However, the actual mechanics of the transfer have not yet been agreed upon or cleared with the Bureau of the Budget. Obviously, the mechanics are very important. In view of the fact that the transfer of the Corporation from RFC to the Board of Economic Warfare should be submitted for your signature, I am suggesting that when the presentation is finally made to you that Jesse and I come in together. Jesse and I are both hopeful that this will result in greater peace in the family . . .[2]

---

[1] The controversy over the Board of Economic Warfare reached its peak in June 1943. Wallace's major letters on the subject, more revealing than his diary entries, are included here.

[2] Jones wrote Wallace on June 2, 1943:

Dear Henry:

I have before me a copy of your letter of June 1 to the President.

I would appreciate it very much if our respective staffs, with you and I approving, could reduce our understanding of Saturday, May 29, to writing and not have someone else undertake it.

As you know, Executive Order 9128 was issued at your instance, without either the State Department or ourselves having seen it, and yet we were expected to work under the order.

At the request of the State Department, the order was later modified in so far as State was concerned.

We have asked for no modification, but have tried to work under it without bothering the President.

Your Order No. 5, issued while the President was in Casablanca, went beyond any reasonable interpretation of Executive Order 9128 and has proved unworkable. This order also was issued without our having an opportunity to discuss it, or even to see it until it was published in the Federal Register, notwithstanding we were expected to operate under it.

We have authorized the expenditure of more than $20 billion in the war effort, at the request of, or by direction of, war policy-making agencies, including OPM, WPB, War and Navy Departments, Maritime Commission, Petroleum Coordinator, Office of Defense Transportation, the Rubber Director, and the Director of Economic Stabilization. Our relationship with all of them except BEW has been both satisfactory and cordial.

We are prepared to proceed in all of the matters, but our respective staffs should get together and reduce the agreements we reached Saturday, May 29, to writing, and not have someone else attempt to do so.

When this is done and we get the approval of the President I will ask Congress to instruct us to make funds available to the U.S. Commercial Company under BEW management . . .

JUNE 3, 1943
HENRY A. WALLACE TO JESSE H. JONES

Dear Jesse:

I am as anxious as you are to work out the problems which were raised in our conference of last Saturday morning.

If a transfer of USCC to BEW is to be made quickly, obviously it must be done under the congressionally prescribed procedure set forth in the First War Powers Act. So far as I know, the Bureau of the Budget is still the appropriate agency for clearing all transfers of this type, and I do not understand your objection to clearance with the bureau of whatever order you and I might jointly agree upon.

Order No. 5 has worked astonishingly well in spite of the obstacles thrown in its way by some members of your staff. It would work excellently if you were to put an end to such obstructionist tactics.

My willingness to go along on a partial transfer to USCC of the foreign procurement and development program assumed that on the work which was not transferred you would fully recognize the responsibility and authority of BEW under Executive Order No. 9128 and that you would willingly cooperate with us.

In view of the surprisingly ill feeling displayed in your last letter, this assumption seems to have been improperly founded. That being so, if any transfer of USCC is to be made, it should, in my judgment, include the entire foreign procurement and development program, as was originally proposed in your letter of February 27, 1943.

Finally, I cannot believe that you want to deal with Congress in the manner suggested by the last paragraph of your letter. We would certainly want to present to Congress our own justification for such funds, as a corporation under our own management might require to supplement those made available at the time of a possible transfer. Complete responsibility for all foreign procurement and development work, with the exception of rubber, now rests with BEW, and so far as we are concerned, it is going to stay there whether we continue operations under Order No. 5 or whether we work out some way of operating with funds which might be made available to us by the Congress . . .[1]

---

[1] Jones replied on June 3:

  Dear Henry:

  Your letter of the 3rd just received.

  The thought I tried to get over in writing you yesterday was that, if those of us in government are to work cordially together, which attitude I accord to you no less than to myself, time and trouble would be saved if the plans, programs, agreements, executive orders, directives, etc., were

JUNE 4, 1943

HENRY A. WALLACE TO JESSE H. JONES

Dear Jesse:

I have your letter of June 3. We certainly would not fully concur in the letter which you sent the President yesterday for the reasons set forth in my letter to you of yesterday afternoon.

Referring to the fourth paragraph of your letter of June 3, I shall

gone over together, and each of us who must cooperate had a clear understanding of interpretations, following the pattern of our joint meeting last Saturday and our understanding that when differences arose we would all get together.

When you asked me about having Wayne Coy arrange for the transfer, I thought I understood that we were to get our agreements written down before submitting it to the Budget. In fact, it had not occurred to me that an Executive Order would be required.

I had outlined to our counsel how I thought the transfer should be made, and stated that I would discuss that part of the arrangement with you, for them to get in touch with the members of your staff and get a written statement as to what each of us was to do, all in line with our Saturday conference.

Prior to receipt of your letter of today, I had dictated a letter to the President, copy of which I enclose, that I thought we might present to him tomorrow.

I had not realized that I displayed any ill feeling in my letter to you, although you have not always been particularly considerate in your letters as far as I am concerned. There is no justification for the first sentence in the last paragraph of your letter, and I could have had no other thought than that the Committee would want to hear from you and BEW executives in considering the authorization. . . .

Jones also wrote Roosevelt that day:

With a view to avoiding conflicts between BEW and RFC in connection with certain of our foreign purchases, and having a clear-cut understanding as to what each agency is to do, I suggested to Henry Wallace, Chairman of the Board of Economic Warfare, that, with your approval, we would transfer the U.S. Commercial Company to BEW management, and that I would ask Congress, in considering our bill now before the committee, to instruct us to furnish the U.S. Commercial Company with funds for its requirements, upon your approval.

Our respective staffs, with the concurrence of Henry and myself, have reached an agreement as to what things the RFC agencies are to do and what BEW is to do. If you approve, we will make the arrangement effective.

U.S. Commercial Company now has ten directors, with representatives from State Department, BEW, Office of the Coordinator of Inter-American Affairs, and RFC. We will rearrange the board, giving BEW seven of the ten directors, with one each from State Department, Office of Coordinator of Inter-American Affairs, and RFC.

The present officers of U.S. Commercial Company will resign and allow the new Board to elect their successors.

This arrangement to continue until changed by your direction. . . .

be glad to examine any written proposal you send us which outlines the details you have given your general counsel as to how the transfer might be made. If you make such a proposal to us, it should include details as to interim financing for USCC under BEW management prior to the time we go before congressional committees to ask that additional funds be made available to carry out our work. The proposal should include in detail compilation of the records, funds, credits, personnel, equipment, office space, et cetera, which would be transferred from the other subsidiaries of RFC to USCC as part of the transfer of functions.

Our interest here is to be sure that work now being done by the various RFC subsidiaries which might henceforth be done by USCC can be continued without interruption to the war effort.

Upon receipt of such a written proposal from you, I shall be happy to resume conferences of the sort we had last Saturday morning . . .

JUNE 28, 1943

I told the President that I brought a message from Bob La Follette[1] namely, that he, Bob, hoped the President would pay more attention to the home front. The President said he was paying more attention to the home front than to the foreign front—that he was giving it plenty of attention . . .

He then started talking about Beaverbrook. Beaverbrook reported on various U.S. publishers to the President. The Beaver said Col. Patterson was not merely figuratively but literally crazy—that his hatred of Roosevelt was so intense it had driven him crazy. Roy Howard, according to the Beaver, could be saved. I told the President that Howard and Clapper had called on me about 6 months ago and that Howard had asked me to visit him the next time I was in N.Y. The President advised me to do it. He then went on to say that he had asked the Beaver who would be the most formidable Republican candidate in '44. The Beaver said, "Willkie." The President replied, "I think Dewey.[2]" The Beaver said "No. Dewey is too far afield on his international views" . . .

I also gave the President a copy of my June 27 *New York Times*

[1] Robert M. La Follette, Jr., progressive Republican Senator from Wisconsin since 1925, when he was elected to replace his celebrated father whose principles he embraced.

[2] Thomas E. Dewey, Republican governor of New York, was to be his party's presidential candidate in 1944 and 1948.

Magazine air article[1] and told him this was written in advance of the time he and Hull and I had talked together. When he finished reading the air memo, he referred to the world map on the other side of the room and said it was there to keep his memory fresh with regard to the airlines of the future. He said some of the air routes would lose money, for example, from the U.S. to Australia and New Zealand. He thought such a route should be government owned. He thought Canada and England might also want to run a route across the South Pacific to Australia. He visioned another route from U.S. to the Philippines and South China. This might make money but the U.S. government should have 51 percent of the stock. Another route might be from Seattle by the great circle route to North China and Japan. He visioned the U.S. and Brazil developing airports jointly at Dakar and Liberia. He visioned routes to South Africa either by way of Belém or by way of Trinidad and Dakar. He would have the British give us a 99-year lease on Asuncion Island, where we have developed quite an airfield. He would let American Export have the route from U.S. to the Mediterranean countries and Pan Air from U.S. to North Europe. I urged the President to talk to General McNarney about Col. Shulgens' air plans. He said he would. I urged air as being the central point in the peace of the future and asked him to give it his closest attention . . .

The President asked what I thought about him making a speech over the air in the near future. I said O.K., if you have your plans worked out and are ready to take the public into your confidence. He said plans had been worked out but he did not think it was time to make a speech. Byrnes concurred. The President referred to how the government had bought all the Cheddar cheese and what a success the program had been. The people had the cheese and the price was reasonable. The government was taking a loss. I judge he likes the idea of the government stepping in and doing the whole job.

[1] In "Freedom of the Air—a Momentous Issue," *New York Times Magazine*, June 27, 1943, Wallace attacked those who argued that "America must rule the air" and attacked, too, their proposals for exclusive American control of strategically located bases around the world, as well as, in extreme cases, for an exclusive American right to manufacture civil and military aircraft and to control all large petroleum fields. He advocated instead working through the United Nations for the use of the airplane to "increase the chance of peace and to guard against the chance of war" and to "accelerate economic development . . . throughout the world." To those ends, he recommended creating an international air authority to regulate air commerce among nations, including the traffic of private commercial carriers; the internationalization of large airports; and the reliance for peace-keeping on an international air force. Those objectives, as he noted, did not preclude limiting to specified routes and landing stations the flights of the aircraft of one nation over the territory of another.

The President spoke about having told Madame Chiang that Formosa and certain other islands off the east coast of China should be returned by Japan to China but that the U.S. should have, subject to Chinese approval, an air base there.

I asked the President what he thought about Russia in the international air picture. He said the Russians were still very suspicious of the rest of the countries of the world, that they did not want us to know what was going on inside Russia, and he doubted if there would be much of a change for 10 years.

I referred to the plans for the English-American air conference at Ottawa in September and said I hoped it would not make the Russians too suspicious. I indicated that Juan Trippe and his backers would probably be standing back of both American and British representatives at Ottawa but especially behind the American.

JUNE 30, 1943

I arrived at Jimmie Byrnes' office about 4 p.m., a few minutes before Jesse Jones came in, and handed over to Jimmie the letter which I had received from him earlier in the day which reads as follows:

June 30, 1943

Dear Henry:

Under Executive Order No. 9347, subject to the direction and control of the President, it is my duty, among other things, to resolve and determine controversies between agencies and departments.

Because of statements appearing in the Press today with reference to relations between the Board of Economic Warfare and the Reconstruction Finance Corporation, I am requesting you and Mr. Jesse H. Jones, Secretary of Commerce, to meet me in my office in the East Wing of the White House at 4 p.m. today.[1]

Sincerely yours,
James F. Byrnes

I said to him that I did not see why he could not have phoned me to come over, that the letter referring to Executive Order 9347 did

[1] For Wallace's detailed statement of June 29, 1943, about the issue, see Appendices. Jones called that statement false. Roosevelt at his press conference then deplored the public controversy between the Vice President and the Secretary of Commerce. After the two principals had met with Byrnes on June 30, Wallace announced that he had not meant to attack Jones personally or to question Jones' patriotism. Wallace went on to call for the complete seperation of the BEW and the RFC, a proposal to which, he said, Jones had no objection.

not make sense to me because of the memorandum which he had put out to the various agencies indicating that it was his function to deal with disputes on the domestic front rather than the foreign. We got hold of his memo and read it over. It read, "Only matters of basic importance affecting the *domestic economy* and the war effort . . ." Jimmie claimed that no matter what the memo said, the important thing was what was in Executive Order 9347. I had a memo from the Legal Department of BEW interpreting 9347 as not applying to the foreign front. However, I did not mention this to Jimmie because frankly I felt 9347 could be interpreted to apply to the foreign front so I merely said to Jimmie, "Is it true that you have not been dealing with disputes affecting the Coordinator's Office, State Department, et al." He said none had come up. A few minutes later he spoke about settling a dispute concerning oil in which the State Department was involved.

I said my purpose in bringing Executive Order 9347 to his attention was to indicate to him that I had assumed, from reading of the order and his explanation of it which he had sent to the various agencies, that he had no jurisdiction over disputes involving the State Department, BEW, etc. Jimmie said in case there was a doubt on this, the order ought to be changed. I told Jimmie that I thought he had not wanted to get into the difficulty between Jesse Jones and myself. Furthermore I understood he had told Milo Perkins when I was in South America, at the time when Milo had attended Lehman's conference at the White House, that he, Byrnes, had told the President that the situation between Wallace and Jones was so hot that he, Byrnes, did not want to touch it. But I said in view of the fact that Jimmie apparently felt that he had authority in the matter, I would not insist that he take the letter back which he had written me. I wanted him to know that I would have been glad to come over in response to a phone call. I also wanted him to know that if he felt he had jurisdiction in this field, he should have gotten into the problem long before this. Although this made Jimmie somewhat mad, it was very useful.

I made it clear to Jimmie that I thought the important thing was getting a constructive answer for the future—and that I thought the only constructive answer was to make BEW separate from RFC in the import field so that Congress would make a direct appropriation to the Board instead of to RFC.

About that time Jesse Jones came in, glowering and glum, saying that Henry Wallace had called him a traitor. I said to Jesse, "I see by the New York *News*, which has a circulation of 2 million, that they think you are going to hit me the next time you see me." I said, "Is that true, Jesse? Are you going to hit me?" Jesse came back to the refrain of his song, "Henry Wallace called me a traitor."

Then he got out a paper on which he had picked out all the different things I had called him and read them over—bureaucrat, backdoor complainer, etc., etc. Jimmie then said, "You don't think Jesse is a traitor, do you?" I said, "No, I haven't called him a traitor and I don't think he is." Jimmie said, "Will you make a statement to that effect?" I said, "I am sure there is no statement which I can make that would be satisfactory to Jesse."

We then went at some length into what McKellar said on June 4. Byrnes said everybody knew that McKellar was irresponsible and that I should not have been stirred up by his statement. I said I was sure that what McKellar said was based on something that Jesse Jones had said to McKellar. Jones pulled out of his pocket a copy of his statement before the McKellar committee. This statement was quite harmless. I still stuck by my guns, however, that McKellar could not have said what he did unless it was based on informattion which he had received from Jesse Jones. I then made the point that the all-important thing was getting constructive work done in the future. Byrnes eagerly took up this thought. I said, "While we are getting a constructive solution, obviously we will have to go along as we have been going, but BEW ought to apply to Congress for independent funds so as to be free from Jesse as soon as possible." I said if BEW were to go before Congress to ask for independent funds for doing its work, we ought to have some assurance that Jesse and his organization would not do what they had been doing the past three weeks on the Hill. Jesse claimed that they had not been doing anything. I did not mention the Flynn memo[1] which had been circulated to certain members of the Senate but I did say that certain members of the Metals Reserve Company had spoken to members of Congress about "my policy on giving preference to foreigners at the expense of Americans." I said that other RFC employees had criticized BEW for being extravagant and engaging in postwar planning. Jesse denied all this.

Jesse left then and Jimmie urged me to issue a statement. I said,

[1] A memorandum by John T. Flynn, an ardent anti-Rooseveltian, incorporated Senator McKellar's contention that the BEW was an extralegal agency, created by the Executive without congressional approval, that spent moneys in an unauthorized manner for questionable purposes and ordinarily without review by the cabinet members on the board. The memo also attacked Milo Perkins as a mystic and a radical, epithets Flynn never hesitated to use also about Wallace.

"Jimmie, you write out the kind of a statement you think I ought to issue." Jimmie wrote out this statement in longhand. I took it, stopped at Milo's office. Milo pointed out there were certain matters of phraseology that would get us into trouble with Congress. I read back the statement as changed to Jimmie. He suggested one change, where I had said, "Mr. Jones agreed to this policy decision." He suggested the phraseology, "Mr. Jones did not object to this policy decision" . . .

Jesse Jones said my attack on him was not Christian. He said he might not go to church as often as I did but that he knew what was Christian and my act was not a Christian act.

Jesse said the purpose of the attack was to destroy him, that Milo Perkins and Morris Rosenthal had had that purpose all the time. He said they had obviously prepared the attack for me. He said Perkins was disingenuous because he, Perkins, on June 7 had written him about the McKellar June 4 attack and he in his reply had cleared the matter up (I remembered Milo as telling me that Jesse had been evasive in his reply).

Jesse's point was that Milo's preparing the attack and having his (Jesse's) letter in refutation of McKellar could not have been honest.

Jesse claimed that he always fought for the President's program on the Hill. Jimmie Byrnes chimed in to say that Jesse had been helpful to the President by lobbying on the Hill for the subsidy and the roll-back. Jesse claimed he always did everything he could to help the President's program on the Hill and that he never fought the President's program. Byrnes wanted me in my statement to indicate that McKellar had quoted Jesse incorrectly. When we dug into this a little bit, it appeared that Jesse got cold feet. He definitely had qualms about what he had done on the Hill although Jimmie Byrnes in his telephone conversation interpreted the matter otherwise.

I endeavored to shape the conference to an agreement that BEW should go direct to Congress for its money to finance importations and that there should be an agreement that Jesse and his organization would not fight such a program on the Hill. Jesse seemed to be in accord. That is why Jimmie Byrnes, in writing down a statement which he proposed I make, wrote it as he did. That is why I put in the sentence saying that Mr. Jones agreed and why Jimmie Byrnes felt it was perfectly all right to put in the sentence but changing it to make it read "Mr. Jones did not object . . ." But while Mr. Jones did not object between 5 and 6 on June 30, he did object most strenuously by 10:30 that night in his release to the newspapermen . . .

JULY 1, 1943

I called up the President and told him I thought he had let me off very lightly in his press conference on June 29, and I wanted him to know I appreciated it. He replied in quite an apologetic way that at the time his press conference was held, my letter to him enclosing the Jesse Jones statement had not come into his hands. In view of the cordial tone of his voice, I then went on to say, "You will remember, Mr. President, I mentioned in my letter of June 10 to you the kind of situation that was brewing." He made some polite statement to this which did not let me know whether or not he had read the letter of June 10. I then went on to tell him about the poll of the Republicans in the House, that 52 of them wanted Dewey as the candidate, 32 MacArthur, 30 Bricker, 13 Willkie, 9 Taft, etc. This seemed to amuse the President and he said, "We shall have Willkie with us yet." I made some statement indicative of distrust of Willkie. On thinking the conversation over, I am not sure whether the President meant that Willkie would become a Democrat in 1944 or whether the President was indicating his judgment that Willkie would be the Republican candidate in 1944 . . .

JULY 6, 1943

Milo's statement in reply to Jesse Jones[1] . . . was issued without consultation with me. I told him I thought it was a fine thing he had made the statement and that I was glad he could not get in touch with me prior to releasing it. Milo told me that Elmer Davis had called him on the carpet about it, and about the firm stand he, Milo, had taken with regard to issuing it. Elmer also criticized me for issuing the statement following the Byrnes conference. Milo said very little in re-

[1] On July 5, 1943, Jones had issued a 30-page statement denying the charges in Wallace's statement of June 29. Milo Perkins, on his own initiative, attacked Jones. The exchange irritated Roosevelt, who found public disagreements among his subordinates personally distasteful and politically embarrassing. Speaking for the President, James F. Byrnes on July 6, 1943, wrote Wallace: "Public recrimination by the head of one war agency against another is bound to hurt the war effort and lessen the confidence of the people in their government. Now that you and Mr. Jones have published your statements I must urge that no further statements or counter statements be made by either of you except in response to a congressional inquiry." Such an inquiry was threatening, for Representative Richard B. Wigglesworth, Massachusetts Republican, had introduced a resolution directing the House Rules Committee to investigate the Wallace-Jones feud. The administration, as Wallace's diary reveals, interceded to defeat the resolution.

sponse to that because he did not want to put Jimmie Byrnes on the spot. Of course, he knew as well as I did that the statement following the Byrnes conference was put out at Byrnes's insistence.

When I left Byrnes' office about 6:20 p.m. on June 30, I did not tell him for sure that I would issue a statement. It was not until I called him about seven o'clock that he knew definitely I was going to go ahead. Nevertheless, according to J. H. Short, correspondent for the Baltimore *Sun*, one of Byrnes' aides announced that I would issue a statement. Jimmie must have read in my attitude that I would issue the statement although I had not said so in words.

On July 6 I received the . . . letter from Jimmie Byrnes. I assume Jesse Jones received a similar one.

Milo consulted with me from twelve to one o'clock, telling me about the Wigglesworth resolution in the House and the fact that Sabath,[1] chairman of the Rules Committee, had announced there would be a vote in the House at 3 p.m. that day with regard to an investigation of Jesse Jones and myself. Milo said that any congressional committee which might do the investigating would be playing politics and that the only way to get a fair investigation was to have somebody from the general public conduct the investigation. He suggested someone like former Chief Justice Hughes heading up the investigation. He also suggested Baruch, Conant, and Compton, former members of the Rubber Committee. I called the President on the telephone at Hyde Park and told him about the House vote coming up at 3 p.m. today and suggested a public committee as the way out. The President suggested I talk the problem over with Byrnes, asking Jimmie to get in touch with Sam Rayburn. He favored the public committee approach, provided we could not beat the Wigglesworth amendment in any other way.

I then called Jimmie and passed on to him the word from the President. Jimmie said, "It ought to be possible to head off the Wigglesworth resolution." I made it clear to Jimmie that I did not fear an investigation, that strictly from the standpoint of BEW, we would welcome an investigation. Jimmie said an investigation by the Rules Committee would be horrible, that Cox of Georgia, Dies of Texas, Howard Smith of Virginia, and Ham Fish of New York would do nothing but play politics.[2] Jimmie said, "Let me work on this problem

---

[1] Adolph J. Sabath, since 1907 Democratic congressman from Chicago.
[2] Of the four congressmen mentioned, Fish was a Republican and the other three —Edward E. Cox, Martin Dies, and Howard W. Smith—were notoriously conservative Democrats.

with Sam Rayburn." A little later Jimmie called back to say he thought he had the situation well in hand, that a meeting of the Rules Committee had been called for 2 p.m. and he thought the Wigglesworth resolution could be defeated. I made the point again to Jimmie, however, that I thought it would be a good plan to have a public committee go into the situation, that BEW would welcome an investigation by any fair committee . . .

JULY 7, 1943

Senator Thomas[1] of Utah came up to see me while I was presiding. He mentioned my talking to him concerning a race riot problem and asked if I had noticed that there had been introduced on July 6, Senate 71, by Senator Brooks of Illinois. He said this resolution, calling for an investigation of the race riots, had been referred to the Senate Judiciary Committee and that Van Nuys had referred it to a subcommittee composed of McCarran, O'Mahoney, and Ferguson. Thomas said he thought the subcommittee was about as bad as it could be from the standpoint of the administration and from the standpoint of the election in 1944. He said he thought the Negro vote would determine the outcome in Ohio, Pennsylvania, and New York and that something ought to be done to prevent the matter from getting into the hands of the President's enemies.

A little later in the day, Charles Marsh called up to say that Gerald K. Smith[2] had had lunch with Dies on Monday, the 5th, and that this was responsible for the introduction of the Brooks resolution. I then called up Miss Tully and dictated a note to her to pass on to the President. In the note, I told the President substantially what I had learned . . . But I did not definitely hook up the Brooks resolution with the Dies[3] and Gerald Smith meeting on Monday.

[1] Elbert D. Thomas, Utah Democrat, was one of the senators most friendly to Wallace. Other senators to whom he referred in the conversation here reported were C. Wayland Brooks, Illinois Republican; Frederick Van Nuys, Indiana Democrat; Patrick A. McCarran, Nevada Democrat; Joseph C. O'Mahoney, Connecticut Democrat; and Homer Ferguson, Michigan Republican.
[2] Gerald L. K. Smith, preacher of a native American fascism that focussed its poisonous rhetoric against radicals, blacks, Jews, foreigners, and New Dealers.
[3] Martin Dies.

JULY 9, 1943

. . . Nelson Rockefeller was seriously alarmed as a result of a conversation he had had with Jimmie Byrnes the day before. Byrnes had told him about a proposal to blend together the foreign activities of RFC, the CIA, Export-Import Bank, BEW, and various other agencies. Nelson believes very strongly that the work with Latin America would be seriously handicapped if it were blended in with an agency of that sort. I said I agreed with him. He wanted to know what to do. I suggested he get in touch with Harry Hopkins and have Anna Rosenberg get in touch with Samuel Rosenman. I said it was my understanding that this consolidation idea had been under consideration for many months, that Judge Rosenman had been working on it for some time.

At cabinet meeting the President said absolutely nothing about the unpleasantness between Jesse and myself . . .

JULY 14, 1943

Along about 6 p.m. I called General Watson on the telephone and said that I was going to be making a speech in Detroit on July 25, in which I would be mentioning among other things labor and race riots, and I thought I ought to get the President's approval of it. I told Pa Watson that I would be out over the weekend and that apparently it would be necessary to see the President either before Friday noon or after Tuesday noon. Pa replied, "Well, I better get you right in tomorrow morning." The following morning word came from the White House to clear the speech with Steve Early. I noticed later on that Harold Smith's name was on the President's appointments on Thursday. I realized then that Milo's off-the-record speech[1] . . . must

---

[1] That speech was to the staff of the BEW, to whom Perkins had said that Wallace's attack on Jones was what "any red-blooded American" would say when he turned over a rock and saw "slimy things crawling" under it. The BEW, Perkins added, would live on. He was wrong. On July 15, 1943, Roosevelt abolished the BEW and placed its responsibilities, along with some of Jones' lending agencies, within a new agency, the Office of Economic Warfare. That office in turn in September was placed with the Lend-Lease Administration within another new and larger agency, the Foreign Economic Administration. The President appointed Leo Crowley the head of the OEW and later the FEA. The outcome was clearly a defeat for Perkins and Wallace and was so interpreted at the time, to the dismay of many liberal Democrats and the gratification of their opponents in both parties. Wallace was angry and hurt. Over the telephone to Harold Ickes on July 16, he said that it looked as if the country was headed for a bipartisan American fascism. To one group of his advisers, he expressed his feelings about Roosevelt characteristically by quoting

have provoked the President to go ahead with the action which he had long contemplated. Apparently there were in with Harold in drawing up the executive order Jimmie Byrnes, Harry Hopkins, Sam Rosenman, and Wayne Coy. Wayne Coy,[1] and Harold Smith are reported by Wayne Coy to have counseled delay. The others were exceedingly eager to push the executive order through at the earliest possible moment.

JULY 20, 1943

The fact that the President himself read my entire speech[2] more carefully than he has read any of my speeches and made several minor changes in his own handwriting suggests his usual technique of being very nice to a person he has just gotten through hitting. However, it must also be said that he is really fond of me except when stimulated by the palace guard to move in other directions . . .

Milo, Tharon,[3] and I talked very little about the recent action of the President. We went over to the garden and talked to my sister Mary. It seemed to me, however, that Milo was very much more bitter toward the President than he had been the first evening. I don't think he has been talking bitter to anyone else, however. The reason for Milo's bitterness is that since the death of his son he has tended more and more to identify his extraordinary efforts with his son. His son's last words to him had been to "stay in and slug," and his son had meant not only from the standpoint of getting materials but also from the standpoint of making Jesse Jones behave, and so Milo subconsciously feels that the President has really dealt a blow to the memory of his son. But Milo has never said anything of this sort and I don't think he ever would.[4]

---

the Bible: "Though He slay me, yet will I trust Him." Wallace continued to do so, but he also felt, as did his supporters in the press, that Roosevelt had betrayed him.

[1] Wayne Coy, competent, versatile, and ordinarily anonymous assistant director of the Bureau of the Budget.

[2] Wallace gave the speech on July 25, 1943, to a labor meeting in Detroit. He began with a generous tribute to Roosevelt, a tribute that signaled the return of official peace in the battle of Washington. The President, he said, was the symbol the world over of the dearest aspirations of the common man for the peace to come. Wallace then attacked Roosevelt's enemies, proponents of an "American fascism," and went on to his familiar themes about a century of the common man and "a capitalism of abundance."

[3] Mrs. Milo Perkins.

[4] That day Wallace also wrote Roosevelt:

A mutual friend has stated that you never received my letter of June 10 . . .

JULY 21, 1943

. . . Leo Crowley came in and said he thought the President had given me an utterly raw deal. Previously he had told the same thing to Milo. Crowley told me that the President in the first instance had told him (Crowley) that he had to get rid of Milo and later on he told his press conference it was up to Crowley whether or not he wanted to get rid of Milo. In other words, he made Crowley the goat for firing Milo and Crowley rather resented it. Of course, Milo resigned before Crowley could fire him which made it much easier for him. I told Crowley that he was going to have real trouble with his export work because State did not understand the mood of the exporters and because the exporters did not like the decentralization plan which had been fathered by State. I gave him a clipping from the New York *Times* to show him how the exporters felt. Crowley indicated that if he had trouble with State on the export front, he would go to the President and tell him to give the work to State. I told Crowley that would be very unfortunate from a political point of view because I felt State

---

Yesterday I sent to Don Nelson my resignation from WPB because Samuel Rosenman in originally notifying me of my membership in the predecessor agency SPAB said my membership was on the theory that I represented the foreign claimants for United States goods (exclusive, of course, of Lend-Lease and the Military). It is obvious that someone else should now take my place on WPB in order that the private claimants in foreign lands be properly represented.

It may interest you to know that on the evening of your recent action, Milo in talking things over with his wife said, "Well, he is still the greatest President this country has ever had." His wife concurred.

I appreciate deeply your having taken the time to read my Detroit speech. The corrections you suggested have been incorporated with one exception. The speech, of course, was written prior to your recent action. Rereading with that in mind, I reached the conclusion that I should move my tribute to you from the last of the speech to the very first and make it much more vigorous. The first question of people about the Detroit speech will be, "What does Mr. Wallace think now about the President?" The Republicans are waiting hopefully. I am going to settle that in the first two minutes.

I shall be in Iowa most of the time in late July and the first half of August . . .

Roosevelt replied on July 28:

It was good of you to write me as you did . . .

I was forced to conclude that under all the circumstances there was no other course for me to pursue. It is needless for me to tell you that the incident has not lessened my personal affection for you.

Your speech was *splendid* and I sincerely appreciate your very generous references to me. It seems to have been well received except in some few quarters and nothing you could have said would have pleased them . . .

P.S. You drew blood from the Cave Dwellers!

would create many enemies. I said . . . the State Department was not a good operating agency and in the very nature of things could not be . . .

Morris Rosenthal is extremely bitter at the President, much more so than Milo. He feels that the President has betrayed the cause of liberalism . . .

II

Witness
Without Portfolio

August 1943-January 1945

II

Witness Without Portfolio

August 1943–January 1945

R OOSEVELT'S ABOLITION of the Board of Economic Warfare probably signified, as many commentators suspected at the time, that the President had decided against insisting, as he had in 1940, upon the nomination of Wallace as his running mate in 1944. The Republican gains in 1942 and the conservatism of the Congress in 1943 also suggested the political advantages Roosevelt might garner from abandoning the most insistent liberal in his administration. Yet Wallace, though he wanted renomination, made no effort to secure it. As he often said, he was no politician. Indeed he abhorred the backroom politics of bargain and intrigue. Further, Wallace believed that as Vice President he had an obligation to rise above politics, and also to serve the President directly and the nation as a symbol of purpose. Most important, in spite of the hurt he felt, Wallace considered Roosevelt the most promising sponsor of desirable domestic and foreign policies and the strongest available Democrat, just as he considered the Democratic Party the best available vehicle for progress. On those accounts he was resolved to take no action that would disrupt the party or weaken the President.

Wallace was equally resolved to continue to work further to develop and promote the postwar objectives he had already defined. He elaborated upon those objectives in speeches he gave throughout the country, and he publicized them in *Democracy Reborn*, a collection of his addresses that was published in 1944. Otherwise he left his political future to the intermittent and unsystematic ministrations of his assistant, Harold Young, and his senatorial friend, Joe Guffey. He concentrated on longer-range and less personal goals.

Now deprived of a portfolio in the war cabinet, Wallace performed instead as a witness to his own selfless purpose. Perhaps he miscalculated, for his goals had become so much identified with his career that political failure foreboded, too, a failure of mission. Still, from August 1943 until the end of 1944, even after he lost renomination, he pursued the only course compatible with his character and tempera-

ment. It apparently never occurred to him, or at least it did not worry
him, that that course enhanced the opportunities of those who were
conspiring to succeed him. His services to the President and to his own
hopes for the postwar period took him halfway around the world to
Siberia and China, across much of the United States as a campaigner
for his party, and ultimately back to Washington as a replacement for
Jesse Jones—an outcome not without irony or justice.

AUGUST 11, 1943

. . . Hugh Cox,[1] whom I have long looked on as one of the smartest, finest people in Justice, told me that the facts in the Joseph Borkin book were true. There might be difference of opinion with regard to the conclusions to be drawn from them. I told Cox I was going to be seeing Borkin and that I was disposed to take up the cudgels with regard to international cartels . . .

I had a very interesting talk with Joseph Borkin. He told me he had written a number of Thurman Arnold's speeches. He said the secret of Arnold's success was the way in which he cultivated newspapermen. He said he thought Arnold had made a mistake by the way in which he prosecuted farmers and workers, that first things should come first, and the international cartel abuses were so infinitely greater than anything in agriculture or labor that there was no question where the action should have been taken. He said, however, that when Arnold stepped into labor, it resulted in Ed O'Neal going to bat for Arnold's appropriation. Borkin said the administration had never given the antitrust division any real support . . .

[1] Hugh Cox, who fitted Wallace's description, had been special assistant to the Attorney General since 1935 and counsel for the Justice Department before the temporary National Economic Commission in 1938–39. He served as assistant Solicitor General (1943–45). An expert on problems of domestic oligopoly and international cartels, Cox rendered a learned assessment of the criticisms of their practices set forth in a book by his Justice Department colleague, Joseph Borkin, in collaboration with Charles A. Welsh, *Germany's Master Plan: The Story of Industrial Offensive* (New York, 1943). Moved partly by Borkin's analysis, partly by the supporting revelations of the Truman and Kilgore committees of the Senate, Wallace had already begun to attack cartels, in one instance in a radio interview in Des Moines on August 5, 1943. "The corporations which need to be watched most closely," he said then, "are those which move in international trade, and those which enter into international cartels respecting markets, prices, and the use of inventions."

AUGUST 17, 1943

I had a long and rather unsatisfactory talk with Herridge. I agree with him in the main thesis that I must hammer continually on full employment. On general strategy we are in complete agreement. On tactics we are in complete disagreement. I told him to prepare 10 pages of what he thinks I ought to say in a speech. He is to spend all Sunday afternoon and evening with me August 29. I don't believe he can write a good speech. His sentiments are fine but when you get beyond a certain point, it is just mere repetition. On broad strategy, Herridge is O.K. but on tactics he is poor. His sincerity is admirable and his broad analysis is sound.

Herridge tells me he saw Eliot Janeway[1] of the Time-Fortune crowd a few days ago in New York. He asked Janeway who would win in 1944. Janeway said, "The Tories will win." Herridge replied, "What do you mean by that?" Janeway came back with the statement, "Oh, Roosevelt and the gang around him will get back in power again." Herridge thinks I ought to stop looking on myself as Vice President of the United States, that I should realize that I am leader of a very important group of people not only in the United States but also in the entire world. He thinks I should speak not as Vice President but as leader of this important group of people. He doesn't like the draft of the speech which I have prepared for September 11 because he thinks it is not on a sufficiently broad basis. I told him I was going to go ahead on that basis anyway but for him to go ahead and prepare the kind of speech he thinks I ought to make.

He believes that I should no longer feel tied to the President's coattails. He thinks the President was a gallant figure in the early days of the New Deal but that he has never known what the economic thing was all about and at the present time he (the President) really represents the forces of reaction. Herridge wants me more and more to break loose from the President altogether . . .

AUGUST 19, 1943

. . . Elmer Davis told me that the State Department had recently prohibited OWI from putting out a statement to the effect that Italy

---

[1] Eliot Janeway, journalist and author, was an admirer of Roosevelt's conduct of the war, especially on the home front. Janeway was an advocate, too, of the views of the armed services in their continuing and successful efforts to control domestic production policies in spite of the attempts of the War Production Board to protect the interests of small business; see Eliot Janeway, *The Struggle for Survival* (New Haven, 1951).

under Badoglio[1] was an ally of Germany. Eisenhower told me that Hull had talked to him for an hour or two to the effect that OWI must not put out anything that had ideology in it. Bob Sherwood asked me if OWI had not made a mistake by distributing three million copies of my Century of the Common Man speech in Italy. I said, "Well, I am afraid there is lots of ideology in it" . . .

Elmer said he had had a heart-to-heart talk with the President last week and the President assured him that he himself was sound at heart with regard to certain matters in which the State Department is involved. This reassurance from the President was a great help to Elmer's morale. I told Elmer I thought the President was sound at heart and that he would demonstrate at the right time in terms of action just where he stood.

At the Bowes-Lyons', Robert Sherwood and Archie MacLeish said to my sister Mary, "We just love your brother, Henry." Mary said, "Why don't you tell him?" Archie replied, "You just can't tell a man like Henry that" . . .

If the Democrats were going to lose, Hull thought it important not to raise the hopes of foreign nations.[2] In other words, Hull is acting as much as possible like a Republican so there will be as little shock as possible in the transition. Hull proclaimed he was against "isolationism, internationalism, and Wallacism."

AUGUST 21, 1943

Sumner Welles told me that he had sent his resignation to the Presi-

---

1 Marshal Pietro Badoglio, the Italian conqueror of Ethiopia, had executed a coup on July 25, 1943, two weeks after the Allied invasion of Sicily, through which he succeeded Benito Mussolini as head of the Italian government. Though Badoglio officially dissolved the Fascist Party, he could not on that account cleanse himself of his own fascist past. Indeed an OWI broadcast beamed from London on July 26 had quoted an American columnist who, with admirable precision, had attacked both the Marshal and the Italian king as fascists. Roosevelt denounced the broadcast the next day. Meanwhile the Allies negotiated with Badoglio for a surrender, which was signed in September, but the German forces in Italy continued to resist. The negotiations with Badoglio, which excluded the Russians, offended those Americans who had previously objected to the Darlan episode and its sequels. Roosevelt and the State and War Departments again defended their policy on the ground of military expediency, but it did not significantly hasten the arduous task of driving the Germans from Italy and it cost the United States much confidence among European, and especially Italian, democrats.

2 So Hull had said, according to what Wallace had learned, to Arthur Sweetser, then deputy director of the OWI and long an ardent supporter of the League of Nations.

dent and that his resignation had been accepted,[1] and that it would be announced when the President came back to Washington on August 26 or 27. Prior to that time he expected to leave town and said he hoped to see me when he got back. I told him I was very sorry to hear he had resigned. He said it was the only thing he could do. I asked him what he was going to do. He said he was going to retire completely, and said that the President had urgently asked him to do some special work and Secretary Hull had agreed, but Welles made it clear that the issue between himself and Hull had been stirred up by Hull and not by himself. He said that the President, with Hull concurring, had asked him to work on the immediate problem of Russian relations. He said he had decided not to do this . . . I asked Welles what Hull's complete domination of the State Department meant in terms of international affairs. He said it meant that England would try to deal with Russia direct and put us in the position of dealing with Russia through England as an intermediary. He said the British had been working on this for a long time.

He said Litvinov was not coming back to the United States; that he had been appointed a vice commissar in Russia. I asked him what this meant. He said he had interpreted it as meaning that Stalin was making a strong effort to strengthen his Foreign Office. Maisky from London and Litvinov from Washington tried to keep Stalin fully informed as to what was really going on in the world. Welles said that Concheso, the Cuban Ambassador to the United States, who was recently in Russia, reported that he had an hour and twenty minutes with Stalin. The first half of the period was spent by Stalin in trying to find out about Latin America. This conference proved that Stalin was completely ignorant of Latin America. Concheso then tried to find out about Russia and her plans. Stalin then said that he felt it was impossible to raise the standard of living in Russia the way it ought to be raised without Russia becoming a part of the "family of nations." I asked Welles if he had passed that information on to the President, as it seemed to be very important. Welles said he had. Welles said, "I am not a communist and I know you are not a communist, but I believe you and I are of the same attitude on Russia." I said, "Yes, I think the future peace of the world hangs on developing collective security in cooperation with Russia." Welles said the English theory was still the balance of power theory—the theory which England has always had except in

[1] Welles' enemies had forced his resignation, Hull by his constant complaints, Bullitt by malicious personal attacks which the President could neither deny nor ignore.

the brief time when she was in the League of Nations. I said, "by collective security you mean the same doctrine Litvinov preached during the latter part of the twenties?" Welles said, "Yes." Welles thinks it is only a matter of weeks until the Russians will determine their course. At the moment the situation looks good, but it could rapidly change for the worse in the very near future. The President received, last week, a long telegram from Stalin indicating willingness for a meeting. It was a well-phrased telegram.

Welles believes in regional organization, and international organization growing out of the regional organization. I asked Welles if he believes in the same kind of regional organization as Churchill. He said, "No." He said Churchill was planning his European regional organization so as to work out a balance of power theory in Europe. He said nearly a year ago he (Welles) worked out his theories on this line and that they had been given to the President, and the President had approved them. I said, "Do you visualize us as being a member of the European regional organization?" He said, "No." I said, "Do you visualize us being a member of the Asiatic organization?" He said, "A member of the North Asiatic group along with Canada, Russia, and China," but that he thought the South Asiatic group consisting of the Philippines, Australia, and the various islands should be separate. I asked him what he thought of the peace committees as they had been set up in the State Department. He said he thought they had been doing good work until six months ago. Up to that time he had been in charge of the political planning committee. When he had charge the method was to bring up the various points at issue, study the facts, and arrive at a decision. Since Secretary Hull had charge the method had been to gather together facts but take no action on them. He said the way Secretary Hull leads the Department it would never decide anything. I asked him if Myron Taylor was doing good work on the planning committee.[1] He said, "Yes, excellent work." He said he had grown in stature enormously. I asked him about Norman Davis. He said he was completely subservient to Mr. Hull and seemed to have no fixed opinions of his own. He said Isaiah Bowman was a tower of strength, and Anne O'Hare McCormick—magnificent.

I told Welles that Enrique de Lozada would be heartbroken to hear of his leaving the Department, that Enrique looked on him and Larry

[1] The State Department's postwar planning committees included, among others, Myron C. Taylor, formerly Roosevelt's personal representative to the Vatican; Norman H. Davis, often a delegate to international conferences and a close friend of Hull; Bowman; and Anne O'Hare McCormick, the talented New York *Times* analyst of foreign affairs.

Duggan as the only liberal sparks in the Department. I told Welles that
the Russian situation was so exceedingly important and eventual danger of war with Russia was so great that he should, by all means, do
what the President wanted him to do. He said he had not declined the
invitation yet, but that he fully intended to do so. I urged him again
and again to reconsider as I thought it was too important from the
standpoint of the future peace of the world. He said that Cordell Hull
was intensely prejudiced against Russia. I said, "Do you mean to say
he has the same attitude as the English Tories have had toward Russia
since 1919—an attitude which has made Russia continue to be distrustful because they know the Tories are doing everything possible to
destroy the Russians?"

Welles mentioned that when he had been out of town Cordell Hull
had had various personal contacts with Arthur Krock and that the
whole newspaper story about Welles had been carefully planned by
Hull and Krock. I ventured to say that while Hull might know very
little about Latin America or Russia, he certainly was a skillful political maneuverer.

I ventured that I had never, at any time, had any question in my
mind about the President's ultimate soundness about foreign affairs—
that I had never had a moment's regret for being in the Democratic
Party or working with Roosevelt. My experiences had been infinitely
happier than my father's. I went on to say that while there are some
evil influences in the Democratic Party, there were many more evil
influences in the Republican Party, that the greedy international mo-
nopolists had much more influence there than in the Democratic Party.
Welles said he agreed one thousand percent. He said he was absolutely
sure of the President's fundamental soundness in his international attitude. He said the President's attitude is like his and mine and not like
that of Hull. I again said, "Then you surely owe it to the President to
help him out on this Russian matter."

Welles said it would be a difficult job to do good work with the
State Department against him.

I then asked Welles if he would read the August 21 edition of my
September 11 speech.[1] He suggested one or two very minor changes
and said he thought it was a very powerful speech, that it was especially powerful because of the specific illustration given. He said, in
his opinion, from what he knows of the President's attitude that the

[1] Wallace delivered the speech on September 11, 1943, to a meeting of the Chicago
United Nations Committee. It followed the lines of his earlier addresses in
1942–43 and included an attack upon international cartels.

President would approve every word in the speech. He said the speech would make Cordell Hull go straight up in the air. I told him that I did not propose ever again to clear a speech with Cordell Hull, but I did think I would let the President know I was making the speech and offer to let the President see it if he would like to do so.

I told Welles I was greatly disturbed to know that Hull was determining his foreign policy on the thesis that the Republicans would win in 1944. I said I could tell him the source of my belief if he really wanted to know. He said he very much wanted to know and so I told him the Sweetser story that my sister had told me. I also told him that Mrs. Hull, according to Mrs. Wallace, had taken the same attitude some six months ago in talking with the Women's Democratic Club. Welles said Mrs. Hull and Cordell both had taken the same attitude with Mrs. Welles in 1940.

Welles went on to say that it had always been Hull's thesis that the administration in its foreign policy should follow after public opinion. On the contrary it was the President's belief, his own, and he believed mine as well that it was the duty of the administration to keep the public informed and to help the public make up its mind.

There is no question but what the Hull approach is safer from a personal point of view. It is better politics. But there is a real question about the safety of the country. The Hull approach will give England and Russia the initiative . . . .

At Mary's party, the most interesting thing was the discussion of the remarks by Clapper and Minister Butler[1] of England concerning de Gaulle. Clapper spent an evening with de Gaulle with about six other people present. He says de Gaulle is a man of great force, that while he was not popular in Algeria, he was marvelously popular in Tunisia. Butler confirmed this, saying that the populace there fairly went into hysterics over de Gaulle. Butler and Clapper agreed that de Gaulle is exceedingly popular with the French people in France. De Gaulle speaks quite good English and joked with Clapper about the United States, saying, "As nearly as I can figure it out, Willkie has taken over the President's foreign policy and the President has taken over Willkie's domestic policy." Clapper says de Gaulle when he wants to put on the charm can put on just as much of it as Roosevelt, that he is a man of very real magnetism and that there is no question but that he has a great deal more force than Giraud.

Neither Clapper nor Butler could figure the reason for the delay in recognizing the French Committee. There seems no question that when

[1] R. A. Butler, then Undersecretary of the Foreign Office.

the Germans have cleared out of France, de Gaulle will come into power by popular acclaim. It seems a mystery why both the United States and England should want to antagonize the man who is going to be the real head of the French people. Clapper probably thinks that de Gaulle has considerable of the instincts of the dictator in him and does not have quite the same admiration for him that Lippmann has . . .

AUGUST 26, 1943

. . . Henry Morgenthau said he wanted to compliment me on the way in which I had behaved on the recent Jesse Jones matter.[1] He said he could not have behaved as well. He says when folks have asked him about the situation, he has said steadily, "Jones ever since April 1942 has steadily fought against the President's April 13 executive order." Henry says that Jones throughout the whole period was really fighting the President not me . . .

Morgenthau wants to weave the Wagner Social Security proposal into his new tax legislation. He says he has talked to some of the CIO chieftains about this and they are agreeable. This, however, is absolutely confidential. The Wagner proposal would take 6 percent out of wages and 6 percent from the employers. The annual amount raised would be something like 7 billion dollars. Of course, large sums would be returned to necessitous workers later on. The Wagner proposal takes in everybody including domestic servants and farm workers.

Henry says he can't understand why the White House places so much confidence in men who come from the legislative branch of the government like Jimmie Byrnes, Vinson,[2] Prentiss Brown, and Marvin Jones. The President has said that these men have influence with Congress. Henry Morgenthau says they don't have influence really with Congress anymore. They used to have it when they were in Congress

---

[1] Wallace had received a more unexpected compliment in an entertaining letter of August 10, 1943, from William Allen White, who wrote: "For a month I have been filling up with good intentions to write to you and tell you I am for you in your fight. Which doesn't mean I am ever going to support you for President or Vice President. You shinny on your side, and I'll shinny on my side. God knows there is plenty for us to do in both parties. And the Conservatives are about as plentiful and as mean on the one side as the other—little fools led by big scoundrels . . . I have upheld the President. . . . But when he is wrong, I am free to say so . . . Between you and me, twelve years is going to get him. I mean get his keen sense of justice, get his quick reaction to evil . . . I just want you to know that you have my blessing and my prayers."

[2] Frederick M. Vinson, Democratic congressman from Kentucky (1923–29, '31–'38), then associate justice of the United States Court of Appeals in Washington, D.C., resigned that post to become director of the Office of Economic Stabilization (1943–45), where he served as Byrnes' right-hand man.

but they don't now. He says the way to have influence with Congress is to have influence with the people. Apparently Henry has considerable contempt for the White House secretariat. Neither can he understand why the President lets Hull and Jones run over him. I told him not to get discouraged, that it was my opinion the President would come to a showdown with Jesse Jones before the end of the year . . .

AUGUST 28, 1943

Pat Jackson[1] told me that a friend of his who is also a friend of Bennett Clark[2] told him that when Bennett was in to see the President the second week in July the President said substantially the following:

"I have had my experience with the professors, the enthusiastic young men, the idealists. They mean well but they are not practical. I am through with them."

I said to Pat, "But that doesn't mean that he really feels that way at heart. He tempers his statements according to the man with whom he is talking."

Pat said, "But Mrs. Roosevelt has the same idea. She talks very frankly to me and she thinks that he is no longer guided by warm, human emotion. He is thinking about his place in history. In his first term this was not true. He acted on impulse then."

I said, "Mrs. Roosevelt's landing in New Zealand was a great surprise to me."

Pat replied, "She did not want to go. She was ordered to go. The Negro situation was too hot"[3] . . .

SEPTEMBER 2, 1943

McAlpin[4] told me how exceedingly popular the President was in England. He wanted to know whether this country was going as far to the right as the superficial observer would gather from the papers.

---

[1] Gardner Jackson, champion of just about every liberal cause since the trial of Sacco and Vanzetti, held various minor federal offices during the New Deal and war years and now and then in that time talked about his hopes and fears with Wallace.

[2] Bennett C. Clark, since 1933 Democratic senator from Missouri.

[3] To be sure, Southerners in particular were attacking Mrs. Roosevelt because of her open sympathy for civil rights for blacks. "Eleanor stories," most of them vile, circulated freely in the South. Her trip to the South Pacific, however, was in fact a substitute the President designed to trade off for her request to visit the Soviet Union and China; see Joseph P. Lash, *Eleanor and Franklin* (New York, 1971), Chs. 53, 54.

[4] E. W. McAlpin, London editor of the Australian Consolidated Press.

I told him I did not think the President was going so very far to the right, that I felt his one concern was to do whatever might be necessary in order to get votes in the Senate for his peace program.

Dick Wilson[1] has spent several months in England and North Africa, and wanted to find out whether or not I had broken with the President. I told him there was nothing to that story, that I had recently had two very nice letters from the President. He suggested that the President had gone conservative whereas I was progressive. I said no, the President was merely thinking about getting votes in the Senate so that he could win the peace as well as the war. Wilson asked, "How are things between you and Harry Hopkins?" I said "Perfectly all right so far as I know. I never had an unkind word with Harry." I said to Wilson that I thought the President had managed things very skillfully from every point of view, that it was quite appropriate that he should be conservative at the moment. It was also quite appropriate that I should be in the position of leading the progressive forces. I said I thought the President was happy to have it this way. Dick said, "Well, here is some gossip I have picked up. I don't know whether there is anything to it or not." The story is that in late July the President asked Clyde Herring to go out to Iowa to sew up the Iowa delegation to make sure I would not have it in 1944. I made no comment whatever on this and started saying, "Is it true that both Mike and John Cowles feel that their number one business in life at the present time is to defeat Roosevelt in 1944?" He said yes, it was true. I asked why it was. Dick said, "Well they feel the New Dealers are very poor administrators." I said, "Who do they mean? Harry Hopkins?" He said, "Perhaps so." I said, "That is quite curious because Harry was responsible for both of them being in Washington." I asked Dick who were some of the other New Dealers they thought were so poor as administrators. Dick then mentioned Morris Rosenthal. I said, "Well, Morris is neither a Republican, a Democrat, nor a New Dealer. He is just a businessman who has been in Washington only during the past year and a half, fresh from business. It is true that he has some liberal ideas but he could hardly be called a New Dealer." "Well, at any rate," said Dick, "John and Mike believe that the only way to have decent government in the United States is to clean out the President and the whole crowd of the administrators that he has brought in." I said to Dick, "I wish you would get this across to John and Mike. When I look at the two

[1] Richard L. Wilson, Washington correspondent of the Des Moines *Register and Tribune* and other Cowles papers.

parties and consider the forces behind the two parties, I am sure that the central group which controls the Republican Party is so under the domination of international cartels that in my opinion it is absolutely essential in order to prevent world disaster to make sure that the Republicans are kept out of power." I emphasized this repeatedly and told Dick I wanted him to make sure that Mike and John understood this. I told him there was no split between Roosevelt and me and there wasn't going to be any . . .

At cabinet meeting the President started out saying, "Hello, Henry. How are you?" I replied, "Fine, Mr. President." Jesse Jones, before the President came in, had put at the President's place a little piece of styrene with a note under it. The President then said after greeting me, "Well, I see here is a piece of polymerized styrene. I bet there is nobody here who knows what that is except Jesse." Don Nelson spoke up to say that it was used to make rubber and Jesse said yes, it was made out of alcohol and is used for rubber. The President said, "What interests me is whether or not it can be turned back into alcohol again." It was rather obvious to me that the President was kidding Jesse and not taking him seriously.

The President then asked Hull if he had anything to bring up. Hull started talking about Russia. Said he had asked Welles back in 1940 to go over Russian affairs very closely, examining every cranny and crevice, while he, Cordell, examined Japanese affairs in the same way. He said he wanted to know whether either of these two powers had any just complaint against the United States even on small items. It was obvious that Cordell was defending himself against the charge of being anti-Russian and trying to put responsibility on Welles for development of Russian policy.

The President spoke about the Russian habit of sending him a friendly note on Monday, spitting in his eye on Tuesday, and then being nice again on Wednesday. He said it took him a while to learn this was Russian technique. He said the first time it happened he was sore. He came back at the Russians which caused them to maintain their disagreeable attitude for a week or two. He later found that when he paid no attention to their disagreeable notes, they straightened out of their own accord the details. It was then that he realized that the Russians were alternately agreeable and disagreeable just as a part of their diplomatic program.

The President then went on to say that it was still a secret that Davies had taken a note from him to Stalin inviting Stalin to meet with him by himself.[1] This, of course, was in the papers at the time and while [it was] not announced officially, Davies had had in a few friendly reporters and had said to them, "Confidentially I am taking a note from Roosevelt to Stalin inviting Stalin to meet with the President." However, the President told us in cabinet that it was a great secret.

The President mentioned that the Americans and British in dealing with the Italians about peace matters had simply forgotten to call in the Russians. They were changing that now and were most happy to call in the Russians. While the President was saying this, I could not help wondering if the Russians might talk peace matters over with the Germans and thoughtlessly forget to call in us and the British. I hope they don't have that kind of thoughtlessness.

The President spoke about the type of recognition given to the Free French Committee. He said it was now arranged that there was to be limited recognition but that government in France was not to be turned over to them as fast as the British-American armies conquered French territory. He said in that case the Free French Committee would not be in position to dictate the form of French government without regard to the will of the French people. He made it clear that the British did not have the same slant on this matter that we had and suggested their motives were unworthy.

Hull then spoke up to say that he had battled with Eden on this point for several hours and had told Eden that he was an opportunistic politician. He went on to say that he himself was on the point of becoming a statesman and then, smiling rather sourly, he said he told Eden, "You know in the United States a statesman is a dead politician."

The President told the cabinet the same story about Molotov that he told me back in June. This is the story about how he found Molotov completely poker-faced, that he could not get anywhere with him all the time he was in the White House until he gave him a lot of liquor to drink, then told him an off-color story. Molotov leaned back in his chair and roared and after that the President got along with him after a fashion. He then told again how Molotov had gone on a trip with one secret service man to New York to have a good time, and how Davies had told this story to Stalin. Stalin had said in Molotov's presence, "The thing that surprises me is why Molotov went to New York instead of to Chicago, where he could have asso-

[1] Joseph E. Davis, former American ambassador to Moscow, had returned in June from a special mission as representative of the President to deliver messages to Stalin, one of which proposed an informal, private meeting of the two heads of state. Instead Roosevelt met with both Stalin and Churchill in Teheran, November 28 to December 1, 1943.

ciated with fellow gangsters." The whole conversation back and forth between the President and Hull suggested to me that the President was appeasing Hull in every way possible . . .

I told the President that the farmers were working hard, they were disturbed about a lot of little things.[1] That they had been told by local government representatives that farmers were in trouble until that man Roosevelt was out of power. I mentioned that Ed O'Neal eight or nine months ago had made a speech in Iowa in which he said that the only difference between labor in this war and labor in the last war was that in the last war, labor wanted only one silk shirt and one bottle of whiskey, whereas in this war they wanted two silk shirts and two bottles of whiskey. I said wherever I had gone I had pointed out to farmers the relationship between their income and the total payrolls of labor and the way in which the representatives of organized labor had helped them in their legislation. I said I felt the feeling of farmers against labor was a national weakness and something ought to be done about it. I said the farmers were working about nine or ten hours a week longer than they did before the war, but that they ought to appreciate that labor also was working longer hours, and that when they took into account the time labor spent getting to and from the factories, labor sometimes was working as many hours a week as the farmers.

Then the President asked me what the farm labor situation was. I told him the farmers felt a little better about it than they did last September, that the high school boys and girls were working now as well as the businessmen working in the evenings, that the farmers were getting a little tired working such long hours and working their women and children so hard. When I told the Ed O'Neal story, the President went off on a tangent, saying something about the need of labor for continuing to have plenty of beer.

SEPTEMBER 7, 1943

I told the President I was going out to Chicago on Thursday. He said, "Fine"; that he was leaving also on Thursday but not for Chicago. I said I was going out to speak on the same platform with Senator Ball on the B²H² Resolution, Senate 114.[2] I said I thought I'd pay my

[1] In Iowa in August Wallace had talked widely with farmers and leaders of farm organizations.

[2] Senator Joseph H. Ball, eager to provoke debate in Congress about the peace, in March 1943 had introduced Senate Resolution 114 (with Republican Senator Harold H. Burton of Ohio and Democratic Senators Carl A. Hatch of New Mexico and Lister Hill of Alabama—thus B²H²). The resolution, bold and

respects to Colonel McCormick. He said, "Fine!" I said with regard
to the Ball resolution that I was not in accord with all of it, especially
the first two sections, but that I thought now was a good time to plug
for the general idea. The President said he, himself, at heart was for
the main part of the Ball resolution but that he couldn't come out for
it publicly because he couldn't get it passed, for the reason, among
others, that Tom Connally was against it.

The President asked if I would send my speech over to Cordell Hull
for him to take a look at it. I said that I couldn't do that. He said,
then, could I send it to him and let him clear it with Cordell. I said
to the President that I was through having speeches cleared by Cordell.
He said he had been having quite a time with Cordell and that I didn't
know what a job he had had keeping the Old Boy sweet. He said the
Old Boy had been suffering from a lot of unfair criticism. He said
that for the general welfare of the country he had to keep Cordell
sweet at the present moment and that he would tell me all about it
some day. I said I had done everything I could to cooperate with
Cordell and that I had gotten no thanks for it and that I was through.
The President said Cordell was not in any thanksgiving mood. I made
it very clear to the President that I valued his judgment at all times
and would like to clear with him personally. He indicated, though,
that this did not get him off his hot spot with Cordell. I finally told
the President I would send the speech over to him and he said he would
talk to Cordell about it.

SEPTEMBER 11, 1943

Mayor Kelly[1] was strategically out of town when I was in Chicago.
Herman Bundesen [2] told me that Harry Hopkins and Kelly were

---

specific beyond the preferences of Roosevelt and Hull, "called for the United
States to ask the United Nations to form a permanent international organization
during the war" with "power to carry on the war, occupy territory liberated
from the Axis, administer relief and economic rehabilitation, and provide
machinery for the peaceful settlement of disputes." That language provoked
Senate isolationists like Burton K. Wheeler and Robert Taft to bitter rejoinders.
Most congressional members of both parties, while anxious to appear sympathetic to a postwar world organization, nevertheless supported Hull's insistence
upon a vague, less binding commitment, at least for the duration of the fighting.
That attitude exactly suited Tom Connally, who in October drafted a bland
resolution of his own that his Foreign Relations Committee reported out. The
B[2]H[2] proponents tried unsuccessfully to add strengthening amendments; see
Robert A. Divine, *Second Chance* (New York, 1967).
[1] Edward J. Kelly, since 1933 mayor of Chicago, and long-time boss of that city's
powerful, pro-Roosevelt Democratic organization.
[2] Herman N. Bundesen, since 1931 president of the Chicago Board of Health.

very close. He attributed the mayor's absence to Harry's influence. He said Harry had been visiting Kelly for a good many years, that Harry's great passion was going to horse races and that Harry, Kelly, and a man by the name of Hertz[1] (I suppose Hertz of the Yellow Cab) were in the habit of going to horse races together. At any rate, according to Bundesen, the Democratic political machine in Chicago did not turn a finger to make the September 11 meeting a success. Neither did the AFL do much. Apparently the greater part of the work was done by the CIO.

According to Bundesen, the strongest political force behind Ed Kelly is Barney Hodes,[2] a Jewish boy of about forty years of age. When Cermak was shot in Florida and Kelly was in on a temporary basis, and had been very severely attacked, Hodes took hold of him (Kelly) under the most unfavorable circumstances and created a favorable public opinion for him. Hodes has control of the famous 24th ward, which is a Jewish ward where the vote for the President in 1940 was 24,000 to 900.

Hodes, while admitting the remarkable crowd that turned out for the Chicago meeting, said that it had been handled in altogether the wrong way. He said the Democratic machine was sore because I had come into Chicago and he was afraid the Democratic machine would be sore wherever I went unless the methods were changed . . .

Hodes told me that from his point of view there is only one purpose in my making speeches and that is to get the nomination for the vice-presidency next July in Chicago. He says I am already looked on as the leader of the liberals, that I should now go out to get other folks as well, and especially I should go over the list of all of the Democratic national committeemen and the potential delegates to the convention, find out just who I can count on. I told Hodes that my object in making the speeches was to make sure that when the peace came it was a lasting one. I told him that I recognized very well that in order to get a lasting peace it was necessary to have the Democrats continue in power. He said, yes, but more than that is necessary. It is necessary, he says, not only to have Roosevelt run again for President but you as Vice President. He said he had been around the White House himself and he knew of a certainty that the crowd around the White House were moving heaven and earth to make sure of a fourth term for the President. He thought they were working

[1] John D. Hertz, founder of the Yellow Cab Company, partner in Lehman Brothers, adviser on wheeled vehicles to the Secretary of War.

[2] Barnet Hodes, former Chicago alderman, since 1935 corporation counsel of the city.

against me for Vice President. He said he was sure that I could work matters out if I went at it in the right way to make it a certainty that I would be nominated for Vice President. I told him I had never gone at matters in that way, that I thought political maneuvering that was being done was being done by Harold Young.

Hodes suggested that some type of national organization be formed, "United Nations for Peace" for example. He urged that it be a nonpartisan organization but that in reality it be my organization.

Unquestionably Hodes meant well in talking to me but I must confess that practical politics of this sort doesn't appeal to me . . .

SEPTEMBER 15, 1943

. . . I talked to Justice Jackson[1] about cartels. He had a number of good ideas and offered to send me some material. He says that the soul of free enterprise is found in the small businessman. He reached that conclusion as a result of his observations living in Jamestown, New York. I asked him what kind of job Justice Frank Murphy was doing. He said he was the most unpredictable man he had ever known, that he did not know how to think for himself but that he generally went along with Hugo Black. He was all right on civil liberties. He said Justice Douglas also went along with Hugo Black. It seems that Justice Byrnes once said to Jackson that in the Senate Hugo Black was a lone wolf and oftentimes could not get anyone to go along with him but that in the Supreme Court he had three votes nearly all the time.

Justice Jackson said that the Chief Justice[2] was deeply concerned about the way in which Bill Douglas was running for President or Vice President. Murphy told Bob Jackson that Tommy Corcoran was in Douglas's office very frequently. Eliot Janeway of the Time-Fortune crowd is working with Corcoran in managing Douglas' campaign. Bob says that Joe Kennedy is also very active. Bob says my disagreement with Jesse Jones has worked out marvelously well . . .

SEPTEMBER 18, 1943

The . . . memo which I released this morning was based on the conference which Berge, Borkin, and I had with Gallagher and Harden

---

[1] Robert H. Jackson, since 1941 an Associate Justice of the Supreme Court, had previously served successively as assistant Attorney General, Solicitor General, and Attorney General, roles in which he turned much of his energy to antitrust policy.

[2] Chief Justice Harlan Fiske Stone.

this morning.[1] Gallagher and Harden came down very strong on the cartel nature of the British business and on the highly cartelized nature of the British oil companies. They were referring to the Anglo-Persian and the Dutch Shell. They said these companies were employing methods which are making it very difficult for them to get along in the foreign field. They said one-half of their business was foreign business. Apparently they feel that they have suffered much more from cartel practices than they have gained from them . . .

Gallagher claimed that the butyl plant at Baton Rouge was really producing about one-third of capacity because of unexpected bugs. They were sure they were going to lick the bugs. Gallagher said that their geologists were sure there was lots of oil along the Urals in Central Russia. Gallagher claimed that fully to rehabilitate their foreign oil business after the war would cost Standard Oil of New Jersey from 750 millions to a billion dollars. He said they did not want to spend this much money if they were going to have to buck British oil cartels.

SEPTEMBER 21, 1943

. . . Leo Wolcott, who is working with Governor Lehman in the Office of Foreign Relief and Rehabilitation, reports the usual difficulties with the State Department. When it comes to approving personnel, passports, etc., the State Department is apparently just as constipated as ever. Wolcott said Lehman had tried to get Morris Rosenthal but that Hull personally had turned thumbs down. Wolcott has great admiration for Governor Lehman but says he is not a very good fighter, says he doesn't know the way things are done in Washington. He

[1] Ralph W. Gallagher, president of Standard Oil of New Jersey, and Orville Harden, a vice president, had come to Wallace to make peace. After Wallace's Chicago speech about cartels, Gallagher had stated that the Vice President should know about Standard's cooperation with various government agencies. Wallace replied in a public statement noting several instances of "subterfuge, concealment, and double-dealing" by Standard in its unhappy history of affiliation with I. G. Farben, a relationship that had retarded the development of synthetic rubber in the United States. Now on September 18, Gallagher, as Wallace then said, had assured him and Wendell Berge, head of the antitrust division of the Justice Department, that "there should be no international agreements to hold prices above competitive levels, and . . . all international agreements made by private parties should be filed with the . . . Federal Government," that Standard favored unrestricted licensing of patents at reasonable prices, that cartels were "against public policy and . . . inconsistent with our principles of free enterprise," and that postwar production should be increased nationally and internationally.

hopes that eventually they will get out from under the heel of the
State Department when OFR&R is changed to United Nations Relief
and Rehabilitation Administration . . .

SEPTEMBER 22, 1943

. . . John Lewis[1] of *PM* wanted to talk about what I thought ought
to be done to make the world safe against cartels. I told him I thought
the first step was a law to provide for putting cartel agreements on
file. I said I was not sure that I agreed with the Department of Justice
that all cartels ought to be destroyed. I said my feeling was that there
ought to be some world organization to supervise cartels and that I
was beginning in my thinking to believe there ought to be something
in the nature of a variable regional organization to handle world affairs.
One group would have a dominating interest in the employment situation, another in food, another in cartel supervision, etc., etc. . . .

SEPTEMBER 25, 1943

. . . Harold Smith wanted me to know that he thought the planning
function of government should rest in the Bureau of the Budget. He
felt that the National Resources Planning Board[2] had rather made a
mess of things and that planning was not something that could be done
in a closet off to one side but was a daily operation of the government.
He would have planning conducted in each of the departments running along with the operations of the departments and the whole thing
finally heading up in the Budget Bureau. There is a great deal to what
he says. It is obvious that Smith doesn't get along with Henry Morgenthau . . .

SEPTEMBER 28, 1943

At the dinner for Claude Bowers[3] . . . Tom Connally, who acted as
toastmaster, dealt at some length on the thought that the quality of the
Senate at the present time was fully equal to that of the times of
Daniel Webster and Henry Clay. He went ahead to say, however,

1 John P. Lewis, managing editor of *PM*.
2 Congress had liquidated the National Resources Planning Board.
3 Claude G. Bowers, journalist, historian, diplomat, ardent Democrat, United
States Ambassador to Spain (1933-39) and since 1939 to Chile.

that the times of today were not such as to call out qualities like those displayed by Webster, Henry Clay, and Patrick Henry. Tom is looking for opportunities such as his forefathers had and apparently is completely unable to see the extraordinary opportunity which is today within his own hands. He doesn't realize that the situation today is one giving opportunity for display of much greater talents than those of Clay, Henry, or Webster. It is time for Tom Connally to roll over in his sleep and wake up.

Ed Stettinius came to the meeting and gave an informal talk, the high point of which was about some American soldiers just landed in Italy with some English Tommies on the shore. The American soldiers began talking about how the war was not going to last long now, they were going to push the Germans back in short order, etc., etc. One of the English Tommies then spoke up and said, "That is the first time I ever heard Russians speaking such good English."

At the conclusion Claude Bowers gave a talk about the politics of Chile and then ended up with a plea that everyone follow the Commander-in-Chief, that the only issue in the campaign of '44 should be (he assumed that Roosevelt would be nominated in '44 as a patriotic duty) "Follow the Commander-in-Chief." He said the Democrats during the campaign should talk nothing but victory, victory, victory, and war, war, war. I gained the impression that Bowers is a very cagey politician. He looked around and saw certain senators present and decided that he would not say anything that sounded the least bit progressive. Barkley also talked nicely but he said nothing even slightly progressive. As a matter of fact, my statement was the only one that had the suggestion of a progressive note in it . . .

SEPTEMBER 29, 1943

At the White House the high point of the meeting was when the President made it clear that he would be most happy to have brought out on the floor of the Senate as soon as possible a resolution such as B^2H^2 or the Fulbright resolution.[1] Barkley asked if the President did

[1] Fulbright in April 1943 had introduced a resolution in the House for the creation of "appropriate international machinery with power adequate to prevent future aggression and to maintain lasting peace." In June the Foreign Affairs Committee redrafted the resolution to make it more compatible to most of the members of the House. The new draft eliminated the reference to preventing future aggression. Fulbright then introduced a revised resolution asking Congress to go on record in favor of the creation of appropriate international machinery with adequate power to establish and maintain peace. Roosevelt was probably referring to that latter version.

not want consideration of the resolution held back until after the conference with Russia. The President made it very clear that it ought to be a good thing to bring the resolution out at once. He said flatly that he thought he, the President, was behind the country and the Senate was behind him. I ventured, "And I suspect, Mr. President, that the Foreign Relations Committee of the Senate is behind the Senate" . . .

The highlight to me of my conversation with Dick Russell[1] was the extraordinary feeling he acquired against the British in his trip around the world. He thinks the British nearly everywhere are cutting our throats. He spoke of the Lend-Lease commodities we furnished nearly every part of the world which the British as distributors handled by taking off our labels or substituting the British flag. He was impressed by the fact that the only news the people get in Egypt, India, and Australia comes through the Reuter's press. He says it costs the United States news agencies much more to get news into these countries than it does the British through Reuter's. He said that all five of the senators including himself, Mead, Lodge, Chandler, and Brewster were of the same opinion . . .

SEPTEMBER 30, 1943

. . . At the dinner at the White House for the sons of the king of Saudi Arabia, Secretary Ickes was the only cabinet member present. Colonel Hoskins[2] was there to interpret for the Arabians. Hoskins is the son of the American missionary who speaks Arabian like a native and who was sent out to Arabia by Berle. The Arabians were dressed in flowing robes . . . Berle was about the only member from the State Department present. Berle has been working on the Arab matter for a long time and apparently felt quite proud last night. It was also a high moment for Hoskins. As to what the whole thing means from the standpoint of the Jewish Zionist movement, I can't figure out. Perhaps Saudi Arabia is not concerned.

[1] Democratic Senator Richard B. Russell of Georgia, recently returned from a much publicized and little productive international jaunt on which his senatorial colleagues had been Democrats James M. Mead of New York and Albert B. Chandler of Kentucky, and Republicans Henry Cabot Lodge of Massachusetts and R. Owen Brewster of Maine.

[2] Colonel Harold B. Hoskins had been sent in October 1942, at Roosevelt's instigation, to find out whether the Jews and Arabs could reach a modus vivendi about Palestine. On returning Hoskins reported pessimistically and recommended freezing the question of Palestine until after the war, while also proceeding at once to help rescue Jews from Nazi-occupied Europe.

On my left sat Felix Frankfurter . . . Felix spoke in very high terms of Milo. This . . . amused me because I had known of the way Felix had run Milo down when there was a possibility that Milo might impinge in some way on his friend Dean Acheson.

Felix expressed concern that Burt Wheeler[1] should have become so emotionally involved that he was no longer a liberal. I said yes, it was very unfortunate when any person became completely dominated by his hatreds. I went on to say that it was a mistake to pay any man the compliment of hating him because in the process of hating him, you give that man power over you. I said in the process of hating Germany, we were in some danger of thereby making ourselves like Germany.

The Arabs spoke of meeting Patrick Hurley[2] out in Arabia. Hoskins showed me some pictures of the king[3] and said he was quite a fine, simple-minded old gentleman. He is sixty-three. The older of the two sons is thirty-eight and is already a grandfather. If the oil resources of Saudi are as great as people say, there is a lot of trouble ahead for these simple-minded Arabians.

OCTOBER 1, 1943

. . . Talked with Bean[4] . . . He asked about the Saudi Arabia boys and said that when Chaim Weizmann, head of the Zionists, visited the President last summer, that the President said to Weizmann that he thought that King Feisal of Saudi Arabia[5] was for sale, that by using $15 million he could get the Jews the opportunity they needed in Palestine. Bean wanted to know if anything of that sort had shown up. I said no, but that I figured the presence of Frankfurter at the President's dinner indicated the possibility of something of this sort. I have no doubt

[1] Democratic Senator Burton K. Wheeler had run in 1924 as vice-presidential candidate on Robert La Follette's Progressive Party ticket. His bitter opposition to American involvement in the Second World War had led him into strangely conservative friendships to a grim dislike of the President, and to rancorous objections to even the mildest proposals for American postwar participation in any international association. Early in September he had urged Roosevelt to act at once to "bring about peace in Europe and establish democracy throughout that war-torn continent"—a suggestion at once wholly desirable and wholly impossible.

[2] Patrick J. Hurley, Secretary of War (1929–33), Roosevelt's special representative to the Soviet Union (November–December 1942) and in 1943 to Egypt, Syria, Lebanon, Iran, Iraq, Palestine, and the Arab States; in 1944 appointed United States Ambassador to China.

[3] Ibn Saud.

[4] Louis Bean.

[5] Feisal II was king of Iraq.

whatsoever that the Feisals would greatly appreciate $15 million to do with as they like. Certainly there is quite a drama going on with regard to Saudi Arabia, Palestine, and oil.

OCTOBER 2, 1943

Morris Ernst said he had written a letter to the President about his proposal to have Simon & Schuster put out four pamphlets on the Four Freedoms.[1] In writing the President he had indicated that he wanted Sumner Welles to do the one on Freedom from Fear (war) and me to do the one on Freedom from Want. He had said in the letter to the President that he wanted to make sure that the project was agreeable to him and that his choice of authors was agreeable. He had also said in his letter that inasmuch as the President had slapped down the men who were really closest to his point of view, it might be well if their point of view, which really was the President's, were put before the public. Morris showed me the President's reply, dated September 21, in which the President spoke of interchanging tidbits with Morris. Apparently, the President feeds Morris gossip and Morris feeds the President gossip. The President in this particular letter fed Morris the gossip that Woodruff of Coca-Cola and Mack of Pepsi-Cola[2] were prepared to raise a lot of money to back Bricker[3] for President if Bricker were nominated. They would not do so, however, if Dewey were nominated because they hated Dewey just like they hated the devil—and the President added in his own handwriting "(or me)." The President concluded the letter by saying in a single sentence that he thought Morris' choice of authors for the Four Freedoms pamphlets was excellent . . .

OCTOBER 8, 1943

. . . Gromyko[4] told me of the fine visit he had had with the President. He said Secretary Hull would be in Moscow on October 16. He said an agenda had been drawn up. Apparently he seemed to feel quite satisfied with his interview both with the President and with Secretary Hull. He said nothing whatsoever that could be construed as being critical of Hull.

The Ambassador referred to Senator Lodge's statement about Si-

---

[1] The four pamphlets under discussion were not written.
[2] Robert W. Woodruff, chairman of the board of directors of the Coca-Cola Company, and Walter S. Mack, Jr., president of the Pepsi-Cola Company.
[3] Republican Senator John W. Bricker of Ohio, in 1944 governor of Ohio, the favorite of his party's conservative wing, and the vice-presidential nominee.
[4] Andrei A. Gromyko, newly arrived Soviet Ambassador to the United States.

berian bases, said that if the Russians put in enough men into eastern Siberia to enable the United States to use Siberian air bases against the Japs, the result easily could be that the Germans, being relieved from Russian pressure, would be able to cost the Americans many hundreds of thousands of lives on the Western Front. It is obvious, of course, that the 400,000 Japanese troops massed on the Manchurian border of the narrow strip of Russian land leading to Vladivostok could pinch off this narrow tongue in two weeks. Undoubtedly Siberian bases would be a very great help to the United States in the attack on Japan, provided the United States and Russians together were in position to hold them without weakening of the fight against Germany. In agitating for Siberian air bases at the present time, the people of the United States are not as well justified as the people of Russia are in agitating for a second front . . .

Senator Brewster took rather strong exception to what Lodge had said about Siberian bases saving a million American lives. He referred particularly to a conversation of Thursday morning which the senators had had with General Marshall at which it was indicated very clearly that a public statement about Siberian bases at the present time would be definitely against the country's war interest. Marshall made it clear also that Siberian bases, militarily speaking, would not be worth what Lodge said they would be. Brewster apparently was very much put out because, after all this, Lodge had gone ahead and spoken as he had. From listening to Brewster, no one could reach any other conclusion but that he looks on Lodge as a very irresponsible and dangerous young man . . .

Senator Johnson[1] of California took issue with Brewster. At the close of Brewster's presentation, he made an urgent plea for the United States making known her attitude with regard to world collaboration. Connally took some exception to this as did Vandenberg. Both are for extreme caution and great slowness. It would seem that the President is right when he says that on foreign collaboration, the President is slower than the people of the United States but that the Senate is slower than the President. It now appears that the Senate Foreign Relations Committee is slower than the Senate and that Tom Connally and Senator Vandenberg are the slowest of all. Senator Johnson gave a speech which started out with "I am against Joe Stalin. I am an American." The old man was so weak and emotional that he choked up and could not continue very long.

[1] Hiram W. Johnson, eminent progressive in the years before World War I, Republican senator from California since 1917, in that role a constant spokesman for American insularity.

OCTOBER 12, 1943

Ralph Ingersoll told me he had been working with some of the generals in London, especially with Lieut. General Jacob Devers.[1] These men have been working especially on the opening up of a genuine second front in France. Ingersoll was greatly concerned about two things and both of these items he had gotten effectively to Harry Hopkins. First, the British have been strongly against a second front and in case there were a second front, they wanted to have control of it themselves, even though the United States were furnishing two or three times as many men as the British. Part of their plan was to get General Marshall over to England serving on a very high level, while the British generals of the 21st Army really ran the show. Ingersoll found, in talking with Harry Hopkins, that he had been aware of this maneuver on the part of the British and it seemed as though effective steps had been taken to prevent General Marshall from becoming a mere figurehead in the stratosphere. It seems that General Marshall will go to England but on an effective and not an ineffective basis. Everyone seems to be agreed that Marshall is the only one who has the necessary combination of real knowledge, guts, and front to handle Churchill. Churchill has enough military knowledge and front so that he is able to talk down most American generals.

Ingersoll had also talked with Hopkins about the shocking lack of landing craft. He told Hopkins that he had briefed the minutes of the Quebec Conference for the American generals in London and he knew that both the British and American navies had in effect lied about landing craft. They claimed there were a certain number, which was correct, but did not mention that one-third of them were out being repaired and another third could not be used for other reasons. Ingersoll said that if it were not for the shocking shortage in landing craft, the landing could have been made in France this fall and the war could have been terminated this year. But the shortage of landing craft was such that the landing would be on such a narrow basis that the Germans would be able to wipe out the bridgehead. No matter how many men we have in England, it doesn't do us any good unless we have the landing craft to land over a considerable area—an area so wide

---

[1] Lieutenant General Jacob L. Devers, then commander of United States Forces in the European theater, was succeeded in that position at the end of 1943 by General Eisenhower. Devers then replaced Eisenhower in North Africa and served, too, as deputy Supreme Allied Commander in the Mediterranean theater. In London Eisenhower took charge of plans and preparations for the cross-Channel invasion of 1944.

that the Germans cannot wipe us out before we get started. The generals talked with Don Nelson about the problem when he was in London a couple of weeks ago and Don said that it was a simple matter to get adequate production of sufficient landing craft; it merely required building one less cruiser or a few less airplanes. Ingersoll said the British are afraid to put on a real second front because they fear the loss of so many men in their ruling class. The British still look on war as a gentlemen's show, with officers gallantly leading their men, which means that a high percentage of officers are killed. The upper-class Englishman thinks that the decadence of England since World War No. 1 has been the result of the loss of so many of their ruling class at that time and for that reason they hate to see anything done at this time which will result in another long period of decadence. Ingersoll's comment on this attitude was that it is high time the British began to look toward the common people as the source of renewal of their strength. Ingersoll feels that the British are still exceedingly superior in their class consciousness. Superficially, they are not as obnoxious as the Prussians but in essence their attitude in some ways is even worse. They are firmly convinced that the English are the chosen race and will stop at nothing in making good on that belief.

At one time the expectation was that the landing would be made in France about the middle of September. It is now put off until next spring. Arrangements have now been made with the Russians so that they can stage a powerful drive at the same time that we start our landing. Ingersoll is convinced that if we had foreseen the need for landing craft and had staged an invasion of France at the same time that the Russians were pushing in the East, the war would have been over in a month or two. Ingersoll mentioned that the United States admiral in charge of landing operations looks on his position as a demotion instead of a unique opportunity. The only way Ingersoll can explain the Navy's singular blindness with respect to the situation is that the Navy has concentrated on the idea of doing a complete job in the Pacific; also, the Navy has never been properly interested in landing craft. Ingersoll apparently feels that while the Navy has apparently been an extraordinarily efficient organization in many respects, in other particulars it is unbelievably blind. Churchill told Devers that the Italian show was important to give the people some victories to cheer them up.[1] Devers told Churchill that the important thing was

---

[1] On September 2, 1943, American and British forces had crossed the Straits of Messina to Italy. On September 9 American troops landed near Salerno and took Naples on October 1. German resistance since then had prevented further advances.

not to give the people victories to cheer them up but to end the war and therefore that we should invade France. Devers speaks bluntly to Churchill and is a very capable man but he doesn't carry enough weight to do anything more than to make Churchill resent him . . .

At the small Sumner Welles dinner were present a Philadelphia cousin of Mrs. Welles, Morris Ernst, the Brazilian Ambassador and his wife. After dinner Welles drew me to one side and told me the President had had him to Hyde Park recently and he spent all one Sunday there. He said the conference with the President had been completely and utterly satisfactory and that the President asked him to go to Russia. Welles gave no answer but the following day he wrote the President giving him in great detail why he believed he should not go to Russia, in effect pointing out that anything he was able to negotiate with Russia would be stopped either by Secretary Hull or by Secretary Hull acting in conjunction with the Senate. Welles indicated that he could not understand why this country went out of its way to prolong the power of the House of Savoy in Italy . . .

OCTOBER 13, 1943

. . . Lord Keynes' conversation indicated to me very clearly that he is following the Churchill line of an Anglo-American alliance. I would judge that Lauch Currie is doing everything that he can to co-operate with Lord Keynes. It was clear to me that Lord Keynes had a very great mental ascendancy over Currie.

OCTOBER 14, 1943

. . . At the White House dinner, the President was exceedingly amiable and asked that I sit beside him after dinner to talk with President Lescot.[1] The President during his toast to Lescot stated that Haiti this year would be furnishing 10,000 tons of rubber (this is wrong; Haiti will not furnish this much until 1945). The President then went on and, very much to my gratification, proclaimed that natural rubber would be cheaper than synthetic rubber and also better, and that the American consumer should not be gouged in the postwar period by a tariff on tires. After the dinner was over, I congratulated the President most heartily on this statement . . .

The President of Haiti gave President Roosevelt some little memento from the time of Toussaint l'Ouverture. I don't think I have seen any

---

[1] President Élie Lescot.

state dinner which the President has so relished giving as this particular one. He looks on Lescot as a real friend and evidently has a real personal fondness for Haiti, which he visited for the first time twenty-five years ago.

OCTOBER 15, 1943

. . . Lord Keynes told me some of the details of what he has been up to here in the United States. He had been working not only on postwar currency stabilization and an international investment bank but also on commodity agreements, buffer stocks, and international controls of cartels. He claimed himself to be enormously heartened at the progress made. He felt the important thing was for the United States and Britain to arrive at certain agreements. He told me that England was willing to agree not to engage in bilateral trade agreements after the war was over. I told him I was very much surprised at this; that I had understood that England was very much alarmed about her balance of payments and that it was customarily assumed that England would find it necessary to engage in bilateral trade agreements. Keynes apparently is willing to take the statesmanlike attitude that the best way out for England is to take steps to bring about worldwide prosperity. He feels that the steps taken in agreement with our officials on currency matters, commodity agreements, etc., are sufficient to lay the foundation for worldwide prosperity. He said that the President and Isador Lubin were strong for an unemployment conference to be held sometime in December or January. He proclaimed himself to be strongly against this, saying that any conference of this sort would be nothing but hot air. Lord Keynes is very proud of himself for using the currency stabilization thing as a front to deceive the newspapers while he met with numerous public officials on all kinds of other matters of importance. He thought that the foundation of an economic modus operandi for the world has been worked out and he is going home enormously encouraged. In working on the problems of buffer stocks and commodity agreements, he said that there were two extremes of thought on the part of the Americans: one, represented by Will Clayton, who took the extreme laissez faire position, and the other represented by Paul Appleby and Les Wheeler,[1] who took the extreme planning position. He said the British took the middle ground between the two positions. Lord Keynes said before

[1] Leslie A. Wheeler, economist in the Department of Agriculture (1926–39), since 1939 director of the Office of Foreign Agricultural Relations.

he came to the United States he had a meeting for two hours with the British cabinet and they went over all the matters which he was to discuss, with the exception of cartels. He said the British had no background of history against cartels such as we have in the United States. They couldn't understand, therefore, why we were so strongly against cartels. He said he could understand it but at the same time, he professed considerable personal admiration for McGowan,[1] the head of Imperial Chemicals. He said that they had been doing some marvelous experimenting which had been very helpful during the war. He said that they had had the benefit also of the knowledge and experience of many of the German Jews who had been responsible for so many of the German inventions.

Lord Keynes said that in most of the conversations he sat in on, Myron Taylor served as chairman. This indicated to me that Keynes sat in on the regular State Department Economic Committee.

This dictation about Lord Keynes reminds me, by the way, of what he said the other evening with regard to the Free French. While he proclaimed himself a liberal, he seemed to think it was the only practical thing to do to work with the House of Savoy in Italy, Salazar in Portugal, Franco in Spain, and the old Civil Service crowd in France. I told him flatly I thought there would come a time when the wrath of the common man would boil over. I asked Lord Keynes what Churchill thought today about the book which he (Lord Keynes) had written back in 1925 about the *Economic Consequences of Mr. Churchill*. In this book Keynes criticized Churchill very severely for putting England back on the gold standard at a time when it was bound to bring nothing but disaster for England. He said Churchill recognized that he was right in his criticism but was inclined to blame it on the bankers for giving him (Churchill) bad advice back in 1925.

Lord Keynes said that he and Harry White of Treasury were in practical accord now on currency stabilization problems and that the Federal Reserve officials, especially Goldenweiser and Gardner,[2] also agreed; that among the members of the board, Ransom[3] was the one most nearly in agreement with him. He said Pasvolsky[4] was in accord

[1] Lord McGowan, an outspoken champion of cartels.
[2] Emanuel A. Goldenweiser, since 1926 director of research for the Federal Reserve Board, and W. Gardner, one of his consultants.
[3] Ronald Ransom, vice chairman of the Board of Governors of the Federal Reserve Board.
[4] Leo Pasvolsky was in 1943 supervisor of the Division of Political and Economic Studies in the State Department. The next year he became executive director of the Committee on Postwar Programs.

with him in the State Department. I said I thought Pasvolsky was an "old dodo." He replied, "Well, he is coming along, he is coming along." With his very great prestige, Keynes has undoubtedly made a lot of hay while he has been in the United States . . .

OCTOBER 16, 1943

. . . Father Masse appeals to me strongly. He is a genuine progressive who is exceedingly keen about solving the problem of freedom and planning in a democracy. He always felt that Thurman Arnold's trust-busting was not enough, that there must be planning. He was a little disappointed in my Chicago speech because he thought it was going too far in the trust-busting direction and not far enough in the planning direction . . .

OCTOBER 17, 1943

At the White House Mrs. Wallace and I ate with Mrs. Roosevelt and Miss Thompson.[1] When Miss Thompson had left and the three of us were alone, Mrs. Roosevelt spoke very frankly. She said the children were all strongly against a fourth term for the President, they had not been very keen for the third term but were all very strongly against a fourth term. I said that some newspaper surveys indicated that if the war with Germany were over by next summer, the probabilities were that the President could not win. She said she had realized that if the war with both Japan and Germany were over, the President could not win, but she had not heard about surveys on the basis of what the situation would be in case only Germany were defeated. She asked very practically what would be done about it. I was amazed when she said that she thought if I were nominated I could win. Of course, I said nothing in reply. She went on to say that the difficulty would be to get me nominated, that, of course, she and the President would be for me as the logical one to carry out the policies of the President. She assumed, however, that the Southerners would be dead against accepting me. I made no comment whatever except to say that I felt the forces behind the Republican Party were such that it would be very dangerous for the Republicans to win in 1944.

We talked some about Willkie and Dewey and I ventured the belief that the situation now was swinging to Willkie, that the moneyed and influential powers in the Republican Party were going to use

[1] Malvina Thompson, Mrs. Roosevelt's secretary and friend.

Dewey to run interference for Willkie and in the final showdown Willkie would win the nomination. Mrs. Roosevelt doesn't think much of Willkie. I said I thought both Willkie and Welles had done a service to the American people by coming out against any partial alliance in their two speeches and standing for England, the United States, Russia, and China serving as a base for building a United Nations approach. She was very skeptical about Willkie on domestic matters.

She said she did not like Jesse Jones. I said he was a very hardworking and able man but I was afraid of what it would mean to the future of the country if he used his abilities in disposing of the billions of dollars in defense plants in a way which strengthened his friends . . .

OCTOBER 21, 1943

The meeting with Sidney Hillman[1] was unusually interesting. He has been in 40 of the 48 states and has been in touch with the Brotherhoods and AFL as well as the CIO. Everywhere he has been working definitely on the job of organizing labor politically. The response has been exceedingly good. Incidentally he says the attitude toward me is unusually fine. He asked me what I thought about [his] taking on Nathan, who he understands has been discharged by the Army because of his bad back. I told him I thought Nathan was the best of the young economists around Washington, that I had the highest regard for him. He asked also about a publicity man. I had no suggestions to make at the moment but told him I would have some names ready when he was in Washington, next Tuesday.

Hillman says that Frank Walker shows every desire to play closely with him. Hillman went especially into the situation in the states of the Northwest from Minnesota out to the coast. He says the Farmer-Labor group is re-forming its line. Sidney says he now has about $200,-000 in his treasury and he knows where to put his hands on $500,000 more. He is very keen to see the President and feels the President needs to be told certain things. He intends to do the telling. It should be said, however, that Sidney did not ask to see the President and had no intention of asking. David Niles[2] had told Sidney that the President wanted to see him.

[1] Sidney Hillman, president of the Amalgamated Clothing Workers of America and former vice president of the CIO, held federal positions in the OPA and WPB and in 1943, not least according to his own assessment, was the most active and influential labor leader in Democratic politics. During October he had been touring the country to prepare his Political Action Committee of the CIO for the 1944 campaign.

[2] David K. Niles, member of the White House staff and close associate of Harry Hopkins.

OCTOBER 23, 1943

Kaufmann [1] wanted me to talk to the Zionist meeting in New York on November 1. I told him I naturally could not make a talk of this sort without a complete understanding with the President. I said since the Jews themselves had become more and more unified on behalf of Zionism I had become more and more interested in Zionism . . . I told him I had spoken to Churchill about Palestine and that Churchill seemed to be quite friendly. This was last May. Kaufmann said Churchill was not so friendly now as he was then. Kaufmann is going to speak to Judge Rosenman to see if he can get clearance from the President . . .

NOVEMBER 3, 1943

At the CIO meeting in Philadelphia on Wednesday, I found that there is considerable dissatisfaction with the President among the CIO leaders. They feel he has been rather reactionary on both the domestic and foreign fronts and they are not going to come out for him for a fourth term. When I spoke to the CIO, however, and mentioned the President himself, I found that the rank and file among the leaders reacted in a way which caused me to believe they are very strong for him.

The CIO now has a membership of over 5 million. At lunch I ate with the vice presidents from unions representing a total membership of nearly four million. Everybody was having a great time kidding Johnny Green about Bridges[2] supporting him for President of CIO instead of Phil Murray. Johnny Green is from the banks of the Clyde and is a grand little Scotchman. A person can't help having a great deal of affection for men like Phil Murray, Johnny Green, and R. J. Thomas.[3]

[1] Edmund I. Kaufmann, Washington resident, president of the chain of Kay Jewelry Stores, and former president of the Zionist Organization of America, asked Wallace to speak on November 1, 1943, to a meeting of Jewish leaders at Carnegie Hall, New York. Through Sam Rosenman, Kaufmann discovered that Roosevelt did not want Wallace to appear. Both Willkie and Dewey spoke. Willkie called for the establishment of a Jewish state in Palestine and Dewey for opening Palestine to Jewish refugees from Europe. "It is interesting to note," Wallace wrote in his diary the day after the meeting, "how vigorously Willkie is going to town for Palestine."

[2] John Green, vice president, and Harry R. Bridges, president, of the International Longshoreman's Association.

[3] Rolland J. Thomas, president of the United Automobile Workers and vice president of the CIO.

NOVEMBER 4, 1943

. . . Herridge and Kaiser clicked amazingly well.[1] Kaiser is very much sold on a four-wheel-drive car which he has worked out weighing around 1300 pounds. He thinks it can be a tremendous service to the average working man and that it can be adapted not only to taking the working man to and from work, but also for plowing and cultivating on his small farm.

Kaiser's most novel idea had to do with marshaling the credit of the country to meet the postwar problem. He would have an agency half private and half governmental take charge of all the life insurance funds, trust funds, etc., etc., so that they could be used as risk capital to get the expansion necessary to prevent unemployment. Kaiser thinks peace is coming on very rapidly and that it is bringing with it problems enormously greater than anyone realizes. He thinks if we don't move rapidly, we will have a bloody revolution. In this Kaiser and Herridge are in complete accord.

Kaiser went at some length into his hospital projects which are described in Paul de Kruif's book. He says the greatest fear of many human beings is being sick for a long time and incurring doctor bills which may take them years to pay off. He has serviced his 70,000 employees at a cost of 7 cents a day. One man has been in the hospital for eleven months and it only costs him 7 cents a day. This 7 cents a day, however, has been sufficient to pay not only for the doctors but also to pay for the hospital and its equipment within two years.

Herridge was much impressed with Kaiser and thought that I ought to work out dramatic ways of using him as an illustration of a means of getting jobs done in abundance in the postwar world . . .

NOVEMBER 8, 1943

Sidney Hillman told me that he had had a very fine visit with the President, 40 minutes in fact, that he kept Roy Howard who was to have lunch with him (the President) waiting 20 minutes. Sidney told the President that labor was losing confidence in the administration and especially in the men who were immediately around the President and that some of the people were beginning to lose confidence in the President himself. Sidney told the President that the only member of

[1] They talked at dinner at Herridge's home where Wallace and Kaiser were guests. Wallace wrote Roosevelt the next day that Kaiser's ideas could be "of great value to the nation."

the President's entourage in whom labor had complete confidence was myself. He told the President the story first told by Eliot Janeway. Someone asked Janeway who was going to win in 1944. Janeway replied, "The Tories." Janeway was then asked, "What do you mean by the Tories?" He replied, "I mean that Roosevelt will win for the fourth term and that will put the Tories who are around him into power again." I did not ask Hillman what the President's reaction was to this blunt statement and Hillman did not volunteer. However, Sidney did say that he came away from the conference feeling better than when he went in. I told Sidney that it was my impression that the President's heart was in the right place but that he had felt it was necessary to surround himself as he had in order to get the best results out of the war effort. Sidney said Hopkins had been wanting to get in touch with him but that he had been rather dubious about seeing Harry. He feels that Harry is responsible for most of the men by whom the President is now surrounded. Apparently Sidney received a green light from the President to go ahead and cooperate with Frank Walker in political organization.

Sidney still feels that the President's sense of timing is badly off. The President told Sidney what a good sense of timing he had and that he felt there was not any hurry. Sidney disagreed utterly. I told Sidney I agreed with him. Hillman apparently is cooperating with Frank Walker in getting the right kind of delegates to the Democratic National Convention . . .

NOVEMBER 13, 1943

Arnold Beichman[1] told of various conversations which he had had with Willkie which indicated very clearly to him that Willkie was a pure opportunist and not really sincere. He said after the passage of the Smith-Connally Act, before the President had signed it,[2] Willkie

[1] Arnold Beichman of *PM*.

[2] In June 1943 Congress had passed over the President's veto the Smith-Connally War Labor Disputes Act, an antiunion measure that proved ordinarily to be ineffectual. It extended the President's power to seize strike-ridden industrial plants useful to the war effort, made it a crime to foment strikes in those plants, and ordered their return to private management within sixty days after normal production had resumed. Before calling strikes, labor leaders in all plants had to observe a thirty-day cooling off period and to obtain a majority vote of union members. On this and other domestic issues of the Second World War, there are excellent accounts in Richard Polenberg, *War and Society: The United States, 1941–45* (Philadelphia, 1972).

had declared this was the test of whether or not the President was a liberal. At that time Willkie was making all kinds of strong statements on behalf of labor. Later on, when Willkie was in St. Louis at the time of his broadcast answering Missouri Republicans, he had a more or less private meeting with some of the big Republican businessmen. On that occasion he spoke very vigorously as to just how liberal labor ought to be handled. Beichman apparently has a number of cases of this sort which cause him to question Willkie's sincerity. He thinks even less of Dewey, claiming that Dewey has absolutely no sense of humor.

Beichman's purpose in coming in to see me was to get me to make a statement against the way in which minorities were being abused in the United States. He referred especially to the anti-Jewish riots in Boston. He said that a Catholic priest had told him that Cardinal O'Connell[1] could stop the riots at any time. He said that the Cardinal, instead of stopping them, salved his conscience by giving $1000 to some kind of racial understanding organization. I told Beichman I had talked with some of my Jewish friends about this matter and I did not think any good purpose could be served at the present time by making a statement.

I must confess that these antiminority manifestations are suspiciously suggestive of the techniques that later led to Hitler's rise to power. They must be watched with great care.

NOVEMBER 15, 1943

Dorothy Thompson[2] felt most vigorously that the time for speech making and writing had gone by and that now was the time for action. The matter she was particularly interested in was to make sure of full employment after the war. She asked me if the government were doing any real planning along this line. I said unfortunately not.

I read to her the speech I was going to make on the New York Herald Tribune Forum.[3] She liked it but said, "What are you going to do about it?" She thinks Germany is going to go communistic. I told her I thought Stalin was against Germany going communistic. She said that might be true and that it might be that [what] Stalin did would do nothing to make Germany go communistic but nevertheless Germany would go that way because she had no other way to go. I told

---

[1] Cardinal William H. O'Connell of Boston.
[2] Dorothy Thompson, trenchant and often gloomy syndicated columnist of the New York *Herald Tribune*.
[3] On the worldwide importance of full employment.

her I thought Stalin would much prefer to see a rather impotent democracy in Germany than a vigorous communism. She agreed to all that but said there was nothing either Stalin or ourselves could do about it. She granted that there might be a rather kind of futile democracy for a time but that its inability to solve the problems of unemployment and full production would inevitably result in a strong swing to a dictatorship of the left. She thinks that Germany and Russia will be drawn together . . .

NOVEMBER 18, 1943

. . . Jack Bell[1] of the AP came in to see me and wanted to know what was the political significance of the speeches I had been giving. I told him there were certain views which I had long held, which I thought were of importance to the general welfare; that with regard to many of these views I had attempted to educate the public while I was editor of *Wallaces' Farmer* and that I had continued to do it while Secretary of Agriculture, and that as Vice President I was continuing to talk, although not quite as often as when I was Secretary of Agriculture. He wanted to know if I thought the President was running for a fourth term. I said I didn't know any more than he did but that I assumed the President would be nominated for a fourth term. He wanted to know, pointblank, if I was running for Vice President. I told him what I was interested in was getting my ideas over. He said, "Well, you could get your ideas over much better if you were Vice President than you could if you were out of public life." He continued, "I suppose you know that some of the men around the White House are against your being nominated again." I said I didn't know that, but that I had understood from general conversation that some of the men around the White House had been quite active in the Jesse Jones affair . . .

NOVEMBER 20, 1943

. . . At the dinner for Mrs. Roosevelt, I talked to her at some length on the future of liberalism in the Democratic Party. She agreed completely that the Democratic Party must be a liberal party. She then said she had been talking about the matter to the President. The President had told her that so far as he personally had been concerned, it had been necessary for him to refrain from furnishing

1 Jack Bell, head of the Associate Press office in the Senate.

liberal leadership until the Democratic primaries were over in the southern states. He did not want a third party put in the field in the South. I told her about Jay Franklin[1] calling on me and wanting me to call a meeting of liberals to discuss the political situation. I said it was my judgment that I should not do so. She said I was right. I then asked her how it would be if certain of the liberal senators would come out vigorously. She said she thought that would be all right . . .

Referring back to the conversation I had had with her the last time I was at the White House, I told her I was completely loyal to the President. She indicated she did not think he ought to run for a fourth term if there was no chance of his winning and she was sure his political judgment was good enough that he would not run if there was any likelihood of his losing. She mentioned again as she had before, the fact that the children did not want him to run . . .

I told Mrs. Roosevelt I thought the three big distracting forces in the Democratic Party at present were: one—the big interests; two—the bigoted Catholics; three—the venomous Roosevelt haters.

I put on some Red Russian army song records for Mrs. Roosevelt and also some Russian rural songs. She seemed to like both. Also I put on several Spanish records. Mrs. Roosevelt put in most of her time knitting a sweater, which was nearly completed and which was very well done. Apparently she has rather unusual facility as a knitter . . .

NOVEMBER 23, 1943

. . . Major Schreiber[2] gave me further information on the approach to the morale problem in the Army and the way in which morale prevents psychiatric disorders of various kinds. It seems that about 5 percent of the men are affected with psychiatric disorders and it appears that the number of psychiatric disturbances can be reduced to one-fifth of what they would otherwise be. The Russians are not seriously troubled with psychiatric difficulties because they believe in what they are fighting for. Many of our men do not believe in what they are fighting for because they do not know what they are fighting for. Schreiber implored me to make more speeches because they are so helpful to the morale of the men . . .

[1] John Franklin Carter, Jr. (Jay Franklin), author and columnist, formerly an economic specialist in the State Department (1928–32) and an official in the Department of Agriculture (1934–36).
[2] Possibly Walter R. Schreiber, formerly of the Agriculture Department, then an officer in the AUS.

NOVEMBER 25, 1943

At the end of the Thanksgiving service at St. Patrick's, I said hello to Archbishop Curley[1] and the Apostolic Delegate, Most Rev. Amleto Giovanni Cicognani, D.D. They were both very appreciative of my having attended the annual service for Latin America. Curley went much further and complimented me on my courage and said he hoped I would continue to fight the way I had been fighting in recent months, that I was doing an unusually good job. I know very little about Curley but his manner suggests that he belongs to the pro-Allied common man group in the church rather than to the Coughlin-Beckman group which is concerned chiefly in hating Russia. I can't help wondering how men like Curley would stand, however, with respect to some of the reactionary movements of the Catholic church in certain Latin American countries where the church, the army, and the big landlords act together to hold back the cause of progress . . .

NOVEMBER 30, 1943

. . . Myrdal[2] told me that he had been working for several years with Carnegie Institute on the study of the Negro problem in the United States. He is now a Swedish senator and wanted to talk to me about the desirability of Finland being independent of Russia. He thinks that if the United States is to be really friendly with Russia, it is necessary for the Scandinavian countries to serve as a sort of bridge between us and Russia. He thinks the Scandinavian countries can serve that function much more effectively if Finland is independent. He recognizes that Finland should perhaps give up a little of her territory to Russia but thinks it would be a great mistake if the island of Hangar in the Gulf of Finland went to Russia. Myrdal was pessimistic about the way things were going both in the United States and in Europe . . .

[1] Archbishop Michael Joseph Curley of Baltimore.
[2] K. Gunnar Myrdal, Swedish economist and lawyer, director of the Study of the American Negro Problem for the Carnegie Corporation of America (1938–42), author of the resulting classic, *An American Dilemma* (New York, 1944).

I had an exceedingly interesting conversation with V. Bush about war secrets. Scientifically speaking, our Navy is not so hot. It is too stiff-minded. The Army is better than the Navy in accepting scientific suggestions. Folks down the line in Navy are O.K. The trouble is with the folks at the top. There is bad organization in the top brackets.

Vannevar Bush told me about the German long-range rocket gun in somewhat the same way as it is described in the New York *Times* of December 5. He said the experiments had been conducted by the Germans on an island in the Baltic and that they had hoped to get into sufficient volume of production to release it with devastating effect against England in September of this year. Churchill himself, however, insisted that the RAF blast the particular spot where much of this work was going on. Curiously enough, the RAF did not want to do it. Churchill got the job done; also the RAF blasted some of the emplacements of these rocket guns in northern France and Belgium. As a result the Germans have now put the rocket gun emplacements so deep that they can scarcely be reached. The guns are carried into place on trucks placed on 32 wheels. A new type of explosive is being used consisting of liquid oxygen and some other liquid gases. The explosive effect is several times as great as ... TNT.

Bush thought that at Sorrento the Germans had quite good results against our shipping with a type of aerial torpedo controlled in the air by radio from a plane. One of these which did not explode was recovered and we know from the model that it was not in production but it was an experimental model; also we know that we have the same kind of thing much better perfected. We have not used it yet.

The danger of the German rocket gun is that a number of these can be released in the daytime and in a few minutes travel 100 miles to London and catch the Londoners unprepared in the streets, killing anywhere from 50 to 10,000 of them.

The preparation of the rockets represents an enormous expense and enormous diversion of priorities. However, there is every indication that the Germans will be ready to strike with a mass attack on London sometime in early February.

Bush described to me the success of the RAF in blasting a (heavy) water plant in Norway. This has enormous significance, which I shall never put down on paper until the war is over. Bush told me in detail about his trip to London and about certain negotiations which he and Secretary Stimson had with Prime Minister Churchill about a matter of very great importance both during the war and during the period after the war.[1] This also I shall not put on paper until after the war is over.

DECEMBER 6, 1943

. . . As I have watched the foreign operations of the different individuals in . . . government and have heard them cuss each other out, I have reached the conclusion that all of them are pretty ignorant from the standpoint of having an overall picture of what the truth really is. It is going to be necessary to have a new type of government servant with larger loyalties and larger understanding. The businessmen who come into government from outside are worse on the whole than those who have been raised in government.

DECEMBER 8, 1943

. . . Harold Ickes was extremely resentful with regard to Harry Hopkins, declared that Harry had tried to knife him with the President for many years. He said that the President could not manhandle him (Harold); if the President pulled any rough stuff with him he would get out at once. He said the President had made many promises to him which he never kept. He referred back to the old Forest Service matter, said that the President had promised to give him FS not only verbally but in writing. Also said that back in 1940 the President was going to make him Secretary of War. But Ickes is sure that Harry Hopkins and Felix Frankfurter between them blocked that . . .

Harold says that if the President gets rid of him (Harold) he will do some serious work writing. My guess is that if he writes he will pay off his old scores with the President and with Harry Hopkins. Harold says he owes his present job to Baruch, that Baruch told the President that Ickes was his best administrator. Harold said that he handled the coal strike altogether on his own without consulting with the President, and that he had had absolutely no word from the President after settling the strike.[2]

---

[1] Those discussions in London in July led to the Quebec agreement of August 19, 1943, signed by Roosevelt and Churchill, relating to the collaboration of their two countries on atomic energy. The agreement provided for a renewed though still incomplete exchange of information; see Hewlett and Anderson, *The New World*, pp. 275–84.

[2] Ickes had worked with John L. Lewis to develop a formula for the settlement of the bituminous coal strike of October–November 1943, one of a series of

Harold said that Jimmie Byrnes was over to see him yesterday and much worried because the President was not coming back as soon as he had been expecting. Apparently he wants to stay in Africa and do some sightseeing and possibly even see Italy. Eisenhower is much worried about it all and thinks the President should get back to the United States as soon as possible. I told Harold that I had had some questions about Bernard Baruch so far as I personally was concerned because of the way Jimmie Byrnes had acted on the Jesse Jones matter. Harold said he did not think that Baruch had influenced Jimmie Byrnes in any way. As a matter of fact, Baruch had never said a thing against me at any time. I said I knew that Baruch had always been a great help to Milo but that I also knew that Baruch was very close to Byrnes. Harold thinks that Jimmie Byrnes is not part of Harry Hopkins' kitchen cabinet but he does think that Jack Hertz, Sam Rosenman, and Hopkins oftentimes plan together . . .

Gradually it became obvious to me that Harold's purpose in talking to me was that it had to do with Harold's ambition to become demobilizer for industry when peace comes. He thinks he has Baruch in his corner. Baruch is doing everything he can to prevent Jesse Jones from taking on the job. Baruch looks on Don Nelson, who is also ambitious for the job, as Hopkins' protégé. My guess is that the line-up is Baruch, Jimmie Byrnes, and Harold Ickes on one side of the fence with Hopkins, Jesse Jones, and Don Nelson on the other side.

DECEMBER 9, 1943

. . . Faymonville[1] said he first got interested in Russia at the time of the other war. He was in the Philippines when the other men left to go to France. He decided there would be activity sooner or later in the Far East and studied Russian. He was stationed for a time in Siberia in 1918. Later on, at the time of the disarmament conference in Washington in January of 1922, the Far East republic which comprised the eastern part of Siberia was unofficially represented and the upshot of it was that he was over there to have a look around. He was

---

strikes by the United Mine Workers that had alienated public opinion, moved Congress to the passage of the Smith-Connally Act, and irritated both Roosevelt and his War Labor Board.

[1] Colonel Philip R. Faymonville, recently recalled to Washington, had been in charge of Lend-Lease in the Soviet Union in 1942–43. There he had operated with a calculated independence from the resentful Ambassador Standley who disapproved of the assumptions and tactics that Faymonville described to Wallace.

a White House aide in 1933. He was sent in 1934 as military observer when our Russian Embassy was opened up. In September of 1941 he was sent over as representative of Lend-Lease. While he has been a colonel in the Army right along, he served Lend-Lease in Russia up until he left there a month ago. He is a great admirer of the Russian people. I asked him about the Russian attitude toward the United States. He said they were very fearful about us on June 22, 1941. He said the Atlantic Charter and the President's declarations allayed this fear somewhat. In January and February of 1942 they were desperate and wondered why we were not sending them help faster. When we eventually complied with our promises, they gained more and more confidence in us. I asked him what was the nature of his difficulty in Russia to which reference was recently made in the press. He said it was a very simple situation. He said he had always told the Russians a very simple story, that we were sending Lend-Lease aid to Russia because we felt by so doing we were helping the United States. He never tried to drive any bargains with Lend-Lease aid. It seems that some of our other government officials wanted to use Lend-Lease aid to get information. Faymonville said he always stuck to his original story and that these U.S. government officials did not like it. Apparently that is the reason he was recalled.

Colonel Faymonville thinks that so far as the future is concerned it is all-important that the United States and Russia stand together. He doesn't like the idea of our standing with England against Russia or playing second fiddle to England in our relationship with Russia. He thinks we should deal with Russia directly. While he did not refer to the State Department, he plainly inferred that there were officials there who believed in playing the British game . . .

DECEMBER 14, 1943

Mrs. Boettiger[1] told me that the labor groups out in Seattle were very anxious to have me come here. She understood that the labor groups in Portland, Oregon, were going to call me and ask me to come to Portland. She thought Seattle was better than Portland . . .

She says that the National Committeeman in Washington is a Farley man and that the State Chairman is a dried-up little lawyer with one stenographer whose heart is in the right place but who has very little energy. In brief, the Democratic Party in Washington doesn't amount

[1] Anna Roosevelt Boettiger, the President's daughter and then the wife of John Boettiger, publisher of the Seattle *Post-Intelligencer*.

to much. The labor influx into Washington from the East has brought a great many people who are Republican rather than Democratic. The program for complete registration may bring about as many Republican registrants as Democratic. Mrs. Boettiger said she thought there ought to be meetings coming out now endorsing her father and myself. She is very liberal in her views. She is in town with her three children so that she can be with the rest of the family when they gather around the President for the first two nights after his return. She said she just could not think of missing those first two evenings. The President's unequaled powers as a storyteller apparently fascinate his children as they fascinate everybody else.

I told Mrs. Boettiger that I thought the President had been playing the international game with remarkable skill. She said yes, that her father long had it on his mind to avoid the mistakes of Woodrow Wilson and she thought he had done it to a remarkable degree. We agreed that it would be a splendid thing if the President would make a report on his trip to the Congress. She thought there was very widespread resentment that the Reuter News Agency had scooped the American press. I said I did not think there was much resentment except among the newspaper men and among those who wanted an excuse to criticize Great Britain or the conduct of the war.

I told her I felt quite good about the situation generally, that I thought things were going to fit together very well by next summer or fall. She herself apparently did not feel optimistic at all. She has no idea whether the President will run for a fourth term or not. She said in 1940 her mother and she tried again and again to find out whether he was going to run for a third term and did not have any luck. Apparently she is going to pump her father again as hard as she can. At the same time she feels her father is quite right in not taking either her or her mother completely into his confidence . . .

DECEMBER 15, 1943

Lowdermilk[1] told me some very interesting things about his experience in northern China, north and a little east of Chungking, just north of Tsinling Shan mountains and a little west of Sian but east of Lanchow. He had three Chinese technicians working with him and he got them pretty well indoctrinated with the principles of soil erosion. He

[1] Walter Clay Lowdermilk of the Soil Conservation Service of the Department of Agriculture had just returned from China where he had served as an adviser to the Chinese government on soil and forest conservation and flood control.

told me that he very much wanted to stop off in Palestine but the State Department refused him a visa to stop there. The State Department is definitely anti-Zionist. Lowdermilk himself feels that the Arabs would greatly profit if the Jews were able to have a free hand in developing Palestine and Transjordania. He is strongly in favor of bringing in water from the Mediterranean Sea by canal to the Jordan River, thus developing power. They could utilize all the streams running into the Jordan River for irrigation purposes. He says there are great possibilities of mining magnesium, bromine, and potassium in the Dead Sea. He says the prosperity created by the Jews would have great effect on the surrounding Arabs . . .

McDougall wanted to talk to me about future plans for food and agriculture and UNRRA as segments of the United Nations organization . . .

Of course I made no commitment whatever on his suggestion that I head up this show. He said he would get in touch with me in early January because no matter what I decided to do, he wanted to get my advice. He asked how it would be to have Roosevelt head up the whole show. I told him the President's name was invaluable and that the President had many excellent characteristics, among others, his acute appreciation of geography. I told him I didn't think the President was a good executive but that nevertheless his methods seemed to get results and that was what counted. He said it was his impression that the President at heart was really an aristocrat. He said the President was infinitely preferable to Churchill, and he got to reminiscing about Churchill in an interesting way. He mentioned how when Montgomery was given charge of the troops in North Africa, Churchill had him in for a talk and asked him if he was fit for the job. Montgomery started out by saying that he got up early every morning and took a run before breakfast; that he didn't smoke or drink alcohol; and that as a result he was 100 percent efficient. Churchill replied, "Well, I don't get up until noon, I start drinking alcohol at once and take it continuously all day, and when I'm not drinking I have a cigar in my mouth; I am 200 percent efficient."

Churchill got to moralizing with one of his cronies, saying, "History is going to be awfully hard on those folks who stood by when they saw this war coming in the thirties and didn't do anything about it; yes, it is going to be awfully hard; I am damn sure it is going to be hard because I am going to write the history!" (McDougall suggested about this time that the smartest thing Churchill could do would be to retire as soon as the war was over because if he did so, he could then rank as one of the three or four greatest Englishmen of all times. If he didn't resign he would be proved by events to be very incompetent.)

Churchill made a crack about Sir Stafford Cripps, just after Cripps left the room, saying, "There but for the grace of God goes God." McDougall says there is some truth in Churchill's observation about Cripps; that he is characterized by too much surface goodness and too great a certainty that he is right . . .

DECEMBER 17, 1943

. . . Baruch dwelt at some length on the great power of the United States and on the need of the United States being strong if this country were to do what she should both for herself and for the world. I asked him if he thought a recession was inevitable after the war. He said, "Decidedly not." John Hancock[1] agreed with him. He said everything depended on our having confidence, confidence that we were going to be living in a peaceful world. Baruch mentioned how strong he had been for Woodrow Wilson and the League of Nations.

Then he went on to speak on the subject which I think he really had on his mind, and that was adequate protection for synthetic rubber. Baruch did not suggest a tariff on rubber although I think that was what was in Hancock's mind . . . Baruch started out by saying, "We have the synthetic rubber plants paying high wages. The British and Dutch don't need to get us down again. We should have a heart for the coolie labor in Java and the Straits Settlements. We should demand that they raise the wages of this coolie labor. I am thinking about the little fellow." I replied to him, "Yes, I know that labor over there is only getting about eighteen cents a day and I will agree that its productivity entitles it to a higher wage. I am sure, however, that a heavy tariff on rubber would make these people much worse off than they are now. I am dead against a tariff." Hancock started to object to my position then stopped. Baruch did not take direct issue but began again to let his heart bleed for the poor people in the East Indies. I said to Baruch, "I am wondering if under the guise of getting their wages raised, there may not be a danger that most of them will lose their eighteen cents and finally get only five cents a day. Aren't you really trying to get these people off of the rubber market of the United

[1] John M. Hancock, an industrial banker, had worked with Baruch in 1942 on the rubber survey and was collaborating with him again on planning for postwar industrial reconversion.

States?" I then suggested that if there were an opportunity to bargain with the British, it might be well to get them to adopt the principle of gradually increasing the wages to at least twice what they were now.

After some more discussion, Milo and Baruch both claimed that we saw eye to eye. I am not altogether sure . . .

Baruch held forth at some length about the butter-mouthed Englishmen all the time advancing hypocritical arguments so that they could get in position to exploit subject peoples. In his argument, I was never quite sure whether Baruch was more interested in getting rid of British competition so American businessmen could make more money or more interested in the subject peoples.

Toward the close of the conference, Baruch was apparently assuming that I was going to be a negotiator at the peace table and urged that he be my "evil partner." He spoke of the firm of Wallace and Baruch and said, "Now when they (I suppose he meant the British although I don't know for sure) ask for things which they should not have and which you can't deny, just send them over to me saying, 'I agree with you but I don't believe I can get this by with that fellow Baruch.'"

The old boy is still a clever operator, apparently placing a small bet on the possibility that I might one way or another eventually be in a position of some power, and he is putting in his bid to work with me . . .

I mentioned to Baruch that the Jews were getting very uneasy about Palestine and the Arabian princes, the oil there, etc. He said he had a solution of his own for that, which he had talked about to the President. It was to have each of the United Nations agree to take a certain quota of Jews. I said that offhand it might sound good but I did not know if it would satisfy the Jews.

Baruch made the point that the biggest card the President had to play was the productive might of the United States. No other nation had the mass production technique of the United States. We had twice saved the world because of our mass production technique. Baruch thinks we are going to furnish immense quantities of produce to the outside world. I asked him to name the top five. He did not name a single one but said that in general we would furnish products that could be made by mass production. Hancock said such as automobiles, refrigerators, etc., etc.

The President opened up cabinet by saying how much impressed he was with Chiang Kai-shek at the Cairo meeting, said he had the most delightful smile on occasion. He went into some detail about what had been promised to China, saying again what has already appeared in the press. The President then went on to say that he tried to get things fixed up so we could give Hong Kong back to China but Churchill was very mulish on the subject.

At Teheran it was apparent that the President and Stalin stood together on the subject of an adequate second front. Stalin and the President finally got what they wanted but not all of it. As a result of this partial triumph over the British at Teheran, the President later on had to give in to them to some extent on agreeing to operations in the eastern Mediterranean. The President thought that the full strength of the landing craft should be used for the Burma campaign but the British insisted on part of it going to the Mediterranean campaign.

With regard to Turkey, the President said he did not know whether they were coming in or not and he did not think it made an awful lot of difference.

The President said that Stalin was very keen about Manchuria going back to China, said that all that he was interested in for Russia was a warm-water port. The President then suggested that Dairen, the extreme southeastern port in Manchuria, be made an open port and that the railroad across from Siberia to Manchuria down to Dairen be put under such management as to permit the Russians free access to the shores of the Yellow Sea. Stalin said he had never thought of this idea and thought it was a splendid one.

The President said that Stalin felt very tough toward both Germany and Japan. The President suggested dividing Germany up into five small countries and two international areas. One of the international areas would include Kiel, Bremen, Hamburg, Lübeck, etc. This area would be made into a series of free ports open to the use of all the nations. Stalin said he had not thought about this . . .

Stalin spoke about access to the Persian Gulf and the President suggested a free port and a railroad that would give Russia the same access to the Persian Gulf as to the Yellow Sea. At this point, the President digressed to speak about what a perfectly marvelous job our soldiers were doing in Iran. He seemed to think there was more poverty in Iran than any place he had ever seen. He said 1 percent of the people were living off the fat of the land and all the rest were sharecroppers. There is bad water there, and many kinds of disease.

Stalin said the thing he was interested in about Germany was to make sure that she would not fight again within 20 years. The President said there had been absolutely no discussion about Palestine.

Apparently the President had a rather hard time with Churchill all the way. He said the British were never keen about the Chinese [being] counted as one of the Big Four. With Stalin it was all right, however . . .

Just before he called on Cordell Hull, the President told how at Moscow[1] Cordell had prepared the way for him. Hull returned the compliment by saying that he had had an easy time at Moscow because they knew the President was coming.

Francis Biddle told about the difficulties with the Japs at Tule Lake. Jimmie Byrnes spoke up and said he thought Dillon Myer[2] was not a strong enough man to handle the Tule Lake situation and recommended that it be put under Francis Biddle. Biddle did not want it and suggested Ickes. Ickes said he did not want it and Jimmie Byrnes said that at the present time it was on the President's doorstep and he did not want it either. Biddle is going to take it. Byrnes mentioned about the various misdeeds of the Japs at Tule Lake. The President suggested that a strong hand be used and it did not make any difference what the Japs in Japan thought about it. I spoke up at once and said, "Wait a minute, Mr. President. It makes a lot of difference to the Americans whom the Japs have in the camps in the Philippine Islands." Jimmie Byrnes took my side at this point and the President backed away.

The President gave it as his opinion that Washington was just like a squirrel cage, that the people in Washington had lost all sense of perspective. He thought the people of the United States were all right but Washington was very bad. He spoke about giving a lecture to Congress . . . A little later on he asked me what had happened among my charges (he always tends to refer to the senators when talking to me as charges), said that when he was in Oran in North

---

[1] At the conference of foreign ministers that preceded the Teheran meeting.

[2] Dillon S. Myer, a veteran official of the Department of Agriculture, had become director of the War Relocation Authority in 1942. At this time he was under severe criticism from the press and the Congress because a group of militant Japanese-Americans at the internment camp at Tule Lake had gone on strike in protest against the lamentable treatment they were receiving. Those and other Tule Lake internees had earlier refused to pledge their loyalty to the United States largely because that pledge would have permitted them only the right to enter the armed services, and would have cost their interned and confused parents their important support. Myer's critics, advocates of repressive measures, understood little about the conditions that had provoked the trouble, which Myer had tried unsuccessfully to dispel. After his failure to do so, the Army took over the camp where a tense quiet merely obscured the still unresolved problems; see Audrie Girdner and Anne Loftis, *The Great Betrayal* (New York, 1969) and especially Dorothy S. Thomas and Richard S. Nishimoto, *The Spoilage* (Berkeley, 1946).

Africa, he smelled something very bad, that he had learned that the southern Democrats were going to start a new party. He asked me what was back of it all. I told him how Senator Guffey had issued a statement after the failure of the soldier vote and that this had touched off Byrd, Bailey and Cotton Ed Smith but I said I did not regard it as too serious.[1] I turned to Jimmie Byrnes and Hull for confirmation and they both agreed. I mentioned the editorials in the Raleigh *Observer* and the Nashville *Tennesseean*. Jimmie Byrnes, in talking on the soldier vote situation, placed all the blame for it on John Rankin of Mississippi and said he thought it was going to work out into a good political issue.

The President indicated that he thought that one of the best things that could happen to the people of the United States would be to have a few German bombs fall here to wake us up.

Referring to de Gaulle, he said that the French people were more and more getting on to de Gaulle and that the people coming out of France were indicating that the people of France did not want de Gaulle. This point of view, which the President has held steadily, is totally different from that which is presented in . . . *The Nation*. It will be most interesting to see which ultimately proves to be correct as to the sentiment of the real French people—the President or the Gaullists.

The President said that England wanted the restoration of the Great France. Stalin said, however, that before France could amount to anything, it would be necessary to get rid of the old French bureau-

[1] Republicans and dissident Democrats had defeated the administration's voting bill. It would have established a bipartisan War Ballot Commission to send ballots to all servicemen in advance of the 1944 election. Congressman John E. Rankin of Mississippi argued that the bill violated states' rights under the Constitution, while Robert Taft feared that soldiers would be intimidated into voting for the President. The Senate, in December 1943, and the House the next February endorsed a substitute measure proposed by James Eastland of Mississippi, John McClellan of Arkansas, and Kenneth McKellar of Tennessee that merely recommended that the states adopt legislation enabling soldiers to vote. Later legislation permitted states to use a federal ballot to that end, but Roosevelt's bill had lost. When it was killed, Senator Joe Guffey had castigated those of his fellow Democrats who helped to defeat it. There rushed to the counterattack doughty southern Tories, including Harry Byrd of Virginia, Josiah W. Bailey of North Carolina, and Ellison D. Smith of South Carolina, with Byrd gladly suggesting the need for a third party of southern Democrats to hold the balance of political power in Congress for the good of their enlightened section of the country. From the first, Wallace had supported Roosevelt's plan. He hoped, he said, that Congress would make certain that servicemen received ballots, for "as a matter of simple justice, every American soldier, sailor, and marine should have an opportunity to vote in 1944."

cracy and the aged, time-serving politicians. According to Stalin, France can't amount to anything until there is totally new blood running the show.

Stalin said there must be a world police force. The President said, "If there is to be a world police force, there will have to be police stations at strategic points." Stalin said, "What are the strategic points?" The President started to list some of them but Stalin spoke up and said, "You will want Dakar, won't you?" . . .

That President said that for three days he, Churchill, and Stalin sat around a very big table, 30 feet or so in diameter, and were not getting anywhere at all. On the fourth day they got results. Stimson spoke up at this point and said he had read the minutes. The results had to do with the establishment of a real second front.

The President mentioned how Stalin was continually ribbing Churchill. The President also mentioned that he wanted to do away with the word Reich. Stalin said, "I don't care what you do with the word. What I want is to do away with the fact."

The President referred to how he had a hard time with Churchill at Cairo on his way back and how he finally had to give in to Churchill and agree to divert 18 landing barges from Burma to the eastern Mediterranean. This was directly in contradiction to what the President had promised Chiang Kai-shek. The President immediately informed Chiang about it who was very much annoyed. All the President could do, of course, was to promise we would manufacture the 18 additional barges in the United States and get them over to Burma as soon as possible.

DECEMBER 18, 1943

At the Big Four meeting at the White House this morning (Jimmie Byrnes was present as well as the President), the President told the same story as he had at the cabinet meeting the preceding afternoon. However, he went into much more detail about the way in which Stalin ribbed Churchill. At the evening banquets the conversations apparently were altogether in the form of toasts.

Stalin said that thinking about the future peace of the world, he decided there could not be any assurance of peace until 100,000 of the leading Prussian army officers had been killed. He might be willing to cut this down to 50,000 but he thought that was as low as he could go. Churchill was annoyed at this and said it had not been the British habit to slaughter prisoners of war, especially officers. The President then proposed a toast and said, "Suppose we compromise and make it 49,000." The President looked on the whole conversation as deliberate ribbing of Churchill by Stalin. However, it seemed that Stalin was more or less serious.

After a while, Churchill got into the spirit of the ribbing and got up and gave a toast in which he began to make a play on the word "rosy." He claimed that everyone coming in contact with Russia had become more or less rosy. The red color was beginning to take effect. After Churchill made a number of smart cracks along this line, Stalin interrupted with a toast, "To the rosiness of humanity, that which indicates a state of perfect health." The President fell into the spirit of the occasion and finally proposed a toast, "To the rainbow, the symbol of hope which contains all the colors." No doubt all of this was taken down with great care and will be available to future historians.

The President again told the story of how he said, "I want to do away with the word Reich." But this time he added the phrase, "in any language." I spoke up and asked the President what did Churchill think of the phrase "in any language." The President said, "I don't think he liked it."

The President then went on to talk about dividing up Germany into five states, a proposal which did not please Churchill but did please Stalin. I interrupted to ask, "Did you propose a customs union for the five German states?" The President said, "No, I would propose a customs union for all of Europe."

At the cabinet meeting I did not get it clear as to the second area which was to be internationalized. The first one, which the President described on Friday, was composed of the old Hanseatic German free ports with a strip of land somewhat wider than the Panama Canal back from the ocean. The second area included the Ruhr and Saar Basin where the iron and coal mines have served as a source of power for the industrialists of both France and Germany, who have from time to time precipitated international conflict. The President defended Stalin's attitude with regard to Esthonia, Latvia, and Lithuania. He said Stalin did not want Finland but did want that part of Finland which was necessary to protect Leningrad and which Russia had obtained in the war against Finland in 1940. The Russian idea about Poland is to take that part of Poland east of the old Curson Line, that part largely inhabited by Ukrainians, that part which Russia had when she moved in in late 1939. Russia, however, according to the President, wants a strong Poland and would give East Prussia to Poland. Russia would give to Poland an area of land from Germany equal to that which she lost in East Poland. In view of the fact that the land which Poland would obtain from Germany would be of better quality than that which she would lose on the east, Stalin thought Poland should be satisfied. This proposal is very much like that which was suggested to me personally by Anthony Eden some six or seven months ago.

Stalin does not want the Dardanelles but he does want the control to be denationalized sufficiently so Russia can have free access from the Black Sea to the Mediterranean Sea. Apparently the President and Stalin spoke each other's language and got along famously . . .

Don Nelson Luncheon Conference

I asked Don about his trip to Russia. He was exceedingly enthusiastic about the Russians. He said we can't judge Russia by Moscow. He spoke of visiting the big industrial centers about Tashkent, Magnitogorsk, and Novosibirsk. He said these cities typically contained only about 200,000 people three or four years ago but now they contained from 700,000 to a million. The workers have been moved out of Leningrad, Stalingrad, Kiev and Kharkov along with the factories to these cities. In this area there seems to be no great food problem. The workers have joined with the cooperative and collective farm groups and do a real job of food production. The factory manager in one of these cities told proudly how many thousands of tons of food he had stored up. In the western part of Russia, there is shortage of food. The shortage will not interfere with military operations but the civilians will go very hungry.

Nelson was enormously impressed with the high sense of participation which the workers in Russia seem to have. Special cash prizes are handed out to the groups which produce the most. Apparently everyone is paid according to his ability. But it is not only on a material basis. For example, when the factory workers were evacuated from western Russia, they evacuated just as carefully the artists because they felt the musicians, et al., were necessary to keep up the spirit of the people. Art is a people's art in Russia.

Don told how he had been laid over for an extra two or three days in Tashkent and how the people who were with him insisted that he go to the opera that evening. He asked what was on at the opera. They said *Prince Igor*. He said he had seen *Prince Igor* and was not interested. An hour or so later they came back and said the program had been changed and they would put on *Swan Lake* ballet for him. This was late afternoon. Don attended the ballet and was amazed how perfectly it was done. He could not see how they could change at such a late hour and yet do a thorough job. Their plane was delayed several more days and he saw several more performances and they were all excellent.

Nelson has the impression that there is in some ways more free enterprise in Russia than here in the United States. He talked quite a while about what would be necessary to maintain the things that we deem necessary in the United States and yet get the driving power of participation by the common man.

I put it this way, "How can we get the profit system to working for everybody?" Don Nelson began to tell me about a plan of his to maintain full employment in the United States after the war. He said the weakest spot in our economy would be in the capital goods industry. He said, "We have a tremendous supply of machine tools, construction machinery, et cetera, hanging over the market. If these businesses go into a tailspin, they will carry the rest of our economy along with them." He, therefore, proposed that we work out a scheme for trading these materials to the outside world for building up huge stockpiles of the basic materials like copper, tungsten, manganese, etc., etc. He would sterilize these stockpiles and release them to the public only when there is a two-thirds vote of both Houses of Congress or a majority vote of both Houses and the signature of the President certifying to a national emergency. This would prevent the huge material stockpiles from creating business depression in the local raw material industries.

Don, like John Hancock, believes that our technological "know-how" in certain lines is the wonder of the world and that it can be made of great service to the world.

Don is very much disgusted with the Washington intrigue and would like to get away as soon as possible. He says Charles Wilson also wants to leave . . . I asked him what he (Don) was going to do. He said he did not know, that he thought he might go with a company which would be working on a worldwide basis on irrigation, flood control, and power projects. I asked him why he did not stay on and work on the problem of reconversion.[1] He replied, "That is Baruch's job." I

---

[1] Nelson was hoping to begin the process of reconversion early in 1944 so that increasing production for civilian use would take up the slack of declining orders for military equipment, and thus sustain full employment and help small business. The War Department considered that prospect potentially dangerous for its supply lines and immediately crippling to civilian morale which, in the military view, should not be diverted from the war. Like the War Department, Charles E. Wilson soon found himself at odds with Nelson over the issue. For an account of the controversy unabashedly favorable to Nelson, see Bruce Catton, *The War Lords of Washington* (New York, 1948).

said I had had lunch with Baruch, Milo, and John Hancock. He spoke up and said Hancock was the worst of all the New Deal haters, that he was so known in New York City, that he hated the President and all the New Dealers. I said, "He looks to me like he drinks a lot." Nelson said that was not true, that he did not think Hancock drinks at all.

With regard to Baruch, Nelson said he had never been able to figure out just what Baruch was really up to. He expressed no feeling either against or for Barney. I told him I had picked it up indirectly, but not from Baruch, that Baruch did not like Nelson because he felt that Nelson was close to Harry Hopkins. Nelson replied, "It is true. I am close to Harry Hopkins. I think a lot of Harry. Harry has never let anything stand in the way of winning the war and winning it as soon as possible. Everything has been subjected to that one objective." I said I thought that that was true, that Harry had devoted every effort even to the extent of imperiling his health to win the war. Nelson ventured that he was under the impression that Jimmie Byrnes was not any too enthusiastic about Hopkins. Apparently, therefore, there is gradually shaping up an inner circle conflict which might conceivably find Harry Hopkins' men, Jesse Jones, Stettinius, and Don Nelson on one side with Baruch's men and Jimmie Byrnes and Harold Ickes on the other.

I told Nelson that I was beginning to think that at the present time Baruch in a sense was a front man for John Hancock. Nelson said that was his opinion also, that Hancock was the action man behind Baruch. Perhaps the situation will simmer down eventually to John Hancock vs. Jesse Jones. Both are power grabbers of the first order.

DECEMBER 20, 1943

Mrs. Emma Guffey Miller[1] came in to push for the amendment to the Constitution—equal rights for women. She wanted me to write her a letter about it. I told her to have her brother, Senator Guffey, fix up a letter and I would take a look at it . . .

---

[1] Emma Guffey Miller, Joe Guffey's sister and the Democratic National Committeewoman from Pennsylvania, had been a devoted champion of women's suffrage, a member of the Consumers League, and a seconder of the successive nominations for President of Alfred E. Smith and Franklin D. Roosevelt. In 1943 she was legislative chairwoman of the National Woman's Party for an Equal Rights Amendment.

JANUARY 1, 1944

De Lozada came around to see me on Saturday to ask if I thought he should give up his fight in view of the State Department opposition. I told him that I had known for many years how he had felt about the policy of the owners of the Bolivian tin mines and that I thought he ought to be true to himself.[1] I said, "For my part, I can't have anything to do with the affairs of other nations. I am influenced solely by what is good for the United States, the Good Neighbor Policy, and the hemisphere." I asked de Lozada about the anti-Semitism comment of Larry Duggan. He said there was a man connected with the former government by the name of Medina who had illegally let some 15,000 Jews into Bolivia, charging them what the traffic would bear. Sometimes he charged as much as $5,000 or $10,000. As a result of this, he had made more than a million dollars personally. De Lozada said these 15,000 Jews, locating chiefly in the two or three larger cities, had created a very difficult competitive situation among the middle-class Bolivians. They were intensely dissatisfied with the illegal action taken by Medina; therefore, the Estenssoro party had gone on record very strongly against Medina. De Lozada said he had talked to influential Jews about this and that the new government had really nothing to fear from the anti-Semitic action. I also told de Lozada that Edgar Mowrer had told me that the new government was being looked on with fear by Chile because of its emphasis on getting a port at Arica. De Lozada said that the new government was not hitting that as hard as Peñaranda did, that Peñaranda talked about Arica and access to the sea all the time.

I told de Lozada that from the standpoint of the people of the hemisphere, it seemed to me the thing for Bolivia to stand for would be making Arica a free port, that I did not think Bolivia ought to imperil the peace of the hemisphere by talking too vigorously about getting Arica back again.

Enrique mentioned a number of things which the State Department had done which indicate that there are certain individuals in the State

---

[1] On December 21, 1943, Major Gualberto Villarroel and his forces overthrew the Bolivian government of President Enrique Peñaranda. Only Argentina recognized the new regime, which most observers considered undemocratic. The State Department decided against recognition on January 25, 1944. In the weeks preceding that decision, de Lozada served as the confidential agent in Washington for the new government. As such, while lobbying for recognition, he argued against the prevalent and reasonable American identification of the new junta with the fascist Ramirez government of Argentina.

Department who will stoop to any level. He said that for the time being, he had blocked their move looking toward a counterrevolution. Larry Duggan had told me he would have much more confidence in the new regime if it included the P I R group led by Antonio Arze.[1] I asked de Lozada where Arze was. He said he had left Mexico for Bolivia but the State Department, using Panagra and the Peruvian government as stooges, had blocked Arze from getting any further than Panama, claiming that the Peruvian government would not give him a visa to fly over Peru, so the State Department is in the curious position of wanting to see the P I R group included in the new government and at the same time of doing everything possible to prevent the inclusion. In other words, the State Department, outside of Duggan, wants a revolution to the right and only gives lip service to the formation of a government which would really help the people of Bolivia get a higher standard of living. De Lozada is convinced that Hull himself is probably all right. He wants in some way to get to Secretary Hull so he can tell him the true story.

JANUARY 3, 1944

. . . Gene[2] began talking about Harry Hopkins. He gave specific details as to how Hopkins had tried to cut my throat at various times. I have no doubt that Gene is absolutely accurate in reporting this. He said he had told the President that he has got to get rid of Harry Hopkins. Gene says the Democratic National Committeemen, when they meet here January 22, are going to demand that Hopkins be gotten rid of before the national campaign. Gene said he had told the President that he has made a great mistake in having Harry Hopkins' friends, Ed Stettinius' friends, and Averill Harriman's friends, et al., at the White House on Sunday evenings when he should be having in senators and congressmen. Gene said, "Oh, yes, I know the businessmen affiliated with the so-called Morgan Banking crowd proclaim themselves as being very friendly to the President and to Hopkins. But when it comes to the final showdown, they won't vote for the President and there aren't enough of them to make any difference anyway."

I told Gene that while I knew that Hopkins had been wholeheartedly against me, that I felt he also had been wholeheartedly for winning the war, and that he had worked with the President to good advantage

[1] José Antonio Arze, leader of the Bolivian left.
[2] Eugene Casey.

to win the war. Gene came back and said, "You are a Christian and
I love you for it. But you are wrong about your attitude toward
Harry. He is selfish and a no-good and I am going to get him" . . .

JANUARY 7, 1944

. . . I told General Marshall about my concern with the Argentine
situation, that I feared that the Argentine military clique and the
fascists' nests were up to no good.[1] The problem is not only an immediate one but a long-distance one as well. I said I thought Argentina
would be a center for fascist infection after the war was over and that
she would endeavor to be so strong militarily at any time that she
could take over Brazil and all the rest of Latin America put together.
I found that the General was quite fully awake to the danger and as a
matter of fact had been putting in a lot of time that morning talking
with [the] State Department about it. He is very much concerned with
the way in which we have furnished military material to the various
Latin American nations.

He also was much concerned with the inefficiency of our own government. He said he had found again and again that the British were
much better coordinated than we. He said the British secretarial system resulted in the British fighting out their difficulties down the line,
then presenting a coordinated front when the time came for meeting
an external problem. Marshall says the President oftentimes takes action and the only way he, the General, learns about it is through the
British.

I did not ask him anything whatsoever about his pronouncement
on the strike situation[2] but he volunteered that he had inside informa-

[1] The Treasury Department, as Wallace knew, gravely disturbed by evidence of
Nazi activity in Argentina, was proposing to freeze Argentine assets in the
United States and to cut British purchasing of Argentine wheat and beef by
substituting American and Canadian supplies. The State Department had long
opposed the former course and the War Shipping Administration and the War
Food Administration found the latter impracticable. The Argentine involvement in the coup d'état in Bolivia, however, so angered Hull that in January he
reversed his policy and agreed to the freezing of Argentine assets. Before the
Treasury could promulgate the necessary order, the Ramirez government conveniently discovered an espionage plot by Axis agents and, on January 27,
severed relations with Germany and Japan. The State Department, with White
House support, then canceled authority for the freezing order. As it worked
out, within another month Axis agents were again freely at work in Argentina;
see John Morton Blum, *From the Morgenthau Diaries*, 3 vols., *Years of War III*
(Boston, 1967), pp. 194–206.
[2] To prevent a threatening strike by the railroad brotherhoods, Roosevelt on
December 27, 1943, had directed the War Department to seize and operate the

tion that the Germans were going to use the American strikes in a strong propaganda drive. The reason he spoke out he said was to forestall the Germans. This did not sound so very reasonable to me but I made no comment whatever.

Marshall is very deeply dissatisfied with the State Department, feels they know nothing whatever about administration. Marshall has an excellent conception of orderly administration and is a very fine man. He makes no pretense of knowing anything about political considerations . . .

The Undersecretary of State for Canada was very strong on lower tariffs and very keen about the idea that the source of prosperity was a larger volume of world trade. McDougall and I took the point of view that the altogether important thing was full employment. McDougall argued for a conference on full employment. Twentyman[1] thought the important thing for the future of the prosperity of the world was to have lower tariffs in the United States. I said I thought the important thing was to have full employment in the United States, that if we have full employment we would import over the tariff walls. Theoretically I agree with Twentyman and have argued that philosophy ever since 1920. However, I am not now as sure as Mr. Twentyman that tariffs are so all-important. Politically it may be impossible to get the adjustment in tariffs which the United States, a creditor nation, ought to make. That doesn't mean the world is sunk provided there is full employment in the United States . . .

JANUARY 10, 1944

. . . At the Big Four meeting, the President seemed to be in excellent spirits. He still showed some evidence of his cold. The President rather indicated that Congress had been lying down on the job and it was time for them to get busy . . .

I told the President I hoped he was paying some attention to the Argentine situation. He said Hull was coming in tomorrow with a plan for our stopping the purchase of Argentine beef. I said, "Do you have a plan also for having the British stop their purchase of beef?" He said no, that the British would not cooperate. He is quite indignant at

---

roads. They were returned to private management three weeks later after the President had successfully arbitrated the outstanding issues. The crisis, potentially damaging to internal lines of supply, so disturbed Marshall that he had considered resigning in protest against labor's demands for higher wages, which he considered unpatriotic.

[1] Wallace probably meant Undersecretary Tweedyman.

the British for their failure to play ball in the Argentine situation. I said I thought this shutting off of Argentine beef would be popular in the Middle West and the mountain states but indicated that the matter which I thought was of the greatest concern was the way in which Argentine was rearming, that the Duperial Chemical Company was bringing about a very rapid production of explosives and that Argentina was rapidly getting into position to clean up South America as she wanted to or at any rate to throw her weight around in the same way Germany did in the thirties. The President promised he would look into this military situation in Argentine . . .

Barkley told a story of how he had been making speeches down in Kentucky and how they had asked him questions about everything under the sun. Finally some one asked him what about the fourth term. Barkley said he answered it in this way. He said it reminded him of a story when Senator Bankhead, father of the present senator, died and Tom Heflin decided he would run for the place. Heflin apparently was in the House at the time. He went down to Alabama and visited around there, came back to Washington. The newspaper correspondents asked him, "Well, how about it?" Heflin replied, "Well, there was so much public clamorment for me running that I guess I will have to do it."

Barkley in many ways is a joy forever. He is loyal and steadfast and has a sense of humor. Undoubtedly he is one of the finest of the Democratic senators . . .

At the Russian Embassy were present Secretary of the Treasury Morgenthau and his wife, Secretary of the Navy and Mrs. Knox, Admiral Leahy, Assistant Secretary of War McCloy[1] and various Soviet army and navy and Purchasing Commission attachés.

The Ambassador started out the evening in the middle of the first course by a toast to President Roosevelt. I responded with a toast to Marshal Stalin. The toasts then became thick and fast. Mrs. Morgenthau gave a toast to the Russian women. There were various toasts to the Russian soldiers, to the American soldiers, to the American and British seamen. Henry Morgenthau, after strong urging by Mrs. Knox, gave a toast to Churchill and the heroic British nation. Mrs. Knox gave a toast to Chiang Kai-shek. General Watson gave a toast to the artillery. Sir Ronald Campbell got up and gave a toast saying, "Here is the Scotch toast: Here's to us. Who is like us? Damn few." He gave this in a broad Scotch accent. Mrs. Knox, who was sitting next to me, said, "That is the toast we always use in the English-speaking Union

[1] John J. McCloy, Stimson's right-hand man.

up in Manchester, New Hampshire." I told Madame Gromyko I thought this toast was an exceedingly aristocratic one. She thought so too and urged that I give a toast for real democracy. So I got up and said I had been inspired by Madame Gromyko to give a toast in Russian. The Russian Ambassador translated the toast almost precisely word for word as follows: "The Vice President drinks to victory and to the realization of new possibilities for the common man of all lands." The absolutely precise translation of what I said in Russian would have been: "I drink to complete victory and to new opportunities for the common man of all countries" . . .

JANUARY 17, 1944
HENRY A. WALLACE TO FRANKLIN D. ROOSEVELT

Dear Mr. President:

. . . the keystone of the German foreign policy is to drive a wedge between Russia on the one hand, and the British and Americans on the other. Such a wedge, successfully driven, represents the only hope the Germans have—barring a secret weapon of unexpected power, which I don't think they have.

The hope of an enduring peace depends in very large measure on closer relationships between the United States and Russia. The Germans are willing to go to any lengths to prevent that from coming to pass.

Another thought suggests itself to me and that is that the German counterespionage may have reached such a high degree of perfection that it may plant certain documents[1] for the specific purpose of promoting dissension . . .

[1] Wallace was replying to a confidential memorandum from the President of January 14, 1944, about an alleged document from the German Foreign Office which proved later to be a forgery. Roosevelt's memo read in part:
The enclosed I am sending to you in utter confidence because I am sure you would want me to. The gist of it is that you talked to brother-in-law, that he passed it on to Switzerland, that then it fell into the hands of the Germans from whom the American secret organization picked it up. Obviously, of course, the story told in it is so utterly untrue that I am sure it could not have originated from your brother-in-law . . .
The enclosure read:
The Vice President's general political comments on the Moscow Conference were the most interesting part of the Swiss Minister's report . . . Now that it is over, everyone who is familiar with the results of the conference is certain that the British and Americans alone must win World War II, possibly even against Russia, and that Russia means to dominate the whole of Europe and has already made substantial progress toward this end. The main outcome of the Moscow Conference is not apparent so much in the

JANUARY 18, 1944

Conversation between the Vice President and Larry Duggan, January 18, 1944

VP said he called on President Alfonso López (of Colombia) yesterday afternoon and spent nearly all his time talking about the peril of fascism by way of Argentina. It may have been indiscreet but that is the way the VP felt, so he laid it on thick . . . The President was friendly to the VP as a person but he apparently thought the idea was unrealistic. Larry said he was surprised; that the State Department had received assurances from Colombia that they would "go along" on measures to protect other countries from Argentine fascism. VP said no doubt they will go along but it is doubtful whether their heart would be in it.

VP thinks the Germans have their minds made up that they have lost this war and they are already preparing for the next one; that they have begun their preparations through Argentina, and that the next war will come via that country. With modern technology backed up by the cartel mechanism, they can work very rapidly. VP has particular reason to be alarmed because of a certain thing he has discovered. One aspect of it is a military secret and VP wants Larry not to speak of it. There are certain resources in southern Brazil that would be of great use to the Germans moving from Argentina as a base. VP would fear Argentine rearmament directed against Brazil, with the idea of getting certain parts of Brazil closest to Argentina under effective control, if not actual sovereignty.

Without mentioning any of the above to the President of Colombia, VP made the prophecy that if we are not exceedingly vigilant German fascism will get the upper hand in South America via Argentina.

VP said he doesn't think there is so much of this in the Bolivian revolution, although there may be some of it . . .

---

resolutions adopted as in the realization that the ideology of a World Revolution is still alive . . .

The report of the Swiss Minister is a valuable supplement to the reports from friendly diplomats which I [the German Minister to Switzerland] sent earlier. The reason that the above report contains so much more concrete information than the data which came to Bern from the American and British government is due to the fact that the Vice President was talking to the Swiss minister, his brother-in-law, in the greatest confidence . . .

To Wallace's dismay, Admiral Leahy, in his memoirs, referred to the fake document as true. After Wallace informed him of his error, Leahy, in a correction to his memoirs, retracted his statement. In the years since, that retraction has sometimes been overlooked by Wallace's critics.

JANUARY 22, 1944

Senator Truman came in to say he will probably be in St. Louis with me on February 13. He is anxious to have me come to meet Bob Hannegan,[1] the new chairman of the National Democratic Committee, at a party which the Missouri people are putting on in the Mayflower tonight. Truman repeated what he said, that he was eager to support me for Vice President again, that he and I had seen things just alike, etc., etc. . . .

JANUARY 25, 1944

. . . I arrived at Drew Pearson's home about ten-thirty and found Sumner Welles, Barnet Nover, Edgar Mowrer, Archie MacLeish.[2] I told them I thought the tendency in the United States now was toward getting our boys out of Europe at the earliest possible moment and then having as little as possible to do with Europe in the future. I said I thought every victory strengthened the growth of this kind of attitude. Then we discussed the article which Welles was putting in the Washington *Post* on Wednesday morning[3] . . . The central thesis in this approach is the mechanism for utilizing regional organizations in a world organization. On the whole, this approach seemed to me to be more promising than any other. In general terms, I myself have come out for the regional approach a year or so ago. Welles had some technical details which appear in this article . . . which make the regional approach somewhat more feasible. I told them I had been trying to get some senator to introduce this article into the *Congressional Record* and that I would talk to Senator Lister Hill about the need for stirring up interest along this line. We discussed quite frankly the danger of Secretary Hull being jealous of any such movement. Welles said that he thought Hull was for this general idea but that his whole

---

[1] Robert E. Hannegan, Commissioner of Internal Revenue, was elected chairman of the Democratic National Committee on January 22, 1944. Then and later, he organized the campaign to nominate Harry S. Truman for the vice-presidency in 1944. On July 1, 1945, Truman appointed Hannegan Postmaster General.

[2] Archibald MacLeish, poet and literary critic, Librarian of Congress (1939–44), had been director of the Office of Facts and Figures (1941–42) and assistant director of the Office of War Information (1942–43). In those roles he constantly urged the President to define and announce specific plans for a liberal peace.

[3] That article provided a preliminary statement about the kind of world organization that Welles described more fully in *The Time for Decision* (New York, 1944).

philosophy was to wait until the people had led the way and not to attempt in any way to form public opinion himself.

JANUARY 26, 1944

. . . Miss Olivarez[1] wanted me to come out with a statement urging the American people both in the United States and in Latin America, and particularly in Argentina, not to be deceived by this apparent change in front of the Argentine government in breaking off relations with the Axis. I called up Berle about it and reached the conclusion that I would say something like the following: "The real question in Argentina is not the breaking off of relations with the Axis but the cleaning out of the Nazi nests which are a center of infection of the whole hemisphere." (Later I decided not to do it . . .)

I also took up with Berle the significance of the Welles statement in the January 26 Washington *Post*. Berle said that Welles had devoted his life to thinking about problems of this sort, and that there was no difference between Welles and Hull so far as he (Berle) knew with regard to this particular matter. Berle said the difference between Hull and Welles was in an altogether different area. I asked Berle pointblank if it would not be helping Hull if public opinion were marshaled behind some such proposal as that of Welles. Berle thought it would. I asked Berle to consider the problem of Tom Connally. He had no suggestions in this field. Berle said the State Department and Hull in particular were quite aware of the need for Argentina going far beyond her present step. I told Berle how delighted I was to know this. I then went on to urge that as the State Department continued to move on Argentina, it should also consider straightening out the situation in Bolivia in terms of the people of Bolivia themselves. Berle immediately started talking against the present government, saying several members of the present government had promoted the overthrow in the office of Perón in Argentina,[2] etc., etc. This may or may

---

[1] Maria Rosa Olivarez of the Office of the Coordinator of Inter-American Affairs.
[2] Colonel Juan D. Perón, an Axis sympathizer, as American military intelligence had reported, still headed the strongest clique within the government of General Pedro P. Ramirez. In February 1944 Perón led a group of colonels in seizing the Argentine Foreign Office and then replacing Ramirez in the presidency with their puppet, General Edelmiro Farrell. The new government released the Axis agents whom Ramirez had imprisoned, nullified civil liberties, and accelerated a military build-up. Those developments persuaded the State Department, which had not recognized the Farrell government, to recall the American

not be true. I still have an absolutely open mind on that subject. It is quite within the realm of possibilities that evidence against the Bolivian government is planted evidence and that Berle has been taken in by it. It is also within the realm of possibilities that Berle has helped to plant the evidence. However, I am inclined to think that with regard to the Argentine matter, Berle is absolutely sincere. At the same time, I cannot help feeling that with respect to Bolivia, he is protecting either the Catholic church interest or the tin interests and that his sincerity may not be altogether complete. In other words, I still don't know whether Berle is completely sound both with regard to Bolivia and Argentina, whether he is sound only with respect to Argentina, or whether he is partially a deceiver and partially a man deceived. Certain aspects about Berle are quite satisfying with regard to the State Department because he does deal in facts and does take a definite attitude. I don't believe he understands the rank and file of the people in South America. I believe on the whole he is governed by certain principles of expediency in the service of his conception of what he believes is right and sound in the world. As to just what that conception really is, I still don't quite know. He is a good technician but psychologically twisted . . .

JANUARY 27, 1944

. . . At Governor Lehman's, Harry White of Treasury told me that considerable progress was being made on international plans,[1] that the final outcome would not look altogether like the procedure which he had advocated nor like the procedure which Lord Keynes had advocated. It would be a compromise but perhaps a little more like the American plan. White is very anxious for me to go to Russia, said Russia was the one country to which we could loan money safely in the postwar period. I told White I would be very glad to go to Russia . . .

Ambassador. For its part, the Bolivian government, which did recognize Farrell, moved away from Argentine influence during 1944 and on that account gained recognition from the United States.

[1] For what was to become the International Monetary Fund.

FEBRUARY 16, 1944

Sidney Hillman told me he had had a long conference with the President that morning and that there was absolutely no question but what the President was actively running and planning for a fourth term. He said the lay of the land was much more certain in this respect in February of 1944 than in February of 1940 . . .

We took [the] Bob Jacksons to the National Symphony concert. Bob told me that David Lawrence,[1] the Philadelphia politician from Pittsburgh, was in to see him and had told Bob without knowing anything about Bob's friendship for me, that I was the only vice-presidential candidate who would strengthen the President in Pennsylvania. Lawrence was looking at the matter in a purely hard-boiled way and was basing his statement on talks with Pennsylvania people.

FEBRUARY 18, 1944

. . . The President was unusually cordial. He immediately asked about the situation in California.[2] Apparently he is much interested in Helen Gahagan[3] running for Congress. He thought she would be an

[1] David L. Lawrence, a rising political broker and member of the Democratic National Committee, was elected mayor of Pittsburgh in 1945.
[2] Wallace had returned from a two-week swing west that took him successively, usually for major speeches, to Los Angeles, San Diego, San Francisco, Portland, Seattle, Milwaukee, Chicago, Springfield, St. Louis, and Minneapolis–St. Paul. In his addresses Wallace put himself unequivocally on his party's left. American fascists, he said in Seattle, were "desperately striving" to control delegates to the state and national conventions. By fascists he meant "those who believe that Wall Street comes first and the country second and who are willing to go to any length through press, radio, and demagogue to keep Wall Street safely sitting on top of the country." Colonel McCormick, he added, in Chicago, was one of them. Everywhere Wallace called for "a general welfare economy" and predicted a "profound revolution" after the war that could be "gradual and bloodless" if the press, politicians, and men of wealth used their influence "on behalf of the public good." The tax system, he said, should give corporations incentives to employ their reserves for innovation and productivity. With "economic abundance" as a national policy, monopolistic practices would no longer have a place in society. Wallace also recommended the establishment of a federal "job authority" to advise the President and Congress about how to achieve and maintain full employment. That objective, he said, would entail cooperative planning by federal, regional, and private groups. His remarks won Roosevelt's public praise.
[3] Helen M. Gahagan, actress wife of film star Melvin Douglas, was, like her husband, an active liberal in California Democratic politics. Elected a National Committeewoman in 1940, she was later appointed by Roosevelt to an unpaid position in the Office of Civilian Defense. Her candidacy for the Congress in 1944 succeeded, but, six years later, running for the Senate, she fell victim to the calculated, undiscriminating, and ferocious tactics of Richard M. Nixon.

offset to Clare Luce. I told him Helen was smarter than Clare Luce and her heart was in the right place. He asked about Melvin Douglas and I said I understood he was in India.

I told the President that a great many people had asked me to transmit to him their warmest regards. He said, "Yes. It makes me cynical. Their interest in me is so that they get re-elected." I said, "That is very natural, Mr. President" . . .

He was very happy about having his veto sustained with regard to the subsidy.[1] He will be sending up a tax veto message in the very near future and expects to have that sustained also. He looked quite rested. He claimed he still had a hangover from the flu, in his shoulders, said that they twinged quite a bit. I said, "Double your dosage of vitamins." He said he was taking a pill now which had in it all the vitamins. I said, "Well, take twice as much."

He spoke with great animation about how he had been planning with Lord Beaverbrook about starting a four-page newspaper in this country after the war. Beaverbrook said he was making more money on his paper since it was cut down to four pages than in the old days. The saving in newsprint more than made up for the loss in advertising. The President said he had been a newspaperman once and he would have no editorials, nothing but straight news and facts. The first page would deal with the world news, news of broad significance. The last page would deal with local news. One of the inside pages would deal with sports and women. Apparently this was Beaverbrook's suggestion. The President asked, "Why do you put sports and women on the same page?" Beaverbrook replied, "One of them is outdoor sports and the other is indoor sports." The fourth page, I think he said, would be devoted to business and economic matters. He would have the publication come out simultaneously at several spots over the country, transmitting the makeup either by radio television or by teletype. He would have the size of the paper midway between the present tabloid and the present newspaper. Beaverbrook assured him that this was very economical in size. I suggested to the President that one page of the paper might vary according to the type of circulation, for example, there could be an edition especially for labor, another for farmers, another for businessmen. The President said the newspaper should be of a sort so there would be absolutely no opinion expressed whatsoever . . .

[1] Congress had sustained Roosevelt's veto of an act continuing the life of the Commodity Credit Corporation but also increasing federal subsidies to agriculture. Those subsidies, the President had noted, would have aggravated inflation. Later legislation merely preserved the CCC.

Stettinius was present at cabinet meeting and the subject for discussion dealt with activities in the House Committee on Foreign Affairs, apparently something relating to the White Paper.[1] Secretary Stimson promptly got into the discussion, saying how dangerous it was now for the House Committee to come out with anything along this line. The President, Stettinius, and Stimson seemed to be in complete accord that the Moslem world was all ready to be set on fire all the way from Morocco to Arabia and the military situation would be imperiled by any action taken at the present time.

Also Stettinius brought up certain difficulties involving oil, having to do with the British and ourselves in Arabia. It seems the British don't like to see us active in oil in the Near East. Mention was made of a particular individual who apparently had called on Ickes, Stettinius, and Jimmie Byrnes with regard to the unfair practices of the British. I have forgotten the name of the man but Jimmie Byrnes said very strongly that if this man's story was made public, it would almost produce a war between the United States and England.

The President said that Ibn Saud, the king of Arabia, was very much insulted because Chaim Weizmann had sent a Gentile archaeologist from England to Saudi and the archaeologist had offered $120 million to Saud if Saud would agree to an independent Palestine. Saud did not need the money at the particular moment and, therefore, proclaimed himself as being greatly insulted and furthermore he said he would never see another Jew until there had been an apology for this insult of offering a bribe.

Stimson called the State Department the wailing wall for the Jews.

At the opening of cabinet meeting, the President said in a very friendly manner, "Well, the Vice President has just returned from a great trip. He found the country was still there. Some of the folks had begun to question it" . . .

[1] The committee had been investigating the deliberate delays, especially those attributable to Breckinridge Long, in assisting the rescue of European Jews threatened by Hitler's "final solution." That investigation revealed Long's anti-Semitism as well as the hideous consequences of his evasions and procrastinations. Prodded by the hearings and by the Treasury Department, Roosevelt in January set up the War Refugee Board to find sanctuaries for European Jews and to facilitate their removal to them. Palestine, the closest and largest sanctuary, remained substantially closed to refugees by the stipulations of the British White Paper that limited Jewish migration there. Until the war ended, the War Refugee Board located temporary sanctuaries outside of Palestine, which Zionists in the United States and elsewhere continued to consider the only appropriate Jewish homeland; see Feingold, *Politics of Rescue*, Chs. 8, 9.

FEBRUARY 21, 1944

At the White House the President started out by reading extracts from his veto of the tax bill.[1] He dwelt at length on the foolishness of Congress in permitting, in the tax bill, the timbermen to count their income from cutting trees as capital gains instead of annual income. Alben Barkley took very sharp issue with him. The debate continued for about an hour. It is obvious that Alben for the first time is thoroughly disgusted with the President and feels that he has been badly treated by the President . . .

When I drove Barkley up on the Hill, he said, "What's the use? I am through." I said, "Alben, we all love you. You have been a pillar of strength." Barkley came back with "What's the use? I can't get the votes in the Senate under the methods that are being followed." It was obvious to me that the President is very much delighted with his veto message and is certain of the soundness of his position and will make no change. Barkley is equally sure of the soundness of his position . . .

FEBRUARY 22, 1944

. . . Krzycki and Kulikowski[2] wanted to let me know about the American Polish Labor Council. Krzycki is from Milwaukee, a member of the CIO, and very eager to see that Polish nationalism in Europe has no effect whatever on Polish voting within the United States. He read from a letter which he had sent President Roosevelt of which he is going to send me a copy. The Polish Ambassador here has undoubtedly been mixing too much in internal affairs of the United States. The Polish language press has been very reactionary. Krzycki claims that this press does not represent the sentiment of the Polish workers. He, therefore, thinks that the American Polish Labor Council is very im-

---

[1] The tax bill fell far short of providing the revenue the Treasury had requested both to finance the war and to combat inflation. The bill also included many regressive schedules that favored business interests whose lobbies had influenced Congress. Educated about the bill's deficiencies by both the Treasury and Byrnes and Vinson, the President vetoed it as providing relief "not for the needy but for the greedy." The timber schedule, as he noted, afforded one example of the bill's deficiencies. It provided for taxing cut timber as capital gains, which would reduce taxes on lumbering companies, instead of as a crop to be taxed at ordinary and higher rates. Only Wallace at the meeting of February 21, 1944, supported Roosevelt's proposed veto. On that veto and ensuing developments, see Blum, *Years of War*, pp. 64–78, and Burns, *Roosevelt: Soldier of Freedom*, pp. 433–437.

[2] Leo Krzycki, president of the American Polish Labor Council, and Adam H. Kulikowski, Chicago publisher of a Polish journal, then with the OWI.

portant. He is trying to persuade Kulikowski to come and work for this council. This council apparently will work parallel with Sidney Hillman's organization but will not be a part of it . . .

FEBRUARY 23, 1944

. . . Senator Barkley's statement was the most outstanding session of the Senate which I ever presided over.[1] After Barkley began speaking, the Senate chamber rapidly filled up. A number of people came over from the House especially from Virginia. After Barkley finished, practically every senator stood on his feet and clapped for about one and a half minutes. Barkley's speech apparently had been very hastily prepared because every few minutes Senator McKellar went out to get for Barkley new typewritten pages. At one time, it looked as though Barkley was about to run out. I wonder if any senator ever received such a spontaneous ovation as Barkley . . .

The news of Raymond Clapper's death came to me while I was on the West Coast. I immediately wrote a letter to Mrs. Clapper. Raymond, in spite of his tendency to swing around every fourth year to the presidential candidate which his paper was supporting, was just about as fine a newspaperman as I ever knew. Undoubtedly he was more independent than 9 out of 10 newspapermen. Most of them as a matter of course are like chameleons, taking on the changing colors of their employers. Clapper did this too to a minor degree in the latter part of each fourth year . . . There are many very fine newspapermen but I do not know of very many who stand up quite as independently as Clapper unless it is Marquis Childs.[2]

While I was talking with Mrs. Clapper, Lister Hill came in and indicated very clearly his sympathies were all with Senator Barkley and that it was time for the President to stop kicking so many people around up on the Hill.

I went into Alben's office. He told me that there was no one to whom he was so loyal, for whom he had so much respect, with the one exception of Woodrow Wilson, as Roosevelt; nevertheless he felt that

[1] Angry over Roosevelt's veto of the tax bill, as were most Democrats in Congress, Barkley resigned as Majority Leader of the Senate, made a speech on the floor that attacked the President's interpretation of the timber schedule, and denounced the President's comment about relief for the greedy as a "calculated and deliberate assault upon the legislative integrity of every member of Congress." Self-respect, Barkley said, demanded a vote to override the veto.

[2] Marquis W. Childs, since 1926 a reporter for the St. Louis Post-Dispatch, had just become a columnist for the United Feature Syndicate.

the Congress derived its power with the people and that the President had not played fairly with Congress, and that he, Barkley, just had to make his statement. I told him undoubtedly the Democratic senators would choose him again as Majority Leader when they met tomorrow morning, and that he, Barkley, would be in a stronger position than he ever had been. He said he had not made his speech with any political motive in mind. I said, "Yes, I know that, but nevertheless it seems to me you can use this situation to get some discipline into the Democratic Party. I think you owe it to yourself, the party, and the country to do this."

I told Hassett[1] over at the White House what a fine attitude Barkley had toward the President and he said he would pass it on to the President. Earlier I had told Grace Tully, before Barkley began to speak, what was in the air. After Barkley finished, I told Hassett about how the Senate had received the speech. Also I told him twice to tell the President not to issue any statement until the President had read Barkley's speech in full. It was obvious during the speech that Senator Byrd and Senator Walsh[2] and the Republicans were getting a great deal of unconcealed pleasure out of it. After Barkley concluded, Senator McClellan of Arkansas, LaFollette of Wisconsin, and a number of others came up to shake hands with him. Barkley more and more is universally beloved in the Senate; even Senator McKellar, who less than a year ago was at daggers' points with him, now seems to be one of Barkley's dearest friends. Guffey is the one now who seems to have the greatest antagonism toward Barkley.

Winfield Riefler told me that his office in London was now a very big thing, that it had to do not only with blockade matters but that both the American and British armies had turned over to it work having to do with picking bombing objectives.

Riefler thinks we are coming into a postwar world of power politics with the world being run by the United States, England, and Rus-

1 William D. Hassett and Grace Tully of the President's personal staff. Roosevelt was at Hyde Park. When Hassett released Wallace's account of Barkley's speech, the President said: "Alben must be suffering from shell shock," but he showed "no word of anger, resentment or recrimination"; see William D. Hassett, *Off the Record with FDR* (New Brunswick, 1958). After talking to Byrnes, Roosevelt sent Barkley a conciliatory telegram urging him to remain as Majority Leader and expressing the hope that if he did resign, his colleagues would re-elect him. On February 25 the Senate overrode the veto, as the House already had. For the first time in American history, Congress had overridden a veto of a revenue bill. That day the Senate Democrats also re-elected Barkley their leader.
2 David I. Walsh, since 1929 Democratic Senator from Massachusetts.

sia. He thinks there is no prospect whatever for any type of League of Nations. I asked him what accounted for the change during the last year and a half. He said the reason was the remarkable progress made by the Russian armies. I asked him what reports he had on the kind of people the leading Russians were. He says they are people who came up by the hard way, who have had very little outside experience. They are competent and capable technicians but are very suspicious toward the outside world, animated by peasant cunning. Riefler said one of our American attachés, who was very friendly to Russia, says the Russians don't want foreigners to see how poverty stricken they are now. That is the reason they keep foreigners out. They will be most happy to show foreigners around 20 years hence when they have been able to do a real job. Riefler thinks Russia will be the most powerful country in the world and that she will dominate all the Slav, the Baltic, and the Balkan states. He thinks that their cultural traditions will be so different from ours that it will be hard for us to get along with them. I told him I thought the thing for us to do was to let England and Russia settle Europe but for us to have direct access to Russia with respect to Asiatic matters. I said I thought our people would ultimately be disgusted if we got into boundary questions in Europe.

Barkley said pointblank to me that the President had been misled by his advisers and he knew who they were. He said they were the same people who had gotten him into trouble with regard to railway labor, folks who were more clever than honest. I asked him who he meant. He hesitated for a moment and finally said he meant Jimmie Byrnes and Fred Vinson . . .

Barkley has drawn the issue clearly for Congress, the President has drawn the issue clearly for the people.

FEBRUARY 24, 1944

. . . David Dubinsky[1] was very frank in describing the affairs of the American Labor Party in New York City as they related to the fight between him and Sidney Hillman. He said Hillman now has control of the communists in the American Labor Party. Dubinksy has been fighting the communists. He said that Hillman in 1942 supported Bennett but that he could not make the American Labor Party vote for him (Bennett).

---

[1] David Dubinsky, since 1932 president of the International Ladies Garment Workers Union, and in 1936 a founder of the American Labor Party in New York.

He says if Hillman, in the primary which is now coming up with the American Labor Party, wins out, the David Dubinsky–Alec Ross–Dean Alfange group will have to set up another party.[1] They will be for Roosevelt and Wallace just the same as Hillman's group, but the David Dubinsky group will find it necessary to denounce the Hillman group.

Dubinsky says that Hillman is doing a good job everywhere in the country except in New York City. Dubinsky says that Hillman is trying to settle some ancient scores in New York City and is doing the President damage there. Dubinsky saw the President recently and told him the situation. The President said he would get in touch with Hillman . . .

He says the communists are very hard workers, that they are fanatics. He says the best workers in his own organization are ex-communists. David says the present communistic front orders come from Oumansky in Mexico City. This checks with my own observations. Dubinsky says the communists today are for the President in the war effort just as strongly as they were against the President and the war effort three years ago. This also checks with my observations as made on my recent trip. The communists in the United States today are not only for the President and the war effort but they are against the class struggle and for Wall Street. The communists are away over to the right of where most workers and union labor are located . . .

FEBRUARY 29, 1944

. . . Crowley is quite stirred up at the attacks on him in *PM*.[2] He thought he ought to talk with Marshall Field.[3] He went into detail about Victor Emanuel. He said Emanuel inherited 25 million dollars from his father and in the twenties went to England and built a castle and became president of the Hunt Club. He came back here in 1930 and settled down. In 1932 he gave $80,000 to help get the President elected. He also gave quite a bit of money in 1936. He gave $10,000 to Leo

1 In May 1944 Alec Ross and Dean Alfange, who had been ALP gubernatorial candidate in 1942, did join Dubinsky in founding the progressive but anti-communist Liberal Party in New York.

2 I. F. Stone was writing that series of articles. One of them condemned Crowley for his failure, while Alien Property Custodian, to take the steps necessary to prevent General Aniline and Dye from reverting after the war to control by I. G. Farben.

3 Marshall Field III, president of the Field Foundation and of Field Enterprises, had established both the Chicago *Sun* and *PM* in New York to assure the availability of a liberal newspaper in those cities.

which Leo personally gave to some one. I have forgotten just who Leo said. Leo says there is absolutely nothing improper about what he has done relative to Victor Emanuel either with regard to the Alien Property Custodian or FEA, that he would be glad to have both agencies examined by congressional committees . . .

Crowley spoke at some length about General Aniline and Dye. This is probably the most effective of the German chemical setups in this country. Crowley said it could be handled in any one of three ways: 1—by negotiated sale; 2—by competitive bidding, and 3—by voting trustees. He thinks only by the last two will it be possible to keep General Aniline and Dye free from German influence after the war. Leo says that General Aniline has about 70 researchers and about 4000 patents. He says they have adopted a program for licensing the use of patents at reasonable rates so that they can be used generally. Superficially at least, his whole program sounded very good.

Leo said that Victor Emanuel was more in accord with the President in his economic views than most of the big businessmen, that he felt Emanuel was definitely more progressive than either Baruch or Jesse Jones. I told Leo that I was glad to know he had such progressive plans in view for the use of patents.

Crowley also went into detail about the way in which he had handled FEA. He said the first thing to do was to get it quieted down. He said his worst trouble was with the State Department. He has a very deep feeling of resentment against Hull and George Messersmith.

He is fully familiar with the way in which Jesse Jones works through Harry Byrd and Senator McKellar . . .

It was interesting to hear Leo pay considerable tribute to Henry Morgenthau. I could not help remembering how Morgenthau a year or so ago brought in to me a terrible indictment of both Crowley and Victor Emanuel.

Crowley claims that he and Frank Walker are the two most prominent Catholics in the administration. I asked him how about Frank Murphy. He says the Catholics look on Frank more or less as a joke. They have no use for a man who parades his religion in the way Murphy does . . .

MARCH 1, 1944

. . . Charles Taft[1] made the observation that the Democratic Party

[1] Charles P. Taft, Cincinnati lawyer and urban reformer, in 1944 in the State Department as director of Wartime Economic Affairs, that night at a dinner given by Secretary of Labor Frances Perkins.

was subsidizing the leading Negro preachers in the country. Madame Secretary disagreed. Taft spoke about a big Baptist Negro congregation in Harlem. Kane[1] spoke up and said he thought the pastor of this congregation, a Mr. Powell,[2] was perhaps more a communist than a Democrat. Madame Secretary said she thought the communists inspired the recent attack on the Bureau of Labor cost-of-living figures. She said Meany is not a communist but she knows the names of two communists who inspired him. I told her I doubted whether the communists inspired this attack because my observations were that the communists were doing everything possible now to support the war effort . . .

MARCH 3, 1944

. . . The cabinet meeting was quite short. The President passed part way around the table a picture of a baby without much clothes on entitled, "The Fourth Term" with a phrase under it, "Oh, God Dammit." It went as far around the table as Frank Knox and Claude Wickard then stopped because they did not want to pass it on to Madame Secretary.

. . . Stettinius indicated that the Argentine situation was still very fluid and that Farrell and Perón were undoubtedly Nazi sympathizers. He said there had been an agreement reached among all the Latin American nations except Venezuela and Chile not to recognize the new government. Secretary Hull did not want to proceed with nonrecognition measures until Venezuela and Chile had agreed . . .

I showed the President after cabinet meeting a two-sentence memo of Stalin's reaction to a presentation made by the British Ambassador on behalf of Churchill with respect to the Polish situation. This memo indicated that Stalin was angry, that he grunted and said nothing. The President said to me with regard to the memo that he was familiar with what had taken place. Then he went on to say, "Did I ever tell you the story of French Indochina? A year or so ago when Churchill was over here, I called his attention to the fact that the French had renounced their claims to Indochina in favor of the Japs six months be-

---

[1] R. Keith Kane, New York lawyer, held various federal positions during the war, in 1944 on the staff of the Secretary of the Navy.

[2] Adam Clayton Powell, Jr., since 1937 minister of the Abyssinian Baptist Church in Harlem, had been in 1941 the first black ever elected to the New York City Council. Then as always an eloquent and aggressive champion of black rights, Powell often sounded radical but he was never a communist. Indeed, during the war, the Communist Party, urging national unity as the best way in which to aid the Soviet Union and defeat the Germans, advocated the postponement of agitation for civil rights.

308 The Price of Vision

fore the United States was attacked by the Japs." The President then continued by saying, "I believe that after the Japs are driven out, the French have no longer any claim to French Indochina and I am sure the Chinese will not want French Indochina." Churchill came back by saying, "Of course, the Chinese will want it." The President then twitted Churchill by saying, "Well, you are speaking for Britain which has been for centuries an imperialistic power and you have several generations of imperialist ancestors behind you. You have never refused a square mile anywhere that you could lay your hands on."

Following this, the President wrote or telegraphed Chiang Kai-shek and asked if he wanted French Indochina. The Generalissimo replied, "No." Later on, at Cairo, the President in Churchill's presence asked Chiang Kai-shek if he wanted French Indochina. The Generalissimo again said, "No." Later on again, at Teheran, the President asked Stalin if he thought France should have French Indochina after the war was over. Stalin said, "No." The President said his idea was that French Indochina should be run for a time under a trusteeship preliminary to the time when she would be given her independence, some 30 or 40 years hence, in the same way as the Philippine Islands will be given their independence. Stalin said that would be fine and came around and shook hands with the President showing how strongly he was for the idea.

Roosevelt said to Churchill, "Well, we are three to one against you on this. You had better come across and we will make it unanimous." Churchill said, "Well, I will have to consult with my cabinet." The President said, "The trouble with you is that you are thinking that Burma might want to be independent, that the Straits Settlements might want to be independent, or the Dutch East Indies might want to be independent after they have gone through an apprenticeship under a trusteeship."

The President said he thought the Poles as usual were handling things very badly, that he thought Stalin's ideas were sound with regard to Poland. Stalin thought that the Poles should have that part of Germany up to within about 30 miles of Berlin including Brandenburg, Pomerania, etc. I said to the President, "I assume you mean the Germans would be moved out of this area and into Germany proper?" The President said, "Yes." He said this part of eastern Germany was much richer than eastern Poland beyond the Curzon Line.

After this conversation, I said to the President, "How would it be sometime during the next month or two if I went to Russia?" The President said, "I think they are going to be shooting at you during the campaign for being too far to the left. My own feeling is that you had better not go to Russia." He continued, "I think it would be better for you to go to China by way of Alaska and Siberia. You could stop off and visit some of the towns in Siberia on your way to Chungking, spending some little time in each of the Siberian towns. The weather is more settled in the Alaska-Siberian country between June fifteen and August fifteen." I said to the President, "How would it be to go on from China to visit the boys in the Southwest Pacific?" He said, "It would be fine if you could find some way of keeping away from the generals" . . .

I mentioned the David Dubinsky matter to him and told him that David wanted me to write him (David) a letter saying the American Labor Party had been doing a patriotic work and it ought to continue to exist. The President said, "Well, let's wait awhile." He said, "I have talked to Sidney Hillman about it and Hillman has agreed to eliminate all communists from running for office but thinks that David Dubinsky is being unreasonable in wanting to exercise some of his personal prejudices with regard to candidates."

I talked briefly to the President about the Barkley situation. The President said when he left for Hyde Park last Tuesday he had no idea anything of that sort would happen. The first word he had of it was the word which Grace Tully transmitted from me about 12:30 on Wednesday. I told the President that it might be well to give the Senators and Barkley somewhat more responsibility than he had given them hitherto. At any rate, it might be good strategy to try out this method for a time . . .

MARCH 4, 1944

Nelson Rockefeller was exceedingly disturbed about the Argentine situation. I agreed with him utterly as to its seriousness. He says the difficulty is with Cordell Hull, that Stettinius is all right. It seems that Hull wants to wait to get all the other Latin American nations seeing things just the way we do. It is interesting to see the extent to which Rockefeller has become completely disgusted with Hull.

The atmosphere at the White House correspondents' dinner was remarkably friendly to the President. They put on an exceptionally good show. I congratulated several members of the press on the unusually fine feeling. Apparently the men felt that this might perhaps be the last time we would have a White House correspondents' dinner with Roosevelt and they were on their best behavior . . . The President got a great kick out of it.

MARCH 6, 1944

. . . I talked to the President at some little length about the Palestine meeting on March 9. He definitely turned down saying anything like the . . . attached[1] in my longhand which I read aloud to him. He said Churchill was a Zionist. Then he discussed the Arabian situation at some length. He also discussed the plans which he has for future handling of the Jewish question. Apparently he intends to get the Jews what they want without setting the Arabs on their ear. He suggested that at the March 9 meeting, I talk about the persecution of the Jews and their need for tolerance . . .

At the White House, I stopped for a moment to show the President a map with a route marked on it showing a proposed trip. He put his finger on the 3300-mile hop from Australia to Ceylon and said that was too much risk to take. He thought 16 hours in the air was too much. He suggested I leave on the trip sometime during June and arrange to get back to Fairbanks, Alaska, about the time the National Democratic Convention begins, say about July 17. He thought it would be about right to leave early in June, thought I ought not to spend much more than three days in Chungking. I told him about my idea of the future importance of Siberia and eastern Asia generally as well as Latin America, saying that this part of the world was going to have the most rapidly growing population, that there was going to be pioneer exploitation of this part of the world, that roads, airports, and railroads would be built, that there would be need for construction machines and machine tools. I said that I felt this area had the very greatest importance to the United States, that technologically speaking we were the leaders with regard to this area. I told him I hoped that my trip to some extent would contribute to this general idea . . .

MARCH 7, 1944

I gave Ed Stettinius the map which I had shown the President and told him the President's ideas about China. Ed confirmed completely Stimson's views that China was a very, very thorny problem right now. Ed thought I ought to go on to India, that I could do an awful lot of good there, also in Australia. Said he felt so strongly about the

[1] Wallace had written but then did not use the following passage: "I am glad to be here tonight—to associate myself in this way with this movement. The homeless Jews of the world have the right to a land which they can call their own. Democracy owes such a home to those Jews whose families have been mistreated beyond all comprehension."

subject he was going to take it up with the President when he saw him the following day to see if he could not induce the President to let me go on to India and Australia. He also said he did not see any reason why I should not go to Moscow. He thought it would be good politics rather than bad politics if I went on to Moscow.

MARCH 9, 1944

Stettinius called up after his visit to the President and told me he was returning the map. He said that the President definitely did not want me to go to India or Australia, that he had his heart set on my going to China and it did not make any particular difference where I went in Siberia . . .

Lauch Currie, Davies,[1] and Fairbank[2] came in to express the opinion that they thought it was very important for me to go to China. They felt that my mere presence there would straighten out certain difficulties, especially difficulties between the Russians and the Chinese. Currie is going to work up for me a tentative schedule in China. Lauch says Madame Sun Yat-sen is a grand person but has been denied freedom of movement by her jealous sisters. Currie thinks the shorter time I spend in Chungking, the better it will be. Currie said a representative of the National City Bank[3] was up in Shensi and S. Lansi, the communistic areas of northeast China, recently, and was quite lyrical about how honest and fine the people were up there as compared with people around Chungking. I asked what the Chinese communists were like and was told that they were agrarian reformers. They want a law passed so interest rates will not be more than 33 percent a year . . .

MARCH 10, 1944

I asked Owen Lattimore to come in because Lauchlin Currie had telephoned that he thought Lattimore would be ideal to go with me on the trip. Lattimore brought on an English translation of the Gen-

---

[1] John P. Davies, capable foreign service officer assigned to the staff of General Joseph W. Stilwell, commanding general of American forces in the China, Burma, India theater. Throughout the war Davies' reporting from China "aroused interest because of its search for essentials, its vividness, and its audacity. All recipients of Davies' memos read them with alert attention"; Herbert Feis, *The China Tangle* (Princeton, 1953), p. 257.
[2] John K. Fairbank, Harvard professor of Chinese history and assistant to Currie on Chinese matters, had recently returned from Chungking.
[3] G. Martel Hall.

eralissimo's book *China's Destiny*, which has not yet been published, and also his own book, *The Making of Modern China.*

Lattimore thinks very highly of Colonel Faymonville, said he met the Colonel in 1936 in Moscow. He understands the internal political situation in China very well and also the situation between China and Russia. He thinks I can render a very great service by going to Siberia and China. He himself would be utterly thrilled to go along . . .

At cabinet meeting Cordell Hull who had just returned from Florida started out talking about Argentina, stating that the latest Ramirez move was an effort to get the Chief Justice of the Supreme Court in as President. Hull said that if it worked it would be fine because the Chief Justice was a friend of the United States. The President spent about ten minutes ribbing Hull on Howland Shaw[1] and the 130 young diplomats whom Shaw had tried to get exempted from the draft. In the paper that was sent over to the President, the claim was made that these men were necessary because of the hard climate. The President, who is an expert on geography and climate, went over the places one by one and pointed out that in most of the places the climate was not hard at all. For example, he stated one man was necessary in Caracas because it was a very hard climate. The President said that everybody knows that Caracas is a perfectly lovely climate all the year round. Hull got a little nettled and said everybody was kicking the State Department around because it was so old, it could not do anything. The President then proceeded to say, "Oh, you are just talking about Arthur Krock." It was obviously a sideways dig at Hull because of the way in which the State Department uses Krock continuously as a stooge to pull its irons out of the fire. The President may have been a little unfair to the State Department but he certainly had a thoroughly good time with Arthur Krock and Howland Shaw.

This precipitated the whole manpower question. Each agency had lost, or was on the point of losing, a large part of its key personnel. The President very vigorously took the side of the Army and the Navy, and said he had to have 1,200,000 men and that the government could not be exempted. McNutt led the opposition to the President, pointing out, for example, that nearly all the personnel in young industries like radar, electronics, etc., are manned by young men, and that obviously there are many of these industries so important to the war effort that no good purpose whatsoever would be served in having these young men fight with guns instead of making radar. McNutt's

[1] G. Howland Shaw, Assistant Secretary of State with special duties relating to foreign service personnel.

answer to the problem is to get the married man, of whom he claims there are plenty.

Stimson claimed there is a great reserve on the farms and that the farmers could get along perfectly all right if it were not for their unwillingness to buy machinery. Of course, Don Nelson, Claude Wickard, and I knew absolutely this was not true. It is amazing how often complete distortions of fact get by unchallenged in cabinet meeting. Of course, Stimson is a fine old man but he doesn't have the remotest glimmering of the farm situation.

The President held forth at some little length about how . . . Stephen Wise and Rabbi Silver[1] were in to see him and how he had started out by attacking them vigorously by saying, "Do you want to be responsible by your action for the loss of hundreds of thousands of lives? Do you want to start a Holy Gehad?" The President continued along this line, quoting his conversation with regard to the danger of attacks from the enraged Arabs. It is exactly the same line he had pulled on Monday when I raised the question. And yet I knew because Silver had talked to me at length the night before that the bulk of the President's conversation had undoubtedly been to cause Wise and Silver to believe that he was in complete accord with them and the only question was the timing . . . The President certainly is a waterman. He looks one direction and rows the other with the utmost skill . . .

Ickes spoke up and said that Wise and Silver were very much pleased with their interview with the President. I did not see Wise myself but Silver told me, the evening of March 9, that he was very much pleased. Silver had also told me that the opposition to Zionism came from the State Department . . .

MARCH 11, 1944

. . . I showed the General[2] the proposed map of my trip. Like Secretary Stimson, the General said the situation in China was very

---

[1] Rabbis Abba Hillel Silver and Stephen S. Wise had seen the President on March 9. On leaving the White House they issued the following statement: "The President authorized us to say that the American government has never given its approval to the White Paper of 1919. The President is happy that the doors of Palestine are today open to Jewish refugees, and that when future decisions are reached, full justice will be done to those who seek a Jewish National Home, for which our government and the American people have always had the deepest sympathy and today more than ever, in view of the tragic plight of hundreds of thousands of homeless Jewish refugees."
[2] George Marshall.

bad. He has no faith whatever in Madame Chiang. He said Churchill was also disillusioned. He said Churchill at first had been completely taken in by the Madame.

He gave quite a different picture of Stilwell's operations in Burma than Stimson had given me recently. Stimson had been very pessimistic; Marshall was optimistic and said it was a question of just how good a job Stillwell had done of training the Chinese troops . . .

I told the General I would like to take Colonel Faymonville with me on this trip. The General went straight up in the air. He said Faymonville was a representative of the Russians, not of the United States. He said Faymonville was more than anyone else responsible for the blowup in Russia which had resulted in Admiral Standley coming back, said there was another Army man, by the name of Colonel Michela,[1] who was also to blame, although Michela had been on the opposite side of the fence from Faymonville. Both of them had been brigadier generals in Russia. Both of them had been demoted to colonel on their return to the United States. The General said the FBI had a file on Faymonville (this probably does not mean a thing because the FBI no doubt has a file, as the President himself has suggested from time to time, on Mrs. Roosevelt, that would make her appear to be the worst person in the United States).

Anyhow, seeing how hot the General was on Faymonville, I shied completely away from that subject. It was rather obvious to me that the General belongs to the school of thought which is fearful of Russia. He is a decisive man and probably about the most progressive man we could have in this key position in the Army. In the broader field of policy, I am afraid he would get lost rapidly. He is a man of character rather than of broad vision . . .

Currie also thinks very highly of Colonel Faymonville. He also thinks very highly of General Marshall. This reminds me too that Owen Lattimore spoke to me in the very highest terms concerning Faymonville.

While I was in Currie's office, I had a visit with John Carter Vincent,[2] who heads up Chinese affairs in the State Department. He has

[1] General Joseph A. Michela, American military attaché in Moscow (1941–43).
[2] John Carter Vincent, a learned, perceptive, charming veteran China hand, had been counselor of the embassy at Chungking (1942–43) and then assistant to the chief of the State Department's Division of Far Eastern Affairs. In 1944 he became chief of that division. Along with Lattimore, Davies, John S. Service, and other relatively young men who gave the United States government the most accurate and trenchant analyses of Chinese affairs available to any government, Vincent, years later, after the communist victory in China, became a scapegoat for the ignorant and suspicious men who temporarily dominated American policy.

spent some time in China and Currie tells me that he is a perfectly splendid man. Currie called up Secretary Hull's secretary about 2:30 to ask if the Secretary was in and whether or not I could stop around to see him. Hull's secretary said he was not in. Currie called again about 4:00 and the report was still that he was not in. Shortly afterward I came down and noticed Secretary Hull's chauffeur in the hall and asked Harty about what time Hull had arrived. He said about 3:30. When I got home, I called Hull on the White House telephone and it was amusing to see how extraordinarily agreeable he was. The old fox knew I had caught him and immediately began to say how the President had sent over a lot of very important work which was going to keep him busy and if I would come around about 6:00 p.m. he would be most happy to see me, etc. I interrupted and said I had been talking with the President about a trip to China and had already talked to Ed Stettinius and I wanted to talk to him about it after he had had an opportunity to talk with his advisers on the subject. He said yes, he had heard something about the trip and that he would be perfectly happy to place at my disposal any of his advisers. His attitude over the telephone was just about the warmest I have ever known it to be and yet apparently he had given his secretary instructions not to let me know that he was in. I guess that is customary office procedure around the State Department. The boys have to keep in practice.

MARCH 13, 1944

. . . I told the President . . . that I had talked to Hull on the telephone with regard to the trip to China and also that I had talked with Stimson and General Marshall. It immediately appeared that the President is much stronger for the trip than I had ever thought. I told him that I told Hull that I did not want to go on the trip unless I could do some real good. The President said, "Oh, you must go. I think you ought to see a lot of Siberia." I said that I had reached the conclusion since he had first spoken to me about going to China and Siberia that he had chosen very wisely in limiting the trip to just those two places and that apparently he had more in mind than I had suspected when he first mentioned China to me. He then said how he had talked to his daughter Anna Boettiger and how she had said that the businessmen on the West Coast were looking forward to a huge trade with Siberia. I told the President about my conversation with General Marshall about Faymonville. The President said yes, that he knew how the General felt, that Marshall felt that Faymonville was a traitor. The President said Faymonville stood pretty low in the Army right now and it probably would be best not to take him with me.

I told the President that Lauchlin Currie was hoping to see him some time tomorrow after press conference and that Lauch thought very highly of John Carter Vincent in the State Department. I told the President I hoped both the Army and the State Department would be for the trip.

When I turned to go and had walked nearly across the room, the President put his hand up to his mouth and whispered in a very loud whisper, "Things went off pretty well, didn't they?" He was referring to the relationship with Barkley . . .

MARCH 15, 1944

. . . Pregel[1] had some pamphlets on Russia, dealing with the mineral resources in various parts of Siberia. It appears that there are especially rich resources in the southern part of the Khirgiz from Alma Ata and Tashkent to Uzbeck and from there on south. There are significant uranium deposits there. The War Department has not had this information and has asked Pregel for it. Pregel told me about a device they have worked out very secretly for using uranium as a source of power by converting the great heat 1800c into energy by using that heat to heat a certain metal alloy inside of a metal tubing. It is my guess that this will eventually make passé oil, coal, waterpower, etc., as sources of power . . .

MARCH 20, 1944

The Ambassador and I talked for some time about Madame Gromyko's health and then began talking about my trip. He wanted to let me know that the Soviet Union would be most happy to have me make a trip to Moscow. I gave him the background of the trip and told him why it seemed inadvisable for me to go to Moscow. The atmosphere was most cordial throughout. He told me a story which the President told him about Stalin's good sense of humor. It seems the President said, after he stopped being President he would like to be a salesman handling Georgian champagne (the champagne at Teheran must have been very good) and Stalin put his finger to his forehead

---

[1] Boris Pregel, a friend and occasional adviser to Wallace, was an expert on radium. His loan of uranium had permitted the first experiments at Columbia University preliminary to the development of atomic energy.

and thought a moment and said, "It seems to me there was a German by the name of Ribbentrop who was a specialist in selling champagne" . . .

MARCH 23, 1944

. . . Oscar Ewing,[1] vice chairman of the Democratic National Committee, said he wanted to make a report to Harold Young and me with regard to the sentiment as he found it among the Democratic organization people in the different states in the west. He said he thought H. Y. and I ought to know the truth even though it was bad news. He said the organization people in Colorado were against me because of some stand I had taken on beet sugar, that there was no enthusiasm at all in Idaho; in Oregon there was a mild enthusiasm; in Minnesota he found them strong for me.[2]

After Ewing left, Harold ventured the opinion that Ewing was trying to be friendly. Ewing made the point that a member of the National Committee could take no part whatever as between candidates. I told him I agreed with him absolutely. I did not tell him that I had heard . . . that Hannegan was passing word around that it was "thumbs down" on me. Ewing said that the Democratic organization people left to themselves would probably pick Sam Rayburn. He said, however, in his opinion the President would handle the situation just like he did last time, that he would wait until the last minute. Knowing the President as he knew him, he thought the President would hesitate to make a change and, therefore, the President would pick me. I said I thought the man who would be picked for Vice President would be the one who gave the best prospect of helping the ticket win in the fall. Ewing said in his opinion the President would make his choice of a man he (the President) felt would make the best Vice President and the man who would make the best President in case anything happened to him (the President). Harold may be right in saying that Ewing's motive was to make a friendly gesture while at the same time displaying no partiality. My own feeling is that there is something else involved although I don't know just what it is . . .

[1] Oscar R. Ewing, New York lawyer, vice chairman of the Democratic National Committee since August 1942.

[2] In comparison, the Gallup Poll, early in March, as the Vice President knew, had found him the strong first choice for renomination among rank and file Democrats in every section of the country. On a nationwide basis Gallup allotted Wallace 46 percent with only 21 percent for Hull, who was in second place, and 13 percent to Farley in third. Others shared fractions of the balance.

MARCH 24, 1944

. . . Pehle and Luxford[1] presented the case of the Treasury against Argentina. Pehle reminded me of the time back last December when we had the meeting on censorship in Frank Walker's office and I had stood out for continuing censorship intercepts because I felt that Argentina would be a center of Nazi machinations against the safety of the hemisphere. Pehle said, after the meeting A. A. Berle had talked to him about how exaggerated my fears were. Pehle also spoke of another meeting later on at which he (Pehle) and Berle were present and at which Berle took the Treasury severely to task because Treasury said that the present Argentine government was a fascist nest. I said, "Well, I have talked to A. A. Berle during the past month or two and he talked perfectly fine about the danger of fascism in Argentina." Pehle said then, "Well, I am afraid Mr. Berle sometimes talks two different ways at the same time."

The Treasury has clear-cut proof that Argentine funds enable the fascists to operate over the whole hemisphere. They think the funds ought to be frozen. They think furthermore that the United States and Britain should clamp down an embargo even though it means that the United States should have to reduce her total meat rations by 10 percent to take care of the British . . .

MARCH 27, 1944

. . . Pehle seems to be an especially capable person. He told me that Secretary Morgenthau was very keen about the War Refugee Board doing a real job. It seems that the Executive Order which was signed by the President was prepared in Treasury. It seems that the order is strong enough to give the Treasury Department a chance to knock the heads of State and War together in order to get the job done. They are approaching the problem solely from the standpoint of saving lives and I am sure from what he said they have saved many thousands of lives and will save many thousands more . . .

[1] John W. Pehle, director of foreign funds control in the Treasury (1940–44) and executive director of the War Refugee Board (1944–45), and Ansel F. Luxford, Treasury lawyer with a special competence in international monetary policy, represented the best of the intelligent, vigorous, and dedicated staff that Secretary Morgenthau had recruited to discharge his department's wartime duties.

MARCH 28, 1944

. . . Lord[1] says he is chief of staff for Eisenhower on handling supplies for the invasion forces. He also seems to be chief of staff for a number of other things. He says Eisenhower is a very fine person, that he is a first-class executive because he places responsibility and then expects results, but if the results are not forthcoming, he places the responsibility elsewhere. Lord thinks Montgomery is a publicity seeker. He says in the initial invasion forces, there will be 20 American divisions and 17 British divisions. After that, there will have to be all American divisions because there are no more British.

I asked if sufficient intensive work had been done with regard to the weather. He said yes, that they had been working on it continuously for more than a year, that they had planes going every day between England, Iceland, and Greenland. He spoke of the very high tides in the Channel and how important it was to have good weather for three days in succession. I asked him why the Italian front had been moving so slowly. He said the truth was we did not have the men to spare, that we had no more men on the Italian front than the Germans. We did have the advantage with regard to airplanes and artillery but this was offset by the advantage the Germans had in position. He said during the past two weeks our air forces had been doing some awfully good work bombing industrial targets in France and Germany. He said prior to that they had done some very poor work on account of bad weather. He said our publicity had claimed good results from some bombing raids on which we had not actually obtained much in the way of results.

Lord says the British are great folks for talk, that they outtalk the Americans every time but that the Americans are better when it comes to action. When he goes into conference with the British, he always arranges matters so that only one person on the American side will do the talking. He says the British always have matters planned out so that they will always be a unit.

I asked about the weather because apparently weather at Cassino balled things up after the big bombing. I had thought the Army was not sufficiently weather-minded.

MARCH 29, 1944

. . . At Morgenthau's lunch were present Marvin Jones and Luxford of Treasury in addition to the Secretary and myself. The subject of

[1] General Royal B. Lord, just returned from London.

the conversation was an effective Argentine embargo. Marvin Jones was dead against it. He said England and the United States needed the food from Argentina. Luxford gave the specific facts with regard to the German backing of many of the Argentine army crowd. I told Marvin flatly that I looked on the Latin American situation as very bad, that I thought the way in which the cost of living was outrunning wages made it possible for the fascist propaganda from Argentina to take hold almost everywhere. It was clear that Marvin, who is a member of the Combined Food Board . . . is afraid to face the consequences of meeting the Argentine situation head on. Luxford, Morgenthau, and I presented some of the other sides of the case, and Marvin agreed to re-examine the problem.

APRIL 5, 1944

I gave Mrs. Roosevelt . . . a realistic survey of the New York City political situation made by one of the CIO men. This survey indicated a very bad situation in the city and indicates quite clearly that as a result of dissatisfaction among the Irish, Italians, Negroes, Polish, and other foreign groups, the Democratic majority in New York City might be reduced to considerably less than 300,000 with the result that the state would go for Dewey rather than for the President. I told Mrs. Roosevelt that I thought the President would win against Dewey if there were 45 million or more votes cast and that we would have more Democrats in Congress than we had now if there were as many as 50 million votes cast. I said I did not think that Hillman's PCA was making quite as much progress in registration as was necessary. She expressed some disturbance about the Dubinsky-Hillman situation in New York City and felt that Hillman had not handled the problem to the best advantage. She said that was getting word of a great many people who were Republican and who did not like the President at all who nevertheless would feel obliged to vote for him if the war continued. I said undoubtedly there were a very great many people of this sort and cited the Des Moines *Register* poll of last January which indicated that even Iowa would go Democratic and vote for Roosevelt against the best possible Republican nominee if the war were on.

It is obvious that Mrs. Roosevelt doesn't like the idea of the President running again but she also feels that he may be forced to run because of sentiment among the people . . .

APRIL 7, 1944

. . . At cabinet meeting most of the time was given to discussion of whether or not coal miners should be exempted from the draft. McNutt held strongly to the position they should be but Stimson was cautiously holding to the position that they should not be, but hiding behind Hershey's [1] skirts. The president played a very shrewd game in between both Stimson and McNutt, saying merely that he wanted to be sure that there was enough coal so that he would not be cold in his house next year. McNutt tried to get him pinned down to an absolute statement that the President would stand behind him in McNutt's recommendations to Hershey. The President refused to do this. Ickes held that the coal miners were just as important to the war effort as soldiers.

After cabinet, without mentioning Ingersoll's name or giving any authority whatsoever, I asked the President pointblank if Stalin yet knew of the fact that the date of the invasion had been postponed for 29 days and that the invasion in the South of France had been called off.[2] The President said Stalin did not know it. I said, "Of course, I don't know of the precise nature of the understanding arrived at at Teheran but I would assume that the understanding was such that Stalin should know what had happened." The President said that the invasion of southern France had not yet been definitely called off but it looked like it probably would have to be for certain reasons which he did not mention.

Then I said to the President, "Well, isn't this situation a little bit like two American Army companies, say Company A is supposed to arrive at a certain point at twelve noon, Company B is supposed to arrive on the other side of the hill at a certain point at one-fifteen. Company B is counting on Company A to carry out its commitment. If the commander of Company B gets to the spot and finds that Company A has not carried out its commitment, then Company B will carry a deep resentment against the commander of Company A." The President said, "Well, I guess I had better get in touch with Stalin myself. Stalin will take it better from me than he will from Churchill." I said to the President, "Then, of course, there is Montgomery's provision that if the weather forecasts for five days after the date of the invasion, and the tide and the moon are unfavorable, that the invasion can be postponed for another twenty-eight or twenty-nine days" . . .

1 Major General Lewis B. Hershey, director of Selective Service.
2 Ralph Ingersoll had so informed Wallace.

When Madame Chiang Kai-shek was staying at the White House, the President said to her, shaking his head, "You are not in my good graces. I don't like you anymore." She replied, evidently much disturbed, saying, "What have I done?" The President then said, "The time when you called Wendell Willkie an adolescent, you said I was sophisticated. I am not at all sure that the word 'sophisticated' is complimentary." The President then said that the Madame was very fast on her feet, and she replied, "Ah, but, Mr. President, I did not say that. It was the fault of the translation. What I really said was that you were very civilized" . . .

The President said he was going away for a while, going to be in a house where no telephone could reach him. He was going to fish. His spirits were excellent but it seems to me his appearance was worse than I have ever seen it. His hands were a little shaky. My guess is that he is now subject to minor irritations in a serious way for the first time. He should come back from this rest thoroughly rejuvenated.

After cabinet meeting, Henry Morgenthau stopped around and said, "Have you read Willkie's speech at Omaha?" I said, "No." He said, "You ought to read it." I said, "Well, what does it say that it is so important?" Henry replied that it was about our foreign policy. I said, "Well, what about it?" Morgenthau said, "Well, Willkie calls a spade a spade."[1]

Henry has long disapproved of the pussyfooting foreign policy of the State Department and his implied approval of Willkie's speech is merely a continuation of his long, deeply felt grievance with regard to the State Department.

I told the President that I had applied to Cordell Hull for someone qualified in Chinese affairs to go with me and that I had arranged for Owen Lattimore of OWI to go. The President said, "Lattimore is a good man." It is obvious that he knows Lattimore and likes him.

[1] Willkie had suffered a catastrophic defeat in the Wisconsin Republican primary on April 4. In that contest, delegates pledged to Governor Dewey won 40 percent of the vote; to General MacArthur, 24 percent; to Harold Stassen, 20 percent; and to Willkie only 16 percent. Two days later Willkie in Omaha delivered the most strenuous indictment of Roosevelt's foreign policy he had yet made. He blamed the administration for failing to state "in plain terms what we stand for and what we are fighting for," for secret diplomacy, for dealing with fascists in North Africa and Italy, and for not establishing a United Nations Council to guide the common effort of all the anti-Axis countries. Following that speech Willkie announced his withdrawal from the race for the Republican nomination.

APRIL 12, 1944

. . . Marquis Childs told me how he was with the President for an hour before he went away and the President was in remarkably good spirits. Childs thought he would come back from the trip to the South very much rested. Childs said I have a great many friends in the country but he thought I ought to give them some more definite idea as to just whether or not I was a candidate for Vice President. I told him there was only one man that counted in this and that was the President himself, and that I was sure that the President himself would not make up his mind until the last minute . . .

APRIL 14, 1944

. . . Major General Leslie Groves[1] presented me with a report on a governmental secret project which is the most interesting report I have ever seen. This is a project about which I have talked with Vannevar Bush for the last two years. This is a project which should result in definitely ending the war within another 18 months at the outside . . .

At the Lord Halifax dinner were present Francis Biddle, Justice Jackson, Mrs. Stettinius, the Archbishop of York, and various British officers and their wives. The Archbishop is a nice old boy. He looked 100 percent better than when he first arrived in this country a week ago. The food has done him good. He says he has enjoyed it enormously, having the feeling always that this will be the last good meal. He spoke very highly of the Russian patriarch and his two archbishops. He said Stalin personally was responsible for the opening up of so many of the churches. When war came on, and so many people were killed, people wanted religious services both for the dead and for the living. Stalin felt his people had made such sacrifices that they should be given what they wanted. If they wanted religious services, they should be given religious services. In this the Archbishop was quoting the Norwegian Minister to Russia who is said to know more about Russia and to have more standing with the Russians than anyone else in the diplomatic corps . . .

[1] Commanding officer of the Manhattan Project, the operation developing the atomic bomb.

APRIL 19, 1944

. . . Kulikowski[1] left the attached concerning the American Polish Congress. He was very deeply concerned and called attention especially to the last two paragraphs, which indicate that the objective of the American Polish Congress is partly to defeat the present administration and partly to stir up the maximum of anti-Russian sentiment. He said he talked to Jonathan Daniels[2] about this. I called Daniels on the telephone. Daniels said he thought the way to handle the situation was to come out with a clear-cut statement of policy, that the Atlantic Charter applied to eastern Europe just as well as to anyplace else. I said to Daniels, "Does this mean that we are going to send an army over to eastern Europe to invoke the Atlantic Charter?" Daniels backed away at once and said that he would take the matter up with the President at once when he returned. I asked him when the President would return. He said possibly the latter part of this week but he did not know for sure. Kulikowski said certain individuals, he thought either Hull or Biddle, should see him at once. I told him anything of this sort would have to be done directly from the White House . . .

I asked Peter Fraser[3] how the broadcasting of the parliamentary procedure over the radio to the people of New Zealand had worked out. He said "Fine," that it had stopped filibustering and it caused the members of the Parliament to talk sense. He said they started on this scheme with considerable trepidation, but now they would not think of going back to the old way. I told him it seemed to me like the first step toward genuine political democracy.

APRIL 20, 1944

Guffey wants to give a garden party for Mrs. Wallace and me before I leave for China, wants to make it clear just where he stands. He

[1] Adam Kulikowski of the OWI had given Wallace a memo about the American Polish Congress and the various organizations and individuals affiliated with it. The congress, which excluded those who did not support the Polish government-in-exile in London, was planning to mobilize public opinion against the Polish government in Lubin, which the Soviet Union sponsored. Kulikowski expected the congress also to attack Soviet policies elsewhere in eastern Europe. As he saw it, the congress and its affiliates would move ethnic groups in the United States in an effort to influence American foreign policy along lines irrelevant to the true national interest.

[2] Jonathan W. Daniels, son of Josephus Daniels and his successor as editor of the Raleigh *News and Observer*, was at this time an administrative assistant to the President.

[3] New Zealand Prime Minister.

says the situation up in Pennsylvania is coming along fine. He says Robert Taft told him that Dewey was going to be the nominee. Guffey thinks the President can beat Dewey quite easily.

Gladieux[1] wanted to tell me about the situation inside of WPB. He said Don Nelson stands very high with labor groups and small business groups and that he is doing everything he can to go to bat for labor and small business. Almost the whole organization is on the other side of the fence, including Charles Wilson of General Electric. Nelson won't admit that he is having a hard time with Charles Wilson but there is no question but that Wilson is trying to cut Don Nelson's throat. I expressed high admiration of Don Nelson to Gladieux . . .

Josephus Daniels[2] is very critical of the President for having men like Stimson and Knox in the cabinet. He thinks the cause for which the President stands is being betrayed inside his own family . . .

APRIL 24, 1944

. . . Wasserman[3] . . . said he had had lunch last week with Willkie, that Willkie was very sore at Dewey, that he preferred Roosevelt to Dewey but naturally he could not say anything about that. This was all a build-up on the part of Wasserman to the effect that the President should appoint Willkie as a special adviser on postwar planning. He asked what I thought about it. I said I thought Willkie would be very unhappy because it was my observation that all people placed in a position of responsibility and doubtful authority got into trouble. I told Wasserman I did not see how Willkie could take a position of this kind because I felt Willkie was smart enough to see the inherent difficulties in such a job. Wasserman says Willkie is very critical of Roosevelt's domestic policy but thinks that, on the whole, Roosevelt has done very well in the foreign field. Wasserman confirmed what I had heard from other sources that Willkie is very resentful of the way in which Stassen[4] has cooperated with Dewey . . .

1 Bernard Gladieux of the WPB, formerly with the Budget Bureau.
2 Josephus Daniels, a Bryan Democrat then in his eighties, had been Secretary of the Navy (and therefore FDR's superior officer) during the Wilson Administration and Roosevelt's Ambassador to Mexico (1933–41).
3 William S. Wasserman, an adviser to the Smaller War Plants Corporation, had been head of the Lend-Lease mission to Australia in 1942 and the representative of the Office of Economic Warfare in England in 1943.
4 Harold E. Stassen in 1943 had resigned as governor of Minnesota to join the Navy which assigned him to the staff of Admiral William F. Halsey. In 1944 Stassen was engaged in the first of his seven successive and futile campaigns for the Republican presidential nomination.

APRIL 28, 1944

Vincent, head of the Department of Chinese Affairs in the State Department, seems to be very glad to go to China with me.[1] He seems like a fine fellow in every way. We talked about minor details of the trip together and I gave him a copy of Chinese extracts of the Confucius Economics on the constantly normal granary. I outlined to him some of the things I might want to say in the only carefully prepared speech I expected to make in China.

I went over with L. Bean the statistical facts back of the importance of export trade and considerably modified the opinion which I had formerly held . . .

MAY 2, 1944

. . . Dr. Wei[2] spent all his time telling me what bad folks the Chinese communists were. He said in his home province in southern China, where they originated, they killed the young people and old people and made the adults join their movement. He says they don't fight against the Japs the way they should, says they are more interested in Russia than they are in China. He says they are conducting a very extensive campaign in the United States. Wei spoke deprecatingly of the *Time* magazine article . . . Apparently he doesn't think much of Ted White.[3] This reminded me that Mrs. Luce had spoken to my

[1] A week earlier, after others had leaked the news, Wallace had announced his plans for his trip to Siberia and China. Newspapers had been speculating about its significance, sometimes interpreting it as a device to boost Wallace's candidacy, more often as a way through which Roosevelt could get him out of the country so as to open the field to his rivals. A few analysts expected the trip to result in unpredictable changes in American China policy. Wallace's statement of April 21, 1944, expressed his real purpose as he saw it then and always:

I am hoping to visit not only China but also that part of Russia which may be called her Wild East in the same sense as the territory west of our Missouri River was called the Wild West in the years immediately following the Civil War. The most significant fact in American history was the rapid opening up of our Great West during the 30 years following 1870. Siberia will have an equally exciting development during the next 30 years. On this trip, I especially want to get acquainted with Russian pioneering and her Great East and Chinese pioneering and China's Great West.

Following the war, the common men of the world will fill up the vacant spots as they try to attain a fuller and deeper life by harnessing nature. This is the kind of a job with which our fathers and grandfathers were fully familiar. We Americans should examine what is going on in the most sympathetic way.

[2] Wei Tao-ming, then Chinese Ambassador to the United States.

[3] Theodore H. White, *Life* correspondent, author of "*Life* Looks at China," had just returned from China where he had developed a sympathy for General

sister Mary about Ted White just returning from China and had asked if I did not want to see him. It also reminded me that Charles Marsh asked me if I did not want to see White. I am not going to see White or Mrs. Luce but this is not saying that White may not be accurate in his descriptions . . .

Benton[1] said that he had read all of my speeches for the past 12 months and he was surprised to find how good they were. He said he had read them because of arguments he had had with some of his business associates who thought that I was a dangerous character . . .

Benton used to be in the advertising business with Chester Bowles[2] of CPA. He says that Bowles is a greater admirer of mine. At the present time, Benton is working with the Committee for Economic Development. He claims that his attitude is somewhat like mine, that is, that our economic function is to bring about the full use of manpower, resources, and skills. He says he has always voted the Democratic ticket. He says the strongest criticism that can be urged against the President in the forthcoming election is the possibility that his health is impaired, together with the fact that his leading advisers have an age of about seventy years, also the fact that Knox recently died under the strain. Benton said if he were fighting the administration he would hammer again and again on the age and physical conditions of the men at the top; therefore, he thinks the President ought to get rid of his old men and replace them by younger men. My guess is that Benton has been sitting in with businessmen who are high up in the Republican circles and knows that they are going to hammer on this day and night. Undoubtedly there are a tremendous lot of stories going around the country at the present moment to the effect that the President is in bad health. Personally, based on my observation of him the last time I saw him, I don't believe this to be true. It is amazing, however, how long his vacation was continued . . .

Stilwell, an understanding of the Chinese communists, and a disdain for Chiang Kai-shek and his government that was common to almost all able American journalists who had covered the area. White spelled out his views in his book, written with Annalee Jacoby, *Thunder Out of China* (New York, 1946).

1 William Benton, at this time vice president of the University of Chicago, had retired from the advertising business in 1936 and was to go on to become chairman of the board of Encyclopaedia Britannica and for a term Democratic senator from Connecticut.

2 Chester Bowles, Benton's former advertising partner, had been head of the Office of Price Administration since 1943 and was to go on to become for a term Democratic governor of Connecticut and in the 1960s Undersecretary of State and Ambassador to India. Bowles did admire Wallace and shared many of his ideas, especially his concern for federal wartime planning to achieve postwar full employment.

MAY 4, 1944

Randall Gould,[1] who is now with the *Christian Science Monitor*, wanted to give me his views on China . . . Gould seems to agree with nearly all the other American newspapermen that the description of China as set forth by Ted White in the *Life* magazine article is substantially accurate. He says he would not go quite as far to the left as Edgar Snow.[2] He does feel, however, that the Generalissimo is not fair to the Chinese communists . . .

MAY 8, 1944

. . . At the White House the President seemed to be in the best of spirits. Apparently the Hill-Pepper primaries had made him more happy. He mentioned confidentially that Barney Baruch had asked him if he felt it was important for Hill and Pepper to win. The President had told Baruch it was important. The President thought Baruch had sent money down to both Hill and Pepper.

The President laughed and laughed about Joe Kennedy's daughter marrying the son of the Duke of Devonshire. The President said he had known the Duke of Devonshire for a long time and that his family were rabid Protestants.

Alben Barkley said he was going up to New York to make an address at the . . . Jefferson Day dinner. He quoted what he was going to say about Dewey and also his remarks about the Republicans who defeated the League of Nations in Wilson's day. He had the word "malicious" in. The President suggested he strike out the word "malicious." The President said he thought Lodge and one or two others were malicious but that the rest were not. The President told a story related by President Eliot[3] concerning Senator Lodge. The President mimicked President Eliot in the way he held his two hands together at the finger tips. "Yes, take it by and large, I think Senator Lodge is the man most lacking in humility of any man I ever knew. There is just one exception and that is the Senator's father" . . .

Alben Barkley said he thought it would be a good thing if various senators and congressmen took some trips to different parts of the world. He indicated he would very much like to go along with me.

---

[1] Randall C. Gould, chief Far Eastern correspondent of the *Christian Science Monitor*, earlier editor of the Shanghai *Evening Post and Mercury* (1931–41).
[2] Wallace had also talked with Edgar P. Snow, then associate editor of *The Saturday Evening Post*, veteran reporter on Chinese affairs, author of *Red Star Over China* (1937), a book more prophetic than it seemed in 1944.
[3] The late President Charles W. Eliot of Harvard.

The President made some statement about my trip to China and how important it was. He spoke of the inflation and the strained relationship between China and Russia and also the state of domestic infelicity between the Generalissimo and the Madame. He said it was up to me to act the part of Cupid to bring them together again . . .

I stayed behind after the meeting broke up and showed to the President my schedule—leaving Washington May 20 and getting back to Washington on July 9. He went into it in some little detail and seemed to be delighted that I was stopping at so many places in Siberia. Apparently he seemed to think the schedule was all right in every way . . .

MAY 9, 1944

Planned with Vincent and Lattimore about the trip. Vincent had read the proposed pamphlet for the IPR.[1] He said he really could not find anything to disagree about in it. He advises that I not submit it formally to the State Department because it would take so long to go round and round. He did not see any reason why the State Department should complain about it anyway . . .

Markell Hall told me the most fascinating story. He was with the National City Bank in Peiping in December of 1941. He had anticipated that the Japs might declare war against the United States and so had made arrangements in such eventuality to move west through the Chinese communist territory. Immediately after the attack on Pearl Harbor, the communists picked him up and passed him westward. In the first instance, he had a positive prejudice against the Chinese communists, but, after living with them for eight months, he came to have a fondness for them. He says they are quite young, decisive, and decent. He says they are not really communists but agricultural reformers. He spoke of the leaders with great affection. The leaders came from southern China. Most of the rank and file of the communists, however, are northern Chinese. Hall says the communists stand first for winning the war against Japan; second, for good government (in which they include agricultural reform), and, third, for a united China.

I said to Hall, "Well, doesn't the Generalissimo stand for exactly the

---

[1] With the help of Vincent and Lattimore, Wallace wrote *Our Job in the Pacific*, a pamphlet published in 1944 by the American Council Institute of Pacific Relations (IPR Pamphlet Number 12). The pamphlet developed themes characteristic of Wallace's speeches. He urged American postwar economic assistance for the industrial development of Asia, a viable trade policy with Asia, the emancipation of colonial areas in Asia, the demilitarization of Japan, and international control of air power in the Pacific.

same thing?" He replied, "The difference is that the Chinese communists do something about it and the Generalissimo doesn't." I said, "This reminds me of what Luis Quintanilla, the Mexican Ambassador to Russia, wrote me. 'People here do every day what the people in the United States talk about on Sunday.' "

Hall replied, "Well, that reminds me of a story of an American communist lady and a British colonel, both of whom were at the dock on a Russian river. The American communist lady looked at the dock workers and said, 'Isn't it marvelous how they work? You can tell by their general attitude that they feel themselves a part of the whole show. Any system of government which can make people feel that way is certainly worthwhile.' At the same time the British colonel was saying, 'Just look at these folks, the scum of the earth. Look at the way they are dressed. Obviously they don't have enough to eat. If anyone needed proof that communism isn't practical, you have got it right here.' "

I then came back at Hall saying, "With what preconception did you approach the Chinese communists?" He said, "I was definitely prejudiced against them."

Of course, Hall may not be telling me the truth but I can't for the life of me figure out what the motive might be in this man who is still employed by the National City Bank taking a very pronounced slant for the Chinese communists. He says he personally tried out with a great many of the Chinese communist army their ability to read and write. Practically all know how to read and write. He made the same trial with the government army and found that every man could not read and write. The communist army is alert, bright, and intelligent. The government army is dumb. The communist army can learn any new thing in a fraction of the time required by the government army.

When Hall got to Chungking, he had a number of talks with different Chinese and found their attitude toward the Chinese communists was exactly like that of the most reactionary Republican businessmen toward the administration. They continually spread poison without any basis in fact. He challenged them repeatedly to produce their facts and they could not. They had none. Hall thinks the Generalissimo means well but he just doesn't know what is going on. Those around him hide the real truth from him.

Hall says the Methodists feel they own the Generalissimo. They take the government side. While he was in Chungking, Hall stayed with an old Methodist missionary. He speaks most highly of Ambassador Gauss and says that Madame Chiang Kai-shek completely pulled the wool over Willkie's eyes when she prejudiced him against Gauss. I said there were rumors of marital unhappiness between the Generalissimo and the Madame. He said, yes, he thought the Generalissimo did have another and younger woman, that that was customary in China and he thought the Generalissimo should not be criticized for it. Hall said, however, that the Madame still had very great influence with the Generalissimo . . .

MAY 11, 1944

. . . Walter White,[1] since Willkie's withdrawal, has swung completely over to the Democratic side and is doing everything he can to get the colored people to vote for Roosevelt again. I was surprised to find how strong he was against Dewey . . .

MAY 12, 1944

. . . L. Bean gave me a memorandum from Alger Hiss[2] with regard to my Chinese trip. The memorandum was excellent. As a result of this memo, I called Hull on the telephone, thanked him for the excellent cooperation which the State Department had given, and asked to see him before I left. I shall be seeing him next Thursday morning at 10 o'clock. He thought I should delay seeing him as long as possible so as to get the last word about the Chinese military picture. He was obviously seriously alarmed about both the military picture and the extent of the inflation in China. Hiss advised that I cultivate Gauss, who, he says, is a very fine man. This checks with what Markell Hall told me. This reminded me that I had met Stanley Hornbeck the night before and Hornbeck had talked in glowing terms of Gauss, saying that while he was not popular with the Chinese, nevertheless, he was doing a very good job of representing us. Hornbeck said China had put on a tremendous campaign to have Gauss recalled simply because Gauss was handling American interests in a firm way. Willkie without much knowledge had lent himself to that campaign.

1 Walter White, since 1931 secretary of the NAACP, of all black leaders probably closest to Roosevelt but still without significant influence, had learned to expect little from the President and less from his staff. Willkie's record on civil rights compared favorably to Roosevelt's. Yet neither had sensed, as White did, the increasing militancy of blacks, particularly black soldiers, about whom White wrote incisively in *A Rising Wind* (1945).
2 Alger Hiss, then serving as a specialist on international organization in the State Department.

MAY 17, 1944

Harriman[1] says, "Is there anything that can be done about the FBI? They are perfectly crazy in the way they call certain people communists." I said that I did not know of anything that could be done about the FBI.

MAY 18, 1944

. . . I . . . called on Hull. He told me how in Moscow they insisted that China be looked on as one of the four great powers at a time when England was dead against China being so recognized and Russia was quite unenthusiastic about it. Hull told me much the same thing as Stettinius had about the progress being made in setting up a world organization. He is working very quietly with certain of the members of the Senate Foreign Relations Committee on this matter. Everyone is sworn to secrecy. The world organization would not have a police force of its own but the members would bind themselves to furnish their armed forces against any nation that was threatening the peace. The new world association would apparently have an executive council composed of five members, of which four would be the United States, England, Russia, and China. The fifth would be a smaller power that would change from time to time. All the nations of the world would belong to the assembly. In its main outlines this is very much like the program worked out when Sumner Welles was Undersecretary.

I then called on Isaiah Bowman. He laid great emphasis on the fact that it was important for the Generalissimo to move in fast and come to an understanding with the Chinese communists, said if the Generalissimo did not do so, Russia would be sure to cause serious trouble in Manchuria and Manchuria might be lost to China.

When I talked with the President,[2] he started out by telling me

---

[1] Averell Harriman, at this time temporarily in Washington on a visit from his post as United States Ambassador to the Soviet Union.

[2] Roosevelt had defined the general purposes of Wallace's trip. He wanted the Vice President, as an agricultural expert, to observe the ways of life in Siberia, Outer Mongolia, and China, and to reach some conclusions about how to minimize sources of conflict between China and the Soviet Union. He wanted him also to influence Chiang Kai-shek to arrange a modus operandi with the Chinese communists in order more vigorously to pursue the war against Japan, to take steps to control inflation in China, and to establish a fair and realistic value for fapi, especially as they were exchanged for the American dollar. So as to prevent embarrassing Wallace in his negotiations with Chiang, the Presi-

what I ought to say to the Generalissimo when the subject of inflation was brought up. He said he thought the Generalissimo ought to call in one person from each province, that they ought to agree to issue a new currency on the basis of $200 worth of it to $1 of the old Chinese yuan. Following this, he should fix prices and really enforce them. I said to the President, "Don't you think I had better talk to Harry White of Treasury about this inflation problem?" He said, "Yes, go ahead and talk to Harry."

Then the President began to talk about how the Generalissimo should handle the Chinese communists. He said the first rule for the Generalissimo to remember was "Nothing should be final between friends." This was the old Bryan statement which the President emphatically endorsed. Then he quoted Al Smith as saying with regard to warring factions, "Let me get them all into the same room with good chairs to sit on where they can put their feet on the table, where they can have cold beer to drink and cigars to smoke. Then I will knock their heads together and we will settle everything."

The President said that he would be happy to be called in as arbiter between the warring factions. He told me to tell the Generalissimo that it might be a good thing if "he would call in a friend." The President referred to Charles Francis Adams when he was ambassador to England in 1861. Adams said that there were some Englishmen who were taking sides but they are friends of the entire United States. The President made it clear that he felt himself to be a friend of all China.

The President then said, "At Cairo I made it perfectly clear that I wanted Manchuria to be Chinese. Later on, I got Stalin to agree to this." He told me to tell the Generalissimo that as far as he knew the plans were still O.K. on Manchuria but if the Generalissimo could not settle the communist thing he, the President, might not be able to hold the Russians in line. The President went ahead to say he knew the Russians would change if the present situation should continue . . .

---

dent told him not to visit the Chinese communists. Further, the itinerary precluded conversations between Wallace and Stilwell, a bitter critic of Chiang, though it included a visit with General Chennault, who was sympathetic to the Chungking regime. Yet Roosevelt also urged Wallace to take with him Owen Lattimore and John Carter Vincent, both informed skeptics about the Generalissimo. The Vice President's party also included John Hazard, chief liaison officer, Division of Soviet Supply, who served as Wallace's interpreter in Russian; Captain Kenneth Knowles as military observer; Colonel Richard T. Kight, commander of the Skymaster airplane, who had also been pilot for Willkie; and the rest of the airplane's crew.

MAY 20, 1944—EDMONTON, CANADA

Gen. Gaffney, born in Massachusetts, raised in Texas, strong for the North.[1] Prefers it to tropics. Likes to hunt. Tells of our unpreparedness in Alaska. Japs could have taken Seward. We had no cruisers up there. Army high command was convinced Japs would not strike at Alaska. Thinks there are great mineral and agricultural possibilities in northwest territory. Prof. Blackfoot of University of Alberta thinks there are enormous possibilities dairying and hog possibilities. Soil marvelous, deep, black . . .

MAY 21, 1944—FAIRBANKS, ALASKA

. . . Took us to visit Alaska University, President Bunnell and Dean Gasser. They told us following—64 million acres agricultural land in Alaska two states size of Iowa capable of producing when cleared of poplar, birch and spruce, fifteen to 20 bushels of wheat. Best variety early sort from Siberia Chugot ripens in 90 days, fine milling qualities— Average yield at station for 30 years 20 bushels—Varieties from Canada and U.S. too late—Swedish select oats—70 bushels. Wisconsin beardless barley yields 50 bushels. Best hay, oats and peas. Also yellow Siberian alfalfa Brome grass best pasture. Blue grass grows well—Brome grass and blue grass just starting to head—Costs $100 to clear an acre—less with a tractor . . . Gasser says cost would be twice that of U.S. $1.30 vs. $0.70 but cost of transportation from U.S. $60 a ton.

Holsteins favorite breed—produces about like in U.S. Saw University pit silo with oat and pea silage good quality. Cows eat 40 pounds a day—10 pounds of hay and one pound feed to 4 pounds of milk . . . Soil when cleared lacking in phosphorus and nitrogen.

[1] On the first day of his trip, Wallace had reached Edmonton, Canada, where General Dale V. Gaffney met him and his party. The Vice President had also begun to keep a record in handwriting in a pocket-size daybook. That record, his diary from May 20–July 5, 1944, also provided the basis for his revelatory book, *Soviet Asia Mission* (New York, 1946). The diary as published here in excised form varies from the original in several ways. To facilitate understanding, Wallace's Russian script, used continually in naming places and people, has been transliterated, and many of his abbreviations have been spelled out. Place names have been inserted in the headings for each date. Insofar as his handwriting offers clear clues, his spelling and punctuation have been retained. Though he kept his diary daily, the selections omit some days of only marginal interest. The selections were chosen to reveal his characteristic observations about agriculture, demography, and culture, and to include all of his important remarks about public policy. The diary as he actually kept it contains a less telling account about Siberia but a much fuller account of China than does his *Soviet Asia Mission*.

Backbone of Alaska will be mining with agriculture to support mines. Ten billion tons of lignite coal south of Fairbanks . . . Biggest placer gold mine in world 8 miles from Fairbanks . . . Tomatoes and lettuce in green houses—Radishes and lettuce just coming up outside . . .

Truck drivers earn more than General Gaffney. Ice cream sodas cost 40 cents Bottle beer 60 cents.

Barn has double windows—equipped with steam heat which is turned on when outside temperature gets down to 30 degrees below zero and inside temperature is 38 above. Has one boiler for house and barn which required only 30 tons last winter which was warmer than usual. Very little wind in the winter . . .

Visited Husky Dog station. Wolf bitch crossed with dog ¼ wolf and ¾ dog—Three pups, ⅜ dog and ⅝ wolf—Siberian dog excellent— Sledge made of birch or hickory . . . Used for rescue work—5 rescues last winter . . .

Rainbow trout 7 pounds to 10 pounds . . . Alaska will have a big tourist, hunting and fishing trade which will bring in more money eventually than mining . . .

Col. Keilor[1] very enthusiastic about the high quality of Russians coming to Fairbanks for P 39s, B 25s and A 20s Very well behaved— Colonel would be proud to pick a bunch of Americans equally good and equally fine and capable in behavior in a foreign country . . .

MAY 23, 1944—VELKAL, SIBERIA

. . . The town was started in 1941 and Semonov[2] was very proud of it. Landing field built of slatted wood—2 by 6"s with 2" inch side up —Several P 39s on field. Probably 300 planes go west thru this field each month.

General Semenov very proud of his 38 pigs—Splendid type Yorkshires—Each in his individual stall. Snow drifts outside several feet thick. Temperature about 35 degrees and snow slowly melting.

Fancy Banquet only about 3 hours after our Nome lunch . . . Col.

1 Colonel Russel Keilor, Wallace's host and escort in Alaska.
2 Major General Ilya Sergeyevich Semenov, commander of the Yakutsk military area, which extended from Lake Baikal to the Arctic Ocean, accompanied Wallace through Siberia, as did Sergei Arsenevich Goglidze, a friend of Stalin and the president of the Executive Committee of Khabarov Territory, under which the Far Northern area was governed. Wallace's other Russian companions were Dimitri Chuvakhin and Gregory Dolbin, both from the Soviet Foreign Office, and Major Mikhail Cheremisenov of the NKVD, the Soviet secret police.

Mazurak[1] very gay at Banquet insisting that Hazard drink much vodka
—champagne and wine. The women helpers at table had been brought
over from Moscow by plane. The winter climate is too severe for
women . . .

Arrived Seimchan 7:15 p.m. local time . . . An elaborate banquet
. . . —mineral water from Caucasus vodka Champagne Red Wine—
excellent bread cheese—caviar—salmon—pork, etc. Ice cream at finish
—Green cucumbers from cold frames—fruit . . .

Long discussion in plane with Chuvakhin about whether the Republicans would win next fall.

He told why Russia did not send more students to U.S. Outside
of Harper at Chicago, Robinson at Columbia[2] and 2 or 3 others the
attitude of the universities . . . was false toward Russia. He felt
papers like New Republic and Nation were edited by men of little
mental grasp. He asked for circulation of papers like P.M. and Chicago
Sun . . .

MAY 24, 1944—SEIMCHAN, SIBERIA

. . . Hospital—sulpha drugs vitamins . . . vitamin pills made locally . . .

Warehouses—Penick and Ford corn oil from Cedar Rapids. Pillsbury
reinforced flour from Minneapolis. All kinds of lend-lease goods.

Kindergarten and nursery combined—43 children also several babies.
One teacher three helpers and a nurse.

Powerful movie on . . . Leningrad siege . . .

At 2 p.m. we got in two C 47s with red stars and went to Magadan,
first flying over the Kolyma river which is Seimchan's source of goods
in summer. In winter Seimchan gets goods via the 560 kilometre highway built from Magadan on the coast.

Took one hour and 20 minutes to Magadan over the high mountains.
Flew at 13,000 feet.

Air port at Magadan 50 kilometres from town. Road . . . was like
a gravel road in Iowa in 1905. Nevertheless we went along in a very
good car at 40 miles an hour.

I rode with Ivan Feodorovich Nikishov, a Russian director of Dal-

[1] Colonel (later general) Ilya Pavlovich Mazurak was one of the pilots who in
1937 had landed Soviet explorers at the North Pole and by virtue of that feat
had become a "Hero of the Soviet Union." In 1944 he served as pilot of the
Russian airplane in which Wallace flew while in Siberia.
[2] Professors Samuel Harper and Gerold T. Robinson.

stroi.[1] The trust has 100 mines coal, lead, gold in which work 300,-
000 people over a wide area extending more than 800 kilometres from
Magadan. Magadan has a beautiful harbor. It receives goods to transmit to interior but the goods produced in the mines goes out by the
rivers.

In 1933 Magadan had two houses. Today it has 40,000 people including its suburbs. Goglidze (who is a close friend of Stalin's) calls
Nikishov a millionaire. As director of the trust, he runs everything. He
looks like an up and coming American business man of 45.

Goglidze says the whole idea of developing the Magadan area was
Stalin's.

Colonel Mazuruk piloted us over and at the dinner that night Colonel Kight and Colonel Mazuruk sat together and I proposed a toast
to the two colonels and the airplane company they might form linking
the two countries together . . .

The trust owns a number of airplanes. It could not do business
without them. Nikishov thinks a railway impractical because of the
effect of the permafrost on the road bed. Airplanes are vital to Siberian development . . .

MAY 25, 1944—MAGADAN, SIBERIA

Went out for a walk in taiga,[2] 7:45 to 8:45. Then breakfast. Then
the port where there was 22,000 tons of stuffs stored. Parts for three
oil refineries which the Japs would not let them ship to Vladivostock.
Then auto repair plant where they make many parts locally which we
would order from Detroit. Complete set of machine tools. Service
1200 trucks and all mining machinery.

Met several Stakhanovites.[3] Ordinary worker gets 1000? or 1200
rubles a month. A Stakhanovite worker gets 2000 rubles a month.

Then visited store. Most smoked fish selling at 17 to 19 rubles a
kilogram. Cheese from America 23 per kilogram. Woman's coat 650
rubles. Woman's wash dress of a sort which sells for two dollars in
U.S., 147 rubles.

Fur store—squirrel, fox, ermine, wolf and bear.

School—1200 students . . . Final exams Physics class . . . Each one
had drawn a question and was subject to oral questioning. We listened

[1] The Far Northern Construction Trust, which Wallace also described as "a
combination TVA and Hudson's Bay Company."
[2] The northern evergreen forest.
[3] Workers so designated for their high productivity.

to the examination of a girl who got 5 the top grade. The Professor
was kindly but thorough in his examination on kinetic energy—speed of
bullets etc.

The principal said school began at 9 and continued to 3. They take
time off for 3 meals in the school dining room—about 15 or 20 minutes
for each meal. Splendid dining room and kitchen.

Ninety percent of the graduates go on to the University of Moscow,
or Leningrad or some other university in the central or western part of
the country . . .

Drove to Collective. Manager is a Tartar. Hog man a Lett.[1] All
hogs an excellent type of English York. They tried the Danish but
found the York could stand the climate best . . .

All grain is shipped in from Vladivostok. They have cleared quite a
bit of land with tractors. The roots of the trees are shallow because
of permafrost.

Season too short for grains. Grow potatoes—rutabagas—and oats for
silage. Use a pit silo somewhat like the one at Fairbanks.

Cows about half Simmerthaler, half Kholmogory. The last breed
came to the Archangel-Murmansk region from Holland about 1710.
Mostly black and white but some brownish red. Very hardy . . .

Great cleanliness with one man in constant attendance, scraping ma-
nure away every time a cow drops any . . . Chickens all white Leg-
horns. Old fashioned incubators for 3800 chicks. Begin taking them
off in January. Best month is February. Worst is June. Begin to lay
when they are 4½ months old. Average production, 118 eggs a
year . . .

In the Magadan House of Culture an excellent concert. I don't think
I have ever seen anything any better put on by the talent of a single
city. Red Army choir, composed of men stationed in Magadan. Non-
professional with the exception of five or six orchestra professionals
. . . Leader has been here past five years. Ballet troops was evacuated
from Poltava in the Ukraine in 1941. It first came to Irkutzk but was
not appreciated there . . .

We saw in the House of Culture the art exhibition, all by local

[1] In a revealing comment about those he met in Siberia, Wallace later wrote: "I
did not find the people of Soviet Asia difficult to understand, and I met persons
in every walk of life, including many native Asiatics . . . All of them . . . were
people of plain living and robust minds, not unlike our farming people in the
United States. Much that is interpreted . . . as 'Russian distrust' can be written
off as the natural cautiousness of farm-bred people . . . Beneath the ideological
talk, the diplomatic protocol, the new urban culture, one catches glimpses of the
sound, wary, rural mind"; *Soviet Asia Mission*, p. 21.

artists. Excellent war cartoons . . . Goglidze says the 700 people in the hall were Nikishov's aristocracy. Nikishov says there are 8000 engineers and economists in Magadan and that in this audience are representatives of workers as well as engineers and economists.

I met N. I. Adagin who has 55,000 miners in his union which covers the whole region. He sent his regards to Hillman and Murray, not to J.L.L.[1]

MAY 26, 1944—KOLYMA, SIBERIA

. . . Gold, coal and lead are the explanation of nearly everything in the Kolyma region. We saw two gold mines—one small, one very large. Placer, surface mining . . . Workers mostly come from old Russia on a three year contract. Wages 2000 rubles a month compared with 800 rubles in old Russia . . .

The Director has a tremendous faith in the future of gold and thinks Russia must have lots of gold. Stalin has made gold mining a preferred war industry and has frozen the men in it.

In every mining town . . . the three buildings which stand out are the hospital, the school and the club. The Director says that because of the hard winter it is necessary to have more entertainment. In the winter the men dig up huge piles of gold bearing rock. They do not work outside when the weather is more than 40 degrees below zero . . .

Nikishov and the director and I went out for a long walk in the taiga afterward. He gamboled about like a calf enjoying the wonderful air immensely. The larches were just putting out their new leaves and the taiga valley looked marvelous with the snow covered mountains 30 miles away . . .

Goglidze proposed a toast to Stalin, Roosevelt and Churchill, referring to the painting of the three at Teheran as made by a local artist. Co. Mazuruk proposed a toast to the modernization of China. Goglidze modified it "May China remain in the war" . . .

MAY 27, 1944—YAKUTSK, SIBERIA

. . . Yakutsk[2] is a autonomous Republic. President is a Yakutsk. Very Indian in appearance.

The permafrost here is 600 feet thick. All the buildings are low—streets are paved with what appears to be round stumps cut off. Larch

[1] John L. Lewis.
[2] Yakutsk had much impressed Willkie.

1 foot long—8 inches in diameter laid on gravel which in turn is laid on the permafrost. Not treated. Will last 20 years.

Along the Lena river, there seems to be quite a bit of cultivation. About 95 percent of the plow land is put in grain crops. Barley is preferred because it is hardier. They grow a 6 rowed, rough awned type. Climate here is about 45 degrees below zero in January but about 58 above in July. About an 88 day growing season. Very dry here, about 10 inches in a year.

Population 25 percent Yakutsk. Remainder Russian and Tartar and other tribes. Mostly Russian . . .

The section of the museum showing development since 1928 was most interesting. The party worker who was an archeologist took us around . . . Production has gone up fully five times. The old fashioned Yakut winter and summer house has been abandoned. We then visited the normal school and sat in several classes. Then the public library with 500,000 volumes, Director a Yakut. Most of the patrons seemed Yakut. About 18 people busy cataloging. We visited the stacks which were primitive but effective. Then visited a public school . . .

At normal school they are proud of their research. The Biological professor is corresponding with some American professors and studies the Biological Abstract. The chemical teacher (a Yakut) is conducting research in vitamins . . .

At banquet, we asked the president what the revolution had meant to Yakut people. First they got a chance to farm. Second they learned to read and write. All the young people know how to read and write and within 10 years everyone will know.

The president was very eager to know about Alaskan agriculture. So was General Semenov. He spoke of the desirability of interchange of information and seeds with Alaska. I suggested the smooth awned barley from Alaska would be of value although it might be too late . . .

Two theatres. One for Yakut folk lore. We went to Russian theatre. Performances four times a week . . . Most of players come from Leningrad. Played there during much of the Blockade. The Russians all seem to look on the defense of Leningrad as even more important than the defense of Stalingrad . . .

MAY 28, 1944—KOMSOMOLSK, SIBERIA

Left Yakutsk about 7:40 and arrived at Komsomolsk about 1:30 p.m. Ten degrees south and 8 degrees east of Yakutsk. All the time on the plane I talked to Dimitri Chuvakhin about the fundamental difference between Trotskyites and Stalinites. He said Trotsky wanted to make peace with the kulaks. That he felt world revolution was vital. Stalin believed Russia must discipline herself and that agricultural and industrial production must be increased and it was not necessary to have world revolution . . .

Komsomolsk city of youth—started in 1932. Now has 120,000 people mostly under 30. Enormous flocks of children. It was Sunday and everyone was out walking in the victory garden. We first visited the shipyard . . . They were just finishing the construction of an 8,000 ton cruiser and three little gun boats. Twenty-five percent of the workers are women . . .

Sixty-five hundred miles from the front they had large numbers of German tanks for scrap. A splendidly equipped machine shop with Cincinnati machine tools received on lend-lease . . .

The refinery gets its oil from Sakhalin. They are making 95 octane gas. The director said 70 percent of the workers were women and that for technical work they were just as good as men . . .

We are living in the rooms of people who have given up their apartments to us. John Hazard was bothered by bed bugs last night . . .

The mayor says his greatest problem is getting manpower and money for streets, streetcars, schools, hospitals, etc. Everything has been sacrificed to the war.

Visited airplane factory employing 13,000 people. Director Timofeev[1] was Mazuruk's mechanic on the North Pole flight. Forty percent workers women. Many boys under 16 years of age. Many Stakhanovites. One a boy of 16 had turned out three times his norm. He worked only six hours a day. The plant is like the old Boeing plant at Seattle. Probably turns out three or four planes a day. Two motored bombers cruising range 3600 miles . . . Plane first put in production four years ago . . .

Give vitamin C to the workers. They claimed only 14,000 man hours per plane. I would guess at least 40,000 hours. They have good machine tools of American make put in before the war. They get aluminum from U.S. Have a month's supply on hand at present time . . .

Plum trees in bloom, absolutely hardy. Pear trees and apple trees fairly hardy. Black currents, hardy. Wild red raspberries larger and tastier than the tame sorts. Black currents yield 3 kgs per bush. Very rich in vitamins.

Steel mill uses army scrap. Enormous numbers of German tanks.

[1] D. A. Timofeev.

Also German helmets. Employs 2200 people, 40 percent women . . . Pay here 900 rubles per month compared with 1500 in airplane factory. Put in here only 48 hours per week compared with 54 in airplane factory. Airplane factory averages 68 percent over its goal.

Wherever we go in the auto, the children exclaim "Amerikantsi."

Visited . . . big concert hall for 2000 people. Large squads of children under five under care of two women. Obviously children of the women in the nearby air factory. They were rather poorly dressed and a little thin but obviously were quite healthy and happy . . .

The young city is dishevelled and run down and the people look overworked. Ten years hence it will be a lovely city. Today they are doing remarkable production job of planes, cruisers, and steel. The roads are pretty bad because they can't take time off from the war work.

MAY 31, 1944—IRKUTSK, SIBERIA

. . . We went to a typical French musical comedy—Garters and ruffles. Voice and choruses excellent. This particular company puts [on] a new comedy every few days. We sat in a box. When I came in the people clapped and rose. I think this must have been organized. Otherwise how could they have recognized me? We got home a little after 11 p.m.

Irkutsk in 1939 had 250,000 population—a year ago 400,000—today 300,000. The refugees from the Ukraine have nearly all gone back home. The atmosphere here is remarkably like Minneapolis. They think this is going to be a great air center . . .

JUNE 1, 1944—IRKUTSK

. . . Visited a collective farm—142 households. Four hundred men in the army. Seventy of the women in war work. Seventy percent of the work done by women. They run tractors. The lady manager . . . says the women do more work than the men ever did.

The fine looking church is used as a grain elevator.

The school house takes care of 200 students. Only a 7 year elementary course. The government pays for school.

The collective farm holds a lease in perpetuity on the land. But the collective has to pay a heavy tax to the government. Sixty percent of grain the government buys at one fourth the market value. The government furnishes tractors and combines . . .

Saw the drama *The Siege of Leningrad* written by a soldier who took part in it. Gave my first speech in Russian.[1] It was well received . . .

JUNE 2, 1944—LAKE BAIKAL, SIBERIA

Went 60 miles by auto to Lake Baikal—took two hours . . . Lake B. contains more ancient forms of water life than any place in the world.

Lake has been as it is now for about 20 million years. Deepest lake in world 1700 meters deep. Some of the fish living at 1,000 meters depth are mammals. They are 50 percent fat.

Many musk deer in mountains. Bears. Elk or something of the sort the horns of which when ground furnish male sex hormone. The scientific station is situated at south western corner of lake where the Angara river flows out. The rapid outflow of the Angara river keeps the lake water always fresh and free from salt . . .

Great need of more people. Population doubled since 1918. Possibly double again by 1970. Birth rate 27 per 1000—death rate per 1000.16.

Eight to ten hectares per person on collective farms. Whole collectives have been transferred from Russia to Irkutsk.

Children of Yakuts and Mongols who have mastered Russian do just as well as Russian children. Are especially good in engineering and medicine.

Before the revolution 50 doctors in Irkutsk area. Now 1500. Three hospitals before revolution. Now 30 or 40. Only 1.5 percent of wounded soldiers turn out to be useless. One half the wounded go back to the front. University was founded after the revolution. Has six faculties—agriculture—mining—medicine—biology and geography. Eighty-five percent of high school students in Irkutsk go on to the University. Students have their expenses paid . . .

JUNE 3, 1944—IRKUTSK

We rested at the comfortable dacha of the commissar overlooking the river. Some discussion with the Russians about the Japs initiated by Vincent. As to what should be done with the Japs after the war they said—"The same as to Germany." Goglidze thinks Japan ought to be confined to her own island . . .

[1] Wallace said that the history of Siberia reminded him of the history of the American Far West. He praised the pioneers of both nations and expressed confidence in the future of the Pacific North in both continents.

JUNE 4, 1944—IRKUTSK

. . . We had a discussion at breakfast about the excellence of the
Russian schools of language. The Chinese school of language at Leningrad is the best in the world. The English school at Moscow is excellent. We have a lot to learn from the Russians. Their world outlook is
broader and more scientific in some respects than ours.

Trinity Sunday which the Russian people are celebrating as a holiday
by walking in the sunshine on the bank across the river. You can hear
them singing. Dimitri Chuvakhin and Vincent got into an argument
about religion. Vincent asked him what church he would belong to
if he belonged to any. He [said] "The Catholic." Chuvakhin is the
most intense Communist of all. I said he was the most religious man at
the table—He said "But it is not the same religion as yours." I said "I
am willing to grant that your religion is doing the world good. Are
you willing to do the same for ours?" He was too intolerant, too intense and too honest to do so. I respected him for his intellectual hon-
esty. We then had a long talk on religion and economics in both the
narrow and broad sense.

We went to see the musical comedy Columbine. Before it began
we talked about the comedy of the fight between the two collectives—
One Jewish raising vegetables and the other Cossak raising rabbits.
The rabbits ate the vegetables. Boy and girl from opposing collectives.
Many Communists can joke and laugh . . .

TUESDAY, JUNE 6, 1944—KRASNOYARSK, SIBERIA

. . . Mr. Goglidze at supper time . . . told us most solemnly of the
opening of the second front. It took away all our appetites. We were
so excited.

After the usual very heavy meal with the usual fine Georgian wines
. . . Vincent, Lattimore and I went walking in the Park. You pay admission to get in. Lots of girls and soldiers strolling around.

JUNE 7, 1944—KRASOYARSK, SIBERIA

We went out to the anti-aircraft factory . . . Half the machines
were brought out from Moscow. In 1929—80,000 people . . . Today
250,000 or possibly 300,000. One hundred twenty thousand came out
because of the war. Of these, 30,000 have gone back. Nearly all the
rest will remain permanently. The iron here comes from Kuznetz—the

coal from Irkutsk. Definitely the war has caused a permanent movement of industry to Siberia . . .

They kidded Major Cheremisenov[1] about having accompanied the various Americans through Russia and someone suggested he write a diary.

He said his heading for the Willkie trip would be "Vodka—Vodka—Vodka" and for our trip would be "Boiled Water—Boiled Water—Boiled Water."

Dolbin spoke up and said Secretary Hull spent his entire time in the house[2] and that the Russians made great efforts to see that the temperature was precisely at 22 degrees Centigrade . . .

JUNE 8, 1944—MINUSINSK, SIBERIA

. . . We got on a beautiful river boat at 6 p.m. and proceeded down the Yenisei on the most beautiful river ride I shall ever take. It is a more beautiful river than the Volga. The river life of Siberia is all important. The towns are on the rivers. We were on an unusually large and luxurious river boat. The Russians sang beautifully . . . A little later Dolbin announced there would be a dance. The waitresses and the two girl radio operators danced with Dolbin, Colonel Kight, Vincent . . . et al. I felt sorry for the girls having to work so hard. Then Goglidze called for tea. It was about midnight. When I got up the next morning at 6, the girls were hard at work. Both the Russian and American men seemed to me rather thoughtless. Everywhere we go the Russian women especially in the country are doing the work.

JUNE 12, 1944—SEMIPALATINSK

Left by plane at 10:20 a.m. for Semipalatinsk—lovely clear day after two showery cool days. It is a very dry spring . . .

I drank three bowls of kumiss with the president in his yurta. Very nicely furnished inside. Made of sheep skins. Draped with rugs inside. Kumiss is mare's milk which has been fermented a day. Contains about same alcohol as beer. Very acid—tastes smoky . . .

These people speak Kazakh which is primitive Turkish. Their blood, however, is Mongolian. They think the present regime is much better than the Czar's. They fought against conscription in 1916. Now they are eager to fight the Germans . . .

[1] Cheremisenov had also accompanied Willkie.
[2] Dolbin was referring to Hull's stay in Moscow.

JUNE 13, 1944—KARAGANDA, SIBERIA

. . . Just north of here 35 miles toward the mountains, the rainfall increases enough to make a fine wheat region. This accounts for big flour mill here. Mine operator from the Don basin son of a coal miner —grandson of a peasant. Chuvakhin pointed to Karaganda and said "This kind of thing saved Russia. Trotsky was against. He thought there had to be a world revolution. Stalin had faith in the moral stamina of Russian people. He said 'We can and we will.' And they did—they created the necessary capital out of their own hides. Russia would have been lost without Karaganda" . . .

Left about 12 for Balkhash. 70,000 people; in 1929, 180 . . . Copper mine—like Chuquicamata in Chile. Produces 55,000 tons a year. Refines to 99 percent stage. Five thousand workers in open pit mine . . . Head of refinery a woman mayor from Leningrad. Her father was a factory superintendent and she brought him out here. Her husband is in the tank corps in the army . . .

JUNE 14, 1944—TASHKENT, SIBERIA

. . . Left at 9:20 a.m. for four hour flight to Tashkent. It now has 1,100,000 people compared with 300,000 in 1929. We stay at a lovely dacha. The Tashkent oasis is much like California but it freezes some in winter so they can grow no oranges . . .

In the afternoon we went over to the pest control station. Central station for plant protection . . . No boll weevil—cotton insects less than with us. They have developed a wilt resistant strain. From central Asia comes the only strain of alfalfa resistant to wilt. They think our Buffalo alfalfa has in it blood of this sort. Our people got seed of it in 1929. The people here are almost completely up to date on latest English and American literature. Full equipment of microscopes and technicians. Have worked out spraying machinery . . .

Had a very jovial banquet with Harriman, American Ambassador to Russia, Quintamilla, Mexican Ambassador to Russia—Chinese Ambassador to Russia[1] . . . They gave me a marvelous Usbek robe. Quintamilla drank large quantities of vodka but held it remarkably well.

[1] Fu Ping-sheung.

JUNE 15, 1944—TASHKENT

Quintamilla told me the story of his visit to Stalin. At first they did not want to let him in but Q. said he had a letter from the President of Mexico and would not deliver it except in person. Stalin said through interpreter "What does he want?" Q. said "Nothing—but does S. want to know anything about Latin America?" They talked 1½ hours. S. is interested only in facts. He goes to sleep on theories. He likes to know facts exactly. He is a very insignificant appearing man but after you talk to him you find he is a genius. He was remarkably informed on all aspects of L.A. but a little vague on some of the geography and he promptly refreshed his mind by consulting a globe . . .

JUNE 17, 1944—ALMA ATA, SIBERIA

Landed in Alma Ata about noon. This is the capital of Kazakhstan. Forty thousand people in 1929. Today 340,000. The completion of railroad line between Tashkent and Semipalatinsk by way of Alma Ata accounts for the increase. Packing plant, canning plant, flour mills, textiles, woolen goods, cigarettes, movie industry . . .

A nice concert—ballet—Red Army chorus. Ballet the best we had seen . . . I gave a farewell toast. Quintamilla says Alma Ata means in Spanish "The Soul binds." Harriman said my trip had done an amazing amount of good. He and Quintamilla and the Chinese Ambassador left at 6:30 a.m. June 18.

JUNE 18, 1944—TIHWA, CHINA

Left about 9:20 a.m. Much interested in the air in looking for the road to Sinkiang and in looking at the last Russian settlements or rather Kazak settlements. Went through the pass and over the blue lake. The road seemed to be in excellent condition with good bridges. Evidences of when the Mohammedans had farmed before the Chinese had cleaned them out 80 years ago. Farming is possible here only with irrigation.

We are now for the first time in the area where the water does not flow into the Arctic. The drainage is simply Central Asia—it does not flow into any ocean.

Tihwa or Urumchi is a town of 90,000. Governor Sheng[1] has a mixed reputation. We were received by a band and soldiers . . . The Russian consul and his assistants were there. Also the British. The only

[1] Sheng Shih-tsai, governor of the northwest province of Sinkiang.

American in Tihwa is the American consul, Horace H. Smith a fine young fellow. After passing through the streets lined with school children we were lodged inside a recently constructed governor's palace with a medieval stockade around it. We were transported in Russian cars—foxier than those used anywhere in Siberia or Central Asia . . . Lincoln body with a Buick motor. The Chinese say the Russian cars hold up much better under rough road conditions than do American cars.

Dr. Wang from Chungking called on me. I told him about the fine work of the Russian experiment stations—about how finely I regarded the work of the Russian scientists. Dr. Wang wanted to know what the Russians felt about the Chinese. I told him I had not asked but I thought John Carter Vincent had talked with them. I said the Russians were very anxious to end the war quickly and that they hoped the Chinese would continue to fight.

He wanted to know if Russia would fight Japan. I said I had not talked to them about that but it was my belief that if the Italian and French fronts went well—the Russians being realists would come in against Japan at the proper time.

Then the Governor came in to talk to me. He told me that in Sinkiang were 4,500,000 people; two million Uighurs speak much the same language as Kazaks and Uzbeks; 400,000 Chinese, 100,000 Mohammedan Chinese; 200,000 Kazaks; 30,000 Uzbeks; 40,000 Manchus; 80,-000 Mongols; 70,000 White Russians.

His policy is to teach the children in the primary grades in their native tongues. He says 60 percent literacy. Main crops are wheat, rice, alfalfa and vegetables . . . He thinks three million acres can eventually be irrigated. Great oil resources. He says the Russians were producing 20 tons of gasoline a day when they took their equipment back to Russia because they needed it in their war effort. He showed no critical bias against Russians whatever. I am told however, that the Russians do not like him at all. Horace Smith tells that while the Governor has done good work on racial minorities and education that he is so much concerned about his own safety that he is quite a tyrant. Complete surveillance of all dinner parties. He puts people in jail under slight suspicion. Uses torture against them. Hanging them by the heels and beating . . .

Everywhere the Russian influence is very strong. All manufactured products from Russia.

We saw an evening entertainment which was poorly put on compared with Russian standards . . .

JUNE 20, 1944—CHUNGKING, CHINA

. . . We go over the desert, see the Great Wall with green on the south side—desert on the north. Come to the deeply eroded areas of loess' near Lanchow. Then we turn south—the land gets very green— it begins to cloud up. We have to land at Chantuk for an hour. This is the B 29 base . . . The boys are full of their June 15 raid. They take us to the chart room and show us full details, including radar pictures . . .

Beautiful farming country at Chantuk. Suddenly word comes that the clouds have lifted at Chungking. We fly above the clouds all the way and break through an 800 foot ceiling with radio direction from the boys on the ground. This is the first rainy weather we have had on the trip.

Gauss, the American Ambassador, introduces me to the Generalissimo and the diplomatic corps. I go to the car where Madame Chiang is seated. We drive to the President's house for a cup of tea. It is about a 40 minute drive. The Generalissimo asks questions and the Madame translates my replies. He asks my opinion of Sinkiang and I tell of my great admiration of the work of Madame Sheng in the schools—express surprise that General Sheng should have put a tardy chauffeur in jail. The Generalissimo laughs. He says "How—how— how" all the time. He has an almost feminine charm.

He asks about my trip in Russia. I pay a strong tribute to Russian science. Describe Komsomolsk. Speak highly of the agricultural work. He wants to know my opinion of the agricultural work in Sinkiang. I tell him I would like to talk to the Minister of Agriculture about it— that I think I may have some suggestions on sheep breeding—but I am not sure yet until I get certain information.

Madame Chiang tells me I have a grandson, born on June 17[1] . . .

At the tea in the very American house are present the four members of my party and T. V. Soong, Dr. Wang, Ambassador Gauss. Madame Chiang complains of her nervous illness. Nervous urticaria. Harrington, the Navy doctor is treating her for it. She looks well, smokes cigarettes, and is animated.

We leave by car for Embassy. T. V. Soong rides with me. I tell him I have not come to China to talk about inflation. He says the Generalissimo wants to bring in by air 2000 tons of cloth a month. I tell him it is impossible to bring in by air enough goods to control inflation. He asks me about Russia. I tell him how deeply impressed I am

[1] Actually a granddaughter, as Wallace soon discovered.

with Russia's science in both agriculture and industry. He wants to know about Russia's attitude toward China. I tell him that Russia wants China really to fight. He says the military situation is not too bad—that even if the Japs take Kweilin,[1] the Americans still have adequate air bases from which to proceed against the Japs. I tell him I think it would be a very serious economic blow to China if the Japs get as far as Kweilin. I tell him there must be no possibility of war between Russia and China.

At the Ambassador's house . . . the Ambassador unfolds the story . . . of Chinese personalities. Madame Chiang has continually been knocking the U.S. ever since she got back from her trip . . .

Gauss says T. V. Soong is O.K. Says that when T.V. spoke frankly to the Generalissimo on his return from U.S. the Generalissimo went straight up in the air. T.V. for a time expected to get shot. The situation is better now.

Gauss says Madame Kung and Madame Chiang through stooges used the U.S. advance of $100,000,000 as a medium of speculation[2] . . . Kung may or may not have been in on it. The Generalissimo found out . . . Kung took the stooges with him to the U.S. and it will be a long time before they venture back.

At the Gauss informal dinner were representatives of the various U.S. Agencies. The military told me the Chinese did not fight. They ran away and the peasants attacked them because they had robbed the peasants. They look on the situation as bad. The Generalissimo has been spreading the propaganda that 17 Jap divisions have been released by the Russian treaty. Our military say they have not been able to identify even one Jap division so released. The Chinese military claim only four. It is true that the Japs have lowered their draft age and now have more divisions and are shipping more divisions to Manchuria and other mainland points.

JUNE 21, 1944—CHUNGKING

Visit the Red Cross. Soldiers. Play a little volley ball with the enlisted men. T. V. Soong calls on me at the Embassy. Tells me of his

[1] At the end of October Japanese advances forced the American troops to destroy their air base at Kweilin.
[2] The United States Treasury had deposited in China's account $200 million of the $500 million credit that Congress voted China in 1942. Though American officials in Chungking suspected that members of the Soong family had used some of that deposit for their personal gain, those suspicions were never proved. Incontestably Kung and others did use American aid unwisely.

precarious position vis a vis the Generalissimo and of his great faith in China. He fears the Gimo does not understand. He is too much the soldier to comprehend the economic forces at work.

Call on Sun Fo and Madame Sun Yat-sen[1] who are both very liberal in their expressions. I give Madame Sun Yat-sen Mrs. Wallace's present. Eat lunch with Secretary of War. Visit the universities. Go out to Gimo's and have first formal conversation with him. I present to him what the President told me verbally about the Communists, and say "There must not be left pending any situation which will lead to conflict with Russia." I hold out the hope of the significant future of a great democratic China with a strong agriculture and strong industry. I point out the part which the U.S. can play and how it is important for American business men that there be peace in eastern Asia.

JUNE 22, 1944—CHUNGKING

. . . On the way back from the station the Minister of Agriculture spent his time denouncing the Chinese Communists just as Ambassador Wei had done in Washington. I told him the U.S. did not propose to fight Russia.

We get to the Gimo's about 6 and plunge into Conversation II. This time Vincent was present and we listen to the Gimo's case against the Communists. It was full of bitter feeling and poor logic. I like the Gimo but fear his lack of vision will doom him to a Kerensky's fate. I was very sad after the second conversation. I told both Madame and T.V. so. They passed it on. The Gimo refused to reply to Vincent on the matter of military observers in Communist China.

T. V. Soong's for dinner. I spent my time talking to the great scholar Tai. He tells me the essence of Buddhism:

1. Love of all life
2. Equality
3. Liberty

He and the Gimo studied together in Japan and had the same housekeeper then which means the same mistress. She had a child which is generally credited to the Gimo although some say it is Tai's. The Gimo recognizes the child . . .

[1] Sun Fo was the son of Sun Yat-sen, the father of the great Revolution of 1911. Sun Yat-sen's widow, his second wife, was the elder sister of Madame Chiang.

JUNE 23, 1944—CHUNGKING

It is still rainy and cool. At breakfast I tell Gimo about my conversation with Tai. I ask Gimo what contribution Taoist monasteries make to China's general welfare. He says none. Buddhist monasteries are worse than useless. Christianity is all right because it is associated with science.

In the conversation after breakfast I open up on strictly military problems and Gimo agrees to military observers. I go to Embassy and find President's wire.[1] I get General Ferris[2] and get the Gimo's confirmation late in the afternoon. We have made some progress. I drive home again and again fundamental thesis. "There must be left pending no questions which will lead to war with Russia."

We have supper with Madame Kung, T.V., Madame Chiang and the Gimo. Strictly Chinese dinner. Only chop sticks. The Madame is sicker than I thought.

The Gimo knows about the President's commitment on Dairen—warm water free port to which Russia might have access.

Madame wants her warmest regards to President and Mrs. Roosevelt and to American people. Vincent takes full notes. I tell Gimo that story was abroad that T.V. was in jail and that it would help dispel the story if T.V. would come back to U.S. with us.

JUNE 24, 1944—CHUNGKING

Gimo says he would appreciate good offices of U.S. in initiating conversations with Russia. He thinks T.V. might come to U.S. later on to work on this matter but not now. With Madame going to U.S. he needs T.V. as a mouthpiece to America.

I am convinced Gimo is headed straight toward being a Kerensky. I like him but I do not give him one chance in five to save himself.[3]

[1] Roosevelt's wire spurred Chiang to the concessions explained in Wallace's diary of June 24, 1944.
[2] Brigadier General Benjamin G. Ferris, one of Stilwell's subordinates, was the senior American officer then stationed in Chungking.
[3] In Chungking on June 24, 1944, Wallace and Chiang Kai-shek issued a joint statement. "Enduring peace in the Pacific," they said, "will depend upon: 1. effective permanent demilitarization of Japan; 2. understanding friendship and collaboration . . . among the four principal powers in the Pacific area, China, the Soviet Union, the United States, and the British Commonwealth of Nations, and among all United Nations willing to share in the responsibilities of postwar international order; and 3. recognition of the fundamental right of presently dependent Asiatic peoples to self-government, and the early adoption of measures in the political, economic and social fields to prepare those dependent

Gimo, through Madame, on way to airport dictates to me 10 points to President.[1]

---

peoples for self-government within a specified practical time limit." The statement also assumed a mutual understanding between China and the Soviet Union and said that "no balance of power arrangements would serve the ends of peace."

[1] Wallace recorded in longhand, often with abbreviations here mostly spelled out, what were actually twelve points. He wrote in pencil but later inserted in ink a few nouns and verbs to make his account clearer. The points follow:

To Pres. from Gimo

1. Attitude of Pres. in Cairo conference, his warmth etc. has immense historic value to people and army of China.

2. Grateful for abrogation of unequal treaties & efforts on behalf of repeal of exclusion act.

3. HAW visit to China as representative of Pres. is to bring about accord with Russia shows great friendship for China.

4. HAW visit at this dark hour will help morale of troops—give hope that American aid will continue.

5. Assure the Pres. that Gimo understands the necessity under which the Pres. acted when he changed plans at Teheran—Nevertheless Gimo foresaw what the change meant. When Gimo sent strong frank memoranda to Pres., it was because he foresaw what is now happening. If the Gimo foresees that China's collapse will come, he must tell the Pres. China has not yet arrived at the collapse state which he predicted to Pres. Things today are not as bad as he feared.

6. Respects greatly Pres. character, views, etc.

7. Deeply touched when I told him about how badly the Pres. felt about Teheran change relative to Gimo personally. Therefore he again appreciated most deeply that I should come out on behalf of Russia-Chinese friendship.

8. China Communist question internal political problem. Would, however, welcome Pres. help. He feels Chinese Comm. are not men of good faith—their signature no good. He would not like to see Pres. blamed for Comm. failure to carry out a commitment. Just the same he happy to have Pres. help if the Pres. after mature consideration decides he would like to do so. He (Gimo) would not consider the Pres. participation as meddling in China's internal affairs, but the Gimo a true friend, who knows the Chinese Communists thru and thru thinks that no matter what Communists say they may do, it will not be carried out—in which case the Pres. prestige would suffer a great loss. Gimo wants President to know that conflict between Communists and central gov't. is not like that between capital & labor in U.S., not analagous.

9. Gimo eager to have closer cooperation and understanding with Pres. How? Too many channels through State Dpt. Churchill has personal representative . . . Both political and military matters. Could Pres. pick a man like this? Could perform an invaluable task. Today military cooperation is very difficult because of personnel. Feels Chenault is most cooperative. Stilwell has improved. Stilwell has no understanding of politics, entirely military in outlook.

10. Gimo has utmost confidence in Dr. Kung. In helping Kung, will be helping Gimo.

11. Gimo is shaping everything toward Democratic path. China Destiny to

We take off at 11:10 a.m. Chungking. First sunny morning in Chungking. Arriving Kunming, we meet General Chennault and General Glenn[1] . . . Play several games of volley ball indoors because of intermittent showers outdoors. Chennault is 54 years old but has trouble with his hearing and a little with his eyes. He is a swell fellow and is looking forward to the day when he can retire on a Louisiana plantation . . .

JUNE 25, 1944—KUNMING

Early in the morning we walk the borders of the rice paddies. A man is leveling a little field with a water buffalo with a baby strapped to his back. His son is leading the buffalo and his wife with a hoe is straightening out the paddy border. The women do all the transplanting of rice. Garden crops are cabbage, Chinese cabbage, egg plant, soybeans. Earlier they had harvested wheat.

Attended Chennault's 8 a.m. staff conference when we had a report on the war in all theatres but with special reference to the Kweilin front. We had a report as to just what precisely some of the B-29 bombers had done which we had seen taking off the preceding evening.

Then we visited the field and went over the B-24s, C-46s, C-47s, the P-40s, the P-51s. It is amazing what Chennault's boys have been able to do with P-40s in spite of their slowness. Visit with the crew protecting the field who can get in to the air in three minutes . . .

In the afternoon, visit the refugee university. The professors nearly all graduates from American universities are very progressive, sympathetic, to the Chinese Communists. They say there is no freedom of speech or press in China. I gave a talk to the University students.

In the evening at the Governor's dinner I give a talk based on the Dragon boat festival. Today is the fifth day of the fifth month. It seems that Chu Yuan on 5th day of the 5th moon jumped into the lake because his advice was not heeded by the prince. I suggested it was even better to live for an ideal than to die for one.

---

get Communists to fall into line. Wants Communists to be a political party. Plans such advance in agrarian program that Communists will have no opportunity.

12. Hopes after war to get interest rate for farmers down to 10%. Hopes to promote land ownership & breaking up of large landholdings.

The reference to Teheran in point 5 related to the decision at the conference there to postpone the invasion of Burma to which Roosevelt had temporarily agreed at Cairo. Chiang's request for having in Chungking a personal representative of the President led later, along with other developments, to the appointment of Patrick Hurley as Ambassador to China.

[1] Brigadier General Edgar Eugene Glenn, Chennault's chief of staff.

Visit to artillery school for Chinese General Waters.[1] A swell job with 75 mm. howitzers packed both on mules and on shoulders of 24 men—or six mules to do the job—3.3 miles an hour. The infirmary. One fifth of the men definitely undernourished. Many die. Scabies. The shoes, straw.

The Chinese infantry school where I talk briefly. The firing range— the Chinese are good marksmen. Here were trained several divisions which are now on the Burma front.

Waters says he is supposed to give Chinese in six weeks what we in U.S. give in three months. Teaching is almost all out of doors practice. They do an awful lot with very little here. At the infirmary they have no vitamins . . .

The Generalissimo, the Secretary of War, etc., have not really supported artillery schools, infantry schools, etc., staffed by American army officers because they know these men will prove very superior to the Chinese trained. They fear the men will upset the static balance of power in China. I am beginning to think they would almost prefer to lose the war rather than to see the old Chinese system upset in any way. Definitely the Chinese and Americans have not combined to do the job that could have been.

Everyone agrees that the enlisted man and the Chinese junior officers are splendid material. I was greatly impressed with them myself. But the damned smiling grafters above? They stand for mediocrity forever continued.

At Kunming I saw the P-38 that photographed the damage by the B-29s on Japan. Several hundred acres of Jap residences were burned out. Only one direct hit on a steel mill—the steel mill was going full blast the next day. On the whole I would say the raid was not too successful. In view of the great danger of cutting off eastern China I cannot help wondering why it is not better right now to use B-29s against Hankow, Canton, etc., which are the base of Jap supplies on this very dangerous full powered Jap offensive.

JUNE 27, 1944—KWEILIN, CHINA

Go to Kweilin which is now the front line air field and the next big objective of the Japs in their drive south. Curious dome-like limestone hills all around Kweilin—like big wigwams. General Casey Vincent is

[1] Brigadier General Jerome J. Waters, Jr.

in charge of air base. General Lindsey in charge of ground troops[1] . . .

[General] Vincent says Japs are advancing from the north at the rate of 15 miles a day. In five to seven days they will be close enough to destroy the effectiveness of his radio network and he will have to abandon this base. He has the air field mined. There are about 1500 troops, both air and land to be taken out by transport plane and railroad. The Chinese generals show me the places on the map where they are going to make various last stands. They say they can hold Kweilin for two months. Vincent says if they can hold Kweilin for two months he can operate on the supply lines with sufficient energy to defeat the Japs.

The Chinese generals are putting great emphasis on the defense value of the caves in these limestone hills. The American generals say the Japs will by-pass Kweilin. The Chinese say they have the troops to attack from the flanks. The Chinese say these troops on the flank are of excellent quality—"The Old Ironsides." Vincent agrees.

The Chinese want artillery. Lindsey says even if we had it—we should not give it to the Chinese because it would fall into the hands of the Japs. He says we have already furnished artillery in their area which has fallen into the hands of the Japs.

T. V. Soong was with us on this trip. It convinced him East China was lost and that he should go to Washington. Lattimore tells me he thinks the whole Soong family is now making its get-away. Madame Chiang and Madame Kung to Brazil—T.V. to Washington. Kung is already in Washington. T.V. swears his trip would only be a short one. I believe him but Lattimore thinks he would not come back to China.

We leave after two hours at Kweilin and go to Chengtu to be officially received by Governor, etc., etc. Dinner by the Governor. Completely the Generalissimo's man but a very nice man. His wife is a very fine woman. This is the center of several Christian universities. I visit in the hospital the two thirds burned survivor of one of the B-29s which crashed. He is from Missouri. It is now 14 days and he will recover. He couldn't see me but he very much wanted to talk.

JUNE 28, 1944—KWANHSIEN

Went up the Min river by auto about 30 miles to Kwanhsien "the Isolated Hill" which was cut through in 300 B.C. by Governor Lee Bin and his son to provide irrigation for this valley. 500,000 acres irrigated land.

[1] Brigadier Generals Clinton Dermont Vincent and Malcolm F. Lindsey.

There are two temples to the Lee Bins at Kwanhsien with appropriate mottos:

"Cut the channel deep—

"Keep the dikes low."

The upper temple is run by the Taoists. Like all the temples, it is located at a nice spot to have a picnic. The abbot is a pacifist, 86 years old. But he thinks it nice that the Americans are doing the fighting for the Chinese. An old pig tail peasant is getting his fortune told by the lottery stick method.

Yield of rice here about 60 bushels an acre. After the rice is transplanted, they give it three rakings to keep the weeds down . . .

Most of the land is rented and the tenants pay the rice crop as rent and get the other crops for themselves. There is lots of tobacco. Soybeans on the borders between fields . . .

Farmers are doing fairly well here although the cost of clothing has gone up faster than the cost of rice.

Road is crowded with rickshaws, wheelbarrows and two wheel carts with old auto tires. China became the ultimate market for old auto tires about ten years ago. More and more hard surfaced highways are built. Pigs are carried to market belly up upon wheelbarrows.

Next after the Nile, this is probably the oldest irrigation system in the world and probably the simplest. Attended a dinner by the nine universities. Miss Wu—a typical, nice, lady of Republican conservative background gave a beautiful little speech. The people here have not the slightest worry about the Kweilin military situation. One man at the table speaks Russian and has lived on the Russian side of the border for three years. Strangely enough, he also does not understand the underlying situation, either political or military . . .

JUNE 29, 1944—CHENGTU

. . . Word comes that Dewey and Bricker have been nominated. I express surprise that it was not Dewey and Warren.[1]

Lunch given by the local General Teng Si-hou, commander of Szechwan province. Both the governor and the general have been very helpful to the military. After the dinner Miss Wu expresses to John Hazard great alarm about the rapid advance of the Russians around Urtebsk. She has all the actions of a very nice reactionary New York Republican. Her kind of people will result in Russia eventually taking over China.

[1] Republican Governor Earl Warren of California.

General gives me a very lovely 300 year old jade belt buckle. We go to the bombing field. I play four games of volley ball. Won three out of four. Talk twice General Gilkeson[1] and Colonel Duncan both very much impressed by the way the Chinese built their B 29 field in less than three months. They feel Governor Chang and General Teng were marvelous. Two hundred fifty thousand Chinese—all hand labor. Both feel the Washington situation utterly screwball in not using B 29s against Jap supplies at Nanking, Hankow and Canton. They believe East China is worth saving.

JUNE 30, 1944—LANCHOW

. . . At dinner Governor Ku had in all the local dignitaries including a "living Buddha" from Tibet and one who had lived in Mongolia but now lives in China. This latter is an old friend of Owen Lattimore— also according to Lattimore a friend of the Roerichs.

Lattimore said "Your friends the Roerichs." I said "The Roerichs are not my friends. They are crooks." Lattimore tells me George Roerich knows Mongol and Tibetan but that he is a phony. He met George in 1934.[2]

[1] Brigadier General Adlai H. Gilkeson.
[2] Nicholas Roerich, a White Russian mystic, and his son, George, had caught Wallace's attention initially because of the older Roerich's promotion of the Banner of Peace, a project to negotiate an international pact to pledge signatories in case of war not to destroy cultural treasures. Wallace's efforts helped in 1935 to effect the signing of that pact by twenty-two nations. Wallace was aware, too, of Roerich's spiritualism and of his knowledge about central Asian agriculture. In 1940 the Republican Party collected letters from Wallace to Roerich, some genuine, some forged, which Westbrook Pegler published in 1948. Those letters contained many mystical references which Pegler intended to embarrass Wallace. By his own account, Wallace had a lifelong interest in spiritual phenomena, but the forged letters gravely distorted that interest. Some historians, including Arthur M. Schlesinger, Jr., in *The Coming of the New Deal* (Boston, 1959) pp. 31–34, have found the Roerich letters credible. Wallace expressed a contrary view in his comments to the Columbia University Oral History Project (Wallace Oral History, pp. 5102–11) where he said:
     I can't think of Nicholas Roerich and certain of his fanatical followers and the relationship of FDR and myself to the Roerich expedition, which began some time in the early summer of 1934, without a strong feeling of disgust. I don't doubt that FDR was moved by the highest motives in authorizing the Roerich expedition, but the actions taken by Nicholas Roerich and his son George were such as to open the door to utterly disgraceful action by others. I know of nothing lower than the actions which some of the fanatical followers of Nicholas Roerich took after I had dismissed Nicholas Roerich and his son, George, from the employ of the U.S. Department of Agriculture in January of 1936.
     The link between Roosevelt and Nicholas Roerich was Roosevelt's mother,

Sara, as well as his own intense interest in central Asia—all the way from Tibet to the Siberian border. The climate, the people, the history, the ecology, and the religion of this area fascinated him. He felt that this area was a breeding place for future wars and the relationship of this area to China, Russia, and Japan intrigued him. Because of his ancestors being linked with China he always attributed a greater importance to China than most people.

He had the idea that the Gobi desert had once grown trees and that when the trees were cut off, the climate had changed . . . He felt the climate might be changed back again by growing trees. I think Roerich had some idea along that line also. Roosevelt also thought that some of the plants of central Asia would be useful to the U.S. I told him that the U.S. Department of Agriculture had previously imported crested wheat grass (*Agropyron cristatum*) from this area and that this wheat grass was serving a useful purpose in our Great Plains area.

At the time of the Dalai Lama in late 1933 Roosevelt speculated with me about an expedition to Tibet—this was one day after cabinet meeting in late December. I told him that the U.S. Department of Agriculture was much interested in importing drought-resistant grasses from central Asia. Both Roosevelt and I knew Nicholas Roerich. I had met him once when I was on my way to Europe in August 1929. Roosevelt had known him when he was governor and referred to him affectionately. I'm sure, however, that the strongest bond between him and Nicholas Roerich was his mother.

In the 1920s Nicholas Roerich traveled extensively in central Asia. These travels were given wide publicity. Roosevelt knew of these travels and we decided to ask Nicholas Roerich to head the expedition. Nicholas Roerich's son was supposed to be peculiarly fitted to travel in central Asia because he had studied many Oriental languages.

Roosevelt directed me to tell Lewis Douglas personally, who was at that time Director of the Budget, to see that the funds necessary for the expedition were provided for in the Department of Agriculture budget.

The expedition began in the summer of 1934. Nicholas Roerich and his son, George, spent the winter of 1934–35 in Harbin, with a White Russian colony. At the time it was a nest of international intrigue. He was bitterly attacked in the White Russian press and in the summer of 1935 articles began to appear in the United States about Roerich. The State Department was seriously disturbed about his being in this troubled spot. As a result, I directed him to proceed southward and finally to northern India.

In January of 1936, I terminated the expedition. All of these actions, which I took beginning in the summer of 1935, were opposed in a gentle way by Roosevelt. He asked why I couldn't be patient with the old man . . .

After I ended the expedition a few of his fanatical followers began to undermine me. They got their first opportunity in 1940 when I was running on the Democratic party ticket for Vice President. That campaign, under cover, was exceedingly dirty. Certain material was being peddled around concerning Willkie's private life and some of the fanatical Nicholas Roerich followers peddled around certain material which I was alleged to have written to Nicholas Roerich. Large sums of money were asked for the material. I never saw the material I was alleged to have written to Nicholas Roerich until quite a while after the campaign when Roosevelt laughingly showed me some photostats of material which had been offered for sale.

The material was composed for the most part of unsigned, undated notes, which I knew I had never sent to Nicholas Roerich, but there were a few letters addressed to Nicholas Roerich signed by me and dated which were

JULY 2, 1944—ULAN BATOR, OUTER MONGOLIA

Arrived in Ulan Bator about noon—over 100,000 people two airfields. We land on one closest to town. Fifteen years ago 50,000 people. Many modern buildings—textile factory, meat slaughtering, southern Outer Mongolia mostly desert. Northern part very good pasture . . . Lattimore says they have improved enormously in last 20 years . . . Russian influence in some ways very marked. In other ways unexpectedly absent . . .

The people of Outer Mongolia are still very religious but they have been freed from the monk racket in large measure. Only one influential monastery in the country now. Museum had an excellent collection of Buddhist images, etc. . . .

JULY 5, 1944

Got up at five and were in the air at 7 a.m. Headed for Seimchan. Due to bad weather at Seimchan, we shifted our course to Yakutsk, flying much of the way at 17,000 feet. Arrived at 12:15 p.m. Took three hours exactly to eat and refuel. Farewell meal with Goglodze and Gubakhin and General Mazuruk.

Many toasts. Goglodze toasted Lattimore and Vincent because they were experts on China and on them rested a great responsibility for the future of China. Goglodze toasts V.P. Wallace coming to Moscow after the war, also toasted President Roosevelt's re-election.

We are now headed for Fairbanks and are flying through the clouds [1] . . .

SUMMARY OF POLITICAL MANEUVERING

When I reached Fairbanks on July 5 I called Joe Guffey. Joe said, "Things are not going well. Some of the people around the White House are saying, 'We need a new face.'" A little later Samuel Rosenman called saying that he and Secretary Ickes wanted to see me at the

---

written in rather high-flown language. None of the material seemed to cause FDR the slightest concern . . .

They tried to peddle the letters in the 1940 campaign and nobody would have anything to do with them, and I'm told that they tried in 1944 and everybody just laughed at them. In 1948 they came out through Westbrook Pegler . . .

[1] With his return from Alaska, Wallace resumed dictating his diary, the text of which is edited hereafter as it was before the Asian journey.

earliest possible moment and wouldn't it be nice if I would eat lunch with them in Secretary Ickes' office on Monday, July 10. The reason for haste was that Secretary Ickes had a date on the West Coast and had to leave the afternoon of the 10th on the train. (Ickes does not fly and so it was proposed that I fly all night in order to make it possible for Ickes not to fly at all.) It was asked that I send a wire when it became a little more certain when I was arriving in Washington.

On Sunday, July 9, I sent a wire to Rosenman from Seattle[1] saying that I thought I ought to see the President before seeing him and Ickes.

After flying all night (leaving Seattle at 5 p.m. Sunday) I arrived in Washington at 9:30 a.m. Monday, July 10, after being gone 51 days and traveling 27,000 miles. At 10 I phoned the President but was informed he was bathing. A little later General Watson called and informed me the President wanted me to see Ickes and Rosenman before I saw the President at 4:30 in an "on-the-record conference."

Therefore I asked Sam and Ickes to lunch at my apartment. After half an hour of polite inquiries they got down to business. Ickes said how much I had grown in his esteem. That I was a true liberal and that he and I were the only two real liberals left in the government. Sam said, "What about me?" Ickes said, "I am talking about liberals in the western sense of the word."

Ickes then made it clear that I had made many enemies, that I was a bone of contention in the convention and that I ought not to let my name be presented.

Before Ickes made this presentation, however, Sam made it clear that the President preferred me as a running mate. In other words Sam created the impression that the President wanted me but he either did not think I could win in the convention nor help him win in the fall.

Neither Sam nor Ickes got very far before I said, "I am seeing the President at four-thirty. I have a report to make on a mission to China. I do not want to talk politics." They beat a hasty retreat.

At 4:30 the President was very cordial. I gave him my report on China. We talked for two hours about it. Then he opened up on politics saying that when I went out I should say that no politics were discussed. He said, "I am now talking to the ceiling about political mat-

---

[1] In Seattle Wallace broadcast a report to the nation about his trip to Siberia and China. He also talked with Harold Young, who reported, as had Joe Guffey, that the Vice President's political prospects looked gloomy. Contrary to some gossip at the time, which Wallace considered fanciful, he did not feel the battle was lost. Rather, almost comforted by the challenge, he moved as fast as he could to repulse it.

ters." He said I was his choice as a running mate, that he was willing to make a statement to that effect. I asked him if he would be willing to say, "If I were a delegate to the convention I would vote for Henry Wallace." He said, "Yes, I would." He then went on to say that a great many people had been in to see him saying that I could not be nominated unless the President did what he did in 1940 and even then they were not sure. I at once broke in and said that I would not want him to do what he did in 1940—that if I had known about it in advance I would not have advised him to do it in 1940. I said I did not want to be pushed down anybody's throat but that I did want to know definitely whether or not he really wanted me and was willing to say so. He was very ready with his assurance. Then the President returned to the theme of his visitors who had told him that I would cost the ticket from 1 to 3 million votes. I said at once, "Mr. President, if you can find anyone who will add more strength to the ticket than I, by all means take him." The President did not say that he believed those who thought I would cost the ticket 1 to 3 million votes. He then said he could not bear the thought of my name being put up before the convention and rejected. I said I had been used to hard situations, that they gave me my best opportunities—that he need not worry about me. He then said, "But you have your family to think of. Think of the catcalls and jeers and the definiteness of rejection." I said, "I am not worried about my family." At this stage of the conversation I was thinking, "I am much more worried about the Democratic party and you than I am about myself and my family." He then asked me to come back for lunch on Tuesday and Thursday. I told him I was going to be seeing Joe Guffey that evening and that I had been out of the country a long time and that I had had absolutely no opportunity to become current. He asked me to take a look around and report the following day.

I got in touch with Charles Marsh and he completed a state-by-state report which looked very good.[1]

For the Tuesday lunch I came in the back way. I presented the President with a glorious Uzbek robe which he liked. (The previous day I gave him some Outer Mongolian postage stamps and money which had cost me $10 but which were probably worth many times that because no Americans have been in Mongolia for 17 years.) We

[1] Marsh's analyses predicted a majority vote for Wallace on the first ballot for the vice-presidential nomination, and predicted, too, victory in November for a Roosevelt-Wallace ticket. Those conclusions drew some support from the latest Gallup Poll, which showed Wallace still the vice-presidential candidate most favored by Democrats.

then talked quite a bit about Siberia. Then he read carefully page by page the Marsh memorandum. Also the tabulation of the vote next fall with and without me. I told him this tabulation was based on work done by some of Sidney Hillman's people. He put a date on it and kept it. He agreed that New York was no better than 50-50. He was doubtful about West Virginia and Kentucky but thought he had an outside chance in Vermont and Maine because of the war situation.

In his Monday talk the President indicated that he meant his fourth term to be really progressive. He was going to get rid of "Jesus H." Jones and Will Clayton and other folks who were thinking only about their own money. The President also told me on Monday how Hannegan was going to send him a letter the following day and how he would accept.

After leaving the President on Tuesday I went over to the State Department and called on Grew and Hull and Stettinius. Then I played two sets of tennis with my son Bob and called up the press to comment on the President's statement (they first having called my office in my absence).

Joe Guffey came around at 9 p.m. He looks on me as a son in this fight. (I forgot to mention that I left with the President, when I was with him at lunch on Tuesday, a statement which Joe Guffey assured me would bring my nomination on the first ballot. The statement read, "It appears the convention will name me. I trust the name with me will be Henry A. Wallace. He is equipped for the future. We have made a team which pulls together, thinks alike and plans alike." The President said he had worked out another wording. But nevertheless he wanted to keep mine.)

The President mentioned how many people looked on me as a communist or worse. He said as a matter of fact there was no one more American than myself, no one more of the American soil. He said some referred to Wallace as that fellow who wants to give a quart of milk to every Hottentot. I said, "You know, Mr. President, I never said that. That was said for me by the President of the National Association of Manufacturers." He was greatly surprised to learn that and then launched into a description of what his defense of me had been.

The secretary to Governor Arnall of Georgia called on me and assured me that Georgia was for me. However, he said there might be trouble holding the delegation after the first vote unless there was some public utterance of preference for me by the President. I told him I was seeing the President on Thursday. He asked me to call him or the Governor after seeing the President.

I made arrangements to meet with Joe Guffey in my office in the Senate Office Building immediately after my lunch with the President on Thursday.

Joe phoned Wednesday morning to say that Sam Rosenman was saying to him that I would get beaten at Chicago. Joe replied with fire. Joe says Phil Murray is going to bat for me.

Charlie Marsh phones that the secretary to Governor Arnall phones him that Georgia Light and Power, operating out of Wall Street, is putting the pressure on the Governor to lay off of me. The Wall Street crowd is beginning to line up as hard as it can behind Barkley. Of course this is not the Rosenman-Ickes-Corcoran game or the Hannegan game. The Hannegan game is to knock me at every possible turn in the hope that Truman will be the ultimate beneficiary. The Ickes game is to have Douglas as the beneficiary.

Hannegan called up my office and came over to see me in my apartment Wednesday morning. He said he wanted to tell me that I did not have a chance. He said I ought to withdraw. I said I would not withdraw unless the President did not want me. And I said the President has indicated he does want me. I said I had never been in favor of the President delivering a fiat to the convention. He said he had been with the President last night and that he thought the President was going to indicate me as first choice and someone else as second choice, and that by so doing this would automatically result in the second choice person getting all the dissident votes and therefore winning. I told him that I had known for a long time that he thought I did not have a chance—that his views were well known and had been freely expressed to many people. I said we might as well understand each other—that I was not withdrawing as long as the President preferred me.

A little later I got word that a newspaperman met Hannegan at the front door of the Wardman and that Hannegan referred to me as a terrible person. Furthermore, Hannegan declared he was not going to Chicago until this vice-presidential thing is settled.[1]

Word comes from several sources that Biddle, Tommy Corcoran's friend, is working very hard for Douglas and very strong against me.

Claude Pepper came in to indicate that while he naturally had ambitions himself, he wanted to cooperate with me on the early ballots at least. He was worried about the fact that with the President

[1] That meeting of July 12 was between Hannegan and one Harris of the St. Louis *Post-Dispatch*, who immediately made a record of the conversation, which he then gave to Marsh.

not available, the party machinery would be left in the hands of those who are unfriendly to the progressive cause. He told about his conversation with Harry Hopkins and how Harry Hopkins had "Yes, butted" me in the highest terms. Pepper said that at a recent party at Joe Davies', Paul McNutt had pulled him off to one side and had said fiercely, "Well, it won't be Wallace this time. I do not give a damn what Roosevelt says."

Sidney Hillman came in at nine Wednesday evening and said he was going to be seeing Roosevelt the following morning. He told me that Ickes had phoned him that I, Wallace, did not have a chance and that they better find a second choice. Sidney had apparently been softened a little by their pressure but on the whole was standing fairly firm. He is revising PAC so as to avoid any legal complications. He has a payroll of $65,000 a month and has a more powerful organization for getting out the vote than the Democratic National Committee and a payroll several times as large. I told him that *Time* was coming out with him on the front page cover (a very Semitic likeness), the idea being to create as much prejudice against Roosevelt as possible the week of the convention. The thought is to make it appear that Jewish labor is running the Democratic party.

On Thursday I came in to lunch the back way at one o'clock. At 1:40 I saw Sidney Hillman's back out of the corner of my eye. He must have been with the President more than an hour. The President started to talk to me about Sidney but I cut in, saying I would like to ask a favor of him, "I would like to have the privilege of putting his name in nomination." He said Alben had asked for that, and in view of Alben's speech against him on the floor of the Senate he thought it was best for Alben to do it. We talked at some little length about the letter Gimo Chiang had sent me and which I had turned over to the State Department with the suggestion that they prepare a reply for the President's signature. Vincent had prepared an excellent reply, which Hull had approved and which I had brought in purely as an expediter. The President referred to Chiang's continual request for a man who had the President's complete confidence who would serve the same purpose as Carton de Wiart serves for Churchill in China. Suddenly the President said, "I think I will send Don Nelson over . . ."

. . . He then told me that he was going to handle the Vice President situation by sending a letter to Senator Jackson, the permanent chairman.[1] He was going to compose the letter that afternoon and send it

---

[1] Roosevelt's letter to Senator Samuel D. Jackson of Indiana, who was to be permanent chairman of the Democratic convention, said: ". . . I have been

from Hyde Park on Friday, July 14. Jackson could release it as soon as he wished, which probably would be Monday but might be Sunday.

In the letter he would say that he had known me a long time, that he thought a lot of me, and that if he were a delegate to the convention he would vote for me. He would also go on to say that he did not wish in any way to dictate to the convention. He wanted to get the wording just right so that it would not seem in any way like dictation but so that it would be just to me.

The President told me about the meeting Tuesday night at which were present Ed Flynn, Ed Kelly, Pauley of California,[1] Hannegan, and some of the other professionals. According to the President they all thought I would harm the ticket. I said at once to the President, "If you think so, I will withdraw at once." He said "I have no basis for a judgment of my own. The only way I could find out would be to drive among the farmers in Duchess County. There is —— —— who is nominally a Republican but mighty independent." He then described a number of men in detail who could give him the basis of judgment he had to have. But, he said he did not have the time to see these men and so he could not say. He said it was mighty sweet of me to make the offer but he could not think of accepting it.

He then went on to say that the professional politicians thought Harry Truman was the only one who had no enemies and might add a little independent strength to the ticket. They thought Douglas might bring a little strength on the West Coast. Moreover he was a picturesque figure because his hair got in his eyes and he had to sweep it out with a gesture of his hand. Jimmie Byrnes was too old and had the handicap of coming from a section which would alienate the Negro vote. He told of a conversation he had recently with Jimmie and of how hot Jimmie was for the job and how he had covered all angles with Jimmie. He said, "Why, you know Jimmie is older than I am? He is sixty-five." He then talked about Alben at some length, his age, his speech, the tax law, etc., etc. I told him about the public utilities swinging in behind Barkley in a big way yesterday. He asked

---

associated with Henry Wallace during his past four years as Vice President, for eight years earlier while he was Secretary of Agriculture and well before that. I like him and respect him and he is my personal friend. For those reasons, I personally would vote for his renomination if I were a delegate to the Convention.

"At the same time, I do not wish to appear in any way as dictating to the Convention. Obviously the Convention must do the deciding . . ."

[1] Edwin W. Pauley, a wealthy Californian oil executive and a promoter of Truman's candidacy, was in 1944 treasurer of the Democratic National Committee.

why. I said I did not know, that I thought Alben was pretty progressive but I guessed perhaps they thought he was conservative compared to me.

I asked the President if he was going to do what Hannegan wanted and give an alternative name. He said no. That would be too much like dictation. I gave him the account of Hannegan's conversation with Harris after Hannegan's visit with me yesterday morning and said in view of the fact that the President would not have a Harry Hopkins at the convention and in view of the fact I could not trust Hannegan, I hoped there would be some method of Joe Guffey getting in touch with him direct. He said Joe could get in touch with him at his railroad car at San Diego by getting in touch with Latta[1] at the White House. The ship which is taking him northward from San Diego has a broken crankshaft and will not be able to leave as soon as he had expected. He said also that he had told Sidney Hillman that he could get in touch with him through Latta.

When I was leaving I said to the President, "Well, I am looking ahead with pleasure to the results of next week no matter what the outcome." As I shook hands with him he drew me close and turned on his full smile and a very hearty handclasp, saying, "While I cannot put it just that way in public, I hope it will be the same old team."

When he referred to Harry [Hopkins] he said that Harry did indeed have his full confidence but that Harry was a very sick man. Harry had eaten lunch with him on Wednesday but could hardly hold his head up for the entire meal and had to go away immediately after lunch to lie down.

The President said, "Even though they do beat you out at Chicago, we will have a job for you in world economic affairs."

CA. JULY 31, 1944 (undated)[2]

RECOLLECTIONS OF THE CHICAGO 1944 CONVENTION

I arrived late Wednesday morning, July 19, at the 63rd Street Station and went direct to the Sherman Hotel. Shortly thereafter I saw Phil Murray, Sidney Hillman, Beanie Baldwin, and R. J. Thomas at the Morrison. Phil told me that on Monday Jimmie Byrnes had told him

---

[1] Maurice C. Latta, executive clerk at the White House.
[2] Wallace wrote this memorandum during the period July 22–31, 1944. He was at the convention in Chicago July 19–21, then in Des Moines, July 22–30, and in Washington July 31.

that I had been of very little service to labor—that he, Jimmie, could be of much better service because he could get into the details of legislation, could persuade legislators, etc. Sidney denied that he had said anything on behalf of Truman. Phil told me later that when Sidney started out opening the door to Truman in a press conference, he, Phil, had shut it uncompromisingly by saying there was no second choice.

When I entered the hall Wednesday evening I was amazed at the friendly reception given me. Joe Guffey told me the following morning that Dave Lawrence, the Pittsburgh boss, was holding out against me in the Pennsylvania delegation, as well as a Phildadelphia man by the name of Clark who was being guided by Frank Walker. Francis Biddle started out against me in the Pennsylvania delegation but swung around to me when he found that Tommy Corcoran's protégé had no chance. Frank Walker stayed steadfastly against me in the caucus, saying to Joe Guffey, "I am loyal to the boss and the boss does not want Henry Wallace." Then came the smoke-out of the letter from the President to Hannegan.[1] Kelly had given a dinner Tuesday evening in honor of Hannegan at which Pepper and Guffey were present. Hannegan worked one end of the table and Kelly the other, saying the President was for Truman but not saying a word about Douglas. Guffey made a public statement which forced Hannegan to divulge his full letter to the press about 6:30 Thursday evening. The effect was damaging to Hannegan's reputation. I realized then that Hannegan had gotten the President to do that which he, the President, had promised me the preceding week he would not do—"introduce a second name." The President's explanation to me doubtless would be that all he meant to say to me was that he would not include a second name in his letter to Jackson.

After the tremendous demonstration for me Thursday evening,[2]

[1] Hannegan had persuaded Roosevelt to write him on July 19, 1944. The President's letter opened the way for the nomination of Truman: "You have written me about Harry Truman and Bill Douglas. I should, of course, be very glad to run with either of them and believe that either one of them would bring real strength to the ticket."

[2] The demonstration, the noisiest of the convention, followed Wallace's speech seconding the nomination of Roosevelt. Wallace said, in part: "The future belongs to those who go down the line unswervingly for the liberal principles of both political and economic democracy regardless of race, color, or religion. In a political, educational, and economic sense there must be no inferior races. The poll tax must go. Equal educational opportunities must come. The future must bring equal wages for equal work regardless of sex or race. Roosevelt stands for all this . . . The only question is whether the convention and party workers believe wholeheartedly in the liberal policies for which Roosevelt has

Beanie Baldwin gave me his size-up of the state-by-state situation. He also told me of a conversation he had had with Paul Porter about the situation in the Democratic National Committee. Paul Porter, according to Beanie, had been shocked by the direct methods used by Hannegan against me. Porter said to Baldwin, "This attitude does not originate with Hannegan but with the President himself."

Friday morning I got word of the strong actions employed by Pauley in trying to get the California delegation to desert me. Word also came that Hannegan, Flynn, and Pauley claimed to be talking with the President at frequent intervals and that he was upbraiding Hannegan for not getting busy to put Truman over in a hurry. Word came that Senator Maloney and Homer Cummings[1] were against me in the Connecticut delegation but that all 16 of the other delegates were for me and therefore these two had to go along. I also heard that when Truman had breakfast with Hillman on Tuesday morning he was pushing Jimmie Byrnes. Leo Crowley, who had come out Monday to work for Byrnes, was working for Truman on Thursday. He said nothing against me personally but claimed that my followers were telling lies. It is said that the President got in touch with Crowley personally so as to get Byrnes to pull out. Hannegan according to Littell[2] had called me a "son of a bitch" because I refused to withdraw. He repeatedly spread stories to the newspapermen that I was about to withdraw. The Minnesota crowd was glorious, also southern California, Guffey, Phil Murray, Tom Miller[3] of Austin, Texas, and Wilson Wyatt[4] of Louisville, Kentucky, and Pepper of Florida, and many others. Gene Casey was working steadily with Ed Flynn to knife me. Ted Hayes, Flynn's man, who used to be very warm to me, was very cold to me in the elevator. I am convinced that some months ago Flynn sold Hannegan to the President and that part of the deal was that large sums of money could be had for the 1944 campaign if the President would only ditch me. The President agreed in spite of his very real affection for me. He tried to wriggle out but could not. The

always stood." Some observers, with whom Wallace came to agree, believed that the convention would have renominated him right after selecting Roosevelt if those running it had not forced an overnight adjournment. In the interim, according to that theory, Truman's sponsors lined up the votes they needed. Though Wallace led on the first ballot the next day, Truman won on the second.

[1] Senator Francis T. Maloney and former Attorney General Homer S. Cummings.
[2] Norman M. Littell, at that time Assistant United States Attorney General.
[3] Mayor Tom Miller of Austin, Texas.
[4] Wilson W. Wyatt had represented the Board of Economic Warfare in North Africa (March–May 1943) and in 1944 was mayor of Louisville.

money boys meant business. After it was all over he felt very remorseful for a brief moment and apparently remembered what he said to me so warmly when I said goodbye to him on Thursday the 13th. At any rate Friday evening on July 21 he wired me, "You made a grand fight and I am very proud of you. Tell Ilo not to plan to leave Washington next January."

Word came on Thursday that Truman had said to the newspaper boys that he had been designated for the job and that he hated to have to beat Henry Wallace. Flynn, Kelly, Hague, Walker, Casey, Jonathan Daniels, and practically the entire White House–National Committee ménage threw everything they had at me, including such picayunish things as not letting the Iowa boys have tickets on Friday (this was Pauley's punishment for the demonstration made on my behalf on Thursday). Baldwin told me that most of the demonstration on my behalf even on Thursday evening was made by people who had gotten in as a part of the Kelly machine but nevertheless were for me. The CIO boys did have 1500 people they wanted to get in on Friday but they simply could not get tickets although the galleries were practically empty. Beanie says the demonstrations for me were mostly by Kelly people and other Chicagoans of no particular affiliation.

Joe Guffey tried to get through to the President on Thursday, using Latta as the President had suggested to me. No luck. Perhaps the blame is Kelly's telephone operators. Perhaps the blame is the President's. I told Joe to tell the President that if the President would write another letter asking me to withdraw, I would withdraw at once. However, Joe did not get through to the President and I am glad he did not.

I shall work for the President's election because I am afraid of what the Dewey alternative means. I shall not speak under the auspices of the National Committee or under the auspices of the CIO. I shall hold the number of speeches down as much as possible and yet do an effective job.

Jim Farley, on his way home from the convention, said to a newspaperman that if either the New York or Illinois delegations had been polled Thursday morning there would have been a majority for me in both delegations.

The *Time* story of July 31 is roughly accurate. Also the Kent and Drew Pearson stories of July 28. Also T.R.B., *The New Republic* of July 31.[1]

[1] *Time* attributed Truman's victory to the influence of the Democratic bosses, especially Hannegan, Walker, Kelly, and Flynn. Frank R. Kent and Pearson

Guffey said on July 31 he was positive that the drive for Truman came from the President and not from Kelly and Hague.[1] He is sure that Hague was telling him the truth the week before the convention when he said flatly he did not want Truman because the nomination of Truman would raise the boss issue. He is sure also that this was Kelly's stand. He is confident therefore that the President forced Truman on the bosses. Personally I think the thing originated with Flynn via Hannegan. Guffey may be right about Hague but I am not so sure about Kelly. The thing may also have had some roots in Hopkins via Kelly. The hard thing for me of course is to reconcile what the President said to me when I left on July 13 with what he later did. What he said to me on July 13 just as I was leaving. Pulling me by the hand so my ear was close to his mouth, was—"Of course, I cannot say it publicly but I do hope it will be the same old team."

On the other hand, there is no doubt in my mind as to his intentions when I returned from Alaska on July 10. (He wanted to ditch me as noiselessly as possible.) And then he apparently changed momentarily when my presentation clearly indicated that he had been lied to by his advisers. Probably the advisers really won at the White House meeting the evening of July 11.

AUGUST 1, 1944

I ate lunch with Alben Barkley Tuesday, August 1. I did not let him talk much about the convention, saying continually to him that the important thing now is to look ahead to November 7, that we must do everything possible to re-elect the President. I told Alben if there was any way in which I could help him get re-elected in Kentucky, I would like to do so.

Alben said he thought Jimmie Byrnes had been worse hurt by the President than anyone. Jimmie talked to him about two hours on Wednesday or Thursday of last week. It seems that Hannegan and Kelly saw the President on Saturday, July 15, when the President went through Chicago. Immediately following this visit Hannegan got in touch with Byrnes and urged him to get into the race. According to Barkley, Jimmie was running like a scared rabbit on Monday and Tuesday, thinking he had the blessing of the President. He was all broken up when he found he had not. Jimmie also told Alben that

and T.R.B. agreed but also emphasized Roosevelt's role in "double-crossing" Wallace. All interpreted the outcome as a defeat for the liberals.
[1] Frank Hague, since 1917 mayor and notorious boss of Jersey City, and since 1922 a member of the Democratic National Committee.

the famous letter to Hannegan about Truman and Douglas was not written on July 19 but was actually written on Friday, July 14. It seems therefore, that the President's letter to Jackson on my behalf and the President's letter to Hannegan on behalf of Truman and Douglas were typed and signed the same day and both within 24 or 36 hours of the time the President told me with such deep feeling, "I can't say it publicly but I hope it will be the old team."

Barkley said Truman talked to him on Monday, that Truman at that time was working hard for Jimmie Byrnes and that he declared with the greatest vigor and apparent sincerity that he did not have the slightest interest in the job himself. On Wednesday, Truman told Barkley that the President had called him on the telephone and asked him to quit fooling around and hurry up and get the nomination for himself. Barkley says if the convention had not been dictated to by the President, I would have gotten the nomination. Barkley says he himself got into the race only when the word was passed around that the President did not want me. Barkley declared that he himself would have been glad to support me if the President had kept hands off.

Barkley says Truman told him he would have voted against the President on the tax bill veto. After Alben got this out of his system, I got him to agree there was only one thing to do and that was to go down the line for the President on November 7. Alben could not help coming back to the theme, however, of "It makes you awfully depressed when you know a fellow will do things like that. He may be a smart politician but how can he go in two different directions at the same time?"

I told Alben I was very happy about the whole situation, that I realized Jimmie Byrnes had been seriously hurt. Alben said Jimmie left the convention to go back to Washington Thursday. Those commentators who say Jimmie was working against me on Friday are probably doing him an injustice. Alben told me he was going to refuse to accept any funds from the Democratic National Committee in his race in Kentucky this fall. I told him that I was going to refuse to appear under the auspices of the Democratic National Committee, that I would pay my own railroad fare.

(I understand at the convention that Frank Walker called up every delegation and said that the President was for Truman.)

AUGUST 2, 1944

I wanted to talk to Harold Smith about the possibility of getting from his organization certain information that bears on the problem of full employment after the war. I told him I wanted to make speeches during the campaign on this subject and would like to have them as sound as possible. He told me that his people were beginning to think it would be necessary to have a national budget of around $25 billion dollars after the war. His people were very much afraid that we were in for an annual unemployment of around 10 million persons.

He then got to talking about the Chicago convention, saying how deeply pained all his people were. He said he thought Jimmie Byrnes was the one originally responsible for getting the President in the frame of mind that he ought to have someone else than me to run with him. Harold said that on Tuesday, July 11, he had lunch with Secretary Ickes, and Ickes told him with some humor of the meeting that Ickes and Sam Rosenman had had with me the day previous. They had been sent by the President to talk to me. After I refused to talk politics, Ickes told with some humor how he had said, "Well, I guess I have to be going. I have got lots of work at my office." Then Sam spoke up and said, "Harold, can I get a ride back with you?" Then Ickes went ahead to say to Harold Smith, "Of course, we both came in the same car and we were both headed direct for the White House." Ickes laughed and seemed to enjoy the hypocrisy of it all tremendously. Ickes then proceeded to volunteer that his wife had said he was a fool to get in a mess like this, that he got exactly what he deserved.

AUGUST 3, 1944

Harry Truman came in this morning. He started out by saying that he was a very unhappy man, that he never spent such an unhappy week in his life as the week at Chicago. He said, "You know, this whole matter is not one of my choosing. I went to Chicago to get out of being Vice President, not to become Vice President." He said they will dig up all the dead horses which he thought he had gotten safely buried and throw them at him. He said, "It will be very hard on my family." I was exceedingly happy throughout the interview and he was very doleful and lugubrious. His whole attitude was that of a man who has not been sleeping. He used the specific phrase that he had not been engaged in any "machinations" for the nomination. He asked for the continuation of my friendship. I said, "Harry, we are both Masons" and smiled at him very sweetly and said I would do everything I could to make the election come out right. I said the important thing was to look ahead and not back. He said he was not a deep thinker like I was and he needed my help on policy matters during the campaign. I made no comment whatever that I would help him, neither did I say I would not. He told me he was going to resign from his committee today although a number of folks wanted him to continue. I told him I thought he was wise in so doing, that he would need all his energies now for the campaign. I said nothing in any way to him which could be interpreted as being anything less than friendly; on the other hand, I made absolutely no commitment to him. I judge he went away relieved and somewhat happier than when he came in. He is a small man of limited background who wants to do the right thing.

When Truman professed such deep friendship for me, I refrained from mentioning to him the fact that three months or so ago, he came out for Rayburn, and on Monday and Tuesday at the convention, he was working hard for Jimmie Byrnes. These actions took place after he had told me on the floor of the Senate that I was his candidate for Vice President, that all he wanted to do was to continue in the Senate. This kind of action convinces me beyond doubt that he is a small opportunistic man, a man of good instincts but, therefore, probably all the more dangerous. As he moves out more in the public eye, he will get caught in the webs of his own making . . .

AUGUST 8, 1944

. . . Phil Murray was getting a bit of satisfaction out of licking Bennett Clark in Missouri.[1] Murray told me that after the Chicago convention, Hannegan had come to him saying how important it was to elect Clark. Phil replied, "Important to who? It is important to us to defeat Clark." Phil said he was going to be seeing Hannegan that afternoon at 2:30.

Phil is not at all satisfied with the treatment he received from the administration. He would like very much for me to head up the new National Citizens Political Action Committee. I said to him, "What is to become of Sidney Hillman?" He said, "Sidney Hillman was only in there temporarily." Phil confirmed my suspicions of Hillman. He said that Sidney on Monday was saying, "We must have a second choice." Phil thinks it quite possible that the President and Sidney cooked up the second choice idea when they were together on Thursday, July 13. Phil says that when he and Sidney had dinner with Hannegan on Monday evening, July 17, Hannegan said, "We will withdraw Jimmie Byrnes if you will withdraw Wallace." This confirmed the statement that was made to me by Barkley that the idea of getting

[1] Clark had lost his campaign for renomination.

Jimmie Byrnes to go to Chicago and run was cooked up by the President and Hannegan when the President came through Chicago on July 15. If it had not been for Phil Murray's straightforward strength, this plan would have succeeded. On the other hand, if Sidney Hillman had insisted that Phil Murray and R. J. Thomas go in with him to see the President on July 13, I am practically certain that I would have won overwhelmingly on the first ballot. I said so to Phil and he agreed.

I also said to Phil that looking toward the future, I was very glad that he and Thomas had not gone in with Sidney Hillman, that the situation was better the way it was. I told Murray that in all of my actions so far I had gone the whole route for the President. I said, however, that I was not going to make any speeches for the ticket until I found as a result of personal conversations with the President just where he stood with respect to liberalism after the election is over.

Phil said that Harry Hopkins had come over to see him earlier in the day, that Harry was much stronger now. Phil said that he had told Harry in the most vigorous kind of language about my unusual strength with the people of the United States. Harry had professed very high regard for me and blamed the Chicago convention results on the President's other advisers, disclaiming all responsibility himself. Phil says Harry still has some New Deal tendencies. I suggested to Phil that he see the President himself and not depend on Harry Hopkins. Phil says that both Dewey and Willkie have made much better statements on wage policy than the President or the Democratic Party platform. Phil thinks the CIO has received a raw deal from the President. He gave me a carefully worked out memo on this subject.

Phil Murray said when he talked with Kelly that Kelly was not against me. He said that Kelly had absolutely nothing against me, that all he was doing was to follow out the desires of the President. The same story has come to me from other folks concerning Hague, that Hague as a matter of fact went out of his way to keep hands off, doing the very minimum which was necessary to comply with the President's wishes. Phil says that word was freely circulated in the Pennsylvania delegation that the Catholic hierarchy was against me. Phil himself had a letter from Bishop Shiel[1] of Chicago saying that he, the Bishop, had a very high esteem for me. Phil Murray says that Frank Walker refused to have any part in the Catholic drive against me which was started in the first instance by Tommy Corcoran and which was continued, so Phil is convinced, by Hannegan . . .

[1] Bishop Bernard J. Shiel.

AUGUST 9, 1944

. . . Don Nelson told me of his great difficulty with General Somervell and Jimmie Byrnes.[1] He says Harry Hopkins' health is getting much better. Apparently Harry is backing Don to the limit. Evidently also Harry has become very liberal all of a sudden . . .

AUGUST 10, 1944

. . . Louis Bean gave me his present size-up of the President's strength. He thinks if the election were held today, the Democrats would get 306 electoral votes and the Republicans would get 225. I remembered the list which Charles Marsh had prepared, which I had left with the President on July 11. I asked for it and compared with Bean's list. Charles' list had indicated that the President would probably have 366 votes and the Republicans only 165 votes, the difference being particularly in states like Minnesota, Michigan, Wisconsin, Iowa, Oregon, Idaho, and Wyoming. Charles had indicated in his list if I were nominated as Vice President, then Michigan, Minnesota, Wisconsin, and Iowa would probably go Republican. Personally I think Iowa would have gone Republican even if I had been nominated. My failure to be nominated, however, probably will make some difference in Minnesota, Michigan, Wisconsin, Indiana, and Illinois, possibly also in Pennsylvania and New York.[2] Both the Bean and the Marsh analysis indicated that New York is probably Republican at the present time. This can be changed but it will take a lot of hard work to do it. Also it will take a lot of hard work to hold Pennsylvania in the Democratic column . . .

AUGUST 12, 1944

. . . CBB said he had a lighthearted comment to make. He was down at the Democratic National Committee the other day and said

[1] Nelson was pressing for the beginning of reconversion, especially for small firms. The War Department continued to believe that any substantial step toward reconversion would damage morale. Though Nelson had a good case, particularly if smaller industry were to have a maximum opportunity for postwar competition with big business, the War Department won the argument when the German counterattack in December halted the Allied advance in Europe. At that point, concern for sustaining public morale overrode the probably sounder considerations about postwar equities.

[2] New York and Pennsylvania went Democratic in 1944.

to Paul Porter,[1] "You had better get over to the White House and straighten yourself out with Anna Boettiger, the President's daughter. She told me (Baldwin) the other day that you are a son-of-a-bitch because of the way you treated Henry Wallace at Chicago." Paul Porter came right back at Beany and said, "You go tell Anna Boettiger, 'So's your old man'" . . .

AUGUST 14, 1944

. . . Chester Bowles indicated he was going to make a number of speeches on CPA. These speeches would be nonpolitical but nevertheless he is going to emphasize as strongly as he can the same theme as I emphasized in my February West Coast speeches—full use of all manpower resources and skills to produce the maximum to raise the standard of living . . .

Frank Walker said that he came up to see me on a purely personal basis, that we had always been good friends and he wanted us to continue to be good friends. He said he had supported Truman at the convention, that he had no apology for supporting him, said he wanted me to know that he had not said anything at the convention against me personally and he did not know of anyone who did. I told him I knew he had not indulged in any personalities and that I had known that he would fight clean. I said one of our mutual friends who had seen some of the fighting which was not clean had told me about how decent Walker himself was. Walker seemed not to be aware of any fighting which was not clean. I told him that, some day 20 years hence, I would appreciate having him tell me why he was against me but I did not care to know now. When Walker got up to leave, I said, "Frank, I want you to know I have nothing whatever against you." I slightly underlined the "you" in my comment. Walker said he thought the President might have a pretty hard time getting re-elected especially with the war over. I said I agreed with him and that I had so told the President. Frank's attitude was fine and decent and I am sure that he was merely carrying out orders for somebody else.

[1] Paul A. Porter was directing publicity for the Democratic campaign. For that purpose, he had resigned as associate director of the Office of Economic Stabilization. After the election Roosevelt appointed him to the Federal Communications Commission.

Vincent told me that the situation in China was not getting any better, that there was a separatist movement starting in southwest China looking toward the loosening of the allegiance of these areas to the Generalissimo. He said that the President had finally decided on Pat Hurley as the man to coordinate America's efforts in China and to serve as the man corresponding to Churchill's man Carton de Wiart. I told Vincent I thought Hurley might do a very good job, especially in view of the fact that I did not see how there would be any oil involved anywhere around Chungking. I said General Hurley made a very favorable impression . . .

Marriner Eccles[1] is very pessimistic and disgusted. I think he would like to see Dewey win. He spoke of a fellow by the name of Elliott Bell[2] who is a past New York *Times* newspaperman and who has been Dewey's Commissioner of Finance. He said he has known Bell for a long time, that he is a sound man, etc., etc. Eccles made this statement when I ventured the opinion that Dewey would do only about 1/10 of what was necessary to meet the postwar difficulties whereas I thought Roosevelt, if re-elected, would do 1/3 of what was necessary and would, therefore, be three times as good as Dewey. Eccles took strong exception to this, claiming that Dewey would probably do a better postwar job than the President.

Eccles says the President is not a liberal anymore, that he does a lot of funny political things. He says, for example, at the present time that the President is sending Leo Crowley around to court Wendell Willkie. I said, "Do you mean that Crowley is not a liberal or Willkie is not a liberal?" He said with great emphasis, "I mean that Crowley is not a liberal."

We spent most of our time talking about the various items in the national as distinguished from the governmental budget, and what is necessary to get full employment and a national product of goods and services of 170 billion dollars at 1942 price levels . . .

Jack Fischer[3] told me how much he wanted to work on behalf of

1 Marriner Eccles, chairman of the Board of Governors of the Federal Reserve System, a champion of the new economics since he had come to Washington in 1934, was especially critical of the Treasury's policies for financing the war.
2 Elliott V. Bell, a financial writer for the New York *Herald Tribune* (1929–39), later on the editorial staff of the New York *Times*, had served as economic adviser to Willkie in 1940 as well as to Dewey. Since 1943 Bell had been superintendent of banks in New York.
3 Fischer had recently returned from India where he had been working for the Foreign Economic Administration.

the liberal cause. He said he has come back to this country permanently and will be working with Cass Canfield on *Harper's Magazine*.
Jack has become thoroughly disgusted with FEA and the State Department. He says Crowley's method is never to make a decision
for fear it may offend someone. He doesn't think FEA can survive
many more months under its current management. He said the best
thing that could happen to FEA now would be to have State Department take over the remnants. He says that for a time both the BEW
group and the Lend-Lease group kept things going on the momentum
of a former organization but that now this momentum is completely
run down. Everything is at a complete standstill . . .

With regard to India, Fischer says the situation is completely hopeless. Since the war began, the population of India has increased by
20 million people. The soil is continually getting worse, and the people
are continually getting more miserable. He says India is the one
country where you can think and think and think and can't possibly
think of any way of improving the situation . . .

AUGUST 16, 1944

Father Sheehy[1] came in mad as a wet hen about the Chicago convention. He denounced Flynn, Kelly, Hague, and Hannegan as crooks
who ought to be in jail and probably would be eventually. . . .

It was obvious to me from what he said both on his own account
and quoting Bishop Ryan[2] of Omaha that the actions of these four
Irish boys at the convention is going to make the Catholic church
stop playing Democratic politics. Sheehy again and again made the
point that these four crooks had no right to speak for the church. I
told him that so far as I personally was concerned, I had been told it
was Tommy Corcoran who had been circulating the story that the
Catholic church was against me. Sheehy then proceeded to denounce
Corcoran, said he was not a good Catholic, that he was utterly unprin-
cipled.

Father Sheehy entered into a long dissertation on the marvels that
the President had done for the country and especially for the war
effort, saying that "history will not speak kindly of anyone who has
not been a supporter of Roosevelt." Then he suddenly switched and

[1] Father Maurice S. Sheehy had grown up in Iowa. Wallace first met him
socially. He found Sheehy, whom he saw with increasing frequency after 1944,
intelligent, liberal, and politically shrewd.
[2] Bishop James H. Ryan.

said "But when Roosevelt double-crossed you, people began to wonder what had happened to the Roosevelt they had known before." He then said he had seen the President at Pearl Harbor, that the President was in terrible shape, that his hands shook so he could scarcely lift his food to his mouth. He thinks the President will be unable to campaign and that he will have to resign from the nomination. I said, "In that case, Dewey will win easily." He said, "Yes. I don't think you should take the nomination even if it were offered to you by the Democratic National Committee." I said, "How about Barkley?" He replied, "I think Jimmie Byrnes would be a more capable man." I said, "He won't be as strong politically because labor and the Negroes are opposed to him." He and I agreed that the fact that Jimmie Byrnes had once been a Catholic and had turned over to be an Episcopalian would not hurt him particularly in the campaign.

It is curious how many people think the President is completely washed up physically. In most cases the judgment seems to be based on his appearance at the time of his broadcast at San Diego and the manner of his broadcast from Seattle. Father Sheehy wanted very much to make the point that no matter what happened I would be in a position of very great influence.

Former Senator Smathers came in briefly to say he did not know whether he and his wife were going to vote this year, said his wife's mother felt the same way this year, said he supposed they would vote but it would not be with any enthusiasm. He said he thought there were millions of folks who might not vote unless the situation were straightened out in some way and he did not know what the President could do to straighten it out.

Norman Littell came in and wanted to gossip about the usual stuff about the convention. It seems Littell doesn't like Francis Biddle at all and wants to get out of the Department of Justice as soon as possible. He thinks I should not make many speeches at all during the campaign, that we should devote all our energies to starting a liberal movement as soon as the campaign is over . . .

Littell and his wife are very close to the President's daughter, Anna Boettiger. He quoted Anna as saying about her father, "He doesn't know any man and no man knows him. Even his own family doesn't know anything about him . . ."

I suggested that Littell keep his criticisms to himself and not make any final decisions for at least six weeks. I think he will work for the re-election of the President but he will be doing it with very little enthusiasm. He feels the President doesn't have enough vigor to be a liberal anymore.

Littell told me that he had met Ernest Lindley[1] Friday morning at the convention and asked him how the convention was going to come out. Lindley said that Truman was going to win. Littell asked how he got that way. Lindley replied, "Yesterday afternoon (Thursday, the 20th) the President got four men on the wire at the same time (presumably Hannegan, Kelly, Hague, and Flynn) and said, 'Tell Hannegan to get the lead out of his pants and put Truman over.' " Littell said it was then that he realized really definitely that the President was a double-crosser. He said a day or so before, he had telephoned his wife and his wife had telephoned Anna Boettiger and that Anna had come out unequivocally for me and said she was sure the President was for me. He thinks Anna Dall is closer to the President than anyone else. I told him that she obviously did not know anything about the letter which he wrote to Hannegan on July 14 or 15.

Apparently all the liberals of the country know about the same things that Littell knows and they will all lie down on the job unless they are given something to believe in. With the situation as it is today, I would say that Dewey would win. Littell said it was becoming obvious to him that it was becoming more and more difficult for the President to have around him anyone except people who were sick or weak or old. He said he thought my real difficulty was that I was vigorous and that people were more and more looking on me as the leader of the liberal movement. This causes the President to want to get rid of me as soon as possible. On the other hand, he will keep those who are weak or old around him as long as possible. Littell then went on to say how remarkable he (Littell) was for picking out to have under him men who are quite capable of taking his job if anything happens to him.

AUGUST 29, 1944

. . . At lunch with the President

The President seemed to be looking quite well, in good spirits and very cordial. He complimented me on the work I had been doing in New England and said they would want me to do a lot of work of

---

[1] Ernest K. Lindley, the journalist and commentator who had written five books about Roosevelt and the New Deal, and was probably closer to the President than was any other newspaperman.

this kind during the campaign.[1] He then started to skate over the thin ice at once as fast as he could, saying that I was four or six years ahead of my time, that what I stood for would inevitably come. I told him I was very happy about what had been demonstrated at the convention and following the convention because I now knew that the people were for me. He said that my difficulty at the convention was that I did not have the reserve strength to throw in, said he was in that same situation in 1932 and found that he had to make a deal either with McNutt or with Garner. While he knew that Garner was an old dear, he also knew that Hearst was behind Garner, so he made a deal with Garner to get the necessary strength after he had used up all his reserve.

I said, "Mr. President, I could have made a deal too but I did not care to do it." I went on to say that I knew just exactly what happened at the convention but that the reason I had come out for him was because his name was a symbol of liberalism not only in this country but in the whole world. He then hastened to say how much he appreciated that and said if everything went well on November 7 I could have anything I wanted in the government with one exception. The exception was the State Department. He said Cordell Hull was an old dear and he could not bear to break his heart. (He started the conversation, by the way, by asking if I had shown Ilo the wire which I had received. I said yes, but that Mrs. Wallace didn't know whether she could earn enough money on the strength of that wire to support me in the style to which I was accustomed.)

The President said he thought the election was going to be very close but in case we won, one of the first things we would do would be to sit down with me and make a list of the folks we were going to get rid of, said the first on the list would be Jesus H. Jones. I said, "Well, if you are going to get rid of Jesse, why not let me have Secretary of Commerce with RFC and FEA thrown in? There would be poetic justice in that." The President said, "Yes, that's right." He said also he would like to have me sit in on some of the international conferences. I told the President if he really wanted me to be Secretary of Commerce, he should let me know because it might influence to some extent the type of campaign I would make, that my inclination in that case would be to emphasize continuously the problem of full

[1] Wallace campaigned for Roosevelt in the South, August 17–22, 1944, and in New England, August 24–29. From August 30 through September 30 he kept almost no diary. In that period he again spent much of his time on the stump, with stops in Virginia, New Hampshire, Pennsylvania, and several in New York. His addresses pursued the themes of his speech seconding Roosevelt's nomination.

employment, that I might be conferring with businessmen in the various localities to find out just how they expected to get full employment. The President then suggested that we go out under the magnolia tree and have lunch with the family. There were present: his daughter Anna, the two grandchildren, who are now quite large, Buzzie and Sistie. Sistie is actually taller than her mother and looks very much like her. Buzzie is almost as tall. Also was present Miss Margaret Suckley, a neighbor of the Roosevelts' near Hyde Park, whom the President from time to time has had on picnics.

The President talked about the Dumbarton Oaks conference,[1] how the Russians wanted to have 16 votes on the basis of the 16 autonomous republics.

The President somehow got started talking about Bill Bullitt . . . He said Bill Bullitt was perfectly terrible. I asked him why. He said because of that awful story he spread all over town about Sumner Welles. He said Bill ought to go to hell for that.

The President then told a story about how his son Jimmie had been approached by a moving picture man who said that if Jimmie would come out with a statement that his father was too old and that he ought to go back to Hyde Park, that he (the moving picture man) could assure Jimmie an undersecretaryship in Dewey's administration. Jimmie insisted on knowing just how the movie man could back up his statement. The movie man finally said, "Talk to Jesse Jones about it."

The President said he did not believe the story but he nevertheless went on to express himself very vigorously about Jesse Jones. He evidently thinks Jesse cooked up the Texas deal. I then told him about what I had learned about the Texas situation and urged him to call up Governor Coke Stevenson[2] directly. I gave him a memo on this subject and he said he would call the Governor.

The President talked about his Alaskan Commission and about how the Army boys wanted to settle up in Alaska.[3] I said I thought it was necessary to do some fundamental scientific work; otherwise there

---

[1] Delegates from the United States, Great Britain, and the Soviet Union had met at Dumbarton Oaks, a handsome mansion in Georgetown, for preliminary discussions about a postwar international security organization. Shocked by the Soviet demand for sixteen seats, Roosevelt had been unable to talk Andrei Gromyko out of it, or to persuade Gromyko to agree that parties to a dispute should not have a veto over decisions pertaining to that dispute.

[2] Coke Stevenson, governor of Texas since 1941, was associated with the more liberal faction of the state's Democratic Party.

[3] The President had returned from a Hawaiian conference with Admiral Nimitz and General MacArthur by way of Alaska where he had talked about the area as a new frontier for settlement after the war by ex-GIs. The Alaska Commission he appointed was charged with facilitating that objective.

would be trouble ahead. I said I thought it was very important for us to get Alaska settled.

We then got to discussing my trip through New England. He told me how he got the French Canadians in New England to voting Democratic just by speaking French to them. He asked what my plans were next. I said I thought in about two weeks I would go out again the same way as I had gone out in New England, give extemporaneous talks, and that I thought I would only give two or three big talks during the course of the campaign. He liked the idea. I said Senator Wagner wanted me to talk at Madison Square on October 31, and Jo Davidson[1] wanted me to speak there earlier in the campaign. Anna then spoke up and said Mrs. Harriman[2] wanted me to appear on an American Unity program from Madison Square on the same program with Wendell Willkie, that Willkie had already agreed to appear if some prominent Democrat would also appear. I asked the President what he thought of that. He said he did not think Willkie was really a liberal. He referred to his letter to Willkie,[3] saying that he did not want to talk to Willkie about international matters but about plugging up the loopholes by which the corporations escaped their taxes. He finally voted for the Jo Davidson meeting and against the Daisy Harriman and the Senator Wagner meetings in New York.

The President said he would be leaving in a day or two for Hyde Park, would be gone over Labor Day, would be back about the 6th and then would be leaving about the 10th for Canada, where he will have a meeting with a distinguished Englishman.[4]

OCTOBER 3, 1944

McDougall said he had talked with Bruce[5] in London and Bruce had

---

[1] Jo Davidson, the talented sculptor whose works included busts of Roosevelt and Wallace, was also an active liberal in politics. Wallace spoke at the meeting Davidson arranged at Madison Square Garden on September 21, 1944. He spoke again at Wagner's meeting at the same place at the end of October.

[2] Mrs. Florence J. (J. Borden) Harriman, Democratic National Committeewoman from the District of Columbia and former Ambassador to Norway, had helped to launch Willkie in 1940.

[3] The letter to Willkie of August 21, 1944, referred specifically to foreign matters and not at all to domestic issues, as had an earlier letter of July 11; see Ellsworth Barnes, *Wendell Willkie: Fighter for Freedom* (Marquette, 1966) pp. 480–86. Ill during much of August and September 1944, Willkie died of a heart attack on October 8.

[4] Roosevelt met Churchill at Quebec for discussions about American Lend-Lease aid to Great Britain for the period after the defeat of Germany and before the defeat of Japan, and about Anglo-American policy toward Germany.

[5] Stanley Bruce (later Viscount Bruce of Melbourne), High Commissioner for Australia.

told him that he should ask me again about heading up the Food and Agriculture Committee. Bruce said, "You should put it up to Wallace on the basis that he could take on this job for three years and then if the liberals of the United States want him in 1948, he could step out of Food and Agriculture and into the United States picture again." "Obviously," Bruce said, "Wallace could not have anything to do with American politics while he was heading up the Food and Agriculture Committee. But he should feel perfectly free at any time to step out and into American politics."

McDougall then began fishing around as to what my future might be. He said, "After Roosevelt is elected, there is obviously only one post you can take." He did not mention the post but evidently meant the post of Secretary of State. I made no comment.

He asked if I would think over his proposition a few days and let him know as to whether there was any likelihood whether I would be interested in the job. He said they would not need to have a final answer until the middle of November but he would like to have a preliminary indication.

McDougall, just before he left, said to me very diffidently, "Might I make one observation and criticism?" I said, "Sure." Then he went ahead and talked on the theme which is very dear to the British heart. He wished I would be a little more careful about putting my name on poorly considered statements. He referred to the pamphlet "Our Job in the Pacific." He did not say so but I am sure he meant page 24[1] . . . Later on I talked with Charles Marsh and asked him if he had had any repercussions from his British friends on the pamphlet. He laughed and said that Flight Commander Dahl[2] (who is now with the British Secret Service) had been very much excited. Apparently while I was gone, the entire British Secret Service was shaking with indignation as well as the British Foreign Office. Dahl said to Marsh at the height of his indignation, "This is very serious. You know Churchill is likely to ask the President to get a new Vice President." Charles replied merely by saying, "Don't be a child. Grow up. Don't you know that the most certain way to be sure that Wallace will continue

[1] Wallace had there called for the postwar "emancipation of . . . colonial subjects" including those in India, Burma, Malaya, Indo-China, the Dutch East Indies, and many small Pacific islands.
[2] Dahl, a talented gossip, saw Wallace and Marsh often during 1943–44 and on occasion wrote them about his sometimes speculative observations of social affairs. Though never a wholly reliable witness, Dahl entertained Wallace, who liked him partly because of his striking physical resemblance to Robert Wallace, the Vice President's younger son.

to be Vice President is for the word to get around that Churchill is against him?"

McDougall, in discussing the relationship of Food and Agriculture to the new world organization, said, "Now as a matter of fact, China just is not one of the four great powers. We should not fool ourselves into thinking that she is. We should base the world organization on reality and not on unreality."

OCTOBER 4, 1944

Don Nelson told me about his trip to China.[1] He thinks very highly of the Generalissimo. Like myself, he and General Hurley worked very hard on the Generalissimo to get him more kindly disposed toward the Chinese communists. He felt that I had made some progress on this front and that they made some additional progress. But right in the midst of their negotiations, General Stilwell came in with a wire signed by President Roosevelt in which the President demanded very curtly the things which Nelson and Hurley had already gotten worked out. One of these points involved sending 14,000 Chinese soldiers at once to the Burma front. General Hurley told Stilwell that this had already been worked out. Stilwell insisted that it was time for the Generalissimo to know who was really running China. He went ahead and presented his cablegram from the President and as a result the Nelson negotiations with the Generalissimo were completely broken off. The Generalissimo refused to meet with Nelson and Hurley any-

[1] Nelson and Pat Hurley had left Washington in August as the President's personal representatives to Chiang Kai-shek. Nelson was also to assist the Chinese in planning and organizing production. The two Americans flew first to Moscow, where they discussed Soviet-Chinese relations with Molotov, who denied any Russian interest in the Chinese communists and urged improvements in the Chinese economy. Hurley so reported to Chiang. Both Nelson and Hurley, in contrast to Gauss, were at that time optimistic about persuading Chiang to devise a mode of cooperation with the Chinese communists in the war against Japan. Hurley hoped, too, to relieve the tensions between Chiang and Stilwell, but the American general, depressed by losses in Burma and at Kweilin, enlisted George Marshall's support for a demand that the Generalissimo put his troops under Stilwell's command. Roosevelt, in conciliatory language, pressed that demand in a cable to Chiang while the G'imo was in the process of negotiating with Hurley about the same question. Chiang subsequently refused either to yield full command to any American, to make any genuine overtures to the communists, or any longer to work with Stilwell. At that juncture, critical for American planning for the final offensive against Japan, Chiang's obduracy provoked the recall of both Gauss and Stilwell, who were replaced respectively by Hurley and General Albert C. Wedemeyer. For a full account of the whole complex development, see Feis, *China Tangle*, pp. 179–99.

more. Just before he left, Nelson managed to patch things up after a fashion.

I said to Nelson I assumed General Marshall prepared the telegram for the President to sign, and that probably Stilwell inspired Marshall as to just what should be said in the telegram. Nelson said, "Yes." I asked him if he had told the President about it. He said he had.

Both Stilwell and Marshall are splendid generals of the highest integrity and very fine in their personal relationships; nevertheless, it is very difficult to figure out just exactly what these generals are up to in China. When I had lunch with Forrestal, and Marshall was present, Marshall was very cutting in his remarks about Chennault, and about the way in which Chennault had gotten more than his share of the goods at Stilwell's expense. Just what Marshall hopes to gain by completely alienating the Generalissimo and losing all of eastern China is hard to figure out. It is as much of a mystery to Don Nelson as it is to me.

OCTOBER 6, 1944

At the Halifax party for the Chinese delegates to the Dumbarton Oaks Conference, Ambassador Halifax at the earliest possible moment started in talking to me about the speech I made at the dinner given me by the Generalissimo, and about the Joint Statement the Generalissimo and I put out. He said he was in London at the time this all broke and that the London Foreign Office was tremendously disturbed, and asked that he make representations to me. I said, sure, that I would be glad to know what their objections were. John Carter Vincent, who was at the party, saw me talking with Halifax and guessed what was up. He told me that Halifax had come over to the State Department and talked with Secretary Hull about it. Hull pulled out from under by saying that my going to Chungking was not a matter of the State Department but was the President's doing. Vincent said that everything I said represented State Department policy and he did not know why Secretary Hull had ducked. Vincent, as a matter of fact, had written both the Chungking speech and the joint statement, and had also approved page 24 of my pamphlet *Our Job in the Pacific*. Vincent says the British don't have a leg to stand on and that if Halifax comes over to see me to tell him that this is just what 999 out of 1000 Americans believe. Undoubtedly the part the British object to in the Joint Statement is that marked in red on page one; the part to which they object in my speech on June 21 is that which is marked in red on page four.[1] Vincent said, "My, what gall the British have!"

Bohlen,[2] head of the Russian Section in the State Department, came up to talk about the Poles and the Russians. He said there is a great deal of unrest now in the United States, especially on the part of congressmen who have Polish constituents because of the way in which the Polish patriots had died at Warsaw. He then told me that the Polish Committee in Moscow had put out over the radio an address to the Poles in Warsaw that the time had come for them to rise. He said the Russian action which had been taken subsequently had been very hard to explain.

I checked Bohlen's statement later and still I am unable to find the full facts. It seems that Knox, a member of Parliament, a man who is very anti-Russian and anti-United States, queried Anthony Eden about the presumed broadcast. Eden would not reply. The question is still open in my mind as to whether this broadcast was bona fide or not. After listening to Bohlen talk, there is no question in my mind but that he is definitely anti-Russian in his attitude.

OCTOBER 7, 1944

Leon Henderson came in to talk to me about allowing the National Committee for Roosevelt and Truman to pay my expenses. I told him I preferred to be independent. I told him that the committee

[1] The parts to which Wallace referred said that enduring peace in the Pacific would depend upon "recognition of the fundamental right of presently dependent Asiatic peoples to self-government . . . within a specified practical time limit." Wallace also referred to a statement of Hull's to the same effect which pointed to the American example in the Philippines.

[2] Charles E. Bohlen had talked with Wallace about the agony of Warsaw. As Russian troops pushed toward that city, Moscow radio, speaking late in July for the Communist Committee of Polish National Liberation, appealed to the Poles to join the fight against the Germans. General Bor Komorowski, who represented the anti-Communist Polish government-in-exile, then ordered the uprising in Warsaw, partly in order to capture the city before the Russians could. Soviet troops, only ten miles from Warsaw, though across the Vistula River, ceased their advance and the Germans crushed the Polish Underground Army, which surrendered after heroic fighting on October 2. Stalin argued that General Bor had not properly informed him about his plans, which Stalin called premature and ill-advised, and that Russian strategy called for an enveloping operation rather than a frontal attack on Warsaw. But Stalin had also refused to permit British aircraft carrying supplies for Warsaw to land in Russian-held territory, a decision that infuriated Churchill. Further, the Prime Minister believed that Stalin had deliberately abandoned the Warsaw Poles because they were not communists. Roosevelt, while also distressed about the outcome, declined to join Churchill in criticizing Stalin.

might be able to help on radio broadcasts and gave him the dates of my major appearances. I asked him where the money was coming from for his committee. He said that a chap by the name of Lew Harris, a raincoat maker, was raising the money and that most of it was coming from wealthy Jews in New York . . .[1]

OCTOBER 29, 1944

HENRY A. WALLACE TO FRANKLIN D. ROOSEVELT

WE HEARD YOUR MAGNIFICENT CHICAGO SPEECH WHILE ON THE ROAD FROM GRAND RAPIDS TO MUSKEGON. YOUR GOAL OF SIXTY MILLION JOBS IS PERHAPS HIGH BUT I GLORY IN YOUR DARING AND AS YOU SAY, AMERICA CAN DO THE SEEMINGLY IMPOSSIBLE. WE ARE PREDICTING THAT YOU WILL CARRY THIRTY-SIX STATES, HAVE A THREE MILLION POPULAR MAJORITY AND A HUNDRED ELECTORAL COLLEGE MAJORITY.[2]

NOVEMBER 8, 1944

At 9:20 on November 7 I called up Western Union and sent the following wire to President Roosevelt:

"Forgive me for having been conservative both in the estimate I made last July and the one I wired you last month. I now double my prediction of 40 Democratic majority in the House.[3] You will now have sufficient majority to put through full employment legislation. H.A.W."

At 9:30 the evening of November 7 I called up the AP, the UP, the International News Service, and National Broadcasting and gave them the following statement:

"Roosevelt until 1948 means a country confident, moving with full steam ahead. The vote constitutes a mandate to Congress to prepare the way for sixty million postwar jobs. Corner apple selling disappeared under Roosevelt. The people have determined to lick the dole. Full employment postwar means prosperity to farm and city alike. Plans will now go ahead for permanent, enforceable peace."

[1] Wallace kept no diary from October 8 to November 7, 1944. He was away from Washington, campaigning for Roosevelt, October 11 to November 3.
[2] Roosevelt replied to this telegram: ". . . I promise to make good on the sixty million jobs if you will do the same on your predictions . . ."
[3] Roosevelt polled three and a half million more votes than did Dewey, carried the electoral votes of 36 states, in all 432 to Dewey's 82, and led the Democratic ticket which produced a margin of 51 seats in the House of Representatives.

When I called the Columbia Broadcasting System they suggested that instead of giving them something to read over the air that I come down and broadcast myself, which I did.

At about 10:45 on the evening of November 7 I made the following statement over Columbia Broadcasting:

The Roosevelt victory tonight forecasts three things:

1. The people have voted a mandate to Congress to legislate a permanent, enforceable peace.

2. The people see eye to eye with the President for his goal of full employment—his goal of sixty million jobs.

3. The Congress majority in both Houses will now go ahead with a fresh and effective majority behind the President as a world leader.

Bipartisan isolationism has been destroyed. Full steam ahead for a people's peace and jobs for all has been ordered. It is now a job for a people's Congress fully to support Roosevelt.

NOVEMBER 10, 1944

At the station, while we were waiting for the President to get off the train, were various cabinet officers, Senator Truman, and myself. Truman was talking with Jesse Jones. I shook hands with Truman but did not offer to shake hands with J.J. but J.J. insisted on my shaking hands with him. It was arranged that I should ride with the President and Truman down Constitution Avenue. Truman asked the President how he wanted us to sit in the back seat. The President said it didn't make any difference to him, so I sat on the left side and let Truman sit in the middle. The President insisted on the top of the car being down although it was raining hard. When we arrived at the basement of the White House, the employees came through and shook hands. First in line was the President, then Mrs. Roosevelt, then Truman, then myself, then Mrs. Wallace. Mrs. Truman wasn't there, she is still in Missouri.

In his conversation with the different people, Senator Truman spent his time boasting how hard he had campaigned. Mrs. Roosevelt told me she wanted to see me.

When I saw Mrs. Roosevelt, she told me that the liberals looked on me as the outstanding symbol of liberalism in the United States. She said that any program they worked up ought to be passed on by me. She said she was going out to the CIO convention on November 20 and she wanted to know whether I would head up a greatly broadened PAC. She felt that Sidney Hillman was not suitable for heading up such a broad liberal organization. She said furthermore that even though I had a position in the government, she thought I could go in on such an organization. She said she knew that I could not answer offhand such a matter. Later in the day I called her up and told her the first thing that occurred to me was that whatever was done should have the complete and enthusiastic blessing of Sidney Hillman. Second, I told her that I felt the only way any liberalism could express itself on a national basis was through the Democratic Party and I felt it would be damaging to the Democratic Party and to the liberalism boys if I should take the position she suggested. In brief, I turned down the proposition flatly but nicely. I can't help wondering, however, to what extent her husband is up to his usual maneuvering tricks.

On the ride down to the White House this morning, Truman said that this was the dirtiest campaign he had ever known. The President agreed, said he was mad during the campaign, he was still mad and was going to stay mad.

The President opened up cabinet by saying that he was mad and was going to stay mad. Later on in cabinet, he referred to the State of Texas not feeling itself to be a part of the Union. He made various other comments and glared at Jesse Jones. It was obvious that he meant no good toward J.J. J.J. was very sweet, however, and said that he had certain things he wanted to see the President about before he got away. When the President showed great emotion regarding J.J., I became conscious for the first time that he had aged very greatly. At the train I thought he looked remarkably well. He has lots of vitality left in his system and he is out to get J.J. Just the same, I would judge from the character and quality of his remarks that his intellect but not his prejudices will now begin to fade pretty rapidly. He will have to take awfully good care of himself to last out the four years in a state of competent leadership.

After he had called on the various members of the cabinet to report, he called on me. I said I had nothing to report. He then said I had been doing an awfully good job of campaigning at every little crossroad, that I had been up in Ham Fish's territory just across from Hyde Park, that I was responsible for defeating Ham Fish. Leo Crowley then spoke up and said I had done an excellent job in Minnesota and Wisconsin. It was the first cabinet meeting I had attended since the Chicago convention. Everything went along as usual in the customary futile way. Real issues are almost never settled in cabinet. The cabinet is a kind of social gathering at which the President rather subtly indicates the trend of his mind and the various cabinet members cautiously bring forward different items in an effort to find out which way the wind is blowing.

Senator Guffey came in to ask me if I would be interested in the position of Secretary of State in case Hull's health was such that he could not continue. I told him, of course, I would but obviously the President would and should stand by Secretary Hull as long as the Secretary wanted to continue his position. Guffey said John Winant was after the job but that he was not for Winant.

I called Miss Tully and told her that Phil Murray wanted me to go out to the CIO convention in Chicago on November 21 and that I had told Phil I would come unless the President had some objection. Miss Tully called back later and said she had checked with the President on the matter and he was very happy for me to go out there.

NOVEMBER 13, 1944

. . . Dillon Myer has been offered Paul Appleby's job in the Budget Bureau. He is not going to accept it. . . . Myer said he thought he himself would stay with WRA because it gave him such an excellent opportunity to battle for racial tolerance in the United States. He is now acquainted at first hand with all the sources of racial intolerance on the West Coast. A lot of it goes straight back to Hearst. There is good evidence, Myer thinks, that Hearst has put money into the American Legion to cause the Legion to take an intolerant stand. Myer thinks there will be a strong flare-up of racial intolerance after this war and that it is important for those who are battling for the right to get into action early. Myer has done a splendid job with the Japs and is to be congratulated for the results obtained by the Jap troops in Italy and in the Pacific. He pressed on McCloy in the first instance the desirability of having the Japs in the Army . . .

At Charles Marsh's home I had an interesting visit with Prince Orizu of Nigeria. He is putting on a campaign to get Nigerians educated in the United States. He says that when Nigerians are educated at Oxford and Cambridge, they are interested in maintaining class distinctions and not in increasing the welfare of the people. He says United States education looks toward increasing the welfare of the people; therefore, he wants more of his people to come to the United States to be educated instead of going to England.

At Biddle's home . . . Hopkins seemed to be in fairly good health but he was very quiet, saying practically nothing. After the buffet supper, the Attorney General called on A. Harriman to give his impressions of Russia, which he did for about one and a half hours. He likened the Russian political system to that of a city boss backed up by the strong arm of the police. Harriman's quarrel with the Russians seems to be with their political system rather than with their economic system. He thinks the United States should oppose the spread of the Russian political system to other nations . . . Biddle interjected from time to time with comments unfriendly to the Russians. Mrs. Reid[1] interjected several times with comments designed to question the Russian good faith relative to Poland. With regard to Mrs. Reid's questions, I would say that Harriman took the Russian side rather than the Polish side. Harriman did not think the Russians acted in bad faith with regard to the Warsaw incident although he admitted the Warsaw uprising has been one of the great tragedies in human history. When I went out after the meeting was over, Harry Hopkins said to me, "There is one thing which the American people should remember, and that is that the common folks of Russia like the system which they have." I replied, "Yes," that it was my impression that the small peoples of Asia felt that they had something better under the Soviet than they had ever had before, that they were for the Soviet system on that account.

During the talk by Harriman, Bohlen of the Russian desk of the State Department also interjected from time to time usually against the Russians but sometimes for them. Bohlen comes from an old Philadelphia family.

Charles Marsh says Harriman is Harry Hopkins' candidate for President.

NOVEMBER 14, 1944

Miss Hedgman and Mrs. Blanshard[2] wanted me to get the backing of the President to get through a permanent FEPC. I told them it ought not to be hard with both parties on record for it. They especially wanted help in the House. I suggested Rayburn. I also suggested Barkley in the Senate . . .

[1] Mrs. Helen Rogers (Ogden M.) Reid, since 1922 vice president and formidable guiding influence of the New York *Herald Tribune*.
[2] Mrs. Paul Blanshard and Mrs. Anna Hedgman, black members of the Committee to Make the FEPC a Permanent Organization.

. . . Lauchlin Currie is disturbed because there is so little planning going forward with regard to postwar employment and with regard to postwar exports. He says there is a little planning being done very quietly in Budget under Gerard Colm and wanted to know if I thought FEA should start some. I told him I felt that the President himself should give the directive and that I thought he did not wish to start very much until Congress was in session. I suggested, therefore, that Currie hold his horses until the middle of December.

Justice Murphy wanted to talk about the election . . .

Murphy said when he was mayor of Detroit back in 1932, he went to the Democratic Convention strong for Roosevelt. Hague of Jersey City and the other bosses were against Roosevelt. Hague came to see Murphy and said to him, "How can you as an Irish boy stand for this fellow Roosevelt?" It seems that the Tammany boys had been working with Murphy without any result and that they had sicked Hague onto Murphy. Murphy said that Harry Hopkins' idea of politics is to be able to get patronage for the big city bosses and to telephone them from time to time to get things done from their end of the line. As I heard Murphy making this analysis, I could not help thinking of a couple of nights ago when Hopkins was present while Averell Harriman likened the Russian government in its politics to the rule of the city bosses in the United States. I told Murphy that I was aware of the fact that in 1940 Hopkins looked on the appeasement of the city bosses as the beginning of political wisdom.

Murphy told me that in June of 1944 Ickes had spoken to him saying that the President was for me. I told Murphy the story of how Ickes and Sam Rosenman came to the apartment for lunch Monday July 11 in an effort to persuade me to retire from the race. Both Murphy and I reached the conclusion that during the latter part of June Hannegan and probably Hopkins between them painted a picture to the President which would make him think I had no standing with the country and especially no standing with the all-important city bosses.

Murphy said that Hopkins had made a statement to the effect that the Catholic church had been against the President in this election. He said that definitely was not true, that if the Catholic church had been against the President, the President would have been defeated.

I told Murphy I knew at the time of the Chicago Convention that some of the so-called Irish Catholics and the bosses had been trying to create the impression that the Catholic church was against me. I said I had checked into this and had found no evidence to that effect. Murphy said he was sure it was not true . . . He said that some of the priests might be against me because of my friendship for Russia but that definitely was not true of the hierarchy in his opinion.

Murphy said that it was under his regime that Pendergast[1] was prosecuted. He said there was no evidence of anything wrong with Truman except that he had been spawned and bred in the Pendergast machine. He said that Hague, Kelly, and Flynn had all made millions of dollars out of being city bosses. He said that Hague had a complete dictatorship, that nobody could succeed in business in Jersey City without being friendly to the Hague machine.

Murphy confirmed the report that came via Guffey that Ickes and Tommy Corcoran were doing everything they could to get the President to appoint Bill Douglas as Secretary of State. Certain others, he said, are trying to get Jimmie Byrnes appointed to that secretarial post. I think he included in this number Felix Frankfurter. Murphy said Joe Kennedy is strong for Douglas because Douglas is his protégé . . .

Curiously enough, right after I had dictated the above, Harold Young wanted me to come in to meet Cy Bevan, Michigan National Committeeman. Bevan started in at once saying how amusing Justice Murphy was. He said he served a useful purpose in his day in Michigan but that he could not get elected to dog catcher now. Said just before the Chicago convention Murphy would get in touch with him as often as twice a day saying, "Of course, I am not a candidate for Vice President but look at the experience I have had: Mayor of Detroit; Governor of the State; Governor General of the Philippine Islands; Attorney General; Justice of the Supreme Court, etc., etc., listing a number of minor items as well. Look at Wallace. Look at Truman. Do they have any experience like mine? Of course, you understand I am not a candidate." Then he would go ahead and enumerate all of his qualifications again. Bevan then went on to say that Murphy is all right but he is such a terrific egotist, has such excessive ambitions that he has absolutely no influence in Michigan.

L. Currie was very much concerned that Lend-Lease assistance to Russia should be kept up. It seems that Admiral Leahy has been trying to terminate L-L to Russia. L. Currie feels it is important in case Russia is going to help us fight Japan that L-L continue after the war with Germany is over . . .

[1] Thomas J. Pendergast, Democratic boss of Kansas City and a political mentor of Harry Truman, had been convicted in 1939 of income tax evasion.

At the 10:30 appointment at the White House, Alben Barkley immediately began talking about how hard he had campaigned in Kentucky, how he had traveled 8000 miles by automobile, how he had made 50 speeches, and how in the last two days he had made 24 speeches. He said his health was fine and that he was in better shape at the finish of the campaign than he was at the start.

Rayburn congratulated me on the vigorous campaigning I had done, saying, "They sent you nearly everywhere, didn't they?" Barkley then spoke up and said, "You didn't campaign under the auspices of the National Democratic Committee, did you?" I said, "No, I campaigned under the auspices of the State Democratic Committees and the independent organizations."

The President seemed to be in unusually good health and spirits. He has lost quite a little weight and I think it has done him a lot of good. He said that for the first time in history the Democratic National Committee had ended up its campaign without a deficit. He said Pauley had done a perfectly swell job. I couldn't help thinking that this meant that Pauley had probably received considerable sums of money from sources which would be expecting a payoff of some kind. I have no confidence in either Pauley or Hannegan. The President, however, is very much delighted with the present situation and expatiated at some length on what a fine feeling it was to come out of the campaign with no deficit. This was brought up in connection with the necessity of doing a real job in 1946. He spoke particularly of beating Clare Luce in 1946 . . .

There was considerable talk about the vast sums of money the Republicans had spent. The President said in Dutchess County the Republicans had spent $40,000. Barkley asked him what he thought the Republicans had spent, directly or indirectly, in the nation as a whole. The President estimated 15 million dollars. Barkley said they had raised $200,000 in Kentucky to beat him. Rayburn spoke of the $200,000 which had been raised by Pappy O'Daniel to beat the President. He said that Dick Kleberg had given $2500, Senator Moore of Oklahoma had given $25,000,[1] etc., etc. Barkley said that O'Daniel had come into Kentucky to campaign against him and against the President.

Then the talk got over onto Jesse Jones and it was obvious that neither the President nor Rayburn had any use for him . . .

There was some talk about the Missouri Valley Authority. Rayburn

[1] Richard M. Kleberg, Texas cattleman and Democratic congressman (1933-45), and Edward H. Moore, Oklahoma oil producer and cattleman, Republican Senator (1943-49).

indicated that he didn't think a permanent Fair Employment Practices bill should come up in this Congress. He thought the next Congress would be much more friendly to it.

NOVEMBER 16, 1944

. . . Milo told me that he had been talking with B. Baruch and that Baruch spoke in the highest terms of my executive ability. Baruch said, according to Milo, that I had been the best executive among all the government people during the Roosevelt administration. He said, however, he did not understand how I could talk as vigorously as I did at times about Wall Street. I told Milo that this proved to me that the President had talked to Baruch the day before about the idea of my becoming Secretary of Commerce and that Baruch had figured that there was a good chance I would be Secretary and, therefore, was trimming his sails to fit the wind. Milo said that Baruch was getting quite old . . .

NOVEMBER 30, 1944
HENRY A. WALLACE TO FRANKLIN D. ROOSEVELT

YOUR CORDIAL LETTER WARMLY APPRECIATED[1] STOP MY MEMORY GOES BACK TO MY CONFERENCE WITH YOU JUST BEFORE LUNCH ON AUGUST 29 WHEN YOU EXPRESSED SIMILAR CORDIALITY AND INTEREST IN MY DEFINITION OF POETIC JUSTICE STOP MY INTEREST IN POETIC JUSTICE IS STRONGER NOW THAN EVER STOP SIXTY MILLION JOBS WILL REQUIRE YOU PLUS PERFECT COORDINATION BETWEEN AGRICULTURE LABOR AND COMMERCE STOP MY JOB SEEMS TO BE COMMERCE STOP ORGANIZATION PLANS SHOULD FOLLOW NOT PRECEDE THESE APPOINTMENTS STOP THANKS IF I MAY SERVE

DECEMBER 5, 1944

. . . At the lunch with Ickes I expressed disappointment in the appointment of Will Clayton and said probably the President had some broader plan in mind which we didn't know anything about. Ickes claimed to be thoroughly disgusted. He had no regrets about having

[1] In a letter of November 27, 1944, thanking Wallace for his assistance in the campaign, Roosevelt had said that both he and Wallace understood the American people had voted for the Four Freedoms and for abundance at home. He was writing, the President concluded, "not only in thanks for your help but to say that I count upon it in the great tasks ahead, to which America has dedicated its purpose and its future."

fought for the President in the campaign against Dewey. He said, however, that if Willkie had run he thinks he might have supported Willkie. At any rate, he would not have been active in support of the President. I told him I didn't feel that way about it . . .

Ickes said the President had told him that he was going to get rid of Will Clayton after the election.[1] I told Ickes that he had told me the same thing. Ickes was very bitter about Hopkins . . .

Ickes then went on to say that Abe Fortas[2] had spoken to him about his going to bat for me with the President. I said yes, Lauch Currie had said something to me about this. He asked if I had told the President I wanted to be Secretary of Commerce. I said yes, I had, both before and after the election. He expressed surprise at this, saying that just before the President went to Warm Springs on November 29 he had been in to see the President and that the President had said to him, "What are we going to do about Henry?" The President also asked Ickes what he thought about Henry Kaiser for Secretary of Commerce. Ickes expressed some question about Kaiser because of his widespread business connections. Ickes showed me a letter which he received from the President, dated August 15, in reply to a hot letter which Ickes had written to the President. In this letter the President spoke very highly of me. The letter from Ickes to the President had criticized Hannegan for misleading the President with regard to my strength with the people. Ickes said that since the election he was the fair-haired boy at the White House and that all the people around the White House were kowtowing to him now. He said this was in marked distinction to the situation which existed immediately after 1940. At that time he went for eleven months without ever seeing the President except at cabinet meetings. The President refused to grant him an appointment. The situation did not change until the President put him in charge of petroleum and then a little later in charge of coal for the war effort.

Ickes keeps all his letters from the President in his left-hand, lower drawer. He has a number of them, of which he seems to be very proud. I judge he is keeping a very complete record of all his contacts with the President with the idea of some day writing them up.

[1] Roosevelt had nominated Will Clayton as Assistant Secretary as one part of a major shakeup of the State Department. Clayton was to administer foreign economic affairs, with authority over some of the functions that had previously fallen to the Foreign Economic Administration or to Jesse Jones. The liberal press and some of the old New Dealers in Washington, troubled by Clayton's conservative view of economic issues, interpreted the nomination as a sop to Jones and an omen of defeat for their own postwar hopes.

[2] Since 1942 Abe Fortas had been Undersecretary of the Interior Department.

Later in the evening Charlie Marsh called me to say that Ickes had
gotten in touch with Drew Pearson immediately after his lunch with
me; that Drew Pearson had told him about it over the telephone. Ickes
had reported that I was very sad (which wasn't true) and that there
wasn't any fight in me whatsoever. (I am glad this is what Ickes reported to Pearson.) Charlie Marsh is probably unjust to Ickes but
nevertheless he is also probably closer to the truth than 80 percent of
the liberals who look up to Ickes as a great hero . . .

DECEMBER 7, 1944

. . . Bill Wasserman[1] came in this morning to say four things: First,
that he hoped I would not accept any position from the President unless I had absolute assurance that I had adequate power to meet the
responsibility and real backing from the President. He hoped that I
would not become Secretary of Commerce unless I had the power of
RFC. He hoped also that I would have FEA but he said RFC was
much more important than FEA. The second point he wanted to make
was that he hoped I would make friends of AFL people. He said some
of them felt that I had high-hatted them and had refused invitations to
address AFL meetings. I told him that I had not been aware of refusal to attend any AFL national meeting except once when I had
another engagement. I said the President told me that Bill Green had
called the White House opposing my continuing as Vice President. I
said I had found the greatest friendship on the part of AFL people
down the line but I questioned whether there was anything I could do
to make men like Green, Hutcheson, and Woll[2] more friendly.

Jim Patton came in to say that up until rather recently he had hoped
I would not remain in government. He now thinks it would be a
fine thing if I could have a job like the Department of Commerce with
Presidential backing. He said Beany Baldwin and Phil Murray had
asked him about Claude Wickard. He told them that the probabilities
were they would get a much worse man than Claude Wickard and
advised them to continue to back Claude Wickard as Secretary of
Agriculture. He thinks the Democratic National Committee would
very much like to get rid of Claude so that they can put in someone
who is satisfactory to the businessmen who contributed to the Democratic campaign. Patton has no use for the Hannegan crowd, the Ickes-

---

[1] In 1944 William S. Wasserman was special adviser to the chairman of the Smaller
War Plants Corporation.
[2] Matthew Woll, former president of the International Photo-Engravers Union
and at this time a vice president of the American Federation of Labor.

Corcoran crowd, or the Byrnes-Baruch crowd. He has his fingers definitely crossed about the President and thinks he cannot be trusted anymore. Apparently the nomination of Clayton as Assistant Secretary of State greatly shocked him. I told Patton I would like to have the position of Secretary of Commerce if I could get the same backing from the President that I had when I was Secretary of Agriculture . . .

Charles Marsh phoned in to say that Beany Baldwin had been to see Dave Niles and that Dave Niles told Beany Baldwin that a man of my very great distinction and high attainments should have something very much more important to operate than a Department of Commerce which had been stripped of all power,[1] and that therefore the boys were working on a cabinet position that would give suitable scope to my creative energies in the field of exports, imports, and postwar jobs. I told Charlie Marsh it sounded very funny to me. As a matter of fact, it sounds very much like the job which Donald Nelson is supposed to operate. Moreover, it sounds like one of the brilliant improvisations which the President so often makes in order to get out of a tight spot. These improvisations nearly always lead to some kind of intra-administration crisis later on because in the process of improvising the President puts the person for whom he improvises in a position to step on a great many toes. The President gives the man responsibilities without power and the man, trying to carry out his responsibilities without inadequate power, inevitably gets into trouble. I think the President gets a certain amount of satisfaction out of improvising in this way and then watching the results of the improvisation without shedding any tears but, in fact, with a considerable amount of quiet satisfaction . . .

DECEMBER 11, 1944

. . . Henry Morgenthau said he was much disturbed about the State Department appointments.[2] He said he had gotten along quite well

---

[1] The reorganization of the State Department had reduced the lending authority of the Secretary of Commerce, which was vulnerable to still further reductions. As Wallace saw it, however, a cabinet post was bound to provide a better source of influence than the anomalous new position of Donald Nelson as a special adviser to the President.

[2] The changes Roosevelt had proposed in the State Department included the nomination of Edward Stettinius, Jr., to succeed Hull, who had resigned, as Secretary of State; the nomination of Joseph C. Grew as Undersecretary; and the nomination as Assistant Secretaries of Clayton, Nelson Rockefeller for Latin American affairs; Archibald MacLeish for public information; James C. Dunn and Brigadier General Julius C. Holmes. Of that list, liberal Democrats approved only of MacLeish, whom Senate conservatives opposed. Senators

with Stettinius—better, in fact, with Stettinius than with Hull. He couldn't understand the Will Clayton appointment, the Julius Holmes appointment, or the Jimmie Dunn appointment. With regard to Holmes he told me substantially the story as it appears . . . in *PM*, with especial emphasis on his association with Murphy in North Africa.

With regard to Will Clayton, Henry Morgenthau said he couldn't understand what the President was up to because, back in 1938 or thereabouts, Henry Morgenthau wanted Will Clayton for a special job involving foreign exchange. Henry had thought that Will Clayton's worldwide business experience would enable him to be helpful to Henry in his dealings with the French on the franc-dollar exchange. Henry put the matter up to the President and the President said not to have anything to do with Will Clayton; that he was thoroughly reactionary.

Morgenthau attributes everything that is going on now to Hopkins. He pointed out to me from his window the place where Hopkins has his office in the East White House office building not far from where Jimmie Byrnes has his office. He says Hopkins reads every day every wire that comes into the White House and every wire that goes out . . .

Henry Morgenthau thinks Ickes is "good troops"; that he can be depended upon. I told Morgenthau I was not quite as certain about Ickes' reliability as he—that there was always the question of the variable quality of the Corcoran influence.

Morgenthau doesn't like Jimmie Byrnes. He said about three months ago Jimmie Byrnes was quite a dominant power around the White House and that the Hopkins influence was very low at the time he last returned from the Mayo Clinic.

Morgenthau is very eager for me to be in the cabinet. He said folks had been talking about my being either Secretary of Labor or Secretary of Commerce. I told him I hoped the President would not ask me to be Secretary of Labor; that I didn't want the post; that I would do everything I could to avoid being Secretary of Labor. I told him I wanted to be Secretary of Commerce. He asked if the President knew that and I said yes, that I had told the President that on August 29 and had sent him a wire recently . . .

Pepper and Guffey led a lonely and futile fight against the confirmation of the others, who struck them as either too closely connected to great wealth or, as in the case of Holmes, with Robert Murphy's tactic of expedient collaboration with fascists. *PM* considered Holmes to be excessively distrustful of the Soviet Union. The Philadelphia *Record* and *The New Republic* also attacked the nominations aggressively but to no effect.

He said he was going to be seeing Mrs. Roosevelt. He asked if Mrs. Roosevelt knew what I wanted. I said no, I hadn't told her. He said Mrs. Roosevelt was very, very strong for me. When he told me this I couldn't help but think that this would make me weaker with the President because I have the feeling that at the present time he fights everything she is for. I didn't care to say this to Henry Morgenthau, however. Morgenthau said he was exceedingly anxious for me to be in the cabinet because he felt otherwise the forces of reaction were in serious danger of taking over the President. He thought Ickes, he, and I could work together . . .

Jack Shelly is an AFL man and a state senator from San Francisco. George Irvine is a Railroad Brotherhood man from San Francisco. Both men were delegates to the convention in Chicago. Shelly took considerable pleasure in telling about a certain meeting which he had with Bob Hannegan, Ed Flynn, Ed Pauley, Frank Walker, and Jack Malone (a California Democratic leader) the evening of Thursday, July 20, in what Shelly called "the sweat box." This is a room under the Speaker's stand in the Chicago Stadium. The Democratic dignitaries had Shelly in, arguing with him while Quentin Reynolds and Helen Gahagan made their speeches. They argued with him for about two hours, Hannegan doing most of the talking, urging him to vote for Truman. Hannegan said, "Don't you know that Truman is going to be nominated and then you will be in bad?" Shelly just replied, "Well, if you are so sure he is going to be nominted why are you working so hard on me?" Hannegan then shifted and said, "Don't you know the President is for Truman?" Shelly replied, "No, I don't; the President is on record as being for Wallace." Then Hannegan laid it on thick, saying, "Don't you know if Wallace wins radical labor will have control of the Democratic Party and of the nation? You don't want radical labor to have things their own way, do you?" Hannegan went on like this and as he did so Ed Pauley, who knew that Shelly was a labor leader, fidgeted in his chair. Finally, Hannegan, gathering from watching Pauley's actions that something was wrong, said, "By the way, what is your business?" Shelly said, "I am a labor leader." Hannegan said, "AFL or CIO?" Shelly said, "AFL." Hannegan then proceeded to say that his remarks applied only to the CIO. Everybody smoothed things down as much as possible but Shelly still made it clear that he was going to stay by me.

Shelly said that undoubtedly I would have been nominated if the vote had been held Thursday evening; that the Hannegan crowd had had it all arranged to put the thing through Thursday evening and then, when the demonstration broke loose for me after the President's speech, they got scared and adjourned the meeting. Shelly told quite an interesting story of his experience as he sat on the platform waiting to make a seconding speech for me—a speech which he never made because both Pepper and Frankensteen[1] grabbed the floor mikes on their own and made seconding speeches for me which had not been planned on. Shelly said they had been very anxious for me to come out to the West Coast during the campaign but they realized that it wasn't necessary.

DECEMBER 14, 1944

. . . Gregory[2] told me more of the details about the way in which Hannegan knifed the St. Louis meeting which I was supposed to address. I expressed surprise at this because Hannegan was one of the ones who wanted us to go to St. Louis. Gregory told how the State Democratic Chairman had been all for the meeting in the morning and then how he pulled off in the afternoon after he got in touch with Hannegan. This checks with information I have had from a number of other places where Hannegan tried to prevent meetings I was addressing from being a success. Gregory also said that the Missouri Bankers Association had at one time employed Hannegan. Gregory is a banker and knew about this from firsthand information. He said Hannegan bought the votes of legislators with money. Gregory's opinion of Hannegan is pretty low. His tendency is to favor the formation of a third party. I called Harold Young in and Harold tried to convince Gregory that that wasn't the best method of approach. I suggested that Young look up the laws in the different states with regard to third parties. Young said as a practical proposition in most States it was necessary for a new party to get a certain number of votes in the preceding election in order to get on the ticket in the following election. He thinks it is much easier to make the Democratic Party liberal than to start a liberal party on its own.

Senator Pepper wanted to talk to me about his fight on the State Department confirmations. I kept hands off and told him he would have to make up his own mind on that. I told him I couldn't figure what the President was up to unless, like a man in a rowboat, he was looking one way and rowing another . . .

1 Richard T. Frankensteen, Detroit labor organizer and president of the Wayne County, Michigan, Labor Non-Partisan League.
2 W. L. Gregory of the Plaza Bank of St. Louis.

Guffey came in to see me and wanted my advice on the State Department confirmations. I told him that I had no advice to offer. He wanted to know what the President was up to and I said maybe it was like the report of the conference between Churchill and Stalin. Churchill is reported to have said to Stalin, "This is what England wants to do in Greece." Stalin replied, "All right, go ahead, it is up to you." Then Churchill said, "This is what we want to do in Yugoslavia." Stalin replied, "All right, go ahead, it is up to you." And so on with several countries. Stalin didn't argue a single point but at the conclusion merely said, "Of course you will have to take into account the people themselves."

I said to Guffey, "Perhaps the President said to Stettinius with regard to each of the appointments, 'Sure, go ahead and appoint them, it is up to you.' At the finish the President may not have said, 'Perhaps the people may have something to say about it,' but the President may have thought it, nevertheless." Guffey said, "I am not sure that this is the situation. Stettinius claims that the President himself appointed these men" . . .

I told Senator Murray[1] how much I thought of his new bill which he will soon introduce. He wanted my opinion on the State Department confirmations. I told him I couldn't get into that fight but that I did look on it as the first skirmish in the fight to make the United States truly liberal. I told him I thought the really important things were going to have to do with full employment as handled in his bill. He wanted to know if I would advocate that the senators filibuster against the State Department confirmations. I refused to give an opinion. I told Murray the same story I told Guffey about Churchill and Stalin, and Murray came back with the same reply as Guffey, to the effect that Stettinius said the appointments of these men were due to the President and not to Stettinius . . .

---

[1] Democratic Senator James E. Murray of Montana was sponsoring legislation to make full employment a stated objective of federal policy and to direct the President to prepare annually a national budget to achieve that end. The bill as introduced in the new session of Congress in January 1945 was also sponsored by Senators Robert Wagner of New York, Elbert D. Thomas of Utah, and Joseph C. O'Mahoney of Wyoming. Its long and complicated legislative history, including the attachment to it of softening amendments, culminated in 1946 in the passage of the Employment Act which incorporated much of what Murray and his colleagues had initially proposed; see Stephen M. Bailey, *Congress Makes A Law* (New York, 1950).

DECEMBER 19, 1944

. . . Sulzberger[1] just returned last week from a 26,000-mile trip to the various islands in the South Pacific, including Saipan and Leyte. On Leyte he was close to the front and on one occasion a sniper bullet came within a few feet of him. His first concern is that there be a working arrangement between England, United States, and Russia. He feels that Roosevelt's great contribution has been in working out this coordination and he feels Roosevelt is best fitted for maintaining it. That is why he supported Roosevelt instead of Dewey. On the basis of domestic issues he would have supported Dewey. He thinks the Republicans will win in 1948. He was intensely devoted to Willkie and if Willkie had run, he would have supported him instead of Roosevelt. Sulzberger was exceedingly friendly, invited Mrs. Wallace and me to come up and spend a weekend with them, saying that he could have Charles Merz[2] and his wife present, and that the six of us would thresh out everything.

Sulzberger is very keen about the spiritual approach to the world's problems. He feels very deeply about the future and obviously wants to do the right thing. He mentioned that he had only interfered with Arthur Krock once and that was when Arthur started to indicate that Willkie would have been against Roosevelt if he had lived. Sulzberger thinks he would have been for Roosevelt if he had lived. I told him I had some evidence from Indiana indicating that Willkie would not have come out for either Roosevelt or Dewey. I also told him about some of Willkie's ideas about the starting of a progressive party in the spring of 1945. I told him I felt it was much better to make the Democratic Party into a progressive party. Sulzberger did not think it could be done. He told me how strong he was for compulsory military training . . . Sulzberger is enormously impressed with the Army but rather critical of the Navy. He thinks MacArthur has done a perfectly marvelous job in the Pacific. He also has considerable admiration for Eisenhower. His worship of MacArthur is most extraordinary. He feels that where the Army and Navy were working together and the Army had top command, a good job is done; but where they are working together and the Navy had top command a bad job is done. Perhaps this is because MacArthur gave him a good sales talk or maybe it is true.

Sulzberger said that our national policy with regard to Russia should

[1] Arthur Hays Sulzberger, publisher of the New York *Times*.
[2] Charles Merz, editor of the New York *Times*.

be to utilize them just as long as they were killing German soldiers and Jap soldiers. He thinks Russia will come in on our side against Japan after Germany has been defeated. He thinks the Russians are not fighting quite as hard as they might right now because Russia would like to see the United States suffer from some heavy casualties. He says that after the Russians have gotten through fighting the Germans and Japs, we should come to a showdown with them. He doesn't think we should fight them. He prays that may not be necessary. He says, however, that the Russians will need lots of help from us as soon as the war is over and that we should not furnish it except under certain conditions. I suspect Sulzberger is probably reflecting the MacArthur point of view.

Sulzberger said my position in the Democratic Party was somewhat like Willkie's in the Republican Party but that I was farther to the left. It seems to me rather obvious that just as Roosevelt was hoping a year ago to use Willkie as a wedge to split the Republican Party so Sulzberger now rather hopes to use me as a wedge to split the Democratic Party. I told him I was very strong for the Democratic Party because it could be made into a liberal party. He claimed it was impossible on account of the returning Negro soldiers in the South to make the Democratic Party into a liberal party. It seems almost certain that Sulzberger will support a Republican in 1948 no matter who runs on the Democratic ticket. He claims that he got a great deal out of his visit with me and was eager that I see him again soon.

I got it on very good authority yesterday that Edgar Hoover continually has Drew Pearson shadowed. Hoover specializes on building up a file against the various public figures and especially against the columnists. He has not as yet built up much of a file against Walter Winchell.[1] Winchell has so far been too smart for Hoover. Hoover is apparently on his way toward becoming a kind of an American Himmler.

DECEMBER 20, 1944

. . . The President started out by opening up a letter from Jimmie Roosevelt and as he went along quoting from the letter saying that Jimmie said he had just won a dime from a fellow soldier on the basis of Dewey getting less than 100 electoral votes.

[1] Both Drew Pearson in his "Washington Merry-Go-Round" and Walter Winchell in the New York *Mirror* and his Sunday radio broadcasts were during the war often critical and more often irreverent about federal policy and many federal officials, particularly in the State Department.

He then got started talking about when he managed Al Smith's campaign in 1924 in New York.

Then he mentioned that one of the newspapermen said, "Is it true that 350,000 votes taken away from you and properly placed would have given Dewey a majority of the electoral vote?" The President replied, "I'll ask you another one. Is it also true that 125,000 votes taken away from Dewey and given me properly placed would have given me all the electoral vote?" I then said, "Yes, Mr. President, during the campaign I said in the Middlewest if the Democratic Party had started organizing a year ago, we could have carried every state in the Union." Of course, I admitted it would have been pretty hard to carry Kansas and Nebraska. The President said, "Yes, the Kansas folks are pretty difficult. I remember back in 1924 when I was acting as manager for Al Smith at the New York convention, the Kansas delegates came in to see me and I sent word out to bring in Al. Al had been attending an Irish wedding. The Kansas delegates looked like Kansas farmers with square-toed shoes, stocky, round-faced men. They all looked just alike." Al came in with his shiny silk hat on the corner of his head, with spats and a cane and a flower in his buttonhole, talking in his broadest "Irishese." The President watched the Kansas boys freeze up and kissed good-by to Kansas right then and there. Al's breezy manner just did not meet the Middlewestern situation.

The President then went on from there to talk about how he got the D.C. vote for a time for Al. After about 45 ballots, the President thought that a break would be a good thing so he asked someone to go around and see what could be done to get the four votes from the D.C. for Al. They agreed to vote for Al if their hotel expenses were paid for the remainder of the convention. Some wealthy lady agreed to put up the money and for three ballots the D.C. voted for Al, whereupon the McAdoo forces raised the ante and they came back into the McAdoo[1] fold.

The President then said to me, "I got your wire. It is all right. You can have Commerce." I said, "I don't want it unless you are really enthusiastic about my taking it in the same way you wanted me to take Agriculture." He said he really wanted me to take the job. I gave him the enclosed copy of my ideas about reorganization of Commerce[2] and asked him to read it. He read over the entire memorandum

[1] Smith's close rival for the Democratic nomination in 1924 had been William G. McAdoo, Woodrow Wilson's Secretary of the Treasury and son-in-law. The deadlock between them was resolved only after more than one hundred ballots by the nomination of John W. Davis.

[2] Wallace's long memo recommended "a new Department of Commerce and a new concept of its work." He proposed closer ties to American business "so

and indicated he was in agreement. He said, however, he had asked
Crowley to stay on at FEA until VE-Day. I would judge, therefore,
that FEA would not go into Commerce. He said he had not yet written a letter to Jesus H. Jones accepting his resignation but would do
so immediately after Christmas. With regard to this letter he was going
to write Jesse, the President said he would put it on the basis of wanting to reduce the average age of his cabinet. He also spoke of Jesse as
being sick. I said I had seen Jesse recently and he looked remarkably
well to me.

I told the President that the idea of using Commerce to make the
most jobs possible intrigued me greatly as well as the idea of dealing
with small-business problems. He seemed to be in substantial accord
with regard to the last paragraph of this memo dealing with relations
with the State Department on foreign commerce.

I told him it was my observation that one of the most fatal things
around Washington was to have responsibility without having adequate authority or power to carry out the responsibility. I said this
after he had given an extensive disquisition regarding the standard of
living of people everywhere over the world, embroidering this with
considerable discussion of the low standard of living of the people in
Africa.

I told the President about the Murray bill for full employment and
it seemed to interest him. He suggested that there be appointed a
committee on which would sit a representative of State Department,
Commerce, Agriculture, as well as a senator and a congressman, and
Henry Kaiser. The purpose of the committee would be to draw up a
program for foreign trade and to suggest the necessary legislation.

The President said, "Will Clayton is not so bad and his wife is a
dear." At one stage in the conversation, I said, "I am sure there will

---

that business opinion and business reality can be injected into governmental
policy," service at home and abroad related to business needs, an emphasis on
federal aid to small business, and a consolidation into one central organization
of all federal agencies to which business might look for its contacts with government, including loans, technical advice, and economic reporting. As Wallace
saw it, the domestic wing of the Commerce Department should include its
existing bureaus and the existing lending agencies as well as those parts of war
agencies that could contribute to reconversion. The foreign wing, he wrote,
should include the agencies necessary to negotiate governmental credits abroad
that affected trade, to control assistance to exporters operating in markets where
other countries limited imports, to purchase materials abroad for federal use
where private business was unwilling to assume the necessary risks, and to sell
federal surplus property abroad. Wallace also asked for authority to restructure
the department and to appoint overseas commercial representatives independent
of the direction of the Department of State.

not be any difficulty concerning my confirmation in the Senate." He said, "No, of course not. But then sometimes you can't tell. Just take the current fight, for example."

Then he mused a moment and said, "I do not trust all six of them either. Take this fellow Holmes, for example, and then there is Jimmie Dunn. Of course, I put in Jimmie just to make Cordell feel good." He then continued, "They will all stand watching, including Will Clayton."

I then said to him, "What do you expect to do with RFC?" He said, "I expect you to take that as well as Commerce."

The President described how Firestone was paying the natives of Liberia 17 cents a day to work on the rubber plantations and how they wanted to get higher wages. Again and again he hit the problem of the low standard of living of the people in the various backward parts of the world. I said, "Mr. President, if you expect to do anything about matters of this sort, we will have to develop international commodity agreements." I said I did not know how Will Clayton stood on international commodity agreements at the present time but I had known that in the past he had been against them, that he definitely belonged in his thinking to the Manchester School of Economics. The President said that we have got to have international understanding about certain problems. He said, "I wish there were some way to get away from the word 'cartel.'" He seemed to think government cartels were all right. I said, "Why not get away from cartel and use the phrase 'international agreement' and use 'international agreement' under government supervision with full protection both for producers and consumers?" He seemed to like that idea. I said, "If you are going down the line on this, you are bound to run into trouble with Will Clayton."

The President talked about the idea of putting Maritime Commission and Civil Aeronautics Board under the Department of Commerce. I told him the CAB was already there in a way although not very definitely so.

I told the President that several years after the war was over, I thought there was going to be the most extraordinary kind of a back lick which was going to bring serious trouble on us and it would be necessary to act with very great comprehension and imagination in planning to avoid this trouble. I said after World War No. 1, Hoover had very big plans for large export trade but these plans as a result of our high tariff policy eventually came to naught. I said we would have to have a very comprehensive and well thought out long-time plan if we were to avoid the same pitfalls which overtook the Republicans in 1930. The President gave an assent to this but I don't think he really understood it. His thinking is completely in other fields.

I told the President that the Commerce function might not amount to an awful lot until the war came to an end. Then I took a second thought and said, "But there certainly should be comprehensive planning long before the war comes to an end and the planning should be started at once."

He said, "You know I am one of those who never has predicted an early end of the war. Churchill said it would end in 1944. Eisenhower said 1944." He continued, "You know all astrologers are agreed that it will not end until 1947." I said, "Well, Mr. President, I disagree with you strongly. I think the German war will end in 1945 and the Jap war in 1946." When the President referred to the astrologists, I judged that he halfway believed in them.

Speaking of small business, I told the President I liked the idea of getting out to the small business groups in the medium-sized towns, to the Chambers of Commerce, etc., etc., and meeting with representatives of labor and agriculture with these Chambers of Commerce and small business groups. He seemed to like the idea.

In discussing Will Clayton, the President spoke at some length about cotton in Brazil. He said that sometime in the late thirties, he had visited with a gentleman by the name of Peñas who owned a marvelous estate formerly owned by the brother of the Emperor of Brazil Dom Pedro, a perfectly glorious palace and estate. The President said to Peñas, "Do you own other land in Brazil?" He replied, "Yes. I own three hundred million acres in Matto Grosso." I was rather aghast at 300 million acres because that represents an area equal to 8 states the size of Iowa. The President said this man cleared 10 million acres of land each year to produce cotton. I interjected to say that this surely could not be true because we only plant 20 million acres of cotton in the United States. The President said Peñas told him also that he could produce the cotton for 4 cents a pound laid down at the port.

The President thinks we ought to stabilize our cotton prices in the United States at around 15 or 16 cents. I said, "Mr. President, as near as I can figure out, this program means an international cotton agreement." I also mentioned that rayon during the past 5 or 6 years had been taking the place of 4 or 5 million bales of cotton and that rayon competition was bound to grow.

A little later the President discussed China, and said Hurley was doing a swell job. He said, "You know, I had a devil of a job with Marshall with regard to Stilwell. I had to say to Marshall, 'If Chiang Kai-shek were only Generalissimo, I would not have to recall Stilwell just because Chiang doesn't like him. But you must remember that Chiang is President of China.' "

The President went on to say that if Churchill would say to him, "You must get rid of Marshall—" then all of a sudden the President backed up and realized that his illustration was going in absolutely the wrong direction and reversed himself and said, "If I found, for example, that Sir John Dill of England were not agreeable to me as representative here, I would expect Churchill to remove him if I complained."

It was obvious to me that the President's mind roams as far afield as ever, that he still talks endlessly about everything under the sun but that he is losing considerable of his old power of focus. His mind isn't very clear anymore. His hand trembles a great deal more than it used to . . .

During the discussion of the full employment bill . . . I told the President that the fundamental idea originally came from Jim Patton, and went through in some little detail with the Simon Kuznets theory of capital formation in its relation to total national production. I then described the bill in course of action and said, "Now suppose, Mr. President, that you found in a particular year, for example, the fiscal year 1947, that 40 billion dollars of capital formation would be necessary to bring about full employment whereas the prospective capital formation from private sources and from local and state governments was only 25 billion dollars. The congressional committee looking at the deficiency of 15 billion dollars and looking at our total debt amounting to perhaps 250 billion dollars would say, 'We can't go into debt anymore.' At this stage of the game, it might be necessary, Mr. President, if we are to have jobs for all, to issue non-interest-bearing government securities, provided a definite stop were put on their issuance to prevent inflation and provided also that they were paid off by the returns from self-liquidating projects.

"The other non-debt-producing alternative would be to bring about huge common stock investments."

I said, "I am in favor of such modifications of the taxation system as would favor capital investment."

I also said to the President that if we were really going to meet this problem, it might be necessary to sooner or later run head-on into the Wall Street setup, that their methods of high interest financing were really one of the blocks in the way of sufficient flow of capital.

The President went to some pains to say that he thought Jesse Jones through his nephew had quite a bit to do with the Texas May convention revolt. Apparently he could not forgive Jesse for being indirectly connected with the Texas regulars. He said he thought Will Clayton was absolutely pure on this score. I did not tell him that Charles Marsh had told me that Anderson of Anderson and Clayton[1] furnished some of the first money to the Texas regulars prior to the May convention.

Evidently the President is a long-time friend of Ed Stettinius. He mentioned back when Ed was president of United States Steel Corporation that he, the President, had spoken to Ed about his desire to take a cruise around the world in economical leisurely manner. Stettinius told him that the way to do it was in the director's suite of the 15,000-ton boats owned by the U.S. Steel Corporation. These boats form what is known as Isthmian line. They are not supposed to carry passengers but friends of the U.S. Steel Corporation can travel in the director's suite by paying $5 a day and signing up as a member of the crew at a compensation of $1.

The President then described in detail how the boats go laden with steel products to Morocco, unload some of the steel and then go on to Bathurst. He then described the scene at Bathurst. While he himself had never made this trip by boat, he visited Bathurst by air and told about his conversations with the British Consul general there. He asked the British Consul general what was the chief export product and he said peanuts. The President had driven out into the open country to our airport and saw the primitive method of cultivating the peanuts and asked the Consul how much return the British empire got out of Gambia for each shilling of investment. The Consul general replied, "About a pound, I would say."

The President then said, "Well, I see some cultivating being done here with a crooked stick drawn by two women. If these people were given more purchasing power, they could buy things from Great Britain to raise their standard of living."

The President then indicated that probably these people should not wear clothes because it had been demonstrated in the Southwest Pacific that those natives who wore clothes succumbed to tuberculosis and those who did not wear clothes did not succumb to the disease.

He then related a story about Miss Suckley's mother, who was very active in the Missionary Society collecting clothes for the Liberians. The President told her that the Liberians who received clothes from the Missionary Society would undoubtedly be murdered. The old lady

[1] Anderson, Clayton and Company, cotton factors in Houston, Texas.

looked up the facts, found they were correct, and stopped her missionary activity.

I mention these matters merely to indicate a few of the many subjects which the President thought had a point when he started telling them but which point he promptly forgot as he went further afield. His whole habit of mind is that of a man who is continually traveling, seeing fresh pictures. His extraordinary discursiveness may have served a very useful purpose as President but as he gets older it makes him less and less capable as an administrator and more and more irritating to administrators . . .

When the President mentioned Henry Kaiser's name, I said I had a great admiration for Kaiser and asked the President how it would be to counsel with Kaiser on what might be needed in the reorganization of the Department of Commerce in the way of new legislation. He said it would be fine to go ahead.

When I left, I asked the President what to tell the press. He said to tell them we had a nice conference, that there was nothing they could ask me that we did not talk about, that we focused particular attention on reforestation in Iran.

DECEMBER 21, 1944

Oscar Chapman[1] started out by saying that he wanted either me or Harold Ickes to call a meeting of some of the key liberals. He had on his list Senator Guffey, Senator Murray, Senator Pepper; plus Dan Tobin of the AFL; Sidney Hillman or Phil Murray of CIO; Henry Kaiser and Aluminum Reynolds,[2] representing business; Jo Davidson, representing Arts and Sciences; Leon Henderson, representing Independent Voters for Roosevelt, et al. I told Oscar I did not think I should call the meeting, that I was a marked man. He asked how it would be for Harold Ickes to call the meeting. I suggested it might be just as well if calling the meeting were to be delayed a little while.

Oscar then started to talk about how much I meant to all the liberals and began to reminisce about the Chicago convention. He said the man who really hurt me more than anyone else at the time when the hurting counted was Tommy Corcoran. He said Tommy really was not for Douglas but was pushing Douglas to beat me. He said Tommy moved in several weeks before the convention on Ickes and convinced Ickes that I had no support whatever in the country. When Ickes, represent-

[1] Oscar L. Chapman, since 1933 Assistant Secretary of the Interior Department.
[2] Richard S. Reynolds.

ing the supposed liberals, and Hannegan, representing the orthodox
Democratic crowd, both told the President the same thing, that I had
no support, the result was fatal, according to Chapman.

Oscar mentioned that he had called on Harry Hopkins on Friday,
July 14, just prior to the convention and had told Harry that he
wanted to know what the President wanted at the convention. Harry
seemed to think that was all right. Chapman also reported that he was
with Harry the week following the convention and he said to Harry,
"Well, I suppose I am in bad with the administration because I supported Wallace instead of Truman at the convention." Harry told
Chapman that those who supported Wallace at the convention were
not in bad with the administration. On Saturday, July 15, Ickes had
Chapman in to his office, and asked him to support Douglas. Chapman
told Ickes he was going to support me. Abe Fortas, the Undersecretary
of Interior, is very close to Corcoran and was serving as a go-
between between Ickes and Corcoran. Chapman threw in parenthetically that Michael Strauss, who is another Assistant Secretary of
Interior, had no use whatever for Tommy Corcoran and has told Ickes
and Abe Fortas to keep Tommy out of his end of the building. Of
course, Harry Hopkins had no use whatever for Tommy Corcoran.
Chapman now reports that Felix Frankfurter is very bitter against
Tommy Corcoran. Chapman said that Wednesday night July 19 Frank
Walker called up the chairman of the Colorado delegation and said,
"This is the Postmaster General speaking. I am speaking for the Presi-
dent and want you to vote for Truman." I have heard this from many
sources.

Oscar was very eager to know what I was going to be doing. I told
him I was not sure yet. He said, "You know, I hoped you would be
Secretary of State. I was in Chicago the day Stettinius' appointment
was announced and, when I came out of a certain building, there were
the headlines. A couple of ladies came by and saw the headlines. One
of them said to the other one, 'Well, the President let Wallace down
again.'" Chapman said that was the way he felt. He said he had been
thinking about what I should do and he thought I could do more for
the liberal cause inside the administration than out and he had been
thinking about the jobs I might hold, said there were only two foreign
jobs that would be good, one was Ambassador to England, the other
was Ambassador to Russia. Concerning the cabinet, he thought it
would be a serious mistake for me to be Secretary of Labor. On the
whole, he thought the best thing, in case Ickes would leave, would be
for me to be Secretary of Interior, either that or Secretary of Commerce. Although he thought there would be less risk looking toward

1948 in being Secretary of Interior. I told him frankly that I would prefer to be Secretary of Commerce because I thought there was a chance from a base as Secretary of Commerce to do some good work looking toward full employment.

When Chapman was holding forth on Corcoran, I asked why it was that Tommy hated me so. Chapman replied, "That is very simple. You did not let him put any of his lawyers in the Department of Agriculture."

Obviously Oscar is not a Corcoran man, nor a Byrnes man nor a Baruch man. It is quite possible, however, that he is a Hopkins man. He specializes in keeping in touch with the various independent liberal organizations which supported the President during the campaign . . . I like Chapman. He seems to be on the right side of things. I would say he might be pretty close to Harry Hopkins, and that Harry at the present time is possibly casting around to find an alliance somewhere in the liberal camp. It is conceivable that Harry may have sent Oscar out as a scout to find out how I was feeling.

DECEMBER 22, 1944

. . . At cabinet the President came in looking thinner than usual. He started in with gaily telling about the lunch he had had with Dick Law,[1] what a fine young man he was, how he would make a good Prime Minister if only he were a little older. He then began to talk about shortage of shipping and about the hardships of the people in Belgium because of the shipping shortage. Jimmie Byrnes said we were planning to build 18 million tons of shipping in the year 1945 and that about half of it would be in Victory ships, which are much superior to the Liberty ships.

Secretary Stimson presented a very serious report, prepared by General Marshall, on the German attack.[2] Eisenhower had wired that

[1] Richard Law (later Lord Coleraine), a Conservative Member of Parliament, head of the British delegation to the 1943 United Nations Conference on Food and Agriculture that created UNRRA, and in 1944 a British delegate to the Bretton Woods Conference that created the International Monetary Fund and the International Bank for Reconstruction and Development.

[2] The surprise German counteroffensive had begun on December 16 in the Ardennes and cut a huge gap in the Allied lines. Eisenhower on December 19 put Field Marshal Bernard L. Montgomery in charge of all forces north of the Ardennes salient and Lieutenant General Omar N. Bradley in command of all forces to the south. He also ordered Lieutenant General George S. Patton, Jr., to attack the southern bulge of the German line and drive on to relieve Bastogne, where the Americans were holding out against a fierce attack. By Christmas the German generals realized they had lost the battle; by the end of January they had retreated from all the ground previously gained. For both sides, the Battle of the Bulge was enormously costly.

Bradley is doing a magnificent job of commanding the American armies. Stimson likened the situation to the German attacks in March, April, May, June, and July of 1915. He doesn't seem to be too much discouraged.

(As he was mentioning this, I could not help thinking of the talk I had the previous evening with Vannevar Bush about a new type of shell[1] which the Americans began to use on December 21 which is three times as efficient as the previous shells because of the time fuse which sets off the explosion just about the ground. Bush said that just 10 days ago he was in that part of Belgium and France where the Germans are now attacking and that our people there had an adequate supply of this new kind of shell, which they are going to start using. These shells might well prove to be a determining factor in holding the Germans back.)

Henry Morgenthau mentioned about closing the racetracks. Both Jimmie Byrnes and Henry were strong for closing racetracks. They said it creates a very bad impression on our soldiers when they come back to Florida, for example, and see hundreds of cars parked around a racetrack and special trains running to the races. Jimmie mentioned that a Pennsylvania train he was taking was held up an hour and a half so that cars carrying four racehorses could be attached to the train. I knew nothing about the background of the racetrack controversy but I somehow had the feeling that Morgenthau and Byrnes were shooting at somebody. The President laughingly referred to Herbert Bayard Swope,[2] who has been active in this kind of business and who is now in the War Department. Leo Crowley seemed to think that there was danger of an attack on racetracks getting into the field of Prohibition and held up very tentatively and carefully a finger of warning.[3] Morgenthau took great pride in the fact that his war loan had amounted to 21 billion dollars when he had only asked for 14 billion dollars.

Stimson indicated that he would need more men. Byrnes said more men would be needed in the building of ships. There was indication everywhere that the recent turn of the war meant that a shortage of manpower would continue quite a while longer. The President took

[1] Wallace was describing the proximity fuse, an important new development both for the Battle of the Bulge and later for use by naval vessels against Japanese suicide planes in the Pacific.
[2] Herbert Bayard Swope, then a consultant to the Secretary of War, had been a distinguished reporter for the New York *World* and later that paper's executive editor. He was also chairman of the New York Racing Commission.
[3] Byrnes ordered all horse and dog tracks closed on January 3, 1945. They were permitted to reopen on May 9, immediately after the war in Europe had ended.

the slant that what we needed now was a continuation of war psychology and no suggestion of peacetime psychology or peacetime planning of any kind. The necessity for maintaining war psychology is that when peacetime psychology gets around, thousands of people immediately leave their war jobs and start looking for peace jobs.

Wickard brought up the question of holidays in the government departments. The President said there was only one holiday and that was Christmas. The President expected the government departments to work on New Year's Day and every other holiday except Sundays and Christmas.

After the President had gone all around the cabinet, he said to me, "And so you see, Henry." I assumed by this statement he meant that it would be necessary to proceed cautiously in planning for peace as long as the war with Germany is on.

The President, referring to the Greek situation,[1] said he thought the best solution was to give both sides in Greece all the rifles and ammunition they wanted and then everybody pull out and let them fight it out.

Jimmie Byrnes mentioned that he was getting the office of OWM and Reconversion established and staffed, and that under the terms of the Act setting up the office apparently it had very wide powers. He mentioned particularly the power to formulate or have formulated such plans as are necessary to meet the problems arising out of the transition from war to peace. He said this power as contained in the Act was as wide as a barn door and about everything could be done under it.

DECEMBER 27, 1944

. . . I told Biddle how much I thought of Hubert Humphrey[2] in Minnesota . . .

---

1 Allied forces had occupied Athens on October 13, 1944, but civil war in Greece erupted soon thereafter. British troops assisted the supporters of the regent, Archbishop Damaskinos, who had been appointed by King George II with Churchill's blessing. The insurgents consisted of leftist factions, some communist, some not. Though the fighting ceased on January 15, 1945, the Archbishop and his British sponsors maintained only a shaky hold on the government while resistance continued to grow. The disaffected groups refused to participate in a general election of March 1946, which the royalists won. In May guerrilla activities prefaced another six months of civil war.

2 While stumping in Minnesota, Wallace had met Hubert H. Humphrey, who was in charge of the campaign in that state for the Roosevelt-Truman Committee. Humphrey took office as reform Democratic mayor of Minneapolis in 1945.

Biddle spoke very highly of Jimmie Byrnes and said he was most cooperative and fine to work with. He asked if I thought Harry Hopkins was behind the appointment of Will Clayton. I said I didn't know. He said he hoped I would be in the new administration and wanted to know if I had any plans. I said I didn't have any plans but that I would very much like to be Secretary of Commerce. He asked if he could be of any help in this matter. I said, "No." He asked if I would be interested in Commerce even if RFC were not included. I said, "Yes," but that I thought RFC was very important to successful operation with regard to full postwar employment . . .

DECEMBER 28, 1944

Lauchlin Currie came in to tell me about a talk he had had with the President. He told the President that the liberals everywhere were very much discouraged about his appointments to the State Department. He said the President was really quite apologetic about it, apparently admitted that Dunn and Holmes were pretty bad, then said to Currie that "Clayton is a pretty good fellow, isn't he?"

Currie then proceeded to develop the theme that the one thing which the President could do that would greatly encourage the liberals would be to appoint me as Secretary of Commerce. The President did not give Currie any direct answer but merely said he thought Currie would like what he was going to do with regard to Commerce. Currie reported with regard to Harry Hopkins, that Hopkins said to friends of mine like Bob Nathan, "Henry is a grand fellow. He helped greatly in the campaign. We must get something for him, etc., etc." But to other people even closer to Harry Hopkins than any of these, Hopkins said, "Yes, Henry is a fine fellow but can you vision him as Secretary of Commerce trying to get an appropriation on the Hill?"

Lauch says that he understands from a third party that Clayton feels I was responsible for the attack on him in the Senate. Lauch thinks that Clayton's operations abroad as revealed by Treasury records were pretty bad. He says, however, that Clayton in his face-to-face contacts seems like a very fine fellow. Lauch reports that there is a great deal of intrigue in the White House. He says the President's original intention was to put in Jimmie Byrnes in the State Department as Secretary. This alarmed Harry Hopkins, who told the President that he would have the same trouble with Byrnes that he had with Hull. Hopkins sold the President on the idea if he was going to be his own Secretary of State, he would have to have Stettinius. Harry and Stettinius are very close and the two of them together worked out the six appointments.

Will Clayton is not really Hopkins' man but Jimmie Byrnes' man and was put in to conciliate Byrnes . . .

Lauch says that Harry Hopkins is terrifically jealous of anybody who tries to get close to the President. He has not only fallen out with Jimmie Byrnes but now has very strained relations with both Sam Rosenman and Steve Early. Lauch thinks the strong man in the State Department will undoubtedly be Will Clayton, which means an indirect triumph, so Lauch says, for Byrnes and Baruch.

Lauch says he has talked with Don Nelson about the current Chinese situation. It seems that Pat Hurley has done a good job over there in getting the communists and the Generalissimo together. He questions whether it will last very long. Lauch says that Nelson is now out of an assignment. He has an office and a staff but nothing for them to do . . .

JANUARY I, 1945

. . . At 6 o'clock in the evening Ed Stettinius dropped by, saying that the President had told him that he wanted me to be Secretary of Commerce. Stettinius was bubbling over with enthusiasm, saying how happy he was about it and how fine it was for the country. He then wanted to talk about the relationship between the Department of Commerce and the State Department on the problem of foreign attachés, mentioning that Hawkins[1] was going to head up the coordination of various economic activities for the State Department in London. I told him that Hawkins was an excellent man and then laid down the thesis that it seemed to me the State Department should be supreme on the policy level and that Commerce ought to be allowed to determine operational matters in its own proper field of activity. I told him my observations concerning agricultural attachés since they had become a part of the State Department and said it seemed to me that if a real job were to be done the agency responsible for operations ought to have the power to hire and fire.

Stettinius said the old-line crowd in the State Department would agree with me on the proposition that it was not the duty of the State

---

[1] Harry C. Hawkins, for many years an official in the State Department, chief of the Division of Commercial Policy and Agreements (January-September 1941) had become Economic Counselor of the American embassy in London in October 1944.

Department to engage in operations. On the whole it seemed to me that there should be no difficulty in arriving at a suitable agreement with Stettinius. He spoke about Milo's being such a fine man and I told him that it wasn't my intention to bring Milo back into the picture. I agreed with him utterly and completely that Milo was an unusually fine person. I told him that when I was Vice President I could not engage in operations myself but that as Secretary of Commerce I wanted to be my own contact man both with Congress and other people in the executive branch of the government, as, for example, with Stettinius. I visioned sitting down with Stettinius and Clayton to work on commercial problems in the foreign field. Stettinius, like Clayton, agreed with me enthusiastically about the need for a big export-import trade. Stettinius said, in a musing way, "How will Jesse like it when he is only in the loan field?" I said the President indicated to me that he was going to give me RFC as well as Commerce. I said of course the RFC would be a headache in many ways but nevertheless if certain things were to be done it seemed to me essential to have RFC.

At the party at Thurman Arnold's . . . Senator and Mrs. O'Mahoney[1] took a very strong anti-Russian stand, claiming that the President had appeased Russia. O'Mahoney also took a very strong stand against the Murray Full Employment Bill, claiming that it was the doorway to totalitarianism. I told him while there were many 'hanges I would make in the Murray bill, I utterly disagreed with him in this analysis and I felt the backwash of the war would make it necessary for the government to step in on the overall fiscal and employment picture in a strong way, trying, of course, to get results through private initiative if possible; nevertheless approaching the problems of peace with the same vigor that it approached the problems of war . . .

JANUARY 2, 1945

The President looked unusually well and was in excellent spirits. He talked at some length about the international situation, indicating his troubles with Churchill. He indicated that when he went on his trip this time, he would meet with Ibn Saud and try to settle the Palestine situation. He said the Greeks were very hard people to get along with, that every one of them was a violent politician.

The President came out very strongly for universal military training. Sam Rayburn indicated this would be very hard to put over.

The President took the page of pictures of the American dead and

[1] Joseph C. O'Mahoney, Wyoming Democrat.

wounded from the January 2 issue of the Washington *Times-Herald* and passed it around. These pictures were entitled "Again and Again and Again," and in essence are probably as treasonable a thing as has ever appeared in an American paper in time of war. The President said nothing but the rest of us spoke our minds pretty freely.

I said to the President there were certain senators who felt that we should get our troops out of France as soon as possible so that we would be in shape to fight Russia later on, that there were some senators who felt that the President was appeasing Russia. The President defended his course vigorously. He said that in England there were certain people who felt the same way, that at Teheran Churchill very much wanted the second front to be opened up on the Dalmatian Coast or some place else in the Balkan states. Apparently the Churchill idea has been that the Anglo-Saxons should open up a sphere of influence in the Balkan states to offset Russia. The President stood fast for opening up a second front in France . . .

The President put in a plug for Senator Fulbright going on the Foreign Relations Committee. Barkley indicated it could not be done, that there were too many sitting senators who wanted positions . . .

At the conclusion of the meeting of the President with congressional leaders I stayed behind for a moment to tell him what a fine luncheon meeting I had had with Mr. and Mrs. Clayton and also about the meeting with Ed Stettinius. I told him it seemed to me as though there should not be any serious difficulty on this matter of the foreign commercial attachés. I told the President it was my intention to meet with Stettinius and Clayton myself and I thought that it would be possible to iron matters of this sort out satisfactorily. I mentioned that I intended to be my own contact man with Congress as well as with men like Stettinius and Clayton. I said when I was Vice President I couldn't do this. The President then asked how Milo was and spoke in glowing terms about him, saying that we must get him back into the picture again. I told him I thought it would be unwise for me to bring Milo into the picture—at any rate, that I shouldn't do so at first.

I said to the President that Stettinius had said, "How will Jesse take it being restricted only to the RFC?" and then went on to indicate that I felt it would be unfortunate to leave Jesse in RFC; that it would prove to be a headache both for him and for me and for the Democratic Party. The President said he agreed absolutely. He asked if I had seen Crowley and I said, "No." I don't know what he had in mind with regard to Crowley because he said he wanted Crowley to stay on until V-E Day. He said Crowley got on well with Congress. He said there would be a question of appointing another man when Crowley got out. I still can't figure out whether he wants FEA to go into Commerce on V-E Day or not.

He said he would write the letter to Jesse Jones accepting his resignation this afternoon if he got around to it. He also said that his plan was to send my nomination to Congress on January 20 so that there would be no interregnum whatsoever.

JANUARY 5, 1945

. . . At cabinet meeting the President spoke about the Greek situation and again referred to the best policy being to give both sides plenty of ammunition and let them shoot each other up while the Allies stayed in boats off the Greek coast. Looking at Jesse Jones, he said that the Greeks were a good bit like Texans, they liked to shoot each other. Then he said, "Well, I guess there have not been any killings in Texas since last spring."

The President said he had been babying Halifax along. He gave it as his general impression that Churchill had slipped greatly in England and was much worried. He said, however, recently he had received a message from Churchill in poetry form and this indicated that Churchill was beginning to recover because a man doesn't write poetry when he is downhearted . . .

The President mentioned, as he always does when the Greek question comes up, that he is a member of the Order of Aheppa but that Greeks love to talk politics and whenever they talk politics they get excited and want to cut each other up. He said he could say this because all the Greeks in the country had voted for him in the last election.

Stimson spoke at some length on the military situation. He referred to the fact that in France the French have 7 divisions, the British 14, and we have about 50. We also have several divisions in England. He said the Germans have about the same number as we have but the German divisions are smaller and not as good. He read from a letter received from General Patton of December 27 in which Patton expressed the belief that this was the decisive battle against Germany. Patton mentioned that the new type of ammunition is working splendidly.

The President said again, as he has said a number of times recently, that he had not heard anyone talking in the past month about reconversion. Apparently he wants all attention fastened on the war effort.

JANUARY 9, 1945

. . . I told Henry Kaiser the President wanted me to talk with him about plans for the Department of Commerce. With Kaiser everything adds up to the question of jobs and establishing the proper working relationship with labor. He says his sympathies are more with the CIO than the AFL although more of his unions are AFL unions. His formula for full employment is what he calls his 3 H's and a T. In other words, Housing, Health, Highways, and Transportation. He would have government financing at low rates of interest of hospitals in connection with in.ustry, the same way he has done out at Vancouver, Washington. In other words, he would have a sort of FHA for clinics and hospitals applied on a nationwide scale. He thinks there would be less opposition to this approach than to the Murray-Wagner-Dingell Bill on so-called federalized medicine.[1] I told him I did not think the Secretary of Commerce had any very direct power in creating jobs but that if I had the right kind of backing from the President and from labor, it might be possible to do quite a lot. Something would depend on who was Secretary of Labor. He asked if I had anyone to suggest. I said I thought it might be important that the Secretary of Labor not be from the ranks of labor but that he be someone who could get along with labor and who could envision the possibility of changing our economy sufficiently to get full employment.

Kaiser said he thought the businessmen now appreciated the absolute necessity of a national income of 140 billion dollars a year or a gross national product of 170 billion dollars a year . . .

At the conference at the White House there were present Speaker Rayburn, John McCormack, Senator Truman, Alben Barkley, and Tom Connally. Sam Rayburn started out by presenting the President with a box of pecans, which caused the President to talk about Jack Garner and the way in which Jack gets his hands stained because he spends his time hulling pecans. The President then talked about how Jack Garner claimed the New Deal was going to ruin him because of low interest rates. It seems Jack Garner had been accustomed to lending his money at 15 percent and didn't like getting only 12 percent.

[1] Senators Robert Wagner and James E. Murray, and Democratic Representative John Dingell of Michigan had introduced an omnibus welfare bill, based upon earlier reports of the National Resources Planning Board, that provided, among other things, for national compulsory health insurance. For a full account of that forward-looking but little supported measure, see J. Joseph Huthmacher, *Senator Robert F. Wagner and the Rise of Urban Liberalism* (New York, 1968) pp. 292–94.

Sam Rayburn said he didn't belong to that school of thought because he was on the borrowing side and not on the lending side.

There was some discussion of the manpower and universal military training legislative situation. Sam Rayburn indicated that he thought the President ought to go slow in pushing for the universal military training and that the boys ought to spend a good bit of their time learning how to be mechanics and learning how to farm. Alben Barkley said this would not do because the colleges didn't like the idea of the boys' getting too much educational training by the government.

In discussing the foreign situation it became obvious that the President anticipated that the next Dumbarton Oaks meeting would be sometime during the latter part of March. Connally spoke about Senator Vandenberg and the Polish question and said they had been quieting Vandenberg by saying that the question of the Curzon Line could be opened up with the United Nations Council fifteen years hence. The President said, "Now, wait a minute! What will I do if I open this up and Stalin doesn't agree?" The President then went on to say that the Russians were insisting on having 17 representatives at the next Dumbarton Oaks Conference and therefore Brazil was going to insist on 26, Canada on 6, and the United States on 48. John McCormack said he understood the Chinese communists were not fighting the Japs. I said that every military man who had returned from among the Chinese communists, no matter what his political opinion, reported that the Chinese communists were doing a good job. The President spoke up to say that the Chinese communists were not communists but were agrarians. I mentioned what Colonel Olmstead had told me the preceding day, which had also been told me in China, that the Japanese soldiers were making quite a bit of money by trading with the Chinese, no matter whether they were government people or communists.

JANUARY 11, 1945

. . . The President started out cabinet[1] by talking concerning the meeting with the eight senators from the Foreign Relations Committee.[2]

[1] This was to be the last of Roosevelt's cabinet meetings about which Wallace commented in his diary. The President left for the Yalta Conference before Wallace was confirmed as Secretary of Commerce and died on April 12, 1945, before Wallace resumed keeping a record.

[2] Tom Connally had appointed a Committee of Eight Senators to confer with the State Department about plans for a world organization. Arthur Vandenberg of Michigan, the most influential Republican on that committee, approved, as did Connally, of Hull's cautious approach to the problem, though Vandenberg was even more hesitant than Hull. The senator considered Roosevelt soft on

He said he was having this prior to his meeting with Stalin and Churchill, which meeting he said was going to be held at the North Pole. The President was pleased with Vandenberg's speech; Jimmie Byrnes spoke up very strongly in favor of Vandenberg saying that he thought the senator's nephew in the air force, General Vandenberg, who was given a great play in this week's issue of *Time* had been working on the senator and that the senator now had a much more enlightened attitude than he had earlier . . .

At the conclusion of cabinet meeting, Henry Morgenthau wanted to see me so we went out for a walk for about 20 minutes. He wanted to tell me the details of a conversation he had had with Ed Stettinius about FEA and about a certain cabinet committee for handling the economic affairs of the United States vis-à-vis the outside world. I told him I would not tell anyone about the details of this matter so I am not even writing them down here. Suffice it to say, I was very much pleased with the proposal as made by Stettinius to Henry Morgenthau. Henry Morgenthau was also much pleased . . .

The President went to bat in a very mild way for Bob Hannegan and his patronage. Apparently Hannegan had been in to the President complaining that Public Works and Housing had not been cooperating with him . . .

The President very mildly in his statement said that he did not think it was necessary to have more than 90 percent of the employees in the government Republicans, that he realized that CPA was largely Republican but he did not see why all the agencies should be so largely Republican. He said maybe the various administrative officials could have Hannegan in and talk to him like a Father. Obviously the President was doing what Hannegan had asked him to do and he was handling the situation as carefully and gently as he could.

Russia and insisted upon the right of Congress to veto any use of force for collective security. Still, on January 10, 1945, in a major speech to the Senate, Vandenberg called for "maximum American cooperation, consistent with legitimate American self-interest" to make a new world organization succeed. He criticized but did not condemn the Soviet Union, and he urged American leaders to persuade Stalin of the necessity of collective security. Vandenberg's generous and genuine motives on that occasion derived as much from his own developing ideas as from any influence of his nephew, Brigadier General Hoyt S. Vandenberg, then deputy chief of the Air Staff; see Robert A. Divine, *Second Chance: The Triumph of Internationalism in America During World War II* (New York, 1967), *passim* but especially p. 262 ff.

JANUARY 13, 1945

. . . Jim Patton told me he is going to be seeing the President next week and that he hoped I would be Secretary of Commerce. I told him I had mentioned to the President his (Patton's) part in forming the full employment bill. Patton says he doesn't trust any of the labor leaders except Phil Murray. He says all the others are indiscreet or will double-cross you. Apparently he means this to apply especially to Sidney Hillman. He says Hillman doesn't like him. He told me that he would very much like to be Secretary of Labor but not to put on any drive for him. I told him I thought I would mention it to Phil Murray . . .

Both Charles Marsh and Morris Rosenthal have reported that Jesse Jones has told a newspaperman (Time-Life-Fortune) that he, Jesse, knew the President wanted to get rid of him and put Henry Wallace in his place. According to Rosenthal, Jesse told the newspaperman that the President would have to blast him out. According to Charles, Jesse said the President would have to dynamite him out. Obviously Jesse is doing his best to put on a warlike appearance. Probably it doesn't mean a thing unless the President is worked upon in some way by Jesse's friends. Of course, there is the possibility that Jesse may try to cause trouble in the Senate. Apparently Jesse has told Harold Smith that he is planning to stay on.

JANUARY 14, 1945

. . . Ernst asked what the President was going to do with Jesse Jones? I said, "Why should he do anything with Jesse Jones?" Ernst replied, "Well, if he takes care of Jesse in some way, it will reduce the amount of discord." I said, "Well, it seems to me it would be better for the President to fight on this issue and get licked than to give Jesse something." In other words, what I was really saying to Ernst was that I would rather not be confirmed by the Senate than to have Jesse Jones still in government[1] . . .

[1] Wallace was almost not confirmed. His diary, which he abandoned temporarily when his term as Vice President ended on January 20, 1945 (he resumed keeping it on April 27) contains no record of the long fight over his nomination as Secretary of Commerce. Senate conservatives, assisted by Jesse Jones, who testified that Wallace lacked the business acumen to run the RFC and other lending agencies, blocked Wallace's appointment until the Administration had no alternative to a two-step compromise. First, Congress passed a bill, introduced by Senator Walter F. George, Georgia Democrat, that stripped the Department of Commerce of all the lending authority Jones had exercised. Then, in March

1945, the Senate confirmed Wallace's appointment as Secretary. Jones' contention was wholly unfounded, for as Secretary of Agriculture Wallace had demonstrated his competence in handling federal funds. Yet Jones' argument served as an excuse for Republicans and southern Democrats who objected to Wallace's positions on the issues which the former Vice President had been stressing for several years. The same Senators who had sided with Jones in the struggle over the BEW, and who had led the movement to dump Wallace from the national ticket, had now punished him again. Still, Wallace had lost another battle without yet losing the war. As Secretary of Commerce he remained an important and potentially essential figure in the ongoing effort to direct federal policy to achieve and sustain postwar full employment, to develop foreign trade in the pattern he had long recommended, and to contrive a peace uninfected by traditional imperialisms or new hostilities.

III

Into the Cold War

April 1945-September 1946

For those who had worked closely with Franklin Roosevelt for many years, his death, a profound personal shock, also created a political dilemma. In different measures, they had trusted him. Each realized that Roosevelt played his subordinates off against each other, phrased what he told each man in a manner calculated most to placate or to encourage him, and kept ultimate control at the White House. Still, each of his close associates had become accustomed to Roosevelt's manner, each felt he exercised influence on some of the President's policies, and all considered him, whatever his limitations, the incomparable national leader in war and peace. Now Truman assumed the presidency. He would want to select his own advisers, some at once, some when it became convenient, as other successors to that office had in the past and would again in the future. But with the war still under way and the problems of peacemaking emerging, Truman needed the experience of Roosevelt's ablest counselors and the continuity they brought to government. For their part, though they offered their resignations as a matter of course, they felt, with few exceptions, an obligation to serve the new President and through him the country for as long as he wanted them to, and as they could accommodate to his unfamiliar and still unpredictable ways. Most of them were anxious about, some suspicious of, those ways. Truman was to prove to be far stronger than many had expected but also at times as devious as the most dubious had feared.

Wallace in April 1945 especially felt the uncertainties that in almost equal measure also troubled Biddle, Ickes, and Morgenthau. More than any of them, Wallace had reason to distrust Truman, who had displayed the devious side of his character in his maneuvering before and during the Chicago convention. Yet Wallace also had a fierce commitment to striving for the kind of peace, domestically and internationally, that he had long advocated. He chose to work with Truman not the least because practically there was no equally promising alternative.

Though Wallace did so with reservations, he also tried to believe in his chief, tried to persuade himself—sometimes to the point of self-delusion—that Truman shared his objectives. He remained in the cabinet longer than any other New Dealer (James Forrestal could scarcely be classified a New Dealer). He attempted, even after intermittent disappointments, to bring the President vigorously to support the domestic programs which the Commerce Department was developing, to re-endow the department with some of the lending authority Jesse Jones had exercised, and to embrace a reconversion and stabilization policy equitable to labor and small business. More important, as Wallace saw it, was the necessity for overcoming the influences on Truman, as well as Truman's own inclinations, militating toward an increasingly hostile stance against the Soviet Union. That question involved many related issues—the role of the military in American life, the control of atomic energy, the future of China, the special relationship with Great Britain, the settlement of boundaries and the direction of politics in both western and eastern Europe. At once hopeful and saddened at each critical juncture in the evolution of American policies on those issues, Wallace shifted more and more to disapproval of Truman's major decisions. As the Cold War developed, Wallace believed that the United States at each stage contributed at least as much to the mounting tensions as did the Soviet Union. After Churchill's Fulton speech, he kept the faith only with visible pain. The Democratic Party, he continued to argue, was capable, as the Republican Party was not, of forging a liberal program at home and a just peace abroad. Truman, he judged, would be the Democratic nominee in 1948. He had to try, he concluded, to cooperate with party and President while he also strove to push them to his own positions.

For Truman, Wallace was both a convenience and a nuisance. So long as he remained in the cabinet, the President knew, the Democratic left would not desert, though it would continue to criticize, the administration. There primarily lay the convenience, though Wallace was also useful as an adventurous proponent of domestic programs Truman endorsed and as a mediator with union labor whose hostility Truman hoped to dispel. Yet Wallace was insistently antagonistic to policies Truman had privately decided to follow. There lay the nuisance. The President intended from the outset to be far firmer with the Soviet Union than Wallace believed wise, and firmness rapidly rose to confrontations, most of them acidulous, between American and Russian negotiators concerned with every question of interest to both countries. As Truman saw it, and as in like manner did his closest advisers—Byrnes, Acheson, Marshall, Forrestal—the Soviet Union was determined to dominate both eastern Europe and Asia, either directly or indirectly. The President moved a long way toward a policy of containment before George Kennan gave that policy a label. In so doing, Truman was provoked again and again by Soviet actions and Soviet rhetoric, but for his part he was equally provoking to his contestants.

Wallace, his access to secret information slimmer and slimmer, understood the latter half of that menacing relationship better than he did the former. His eagerness to reach a genuine détente with the Soviet Union made him generous beyond Truman's tolerance in his interpretations of Russian initiatives and responses. From the beginning the two men were moving apart. That movement accelerated in the spring of 1946. Their tenuous official relationship snapped in September.

Then and earlier, Wallace, by no means either wholly naive or wrong in his assessment of Truman's policies, was honest with the President, a courtesy Truman only sometimes reciprocated. The President may often have felt honest when he was in fact dissembling, for he tried, as Roosevelt had, to please each of his associates as he talked to him. But in the case of their conversation about the Fulton speech, as Wallace later learned, Truman lied to him. So too did the President wriggle past the edge of prevarication in his public remarks about Wallace's September Madison Square Garden speech, the episode that provoked their final break. But as Wallace's diary discloses, that break would have come soon had it not occurred when it did. Though both men kept their tempers under admirable control, though both practiced an amicable civility in their meetings, Truman and Wallace on questions of international policy had become irreconcilable months before the President asked his Secretary of Commerce to resign.

※

and to South America. With regard to China I mentioned the objective of my trip over there and suggested that the President get in touch with John Carter Vincent. I also mentioned that there were a number of people in both China and Poland who would like to see the United States get into war with Russia. He said, "That must not be." [H.A.W. footnote] I said the reason I had been brought in to the Board of Economic Warfare was because there were misunderstandings between State and Treasury and the President apparently thought that I was the only one untangling both cabinet officers.

APRIL 27, 1945

President Truman was exceedingly cordial. He started out talking about the surplus property disposal, how he thought it belonged in Commerce. I said it was going to be quite a headache but we would do the best we could with it. I told him that Al Schindler[1] was going to have complete responsibility of supervising the administration and that he was going to operate it from a business point of view and not a political; that when he appointed people he would let the senators know about it in advance but that he would be influenced by only one consideration and that was efficiency. He said that was just the way he believed in operating. I said that Joe Guffey had wanted us to name a certain political figure and that Mr. Schindler was calling up Senator Guffey and gently saying that we couldn't use the person for a variety of reasons. President Truman said that Joe Guffey was terrible on patronage; that Senator Guffey, Dave Lawrence, and other Pennsylvania boys had called on him the day before. President Truman said that he had been rough with them in a nice way, indicating that they had gotten more patronage than they were entitled to.

I told him that as Secretary of Agriculture I had always had the closest relationship with President Roosevelt; that I had served him loyally and he had backed me up completely. The only two disagreements we had had were on the purge campaign in 1938 and the question of the transfer of forestry from Agriculture to Interior. Truman interposed to say that I had done a magnificent job as Secretary of Agriculture and that he had said so many times both privately and publicly. I then went on to say that in 1940 the President had really wanted Jimmie Byrnes as Vice President and that after the election he continually used Jimmie Byrnes as his liaison with the Senate rather than myself. The President had seemed to look on me as a man for doing special jobs. I described in some little detail the trips to Mexico

[1] Alfred Schindler had worked in the Federal Loan Administration and the Defense Plant Corporation. Wallace had just arranged for his appointment as Undersecretary of Commerce.

and to South America. With regard to China I mentioned the objective of my trip over there and suggested that the President get in touch with John Carter Vincent. I also mentioned that there were a number of people in both China and Poland who would like to see the United States get into war with Russia. He said, "That must not be." [H.A.W. footnote.] I said the reason I had been brought in to the Board of Economic Warfare was because there were misunderstandings between State and Treasury and the President apparently thought that I was the only one outranking both cabinet officers who could step into the position. The same situation existed in the War Production Board between Knudsen and Don Nelson. I referred to the Jesse Jones incident of July 1943, and said that this surprised me greatly. Truman said that it surprised him too; that he was in my corner at the time. I spoke highly of Milo Perkins and he spoke just as highly. I said that while my relations with Roosevelt had been of the finest, yet there had been some people about Roosevelt who apparently were conniving against me. I told him I was prepared to serve him as loyally as I had Roosevelt, provided he wanted me to do so. He was very emphatic in saying that he did. I then said that there were folks around Roosevelt who apparently had connived against me. I told him that I didn't care to go through that kind of thing again and that if I were to continue I would expect him, himself, to let me know when there was need for change in policy or attitude. He spoke very vigorously about connivers, saying that he was against them and that he was going to get rid of them as soon as he could. No names were mentioned.

After I had mentioned that the only disagreements I had had with Roosevelt as Secretary of Agriculture were on the purge and the forestry matter, he said he wouldn't give two cents for a man with whom there weren't disagreements from time to time, but he said he certainly would be above board with all the cards on the table.

Secretary Stettinius called up while I was there and after the conversation ended he spoke very emphatically against the Russians, saying that it was always the custom to have the host country furnish the presiding officer. He said that at the insistence of the Russians we had arranged to have the four main countries alternate with the presiding officer. Truman and Stettinius, however, had insisted that Stettinius be the senior of the four. The President had just told Stettinius to stand pat on this and if it was not agreeable to Molotov to "tell him to go to hell."[1]

[1] The United Nations Conference on International Organization had opened in San Francisco on April 25, 1945. Stettinius was head of the American delegation.

I said that now that Germany was about to be defeated there would be things happening very rapidly on the home front and that full employment would be the most important single objective. He said he agreed. I said that of the old-line departments Commerce and Labor would be especially involved.

He told me very confidentially that he was going to have Lew Schwellenbach come in as Secretary of Labor[1] and that he hoped to have him in before the end of May. He also told me confidentially that he thought Hitler was dead and that Germany would give an unconditional surrender either today or tomorrow.[2] He said he had found there was no one to whom he could tell things in absolute confidence; that the congressmen and senators invariably leaked if he told them anything but that he had confidence in me. I told him that as soon as Schwellenbach came in I thought it would be a splendid thing if he could have Schwellenbach and his right-hand man, myself and my right-hand man, and Judge Vinson and Bob Nathan get together so that a program could be worked out. I said there was no time to lose. I spoke very highly of Vinson and Bob Nathan. He also spoke highly of both. He said Bob Nathan had worked closely with him when Bob was in the War Production Board.

Truman was exceedingly eager to agree with everything I said. He also seemed eager to make decisions of every kind with the greatest promptness. Everything he said was decisive. It almost seemed as though he was eager to decide in advance of thinking.

On leaving I mentioned the air problems and he said he was very much interested in that. He feels that international air is, together with reparations, the most important postwar international problem. He said he wanted to have another talk with me when we could go into these things more in detail. He thinks the Civil Aeronautics Administration should be in the Department of Commerce rather than outside. He says he has given international air a lot of study.

After I left, the newspaper boys asked me a variety of questions. I

The United States and the Soviet Union immediately opposed each other on a series of issues. The first was symbolic. Though the host nation traditionally supplied the chairman for international conferences, Molotov insisted that the leaders of the delegations of the Big Four (the United States, the Soviet Union, Great Britain, and China) rotate in the chair. Anthony Eden proposed an acceptable compromise, according to which the rotation would occur at plenary sessions but Stettinius would preside over the more important Steering and Executive committees.

[1] Lewis B. Schwellenbach, Democratic senator from Washington (1935–40), then United States District Judge, was appointed Secretary of Labor in May 1945.
[2] The German surrender was actually ten days away. Truman designated May 8, 1945, his birthday, as V-E Day.

told them merely about surplus property disposal. They asked me if I had any comments to make on the Pennsylvania delegation, including Joe Guffey, Emma Guffey Miller, and Dave Lawrence, stating to the newspaper boys that they had just been in to assure President Truman of their support in 1948. I said, "No comment." They asked what kind of visit we had had and I said we understood each other perfectly.

MAY 1, 1945

. . . Harold Smith was thoroughly alarmed about the fascist-minded proposal of Vannevar Bush, spearheading for the War Department and the Navy to set aside $100 million for research which would not go through regular Congressional channels.[1] The more Smith talked about this the more alarmed he became and the more I shared his alarm. I like Vannevar Bush, but he really knows nothing about genuine democratic government. He believes in government for scientific aristocracy.

Smith talked to me in some detail about what they call in the Budget Bureau the "Manhattan Project." I told Smith I thought this definitely was involved in Bush's proposal. Smith told me that he had recommended to President Roosevelt the stopping of the Manhattan Project, but that Roosevelt felt it should not be stopped. I told Smith I questioned whether it should be stopped, but that I thought the peacetime implications should be examined very carefully.

MAY 2, 1945

. . . Will Davis[2] and I had an excellent talk with Attorney General

[1] Eager to preserve independence in research for American scientists, and without confidence in the willingness of Congress to do so, Bush had recommended replacing the wartime Office of Scientific Research and Development with a Research Board for National Security. The board was to consist of Army and Navy officers, an equal number of civilian scientists and engineers to be selected by the National Academy of Sciences, and members of Army and Navy organizations. Stimson and Forrestal had established the board early in 1945, but Harold Smith refused to release funds to support it. Smith was not against science. Rather, entirely apart from his anxieties about excessive military influence, he insisted upon proper channels for appropriating the growing funds necessary to support scientific activities. Bush then put forward a new proposal, similar to his previous one, described in detail in his July 1945 report to the President, "Science, the Endless Frontier." Again he advocated keeping scientific research under the control of scientists and free from the interference of politicians, though again he seemed not to consider military officers a problem; see Richard G. Hewlett and Oscar E. Anderson, Jr., *The New World 1939–1946*, pp. 409–11.

[2] William H. Davis, New York patent lawyer, since 1942 chairman of the National War Labor Board.

Biddle about the Patent Committee. Biddle expressed his alarm about Vannevar Bush and Kettering.[1] It was finally agreed that Davis would take Walton Hamilton of the Justice Department on his staff as well as Houston Kenyon.[2] It was also agreed that both the Attorney General and I would sit in on the committee from time to time. Davis has great confidence that something constructive will come out of this Patent Committee . . .

MAY 3, 1945

. . . At the conclusion, just before he was leaving, Adlai Stevenson[3] told me personally how much disturbed he was about the conference at San Francisco. He said the Russians were right with regard to Argentina and that many people in the State Department realized this to be the case. It happened, however, that Nelson Rockefeller placed the unity of the hemisphere above the unity of the world and that he felt it was more important to bring in Argentina than to work out a satisfactory world formula. This may not be stating it quite fairly to Nelson Rockefeller. The only conclusion I could reach, however, from

[1] Bush and Charles F. Kettering, vice president of General Motors, where he had been general manager of the Research Laboratories, had clashed over federal patent policy with the Justice Department, Harold Smith, and Democratic Senator Harley M. Kilgore of West Virginia. Smith and Kilgore especially advocated a departure from previous policy in order to assure that research sponsored by government funds would be free from patent restrictions. Bush and Kettering considered the existing patent system essential as an incentive to private organizations engaged in government research. The Patent Office lay within the Commerce Department, where Wallace, eager for patent reform, had created a committee on the problem with Davis as its chairman.

[2] Walton H. Hamilton, Yale law professor, one-time member of the National Recovery Administration Board, author of many books about antitrust law including *Patents and Free Enterprise* (1941); and Houston Kenyon, also an expert in patent law.

[3] Adlai E. Stevenson, who had served under Wallace in the Department of Agriculture, was a special assistant to the Secretary of State and a member of the American delegation to the San Francisco Conference. He was upset over Stettinius' decision to press for the admission of Argentina to the United Nations. That decision had broad ramifications. Truman had approved the Soviet demand to seat White Russia and the Ukraine. The Latin American nations, whose votes were needed for that purpose, insisted in return on the admission of Argentina. Molotov protested on the ground that the conference had refused to admit Poland under the Lublin government and yet was accepting Argentina, a fascist country that had not fought against the Axis. The Executive Committee voted unanimously to seat the Soviet Republics and divided, 9 to 3 with 2 abstentions, in favor of Argentina. At the plenary session Molotov challenged that outcome, but Argentina was admitted by a vote of 32 to 4, with 10 abstentions. Stettinius and Rockefeller mustered the Latin Americans for that vote, an action that Stevenson and others considered a moral defeat for the United States.

Stevenson's statement was that we had definitely entered an era of power politics with the United States on one side and Russia on the other. As Stevenson put it, Russia will look at the United States and say, "There is the United States with twenty American republics plus Liberia plus the Philippines, representing a total of twenty-three votes in the Assembly. Add in the other Latin nations and the British Commonwealth and where does it leave Russia?" Stevenson said that under such circumstances the Russians necessarily would tend to play their own game, not trusting the world organization. They would see themselves outvoted again and again in the Assembly. I must confess that Stevenson's analysis of San Francisco made me feel very much depressed concerning a constructive outcome on behalf of world peace. It begins to look like he is right in suggesting that we are entering an era of power politics rather than world organization. Of course the superficial appearances may indicate to the contrary.

MAY 4, 1945

. . . At cabinet meeting President Truman opened up by calling attention to President Roosevelt's orders with regard to not engaging in interdepartmental fights. He was very vigorous, decisive, and hardboiled in presenting his viewpoint, saying there was nothing which had happened but that he was saying this merely to prevent interdepartmental difficulties from breaking into the papers in the future.

Undersecretary Grew stated that he had just talked with Secretary Stettinius and that everything was going along very well at San Francisco. The most significant thing at cabinet meeting came when President Truman told Grew and Ickes to go ahead and take possession in the name of the United States of the continental shelf out from the shores of the United States beginning at low tide.[1] This means that Ed Pauley has lost out. Ed Pauley had tried at various times practically to bribe Ickes on this matter for the sake of the oil industry in California. This is an indication that the new President will not fall for some of the obvious machinations concerning which many people feared at the time when they saw Pauley for such a long time in Truman's car on the funeral train coming back from Hyde Park . . .

Truman's decisiveness is admirable. The only question is as to

[1] The tidewater areas were rich in oil along the Gulf and Pacific coasts. The Eisenhower administration later delighted the oil industry by turning control of the tidewater beds over to the states whose coastlines adjoined them. Most of the states then welcomed the oil companies into the fields.

whether he has enough information behind his decisiveness to enable his decisions to stand up. Thus far I would say the evidence would indicate a net plus on small things and even on medium-sized things. The query is as to whether his decisions in the international field have been wise. On the whole it seems to me that his attitudes have been such as to increase the liability of disagreement with Russia. In this connection the June 24, 1941, New York *Times* story may furnish the key to his fundamental slant. According to this story Truman said, two days after Russia was invaded by Germany, "If we see that Germany is winning we ought to help Russia, and if Russia is winning we ought to help Germany. And that way let them kill as many as possible, although I don't want to see Hitler victorious under any circumstances. Neither of them think anything of their pledged word."

The fear I have is that his instinctive attitude toward Russia may prevent Russia from coming into the war at the right time against Japan. Russia, in view of the attitude we are now taking, may reach the conclusion that it is desirable to see as many Americans and Japanese killed as possible.

President Truman asked me to remain after cabinet meeting. He wanted to talk about patents. Will Davis and the Attorney General also remained. Truman indicated he had read my *Reader's Digest* article and that he agreed with it. He said he thought the great difficulty with patents was in the contracts. I asked him if this meant that he thought there should be no new patent legislation. At first he didn't seem to be altogether clear on this point. As we discussed the matter he agreed to the idea that we should get a report to him by the middle of June. Vinson interjected, saying that the present patent laws were very contradictory and that it was time they were straightened out. Davis spoke very highly of Conway Coe, the present Commissioner of Patents,[1] and the President concurred. The Attorney General questioned whether Coe was quite such a good man. I pointed out that Coe had offered his resignation to President Roosevelt. Truman said he hadn't seen it. Davis said Coe was one of the best Commisisoners of Patents the Department had ever had. I referred to the fact that the House Patent Committee had been in to see the President and asked if that had in any way changed the directions the President wanted to give us. He said no; that he still felt like he had always felt and that he thought my ideas were exactly the same as his. I then mentioned that Harold Smith had talked to me about scientific research and governmental patents and asked him if he wanted our committee to go ahead and

[1] Conway Coe resigned later in the month.

look into this question of governmental research and governmental patents after we had finished up with the work on patents legislation. He said yes, to go ahead. I told him I thought the matter was very important because we had to get into this problem in order to keep up with England and Russia. The President said we ought not only to keep up with England and Russia but we ought to be ten years ahead of them. I said I thought the greatest shortcoming of the New Deal was that it did not back scientific research the way it should have. The President mentioned that Harold Smith had talked to him about this problem that morning. Fred Vinson also spoke up and said that Harold Smith had talked to him.

Spruille Braden[1] was exceedingly vigorous in his statements about actions of dictators in South America. He said Batista[2] had grafted to the extent of about $20 million in Cuba and his wife had another $10 million or so. He said he had come to this country and hired a publicity agent and was going around making talks trying to impress people with his liberalism.

He said that Grau San Martín was honest and a liberal but rather impractical. He told about the coup the Cuban army had tried to stage to prevent the election of Grau San Martín. Apparently Spruille Braden himself by the action he took was responsible for the victory of Grau San Martín in the last Cuban election.

Braden also paid his respects very vigorously to Dictator Trujillo[3] in Santo Domingo and Somoza[4] in Nicaragua. He said the United States had a lot to answer for in the way it played ball with the dictators. I was more impressed with Spruille Braden than I had ever been before. He is going to move cautiously in Argentina but it is obvious to me that he is going to throw his full weight on the side of democracy in the hemisphere . . .

MAY 5, 1945

. . . Tim Campbell[5] told me a most interesting story of the visit he had had with the colored people on the Gold Coast, Nigeria, the Bel-

---

[1] Spruille Braden, American ambassador to Argentina, former ambassador to Colombia and to Cuba.
[2] Colonel Fulgencio Batista, elected president of Cuba in 1940, lost his campaign for re-election in 1944 to Ramón Grau San Martin. Batista regained power in a coup d'état in 1952 and held it until Fidel Castro overthrew him in 1959.
[3] Rafael Leonidas Trujillo had controlled the Dominican Republic since 1930.
[4] Anastasio Somoza, president and dictator of Venezuela since 1937.
[5] Timothy M. Campbell of the Tuskegee Institute, also an Extension Field Agent of the Department of Agriculture.

gian Congo, and various other spots in Africa. He says the British attitude toward the colored people in Africa is rather better than the American attitude toward the colored people in the United States. The economic condition of the colored people, of course, is very bad. He thinks the British have consciously prevented the Negro people from learning up-to-date methods of taking care of their crops. He had a number of very interesting pictures. Tim Campbell, who is a colored man, himself, thinks there is marvelous opportunity for agricultural extension in Africa.

At the Pinchots' were present three members of the French underground, one a girl of about twenty-four who had gone back and forth between England and France under the most trying conditions. On her return trip to France she usually parachuted at night, sometimes landing in the top of trees.

The three different members of the French underground all had the same attitude with regard to Germany but their attitude with regard to the French collaborationists differed greatly. After listening to them I couldn't help thinking that France was going to be the same divided, inefficient, rather decadent country in the future that she has been in the past. The individual French are very attractive but the nation is trying to sit on two or three different stools at the same time. It doesn't know where it is going and it can't find out.

MAY 6, 1945

At the picnic at the Burlings'[1] on Sunday several people spoke in horrified tones of Russia and especially of the disappearance of the sixteen members of the Polish underground. More and more it begins to look like the psychology is favorable toward our getting into war with Russia. This must not be. It seems incredible that our people should drift toward this whirlpool which will inevitably end in world communism. Among those present at the Burlings' picnic were Will Clayton and Robert H. Brand, who used to be with the British Food Mission but who now is head of the United Kingdom Treasury Delegation. I mentioned about how tight the food situation would be and how important I thought it was for us to re-examine it to see whether we couldn't increase the amount of food we would send to Europe. Brand said he thought this was a very important thing to do; otherwise, the European countries would go communistic.

[1] Edward B. Burling was a leading Washington lawyer and a partner in the city's best-known law firm, Covington, Burling, Rublee and Acheson.

MAY 7, 1945

. . . Harold Young brought in Creekmore Fath.[1] Creekmore reported that when Nelson Rockefeller was recently back here for a few days, justifying his budget with the subcommittee of the Appropriations Committee under Louis Rabaut,[2] he insisted that the full committee be called together and also any members of the Senate Foreign Relations Committee who might be in town. After this dramatic move, according to Creekmore Fath, Rockefeller laid before the group his need for having three or four million dollars for work in the hemisphere so that the hemisphere might present a solid front against Soviet Russia. He prided himself that Argentina was now in the hemisphere bloc and claimed that Argentina was especially important because Argentina had the most determined attitude of all against Russia. I would have been inclined to question this statement of Fath's except for the fact that it agreed in considerable measure with a story told me by Adlai Stevenson. Apparently Rockefeller, in his vigorous endeavor to get hemispheric unity, is bent on provoking the type of world disunity which will inevitably produce war. Fath thought the information was so important that it should be gotten to President Truman. I told him that I didn't feel disposed to take the initiative in the matter. He then said, "How about Harry Hopkins getting into it?" and mentioned that Dick Gilbert[3] was close to Harry Hopkins. I then said, "I will put you in touch with Dick Gilbert and you can pass the story on to him."

Fath spoke at some little length about the speed at which Colonel Donovan's outfit is growing reactionary. It seems that the few liberals which the President put in OSS are being let out as of June first. I asked Fath how he managed to survive so long in OSS and he said it was because the President sent a letter over to Donovan placing him there. Both Fath and his immediate superior, Mr. Muehle, are being let out as of June first.

Donovan is pushing full steam ahead with his plan for having an integration of international intelligence services under his direction.[4]

---

[1] Creekmore Fath, a friend of Wallace's, at this time on the staff of the Office of Strategic Services.

[2] Louis C. Rabaut, Democratic congressman from Michigan since 1935, member of the House Committee on Appropriations and chairman of the subcommittee for the Departments of State, Commerce, and Justice.

[3] Richard V. Gilbert, an economist, who had assisted Harry Hopkins while he was Secretary of Commerce, had worked with the OPA during the war. He arranged an appointment for Fath with Hopkins.

[4] The National Intelligence Authority was established in January 1946 and suc-

This has in it many dangerous implications. I can't believe that State, Army, Treasury, Navy, FEA, and Commerce will agree to it. It seems that last October when Colonel Donovan pushed the President for a move of this kind the President told him that he should first get clearance from the agencies I have just mentioned . . .

MAY 8, 1945

We arrived at 8:15 at the White House, stood around in the Cabinet Room for ten or fifteen minutes, and then went into the Press Room where the President held a press conference which consisted in reading to the press the statement he gave later over the radio.[1] Then we went down to the Radio Room, where we listened to the President's speech and, following that, the speech of the Prime Minister. At the conclusion, the President said he would like to talk to me about the problem of handling social security to take care of workers who lost their jobs between V-E Day and V-J Day. I asked him if he wanted me to stay then or to come in later. He suggested that I come back later . . .

Eberstadt came in to talk about investment policies. He said if we are going to have the maximum flow of private investment it would be necessary to speed up the processes in the Securities and Exchange Commission. I . . . said we would look into it.

Bill Wasserman came in with the flat statement that our relationship with Russia was never worse, and that Stettinius and Averell Harriman had handled the situation in a very bad way in San Francisco; that we are headed straight for war with Russia, and we must do something very concrete and definite about it. He thought I should sell the President on the idea of me, myself, going to Russia as head of a commercial mission with very prominent names from General Electric, Westinghouse, U.S. Steel, the House of Morgan, etc., going along with me, and coming back from Russia with a big volume of orders and a plan for importing large quantities of goods from Russia . . .

MAY 9, 1945

. . . With the President . . . I said the Department of Commerce was not reaching out to get any function belonging to any other

---

ceeded in July 1947 by the Central Intelligence Agency. The latter office, unlike the former, was organized along the lines Donovan had recommended.
[1] Announcing victory in Europe.

agency but that I realized that sooner or later the question of export controls would probably be coming to the department and that we did believe the question of controlling the volume of exports had a pronounced bearing on full employment, on the one hand, and taking adequate care of the domestic consumer on the other. The President was very emphatic in saying that he thought export controls ought to be in the Department of Commerce.

The President was delighted to know the Census Bureau was in shape to furnish monthly data on a sample basis on unemployment. He also indicated that he was much interested in the presentation which Bailey of Arkansas had made to him with regard to patents and monopoly. On everything he seemed to take the right slant; so much so, that I was moved to say that I hadn't yet found anything concerning which I had disagreed with him. He is definitely liberal on the patent thing.

When I told the President that the first and all-important thing in determining what might be needed in the way of unemployment benefits to tide the workers over the prospective period of unemployment was to get from the Army their real ideas as to the cutback, he said he agreed with me. I said I saw according to the morning paper that the Army estimates an expenditure of 52 billion dollars for munitions this year as compared to 58 billion last year. I said my guess would be that they would actually spend around 37 or 38 billion dollars. He said his estimate would be around 35 billion dollars. I said I thought he ought to get from the Army, not for publication but for his own information, their true estimate as to what their expenditures would actually be. He said he was going to get it. He said I knew how he felt with regard to the danger of too much domination by the military . . .

MAY 10, 1945

. . . At the Symington dinner . . . I told them[1] that none of their plans were any good unless we could be sure of peace between the United States and Russia; that at present it looked like the United States was getting ready to embark on an era of power politics and imperialism in international affairs.

Senator Morse[2] spoke up very vigorously to say that in the cloak-

---

[1] A group of men from the National Planning Association were preparing for a meeting of that enlightened, private organization later in May, at which they expected to announce comprehensive plans for an expanding economy.

[2] Wayne L. Morse, then still a Republican, had just begun his long tenure as senator from Oregon.

rooms on the Hill there was an immense amount of anti-Russian talk. Holme[1] said that General Electric had already sold to the Russians equipment to take care of nine units of the Dneprostroi dam. In the first dam General Electric had equipped five of the units and the Russian government had equipped four. General Electric apparently feels very proud that it has been called on to do the whole job this time.

I suggested it might be a good thing if the top men from General Electric, Westinghouse, United States Steel, J. P. Morgan, etc., would go to Russia and come back with orders and also with a plan regarding the imports we would be willing to accept from Russia. I said a tangible action of this sort would mean more than a thousand speeches.

MAY 12, 1945

. . . At the luncheon, Don Nelson spent all his time talking about Russia. He said the way we were going we would certainly have war with Russia, and there was absolutely no need of it. He said he knew exactly how the trouble arose. It appears he put the responsibility chiefly on Averell Harriman. He said that Averell last August began with his policy of getting tough with Russia. Don said that Averell really knew nothing about Russia, that he didn't know the Russians, that Russia could get along all right without us, and that our methods of dealing with Russia were just no good—they were not factual. He also said that there was a faction in the Army that was looking toward war with Russia. He said this also was utterly foolish—that the Russian Army was better than our Army because the Russian soldiers would put up with more hardship; that they were more flexible and more ingenious. Don also spoke about Ed Stettinius going along with Averell Harriman. . . .

Don said Averell Harriman was an awfully nice fellow. I said, "And so are Ed Stettinius and Nelson Rockefeller." Don said that Averell Harriman, in a press conference at which Walter Lippmann and Raymond Gram Swing[1] had been present, had said, "The aims and purposes of the United States are irreconcilable with those of Russia." According to Don, Ed Stettinius, in a press conference at San Francisco, after the seating of Argentina, spoke of our gaining a "victory over Russia."

Nelson really felt very strongly with regard to both Stettinius and Harriman—feeling that while they were both exceedingly pleasant people and well-meaning people, yet their ignorance was such as to make them very dangerous to the peace of the world at the present time.

1 Stanley Holme, a General Electric executive.
2 Raymond Gram Swing, the notable radio commentator on foreign affairs.

He felt that unwittingly they had taken a stand at San Francisco which was leading us toward a conflict with Russia.

He said he hoped to see the President early next week, and that he had a memorandum worked out which he would leave with the President, concerning the kind of trade we might have with Russia. He thinks that President Truman might have the same interest in this which Roosevelt had had, and it might be possible with Truman to prevent Harriman from blocking things . . .

MAY 16, 1945

. . . Anna Boettiger told of the meeting she had had that afternoon with President Truman. She said that Truman said that all his advisers had urged him to be hard with the Russians. I said to Anna Boettiger, "How does the President feel this has worked out?" Anna Boettiger said the President now feels that it was a mistake. This means to me that Don Nelson had a very deep effect on President Truman.

Elliott Roosevelt claimed that our bombing in Germany had caused three or four million German civilians to lose their lives. Everyone else questioned Elliott's figures. Elliott claimed that our objective in Japan should be to keep on bombing until we have destroyed about half the Japanese civilian population.

John Boettiger still clings to the idea of an early and an appeasing peace with Japan.

Anna Boettiger feels that one of the great contributions by her father was holding relationships with Russia on a constructive and stable basis. It was obvious she feels the new President has not done well on this front.

Grace Tully, when she was talking to me alone, kept saying again and again, "I just can't call that man President."

MAY 17, 1945

. . . At the Russian reception there were almost no high-ranking Americans. The Russian personnel also had changed. The whole atmosphere reminded me somewhat of that which existed back in 1940, when Russia was so unpopular in the United States. Madame Gromyko expressed to me the most vigorous opinion that everything depended on me to maintain friendly relationships between Russia and the United States. I told her I would do everything I could.

At my sister Mary's were Henry Morgenthau and Senator Aiken.[1] Secretary Morgenthau held forth very vigorously on the idea that it meant a great deal to the United States to get Russia into the war so as to clean up Japan quickly. He took very strong issue with those who play up minor points to stir up discord between the United States and Russia. My brother-in-law and sister took a slightly anti-Russian bias.

Henry Morgenthau told me again how happy he was that he had had the privilege of spending the evening of April 11 with the President—the last evening the President was alive. He said the President was in the best of spirits; that he ate very heavily, especially of some caviar which had been given him; that he drank two cocktails. The President's mental processes were exceedingly clear. The only thing which disturbed Henry was that the President was unable to pour accurately from the cocktail shaker into the glass and Henry had to do the pouring for him . . .

MAY 18, 1945

. . . The cabinet meeting was very routine. Francis Biddle indicated he thought the government would lose the Montgomery-Ward case in the lower court. The President came out flat for carrying it up to the Supreme Court.[2] Biddle said he thought it might be serious if we lost it in the Supreme Court because it would undermine the President's power in time of war. Vinson said in any event he thought the President ought to know just how much power he had in time of war. And so it was Vinson and Truman against Biddle. It seemed to me rather obvious that Truman wasn't too enthusiastic about Biddle.

Bob Patterson dwelt at some length on the very high qualities of the American soldier and the American Army in Europe. He said they had made an extraordinary record and had just reached the peak of their striking power when the European war ended.

I mentioned in cabinet that the Business Research and Statistics boys in the Department of Commerce figured that by 1947 the total output

1 George D. Aiken, internationalist Republican senator from Vermont since 1941.
2 Roosevelt had taken over Montgomery Ward first in April and again in December 1944 because the company's anti-union president, Sewell L. Avery, had refused to comply with orders of the War Labor Board. In January 1945 a United States District Judge disallowed the seizure but permitted the government to retain control pending appeal. By a vote of 2 to 1 the Circuit Court ruled that the War Labor Disputes Act authorized the seizure. After Montgomery Ward appealed to the Supreme Court, the government withdrew. In October Avery returned and resumed his fight against the union.

of goods and services in the United States would be about 40 billion less than for the year 1944, and that this would mean something in the neighborhood of 7 million unemployed. I said the boys in the Department of Commerce figured this was not too disturbing a situation. I said I thought it was pretty disturbing. General Fleming[1] said he thought it was very disturbing. The President said he felt that way about it, too. He said he hoped I was working on the problem and that he knew I was. I said I hoped that it would be possible for our boys to get together with Bob Nathan and then perhaps at some future date we could make a presentation of the nature of the problem to the cabinet.

I then went on to mention the fact that there were exchange controls in thirteen of the Latin American countries and that these controls were used in considerable extent to make sure there was an excess of exports over imports; that this was a matter which interfered with free movement of trade.

The President indicated that in future cabinet meetings he would bring up particular subjects for discussion in order to get the judgment of the various members of the cabinet. He said he would have done that before this but had been so pushed by a variety of things that he had been unable to do so; that he had found that a lot of matters had not been handled during the months prior to the President's death because the President had not been in good health at the time.

At the close of cabinet meeting I told the President that at the Spanish lunch which I attended every Friday one of the members had called my attention in Spanish to the article in the New York *Times* indicating that the United States, Britain, and France were lined up against Russia and China. The President mentioned how sorry he was that he couldn't speak Spanish and then went on to say the Russian situation was causing him a lot of concern. I said there was just one point I wanted to make and that was I hoped he would not accept the representations made to him by the State Department without looking at them twice. He said he had no confidence in the State Department whatsoever and that he was going to get new leadership as soon as possible. He said as soon as he got new leadership in the State Department and Labor Department he thought we would have a fine team. He said there might be one or two other little changes that ought to be made. I suspect he was thinking about Francis Biddle. He said he hadn't told anybody else about his plan for reorganizing the State Department.

[1] Major General Philip B. Fleming, since 1941 Federal Works Administrator.

He said that President Roosevelt had obviously been sick for the last month of his life; that there were a number of wires from Stalin which had not been answered. He said the Russians had not kept their agreements which they made at Yalta.[1] He said they had put the sixteen Poles in jail. I said I had heard that the sixteen Poles had been killed. He said that wasn't true; that there was one general who had been killed but the other fifteen were alive.

The President said that all of his wires to Stalin had been couched in the most friendly language. He also said that Russia would not let us send people in to Rumania, Bulgaria, Austria, Hungary, and Berlin. I couldn't quite understand this because it is my understanding that we already have people in some of these places or soon will have.

The President said the Russians were like people from across the tracks whose manners were very bad. He said, however, that his one objective was to be sure to get the Russians into the Japanese war so as to save the lives of 100,000 American boys. Apparently, Lend-Lease is still being continued to Russia[2] via Vladivostok or Magodan. My guess is that it would have to be via Magodan because the Japanese surely would not let further supplies through to Vladivostok.

The President said his great fear was that one of the Russian generals would take over, acting like a Napoleon. It seemed to me that Truman was still committed to the doctrine of acting tough with Russia and that neither Don Nelson nor Anna Boettiger had as much of an effect on his mind as they thought.

[1] At Yalta Roosevelt and Churchill had rejected Stalin's proposal for recognition of the Lublin government, then in power in Warsaw. After lengthy discussions, the three agreed instead on a reorganization of the Polish government to include noncommunist leaders. The reorganized government was then to hold free elections. Most London Poles denounced the agreement and declined to participate with the Warsaw Poles in forming the proposed new government. The Russians refused to accept the credentials of still other noncommunists. Further, Moscow negotiated a mutual assistance treaty with the Warsaw government, and turned over to that government the administration of Danzig and parts of Silesia which Germany had held before the war. The Russians also imprisoned sixteen leaders of the Polish underground who had fought the Germans during the abortive Warsaw uprising. By mid-May 1945 those developments had made Poland a major issue of controversy between the United States and Great Britain, on the one hand, and the Soviet Union, on the other. They had also provoked the unprecedented and severe scolding that Truman had given Molotov in Washington on April 23, 1945.

[2] Pursuant to the instructions in the Lend-Lease Act of April 1945, Truman had cut off Lend-Lease shipments to the Soviet Union on May 8, with the end of the war in Europe. The abruptness of his order, as well as the cessation of American support, angered Stalin, who interpreted the move as hostile. The United States did continue some shipments to Siberia, as it had promised to do, to assist the build-up there for Stalin's promised entry into the war against Japan.

In the talk I had with the President after cabinet meeting he made it very clear that he felt that during the time when he was Vice President, President Roosevelt had not taken him into his confidence about anything. He said rather plaintively, "They didn't tell me anything about what was going on."

Joe Guffey came in to say that Averell Harriman had been up meeting with the senators at lunch and that he had made a very favorable impression. Harriman among other things made it clear that Russia would not fight. Apparently, the tough doctrine that Harriman has sold to the President is based on Harriman's belief that the Russians will not fight . . .

MAY 22, 1945

. . . At the White House, the President immediately signed a proposal that would give the Coast and Geodetic Survey the right to go ahead preparing charts for civil aviation.[1] The Army Air Force has been trying to take this right away from the Coast and Geodetic Survey.

The President made it clear that General Marshall agrees with him entirely that in time of piece the Army should not get into certain functions which definitely are civilian functions. The President also made it clear that the Services of Supply, in other words, General Somervell, does not have this idea. In other words, the President feels that Marshall is right, but that Generals Arnold and Somervell are wrong in their slant with regard to certain problems involving civilian life.

The President said he knew that I knew how he felt about these matters when he was in the Senate. I told him about our visit to Langley Field the day before, and he told about his visit there a couple of years ago. We had a little talk about the early history of the NACA—how it started on such a modest scale with only a five-thousand-dollar appropriation in 1915 and of the very significant service it had rendered to the war effort, in the development of different types of planes.[2] I suggested that this same approach might be used with regard

[1] The Coast and Geodetic Survey was under the Commerce Department.
[2] The National Advisory Committee for Aeronautics, established by Congress in 1915, was composed during World War II of both military and civilian members appointed by the President. Its successive wartime chairmen were Vannevar Bush and Jerome C. Hunsaker. They directed the committee's fundamental research, its primary responsibility. The armed forces incorporated in American military aircraft virtually all of the designs the committee developed.

to developing other scientific programs. The President said he thought there were many government agencies involved in this. I said it should not be left with the Army and Navy; that there was one project which I could think of (I could tell from a little exclamation which he made that he knew exactly what project I referred to) that should not be left with the Army because it had such profound peacetime implications. The President asked how everything was getting along over at Commerce. I said very well, but I thought the day was not far distant when we should get to work in more clear-cut fashion on the unemployment problem. I said it was going to be necessary sometime within the next thirty days or so to assign certain responsibilities more definitely. The President said he recognized that, and he wanted to have a straight line flow of responsibility where there would be no opportunity for conflict between agencies . . .

Ralph Ingersoll is a Lt. Colonel and has been serving on General Bradley's staff. General Bradley is a great hero to him. He thinks Bradley is much better than Eisenhower. He says Eisenhower caters continually to the British, and that the British picked him with that in mind. For example, he said that under the Yalta Agreement the American troops were never supposed to be at the Elbe; that they were supposed to be about 50 miles further west. Churchill, however, had a conference, face to face, with Eisenhower and Bradley and suggested that the American troops stay 50 miles further east than they were supposed to. Churchill's argument was if the troops would stay this much further east the British and Americans under the doctrine of possession being nine points of the law would have a bargaining point with the Russians.

It sounds to me like this is where a large part of our trouble with the Russians may have originated. Churchill was using the Americans as a spear-point with which to needle the Russians . . .

MAY 29, 1945

When I went in to see the President I said I thought Stettinius had made an excellent speech last night. The President said he thought so, too. I commented that it seemed to me very important for the world to look on the President not as a spokesman for Anglo-Saxondom or for Pan-Americanism. He said he felt that way very strongly and that he was glad Stettinius had put Argentina in her place in his speech last night. He said Stettinius had conferred with Hull on that section of his speech.

I said the world was hungry for leadership and Stalin couldn't furnish world leadership because the Latin nations and China, as well as England, distrust him; that Churchill couldn't furnish it because Russia, China, and many of the so-called "subject" peoples distrust him. I said it was important for the President to get into the position of being a moderator because in China we stood better than either the British or the Russians and in Latin America we stood better than the British. Many of the so-called "subject" peoples look to us. The President said that he agreed.

When the President started reading my Churchman Award speech[1] he stopped at the sentence where I said no President had done so much to promote good will as President Roosevelt, and said, "And that is right." When I came to the sentence saying, "I am satisfied this is the policy of President Truman," he said, "It is." I then suggested that I change the sentence to read, "I know this is the policy of President Truman." He liked the stronger statement. Again, in the following paragraph where I said, "President Truman is following the Roosevelt policy," he said, "I certainly am. I have conferred with all who knew anything about his policy, including the immediate members of his family, and I am doing everything I can to carry it out." I therefore suggested changing the sentence to read, "President Truman is following the Roosevelt policy to the letter." He liked this change.

When I came to the religious note in the third to the last paragraph he said, "It is right to say that abundance is not enough and peace is not enough." I said that I would be glad to modify the speech in any way that would be more helpful. He said he thought it was fine the way it was and he would stand behind me on it.

I called his especial attention to the statement that Roosevelt could still say today, as he did three years ago, "The road ahead is dark and perilous." I said that since Stettinius' speech of last night I felt that the road ahead looked much brighter than it had previously. Truman said, "No, you were right the way you had it. The road ahead is still dark and perilous. There still are many enemies of the peace." He made special reference to Bob Taft, who apparently has broken his truce with Truman and Truman resents it.

Truman said that by sending Harry Hopkins to Moscow he had straightened out a fundamental misconception of Stalin and that Stalin was going to come along all right now.[2]

[1] On May 28 Wallace was officially voted the Churchman Award of the Protestant Episcopal Church for his constructive role in international relations. He accepted the award in a speech on June 4.

[2] At the urging of Bohlen and Harriman, Truman had sent Hopkins to Moscow to talk directly with Stalin about the growing problems in Russian-American

I called his attention to the part of my speech where I said, "The United States is the great world leader of political democracy based on freedom of religion, freedom of information, freedom of expression, and the right of small nations to separate existence." I said the phrase, "the right of small nations to separate existence" might be interpreted as a poke at the Russians. He said, "No, that is all right to say. I also am going to take a little poke at the Russians when I speak out in San Francisco." It was obvious, however, that Truman now feels much more kindly toward the Russians than he did before. Apparently, Harry Hopkins has been really helpful in Moscow.

I called his attention to the sentence where I said, "Roosevelt was willing to give up a little sovereignty for a lot of peace." Truman liked that sentence.

I told him a little about the background of the Churchman Award and said that I had hesitated to take on awards of this sort since the war was on. He said I shouldn't be; that no one deserved an award of this kind more than I, myself.

Truman said he realized that our relationship with Russia had to be solved before we could go ahead with satisfactory planning of domestic affairs. He also mentioned that he had refused several times to meet with Churchill because he felt he ought to meet with Stalin first.

We talked briefly about the time when Schwellenbach, Vinson, and I would get together with certain technicians and arrive at a fundamental policy with regard to the full employment problem. He thought we ought to wait until Schwellenbach was confirmed . . .

MAY 30, 1945

. . . Charlie Ross[1] . . . said with my permission he would tell President Truman that I had 'phoned him and that I concurred in the suggestion that it would be well for the President in closing the conference at San Francisco to make a strong, courageous statement in support of the economic and social, as well as the political, objectives of the Charter. Ross said his own feelings ran in exactly the same direction as mine.

---

relations. Bohlen and Harriman accompanied him on the trip and at his meetings with Stalin and Molotov. Emphasizing American good will toward the Soviet Union, Hopkins raised questions about Lend-Lease, Poland, Argentina, Soviet participation in the Pacific war, and Allied policy toward Germany. They also discussed the forthcoming meeting of Truman, Stalin, and Churchill at Potsdam. Though nothing was settled, Stalin and Hopkins got along well, and early in June Hopkins left encouraged; see Robert Sherwood, *Roosevelt and Hopkins* (rev. ed., New York, 1950), pp. 885–916.

[1] Charles G. Ross, Truman's press secretary.

MAY 31, 1945

. . . Cordell Hull had apparently gained about fifteen pounds. He was a little pale but his mind was functioning clearly. He was very disdainful of the way in which "Little Rockiefeller" had handled the Argentine situation. He indicated that Rockefeller from the very time he got in as Assistant Secretary, had gone out of his way to appease Argentina. He referred to Avra Warren[1] with the same disgust. He spoke in the very highest terms of Pasvolsky and Jimmie Dunn. I judge he gets his information from them and from two or three others who visit him quite continuously. He indicated that he wanted the President to take Jimmie Dunn and Pasvolsky to Yalta and apparently he was very much disappointed when the President didn't take them. His mind went back to the Atlantic Charter meeting in August of 1941 when the President took Sumner Welles. His hatred for Sumner Welles remains as deep as ever. He says he is not honest.

Cordell Hull spoke about how he and Roosevelt had the same ideals but oftentimes the President took hasty action which Hull had to patch up. At the time of the Atlantic Charter meeting, for example, Churchill sold the President on the idea of taking very decisive action against Japan. Hull said this was all very well and good for the British because they had neither military nor naval strength in the Pacific. Strong action against Japan would mean that the United States would have to carry the load all by herself. When Welles returned to Washington, therefore, wanting to get out within a few hours a strong statement against Japan, Hull would not permit it. He pigenholed the proposal which President Roosevelt and Churchill had agreed on.

Cordell referred at some little length to the unwise action which the President and Henry Morgenthau had initiated at Quebec. He said that Henry Morgenthau and the President had agreed to let England have three billion dollars under Lend-Lease for postwar construction purposes and three billion dollars for certain other purposes without exacting any quid pro quo.[2] Apparently Cordell took a great deal of pride in having upset this agreement.

[1] Avra M. Warren, foreign service officer, in 1945 director of the Office of American Republic Affairs in the State Department.

[2] The Quebec agreements, less precise by far than Hull suggested, did provide for diminished American Lend-Lease to Great Britain during Phase II, the period from the German surrender to the end of the war against Japan, and for probable but still smaller American aid thereafter. Details for both periods needed careful working out in Anglo-American negotiations, which in the end made no provision for the latter period. In some respects, the Quebec assurances about Lend-Lease explained Churchill's temporary endorsement of the

He then dealt at some length on how he had tried to take foreign policy out of the political campaign in the fall of 1944. He mentioned how he had had Dulles down to talk with him hour after hour. He told how he had worked himself completely out and then, when he had gotten so low that he felt he couldn't go along, the President came out to see him to try to persuade him that he shouldn't resign. Cordell said the President remained with him for an hour and forty minutes and that he felt like he was practically dead when the argument began and he felt like he was really dead when the argument ended; that then the President send Admiral McIntire[1] out to argue with him and he argued for forty minutes.

He called the Argentine government all kinds of names and referred to the way in which they had cooperated with Hitler and the Nazi methods which they had used inside their own country. He said no wonder the Russians reacted the way they did when we took up the cause of the Argentines . . .

Hull said Truman had gotten along pretty well so far but that he had not got out into deep water yet. It is obvious that Hull feels Truman is pretty ignorant of foreign affairs.

JUNE 1, 1945

. . . At the cabinet meeting, which lasted only half an hour, only two significant things took place. First, Henry Morgenthau took a pot shot at WPB for breaking that that there would be 1,800,000 unemployed at the end of the year. He said he didn't think anyone knew how many would be unemployed a year hence and that such statements were bad for the bond drive. Jim Forrestal spoke up and said he thought there would be fewer people unemployed two years hence than there are today. Paul McNutt spoke up and said that there would be no unemployment at any time in the next ten years. I then suggested that it would be wise to take another look at the situation after the bond drive was over.

At the close of the cabinet meeting, Ickes, Biddle, and I were standing together waiting for our cars and laughingly said how fine it would be if there would be no unemployment. We thought it amusing to see the Democrats engaging in the same Pollyannish performance as

Morgenthau Plan for Germany. It was that plan, not the Lend-Lease agreements, that Hull successfully attacked after the conference; see Blum, *Years of War*, pp. 316-414.
[1] Admiral Ross T. McIntire, White House physician (1933-45).

the Republicans, refusing to admit the truth of a prospective situation for fear it might interfere with some particular project. At the conclusion of the unemployment discussion, President Truman made a statement indicating that he wanted no public statement with regard to the extent of prospective unemployment. He was very incisive and hard-boiled about it. This tendency toward an incisive and hard-boiled attitude has its advantages but sooner or later it will result in obscuring the truth and then there will be trouble.

Ickes mentioned in cabinet meeting that there was still extensive unemployment in the anthracite area, the miners saying they would not come back to work until the National Labor Relations Board did certain things. The President took a prompt and emotionally hard-boiled attitude, saying the miners could stay out of work until next Christmas as far as he was concerned . . .

JUNE 8, 1945

. . . In our meeting with Mrs. Roosevelt and her daughter, Mrs. Anna Boettiger, Anna said she had it from Mrs. Ickes that Harold had written the President about certain matters having to do with the Philippines and the President had not replied. Whereupon, Ickes had sent quite a sharp note to the President. When Harold then called on the President the President started out by saying to Ickes, "I want you to feel perfectly free to come over here at any time and call me any kind of an S.O.B. you want to." This cheered Harold up enormously.

Mrs. Roosevelt also reports that Jim Loeb[1] and the other liberals of New York want her to find out from me any instructions which I have for them. They are . . . waiting for me to give the word . . .

JUNE 9, 1945

. . . Sam Rayburn displayed considerable feeling against the Bureau of the Budget and against Harold Smith, saying that they wanted to get into matters of policy which were none of their business. I said it seemed to me the proper way to handle these questions of policy about which continual action must be taken would be—in the case of domestic matters—to set up a committee composed of the Director of

---

[1] James Loeb of the Union for Democratic Action, a New York liberal whom the Communist Party had denounced, and others of his views were worried about Roosevelt's seeming drift to the right in 1944-45 and Truman's apparent leanings in that direction. Wallace, also worried, nevertheless remained convinced that he could most effectively influence national policy from within the cabinet and the Democratic Party. He had no "word" for the New York group.

War Mobilization, Fred Vinson; the Director of the Budget, Harold Smith; the Secretary of Agriculture; the Secretary of Commerce; and the Secretary of Labor. It would be ideal, I said, if the President would serve as chairman of this committee, and meet with the committee for an hour once a week. I said there might be certain situations that would make it advisable to have in the Secretary of the Treasury as well; others where it would be desirable to have in the Secretary of the Interior. But, I said, if rapid action was to be obtained with a minimum of disturbance it seemed to me the three cabinet officers, plus the two directors, would be ideal. I said, of course, if the President couldn't afford the time it would be advisable to have the Director of War Mobilization serve as chairman. Rayburn seemed to think this was an excellent idea.

Rayburn said the new President was getting off to an excellent start. I said he seemed to be making his decisions with great speed. Rayburn said yes, he certainly is, but I am afraid one of these days he will make a decision based on inadequate information. Rayburn said that Franklin Roosevelt would go down as one of the great men of history. He said, however, he was a terrific waster of time.

He said when he and Alben Barkley and John McCormack and myself used to go down to meet with the President in the Big Four meetings, the President would gossip along saying not much of anything for an hour and a half. He said with Truman they get more decided in fifteen minutes than President Roosevelt used to decide in an hour and three quarters . . .

JUNE 11, 1945

. . . We showed Wright Patman[1] the plan for reorganizing the department. He immediately started in criticizing the department for the stand which it had historically taken in favor of chain stores as compared with the small, local merchant. He said he thought the small, local merchant should be given every break possible. He didn't like the idea of having an Assistant Secretary in charge of Small Business because he felt the department had not been friendly to small business. Then he changed his phraseology and said that he would have an open mind. Maury Maverick[2] is a close friend of Wright Patman's and it was to be expected that he would take the attitude

---

[1] Wright Patman, Democratic congressman from Texas since 1929, chairman of the House Banking and Currency Committee, self-appointed scourge of big banks and big business.

[2] Maury Maverick, former Democratic congressman from Texas, since 1943 chairman of the Smaller War Plants Corporation.

which he took. I told him the question was whether after the war there would be a big Department of Commerce in charge of small business or a small Department of Commerce in charge of big business. I told him I thought there ought to be one Department of Commerce and not two competing Departments of Commerce.

We showed Senator Pepper the plan for reorganization and he seemed to like it.

Senator McKellar's chief comment on the reorganization plan was that it would cost several thousand dollars more to pay for three new Assistant Secretaries than it had heretofore cost. McKellar was really quite friendly but I never before realized how exceedingly small he is with regard to sizing up an overall picture. His habit of mind has been formed by taking budget bills and examining them item by item. He has suddenly become much older. His general attitude was exceedingly friendly.

Alben Barkley had no particular comment to make on the plan for reorganization. In general he seemed to think it was all right.

JUNE 12, 1945

. . . At the Export-Import Bank meeting the question up for discussion was the purchase of the Mexericsson Telephone Co. by Mextelco, which is the Mexican branch of International Tel. & Tel. The Export-Import Bank would advance 23 million dollars to International Tel. & Tel. to buy out Mexericsson and Mexericsson's holdings of Mextelco. The interest rate would be 4 percent. There would in effect be an understanding with the Mexican government that would make it possible for the united company to charge higher telephone charges to the consumer. With the help of these higher charges and economies resulting from the united operation, it would be expected that beginning four or five years after the transaction was completed it would be possible for the united company to pay 4 percent interest on the loan and enough on the principal to retire 75 percent of the loan within 20 years.

I told them I would very much like to get the opinion of the Federal Communications Commission. It was obvious that the staff of the Eximbank was doing everything it could to put the loan through at the earliest possible moment. When I bucked and the Treasury representative, Mr. Ness,[1] bucked, there was a lot of fluttering in the dovecote. I told them as far as I was concerned they could go ahead

[1] Norman Ness.

and tell the Mexican government they were going to give the loan but that the loan was being granted in spite of the opposition of the Secretary of the Treasury and the Secretary of Commerce. They said that the loan had the approval of the Mexican government. I said, "Just who in the Mexican government?" They said, "The Minister of Communications." I said, "Just who is the Minister of Communications?" It then developed the Minister of Communications was Maximino Avila Camacho, the brother of the President, who is now dead. It was obvious the State Department was very keen about the deal and Collado said Messersmith very much wanted to have the matter approved by the Eximbank for the sake of strengthening his hand when he returned to Mexico City. The State Department people were not at all shocked at the idea that the United States government should use its power to help one of our utilities to raise its rates in a foreign country in order to make a loan good which had been made by this country. It seems this kind of thing has been done again and again by the State Department working with private corporations . . .

JUNE 13, 1945

. . . At the staff meeting Mr. Waring[1] gave a most interesting presentation on his experiences at San Francisco. He told how certain members of the delegation had leaked again and again to Scotty Reston[2] of the New York *Times* and how one of the delegates one morning said, "I have been studying our agenda for the day and find it differs in certain particulars from what appeared this morning in the New York *Times*. I should like to inquire which is the official version."

He mentioned that on Saturdays the schoolchildren swarmed over the place getting autographs and one delegate reported that he had heard one of the children saying, "I'll trade you six Tom Connally's for one Anthony Eden." He told about the high quality of the Russian delegation and his picture was totally different from that which would be gathered by reading the newspapers. I am more and more beginning to reach the conclusion that it is a mistake to read the newspapers about any controversial matter because they so often give an absolutely inaccurate picture. Undoubtedly the newspapers should be read so far as possible with the idea that account should be taken of the bias. It is just as important to take account of the bias of newspapers as it is to take account of the directions of the wind when flying an airplane.

[1] Frank A. Waring.
[2] James B. Reston, since 1941 in the Washington bureau of the New York *Times*.

JUNE 15, 1945

At the White House we showed the President the chart on the re-organization of the Department of Commerce and he was much pleased with it. I explained it to him just like I had to the different senators and congressmen. He was very keen about moving Smaller War Plants into the Department of Commerce right away. He said Maury Maverick had been in to see him and had given him advice on everything under the sun except small business. He said Maury was so good at giving advice about these various countries such as Italy, Germany, Russia, Africa, and all the other countries of the world that he thought he would just give him a chance to try out one of those countries. He said he had had people working with Wright Patman on a problem. I told him about our conversation with Wright Patman. Also I told him that Maury had seen one of our people and had gone straight up in the air. He said also that some of the conversations I had had with some of the senators had gotten back to Leo Crowley and he was very much disturbed. The President seems to be very keen about putting these various war agencies back into the departments.

The President was very humble about his own ability, saying that he knew he didn't have much in the way of brains but that he did have enough brains to get hold of people who were able and give them a chance to carry the responsibility. I told him that we wanted to be sure to push hard enough on the reorganization but on the other hand we didn't want to push too hard. He suggested that we hold up a little while on the Assistant Secretary in Charge of International Trade and the Assistant Secretary in Charge of Industrial Economy. Apparently he wants to wait until Schwellenbach gets on the job before he moves on this front. Also, he will want to get back from his trip to the Big Three meeting . . .

JUNE 18, 1945

While we were waiting at Speaker Rayburn's office for General Eisenhower to appear, Madame Perkins and Admiral Leahy got into quite an extended discussion of Russia. They both agreed that communism was a kind of religion that people were glad to die for. Admiral Leahy made the rather astonishing statement that whenever there was a religion anywhere else in the world that people were ready to die for, the United States must of necessity be deeply concerned and be ready to defend itself against the onslaught of such a religion. It was obvious to me that Admiral Leahy is among those who are vigorously getting ready to fight Russia . . .

At the Eisenhower dinner I sat at a little table with Senator Austin, Major General Bedell Smith,[1] Assistant Secretary of State Julius Holmes, and Admiral Hewitt.[2] Senator Austin told a most interesting story about how his boy in the Tank Corps had been wounded three times. I told General Bedell Smith how highly I thought of General Bradley as well as of General Eisenhower. Bedell Smith and I both agreed it was a shame that Bradley had been put in charge of the Veterans Administration. We both felt that he would be more useful elsewhere. Bedell Smith also thought it was a shame that Eisenhower was taking on the civil administration of Germany.

JUNE 22, 1945

. . . Richard Patterson[3] told quite a horror story about Tito and the Russians in Yugoslavia. He said he had a friend who knew that 600 people were killed by Tito in Zagreb. (The evening of June 22 I met with André Visson, one of the employees of the *Reader's Digest,* at the Wassermans'. I asked Visson if he had talked to Patterson and he said he had. I asked him if he believed Patterson's horror stories. He said Patterson was green in the country and had only a part of the picture.) Patterson thinks that Tito is killing off certain of the people in Yugoslavia at the suggestion of Moscow. Apparently the Russian army is out of Yugoslavia at the present time. Patterson thinks there will be quite complete expropriation of American properties throughout all the Balkans and that it will be necessary to make very strong representations to get them back. The Standard Oil Company is particularly affected.

Pawley[4] went into detail about his airplane plant, which is located in the highlands just west of Madras in India. He said as the result of a good diet he was able to make this plant very efficient, getting as good results from the Hindus as he would from an equal number of Americans. He had made arrangements where all the Hindus, no matter what their caste or faith, could eat in the same cafeteria. He reinforced the vegetables with vitamins so that those who were vegetarians would

1 Major General Walter Bedell Smith, Eisenhower's chief of staff.
2 Vice Admiral H. Kent Hewitt had been in command of the naval forces during the landings at Morocco, Sicily, and southern France.
3 Richard C. Patterson, Jr., New York broadcasting executive and Democrat, then American ambassador to Yugoslavia.
4 William D. Pawley, corporation executive, then American ambassador to Peru.

have a good diet. Pawley said that the British were gravely concerned about the success of this airplane plant and wanted to kill it off. He told about the methods which they used in killing it off. Pawley says the British are so shortsighted in their efforts to keep India a purely agricultural country without industry that they will inevitably throw the Hindus into the hands of Russian ideology.

Pawley told also about his experience in getting a sulphate of ammonia plant established and the way in which the British tried to sabotage that. He agrees with me that we must find some way to get the British interested in big things instead of in small, mean, dirty pilferings. Pawley is really friendly to the British but he is certain that the methods which they are using will bring disaster to themselves and to the world . . .

JULY 5, 1945

. . . Claude[1] spoke at some little length about his disillusion about the way things were going. He seemed to think there was danger of the present administration making many of the same mistakes that the Harding administration made. He seemed to be especially disillusioned with the appointment of Tom Clark and Jimmie Byrnes.[2] He said that Francis Biddle had told him that one day Steve Early called him up and said the President would like to have his resignation within twenty-four hours. Biddle immediately replied, saying, "Why doesn't the President speak to me himself?" The upshot of it was that the President had him over and Biddle said, "Of course, Mr. President, you can have my resignation, but why didn't you speak to me about it rather than have Steve Early call me?" The President said, "I thought maybe it might be embarrassing." Biddle came back by saying, "Well, you see, it is really very simple." He then said, "May I inquire, Mr. President, whom you are going to appoint in my place?" The President said, "Tom Clark." Biddle then said, "Whom have you checked with with regard to Mr. Clark?" The President replied, "Sam Rayburn and Bob Hannegan both think highly of him." Biddle then replied, "Mr. President, they have quite a record on Mr. Clark both in the Justice Department and in the Office of the Collector of Internal

---

[1] Claude Pepper.
[2] As he had been planning to, Truman had appointed Thomas C. Clark, a Texas Democrat and friend of Hannegan, as Attorney General, and James F. Byrnes as Secretary of State. The President had waited to replace Stettinius until the end of the San Francisco Conference. Byrnes preferred a harder line toward the Soviet Union than had Stettinius, while Clark preferred a softer policy on antitrust than had Biddle.

Revenue." The President said, "Well, I didn't know about that" . . .

Claude thinks that Hannegan's game is to set up a national administration based on the "city boss" idea, under which everything is controlled with an iron hand. Claude's counteroffensive is to call the liberals together in a meeting to get them unified behind a program for full employment.

Claude indicated he very much questioned the sincerity of Truman's humility. He said that during May and June 1944, just prior to the convention, Hannegan had arranged for Truman to make a very large number of speeches in many different states. These were not large speeches but he said he knew that Truman made at least five speeches in Florida during this time and that in his opinion Truman and Hannegan were working a very astute game during the two months just prior to the convention.

I told Pepper that the Democrats would lose control of the House in 1946 unless we got out a big vote and that it was going to be necessary for Democrats of all kinds to work together to get out the vote. I said so far as Hannegan and Kelly and the other bosses were concerned, the future would take care of the situation and they would eventually stand revealed to the American people for exactly what they are. I told Claude I thought he was doing a very wise thing in forgetting all about gossip of this kind and concentrating his attention on rallying the progressive forces behind full employment.

JULY 6, 1945

Al Schindler came in to say that one of his Missouri friends was saying that it was common talk in the Midwest now that the "Missouri gang" was taking over the government. Al furthermore said that it was commonly believed that he, Al, was part of the gang. Al protested that he had been appointed by President Roosevelt. Nevertheless, Al's friends continue to push him by saying that the public looked on him as part of the "Missouri gang." Apparently this has gotten under Al's skin and he advocated that we check things over once a week to decide when would be the best time to get out. I suspect perhaps the Morgenthau resignation[1] had something to do with that state of

---

[1] Morgenthau's personal loyalty to Roosevelt and Truman's disapproval of the Morgenthau Plan for Germany had made the question of Morgenthau's resignation only a matter of time. The President had wanted to delay acting on a new Secretary of the Treasury until his return from Potsdam, but when Morgenthau asked for assurances that he could remain in office until the end of the Pacific war, Truman precipitated his resignation and appointed Fred Vinson in his place.

mind. I agreed with him that it would be a good thing to check things over once a week but I said I felt it was our duty to stay by the ship as long as we could do a good job for the general welfare . . .

Helen Gahagan told me that there were 85 congressmen backing the Patman-Murray Full Employment Bill. She said that they would be willing to back any legislation which I felt to be necessary . . .

. . . At cabinet meeting the chief subject up for discussion was the shortage of coal. Secretary Ickes wants the armed forces to release 100,000 coal miners. Bob Patterson took the stand very strongly that nothing should be done to break over the point system which is being used in the Army. The President sided with Bob Patterson. I mentioned that Jouhaux, a French labor leader, had told me they were only feeding the French coal miners half the number of calories necessary for this kind of work. Clinton Anderson[1] said that there were sugar beets in France that were not being processed into sugar because of shortage of coal. It was obvious to me from the discussion, as well as other information, that this coming winter is going to be the worst winter Europe has ever experienced. The Army's hard-boiled attitude is going to be responsible in considerable measure for the great difficulties that will exist in Europe this winter. The Army is not looking at this coal situation realistically. The production of coal is really a part of the Army job and the Army is not cooperating.

This was the first cabinet meeting at which Jimmie Byrnes, Tom Clark, Clinton Anderson, and Lew Schwellenbach were present. Henry Morgenthau was present, obviously somewhat downcast. It is my guess that when he precipitated matters with Truman he expected to have Truman back him up. Instead, Truman let him down and now he is out. It probably is a very fortunate thing for him that he is out at this time. The public will give him credit for having made a great success in financing the war. The methods which he used were definitely somewhat inflationary in nature but this will not fully appear until a year hence. I have always found Henry Morgenthau a very good friend and do not care to criticize him in any way. His heart usually led him in the right direction and he courageously stood for the right things except when his intellect was not equal to the occasion and his bureaucracy led him in the wrong direction. I really am sad about Henry Morgenthau's going.

Bill Stone[2] has just returned from Germany. He says there are two

[1] Truman had appointed Clinton P. Anderson, Democratic congressman from New Mexico, Secretary of Agriculture in place of Claude R. Wickard. Only Stimson, Forrestal, Ickes, and Wallace now remained from Roosevelt's cabinet.
[2] William T. Stone had been successively assistant director of the BEW (1942–43), director of the special areas bureau of the Foreign Economic Administra-

castles there, one known as "Dustbin" and the other as "Ashcan." In the "Dustbin" castle are those Nazis who may not be quite bad enough to rank as war criminals. In the "Ashcan" castle are those Nazis who are definitely criminals. The smartest of all the Nazis, according to Bill Stone, is Albert Speer. Stone has met these various Nazis. He says Speer is about forty-two years of age and is a very capable citizen. He is one of the "Dustbin" Nazis who has decided to tell "all." Apparently Speer, during the five days before Hitler's death, decided to buck Hitler. He went on the radio against Hitler and urged the German people not to engage in the "scorched earth" policy which Hitler was advocating. Schacht also inhabits the "Dustbin" castle. Bill Stone says that his people got a wealth of documents from I. G. Farben and among those documents is one which indicates that the Germans felt that in trading with the Standard Oil Company of New Jersey they definitely got the best of the deal. This is amusing because the Standard Oil Company of New Jersey has always claimed that in their trading with I. G. Farben they got the best of the deal. Both outfits claimed that in their trading they served the war effort in their respective countries. Stone has a copy of the precise German document. It will eventually make uncomfortable reading for the Standard Oil Company of New Jersey, so Stone claims.

JULY 18, 1945

Harold Young brought me in this morning a memorandum on H.R. 3771, the bill which was passed by the House and which provides for increasing the lending authority of the Export-Import Bank, and which also revises the organization of the Export-Import Bank by vesting the management in a board of directors consisting of the administrator of FEA, the Secretary of State, and three persons appointed by the President of the United States, two of whom would have to be Republicans. The Secretary of the Treasury and the Secretary of Commerce, who at present are on the Export-Import Bank board, are left off. It seems like it is a definite gang-up between Crowley and Jimmie Byrnes. In calling up Bob Wagner I suggested that either Section 3 be deleted or that the Secretary of the Treasury and the Secretary of Commerce be added to the board of directors. Bob said that there was great pressure to get the bill through at once in order to have money available and that if any change were made in the House bill it would be impossible to get the legislation through both houses be-

tion (1943–44), and director of the Economic Warfare Division of the American embassy in London (1944–45).

fore next fall. He said there was great pressure not only from Crowley but also from the White House. He said he no longer got "worked up" about things. In other words, Wagner is a good little boy. He said Vinson had called up disturbed because the Secretary of the Treasury was left off. As a result of what Bob told me I decided to write a letter to President Truman.[1] . . .

Ernest Lindley wanted to get gossip on what I intended to do as Secretary of Commerce. I didn't give him much satisfaction. I told him there wasn't much that could be said until the President had made a decision as to just what responsibility and authority to give to the Department of Commerce. I told Lindley that I had put the full employment problem up to the President several months ago and that he had suggested holding off talking about it until Schwellenbach was confirmed as Secretary of Labor. After Schwellenbach was confirmed, of course, the President went to Europe. I told him that it seemed to me this should be one of the President's number one problems when he returns.

JULY 19, 1945

. . . Baruch was especially interested in showing me a document he wrote under date of April 20 for President Truman reporting on his trip for Roosevelt to England in early April. He got Churchill to go along on Bretton Woods, although Churchill had no faith whatever in it. Churchill asked merely that it be held up until after the British election. Churchill says the Tories are very much against Bretton Woods. Baruch reports that Keynes and others wanted to borrow from the United States from $5 to $8 billion from U.S. peace Lend-Lease. Baruch told them they needed only what he called a "cylinder head" loan amounting to $1 billion. Baruch says the British were wavering between tearing down Germany (to be safe from Germany) or building up Germany to be safe from Russia. Baruch came in on the Russian side. Baruch's great worry is about World Wide Cartellization vs. free enterprise. He sees Russia as a single buyer and seller. He sees England using cartel practices and asks where the small businessman in the United States gets off.

He presented his report to Truman and Truman told him he was

[1] On July 18 Wallace wrote Truman to repeat and elaborate the points he had made to Wagner. Truman, replying from Germany on July 27, said he would like to look into the matter when he returned. The legislation passed without alterations.

for it and asked him not to leave it with anyone. He showed it to both Stettinius and Byrnes. I was the fourth to whom he had shown it. The essence of the report was that the United States had a limited amount of certain very essential materials which the rest of the world needed and that the United States by conferring priorities could determine which countries would develop first. He felt Truman and Byrnes should play a hard bargaining game in deciding the priorities. He felt the first thing was to make sure of full employment in the United States.

He advocates inside the United States a President's Peace Council and for Europe a Supreme Peace and Reconstruction Council. Truman, after expressing himself for these things, has not consulted him further. Jimmie Byrnes told Baruch there was nothing new in what he proposed. Baruch has it in for Byrnes. He says back in 1939 Jimmie wanted to resign from the Senate to become a circuit judge but that now he has his sights very high. He says Byrnes is power-crazy—that he wants to decide everything himself but that he doesn't know how to get things done. Baruch doesn't think much of Byrnes' man, Don Russell.[1] He says Ben Cohen[2] is weak. He speaks highly of Miss Cassie Connor, Byrnes' secretary, who, he says, has saved Byrnes from many mistakes. He has no use whatever for Hannegan, who, he says, has insulted him. Baruch in return called Hannegan a liar.

Baruch wants to play up to the small businessmen after this war in the same way as he played up to the farmers after the last war.

He spoke very highly of me and said he wanted to keep in touch with me and to help me.

He called Jesse Jones a rascal. I asked him what Jesse was doing now. He said, "Lying in the long grass with a long knife." He said he had a great respect for Jesse because he was so slippery. He said Jesse tried to sabotage his rubber program and told how he jarred things loose by saying to Jesse, "I am going to cut your throat."

He also told Don Nelson the same thing. He said the President offered him in writing the job of being head of War Production Board. Baruch suggested to the President Bill Douglas. However, Bill Douglas told Baruch the President never offered it to him.

Baruch is obviously put out with both Vinson and Byrnes—thinks they are "fixers" and not men of action.

[1] Donald S. Russell, long one of Byrnes' assistants, had become deputy director of the Office of War Mobilization and Reconversion on January 1, 1945.
[2] Benjamin V. Cohen, one of the wisest of the New Dealers, had been general counsel of the OWMR since 1943.

At the moment Baruch is antilabor and pro–little business. He thinks labor has overplayed its hand. He is very proud of what he did in World War I and thinks he did a better job of controlling prices than has been done in this war. He saw Harry Hopkins and Mrs. Roosevelt this week. Harry looks very well and is being paid a fantastic sum for his memoirs. He told how Harry and Jimmie got at outs in 1943. Jimmie reached out for too much power and President Roosevelt did not like it. Jimmie fell out with Roosevelt three times, once in 1943, once in 1944 at the time of the convention, and again when Stettinius was appointed Secretary of State. I would say Baruch is definitely out to teach Jimmie a lesson and he would very much like to use me in his machinations.

JULY 24, 1945

. . . Don Stone[1] wanted to talk about the reorganization of the Department of State which had been requested by Jimmie Byrnes. I listened to him. He will come back and see me again later. I told him part of the difficulty in the State Department was due to the fact that nobody ever knew exactly what the policy was. I told him that Secretary Hull, all the time that he was Secretary of State, always felt uncertain because he thought the President was operating directly through Sumner Welles. For somewhat other reasons Sumner Welles also felt uncertain. Stone commented that Cordell Hull created in the State Department exactly the same situation which President Roosevelt created with respect to Hull; in other words, Hull would operate oftentimes not through his regular channels but through his particular pets. Of course, this type of relationship between the State Department and the President has characterized nearly all of the administration. Moreover, in nearly all departments there has been a tendency for the Secretary to use certain men in whom he had confidence as staff officers . . .

. . . Mrs. Grew said apropos of the probability of Russia attacking Japan in Manchuria, "Well, in that case we must now begin to think about strengthening Japan." Mary was horrified at Mrs. Grew's indiscreet frankness. Of course, a statement of this sort merely confirms one's belief that a high percentage of the State Department is composed of "*the* people," who want to make sure that "*the* people" come out on top everywhere in the world. Therefore, they have a great deal spiritually in common with Nazis and fascists wherever they may be . . .

[1] Donald Stone of the Budget Bureau.

AUGUST 7, 1945

With nearly everyone who came in to see me on August 7 the first topic of conversation was the atomic bomb.[1] Everyone seemed to feel that a new epoch in the world's history had been ushered in. The scramble for the control of this new power is going to be one of the most unusual struggles the world has ever seen.

AUGUST 8, 1945

Boris Pregel came in to tell me about his early work with radium, uranium, etc. He states that Arthur Compton,[2] in the presence of several other people, said that if it hadn't been for Pregel's foreseeing the possibilities of uranium and doing some stockpiling purely on his own, the progress toward the bomb would have been delayed by a year or a year and a half. He told how Howe,[3] the Canadian Minister of Munitions, was trying to squeeze him out of the ownership of his mine up in Canada.[4] Howe had been conducting an undercover campaign to try to depress the price of his stock and had forced the price down from $1.80 a share to $.95 a share. As a result of the announcement the other day the price had bounded up to more than $2.00 a share. Pregel told me that he thought General Leslie Richard Groves, who is anti-Semitic and anti-foreigner, had been inspiring the Canadian campaign against him. He showed me a letter from General Groves invoking the espionage act and directing Pregel to keep his mouth shut. At the same time Groves apparently is scheming with the Canadians to eliminate Pregel. What Pregel told me rather agreed with my own estimate of Groves when he came in to see me about a year ago. Groves is slightly pathological and the recent publicity will

[1] As Truman announced, the United States had dropped the atomic bomb on Hiroshima on August 6, 1945, the previous day. That bomb, a weapon of a type used on only one other occasion, the test at Alamorgordo, weighed about 9000 pounds, had the effect of about 20,000 tons of high exj osives, and had virtually destroyed the city that was its target. Truman's announcement repeated the ultimatum delivered to Japan after the Potsdam Conference, and promised that recommendations to Congress about control of atomic energy would be forthcoming.

[2] Arthur H. Compton, eminent American physicist, had organized the Metallurgical Laboratory of which he was director (1942–45). That agency authorized and supervised the experiments that resulted in the chain reaction essential to the development of the atomic bomb.

[3] Clarence D. Howe, American-born engineer, Canadian Minister of Munitions and Supply, member of the Combined Policy Committee for the development of the atomic bomb.

[4] Pregel was president of the Canadian Radium and Uranium Corporation.

probably make him more so. Pregel appeared to me as a rather badly scared Jew. Undoubtedly, he anticipated what happened on August 5. Undoubtedly, he had stockpiled uranium for the specific purpose of making it possible for the United States to do this thing. Undoubtedly, he played a much more important part than most of the people who are getting the publicity. Probably there are a group of businessmen in the United States who would like to get Pregel and who might very well cooperate with General Groves in the effort. Pregel, himself, didn't hint at anything of the sort to me, but from what I know of both Groves and Pregel I am sure this must have been running through Pregel's mind. Pregel claimed to have spent several sleepless nights thinking of the possibilities which the atomic bomb opens up to the worst type of dictator. Pregel says the Army doesn't realize that Russia has vast stores of uranium. Pregel says the three men who did the most significant work were Leo Szilard, who worked with Arthur Compton, Enrico Fermi, the Italian physicist, and Dr. Niels Bohr, the Dane.[1] Fermi's mother was Jewish and he is married to a Jewess. Both Szilard and Bohr are Jews. Of course, Dr. Lise Meitner[2] is a Jewess.

When Pregel spoke of all this my mind couldn't help running back to the time when General Groves told me how important it was to get the foreigners out of the uranium business, obviously referring to the Jews but not saying so.

I suggested to Pregel that I thought it was important to begin thinking of the peacetime uses of the product . . .

AUGUST 9, 1945

Altmeyer[3] came in to see me to let me know how much Garcia Tellez[4] and President Camacho thought of me. He had been attending a Social Security conference in Mexico and had sat next to various Mexicans who wanted him to convey to me their warmest regards. He also told me how much disturbed he was about Messersmith, who seems to be completely out of touch with the Mexican scene. He

---

[1] Szilard, Fermi, and Bohr had all provided theoretical information indispensable to the initial organization of the project to develop the atomic bomb, and had all also played major roles in that development. All three were gravely concerned about peacetime controls.

[2] Lise Meitner and her nephew, Otto R. Frisch, had contributed to Bohr's early calculations about the feasibility of developing the bomb.

[3] Arthur J. Altmeyer, since 1937 chairman of the Social Security Board.

[4] Ignacio Garcia Tellez, for twenty years, in a succession of different posts, an influential Mexican public official.

speaks in the most slighting terms of progressive Mexican leaders. He wants us to own the Mexican telephone system so we can tap the Mexican wires and hear the conversations of various Mexicans. Messersmith claims Toledano is a communist because he has listened in on conversations which Toledano has had with certain Cuban labor leaders. Messersmith was furious because I had blocked the sale of the Mexican-Ericsson Swedish Telephone Co. to IT&T which was proposed to be made by means of a loan through the Export-Import Bank. I used to think very highly of Messersmith because of the stand which he took against Naziism when he was in Europe. The more I see of his operations the more I realize now that he is spiritually a Nazi himself, or at any rate a narrow-minded martinet with a 19th-century outlook . . .

Dave[1] wanted to know specifically whether Roosevelt knew that Russia was coming into the war against Japan.[2] I told him that Roosevelt had twice told me in the spring of 1944 that there was no question about Russia going into the war. Also I had found when I was in Soviet Asia in June 1944 that there was no question about Russia coming into the war. The truth of the matter probably is that there was no way of keeping Russia out of the war with Japan once the war with Germany was over. She undoubtedly started preparing at once for the war with Japan and the four-month interval was the minimum that could be allowed in view of the great distances involved . . .

AUGUST 10, 1945

. . . The President, who usually comes to cabinet not later than 2:05, came in about 2:25 saying he was sorry to be late but that he and Jimmie had been busy working on a reply to Japanese proposals.[3]

---

[1] David Kerr, one of Drew Pearson's staff.

[2] The Soviet Union had declared war on Japan on August 8 and at once invaded Manchuria from Siberian bases.

[3] On August 9 the United States had dropped another atomic bomb, this time "fat man," a type using plutonium instead of uranium and triggered by implosion rather than a gun mechanism. The bomb hit the Japanese city of Nagasaki. It was a larger weapon than the Hiroshima bomb but of about the same destructive force. That second drop and the Russian declaration of war, which had surprised the Japanese government, set off discussions within the Japanese cabinet about acceptable conditions for peace. On August 10, with the Emperor's approval, Japan informed the United States that the Potsdam terms were acceptable provided they did not prejudice the Emperor's prerogatives as sovereign. Stimson considered that proposal satisfactory, while Byrnes favored unconditional surrender and Forrestal suggested a middle course. Truman then directed Byrnes to amend the Japanese offer so as to make the

Byrnes then read very slowly the Japanese proposal just as it was printed in the press late in the afternoon . . .

He then read the reply which Truman indicated had been worked out by Byrnes, assisted by Stimson, Leahy, and Forrestal that morning. These are the proposals that were made public property August 11.

Byrnes stopped while reading the proposal and laid special emphasis on the top dog commander over Hirohito being an American. They were not going to have any chance for misunderstanding as in Europe. They said the proposal had been transmitted to the other Allies and that they had already heard from Bevin[1] and Bevin was in accord. Truman then interjected most fiercely that he didn't think we would hear from the Russians but that we would go ahead without them anyway. Stimson said the Russians were in favor of delay so they could push as far into Manchuria as possible. Truman said it was to our interest that the Russians not push too far into Manchuria. He said there was no agreement with Russia about Manchuria. This surprised me because I remember what Roosevelt used to say in the spring of 1944 about his agreement with Stalin on access to Dairen.

Truman said he had given orders to stop atomic bombing. He said the thought of wiping out another 100,000 people was too horrible. He didn't like the idea of killing, as he said, "all those kids."

Referring to hard and soft terms for Japan, Truman referred to 170 telegrams precipitated by the peace rumor of August 9. 153 of the 170 were for hard terms—unconditional surrender. They were free-will telegrams—not inspired—and were mostly from parents of servicemen.

Abe Fortas, the friend of Tom Corcoran who sat next to me in Ickes' chair, said they were getting together a report on the uranium supply. Also they were drafting legislation. Vinson said the legislation ought to be cleared with Justice. Tom Clark said they also were drafting legislation.

Emperor's authority to rule subordinate to that of the Supreme Commander of the Allied Occupation (who was to be General Douglas MacArthur). While fighting in the Pacific continued, Truman forbade the use of a third atomic bomb without his express prior permission. Great Britain and China immediately assented to the new American formula for Japanese surrender. The Soviet Union, at first hesitant, also agreed in time for Byrnes to reply to Japan on August 11. Though some of the Japanese military dissented, the Emperor endorsed the terms and Japan surrendered on August 14.

[1] Ernest Bevin, Foreign Minister in the new British Cabinet which Prime Minister Clement R. Attlee had formed in July after the Labor Party won the general election.

Clint Anderson said the agricultural problem would be very great the moment V-J Day came and that it would cost the government a lot of money to carry out its commitments to the farmers.

I suggested that the government should make a survey of thorium as well as uranium, not only in the United States but also in the whole world. Fortas, Truman, and Stimson then spoke up in a chorus saying they were doing that.

At the close of cabinet the President called me by my first name and came around the table to see me. I complimented him on how well he looked. He said he had bad headaches every day. I replied, "Physical or figurative?" He said "Both"—that he had had to read a million words. (His eyes have always been weak.) I asked him if he was taking complete vitamins and he said yes. I said I would like to see him soon after V-J Day. He said, "Come in early next week." He said it would be good to have in Schwellenbach also. I suggested then the addition of Anderson and Snyder . . .

One very amusing incident: Truman said to Byrnes, "Tell them what it was Stalin called you." Jimmie smiled in a wry way and said, "The most honest horse thief he had ever met."

It is obvious to me that the cornerstone of the peace of the future consists in strengthening our ties of friendship with Russia. It is also obvious that the attitude of Truman, Byrnes, and both the War and Navy Departments is not moving in this direction. Their attitude will make for war eventually . . .

AUGUST 17, 1945

At the White House I submitted to the President the sheet of paper entitled "Specific Items for Approval by the President to Revitalize the Department of Commerce." He went over the eight items and approved them. He said that of course all of them might not work out precisely as I had them down but in general he was for them. He indicated particularly he was for Items 2, 3, and 4.[1]

[1] Those items were: 1. The general program of the Commerce Department was "to help business and industry to maintain high levels of production, sales, investment, and employment." 2. Reorganization of the department was to include provisions for three new assistant secretaries, one each for international trade, small business, and industrial economy. 3. Transfer to the department of all nonfinancial activities of the Smaller War Plants Corporation. 4. Transfer also of those activities of the Foreign Economic Administration relating to the promotion of foreign trade, procurement, export control, and economic planning, as well as the designation of the Secretary of Commerce as chairman of the Export-Import Bank. 5. Transfer to the department at once of the research

I talked at some little length about the Export-Import Bank and told him that down the line in the State Department there were men who didn't want me on the Export-Import Bank. I went into the details of the proposed loan to enable the IT&T to buy out the Swedish Ericsson Company in Mexico and told him that I was against the loan as originally proposed because it would have involved our standing responsible in the eyes of the Mexican people for an increase in the telephone rates in order to make the loan good. The President said he agreed with me in my attitude. I also mentioned that Messersmith was interested in the transaction because he wanted a telephone company set up which would enable the United States to listen in on Mexican telephone conversations. I told the President I didn't know all of the details of the conniving that had been going on but that I had a hunch. The President said he was embarrassed by the legislation that had recently been passed with regard to the Export-Import Bank.

I spoke at some length about the desirability of the Department of Commerce keeping posted on the development of atomic power. I referred to our interest through the Patent Office and through the Bureau of Standards. I said undoubtedly the future development of atomic power would have an influence on the expansion of commerce and that whoever might be Secretary of Commerce ought to be present on any board concerned with the development of atomic power. The President spoke up at this moment and said that as long as he was President he wanted me to be Secretary of Commerce. I told him about Pregel and his connection with the uranium used in the atomic bomb. He said he couldn't remember ever having met him. I told him that Arthur Compton had said that if it hadn't been for Pregel's foresightedness we would have been at least a year later in the development of the bomb. I told him that Pregel had been much interested in the election of Roosevelt and that I hoped someday he would meet him. I mentioned that Pregel was quite familiar with the scientific work going on in Russia. I told him that if the future world situation was going to be so bad as to warrant continuous universal military training, then, in view of the atomic bomb, it would be wise to decentralize our industry and our population and build a good many

and development and the labor-management committee of the War Production Board, and later of that board's activities relating to statistics, economic planning, and industry committees. 6. Supplemental appropriations for fiscal 1946 and increased appropriations for fiscal 1947. 7. Representation of the department in any central agency on scientific research and its support. 8. Organization of a cabinet committee for reconversion and economic policy, with the President as chairman and the Secretary of Commerce as one member. (Items 2, 4, and 6 required congressional action.)

of our industrial plants under the Rocky Mountains. He seemed to agree; he said he wasn't sure, however, that we needed universal military training; that he was working on a formula which was somewhat of a compromise . . .

The entire cabinet meeting was devoted to discussing the agenda which the President had sent out that morning. The first point on the agenda was the discussion of what ought to go in the President's message to Congress.[1] Most attention was given to just what he should recommend with regard to Selective Service now that the war was over. Patterson and Forrestal were very keen about continuing Selective Service. Leo Crowley was against it. I said that Selective Serivce might have to be continued as long as necessary to get men for the occupation forces. I said I hoped, however, that we would now begin to make it possible for the young men who would be taking scientific training to go to school. I said we would be outdistanced by other nations unless we took care of this. I laid it on very thick.

Jimmie Brynes thought the President's message should deal exclusively with domestic affairs. There was considerable discussion of taxes. The point I made was that taxes should be adjusted to bring about the maximum of consumption with the greatest possible amount of investment; that if both objectives were kept in mind no serious mistake would be likely to be made this coming year.

At the close of the meeting Leo Crowley again laughingly spoke to me, saying, "And these are the guys who said some weeks ago that there would be no unemployment problem!" . . .

AUGUST 18, 1945

. . . The following inspired story, which appeared in the August 18 issue of the *Times-Herald*, is interesting because it indicates the probable attitude of the Hearst-McCormick-Patterson press.[2] In this

---

[1] Truman sent his recommendations to Congress in a special message of October 22, 1945. He proposed a system of universal training as one basis for a postwar military organization which was to consist of a relatively small Army, Navy and Marine Corps; a strengthened National Guard and an Organized Reserve; and a general reserve of all males who had received training. Only an act of Congress would be able to mobilize the general reserve. Congress rejected the proposal; see Harry S. Truman, *Year of Decisions* (Garden City, 1955).

[2] Walter Trohan reported in the Washington *Times-Herald* on August 18 that Truman had "bested" Stalin and made the United States "boss of the Pacific." Trohan claimed that he had received secret reports about the Potsdam Conference from American representatives who attended it. His story stressed Truman's firmness with Stalin, especially about Manchuria and Korea, and the President's determination to protect American security in the Pacific.

attitude are the seeds of what may possibly turn out to be World War III. On the other hand, much of the story is as stale as can be and is merely a reflection of what Stalin and Roosevelt agreed on at Teheran. I know that Roosevelt told me in May of 1944 that Russia had agreed not to take Manchuria but that Russia was to be given access to the port of Dairen. The dangerous thing in the whole story is the suggestion that Truman is going the whole way with the Generalissimo. This means unless the Generalissimo shows a more enlightened attitude than he did to me in June of 1944, there will sooner or later be revolution in China and the United States will lose influence there and Russia will gain.

AUGUST 22, 1945

. . . At the White House dinner for de Gaulle one of the Frenchmen spent all his time talking to me about plans to get French Indo-China back. He claimed that France was working out a new system of governing her colonies, under which she would give the colonies much more democratic opportunity to govern their own affairs.

After the dinner at the White House was over and we were all standing around talking, the President came up to a group of us, including Secretary Schwellenbach, Secretary Ickes, and several others. He seemed to be in a very jovial mood and started out by saying that what he really ought to have been was not a President but a piano player in a whorehouse. Secretary Schwellenbach spoke up and said, "That would have been too bad because then we never would have known you!" The President rejoined, "Why be so high and mighty, as though you had never been in a whorehouse!" Schwellenbach seemed to be genuinely shocked . . .

AUGUST 23, 1945

. . . On parting from de Gaulle he [de Gaulle] said to me in English, of which he speaks very little, "The century of the common man is assured because we have won the war." I merely said to him, "Is it?"

AUGUST 29, 1945

. . . At the luncheon with Schwellenbach he said the idea of the labor-industry meeting did not come into full flower until the meeting in the President's office on Friday, August 24, at which meeting the

President, Eric Johnston, Ira Mosher,[1] Bill Green, Phil Murray, and Schwellenbach were present. The President apparently indicated that there should be another meeting, at which I should be present, and at this meeting an agenda committee would be picked. Schwellenbach said he wanted Paul Douglas, formerly of Chicago University and now in the Bethesda Naval Hospital with serious wounds, to serve as chairman. I told him that was fine; then he modified the statement and indicated he thought there ought to be a co-chairman from industry, who would represent the public but who would have somewhat more the industrial point of view than Douglas. It was decided to hold the next meeting on September 6, at which time we would pick a committee of seven to work on the agenda and to pick a larger committee of about thirty which would participate in the final meeting. I asked Schwellenbach what he hoped would come out of the final meeting. He listed the following five points:

On Industry Side

1. Complete recognition of principle of collective bargaining.
2. Development in industry of a pattern whereby responsibility and right of decision on labor policies could be extended to those who actually deal with the unions.

On Union Side

1. Adoption of system of voluntary policing and settlement of jurisdictional disputes.
2. Strengthening of relationship between national and local units in labor.

Both

Recommendation for the establishment of some system of voluntary arbitration.

I told Ira Mosher that with regard to labor-industry relationships my formula was that I wasn't for anything for labor that wasn't good for business and that I wasn't for anything for business that wasn't good for labor, and that I wasn't for anything for either one of them that wasn't good for the consumer and the farmer. Mosher said he could make it even simpler than that; that he would not be for anything for labor and business that wasn't good for all the people. He

[1] Ira Mosher, Massachusetts business executive, former vice president and general manager of the American Optical Company, in 1945 president of the Russell Harrington Cutlery Company.

also said he was for full production by both labor and industry. You would have thought his heart was God's little garden to hear him talk . . .

AUGUST 31, 1945

Ellis Arnall tells me that the President urged him to take the job of Solicitor General. He wanted my judgment on the matter. I urged him to take it. He very much has his fingers crossed about the present administration setup. If he takes a job he will undoubtedly be completely loyal. He feels, however, that the world is definitely going to the left and that Truman, Hannegan, Clark, etc., do not fully appreciate that. Arnall is a very smart man and liberal-minded. At times he may be a little overpolitical but perhaps that is because he is so smart.

At cabinet meeting the President read a first draft of a statement which he had written with regard to military policy. He said he had put everything in it but the kitchen stove. Everybody complimented him on what a fine statement it was. When it came my turn to talk I asked him if he would care to have me say something about the kitchen stove. I then went on to suggest that a real military program for the country must of necessity be based on science, both in increased scientific personnel and also more laboratory equipment. Second, I said that if the world situation was as serious as Secretary Patterson had indicated, it would be desirable to have the Secretaries of War and Navy cooperate very closely with the Public Works Administrator to bring about a decentralization of our industry and population. Third, I indicated the desirability of having some standing committees which could throw us into mobilization more rapidly . . .

SEPTEMBER 5, 1945

The interesting thing about General Groves' presentation[1] was the point he made that atomic energy would not be practicable for peacetime purposes for many years, probably after all of us at the meeting were dead.

[1] Groves was guest speaker at a dinner that night of the Business Advisory Council of the Commerce Department.

SEPTEMBER 18, 1945

Jim McCamy[1] told me the situation in Austria is quite desperate. People are getting less than 800 calories and there is going to be much starvation this winter. I am convinced that the American people are going to be ashamed of themselves next spring when they look back and realize they took off rationing at a time when many parts of Europe were on the verge of starvation . . .

We talked at some little length about atomic energy. The President took the stand that while we should keep the secret of the atomic bomb we should inform the United Nations about atomic energy. Secretary of Agriculture Anderson took strong dissent to this view on the ground that 80 percent of the people, according to the Gallup Poll, were strong for the United States maintaining the secret of atomic power. Jim Forrestal took the same view as Anderson. Secretary Stimson and I supported the President. I made the point that if we maintained utmost secrecy we would be blamed by the world for a dog-in-the-manger attitude while at the same time countries like England, France, and Russia would go ahead with atomic power developments and would surpass us. I said there was danger of developing a type of "Maginot Line" attitude which would give us a false confidence while other countries would surpass us. I said it was impossible to bottle scientists up in the way some people seem to think.

SEPTEMBER 20, 1945

. . . At the meeting of the United States Financial Group the whole time was spent considering the problem of blocked sterling.[2] I suggested that we ought to get as much detail as possible from the British with regard to how much they expected to export and to what nations they expected to export. In the final analysis the only security for our loan to the British would be the matter of their exports and it is a matter of interest to us to know where they expect to send these exports . . .

[1] James McCamy, the economic adviser in Austria of the Foreign Economic Administration.
[2] Negotiations for an American loan to Great Britain were then under way. The meeting at the Treasury Department about that loan addressed itself, as the Treasury continually had during the war, to the question of the probable impact upon American exports of sterling assets accumulated by the British Dominions but confined for use within the British Commonwealth—that is, "blocked sterling."

At the cabinet meeting the one subject up for discussion was the atomic bomb and the peacetime development of atomic energy.

The President asked Secretary Stimson to open the meeting, which he did in an unusually fine and comprehensive statement. He said that all of the scientists with whom the War Department worked were convinced that there was no possible way of holding the scientific secret of the atomic bomb and that, therefore, they felt there should be free interchange of scientific information between different members of the United Nations. He said that the scientists told him that the bombs thus far dropped were utilizing only a very small fraction of the power of the atom and that future bombs would be infinitely more destructive—perhaps being as greatly advanced over the present bombs as the present bombs are over the bombs which existed prior to 1945. He said some of them were afraid they would be so powerful as to ignite the atmosphere and put an end to the world. He said he recognized that any interchange of scientific information with the other United Nations would bring into the foreground the problem of Russia. He then entered into a long defense of Russia, saying that throughout our history Russia had been our friend—that we had nothing that Russia wanted and that Russia had nothing that we wanted. He said our relationship with Russia during recent months had been improving. President Truman agreed to this.

The President then called on Dean Acheson, who indicated that he agreed with Secretary Stimson.

The President then called on Fred Vinson, who disagreed with Secretary Stimson and expressed great distrust of other nations. Secretary Stimson had said it was conceivable that some of the other nations could learn the secret of the atomic bomb without any help from us within three years, and almost certainly within five years. Vinson rather questioned this statement.

Tom Clark took very much the same attitude as Secretary Vinson.

Secretary Forrestal took the most extreme attitude of all. He had a memorandum which had been prepared by his admirals, which he read. It was a warlike, big-Navy, isolationist approach.

Bob Hannegan spoke very briefly but took the side of Secretary Stimson. The President had said enough in his opening statement to indicate he was substantially in accord with Secretary Stimson, and it was obvious that Bob was backing up what he thought were the President's views.

Secretary Anderson took in some ways an even more extreme view than Secretary Forrestal. He was passing his judgment merely on what people thought. He said he had talked to a great many people in the Middle West and they were all against our giving away the secret of the bomb to any other nation. Of course, that was not the subject up for discussion but Anderson assumed it was simply because that was the way he had talked to the people in the Middle West. He said he had been at a meeting in Decatur, Illinois, the previous night, and he asked the people how many were in favor of giving away the secret of the bomb and they were all against it. He said he thought it was a very precious thing to maintain the President's prestige and it should not be sacrificed by going against the will of the people. Anderson was quite violent about Russia, saying that Russia was taking over Mongolia and Manchuria and various other spots.

Abe Fortas, who was sitting in place of Secretary Ickes, briefly took the same view as Secretary Stimson.

When I started to speak, I asked what specifically was the subject up for discussion. The President said that the subject up for discussion was whether or not the scientific information regarding atomic energy should be shared with the other members of the United Nations. The subject to be discussed did not include the sharing of factory technique or "know-how." I mentioned that all those who were seated on the President's right who had thus far spoken had taken what the people would interpret as the "Left" view and those seated on the President's left had taken what the people would interpret as the "Rightest" view. I laughingly said that when the subject of Russia was introduced into an American discussion it seemed to have about as much effect on the people involved as the atomic bomb. I referred to the lattice piles used in developing atomic energy from uranium oxide and said perhaps we should find the equivalent of the slowing-down strips to enable us to discuss more reasonably problems where Russia was involved. I then went at some length into the whole scientific background, describing how foreign Jewish scientists had in the first place sold the President in the fall of 1939. I indicated the degree to which the whole approach had originated in Europe and that it was impossible to bottle the thing up no matter how much we tried; if we took the attitude of being dogs in the manger with regard to scientific information that we would develop for ourselves a scientific Maginot Line type of mind, thinking we were secure because of our past attainments, while at the same time certain other nations were going beyond us. I advocated strongly the interchange of scientific information but not the interchange of techniques or "know-hows." I also advocated that in case scientific information were made freely available to Russia that we have as a quid pro quo the proviso that there be as much freedom for American scientific workers to work in the Russian laboratories as for the Russians to work in American laboratories.[1]

I then took up Anderson's statement about Russia and said it simply wasn't true that Rusisa was taking over Manchuria; that back as far as 18 months ago Roosevelt had told me what the arrangements were with regard to Manchuria and that Russia was living up to the understanding at that time. President Truman interjected to say that that was true. I said with regard to Mongolia that the Mongolians were livestock people and that there had always been misunderstanding between Mongolia and China because the Chinese were a sedentary, agricultural people; that the Mongolians wanted Russian scientific information regarding animal diseases. I told of my visit to the animal disease laboratory in Mongolia and of finding there the 37 Mongolian technicians who had been trained in animal disease work and to produce vaccines against animal diseases. I said it was perfectly natural under the circumstances that the Mongolians would look toward Russia as a source of progress rather than toward China.

In conclusion, I spoke very strongly on behalf of freedom of science and urged that we not take a stand which would finally result in our becoming essentially another China.

Secretary Schwellenbach, who sits on the President's left, said that he had departed from the views of the others who sat on his side and that he agreed with those who sat on the right of the President. In other words, he agreed with Secretary Stimson.

So also did General Fleming.

Krug[2] said he was in favor of delay.

Senator McKellar agreed with Krug.

[1] Wallace's position at this meeting became an object of public controversy after a distorted version of his remarks was leaked to the press. Newspapers hostile to him and to his views about atomic energy accused him of advocating the release to the Soviet Union of the "secret" of the atomic bomb. Though Truman denied that allegation, and though Wallace had struck a position almost identical with that of Henry Stimson (who was attending his last cabinet meeting), the distortion of Wallace's ideas remained a target for continual conservative attack. Wallace provided the fullest and clearest statement of his opinion in his letter to Truman of September 24, 1945 (published below), a letter based not only on his own reflections but also on advice he solicited from four atomic scientists, who reinforced his opinion. Those scientists were Szilard, Fermi, James Franck, and Farrington Daniels.

[2] Julius A. Krug, at that time chairman of the War Production Board.

Leo Crowley took no definite stand one way or the other, but seemed on the whole to back Stimson.

John Snyder[1] backed Stimson.

SEPTEMBER 23, 1945

The newspapers in Chicago[2] were eager to find out what I had to say about the atomic bomb. I refused to talk. The word had already been leaked out by the President's press secretary that I favored giving the atomic bomb to Russia. The question is why he said such a thing; also, why he should have talked about a cabinet meeting at all.

SEPTEMBER 24, 1945
HENRY A. WALLACE TO HARRY S TRUMAN

Dear Mr. President:

You have asked for the comment, in writing, of each cabinet officer on the proposal submitted by Secretary Stimson for the free and continuous exchange of scientific information (not industrial blueprints and engineering "know-how") concerning atomic energy between all of the United Nations. I agreed with Henry Stimson.

At the present time, with the publication of the Smyth report and other published information, there are no substantial scientific secrets that would serve as obstacles to the production of atomic bombs by other nations. Of this I am assured by the most competent scientists who know the facts. We have not only already made public much of the scientific information about the atomic bomb, but above all with the authorization of the War Department we have indicated the road others must travel in order to reach the results we have obtained.

With respect to future scientific developments I am confident that both the United States and the world will gain by the free interchange of scientific information. In fact, there is danger that in attempting to maintain secrecy about these scientific developments we will, in the long run, as a prominent scientist recently put it, be indulging "in the erroneous hope of being safe behind a scientific Maginot Line."

The nature of science and the present state of knowledge in other countries are such that there is no possible way of preventing other nations from repeating what we have done or surpassing it within five or six years. If the United States, England, and Canada act the part of

1 John W. Snyder, at that time director of the OWMR.
2 Wallace had gone to Chicago to confer with atomic scientists there.

the dog in the manger on this matter, the other nations will come to hate and fear all Anglo-Saxons without our having gained anything thereby. The world will be divided into two camps with the non-Anglo-Saxon world eventually superior in population, resources, and scientific knowledge.

We have no reason to fear loss of our present leadership through the free interchange of scientific information. On the other hand, we have every reason to avoid a shortsighted and unsound attitude which will invoke the hostility of the rest of the world.

In my opinion, the quicker we share our scientific knowledge (not industrial and engineering information) the greater will be the chance that we can achieve genuine and durable world cooperation. Such action would be interpreted as a generous gesture on our part and lay the foundation for sound international agreements that would assure the control and development of atomic energy for peaceful use rather than destruction.

The announcement of our policy of disclosing all scientific information relating to atomic energy could be made in conjunction with other steps designed to arrive at international regulation relating to atomic weapons. I would regard this as indispensable for our own security and international peace.

I should like to stress that the present situation is a dangerous one and calls for early action.

The danger will increase and our position and that of international security will further deteriorate if we continue to follow our present course of maintaining useless secrecy and at the same time building up a stockpile of atomic bombs.

So far as Russia is concerned, I would hope that we could make arrangements for as many Americans going to Russia to study or work in the laboratories and universities as there are Russians coming here. We cannot have a truly effective scientific interchange unless this is done. Hitherto the Russians have learned much more from us than we from them. This is chiefly because we had much to teach but it is also because we didn't take sufficient advantage of the invitations extended to us. The Russian scientific progress is certain to be very much faster in the future than in the past. Russia has all the potentialities of a young and vigorous nation. To maintain peaceful relations with her we must keep in the closest possible touch with her scientific, agricultural, business, and cultural development. In this way we can both guard ourselves and gain a true friend.

After writing the above I have had the opportunity to listen to discussions of a large number of the outstanding scientists in this field. The views which they expressed are similar to those at which I had arrived independently, as is indicated by the enclosed statements from five American scientists, three of whom are Nobel Prize winners, and four of whom were intimately connected with the atomic bomb project. The statement by Dr. Szilard, who together with Dr. Fermi and Dr. Einstein was most responsible for moving President Roosevelt to action on the atomic bomb in the fall of 1939, emphasizes even more than the statement by Dr. Fermi the destructive possibilities of atomic energy. Dr. Franck's statement accurately reflects the consensus of the scientists who discussed the subject at the meeting which I attended. Dr. Daniels' observations illustrate the types of problems with which the scientists are now concerned.

In light of the above, I support Henry Stimson in his proposal for the free interchange of scientific information concerning atomic energy . . .

OCTOBER 1, 1945

On October 1, at the luncheon given by Dean Acheson, Dean said it was utterly amazing the way in which the cabinet meeting had leaked. He said he had never seen anything like it. I asked him who he thought had leaked. He said he thought Forrestal had leaked; or those in the Navy to whom Forrestal had talked.

At the meeting with the President, Wright and Burden[1] presented very fully their views on the development of aviation. The President seemed very agreeable to everything they said. At the close of the meeting, I stopped for a minute and told the President that the relationship between Symington[2] and Schindler was not at all good and I strongly advocated, as I had previously, August 17, the transfer of Surplus Property disposal from Commerce to Symington. I said it was an impossible situation as it was. The President said to take the matter up with John Snyder.

OCTOBER 3, 1945

Surprisingly enough, Symington agreed with us on transferring Surplus Property disposal to him. Symington is a nice fellow but the

---

[1] Theodore P. Wright, head of the Civil Aeronautics Administration, and William A. M. Burden, Assistant Secretary of Commerce.

[2] W. Stuart Symington, then head of the Surplus Property Administration.

more I see of him the happier I am to get out from under his direction. He is a hard-hitting, go-getting type, who doesn't know too much about government . . .

OCTOBER 11, 1945

. . . At the meeting of the U.S. Committee on the British loan it was decided to make the loan on a basis which would involve the British paying 31 million dollars for each billion dollars borrowed, payments beginning five years after the loan was negotiated.[1] It was decided to give the British credit up to a certain amount rather than a definite loan. The British would be allowed to draw on this credit up to a four- or five-year period. There was difference of opinion as to the maximum amount of credit. The Treasury and the Federal Reserve apparently felt it should not be more than three billion dollars . . .

Tom Connally was present at the dinner and spoke to me in very critical terms of Spruille Braden, said he ought to have the cockleburs combed out of his hair. It is Tom Connally who has been holding up Braden's confirmation.[2] Tom Connally in some respects is the lowest type of senator we have. He loves to get at cross purposes with the White House and bluster around. He is essentially a demagogue with no depth of perception, no sense of the general welfare, and no interest in it. He has a high sense of personal dignity and is likable personally . . .

OCTOBER 12, 1945

At the cabinet meeting Friday morning there was very little discussed. There was some discussion of the labor problem and some of Food and Agriculture. Clinton Anderson wanted to get instructions from other members of the cabinet as to whether the man appointed to head up Food and Agriculture under the Economic and Social Council of the United Nations Organization should be an American or a foreigner. He said the Chinese very much wanted the man appointed to

[1] The American negotiators decided on a credit of $3.5 billion. The British had come down from their original request for $5 billion to $4 billion. Truman interceded to split the remaining difference and offer $3.75 billion with the entire sum to bear interest at 2 percent but with a four-year period of grace before payments were due. That made the effective rate 1.63 percent, only slightly higher than the British had hoped for.

[2] Braden's appointment as ambassador to Argentina was confirmed.

be an American but he knew there were five other branches of the Economic and Social Council and that it might be more important to have Americans in some of those other branches. He mentioned that I had suggested the possibility of Frank McDougall, the liberal-minded Australian. After cabinet meeting we went out on the White House lawn to see the President pin Distinguished Service Medals on the soldiers.

At the broadcast Friday night,[1] as we sat around talking in advance, Dick Wilson mentioned that the President's honeymoon was over and that from now on there was going to be continual criticism. He said the President's personal habits would come up for criticism, and spoke about his winning $52 shooting craps at Jefferson Island. Marquis Childs spoke up and said the President didn't shoot craps; that he won the money playing poker. I then remembered that at one of the cabinet luncheons two or three weeks previous Clinton Anderson had spoken about the President's great skill at playing poker and how he had won $52. The significance of it all was that the press is now getting ready systematically to criticize Truman. This should close the ranks of the Democratic Party and end some of the sniping which has been going on from within.

OCTOBER 15, 1945

My conference with the President was most interesting. I gave him the accompanying material to read[2] and he read it, sentence by sen-

[1] Wallace broadcast on "Meet the Press" with four reporters as his interrogators, Alfred Friendly of the Washington *Post*, Richard L. Wilson of the Des Moines *Register and Tribune*, Walter C. Hornaday of the Dallas *News*, and Marquis Childs of the United Feature Syndicate.
[2] Entitled "The Significance of the Atomic Age," it read:

> When many nations have atomic bombs and some of them are held back only by fear of retaliation, suspicion and apprehension will eventually mount up to a point, under the encouragement of the yellow press or the controlled press, which will require only the smallest spark to set off a worldwide, humanity-destroying explosion. Steps should be taken at once to call into being a vital international organization based on the elimination of all weapons of offensive warfare, the pooling of the constructive aspects of atomic energy, and the adoption of the principle of international trusteeship for certain areas of the world . . .
> With regard to the atomic power commission, the President himself should have the power to appoint the director by and with the consent of the Senate. Any board should serve in a consultative fashion and should represent equally the governmental, the scientific, and industrial, the labor, the agricultural, the military, and the consuming public point of view. The

tence. He said he agreed with it throughout. He said this was what he had been trying to say right along in the statements which he had made.[1] He said he had been having a hell of a time with the State Department. He had been wanting to call a conference with England and Canada on the bomb, preparatory to having conferences with Russia. He said Stalin was a fine man who wanted to do the right thing. I said that apparently the purpose of Britain was to promote an unbreachable break between us and Russia. The President said he agreed. I said Britain's game in international affairs has always been intrigue. The President said he agreed. I said Britain may have plenty of excuse for playing the game the way she does; it may fit into her geographical position, but we must not play her game. The President said he agreed.

The President, in speaking about Stalin, said he wasn't well at Potsdam, and he wasn't well now; and he was afraid that he was so tired he wanted to retire. He said this would be very unfortunate both for Russia and the United States, because then it would be a struggle for power between Molotov on the one hand and Zhukov[2] on the other. He didn't like the prospect with either one of them. He returned to the fact that Stalin is an honest man who is easy to get along with—who arrives at sound decisions . . .

I brought up again the question of a cabinet economic committee composed of the Secretaries of Agriculture, Labor, and Commerce,

---

commission with its director should deal primarily with the practical engineering development and civilian use of atomic power under appropriate safeguards. Most of the fundamental scientific work should be carried out by scientists in governmental, university, and private laboratories under the encouragement of some such scientific research foundation as that set up under this revised Kilgore-Magnuson bill.

It is time for the military to release the scientists from restraint so that we may have genuinely free public discussion at once.

[1] Truman on October 3 had sent Congress a message about the control of atomic energy. Drafted at Acheson's request by Herbert Marks in the State Department, the message, while cautious and unspecific, followed Stimson's approach to the sharing of atomic information. The President proposed the appointment of a commission to control all sources of atomic energy, all research, materials, plants, production, and licenses. That control was to involve "minimum practical interference with private research and private enterprise." In international policy, Truman had noted, it would be futile to attempt to keep a scientific secret. To avoid "a desperate armaments race," he recommended negotiation of an international agreement "under which cooperation might replace rivalry in the field of atomic power." Truman contemplated no exchange of information about weapons. He did not mention the Soviet Union by name.

[2] Marshal Georgi K. Zhukov, the foremost Russian general during the Second World War, had had, in the informed opinion of Dwight D. Eisenhower, "a longer experience as a responsible leader in great battles than any other man of our time."

with John Snyder and Harold Smith sitting in. I said it would be a fine thing if such an economic committee meeting could be held weekly under his chairmanship. The President agreed. He said he had been unbelievably busy—so busy that he didn't know where he was and, therefore, he hadn't done some of the things he wanted to do.

In leaving the statement on "The Significance of the Atomic Age" with the President, I asked him not to pass it on to anyone because people couldn't be trusted. I said that the experience at the September 21 cabinet meeting had been very surprising to me, and said that undoubtedly there was a lying leaker in the cabinet. He said "Yes-undoubtedly there was." He said he was as much disturbed about it as I was. I thanked him for knocking the story down . . .

The President started to say who he thought had leaked and then hesitated, saying, "Well, it won't do any good to talk about personalities."

I told him that as long as there was a lying leaker in the cabinet it would be impossible to have frank discussion on controversial questions. He agreed and said that at the next cabinet meeting he would bring the matter up.

In leaving, I told him that there was evidence that certain of the newspapers were going to start a drumfire against him. I said I had appeared on a radio program with Dick Wilson, Marquis Childs, and some others and that before that program took up Dick Wilson indicated that drumfire was getting ready to start. The President said he thought so, too, and then added, "Well, you and I know how to take it, don't we?" . . .

Marquis Childs came in to develop somewhat the same thesis that Dick Wilson had developed the previous Friday night. His discussion, however, was concerning Pauley.[1] He said in case Pauley came in as Secretary of the Navy could I remain in the cabinet in view of what I knew about Pauley? I said it might perhaps make the situation somewhat similar to that which my father had when he was in Harding's cabinet. He asked what my relations were with the President and I said they had been the most friendly; that the President had cooperated with me in everything I had wanted. Childs rejoined, "Well, that is one of the great difficulties with the President; he does that way with everyone" . . .

[1] Washington rumors then had Truman about to appoint Pauley Secretary of the Navy. Liberal Democrats objected to Pauley's connections with large oil companies and his advocacy of turning tideland oil rights over to the states for their alienation to private exploitation. Truman did appoint Pauley, but Ickes led the opposition that grew sufficiently strong in the Senate to persuade Pauley, during the debate over his confirmation, to withdraw.

OCTOBER 16, 1945

. . . The President said there were two things he especially wanted to emphasize: One had to do with the cabinet meeting which had been held some time ago following which there was a leakage which had taken place, he knew not through any members around the luncheon table. He said he thought he knew who had leaked and he thought that man would not be in the cabinet any more. I suppose he was referring to Crowley. The President said that I had not taken nearly as vigorous a stand as either Stimson or Schwellenbach. He didn't say, as he should have said, that the question of giving the atomic bomb to any other nation had not even been discussed. However, he was obviously doing his best to straighten out what he considered to be an injustice . . .

OCTOBER 17, 1945

When I walked downtown this morning with Wing Commander Dahl I asked him what his present job was and he said he was still with the British Secret Service. He said he was now something of a Russophobe. I said, "Well, if you fear the Russians it won't be long until your fears are well founded." I am convinced that the British slant is to stir up the maximum of distrust between the United States and Russia. He spent most of his time trying to convince me that the United States should continue the Donovan secret service setup. He told of the very close friendship which had continued since the beginning of the war between Sir William Stephenson, his chief, and General Donovan. He said that of the 20 German saboteurs discovered by the FBI 17 of them had been apprehended because of advance information given by the British Secret Service to the FBI. In other words, the British knew when the saboteurs left Germany to come to the United States. Dahl was very complimentary about the high quality of the work done by the OSS under Donovan. He thinks a combined American-English Secret Service is necessary to prevent destructive possibilities of the atomic bomb. In other words, Dahl visions the United States and England working together to prevent Russia from blowing up Anglo-Saxon civilization and wants an American Secret Service organization which in fact will be under the thumb of the British Secret Service organization. He is a nice boy and I am very fond of him but necessarily he is working out problems from the standpoint of British policy, and British policy clearly is to provoke the maximum distrust between the United States and Russia and thus prepare the groundwork for World War III . . .

At the meeting in Secretary Vinson's office the chief subject up for discussion was how much money to loan the British. The Treasury took the low side, figuring that the maximum ought to be about $3 billion. Will Clayton took the high side, figuring that the maximum might be $5 billion. Eventually a compromise was arrived on which was a little closer to the Treasury than to State. The British have come out flat with the idea that they ought to be given $2 billion and they would be willing to borrow $3 billion with not more than $100 million a year paid in repayment beginning five or ten years from now, at the rate of $30 million for each billion borrowed, and continuing for fifty years.

At the luncheon in Secty Ickes' office Phil Murray said that the steel negotiations were not getting anywhere and that the steel boys were going to go out on strike. He indicated that he had lost faith in the administration because they had not grappled courageously with the wage and price problem. Bob Nathan said that due to elimination of overtime it would be possible for businessmen to pay 10 percent more in basic wage rates next year than this year without diminishing their profits or raising their prices. He said that after the last war increased efficiency in manufacturing had raised profits 10 percent for two years and that he expected the same increase after this war. Nathan says that in 1946 the total wage bill of the country will be about $60 billion as compared with $80 billion in 1944. This reduction of $20 billion in the take-home pay of labor is bound to have a severe effect on the whole economy. He thinks that neither Truman nor Snyder fully understand the situation . . .

I sat in at a most interesting meeting at the Statler Hotel as a guest of Watson Davis of Science Service, with Harlow Shapley presiding. A number of the leading atomic bomb scientists were present, including Oppenheimer, Curtis, Szilard, Fermi, Condon, et al.[1] There were also

---

[1] Watson Davis was managing editor and director of *Science Service;* Harlow Shapley, an eminent American astronomer, was director of the Harvard Observatory, a trustee of M.I.T., and an articulate advocate of sharing scientific information with the Soviet Union. Among other scientists Wallace mentioned, J. Robert Oppenheimer had been and then still was director of the laboratory at Los Alamos where the atomic bomb was perfected; Harley L. Curtis was the principal physicist at the Bureau of Standards, and Edward U. Condon, a theoretical physicist, had worked on the problem of U-235, had been associate director of the Westinghouse Research Laboratory, and was about to be Wallace's candidate for appointment as Director of the Bureau of Standards.

present Senators Kilgore, Taylor, Murray, Tobey, Smith, and Mc-
Mahon.[1] The scientists presented in very vigorous terms the peril in
which the United States now finds herself.[2] They centered their attention chiefly on the threat to peace. This interested Tobey greatly. He
was enormously impressed and insisted that there be another meeting of
the atomic scientists Wednesday night of next week. Everybody
agreed to meet again at the Statler Hotel. Oppenheimer said he very
much wanted to see me and I made arrangements to walk down with
him Friday morning.

OCTOBER 19, 1945

At cabinet meeting the subject up for discussion was wage and
price policy. The President started out with John Snyder and then
shifted to Schwellenbach. He then called on Chester Bowles, who
usually doesn't sit in on cabinet meetings. Bowles took the position
very strongly that prices should be held rigidly on a 1942 basis; that
there should be no break in the price front; and that the situation in
each industry should be taken up by some prominent arbitrator. He
pointed out that the problem was so detailed that he couldn't handle it
properly in OPA. The President then called on Clint Anderson, who
presented the agricultural situation very vigorously and claimed that
with agricultural prices going down the farmers couldn't stand to see
an increase in wages.

The President then called on me, but Ickes, whose hearing is none
too good now, thought he was calling on him. He talked at some

1 Harley M. Kilgore, West Virginia Democrat; Glen H. Taylor, Idaho Democrat; James E. Murray, Montana Democrat; Charles W. Tobey, New Hampshire Republican; H. Alexander Smith, New Jersey Republican; Brien McMahon,
Connecticut Democrat.
2 That day Wallace sent Truman a list of observations that had been made by
leading scientists and public administrators about the pending Johnson bill.
Those comments pointed out the enormous powers the bill gave to the Administrator and the Atomic Energy Commission. One paragraph, as Wallace put
it, conferred "the strongest controls over citizens not in the military service, in
either time of peace or of war, ever proposed in federal law." Wallace particularly noted another paragraph granting the commission authority to establish
security and secrecy rules and penalties for violating them. The bill provided
that those security rules should apply not only to all persons who par-
ticipated in the development of the atomic bomb, either directly or through
employment by a contractor, but also to all persons who had at any time
experimented with the release of atomic energy in amounts which the commission might retroactively establish as "constituting a national hazard or being of
military or industrial value."

length about the political significance of failing to meet the challenge of the present situation.

When the President called on me I pointed out that according to Bureau of Foreign and Domestic Commerce estimates there would be, as a result of the termination of the war, a total cut in the gross national product of about $40 billion in 1946 and a total reduction in wages of $20 billion, and that a reduction of this kind meant seven or eight million unemployed people next spring, which represented a great increase over the present unemployment. I said that a reduction in income of this kind and an increase in unemployment would have the greatest repercussions not only with regard to labor but also with regard to agriculture. I said very emphatically that some of the farm organizations were taking a very blind attitude and then I threw in parenthetically that I didn't want this statement quoted to the press and that if it were quoted to the press, I would not again speak on controversial issues in cabinet. The President said at this point that he felt the same way I did and that people shouldn't communicate to the press that which took place in cabinet meetings. I said that I would be most happy, in case there was a leak to the press, to communicate my views to the President, either by memorandum or face to face. I then went on to say that by one means or another there should be an average increase in basic pay rates of around 15 percent and that an increase of this sort would mean that the total shrinkage in wages for 1946 under 1945 would be only about $10 billion instead of $20. I said that the take-home pay of industry after payment of all taxes in 1946 would be about as great as in 1945. I said, in fact, that I had been told by OPA that the Treasury estimate was that the income of the corporations after paying taxes would be around $11 billion as compared with $10 billion in 1945. Vinson said he thought $11 billion was a little high. Everyone agreed, however, that the income of corporations after paying taxes would be twice as great as before the war.

The President then called on Jimmie Byrnes. As a result of several interchanges of conversation during Jimmie Brynes' presentation, it appeared that as a result of the elimination of overtime, industry could pay labor an increase on the average of about 9 or 10 percent without any advance in prices. I interjected to say that the increased efficiency of labor growing out of new technologies would make it possible to increase wages more than that without any increase in prices.

The President then called on Secretary Vinson, who took the point of view that Bowles could really do the job if he utilized the full powers under the Act. Judge Vinson seemed willing to see that there be some price increases. I pointed out that since 1940 there had been practically no increase in steel prices, whereas farm prices at the farm had gone up about 90 percent. Vinson thought that the automobile folks could make an advance of at least 15 percent in wages without reducing the profits below the prewar situation. Bowles showed me some figures indicating that in 1946 there would be produced about 85 per cent more cars than before the war but with only 35 percent more labor employed . . .

Re: 8:00 a.m. appointment with Dr. J. R. Oppenheimer, atomic scientist.

Oppenheimer told me that last spring before the first atomic exhibition took place, the scientists were enormously concerned about a possible eventual war with Russia.[1] A plan had been worked out while Roosevelt was still alive to communicate with Russia regarding the atomic bomb. Oppenheimer thinks this plan was tentatively presented to the British but that the British turned it down. He says Stimson had a most statesmanlike view of the whole matter and that the last thing he did before departing as Secretary of War was to write down this view. In this statement he fully considers the peril of the threat of the bomb to Russian-American relations. Apparently Stimson advocated turning over to Russia as well as to other nations the industrial know-how as well as the scientific information. I told Oppenheimer that this phase of the matter never appeared in cabinet meeting.

I never saw a man in such an extremely nervous state as Oppenheimer. He seemed to feel that the destruction of the entire human race was imminent. Apparently there is a very intense jealousy between him and Szilard. He spoke in the most slighting terms of Szilard. He has been in charge of the scientists in New Mexico and says that the heart has completely gone out of them there; that all they think about now are the social and economic implications of the bomb and that they are no longer doing anything worthwhile on the scientific level. He wanted to know if I thought it would do any good for him to see

[1] In March 1945 Szilard had written a memorandum about the necessity for international control of atomic weapons. At his request, Albert Einstein attempted, without success, to arrange a meeting for him with President Roosevelt. After Roosevelt's death, with anxieties rising among atomic scientists at Los Alamos and Chicago, Compton introduced Franck to Wallace. Franck gave Wallace a memo from the Chicago group explaining the restiveness of the scientists with military security restrictions and the futility of permitting statesmen to make international policy without precise scientific information. Stimson said as much to Truman. Oppenheimer's remarks to Wallace revealed a misconception about exactly what had happened during Roosevelt's lifetime; see Hewlett and Anderson, *The New World*, pp. 342 ff.

the President. I said yes, and he is going to try to get either Secretary Patterson[1] or Senator Kilgore to make an appointment for him. He told me that the President's statement to Congress had been written by Dean Acheson's assistant, a Mr. Herbert Marks, and that he had had something to do with helping Marks on the message. He says that Secretary Brynes' attitude on the bomb has been very bad. It seems that Secretary Byrnes has felt that we could use the bomb as a pistol to get what we wanted in international diplomacy. Oppenheimer believes that that method will not work. He says the Russians are a proud people and have good physicists and abundant resources. They may have to lower their standard of living to do it but they will put everything they have got into getting plenty of atomic bombs as soon as possible. He thinks the mishandling of the situation at Potsdam has prepared the way for the eventual slaughter of tens of millions or perhaps hundreds of millions of innocent people.

The guilt consciousness of the atomic bomb scientists is one of the most astounding things I have ever seen.

OCTOBER 23, 1945

As I listened to the President giving his message to Congress on universal military training and heard him speak about preparing the United States to meet any aggressor nation, I couldn't help thinking about the effect the message would have on Russia. It was almost like the prelude to the declaration of World War III.

As I walked out I said to Lew Schwellenbach, who was walking along beside me, "I wonder what effect this will have on the United Nations organization?" Somehow it frightened me.

Les Biffle[2] asked a number of us to stay to a luncheon in the dining room of the Secretary of the Senate. It is the place where since time immemorial the senators have gathered, especially senators of the Majority, to drink and settle things off the record. In addition to the Democratic senators and cabinet officers there were present Senator Taft, Senator Vandenberg, Senator Wallace White,[3] and Joe Martin. Jimmie Byrnes and Vandenberg were talking about the Polish question. Vandenberg was very savage against the Russians. Jimmie Byrnes was taking rather a judicial attitude. Byrnes mentioned that the great

---

[1] Robert P. Patterson had succeeded Stimson after the latter's resignation in September.
[2] Leslie L. Biffle, since 1937 secretary of the Senate.
[3] Wallace H. White, Jr., since 1931 Republican senator from Maine.

dispute he had had with Molotov was that Molotov insisted that all of the prisoners which the Allied armies took of former Russian nationals who had served in the German army should be turned over to the Russians. Byrnes' point was that Poles who came from that part of Poland which was east of the Prussian line should have the right to continue to be Poles. On this point it seemed to me that Jimmie was sound.

As the President left Biffle's office on his way to the White House he shook hands with me and I told him very briefly about Shapley's proposal to bring over some Russian astronomers. He seemed to be much interested . . .

The really significant conference of the day was with James Newman[1] and Creekmore Fath of OWMR. They referred to the memorandum which I had given to the President on the Johnson-May bill and said that they had also given a memorandum to John Snyder which he had passed on to the President . . . Newman says that Snyder has been assigned the duty by the President of following the atomic bomb legislation; therefore, he has the right and duty to call together various departments that would be affected by the legislation to consider whether changes should be made. Newman says that the Johnson legislation could now be defeated in the Senate and that it is essential for the administration to rewrite the bill.

Dr. Condon left with me a most interesting memorandum[2] with regard to the next step in the international control of the atomic bomb. The more I see of Condon the better I like him. He mentioned that he was recently taken to a luncheon in the Pentagon Building by Kenneth Royall[3] and a number of others in the War Department who have been active in drawing up the Johnson bill. When Royall was asked why Secretary Wallace had not been consulted about the legis-

---

[1] James R. Newman, assistant deputy director of the OWMR, was also special assistant to the Senate Commission on Atomic Energy. Newman and Harold Smith, among others, persuaded Truman to oppose the pending May-Johnson bill on atomic energy and to support the substitute and ultimately successful bill of Senator McMahon.

[2] Condon's memorandum stated that "the international situation is deteriorating day by day." He suggested the President "call a Big Three conference of an exploratory character designed to bring out the terms of an international agreement leading to renunciation of the making of bombs together with development of a scheme of cooperation through mutual inspection which would satisfy all parties to the agreement that it was not being violated . . . Because of public confusion over the question of whether we shall 'give away the secret' it should be made clear that matters of this kind will not be discussed, that the subject matter is restricted technically to a study of adequate control measures and politically to means of expressing them in an effective document."

[3] Kenneth C. Royall, recently appointed Undersecretary of War.

lation he dismissed it rather airily, as though to say, "It is not necessary to consult with Wallace anymore." (There is a bare possibility this conversation came from Newman rather than Condon.)

Mrs. Roosevelt was looking exceptionally well and seemed to be in good spirits. She seems to have the same slant on the various international and atomic bomb issues that I have. She says Mrs. Bethune,[1] the colored woman leader, has been trying to get in to see Truman but Truman won't give her an appointment. Mrs. Roosevelt thinks Truman is a good man who has very poor advisers about him. She thinks it would be terrible if Pauley were appointed Secretary of the Navy. She says that Hannegan very much wanted Pauley as Assistant Secretary of the Navy when Roosevelt was still alive and that she herself intervened with Roosevelt against Pauley.

OCTOBER 24, 1945

The luncheon with Smith and Gromov[2] was most interesting. Smith had practically nothing to say except he wanted me to talk at the American-Soviet Friendship meeting at Chicago on November 16. I told him I didn't think I could do it. Gromov did most of the talking. It was obvious from what Gromov said that the Russians are deeply hurt at the various actions of the United States relative to the atomic bomb, Great Britain, Argentina, and eastern Europe. He can't understand why we are getting ready to loan so much money to Great Britain and are not prepared to loan much to Russia. He was very critical of Jimmie Byrnes. I told him Jimmie Byrnes had defended Russia against Senator Vandenberg and he found that hard to believe. He wanted to know why Jimmie Byrnes played England's game so exclusively. I told him it was traditional for Southerners to be friendly to England because England had been friendly to the South at the time of the Civil War. He was very critical of our letting Argentina into the San Francisco Conference. He cannot understand why we let Argentina get away with all kinds of anti-democratic programs while at the same time we insist on democracy in the Balkan States.

Alexander Sachs[3] went into great detail concerning his relationship

---

[1] Mary M. Bethune, a friend of Mrs. Roosevelt and a leader in black women's organizations, had served since 1934 in a succession of federal offices.

[2] Edwin S. Smith, director of the National Council of American-Soviet Friendship, and Anatola B. Gromov, First Secretary of the Soviet embassy in Washington.

[3] Alexander Sachs, while an economist with the investment house of Lehman Brothers, had helped to organize the original effort to interest Roosevelt in atomic research. There exists no known documentary record of what he told Wallace he had agreed upon with Roosevelt about the use of the atomic bomb.

with Roosevelt and the atomic bomb during 1939, 1940, and on up through the year 1944. He thinks we made ourselves morally culpable when we dropped the bomb on Hiroshima. He said the way he had planned it out with Roosevelt was that the first bomb would be dropped with representatives present from all the neutral nations, including those neutrals who leaned toward the fascists. The results of their findings would be publicized and then the second bomb would be dropped on an island off the coast of Japan, after the Japs had been warned to vacate all their civilian population. Sachs said our moral prestige in the world is very low as a result of the way we used the bomb. He also said that during 1940 and 1941 the War Department had absolutely no faith in developing the bomb. He says he was responsible for the President's appointing Vannevar Bush but he says that Vannevar Bush is definitely a tool of the big corporate interests. I was amazed that he should also say this was true of Conant. He described General Groves as very ambitious, intelligent, and a fascist. He said General Groves was in the pocket of Carpenter[1] of du Pont. Sachs says that our own foreign policy is very, very bad; that we are being too much guided by the concepts that guided us at the first peace conference. He said the realistic approach was to look on the world now as being dominated by three great nations. In the main his views were the same as the other scientists. He told me he had dropped his connection with Lehman Brothers the minute he started to work on the atomic bomb and that since that time had been a consulting economist . . .

OCTOBER 25, 1945

. . . The last time I had seen Joe Alsop[2] was in Kunming when he was serving as a press agent for Chennault. He now weighs 157 pounds as compared with 249 when he was at his fattest nine or ten years ago. At that time he weighed 70 pounds more than I and now he weighs about 30 pounds less. Joe is getting ready to start up his column again in partnership with his younger brother . . . He is violently against Stilwell and Stilwell's publicity man, Joe Davies. He is equally violent against Russia. He is for Generalissimo Chiang Kai-shek. His ideal apparently is T. V. Soong. He is violent against the

---

[1] Walter S. Carpenter, Jr., president of the du Pont Company which had, under government contract, played a major part in the development of the atomic bomb.

[2] Joseph W. Alsop, Jr., journalist and author, had been an aide to Chennault.

Chinese communists and apparently has no comprehension of what the average Chinese farmer is up against. He was very skeptical about Truman. He thinks Truman gets too much of his advice from his military aide, General Harry H. Vaughan, and his naval aide, Commodore J. K. Vardaman. He is a strong admirer of Jimmie Byrnes and thinks the present State Department setup is excellent. He described his own position as a man well left of center but not a communist. I said that was my position also but that I didn't agree with him about the violent attitude against Russia. I said if I felt like he did about Russia I would advocate immediate war with Russia. I said if we were not going to have immediate war with Russia we had better be friends with Russia. Alsop concluded by saying that it was inevitable that all the world would be communistic within a relatively few years. I said that on the contrary we could work hard to make friends with Russia and to build up a really strong United Nations organization; that we didn't need to have the fear of Russia hanging over us like we had the fear of Nazi Germany hanging over us . . .

OCTOBER 26, 1945

At the cabinet meeting Jimmie Byrnes reported on the London meeting.[1] His method was the chronological one. First, he dealt with the question of Italian rearmament. It seems that the Russians wanted to let the Italians rearm as much as they wished. The United States led most of the other nations in the view that the Italians should not be allowed to rearm; that it would be bad for them; that they didn't have the wherewithal to enable them to develop a substantial army and navy; that they had no business having them anyway. Byrnes said the real reason for the Russians wanting the Italians to rearm was to set a precedent for the Greeks to rearm. He said that the Russians believe they are going to get the upper hand eventually in Greece and that they want to have an armed Greece to offset British influence in the Mediterranean.

Byrnes dealt with a great many points one after another, each designed to show the Russians up in a bad light. I have no question as to the truth of his report but neither do I have any doubt that Jimmie was rather anxious to have the Russians shown up in a bad

[1] Byrnes had recently returned after several exhausting weeks of negotiations at the first meeting of the Council of Foreign Ministers, set up by the Potsdam Conference.

light. Jimmie said that he never lost his temper in dealing with Molotov but that his temper had never been so sorely tried.

At the conclusion of the cabinet meeting the President made the point that we were not going to let the public know the extent to which the Russians had tried our patience but that we were going to find some way to get along with the Russians.

At the close of the cabinet meeting I spoke to the President about when he was going to send up Condon's nomination to be Director of the Bureau of Standards. He said he would do it early next week. I also gave him a nice letter for him to send to Briggs, the retiring Director of the Bureau of Standards.[1]

I then spoke to the President about Harlow Shapley's proposal to bring over fifty Russian scientists to the United States. He said that would be perfectly splendid and that he would like to see Harlow Shapley. I then gave the President the attached memorandum dated October 19 which had been prepared by Condon. I didn't tell him Condon had prepared it. I merely said that it had been prepared by a scientist not in the Department of Commerce. He glanced at it but didn't read it all. He saw enough of it, however, to be moved to say that he was planning to have Bevin and Attlee over here soon to talk with them about the atomic energy matter preliminary to talking with Russia. I told him I thought that was fine; that at the moment the prestige and leadership of the United States were definitely on the skids and that it was necessary for him to move out very decisively. He said then he was going to clear all that up in his New York speech. I remembered then that he had referred to his New York speech the last time I had seen him. I told him that his Reelfoot Lake pronouncement had had a very unfavorable effect on both British and Russian public opinion;[2] that in some safe way he must get the moral burden of

[1] Lyman J. Briggs had held that post since 1933.
[2] At Reelfoot Lake, Tennessee, a fishing resort, Truman had had "an old-fashioned bull session" with the reporters there with him. He had said that scientific knowledge, by its very nature, could not be withheld, but that he had no intention of sharing engineering secrets. The United States alone of all nations, he added, had the industrial capacity and resources necessary for producing the bomb. To his audience, as they reported his remarks, he seemed to be minimizing the importance of international control of atomic weapons. In New York on October 28, in his Navy Day speech, Truman made his intentions clearer. The United States, he said, would open discussions about the control of atomic explosives with Great Britain and Canada, and later with other countries, before the formal organization of the United Nations. Those talks would look to the free exchange of fundamental scientific information, though they would not relate to manufacturing the bomb. American possession of the bomb, "a sacred trust," constituted, he said, no threat to any nation. The following week the White House announced that Prime Minister Attlee would be in Washington November 11 to begin the talks, as the President had promised.

carrying the atomic energy secret over on the United Nations organization; that as long as we were following our present policy we would be looked on with suspicion and fear. I pointed out at some little length the dangers of playing a one-sided game on the side of the British; that it was advisable when we safely could make the loan to make the Russians a loan proportionate to their needs comparable to the loan made to the British.[1]

I pointed out that the Russian attitude in the Balkan States was not so greatly different from our attitude with regard to Mexico and Cuba. I referred to my trip to Mexico in December of 1940, stating that in all probability Almazan would have been elected but that the United States had finally decided to back Camacho and that I had been sent down there to serve as a front for the United States to help prevent what otherwise might have been a revolution.[2] President Truman said he had not been aware of that situation. I then referred to the way in which Spruille Braden recently in Cuba had thrown his weight around to make certain that Dr. Roman Grau San Martin became President, in spite of the fact that there were revolutionary forces brewing in Cuba which without our intervention would have prevented San Martin from becoming President.

I said that Russia, with her more or less illiterate neighbors, untrained in democratic processes, would inevitably take, in terms of her situation, steps somewhat corresponding to those which we have always taken with regard to our more or less illiterate neighbors with poorly established democratic processes. Truman replied that yes, Russia was always talking about a cordon sanitaire. He talked as though he completely agreed with me and as though the thing he most wanted in the world was an understanding with Russia which would make impossible a third world war.

I said to the President there was grave danger that during the next ten years Russia might hang as a specter over the world economy in the same way as Nazi Germany did during the decade of the thirties. I said it would be possible to prevent that and we should do everything possible to prevent it. I said if we didn't prevent it we would inevitably have from five to ten million people continuously unemployed because of the fear of World War III that would be engendered in the hearts of the businessmen and especially the investing public.

1 Truman and Byrnes had already substantially decided against making a loan to Russia.
2 Manuel Avila Camacho had won a tense election in 1940. He was a more conservative reformer than his predecessor President Lazaro Cárdenas or his rival of 1940, Juan Andreu Almazan, whom organized labor had supported.

Friday night at Hot Springs, Virginia, General Marshall gave a talk to the Business Advisory Council, the fundamental essence of which was that we were demobilizing too fast and that we should go all out for universal military training. The businessmen loved it.

OCTOBER 30, 1945

I testified for seven hours before the House Committee on Expenditures with regard to the Full Employment bill. Then in the evening I gave a talk before the American Society for Public Administration and answered questions for an hour. This made it a busier day than usual.

At the Edward C. Carter[1] meeting Carter made a most interesting talk with regard to his trip to Russia. He said he was in Moscow at the time the atomic bombs fell on Japan. He said that Litvinov told him after the second atomic bomb fell, "Those are the only two atomic bombs that will ever fall. With this power in the hands of the United States it is bound to be used for peace and not for destruction." Later on, after the President made his Reelfoot Lake statement, the whole attitude in Russia changed. Carter seemed to think that the change in attitude between the time the President sent his atomic bomb statement to Congress and the time he made his offhand newspaper statement had a pronounced effect on international affairs and especially on Russia. Unfortunately, I had to leave early and did not hear Carter's complete statement.

NOVEMBER 1, 1945

. . . At the dinner with the Luces, Bill Benton and his wife were also present. Most of the time was taken up by Henry Luce telling in a very slow and rather halting way about his 31-day trip around the world. Luce is a very strong admirer of the Generalissimo, who he thinks is a heroic figure. He has no use whatever for the Chinese communists. It seemed to me that Mrs. Luce was more realistic about the Chinese than Henry. It seemed to me as though Henry were continually modifying his sentences so as to make sure that all of them contributed to the utmost to make the Generalissimo a hero. He was in Kunming at the time the Generalissimo deposed Governor

[1] Edward C. Carter, secretary-general of the International Secretariat of the Institute for Pacific Relations.

Lung Yum. He thought the Generalissimo had shown unusual astuteness in picking a time when Lung's army was out of the way.

Luce thinks that the Chinese communists have received too good a break from the American press. He said the hottest spot in China right now was in the province of Shantung. He referred to that as his "native province." Apparently he was born there.

Luce wanted to know my opinion as to what could be done for China. I told him in my opinion the first thing to do was to stop inflation and get in a considerable quantity of textiles. From a longer range point of view I urged that we get in various types of technicians, especially men who could get really practical information to the Chinese farmers. I suggested that from the immediate point of view he get in touch with Tom McCabe,[1] who has charge of army surpluses abroad.

Throughout the evening Bill Benton was very reverential toward Henry Luce, acting toward him as though he were an oracle speaking words of the utmost wisdom. Mrs. Luce also was very deferential toward her lord and master, although it was rather obvious that her brain worked twice as fast as the slow-spoken Harry's. Harry was under the continual necessity of trying to twist the truth in order to make it come out with the answer he wanted. Mrs. Luce was enjoying the luxury of saying what popped into her mind first. Mrs. Luce freely confessed that she hated Russia. Henry Luce probably hates Russia even more but he concealed it more skillfully in order to give his reportorial comments greater weight.

On the atomic bomb thing Mrs. Luce seems to be right in many particulars. She says that as much as she hates Russia, she is convinced that Russia will have the secret within a very few years and that, therefore, it is especially important to get the whole thing under the control of the United Nations Organization as soon as it can be got there effectively. Just as I was leaving Mrs. Luce said she was sorry that the season was so far along; that she would like to play tennis with me . . .

NOVEMBER 5, 1945

Just before the meeting in Secretary Vinson's office I asked Will Clayton what he felt the Russian needs for a loan were as compared with the British. He said he didn't think the Russians had anywhere

---

[1] Thomas B. McCabe, president of the Scott Paper Company and since February 1945 Army-Navy Liquidation Commissioner.

near so great a need for a loan as the British. I said I understood Mr. Kaplan in FEA had estimated the Russians needed a loan much larger than the British. Clayton then said he thought the British needed the loan in order to import more goods to sustain their standard of living and to prepare themselves to engage in world trade. Harry White interjected to say that he felt the Russians had just as much need for a loan to sustain their standard of living as the British and that as a matter of fact the Russian standard of living was far lower than the British; that it was much lower than before the war . . .

Just before I swore in Condon, Brian McMahon called up to say that the FBI and the War Department claimed Condon was a "pink." I told McMahon that if Condon was a "pink" then he, McMahon, was a "pink" and so was I. I might also have said, although I didn't, that if Condon is a "pink" the FBI and certain segments of the Army are Nazis. McMahon said that General Groves and someone from the FBI were coming up to see him and that he would let me know their story later on.

NOVEMBER 6, 1945

At the cabinet luncheon the President asked Jimmie Byrnes to talk about the Chinese communist situation. The President said, "Tell the cabinet what Stalin said about the Chinese communists." Jimmie replied by saying that Stalin at Potsdam had called the Chinese communists a "bunch of fascists." Stalin also had said, according to Jimmie, that the only chance he saw for stable government in China was the Kuomintang around the Generalissimo. President Truman said that the Chinese communists had worked with the Japs. Jimmie Byrnes said that President Roosevelt had followed a policy throughout of backing up the Chiang Kai-shek government. I couldn't help remembering what the President had told me before I left on the trip to China; also what Lauch Currie had told me about the President's attitude. Perhaps I should have spoken up but I didn't say a word. It seemed as though the President and Secretary Byrnes had made up their minds as to the course they were going to follow and that any effort to speak about the true situation in China would be misunderstood. I think it is undoubtedly true that the Russians don't look on the Chinese communists as communists. But that doesn't mean that they don't have a great deal of sympathy among the masses of the Chinese people. President Roosevelt, of course, did his best to get the Generalissimo and the communists together. Apparently this has been hidden from Jimmie Byrnes and President Truman. It is my observation that the Russians wished Generalissimo Chiang Kai-shek well but wondered why he had so many rascals around him.

The President called attention to the fact that this was the first time he had met with the entire cabinet and no one but the cabinet. He said he had complete confidence in every man present. He said in the future he was going to keep his afternoons free for conferences with the members of the cabinet. He said he wanted the greatest harmony among the members of the cabinet . . .

NOVEMBER 7, 1945

. . . At Secretary Byrnes' office we discussed British counter proposals on the loan. Strangely enough, the British have come back to the proposal which I suggested in the first place, a month ago, namely, that their payments be deferred in case their exports and invisible balance should fall below a certain level. In the first instance the British had been very unfavorable to this approach.

At Ambassador Davies' luncheon there were present two Poles, Janusz Zoltowski, Chargé d'Affaires of the Embassy, and Stanislaw Mikolajczyk, Vice Premier and Minister of Commerce of Poland. I asked Mikolajczyk what truth there was to these stories which Senator Vandenberg was telling about the way the Russian army was abusing the Poles. He said there were certain marauders in Russian uniform who didn't belong to any of the units officially stationed in Poland who were causing a lot of trouble. Mikolajczyk had spoken to Stalin about it and Stalin had said he would straighten the situation out. Apparently the situation is not at all what Vandenberg says it is. However, there is still a lot of confusion. These two Poles were very eager to work out a friendly relationship with Russia. They went into some detail describing the great problem ahead of them in getting the population properly placed. I was amazed to have them tell me how nearly East Prussia had been vacated by the Germans.

At John Snyder's office we went over the way in which the Office of War Mobilization and Reconversion could change the Johnson-May bill. They had the original version in one column and their suggested changes in another. Kenneth Royall, the Undersecretary of War, carried the battle for the War Department, although Bob Patterson was present. It seems that Royall and another army officer by the name of Marbury[1] drafted the Johnson-May bill under the supervision

[1] Wallace had in mind William L. Marbury, a Baltimore lawyer, whom Patterson had made chief counsel on War Department contracts.

of Conant, Karl Compton, Vannevar Bush, George Harrison,[1] Jimmie Byrnes, and several others. Kenneth Royall started out by saying how after the bill had been drafted it had been cleared by the State Department, the Attorney General's office, and the Department of the Interior. I asked them why they had not cleared it with the Department of Commerce. He had no defense. Later on I asked Bob Patterson the same question. He also had no defense. I said, "Well, I take it you cleared with Secretary Ickes because you thought he had a higher nuisance value than I did." Ickes and I carried the ball against the War Department. Royall told how they had tried to get in touch with the various scientists who had been criticizing the bill but the scientists would not see them. He qualified his statement by saying that they had tried to get in touch with everybody but Szilard and indicated that the War Department didn't think much of Szilard . . .

I exchanged telephone views with Harold Ickes and we both have the idea that a certain small group of scientists which works pretty closely with a certain small group of industrialists, who in turn work very closely with the War Department, are trying to control the atomic energy thing in their own way. Pregel says the only way the atomic energy thing can be made safe for the world is to develop its peacetime potentialities as rapidly as possible. After noting the way in which the Army has spread rumors about Pregel, Szilard, and Condon, I am inclined to think they will knife anybody who, directly or indirectly, fights the legislation which they are pushing. The war psychology has gotten into their blood and the ends justify the means. I am expecting them to circulate the most absurd stories.

NOVEMBER 8, 1945

. . . When Henry Hart of *Fortune* came in he started out in a way which led me to think he wanted to drive a split between me and the Truman administration. He is writing a story illustrated with color photographs on each of the cabinet members for the January *Fortune* magazine. I told him I was very happy at my work and that I felt it was possible for the Secretary of Commerce to make some contribution toward preventing the debacle which came after World War I. When he went out he said, "Well, I hope I can vote for you in 1948." I said, "Don't you think you had better make it 1952?"

[1] George L. Harrison, New York banker, had been a special consultant to Stimson on the Manhattan District and was co-chairman of the Interim Committee on postwar atomic policy.

Dear Mr. President:

Immediately after the cabinet meeting this morning, John Snyder suggested to me that I write a letter to you giving my impressions of the analysis of the May-Johnson Bill made by the Office of War Mobilization and Reconversion.

Before taking up the OWMR recommendations, I should like to say that the cabinet discussion this morning was very much to the point in that it had a direct bearing on the control features of the proposed Atomic Energy Commission. You, and many of the rest of us, were concerned because the House and the Senate had exempted some 10 or 14 agencies from the Reorganization Bill. The point was made that some agencies had strong lobby power, stronger in fact than that of any cabinet member, or even the President. The point that I should like to make is that the Atomic Energy Commission as proposed in the May-Johnson Bill has potentially the opportunity to become much more powerful than the Interstate Commerce Commission, the Federal Deposit Insurance Corporation, the Federal Trade Commission, or even the Army Engineers.

It seems to me all important, therefore, that the administrator of an Atomic Energy Commission—the person who would be most responsible for directing the development of this great new force—be brought immediately under the control of the President and that he not be placed under the commission. I am confident that with the May-Johnson Bill as it now stands it would be easily possible for certain groups that definitely do not stand for what you and I stand for to gain an astonishing amount of control in an amazingly short time.

The OWMR analysis of the bill recognizes this all-important matter of assuring democratic control of the Atomic Energy Commission. I should like wholeheartedly to endorse the OWMR recommendations which would remove the restrictions on the authority of the President to assume responsibility to the people for the activities of the commission. Provisions should be made in the bill to enable the President to remove members of the commission when he deems it necessary in the national interest, and for the administrator to be appointed by the President with the advice and consent of the Senate, with tenure, as in other major appointments, at the President's pleasure.

Of major importance also is the OWMR recommendation that the bill be revised to place at least as much emphasis on atomic energy for peaceful purposes as for national defense. In my opinion it is important to place *much more* emphasis on the peacetime development of atomic energy. We must recognize that the development of atomic energy for industrial purposes may soon be of much greater concern to the nation and have greater effect on our economy and our way of life than further improvements of the atomic bomb. It will of course continue to be of the greatest importance to find the road to international peace, but while working in this direction we must be mindful of the industrial peacetime implications of atomic energy. I endorse, therefore, the specific recommendations made in the OWMR analysis with respect to the basic policies and objectives to be pursued by the commission.

I am not in accord with the OWMR recommendation that members of the commission should be full-time personnel if the administrator is responsible to you. If the administrator is made directly responsible to the President, it seems to me that members of the commission should serve on a part-time basis; and that in addition to representatives of the various elements of the American people, they could also include representatives from the various cabinet departments most concerned with this vital problem. Such an arrangement would result in better integration of federal activity in respect to atomic energy development and control and further strengthen the principles of democratic responsibility in the administration of the commission.

Atomic energy is potentially the major factor in our domestic, economic, and political life. This leads me to concur in the OWMR recommendation that it would be more in keeping with American democratic principles and traditions to provide that neither the administrator nor the deputy be an active member of the armed forces.

The recommendations made by the OWMR as to research in the field of atomic energy are also in the public interest. Especially important is the recommendation for provision to secure to the public the fruits of inventions or discoveries resulting from the expenditure of public funds . . .

In agreement with the OWMR recommendations I regard the provisions of the May-Johnson Bill as extreme in the matter of security regulations and violations. The recommendations made by the OWMR should receive your complete support. Moreover, positive emphasis should be placed on the importance of maintaining complete freedom in research endeavor to assure a climate in which science can best develop. The continuation of wartime security regulations, such as those imposed in the development of the atomic bomb, into peacetime research activities would greatly retard scientific progress and would probably drive many of our most talented scientists into other fields.

I am in full accord with the recommendation by the OWMR for complete nationalization of production, processing, and ownership of fissionable materials. As you yourself have indicated, atomic energy is a force too revolutionary to be dealt with in the framework of old ideas and I cannot conceive that the materials from which this force may be drawn should ever be in the hands of any but the government representing all the people of the country. It would seem to me just as dangerous to permit private interests to own, produce, or process fissionable materials in significant quantities as to permit, say, any private group to raise its own military force or to store its own arsenal of weapons.

The OWMR recommends that the same policy extend to the development of devices which may be used with atomic energy. I do not agree, and I strongly urge that the development and utilization of atomic energy for industrial purposes be placed in the hands of free private enterprise as far as can be consistent with public safety and security. Government controls or government monopoly of uses of atomic energy should be restricted as much as possible and should be accepted only when necessary to public welfare. I favor a policy of nonexclusive licenses for all important economic applications of atomic energy, with the government reserving only the right to establish safety and security regulations to govern such licensees. Inventors of devices for the economic use of atomic power should secure a reward for their genius in the form of reasonable royalties under such nonexclusive licenses.

In light of the major way in which atomic energy can affect our economic, social, and political life I cannot too strongly urge the importance of effecting modifications of the May-Johnson Bill along the lines indicated by the OWMR recommendations and the further suggestions made above . . .

NOVEMBER 9, 1945

At the cabinet meeting the President started out by saying that the Republicans were getting ready to open up a real attack on us . . .

. . . I presented . . . charts[1] to the cabinet. The President seemed

[1] The charts expressed predictions of the Department of Commerce about gross national product and national income. They revealed the importance of generating more consumer buying power to prevent a recession. To the same end, and on the basis of related statistics, Wallace had announced his belief that the automobile industry could raise wages 15 percent in 1946 and another 10 percent in 1947 without jeopardizing profits.

quite interested in these charts and stopped around to talk to me about them after the meeting was over. I told him that our objective should be to get $30 billion more consumer dollars; that we should have $130 billion consumer dollars instead of $100 billion. He said yes, we must get full production as soon as we can. He said, smiling very whole-heartedly, "We can get thirty billion more consumer dollars." He takes matters of this sort very confidently and lightheartedly; I hope he has a firm basis for his confidence . . .

NOVEMBER 13, 1945

. . . I sat at the left of Prime Minister Attlee at dinner. He is a rather mousy little man who speaks without spark. He made it clear that the socialism of England is derived from William Morris and that it has a Christian base in contradistinction to the Marxian socialism of the Continent. He feels like he is preaching pure Christian doctrine when he preaches socialism. I told him that if socialism were to gain in the United States it would have to have the same kind of base as in England; that the Marxian socialism would never appeal to the rank and file of the common people of the Middle West who had a Christian background. He said, "You know we have a great many Catholics in our party in England. They are not offended by our type of socialism. There are a number of Catholics in my own constituency in Lime-house."

Attlee is very enthusiastic about the idea of having full employment in the United States and England as a method of preventing worldwide revolutionary disturbances. On the whole, everything considered, I would say that Attlee's administration will probably be more conservative than Winston Churchill's would have been. Certain very large industries may be nationalized but they will be nationalized in a very conservative way . . .

After dinner I talked to Admiral Somerville[1] . . . He was much disturbed about atomic energy and claimed that the only safe thing to do was to outlaw it so that it would not be used either for munitions or any other way. About this time Lord Halifax came up. Lord Halifax told the Admiral that he was completely unrealistic about atomic energy. Lord Halifax spent some little time going over the diplomatic history from 1930 to 1940. He claimed that Chamberlain could not have done anything else at Munich. He said that Churchill in 1939

[1] Admiral Sir James Somerville, head of the British Admiralty delegation in Washington.

had gone to him and said, "The thing you ought to do is to make friends with Russia." A year or two later Halifax asked Churchill, "Do you think if we had given Stalin everything he wanted in 1939, including the right to have his way in the Balkan States and in Poland, that he would have come in with us against Hitler?" Churchill answered, according to Halifax, that looking back on Stalin's problem he thought he would not have come in at the time for the simple reason that his army was not prepared at that time properly to resist the German army. Stalin, knowing the facts, simply had to play for time and use any method he could.

I then said to Halifax, "Well, when was it that you did make your mistake, then? Was it in Manchuria in September of 1931? Was it when Mussolini went into Abyssinia in 1935? Was it when Hitler went into the Rhineland in 1936? Or was it when Hitler went into Austria in April of 1938?" Halifax shied away from meeting the Manchurian issue; I thought he definitely was not frank on that. With regard to Italy going into Abyssinia, both he and Somerville agreed that if the British had taken a strong stand to close the Suez Canal to Italian shipping, the Italians couldn't have gone ahead with their Abyssinian venture and that they would not have called the British bluff. I raised the question of the extent to which we were now promoting economic situations which would result in the rise of other madmen at some future period. As I listened to Halifax and Somerville I couldn't help thinking, "Yes, there will always be a Britain—there will always be a Britain doing her part to perpetuate economic and political injustice in a way that will result in a war every generation."

The British are very likable people but it seems to me their whole attitude inevitably leads to causing the other peoples of the world to feel inferior and fearful and therefore willing and anxious to strike out in a violent way as soon as they think they can do so with some chance of success. The United States is the only country which has gotten away in a big manner with resisting the British. British policy in my opinion will be to try to set us in the United States against the Russians as much as possible . . .

NOVEMBER 15, 1945

. . . Joe Alsop was on a fishing expedition. He said that both Vinson and Hannegan were disgusted with the small-caliber men immediately around the President and they were putting forth pressure on the President to get rid of such little fellows as General Vaughan, Commodore Vardaman, George Allen,[1] et al. He wanted to know whether I felt the same way and whether I thought they would succeed. I didn't make any statement myself but said that I understood that Bob Hannegan felt this way very strongly. I didn't know about Vinson. As to whether they would succeed I said that it was my opinion that Truman was very loyal to his friends and therefore I wouldn't care to predict. I said that those immediately around the President were inevitably shot at and said this was true in Roosevelt's day also. Alsop interjected to say, "Ah, but they were giants in those days compared with these little men" . . .

At the dinner at Sumner Welles' home the chief subject of conversation was the 9-point declaration on the atomic bomb by the President, Attlee, and King.[2] I took Evatt[3] to the dinner and back again. He spoke very freely on Jimmie Byrnes, whom he looks on as a double-dealing reactionary who doesn't read anything and doesn't know anything. He looks on the British Foreign Minister Bevin in almost exactly the same light. He thinks Attlee is a sincere man but of very limited outlook.

The others present at the Welles dinner were Senators La Follette, Ball, McMahon, and Fulbright; also the Mexican Ambassador; Dr. Shotwell,[4] Marquis Childs, and Clark Eichelberger. Senator McMahon criticized at some length the first sentence in Section 8 of the declaration, which reads as follows:

[1] George E. Allen, professional friend of generals and Presidents, an entertaining and sometimes influential Washington wheeler-dealer.

[2] The declaration, signed that day by Truman, Attlee, and Canadian Prime Minister W. L. Mackenzie King, observed that no single nation could have a monopoly on atomic weapons, and called for using atomic energy to benefit mankind, instead of for destruction, and for the prevention of war. The signatories declared their willingness to exchange fundamental scientific information and to encourage free interchange of scientific ideas. To those ends, they promised they would make further basic information available from time to time. They also maintained that the release of military information would retard rather than assist the development of international safeguards against use of the bomb. They recommended the establishment of a United Nations commission to prepare recommendations for preventing military use and encouraging civilian use of atomic energy. The work of that commission, they said, should proceed step-by-step, with each stage instilling confidence for movement to the next. The United Nations, they concluded, with its commitments to the rule of law and to the banishment of war, afforded the best hope for world peace.

[3] Herbert V. Evatt, Australian Foreign Minister.

[4] Professor James T. Shotwell of Columbia University, an authority on international organization.

The work of the commission should proceed by separate stages, the successful completion of each one of which will develop the necessary confidence of the world before the next stage is undertaken.

He said this was evidence of the hand of General Groves. He thinks this is likely to lead to wrangling and misunderstanding. There was also the question of who would serve on the United Nations Commission. It was also noted there was no statement as to whether the matter was to be dealt with by the United Nations Security Council or the Assembly.

McMahon, during the dinner, took a number of cracks at J. Edgar Hoover. McMahon was assistant to the Attorney General under Homer Cummings. He said that Homer Cummings allowed Hoover to operate on his own too freely. He said that Hoover was taking a lot of credit for things that he had no right to take credit for.

Evatt in discussing China criticized the Chiang Kai-shek regime as fascist. He said it was a horrible military dictatorship . . .

NOVEMBER 16, 1945

At the start of cabinet meeting the President indicated that he thought Attlee, King, and himself had done a pretty good job in the declaration which they put out on November 15, the previous day. He said he wanted to get the opinions of everyone there about it. Vinson said he thought it was good. Acheson said the same; so also did Tom Clark, Patterson, Forrestal, and Hannegan. Ickes and Anderson were not there.

I said that the President knew from his conversations with me that the declaration carried out the points which I had made . . . I read the first paragraph of Section 6 and said I was sure that the second sentence of this paragraph was true.[1] I said, however, that this sentence was used in a rather deceptive way; that the paragraph had to do with the peacetime application of atomic energy and therefore the way the second sentence should have read would be "The industrial exploitation of atomic energy depends, in large part, upon the same methods and processes as would be required for military use." I said that for peacetime use it was not necessary to go nearly as far as in military use. I said that I had not had opportunity to talk with any

---

[1] That sentence read: "The military exploitation of atomic energy depends, in large part, upon the same methods and processes as would be required for industrial use."

of the scientists about this matter and that Condon was out of town. I said that I thought a number of the scientists would feel that the argument used in Section 6 was somewhat deceptive. The President said that the particular section to which I referred had been drawn up by the scientists. I said that Vannevar Bush didn't necessarily represent the view of all the scientists at the present time. The President said that Oppenheimer was in on it. I said, "Neither does Oppenheimer altogether represent the view of the scientists at the present time." Then I went on to talk about Section 7, saying that I noted that the international commission was to be set up under the United Nations Organization to prepare recommendations for submission to the Organization. I said I assumed this meant that this action was to be taken by the Assembly of the United Nations and this meant that the small nations would be in on it in a big way. I said no doubt this problem had been fully considered but it seemed to me that the small nations, as they considered the commission and its recommendations, would conceivably create considerable confusion.

I then dealt with Section 8, and particularly the sentence saying, "The work of the commission should proceed by separate stages, the successful completion of each one of which would develop the necessary confidence of the world before the next stage was undertaken." I said this sentence suggested that Russia would have to pass the first grade in moral aptitude before she would be allowed to enter the second grade in moral aptitude. I said I thought there was a fifty-fifty chance that Russia might accept. The President said that this step-by-step procedure is one which we have found is best in dealing with the Russians. I did not say so in cabinet meeting but I suspect the Russian agreement to come along will depend on just how far along her scientists are. If they have made a really great advance they may not care to accept England, the United States, and Canada as their teachers in international morality.

Schwellenbach, General Philip Fleming, Jack Blandford,[1] and John Snyder all agreed that the statement was excellent . . .

After the meeting was over Schwellenbach was rather slow coming around because he was waiting for John Steelman to come in. John Steelman[2] is the newest presidential adviser. At that time I gave the President the letter . . . with regard to the Export-Import Bank.[3] The

[1] John B. Blandford, Jr., then administrator of the National Housing Agency.
[2] John R. Steelman, then director of the United States Conciliation Service.
[3] The letter repeated Wallace's arguments for making the Secretary of Commerce a director of the Export-Import Bank.

President said that he had had a terrible time with the Export-Import Bank; that there had been some lobbyists in town who under the old setup had been making a lot of money out of getting loans for certain foreign countries from the Export-Import Bank. He said in trying to break up this bad situation he had been exposed by the Republicans to the necessity of appointing two Republicans on the board. He said the only position he had left was a position for a Republican. I told him that the work in FEA was such that the Department of Commerce should have a representative on the board and said we might see if we couldn't get someone in the Department of Commerce who was a Republican. He said that when he revised the board that Jimmie Byrnes had given him the devil of a time because of certain State Department attitudes. The way he said this indicated to me that the situation between the President and Jimmie is not at all happy. Apparently the President has heard some of the cracks Jimmie has taken at him in some of his press conferences.

Before the cabinet meeting took up I said to Bob Hannegan, "I understand that you are now looked on as one of the most progressive members of the cabinet." Bob said, "Does this mean that you think the cabinet is so reactionary?" I said, "No, not at all." Bob then thawed out quite completely and told me how he had been working with Sidney Hillman and that Sidney Hillman had told him that the number one business from the standpoint of the CIO people was the minimum wage bill[1] . . .

Hannegan, during the time I was talking with him . . . indicated that the President now had a number of advisers who were continually referring to his progressive friends as "Reds," saying to the President, "Don't pay any attention to what those 'Reds' want you to do."

NOVEMBER 21, 1945

. . . I had quite an extended talk with Spruille Braden and Carlos Montero Bernales, the Minister of Finance of Peru. They both claimed that the communists in Latin America played with the dictatorships. They said that Prado of Peru had an alliance with the communists, that Medina of Venezuela had such an alliance, that Batista of Cuba had had it, and also Vargas of Brazil. Braden claimed that the objective of these alliances was to drive a wedge between the United

---

[1] With Truman's support, Wallace had testified in behalf of the bill raising the minimum wage to 65 cents an hour.

States and the Latin American countries. The Finance Minister made the same claim even more emphatically . . .

Spruille Braden, who is very thick-set and weighs about 260 pounds . . . was extraordinarily vigorous in his statements about the communistic activities in Latin America. After I had heard both Braden and the Finance Minister talk at some length, I made the statement that their observations led me to think that it was very important that we have an understanding with Russia so that we could develop our inter-American relations without the danger of the communists continually stirring up trouble. I said it seemed to me that there might be a number of quid pro quos on both sides and there was a possibility that Russia might feel about the Balkan states in somewhat the same way as we feel about Latin America. At the conclusion of the luncheon I suggested we stop over and see Joe Davies. Spruille Braden told Joe how he felt about the matter. Braden went on to develop the thesis that he didn't like it when the communists in Latin American countries tried to make it so difficult when a democratic government took the place of a dictatorial government. Davies made the point that there are many definitions of a democratic government. Davies proclaimed that his real interest in the Russian affair was to be sure that we got a basis for an enduring peace. I could see that he was not so much impressed by Braden's presentation. I could also see that Braden was not in the least impressed by Davies. After listening to Braden I am beginning to think that perhaps he was brought in by Jimmie Byrnes as much because of his vigorous stand against communism in Cuba as because of his vigorous stand against fascism in Argentina . . .

NOVEMBER 23, 1945

At the cabinet meeting the chief subject up for discussion was strikes. Schwellenbach said that recent events had changed his opinion and that he is now convinced that the administration ought to step in and step in in a very decisive way. He pointed out that both the unions and General Motors were very recalcitrant and thought the government had to carry the ball. Jimmie Byrnes and Vinson expressed their opinions. I expressed briefly most of the points dealt with in the memorandum which appears herewith.[1] I said there would be some

---

[1] Wallace's memorandum, while defending the right of labor to strike, advocated legislation to create a fact-finding organization, a mediation and conciliation service, and compulsory arbitration in cases where labor and management could not agree. He also suggested arbitration of jurisdictional disputes and the prohibition of separate unions for supervisory employees.

difficulty in getting set up in law a fact-finding commission because the large corporations with great profits did not want their profits looked into. I said, however, it should be possible to have as a part of the facts for the public the general profit situation in industry . . .

The President, in shifting from consideration of domestic to foreign affairs, said, turning to Jimmie Byrnes, "I am sure you agree with me, Mr. Secretary, that if we can't straighten out these domestic affairs we shall not be able to have the influence we should have in international affairs. The people of the world won't have much respect for us if we allow ourselves to get engaged in a lot of internal disagreements."

Jimmie Byrnes discussed at some little length the Iranian situation.[1] He said that he was sure that the disturbances in Iran had been fomented. He called the attention of the President to the fact that at Potsdam he and the President were on record to the effect that we were in position to get our troops out of Iran within thirty days. He said the British were as bad as the Russians in wanting to hold their troops in Iran. He thought the only thing for us to do was to act at once and get our troops out. He said there were still 5000 men there but they were service men and not combat troops. Patterson agreed with Byrnes that we ought to get these men out at once . . .

NOVEMBER 27, 1945

. . . The cabinet luncheon started out by the President walking in with a roll of teletype yellow paper in his hand, saying, "See what a son-of-a-bitch did to me." Then he proceeded to read the story of Pat Hurley's resignation as it had been given out just a half hour previously.[2] He said that Pat Hurley had assured him just the day before that he was going back to Chungking. Pat Hurley's statement as read by the President over the teletype was a marvel of political demagoguery, appealing both to the British-haters and the communist-haters

[1] In September 1945 the United States, the United Kingdom, and the Soviet Union had promised to withdraw their troops from Iran. On November 18 a communist rebellion broke out in the province of Azerbaijan, and Soviet troops remained in Iran as one device for preventing the Iranian government from suppressing the rebellion. British and American oil interests in Iran added tension to the crisis. It was resolved the following spring. In March 1946 Iran protested against Soviet activities to the United Nations Security Council. In April the Soviet Union agreed to withdraw its troops in return for various political reforms in Azerbaijan and the creation of a Soviet-Iranian oil company. The Iranian parliament later blocked the latter project.

[2] At the National Press Club that noon, Hurley had attacked the administration, the State Department, and its Foreign Service officers as lacking any policy for China and, by innuendo, being soft toward the Chinese communists.

as well as to all those who don't like the State Department. I immediately thought it was some high Republican masterminding.

Bob Hannegan said that Hurley had called him up at 11:30 today saying that he very much wanted to see Bob and indicating that he was going back to Chungking. Bob Hannegan said that Hurley spoke in the very highest terms of Jimmie Byrnes and the President, saying that the President's Navy Day speech was absolutely perfect and that Jimmie Byrnes had given him absolutely splendid backing in every way.

Jimmie Byrnes said that Hurley had also assured him that he was going back to Chungking. Apparently, Hurley has had a violent attack of hatred against two State Department men, one by the name of John Service and the other by the name of George Atcheson.[1] He spoke most violently against them both to Jimmie Byrnes and to Bob Patterson. He claimed they were "Reds" going against the policy of the President continually . . .

The subject then shifted over to the desperate state of affairs in China. The President read a wire from Ed Pauley indicating that the Russians had taken all the machinery out of the factories in Korea and Manchuria. The President said that both England and Russia wanted a weak and divided China. He said we were the only big nation that wanted a united democratic China. The President said that unless we took a strong stand in China, Russia would take the place of Japan in the Far East. I thought to myself, "This (the President's attitude) means World War Number 3." Byrnes said that the Chinese Nationalists have informed the State Department that the Chinese communists now have lots of Russian tanks and guns. I couldn't help remembering that when I was in China in June of 1944 the Chinese Nationalists were continually claiming that the Russians, as the result of their pact with Japan, were pulling out their troops in a way to permit Japanese troops to fight against the Generalissimo. I found that the American

---

[1] John S. Service and George Atcheson, neither of them a communist, had offended Hurley and other uncritical supporters of Chiang Kai-shek by their honest but devastating reports about the weakness, corruption, and disingenuousness of the Generalissimo, his entourage, and his party. The previous March Hurley had arranged the transfer of Service and Atcheson from Chungking. He and Chiang were both distressed when Atcheson was assigned to MacArthur's staff in Tokyo. Service went temporarily to the personnel office in the State Department. In his letter of resignation, Hurley, still angry, accused them of siding both with the Chinese communists and with "the imperialistic bloc of nations whose policy is to keep China divided." Those paranoid observations were only the first of a long series of harassments to which the China lobby, the Luce publications, the Republican Party, and many misguided Democrats subjected the country's ablest experts on China.

Embassy people didn't believe the Chinese claims. Pat Hurley, however, is much more sympathetic with the Chinese Nationalists than Ambassador Gauss was.

Jimmie Byrnes also said that the Chinese Ambassador in Moscow had asked the Russians to remain in Manchuria until January. Apparently they feel that if the Russians pull out too soon the Chinese communists will take over. It all sounded to me like the Chinese Nationalists were playing the game which I suspected them of when I was there in June of 1944, namely, "Doing their dammdest to provoke a war between the United States and Russia." With all our superiority in material things I am inclined to think that the Chinese are smarter than we are in the psychology of diplomacy.

Jimmie Byrnes outlined his policy as being one of using our armed forces to disarm the Japs in China and Manchuria. He said we were obligated under the Japanese surrender terms to do this; that we were supposed to assure the Japanese troops on the mainland of transport to Japan so they could engage in civil peacetime pursuits. He thought we ought to carry out this assurance and in doing it make it possible for the Chinese Nationalist troops to take over as fast as the Japanese troops were withdrawn. He seemed to think there are about 200,000 of the very best Japanese troops, fully armed, guarding certain key railways in northern China and Manchuria. Altogether in Manchuria and China there are still about 720,000 Japanese soldiers and about 120,000 Japanese civilians. These are being moved out of Korea at the rate of about 8000 a day. At the conclusion of getting the Japs out Jimmie Byrnes thought the United States should stand pat and not give Chiang Kai-shek anything whatsoever until he agreed to come to terms with the Chinese communists and give them some places in a combination cabinet. Jimmie Byrnes again quoted what Stalin said to the President at Potsdam about the Chinese communists. It appears that Stalin called them brigands, robbers, and fascists. He also said that Stalin was for backing up the Generalissimo, thus furnishing the only hope for a strong central government in China. The various statements seemed to be as utterly contradictory as Hurley's own actions of the past month.

Jimmie Byrnes spoke at some little length about Bob La Follette, how exceedingly anti-Russian he was and how he believed that Russia was going to take over all of China. Bob La Follette advocated, according to Jimmie Byrnes, that the United States keep her troops more or less indefinitely in China until a stable government was really assured. It is amusing to see the way in which La Follette has now swung around to become an interventionist. Apparently those who had a large German constituency were for a strong America First policy prior to 1942, whereas today the same people are strong interventionists and anxious to follow a policy which would eventually get us into a war with Russia.

Clinton Anderson urged that General Marshall be appointed at once as ambassador to take Hurley's place.[1] The President said he planned to put General Marshall in as head of the Red Cross. This job would not be open, however, until March. When we left the cabinet luncheon the President and Jimmie Byrnes were getting ready to get hold of Marshall to talk him into going out to China. It was also suggested that he stop off in Moscow on the way. Marshall is very strongly anti-Russian and if he takes the job this may produce a rather unusual situation.

I suggested that former Ambassador Gauss be consulted with regard to the Hurley matter. Hannegan spoke up and said that Gauss, who was a Republican, was being recommended both by Senator Hart[2] and Senator McMahon as the man for the Republican place on the Export-Import Bank.

I mentioned that when it came to getting the Generalissimo and the communists together they might have a pretty hard job and cited the conversations I had had with the Generalissimo in June of 1944 in Chungking.

Somebody mentioned that there was great need for educating the American people with regard to the true situation in China. Jim Forrestal said that the New York *Times* and the United Press could be counted on to carry the ball from the administration point of view.

NOVEMBER 28, 1945

I gave the President my speech on "Peaceful Atomic Abundance."[3] He started out by saying that he liked the title very much. I called his attention particularly to the sentence which reads, "Thank God the key to the atom is owned by all the people and not by those creatures of special privilege who would hide behind a military or industrial

---

[1] Marshall agreed that afternoon, as Truman announced at once, to go to Chungking as the President's personal representative.

[2] Thomas C. Hart, retired Rear Admiral, recently appointed Republican senator from Connecticut to complete the unexpired term of Francis T. Maloney.

[3] Wallace delivered the speech at Madison Square Garden on December 4, 1945, to a meeting of the Independent Citizens' Committee of the Arts, Sciences and Professions.

cloak to use this new device to bring the peoples of the world into subjection to Atomic Imperialism." He liked the sentence and said that was just the way he felt. Again I called his attention particularly to the paragraph dealing with the methods of developing atomic energy for peacetime purposes.[1] Here again he agreed enthusiastically and wholeheartedly.

I called his attention to the paragraph dealing with commendation of the scientists for condemning the destruction of the Japanese cyclotrons. He said he agreed with me on the sentence but said he thought that might cause him some difficulties with MacArthur. I told him I would be most happy to take this sentence out.

When I first came in I referred to the broad general memorandum which I had left with him on atomic energy and he said that had been very useful to him; that he had used it in his conversations with Attlee and King.

I then told him I would like to talk with him briefly about the foreign situation. I told him that for the past 200 years there had been a continual race between the British Empire and the Russian Empire; that this was a matter of geographical position and historical tradition. I told him it was not our business to take sides in this race but that at the present time it appeared we were playing the British game and a fascistic game. I told him that the British actions in Greece had been pretty bad. I was going to list some others but he interrupted to say he agreed with me. I then said I was afraid that one of the troubles was with Jimmie Byrnes; that it was a part of the tradition of people raised in the South to play up to England. This is partly a tradition carried over from the Civil War and partly due to the fact that the South looks to England as its chief market for cotton. They are not familiar with the Russian language, the Russian background, or the Russian situation. I then said I didn't think Jimmie really understood just what was going on. He said he agreed with me entirely; that he didn't realize that I had watched the situation so closely as to catch what he was up against. He said the grand thing about the Hurley resignation was that it was going to give him a chance to get into the State Department to straighten it out.

I talked at some little length about the relationship between Russia and China on that long border and especially about the situation among

[1] The paragraph pointed to the extraordinary future possibilities of atomic energy as a source of power and of radioactive materials as research tools in biology, agriculture, and medicine. Returning to those ideas later in the speech, Wallace linked them to his vision of a future of shared abundance.

the Mohammedan tribes that move back and forth across the border. I told him that President Roosevelt had been his own Secretary of State and that, as I looked at the current situation, I felt that he also would have to be his own Secretary of State; that I didn't see any hope in the foreign situation unless he did take over. He professed himself to be much baffled by it all. He said he very much wanted to talk with me at greater length but now he had to go and eat lunch with his mother-in-law. I told him I would be happy to help him.

Just before I started to talk about the foreign situation I said to him that a number of newspapermen had been coming in, some of them apparently representing the extreme right and others the extreme left, saying that they understood I was going to resign. I told him that I had told them all that President Truman had given me 100 percent co-operation every time I had approached him on anything. He said, "I don't want you to resign and that comes from the heart" . . .

The President expressed considerable disquietude that the peacetime utilization of atomic energy would so shorten the hours of labor that the people of the United States would get into mischief. I said I could understand how he felt but it seemed to me that abundance should be made into a blessing rather than a curse; that I recognized that it took more spiritual strength to live with abundance than with scarcity . . .

After the luncheon given by Juan Chavez, the Peruvian minister, Harry White said he would like to see me. We drove over to the Treasury in my car. The point he wanted to make was that everyone recognized that the administration was very rapidly going to pieces on both the domestic and the foreign front. He thought I ought to come out in the very near future and make a very forthright speech in order to dissociate myself as nearly as possible from the impending wreck. He said the businessmen in New York City felt very strongly that things were going to pieces . . . I told White that the situation was so critical now that I thought I should do what I could to help the President and that I had found the President had expressed himself as willing to be helped. White broke out rather impatiently, saying, "Yes, that is the trouble, the President always uses good words but never does anything, or if he does act he acts weakly or on the wrong side." Harry White apparently is not [a] great admirer of his present chief, Vinson. Apparently he feels he is quite opportunistic.

Harry White told me that he was very much alarmed about Marshall's appointment to China because Marshall was anti-Russian and the Russians knew he was anti-Russian. He felt the Russians would place a very unfortunate interpretation on our sending our top military man to this post at this time.

After the staff meeting Condon wanted to tell me about the progress of the investigation by the Senate Committee on Atomic Energy. He showed me a Senate Atomic Energy Manual. This he said had been given to General Groves. General Groves had indicated the questions which he would and would not answer. With regard to the question dealing with British-American-Canadian cooperation Groves said he would not answer because his answers would reflect on President Roosevelt. He indicated that he had used his own judgment and had acted deliberately against directions from President Roosevelt. In view of Groves's disloyalty to President Roosevelt, Condon felt that it was very important that one broad question be answered, "In whose hands is the control of the present stockpile of bombs? Are they completely assembled and ready for use? Can the War Department furnish assurances that there is no possibility of our stock of bombs falling into the hands of unscrupulous persons?"

Condon told me that he felt now that Groves definitely was a fascist and that there was serious danger of a certain element in the Army at a certain stage of the game launching a bomb against Russia. He felt, therefore, that the stockpile of bombs should be under a type of lock whereby it would be necessary in order to get them out to use a series of keys coming from the President, the members of the President's cabinet, the president of the Senate, and the Speaker of the House. The danger of unscrupulous use is such that the United States for the first time is in danger of the kind of military coup d'état which happens so frequently in Latin America.

Condon went into some detail as to Senator McMahon's characteristics. He says that he has a very disorganized mind; that his office is a mess; that his instincts are good but that his capacities are small . . .

John Carter Vincent brought me up to date on the Chinese situation. As nearly as I can discover, he is absolutely sound in his views. He says the State Department has definitely been playing a pro-British game and that it has taken all that he and Dean Acheson can do to hold the scales even halfway level so far as Byrnes' actions are concerned. He is optimistic about the outcome of the Hurley affair. He welcomes the Marshall appointment but is deeply concerned about the underlying trend both in the direction of helping British imperialism and with regard to the State Department itself. I cheered him up by saying I thought the President was definitely susceptible of education. He made the same point as Harry White to the effect that the President oftentimes seems to use the right words but not to do anything effective.

NOVEMBER 30, 1945

The President opened the cabinet meeting by asking Schwellenbach for a report on the Labor-Management Conference. He called attention to the three united reports and indicated the split on the other three was not as great as might appear and said that apparently the conference was going to be just about what Henry Wallace had said it was going to be two weeks ago, namely, that a number of fine resolutions would be agreed upon but that none of them would apply to the present situation. When the President called on me I gave him very briefly the essence of what appears in the attached memorandum,[1] saying that this program would not meet with the approval of either management or labor but that such a program might be necessary in order to prevent Congress from doing something more drastic. McKellar said he didn't think the Senate would act suddenly or drastically . . .

DECEMBER 3, 1945

. . . I didn't go to the dinner . . . given by Secretary Byrnes to the senators for the purpose of discussing the British loan. But I did get in immediately after the dinner. From the Executive Branch were present Jimmie Byrnes, Fred Vinson, Dean Acheson, Will Clayton, Marriner Eccles, Tom McCabe, and myself. The senators present were Tom Connally, Walter George, McKellar, Wallace White, Austin, Vandenberg, Tobey, and Wagner. Connally said that if there was going to be a loan to England there ought to be a loan to Russia also. Vandenberg said that he was against the loan to England because he thought that meant a loan to Russia. He said the Senate with misgivings would vote to give a loan to England but would not vote to give a loan to Russia; that Russia would therefore be offended and that would mean war; that therefore a loan to England would mean war. He didn't phrase it quite this brutally but that was what he meant.

Connally didn't think England would ever repay the loan. George claimed England was bankrupt and ought to be given a bigger loan. George was pretty "tight" and at the start was brutal in his treatment of both Fred Vinson and Will Clayton. Dean Acheson told me after

---

[1] Predicting a failure of agreement at the Labor-Management Conference, Wallace in his memorandum repeated his earlier recommendations about fact-finding, conciliation, and arbitration.

the party was over that he never saw such stupendous ignorance in his life as that displayed by the senators. Tobey and Austin showed some comprehension of the nature and magnitude of the problem.

I agreed with Tom Connally that a loan to England meant there should be a loan to Russia. Fred Vinson, after the show was over, expressed disappointment that Jimmie Byrnes didn't carry the ball more. He thought Jimmie did a poor job of selling. Probably the senators were just blowing off and the situation was not nearly as bad as Dean Acheson thought. Will Clayton did, as usual, a good job of making a presentation.

DECEMBER 4, 1945

At the cabinet luncheon the President mentioned that Brian Mc-Mahon, who usually is a reasonable fellow, seemed to be going off on a tangent.[1] He said he thought it must be because of the advice he was getting from the scientists. I suppose he was referring to Condon and Newman and that his statement reflected something that Bob Patterson had told him. I asked who had control of our stock of atomic bombs. Bob Patterson interjected to say that there were not any atomic bombs; that the material out of which they were made was available but that the material was not assembled in bomb form. He did say, however, that they could be assembled in less than a day. He said General Groves was in charge. I said that it seemed to me that no one man should be in charge. I said that the material should be held under some kind of lock and key where it would be necessary to get the permission of the Secretary of the Navy, the Secretary of War, the Secretary of State, and the President in order to make the material available. Bob Patterson spoke up rather sharply to say, "I don't want control of this material; you can have it if you want it." I merely repeated that the President himself should have the supreme authority . . .

[1] Truman had assisted disaffected senators and scientists who opposed the May–Johnson bill, which was dead by this time. McMahon for his part had managed to become chairman of the Senate Special Committee on Atomic Energy. During December he permitted hearings to ramble on while he waited for James R. Newman of the OWMR and his associates to complete drafting a new bill, which McMahon was about to introduce. Wallace, the Chicago scientists, and others who had disagreed with Bush and with the May-Johnson bill were pleased by McMahon's measure, but the War Department hesitated to endorse it.

The cabinet luncheon was held on the *Williamsburg*, of which the President is very proud. It is by far the fanciest presidential yacht which has ever been in use. The skipper told me that it could go to Europe and back. The various rooms are fixed up in grand style . . .

The President brought up the subject of Alaska for conversation . . . I made the point that in order to develop Alaska the way it should be developed it would require much more governmental action than was necessary in places farther south. I said the individual farmer would not have much chance in Alaska. The President suggested that Ickes, Anderson, and myself get together to work out a program for Alaska. In view of the fact that the President mentioned Ickes' name first I very much doubt if anything will come of the suggestion.

Anderson brought up the question of sugar quotas. It seems the President out of the goodness of his heart gave the Philippines a quota of a million tons, feeling the Filipinos had done such a magnificent job fighting for us that they ought to have anything they wanted. Anderson told the President this had created great confusion in our negotiations with Cuba. I suggested to the President that he have an open mind with regard to the question. He said he had already made his decision. I said that it was important that anything we gave the Philippines got back to the Filipinos who were actually doing the work and suggested that if he would reopen the matter with the Filipinos on the basis of making sure of this point it might be possible to take care of the legitimate needs of the other sugar areas as well.

It is more and more evident that the President arrives at his decisions on the spur of the moment on the basis of partial evidence. He does *so* like to agree with whoever is with him at the moment . . .

I first told the President I was seriously disturbed about the way in which the atomic bombs or atomic bomb material were being held by General Groves and five people under him. I urged that he at once make arrangements whereby this material be put under the control of a man appointed by himself, by the Secretary of State, Secretary of War, and the Secretary of the Navy as a very minimum. I told him that General Groves was a Roosevelt hater and a Mrs. Roosevelt scorner. (Condon had told me that Groves in 1943 at Los

Alamos had called Roosevelt a son-of-a-bitch and had told two off-color stories about Mrs. Roosevelt.) I told the President that Groves felt that Roosevelt had made some blunders with regard to the international handling of atomic energy and that he, General Groves, would straighten the matter out on his own. (This statement was based on what Groves told Senator McMahon about two weeks ago.) I said, "It may be that Groves was altogether right and Roosevelt was wrong." President Truman interjected to say, "We can't conclude that because Roosevelt isn't here." I told the President it was important to move and to move fast . . .

I told the President the point I was making was merely that there was always a certain group in the Army who had their own ideas as to what constituted national security and that if the situation either on the national or the international front got bad you couldn't tell what they would do, especially if they had something like the atomic bombs at their disposal . . .

We then talked about the labor situation.[1] The President said he thought Phil Murray had not done right by him. He said that, last August 14, Phil Murray, Kennedy of the Mine Workers, and "that clothing man, let's see, what is his name?" I said, "Sidney Hillman." He said, "Yes, Sidney Hillman has the best brains of the lot." He said, "They sat here and told me they wanted the War Labor Board continued with the no-strike pledge up until January first. Now see what Phil Murray is doing to me, calling me a thief, etc." I told him I couldn't account for the violence of the CIO statement. I also told him that I hadn't seen any of the CIO people but the Electrical Workers, who had talked to me about another matter altogether. I asked his judgment as to whether it would be a good plan for me to see the CIO people in order to find out just what accounted for their very strong attitude. He said he thought it would be a good plan for me to see them if they made the inquiry but that I should not ask to see them . . .

The President got out the atomic bomb documents that Jimmie Byrnes was taking with him to Moscow and read a page or two about the commission which would be set up under the UNO. He also told

[1] On December 3 Truman had asked Congress to pass legislation establishing fact-finding boards to investigate labor-management disputes and providing for a thirty-day cooling-off period while those boards conducted their inquiries. Pending that legislation, which was not passed, he issued an Executive Order creating the boards. He hoped thereby to settle the ongoing automobile, oil, and meat-packing strikes and to forestall a threatening steel strike. His order provoked quick, angry protests from the UMW and the CIO.

me about the personal letter that he had sent Stalin and how he had
gotten a reply from this personal letter transmitted by wire within
two hours. This indicated to Truman that Stalin was very anxious for
the conference.

DECEMBER 14, 1945

. . . At the cabinet meeting the President asked where Jimmie
Byrnes was and Acheson said bad weather had forced him to stop
at Frankfurt. The President then mentioned that the Senate Committee on Atomic Energy was very anxious to see him (the President)
before Byrnes got to Moscow. The President thought they wanted
to see him in order that the President might get to Byrnes a caution
to hold back on giving the Russians any information about atomic
energy. The President said he was convinced they were wrong; that
the Russians had just as good scientists as we had; that the scientific
information was now available to everyone and that it was important
that we help create an atmosphere of worldwide confidence. Mc-
Kellar took quite violent exception to the President's statement.
Patterson stated that the Senatorial Committee had been egged on by
the scientists (meaning Condon and Newman) to ask General Groves
how many atomic bombs there were. Patterson said the senators themselves really did not want to know. The President at this moment
chimed in to say that he didn't really want to know either. I promptly
intervened to say with the greatest earnestness, "Mr. President, you
should know; also the Secretary of War should know, and the Secretary of the Navy." I said I agreed that giving any information of
this sort to the senators, especially to senators in executive session,
would promptly result in a leak, and returned to the original theme
and hammered with all the energy I could to the effect that the
President himself must have this information. The President retreated
in some confusion and said he guessed he should know and then
covered up by saying, "I do know in a general way." Jim Forrestal
agreed with me, saying that while he, himself, did not want the information he felt definitely the President should have it; that it was
a necessary protection for him in case any investigation ever were
made. I thought it was utterly incredible that Patterson and the
President should be willing to trust full information and responsibility
on this to a man like Groves and his underlings without knowing what
was going on themselves.

The President then turned to Secretary Schwellenbach and said.

"Well, how is your atomic bomb, the steel strike, coming along?" Schwellenbach gave the current details, giving it as his opinion that there would not finally be a steel strike. The President said he had been over the profits of the steel companies since 1890. He said they felt that they could afford to grant a wage increase if they got an increase of seven dollars a ton in their prices. I asked the question, "At what volume?" He replied, "Operating at sixty percent of capacity." Judge Vinson intervened to say that he thought they would be operating at more than 60 percent of capacity and therefore they would not need this much of an increase.

The President indicated that he had made a number of mistakes in taking off controls too soon and that he was now prepared to back up Chester Bowles to the limit. Judge Vinson then brought up the status of the full employment legislation.[1] He made the same presentation as he had made to me late Thursday night over the phone. He said the Senate bill had not been discussed in the committee and therefore it would be impossible to get it favorably considered on the floor of the House. He thought the thing to do was to pass the weak House version and rely on getting the matter straightened out in committee. I spoke up and said that following Secretary Vinson's conversation with me last night I had gotten in touch with Outland[2] and that I had undertaken to tell Outland in confidence the nature of my conversation with the President Thursday noon. The President said that was all right. This means, therefore, that the President is definitely prepared to come out with a statement on behalf of the Senate bill once the House bill is passed and before the conferees meet. I told the President that Outland was rather disturbed at the way in which Manasco and his colleagues were calling the Senate legislation socialistic and communistic. I said Outland was surprised at their indulging in such epithets in view of the fact that Republicans like Vandenberg had voted for the measure. The President then kidded McKellar on the Senate being a bunch of communists. Bob Patterson spoke up to

---

[1] The Senate had passed an employment bill that Vinson and Wallace considered satisfactory. Representative Carter Manasco, Alabama Democrat and chairman of the House Committee on Expenditures, opposed the whole concept of the Senate bill and was moving his committee to prepare a substitute measure. It eliminated a declaration of the right to employment opportunity, of federal responsibility for full employment, and of the pledge of federal resources to achieve that end. For a detailed account of the legislative history of the Employment Act of 1946 at this and other stages, see Stephen K. Bailey, *Congress Makes a Law* (New York, 1950).

[2] George E. Outland, California Democrat, a leading supporter in the House of the Senate's employment bill.

say that he was being attacked for having ordered the destruction of the Japanese cyclotrons. He said actually he hadn't been aware of signing the order but that the order had been put out in his name. He said Groves was responsible for the action. He said, however, that he was going to stand behind Groves; that he thought that a cyclotron was just as much an implement of war as a pistol. He said, "I know Henry Wallace doesn't agree with me." I said, "I most certainly do not. I think the destruction of the Japanese cyclotrons was an act of barbarism—as barbaric as the destruction of the library at Louvain." I said it was more proper to look on the cyclotron as a piece of iron than as a pistol; that it was more important in research than in making bombs and with the Japanese in their position it could not be used in making bombs. When I referred to iron, Bob Patterson interjected to say that he didn't think either Germany or Japan ought to be allowed to have much iron. I replied, "Well, iron is necessary to make agricultural implements."

Bob Patterson took violent exception. Senator McKellar said it was the Japanese who had committed an act of barbarism when they attacked us at Pearl Harbor. Later on Bob passed some rather humorous notes over to me, saying that he had ordered the destruction of the Japanese cyclotrons on the advice of the Secretary of Commerce. After the meeting was over I talked with Bob a little bit telling about the way in which cyclotrons were used in the construction of tagged atoms, which were very useful in conducting biological research. It was obvious that Bob knew nothing whatever about cyclotrons or about atomic research. He is merely in the hands of the generals. He promptly resorted to the position that both the Japanese and the German people were very wicked and he was going to do everything he could to see that they did not have anything with which to make war. Bob is a fair-minded person and a decent person but from a scientific point of view very ignorant. His instincts are of the highest but he is one of the most narrow-minded men I have ever met.

At the conclusion of the cabinet Dean Acheson came up to Bob Patterson and said, "I don't think we ought to continue making atomic bombs." Bob replied, "Well, if anyone forces me to reply to the question I could say, 'We don't have any atomic bombs.'" Then he added, "But we do have the materials all ready out of which we can make atomic bombs almost immediately. They just are not assembled." Patterson said, "We are keeping the plants running because if we closed them down we couldn't get them going again. Actually they are going to spend something over a half a billion dollars this year for making atomic bombs." Acheson's point was that as long as we were doing this the other nations of the world couldn't trust us. He said it was the old hen-and-egg proposition. We would not trust the other nations until they trusted us and until they trusted us we would not stop making atomic bombs. On the other hand, the other nations could not start trusting us until we stopped making atomic bombs. Arguments of this kind have absolutely no effect on an opaque mind like Bob Patterson's. It is a shame that Secretary Stimson could not have continued as Secretary of War . . .

DECEMBER 15, 1945

. . . In view of the comments I made Friday, December 14, about Bob Patterson and the cyclotrons, it is only fair to say that Bob apparently was influenced by the discussion in cabinet meeting and on Saturday morning called me on the phone to say that he had admitted it was a mistake.[1] . . . It appears, therefore, that my comments regarding Patterson on Friday were too harsh. It also should be said, however, that if I had not come out vigorously Patterson would probably not have taken the action he did.

DECEMBER 18, 1945

John Beecher[2] told an amazing story of his experience at Stuttgart, Germany, and Antwerp, Belgium, running UNRRA affairs in cooperation with the British. From what he tells me the British performance has been absolutely disgraceful. He claims that the British by their black market methods have siphoned off tens of millions of dollars' worth of UNRRA materials from the docks at Antwerp. He had the matter up with the British authorities there and they tried to scare him by a pseudo court-martial. He also told about his experience with the British in handling displaced persons at Stuttgart. The Army had asked him to process and sift out the Ukrainians who were supposed to go from the Stuttgart area back to that part of the Ukraine east of the Curzon Line. When he started to work on the problem there was a great uproar in camp and it appeared from the uproar as though none of the Ukrainians wanted to go back. The next day he took out

[1] Patterson regretted, as he told Wallace and Karl T. Compton, that he had not consulted leading American scientists before ordering MacArthur to destroy the Japanese cyclotrons.
[2] John Beecher, former editor of the Montgomery *Advertiser*.

of the group those Ukrainians who had on them the Free Ukraine buttons that had been supplied by Hitler. When they were taken out and put in a separate place he found that all of the remaining Ukrainians wanted to go back to Russia, so he loaded them up in trucks and took them to the place where the displaced Russians were. The Russians went over them one by one and accepted them all. Then they brought in as the last truckload those who had the Free Ukraine buttons on. They all turned out to be Poles. They were London Poles masquerading as Ukrainians and out to create the maximum of disturbance.

Beecher had a number of other illustrations dealing with the activities of the British and the London Poles. He said the British were training the London Poles so that they would fight against Russia to obtain the disputed territory east of the Curzon Line and west of the Russian line as it existed prior to 1941. Everything he said confirmed me in the view that there is grave danger of the United States' playing the British game and getting into all kinds of trouble in eastern Europe. Beecher said the Russians were absolutely correct in their handling of every situation that he had anything to do with.

I mentioned this situation a little later in the day to Gladieux[1] and Gladieux said that when he was with UNRRA he found exactly the same problem. He had a wealth of details about it. Apparently the British and the London Poles in their operations in Europe are first-class sons-of-bitches and many of the United States people are suckers in falling for their game . . .

Marquis Childs came in all hot and bothered about the atomic bomb. He had already written a story which had been sent off earlier in the day and therefore what he was asking of me was not for quotation. He shared my views that the all-important thing to the future of the world had to do with Russian-American relations, with the British situation as a corollary to that. Apparently he had been talking to some of the senators on the Atomic Committee up on the Hill who were very much worried because we were still making bombs and the bombs were under the control of General Groves. He wanted to know how I felt about that. I told him the bombs ought to be more directly under the control of the President; that the control definitely ought to be lifted to a higher notch than it was now. Childs said that he had found some very level-headed senators were of the view that if we were unable in the present conference to come to an agreement with the Russians with regard to inspection of their establishments

[1] Bernard L. Gladieux, Wallace's executive assistant.

along the principles laid down in the document signed by Truman, Attlee, and King, we should immediately declare war against Russia and drop bombs on her. He said the senators told him that we now had bombs which were 100 times as powerful as those which were dropped on Hiroshima. I told Childs that if the United States became an aggressor nation on this basis it meant our complete moral bankruptcy; that it meant that we, like the Germans, were going out on the basis of a superior race to dominate the world with a beneficent dictatorship. I said I just couldn't imagine the United States doing a thing of this sort but if the United States did that I would be very much tempted to leave the country; that I couldn't reconcile myself to living with fascists. I then closed on the optimistic note, saying I just couldn't believe the United States was a nation of fascists; that I couldn't believe these senatorial members of the Atomic Bomb Committee, level-headed though they might be, represented the views of the American people . . .

DECEMBER 29, 1945

. . . My brother-in-law, Charles Bruggmann, told me about some friends who were in Dublin, Ireland, recently. At a social gathering were present several Jesuit priests who indicated that one of their supreme purposes was to bring about a war between the United States and Russia. Later on I began to speculate about the forces that are interested in trying to bring about such a war. In addition to a small group in the Catholic hierarchy there is also a small group among the English Tories and a small group in the American Army . . . a small group among the American big-business hierarchy, a substantial group among the Chinese Nationalists, the London Poles, and in general the more wealthy people who live in the countries close to Russia. Also there is a small group in the Navy (note for example Admiral Stark's[1] statement in the Pearl Harbor hearings with regard to communism being a greater danger than Naziism); also there should be included in this group a very strong element in the Republican Party. All of these people feel that it is only by the United States whipping Russia that they have a chance to maintain their present position in life. Against this group is found the peace-loving people everywhere. Unfortunately, the love of peace is a general sentiment and doesn't bind people together in the same way as hatred binds together those who are intent

[1] Admiral Harold R. Stark had been Chief of Naval Operations at the time of Pearl Harbor. He commanded United States Naval Forces in Europe (1942–45).

on producing war between specific countries. The bulk of the Catholics, the bulk of the British, and the bulk of the common people everywhere do not want a third world war. These various groups that want a third world war in order to lick Russia are not at the present time working together but as time goes on they will tend more and more to coalesce. This is the great danger of the future.

JANUARY 2, 1946

. . . The dinner at Joe Alsop's was most interesting. There were present Ben Cohen, Justice Black, Grace Tully, and Mr. and Mrs. Gaud. The Gauds come from South Carolina but are now living in New York. Apparently Gaud was in China for a time, I suppose with the Army. He is a lawyer and violently anti-Russian.

Immediately after we left the ladies the Russian subject opened up. Alsop and Gaud were vigorous proponents of the thesis of getting tough with the Russians. Justice Black and I took the other side. Gaud said we ought to "kick the Russians in the balls." He said we ought to check them at every opportunity. I said I thought the Russians were entitled to free access through the Dardanelles; that they had been promised this in World War I. Gaud said this was "crap"; I replied that his statements were "crap." He said, "Well, then, we are even." Alsop said we ought to know what the Russian intentions were. He said as to Russia we had no intentions. He said that a democracy like ours never had any intentions. Nobody else knew where we were going and we didn't know ourselves. I said to Joe, "In other words, you look on Russia as a young man and think that he ought to declare his intentions regarding the young lady. You assume that the young lady has no intentions of her own at all." Ben Cohen took somewhat the same slant as Justice Black and myself and Alsop called his statements "a barrel of horse-shit." Alsop's point of view was that the Russians had a government just like Germany's; that they were expanding just like Germany, and that the situation was just like that of Germany when Germany moved into Austria. He said he was one who believed that we should have gotten into the war when Germany moved into Poland. I said it was apparent to me that both Alsop and Gaud belonged to that group who believed that war with Russia was inevitable and the quicker it came the better. I described that group as consisting of certain Chinese, the London Poles, the more well-to-do people in all the countries immediately surrounding Russia, certain reactionary business groups in the United

States, certain generals in the United States, et al. I didn't include any mention of the Catholic church as I had in my thinking of yesterday. I did include the Tory English and said that it seemed to me that what Alsop and Gaud proposed was really pulling chestnuts out of the fire for Britain. I said it seemed to me that the cost of a war with Russia was so infinitely greater than the value of any oil in the Near East that we should not consider getting into war with Russia over Azerbaijan, access to the Dardanelles, or Rumania. Alsop began to shift ground because he did not want to be accused of wanting war with Russia. He finally centered on the thesis that we had to know the Russian intentions. Justice Black made the point that we had no more business messing in Rumania and Bulgaria than Russia had messing in Mexico and Cuba. He said that we would no more tolerate an unfriendly government in Mexico than Russia would tolerate an unfriendly government in Rumania. I advocated that the proper way to handle the situation was to raise the standards of living of the people in the Near East; that from the standpoint of the peace of the world and the welfare of humanity water for irrigation for the people in the East was more important than oil for the navies and the war machines.

About this time Chip Bohlen, head of the Russian desk at the State Department, came in. Joe Alsop turned joyously to me and said, "Now we have a real expert on Russia." He was confident, apparently, that Chip Bohlen would sustain his point of view. Bohlen started out by saying that Russia had gone back to the eighteenth or even to the seventeenth century. He said nowadays when you come into the Kremlin you find hanging on the walls in a most prominent position portraits of Generals Suvarof and Kutuzof. The pictures of Marx and Lenin are well down the hall in a much less conspicuous place. The Russians are again worshipping at the shrine of Peter the Great and Ivan the Terrible. They are making out that Ivan the Terrible was really good for Russia; that he carried on against the Boyars who were creating disunity. Bohlen says he is thankful the communists are in charge at the present stage of Russian history rather than an imperialistic Czar of the old-fashioned type. Bohlen's attitude was frankly one of pulling chestnuts out of the fire for England. He says it is not to our interest to let Russia cut the lifeline of England to the Far East too thin. Bohlen had not been in the room when Alsop had been so vigorously proclaiming that the United States had had no policy and could have no policy. It is very clear that the policy of the United States, judging from Chip Bohlen's statement, is to maintain the lifeline of the British Empire, even though it means disagreement with Russia. From what Ben Cohen said, I would say, however, that his influence is on the side of making certain that this policy is not carried to a point where it means war with Russia. Bohlen mentioned that just a week ago yesterday he and Ben Cohen had been talking with Andrei Vishinsky, Vice Commissar of Foreign Affairs, [about] the fundamental nature of freedom in a democracy. Bohlen had been serving as interpreter for Ben. Both Bohlen and Ben agreed that Vishinsky was a very smart man. He said he agreed fully in principle with Ben with regard to the nature of political freedom and the desirability of it.

There is only one logical action that can be taken if the Alsop point of view is adhered to and that is to provoke a war with Russia as soon as possible. The Alsop point of view is that within twenty years Russia will be enormously stronger than we are and that she is an aggressive nation. If the Alsop-Gaud point of view is followed and we get tough with Russia we certainly should be prepared to go to war with her. Otherwise, getting tough with Russia now will leave sore spots and produce a war at a time when Russia is much better prepared than we are. I sketched out in detail to Bohlen my belief, which was the belief of President Roosevelt, that the key to the problem was cooperation between the three nations in developing the water resources of the Near East, but with the United States taking the lead as we are prepared to do because of our superiority in capital resources and equipment. Bohlen seemed to be rather impressed with my approach.

Bill Gaud recently became executive assistant to Bob Patterson. He was with Lend-Lease during the war and for a time was on Stilwell's staff in China and then went down to India, where he was on the Sultan's staff. Alsop looked on him as one of the smartest and nicest men in the Far East. Alsop, apparently getting his information from Gaud, says that the Army is insisting on complete encirclement of Russia, with air bases in Iceland, Greenland, the Aleutians, and Okinawa. The Navy is standing for much the same thing. Alsop says frankly that if he were Russia, seeing this going on, he would declare war on the United States at once. Joe says that the United States free enterprise system is no good to meet the competition it will have to meet in the future; that we will have to have a more centralized form of government. In other words, Joe believes in totalitarianism for the United States to meet the totalitarianism of Russia. He is, to use his own words, "disturbed as hell." This has to be said for Joe—he does get around. His family has long had contacts with people in high positions. He can get the current gossip from many of the well-placed people in the departments of the government.

JANUARY 8, 1946

. . . Berle says the communist line in Latin America . . . has been to cause as much embarrassment to the United States as possible. He says that since Moscow there may be some modification of this. He says the communist strength has developed especially in those areas where the United States is trying to establish bases. In other words, it seems to be a struggle for world power between the United States and Russia, with Russia looking on very suspiciously everywhere the United States is trying to establish military bases and vice versa . . .

JANUARY 11, 1946

At the cabinet meeting most of the time was taken up by discussing the demonstrations on the part of the soldiers abroad. Secretary Vinson was most indignant about the situation and Secretary Ickes was a close second. Bob Hannegan took the part of the boys. Undersecretary of State Acheson felt that the effect of the demonstrations was seriously to undermine State Department policy and to weaken the United States in world affairs. The President spoke of his recollection of how the boys felt in 1919. He said he thought we had done a remarkably good job of getting men back from overseas so promptly. Secretary Forrestal said that he felt the situation after this war was more serious than after World War I because so many of the boys had been in for three, four, and even five years. The President called attention to the Gallup poll . . . He took a great deal of comfort out of the fact that the people of the United States seemed to be behind him in the speech he gave on January 3.[1] Bob Hannegan thought we ought to get out and hit harder for the President's seven-point program. Ickes was very critical of the columnists and com-

---

[1] The most recent Gallup poll indicated that a majority of Americans supported six of the seven proposals Truman had made to Congress in his State of the Nation speech of January 3, 1946. Those the voters favored called for fact-finding boards and cooling-off periods before strikes, for one year of universal military training, for an increase in the duration and amount of unemployment compensation, for a 65 cent minimum wage, for a pay raise for federal employees, and for the extension of price controls. Opinion was about evenly divided about extending the Fair Employment Practices Commission.

mentators. The President said he had paid his compliments very vigorously to one of the columnists. We all assumed he was referring to Drew Pearson . . .

JANUARY 14, 1946

. . . Phil Murray called up very anxious to see me. Schwellenbach and I went over to his room and he told the history of his negotiations with Snyder, Steelman, Fairless,[1] and the President last Saturday. He was very angry with Steelman and Snyder. He claims Steelman is a stooge for John L. Lewis. He felt on the whole he had gotten a raw deal from the administration, although he was not critical of Truman. He did say, however, that Truman started out talking like a wild man. He felt Truman had been misinformed by Snyder and Steelman. He went into the details of the figures . . . Murray felt definitely that Snyder was continually representing the point of view of steel. He did not make the point that George Allen, one of the confidential advisers to the President, was a director of Republic Steel but it was easy enough to read his feelings with regard to this between the lines of his statements. Schwellenbach and I said that we would see that his point of view was presented to the President.

Schwellenbach and I saw the President at 4:30 in the afternoon and presented to him Phil Murray's point of view, saying that even after the increase of 19½ cents an hour in wages, the net profit of the steel companies (taking into account the elimination of overtime, downgrading, elimination of excess profits tax, etc.) would be more than twice what it was during the four years before the war. The President said that the companies had had rather serious losses in the fourth quarter. I said, however, that this did not indicate what they could do in 1946. I also pointed out that under the insurance against loss provision in our tax structure the less efficient companies would be assured of their prewar profit position even though they did practically no work in 1946. I said the liberals in Congress would point out the way in which the government had taken action to protect business by removal of the excess profits tax and by this payback provision, thus in effect insuring the companies against loss if they wanted to fight the unions to a showdown. I told the President that Phil Murray did not show any animus against him but that he did feel strongly with regard to Steelman and Snyder. Schwellenbach concurred in everything I said. We both agreed that the settlement of

[1] Benjamin F. Fairless, president of the United States Steel Corporation.

the steel strike was the issue on which probably hung the outcome of the 1946 Congressional elections.[1] The President agreed to that. When we left he thanked us most heartily for coming over and urged us to come again . . .

JANUARY 16, 1946

. . . The AVC boys are three of the finest boys that could be found anywhere.[2] They reminded me of the talk I had with them a couple of years or so ago when all they had was an idea. Now they have about 15,000 members and they actually think they may have as many as a half million members a year from now . . .

At the Business Advisory Council Bill Elliott and Marion Folsom[3] and others discussed Russia. Elliott and Folsom had been on a trip to Russia with some congressmen. They both were quite critical of Russia but Elliott much more than Folsom. Elliott was really a special pleader for Germany. In the first part of his remarks he told how people in Paris were getting about 1800 calories a day, which was not quite enough, he thought, and then went on to say that in Belgium they were getting about 2000 calories a day, which was adequate. Still later he referred to the German workers as getting 2000 calories, saying that certainly 2000 calories was inadequate for the Germans. I don't think he ever realized that his talk was so obviously special pleading for the Germans. I suspect his special pleading for the Germans was occasioned by his rather recently acquired fear and hatred of the Russians. Apparently he would have the United States do what the British did after World War I—build the Germans up as a barrier against the Russians . . .

JANUARY 17, 1946

When I was at the Brazilian Embassy Thursday night, the President phoned me to say they decided on the 18½ cent proposal; that he thought that was fair and that it was just midway between the original proposal of the steel company of 12 cents and the union demand of 25 cents. The President also told me that the steel workers were

[1] The steel strike began on January 20, 1946.
[2] Charles G. Bolte, Gilbert A. Harrison, and Samuel Spencer of the American Veterans Committee, a new and liberal veterans' organization.
[3] William Yandell Elliott, Harvard professor of government, and Frank Marion Folsom, business and radio executive, were then members of the Business Advisory Council.

prepared to go along but that the steel companies were still bucking. He asked if I would do anything I could to get the steel companies to go along on the 18½ cent proposal. I told him I was not in very good position to speak to these gentlemen directly but that I had some indirect methods that might perhaps help . . .

JANUARY 18, 1946

. . . I raised the Swiss watch question in cabinet, saying that in the first instance I had become a Democrat because I believed it was essential for a creditor nation to prepare eventually for receiving imports with a value greater than exports; that I believed that any creditor nation which continually raised tariffs to prevent imports was bound to run into trouble and that any party that stood for such a policy was headed for ultimate extinction. I said that my brother-in-law was the Swiss Minister and that my views, therefore, were perhaps colored but that I had really believed in freer trade always; that I had stood for the reciprocal trade agreements in the President's cabinet from the very beginning and that I had been against Jack Garner at that time; that I had testified again and again before congressional committees in favor of the agreements and that I had made many speeches in behalf of reciprocal trade agreements. I said it pained me deeply, therefore, to find the State Department prepared to denounce the Swiss treaty unless the Swiss would put a quota on exports of Swiss watches to the United States.

Dean Acheson promptly beat a hasty retreat and said the idea of putting on a quota had now been abandoned. I pointed out that as far as both businessmen and workers were concerned that there was a sharp difference of opinion on the matter because there were more workers and more businessmen associated with the Swiss import trade than there were with the making of watches in the United States.

Dean Acheson was very critical of the Swiss because they refused to export watch-making machinery to the United States. Secretary Vinson was critical because the Swiss had not joined up at Bretton Woods. Senator McKellar came to the support of the Swiss, saying that the Waltham, Elgin, and Hamilton people were trying to use the State Department action as a basis for making a killing. For his part, he thought there was no sense in a quota. It appears that the main people pushing for quotas are Senator Guffey, Senator Lucas, and Senator Saltonstall.[1] Senator McKellar and Senator Taft are against quotas.

[1] Senators Scott W. Lucas, Illinois Democrat, and Leverett Saltonstall, Massachusetts Republican.

It all reminds me of the old saying "The tariff is a local issue." These particular senators are not acting on a matter of principle in any way. Perhaps we should say the tariff in practice is a local issue, but it really should not be; it should be handled from the standpoint of the general consumer and to promote the peace of the world and a higher standard of living for the world.

General Royall, the Undersecretary of War, did not speak up. I had been informed by Congressman Celler that he would speak up if I opened the matter in cabinet.

After the cabinet meeting was over, I was talking with Senator McKellar and Undersecretary Royall, and Royall then told McKellar that the word had gotten out, as a result of a statement somebody down the line in the War Department had made, that the War Department was in favor of a quota on Swiss watches. He said he had called up Dean Acheson the day before, saying that the War Department was not in favor of a quota on Swiss watches. We all of us agreed that this was a battle between two groups in business and two groups in labor.

Secretary Vinson took a rather strong position against the Swiss, saying that they should have joined Bretton Woods and that in order to maintain our trade agreements it was oftentimes necessary to give in to our opponents. I took rather sharp issue with Secretary Vinson on this. I don't think he ever sounded more opportunistic . . .

JANUARY 24, 1946

As I read the . . . press this morning[1] . . . I couldn't help thinking about the statement made by General Marshall at Hot Springs, Virginia, on the evening of October 26 to the effect that the United States Army had made every possible effort to occupy the southern half of Korea in order to shut off the Russians there. The Army undoubtedly is following the same policy as Arthur Sulzberger of the New York *Times*—"Be tough with the Russians." This means that it is impossible to believe in the press anything inspired by the American Army or by the Soviets. Both of them will lie with equal facility.

JANUARY 25, 1946

The only thing of any importance that took place in cabinet meeting was the presentation by Acheson with regard to the amount of

[1] The Associated Press had reported a statement of General MacArthur rebuking the Russians for allegedly fomenting revolution in Japan and South Korea.

starvation that would take place in Europe this winter and the presentation by Clint Anderson with regard to the tight wheat situation. It caused my memory to go back to the telephone call I made to Roy Hendrickson[1] last fall with regard to the food situation in Europe. At that time he assured me that the situation had improved greatly and that there was no great danger. I don't know whether Roy Hendrickson is incompetent or whether the incompetence is general everywhere in UNRRA. Someone's judgment was very, very bad last fall. Hannegan and I pushed on this situation and as a result the President appointed a committee with Clint Anderson as chairman, Dean Acheson (or Byrnes), and myself as the other members, to report back to the next cabinet meeting with regard to what might be done to handle American wheat and the European starvation situation to the best advantage. I was rather surprised to find Hannegan taking an interest in a problem of this sort.

JANUARY 28, 1946

. . . Senator Pepper gave a very interesting account of his trip to Europe. He dealt chiefly with Russia and was very complimentary both to Russia and to Stalin. He said that he talked at great length with Stalin and Stalin told him that Russia's great aims were reconstruction and peace but that she was determined to control the area which she had prior to World War I. Pepper said he didn't think Stalin's power was as absolute as some folks inferred. He noticed on certain occasions Stalin was very careful to shake hands with all the members of the Politburo, treating them with the same deference that a cabinet officer would treat the chairmen of important senate committees.

JANUARY 30, 1946

. . . Casper Ooms[2] told me that certain patent legislation urgently desired by the State Department so as to straighten out the situation between us and the British had been killed by the House Patent Committee as a result of the activities of the NAM. Some of the boys in the NAM boasted to Ooms that they had done it. If the NAM has done this, they have given an outstanding example of shortsighted action of the type which will eventually make the United States anathema

[1] Roy F. Hendrickson, deputy director of UNRRA.
[2] Casper W. Ooms, Commissioner of Patents.

throughout the world. I hold no brief for the British but you can't be unfair in the way the NAM crowd has made the House Committee on Patents perform. Boykin of Alabama and Lanham of Texas[1] seem to have been the worst. Perhaps we should be charitable and call them ignorant prostitutes.

FEBRUARY 5 ,1946

At the cabinet meeting the only subject up for discussion was the problem of food for Europe. It is quite clear that our present failure to contribute as we should is due in considerable measure to the lack of foresight on the part of Marvin Jones and the OPA officials and the OWMR in the spring of 1945, combined with the inability of the Department of Agriculture in the late summer and early fall of 1945 to understand just what the cold weather of May, June, and early July meant to the corn crop. It is apparent that the Department of Agriculture is now much more susceptible to influence from the processing trades than it was in the old days . . .

FEBRUARY 8, 1946

I called up the President this morning and . . . suggested that among the scientists there was some criticism of the forthcoming naval atomic bomb test and said that this might be obviated in some measure if he would appoint a civilian committee. I offered to send him a memorandum and he said he would be glad to get it. This memorandum appears herewith.[2] It was prepared by Condon.

Then I suggested with regard to the full employment bill that it should be called the "Maximum Employment Bill"[3]; that "maximum employment" was really more radical than "full employment." I then pointed out that this bill would leave his own office in a somewhat difficult administrative position, somewhat in the nature of a three-headed monster, namely, the three economic advisers set up by the maximum employment bill in the Executive Office; the Office of War

1 Congressmen Frank W. Boykin, Alabama Democrat, and Fritz G. Lanham, Texas Democrat.
2 The memo emphasized "the desirability of the President's having an independent critical review" of the Navy's plans for the tests at Bikini Atoll in July and for their evaluation. Scientists were to be present at those tests.
3 In the House-Senate conference committee on the bill, Senator Tobey had also suggested the phrase "Maximum Employment," which the committee endorsed. The measure ultimately carried the title "Employment Act," but the declaration of policy in its second section designated maximum employment as its objective.

Mobilization and Reconversion; and the Budget Bureau. I said that I had a very high regard for Harold Smith and suggested that this situation might be to some extent solved by appointing Harold Smith as the head of the Council of Economic Advisers as well as having him continue as Director of the Budget. This would result in satisfactory consolidation because the Office of War Mobilization and Reconversion would be passing out of the picture in the not too distant future anyway. The President agreed with everything I said and said he thought it was a "solid suggestion." I spoke most highly of Harold Smith and the President agreed[1] . . .

FEBRUARY 12, 1946

Oscar Chapman came in to tell me very confidentially that Secretary Ickes had sent his resignation to the President today[2]; that it was a very fine resignation, and that he was going to hold a press conference tomorrow at eleven o'clock to announce the resignation unless the President acted in the meantime. Chapman said there was no question in his mind that Pauley would not be confirmed. Chapman said that Pauley in all his contacts with him had been perfectly proper but that he knew Pauley had made certain propositions to Ickes because Ickes had told him about them at the time. He is sure that Ickes has been absolutely sound and right on the whole matter. Therefore he wondered if he shouldn't resign at the present time. I told him that in view of the fact that there was no other Undersecretary of Interior and no Assistant Secretary it was his duty to continue until such time as the President had designated a new Secretary. I said I assumed the President would not designate him as Secretary. He said there was no danger of that. He thought the President might designate Bob Kerr of Oklahoma.[3] He said that would really be very bad because Kerr had so many public land oil leases. He said he would have to resign if Kerr were named . . .

. . . I had a very interesting luncheon with Bill Bullitt, who is very anti-Russian and who obviously had me in to try to make me anti-

---

[1] The bill called for a Council of Economic Advisers of three members to be appointed by the President with the consent of the Senate. Truman, after consulting Harold Smith, named to that council no one with other federal responsibilities.

[2] Ickes had resigned in protest against Truman's nomination of Pauley as Assistant Secretary of the Navy. Truman appointed Julius A. Krug Secretary of the Interior.

[3] Governor Robert S. Kerr of Oklahoma, oil man and Democrat, later United States senator.

Russian also. Of course Bullitt's attitude toward Russia has been obvious for the last seven or eight years . . .

Bill . . . proceeded to get down to the business of attacking Russia
with the greatest speed possible. He said he was a good Democrat and
he felt my domestic policies were marvelous. He thought my foreign
policy was pretty bad. He said he thought I shared some of the ideas
of Joseph Davies; I said I certainly did. I told him my foreign policy
was based fundamentally on the idea of avoiding World War III and
doing our part towards raising the standard of living in the backward
areas of the world. He was very critical of Stalin's recent speech.[1] I
told him that I thought this was accounted for in some measure by
the fact that it was obvious to Stalin that our military was getting
ready for war with Russia; that they were setting up bases all the way
from Greenland, Iceland, northern Canada, and Alaska to Okinawa,
with Russia in mind. I said that Stalin obviously knew what these bases
meant and also knew the attitude of many of our people through our
press. We were challenging him and his speech was taking up the
challenge.

Bill described the Communist Party as a privileged, persecuting minority group of the same type as the Spanish Inquisition. He described
the Russian people as perfectly lovely people for whom he had the
greatest admiration. He said that while he was Ambassador to Russia
he had taught the Russian army to play polo and the Russian factory
workers to play baseball. He just loved the Russian people but, unfortunately for the Russian people, they were held completely in subjection by this privileged, persecuting group known as the Communist
Party . . .

He said these Bolsheviks are charming people. He spoke of Stalin as
a man of extraordinary intelligence. He says he has brown eyes with a
bluish film over them. He says he has extraordinary intuition; that
when you talk with him he seems to be reaching out all over the room

---

[1] Stalin's speech of February 9, 1946, had also alarmed Dean Acheson and George
F. Kennan. The address, a reiteration of standard communist themes familiar
for decades, attributed the causes of World War II to the dialectical necessities
of capitalism. Those same forces of capitalism, monopoly, and imperialism,
Stalin said, were still in control outside of the Soviet Union. Accordingly he
saw no possibility of peaceful international order. Stalin called for increased
output in the Soviet Union of materials essential for national defense, even at
the cost of consumer goods. Responding in part to the address, Kennan sent his
celebrated long cable from Moscow to Washington, a cable that predicted
Soviet policy would attempt in every way to infiltrate, divide, and weaken the
West. The speech and the cable, taken together, marked a significant escalation
in the tensions as well as the rhetoric of the developing Cold War.

with his mind in a dozen different directions; that he can follow half a dozen different conversations simultaneously. He said, "Stalin at one time was very affectionate toward me. At one time when he had had a little too much to drink he kissed me full on the mouth—what a horrible experience that was!" He spoke about the different people whom Stalin had shot—people who at one time were close to him. He said the Russians were like an amoeba, sending out pseudopods, surrounding that which they could digest and avoiding that which they could not digest. He then proclaimed that the proper policy of the United States was to put indigestible particles in their path. He said because of the fact that the United States had the atomic bomb we could come down firm with Russia and get away with it. I said I thought that was where the trouble had begun; that after we got the atomic bomb and acted the way we did, the Russians felt it necessary to enter upon an armaments race with us; that since we proposed to have bases clearly aimed at Russia, a large number of atomic bombs, and a large Navy, the Russians could feel that we were aiming the whole thing directly at them. I asked Bullitt what he would propose doing. He suggested setting up a Western European Federation of all the countries which have democratic forms of government. I said I thought that sounded like a good idea. He said, "Well, the Russians won't be for it." I said I didn't think that they would be against it provided the federation was not directed against the Russians; that it was all a question of attitude . . .

Bill and I both agreed that the UNO should be built up; that it was a healthy thing to have differences aired in the UNO. We both agreed with regard to Latin American policy and apparently as to Chinese policy. I told him I thought the best way to handle the Russians was to demonstrate to the countries surrounding Russia that our system would furnish the common people in these countries more good things of life than the Russian system. We should have a friendly competition to see who could do more for the common man. I said with regard to the Near East we should move in and help the people there establish irrigation systems and industry. Bill said, "Yes, I agree with you on that but we must go beyond that and be prepared to go in and stop Russia with a strong hand before her strength gets too great for us." I said to Bill, "It seemes to me that that way leads to World War III— not at once but in the long run." I said that I didn't think the Russians really wanted to impose their system on the rest of Europe; that as a matter of fact they would prefer not to. Bill said, "In the long run they do." He said the Soviet foreign policy is thought of in purely military terms; that they establish fronts and conduct a war of nerves on these diplomatic fronts in the same way as they would actual warfare. I said, "Well, it seems to me, then, that the all-important thing is for us to come to a complete and continuous understanding as rapidly as possible in the UNO. Let's carry frankness to a point where both sides have to come absolutely clean." I said the Russians were not the only ones who were engaging in a considerable amount of double-dealing, infiltration, etc. Bill said that Litvinov in 1935 had said to him, "Why worry about Bessarabia? Why take two bites to a cherry? One of these days a war will come along and we shall have Rumania as well as Bessarabia." Bill claims that Russia now has Rumania.[1] I told him I didn't think so. He then said, "Well, you wait and see—Russia will take over 130 million people in addition to her own in eastern Europe. It will take her some time to digest them but this small, privileged, persecuting class known as the communists will accomplish the digestive process in due time."

I said it seemed to me that the Balkan states were in an entirely different category from Estonia, Latvia, and Lithuania; that the Balkan states had never been a part of Russia and that I certainly did not think it was communist policy to impose the communist economic system on the Balkans.

Bill says Russia is going to take over Manchuria.[2] Bill's final clinching point is that it is good internal politics to be against Russia. I told him that it might be good politics but that I didn't think it was sound statesmanship; that I thought what he called "good politics" led directly into World War III . . .

FEBRUARY 13, 1946

. . ., At the meeting with General Arnold, General Arnold said that he thought it would be a great benefit to the CAA if the Army maintained continuously a transcontinental transportation service of about a hundred planes. The Army could try out all the new gadgets and take risks which the CAA could not. This Army line would fly only Army people. Arnold claims that the Army has learned how to land

[1] The Rumanian government had clear pro-Russian leanings but still included some noncommunists. It was 1947 before the communists affected an overt takeover of the country.

[2] The Russians already dominated that area, from which they had promised to withdraw. They had just made withdrawal conditional upon terms Chiang Kai-shek resisted. His continuing refusal to meet even those conditions that General Marshall considered reasonable gave the Russians an excuse for continuing their control while Chinese communist forces gradually moved in to take over.

its planes in all kinds of weather and that the CAA is very backward. Arnold also came down strong for the Army being in the transport service in a big way in order to be ready for the next war. I asked him who he was going to fight. He didn't answer this question but later suggested how important it was to have a continuous line flying all the time between Greenland and Alaska. Undoubtedly such a line would be directed specifically against Russia and would be so interpreted. Obviously there is no commercial traffic between Greenland and Alaska. Apparently the Army feels that there are going to be raids from Moscow via the North Pole or they want to be ready to raid Moscow via the North Pole. I hadn't realized before what a direct threat our air bases at Fairbanks and Greenland are to Russian security. I read over Stalin's speech last night and was impressed at the vigor with which he was taking up the various challenges which we have been making all the way from the President on down.

FEBRUARY 14, 1946

As I listened to the broadcast of Secretary Ickes' press conference yesterday and also his ten o'clock ABC speech, I couldn't help thinking back to the various conferences I had with Secretary Ickes on the funeral train when we were going up to Hyde Park to bury President Roosevelt on April 14–15, 1945. I remember that when I went forward to pay my respects to Mrs. Roosevelt, on the way back both Pauley and Allen were in President Truman's car and that the presence of these two gentlemen caused Ickes grave disquietude. He told me that Pauley had again approached him with regard to the matter of the tidelands oil on the train. Ickes went into some details on the subject with me and also, as I remember, indicated that at one time he had been friendly with Pauley. I couldn't help also remembering that at one time I left a memorandum with President Roosevelt against Pauley two or three years ago. At that time I was placing my criticism of Pauley largely on the basis that sooner or later he would be attacked and would gravely embarrass the party.

Someone has jokingly said that Ickes resigned because President Truman admitted that there might be other honest men in Washington besides Ickes . . .

Marquis Childs came in to talk about the same thing that Beany Baldwin had talked about. He also had heard that Ickes was maneuvering in every way possible to become head of PAC. Childs has great admiration for Ickes but we both agreed that Ickes would probably do the liberal cause more harm than good if he went in as the head of PAC. He is too much a prima donna and not good enough as an organization man. His temperament would alienate certain types of people with whom it is necessary to cooperate . . .

FEBRUARY 15, 1946

At the cabinet meeting about the only subject up for discussion was the nature of the atomic bomb tests against the Navy. Forrestal indicated that Admiral Blandy [1] had chosen Karl Compton of M.I.T. and Bradley Dewey to advise him. The President said some people had mentioned Bob Hutchins of the University of Chicago. I said Hutchins' selection would be reassuring to many people who felt that the atomic bomb test against the Navy was not on the square. Forrestal objected to Hutchins . . . Bob Patterson also objected . . .

At the close of the cabinet meeting . . . the President . . . spoke of the Ickes situation with some feeling. He said that Ickes had told him personally that Pauley was a good man. He said he knew there had been no disagreement between him and myself but he hoped that if at any time in the future anything of the kind should arise that we could sit down and talk things over. He said he thought I believed that he (Truman) was an honest man. I said, "Yes." The only reservation I had in my mind when I said it was the recollection of his telling me twice about six months prior to the Chicago convention that he was for me for Vice President, only to find him later coming out for Jimmie Byrnes. I also couldn't help remembering the interview with Houston of the New York *Times* which was printed on January 10, 1945. In the sense in which Truman was using the word "honest," however, I could honestly say that I thought he was honest . . .

The President said he had always had the highest regard for me and still had the highest regard. He thought that we understood each other and he hoped that I would not resign like Ickes. I said that I had an entirely different temperament than Ickes . . .

[1] Admiral William H. P. Blandy was in command at Bikini. His scientific advisers did include President Karl T. Compton of the Massachusetts Institute of Technology and President Bradley Dewey of the Dewey and Almy Chemical Company, both of whom had been involved in the Manhattan Project. President Robert M. Hutchins of the University of Chicago was not one of Blandy's advisers.

FEBRUARY 21, 1946

. . . . Clint Anderson said that he had been in the Middle West and at Chicago on Monday of this week he had been told by a man who was rather unfriendly to Secretary Wallace that Wallace's stock had gone up amazingly because of the fine way he had stood by Truman in the recent crisis. Anderson reported that this man said that when Wallace indicated that he was not going to run for President if Truman was a candidate and that he was not going to resign, it helped the situation amazingly.[1] Truman then said that he always knew he could count on me; and then, as a sort of an afterthought, he said he had always thought he could count on Ickes, too. He said Ickes had deceived him; that he had more or less indicated that Pauley was all right with him . . . .

FEBRUARY 28, 1946

I took Condon and Newman in to see the President with regard to the situation in the Senate Atomic Energy Committee.[2] We first said that there was grave danger of the McMahon bill, which he had supported, being defeated. He agreed that there was and said that a lot of hard work would have to be done. I asked him if he was still for the McMahon bill. He said emphatically that he was; that he had already said so several times. We told him about the drive in the committee to put four military men on the Atomic Energy Executive Committee and to make every decision subject to a veto by the Chief of Staff. I said flatly that this would lead toward a military dictatorship and the domination of our foreign policy by the military. I

[1] At a CIO cinvention in Cleveland on February 19, 1946, Wallace had said that he expected Truman to run in 1948 and to select a vice-presidential candidate from some part of the country other than the Middle West. For his own part, Wallace said he was not a candidate for either place on the Democratic ticket, and he was not planning to resign from the cabinet.
[2] During the February hearings on the McMahon bill, Secretary of War Patterson had attacked clauses excluding the Army from any role in developing atomic energy. He advocated various amendments, including two to permit the armed services to engage in research on atomic weapons, and to direct the commission continuously to consult the War and Navy Departments. Patterson also privately opposed Truman's directions to McMahon to have the commission consist only of civilians. General Groves stood adamantly for retaining his own system of military security in atomic research. He emphasized that point during hearings on February 27. Those hearings followed the revelation on February 16 of the arrest by the Canadian government of spies who had delivered secret data about atomic energy to the Soviet embassy. Groves also stressed his arguments for including military personnel on the commission.

referred also to the drive being put on by General Groves to prevent peacetime utilization of atomic energy. I said that I thought Groves' testimony was damnable. The President said he agreed. The President went over the personnel of the Committee one by one. He is proposing to work through Tom Connally and Millard Tydings, Dick Russell and Senator Austin. He asked Condon and Newman not to resign from the committee and said that we would check in on this matter again later on.

After Condon and Newman left the room I told the President I would like to talk a little politics with him and suggested that it might be helpful in looking toward a large vote next fall to try to stir up interest in getting out a large Democratic vote in the primaries. He said he would take the matter up with Bob Hannegan. He said that Bob Hannegan was in much better health now; that since he had had his teeth out his blood pressure was going down. I said that it would require about 40 million voters next fall to insure a Democratic Congress and that we couldn't get out 40 million voters unless some issue could be used which would thoroughly arouse the people. He mentioned with some feeling the way in which some of the Democrats had ganged up with the Republicans to prevent adequate funds for both OPA and Civilian Production Administration. I said that some of the Republicans were essentially fascist-minded and that they would like to see a military dictatorship in this country in order to maintain just the kind of status quo they wanted. He said he agreed and said that some of the Democrats belonged in the same category as the Republicans. This statement just referred to I made in a different context while Condon and Newman were still in the room. Just as I was leaving the President he said he didn't think he had made any mistakes. In reply to this I had to be honest and said, "Well, I am inclined to think that John Snyder made a mistake when he advised you to take off the controls last summer." His reply to that was that the various business and labor leaders had given him assurance at that time that they would all go along. He said he regretted that he had not taken down in writing the assurances that they had given him. If I had been completely frank with the President I would also have referred to the character of some of his appointments. His complete self-confidence and assurance is amazing . . .

MARCH 1, 1946

. . . Al Black[1] told me about the situation in Iran. The upper class Iranians are mostly crooks who oppress the poor. The poor peasants cannot read or write and 90 percent of them are affected with malaria. Black says the situation has been one which is favorable to revolution for many years but he is sorry that the present revolution is inspired by Russia rather than arising from the people themselves. I asked him for further information about this and he said that actually the revolution in Azerbaijan had been started by some Azerbaijanians who had gone across the border into Russian Azerbaijan and then had come back. I said, "Well, perhaps they feel the people in Russian Azerbaijan are living better than those in Persian Azerbaijan." Black says there has been rivalry between England and Russia with respect to Iran for more than 100 years. He says within the last 30 or 40 years the English and Russians entered into a treaty carving out spheres of influence, with Russia having as her sphere of influence the territory reaching several hundred miles south of Teheran. The British now would very much like to forget this agreement. It begins more and more to look as if the backward areas of the world would have to be led toward a higher standard of living either by way of American organization, British organization, or Russian organization. Neither the British nor the Russians really care much for raising the standard of living of the people. The British raise the standard of living merely as a by-product of exploitation. The Russians raise the standard of living as a part of their effort to enlarge the field of influence of the communistic doctrine . . .

At the meeting of the Food Relief Committee everybody kowtowed in the most amazing way to Hoover.[2] Hoover came out very vigorously for approaching the food problem on a purely voluntary basis. Anderson has the same slant. There will be a lot of publicity but I am afraid all that it adds up to is that there will be business as usual, consumption as usual, and not much change in the amount of food available to Europe. There will be some food saved as a result of the

[1] Albert G. Black, agricultural adviser to the Iranian government, had held several major positions in the Department of Agriculture while Wallace was Secretary.
[2] Truman had appointed former President Herbert C. Hoover honorary chairman of a new Famine Emergency Committee. That committee recommended federal measures to increase food export and, in keeping with Hoover's characteristic emphasis on volunteerism, individual efforts to conserve food. Truman endorsed both proposals.

80 percent bread and the reduction in the amount of grain going into liquor to the 1940 levels. The American people will get a nice glow out of pretending to do something for the starving but undoubtedly there will be several million people in the world who will starve to death in the next four months who could have been saved if we had used more vigorous methods. Anderson and Hoover will get great acclaim. Anderson is a nice fellow but I am beginning to think that he is more to blame for the food difficulties than I had heretofore thought.

MARCH 4, 1946

. . . Chester Bowles told me the story of his conflict with Snyder.[1] He told President Truman exactly what he thought of Snyder in a letter of resignation which he sent to the President. After Ickes resigned, Bowles, at the request of the President, stayed on because he did not want to hurt the administration. He doesn't want to stay on more than a few months. He says, however, that he will not get out without consulting me. He had a lot of details which I can remember only in part. He mentioned, for example, that Snyder, Vinson, Baruch, and Jimmie Byrnes have been conducting negotiations with the steel companies as to the degree to which prices should be raised. Bowles did not know anything about this. He also mentioned that when the new formula was worked out he was brought in with Snyder, Vinson, Schwellenbach, and a number of the other boys (he said everybody was there but the Secretary of Commerce), and the President pointed to each one in turn and said, "Are you for it?" Bowles was definitely put on the spot. He did not think it was wise to resign at that time so he went along. I told Bowles that the President felt very definitely that he had had commitments from labor at the time the controls were removed after V-J Day. Bowles said yes, the President had mentioned that on various occasions and in his talk always pointed to the specific chair in which Phil Murray had sat. Bowles said he had talked to Eric Johnston about it, who was in on the particular meeting. According to Eric, as reported by Bowles, Phil

[1] Yielding to pressure from the steel industry, Snyder had agreed to an increase of seven dollars a ton in the price of steel. That increase, the industry had argued, was necessary to cover the larger labor costs imposed by the settlement of the steel strike. Bowles had concluded that the largest fair increase was two and a half dollars. Bowles therefore wrote a letter of resignation, but Baruch, Byrnes, and Truman persuaded him to stay on as head of the Office of Economic Stabilization with Paul A. Porter succeeding him as head of the OPA. Bowles resigned the following June when Congress stripped OPA of its effective powers; see Chester Bowles, *Promises to Keep* (New York, 1971) pp. 138–42.

Murray had given no commitment of the sort which the President claims. The only conclusion which anyone can reach is that it is just another one of those things which are so frequent in Washington—government by rumor, guess, and hazy recollection . . .

MARCH 5, 1946

The most significant event of March 5 was the dinner given by Dean Acheson at which were present Dick Casey, the Australian minister to the United States, and his wife, Walter Lippmann and his wife, and Chip Bohlen and his wife. Before we sat down to eat the subject for discussion was Winston Churchill's speech.[1] Mrs. Acheson spoke in lyrical terms about it. She has always admired Churchill and never more than yesterday. I asked what he had said and she said he advocated a military alliance between the United States and England against Russia. Mr. and Mrs. Casey became glowing in their comments. I promptly interjected that the United States was not going to enter into any military alliance with England against Russia; that it was not a primary objective of the United States to save the British Empire. At this point Mrs. Casey became almost fanatical, perhaps I should say frenzied. She said it was to save the world, not the British Empire. Casey spoke of the Russians as being beasts. I said instead of talking about military alliances it was high time to talk about an effective method of disarmament. I said it would destroy the United Nations to have two of the chief members of the United Nations ganging up against a third member. I said what we ought to have would be effective disarmament with complete inspection on both sides, including inspection of all atomic bomb facilities and supplies. Casey interjected very brusquely, "We might as well talk about a trip to the moon." Then suddenly everyone became very polite and the matter did not come up again until after dinner . . .

We then got to talking about Russia again and it was apparent that Bohlen, Acheson, and Casey all think that the United States and England should run the risk of immediate war with Russia by taking a very hard-boiled stand and being willing to use force if Russia should

[1] At Westminister College, Fulton, Missouri, with Truman on the platform, Churchill had that day delivered his famous "iron curtain" speech. The former Prime Minister called the Soviet Union a "shadow which . . . falls upon the world." Communist parties, he said, constituted "a growing challenge and peril to Christian civilization." He therefore called for a "fraternal association of the English-speaking peoples," in effect for a military alliance, and he warned against releasing the secret of the atomic bomb.

go beyond a certain point. Bohlen part of the time claimed that Russia was resuming the tactics she had used in the 17th century and part of the time that she was using the tactics advocated by Lenin. I asked him what were the tactics used by Lenin. He said to drive a wedge between the capitalistic countries and then pick on the weaker ones of the capitalistic countries. I advocated as a program that we have an agreement on disarmament and that the United States and Britain then proceed to show backward peoples of the world that their system would give them a higher standard of living than the Russian system. I said that what Russia feared was encirclement by the United States and England; that she saw us busily setting up military and naval bases whose only object could be to attack Russia. Bohlen made fun of this idea and said that it was not the United States which was on the offensive; that it was Russia. I said it was very unfortunate that Churchill had made the kind of speech he was reported to have made, because he was the one who back in 1919 was calling the Bolsheviks such names and doing everything he could to assemble an Allied force to destroy the Bolsheviks. I said I didn't see how these warlike words of Churchill now could have any more real influence on the Russians than his warlike attitude toward the Bolsheviks had in 1919. I said the American people were not willing to send American boys anwhere to fight now; that certainly the Russians did not want to fight anybody now; that in all probability the situation would finally work out on a basis that would cause the Russians completely and utterly to distrust us; that it would cause the Russians to engage in a race with us in the making of atomic bombs; that while they might be a long way behind us at the present time they would have enough bombs to destroy us fifteen years hence; that with the Russians completely distrusting us because of the way we had handled them they would not scruple fifteen years hence to drop bombs on us without warning; that they would have no hesitation in continuing their fifth column activities in all the nations of the world; that they could use these fifth columnists effectively to destroy our form of government.

On the way home Mrs. Wallace told me that Walter Lippmann and Mrs. Lippmann agreed with me,[1] though they said practically nothing . . .

---

[1] Lippmann condemned Churchill's speech in his next column. An Anglo-American alliance, he wrote, was not workable, for it would commit the United States to underwrite the status quo in the British empire.

MARCH 12, 1946

When I sent to the White House at 12:30, I started out by telling
the President that I had been on the Hill testifying for the British
loan; that I had said that I thought it would be good business for the
United States if we made a gift of the necessary money to get England
on her feet again. I said that at the conclusion of my testimony Senator
Mitchell[1] of Washington had said to me, "Do you think the purpose
of the loan is to bring about a military alliance between the United
States and Britain?" and that I had replied to Senator Mitchell by saying that if I thought that were the purpose I would be against the loan.
The President immediately said that he had not seen Churchill's speech
in advance.[2] He went into the details of just how he had been sucked
in and how Churchill had put him on the spot. I told him I thought
Churchill had insulted him by coming out with a proposal of this sort
in the United States with him on the platform. I said that the peace
of the world hinged on the United States and not on a military alliance between Britain and the United States. He said he agreed. I told
him that I had sat in on a conference between Roosevelt and Churchill
at which Churchill had proposed an Anglo-Saxon alliance but that
Roosevelt had not risen to the bait. I told him that I had vigorously
opposed Churchill and had said that an Anglo-Saxon alliance would
inevitably cause the rest of the world to react against us, and that I
thought it was sounder policy for the United States to develop a regional sphere of influence in cooperation with her Latin American
neighbors. I said that Churchill had turned up his nose at this and said
that as a painter he knew that when you mixed the colors you got a
dirty brown. Truman said it was just like Churchill to make a crack
like that.

I said granted that Russia is wrong on every stand which she is taking at the present time, the fact still remains that the proper policy
for the United States is to serve as an intermediary between Britain
and Russia and not as a defender of England. Truman declared up

---

[1] Senator Hugh B. Mitchell, Washington Democrat.
[2] Truman had also told his press conference on March 8 that he had not known
beforehand what Churchill was going to say. Among others who were skeptical
about that claim, Marquis Childs in his column of March 8 stated categorically
that the President had gone over the text of the speech before Churchill delivered it. As Wallace discovered in 1947 (Oral History 4621), Childs was
correct. In any event, Truman's remarks to Wallace on March 12 were
disingenuous, for by his own later account, the President had privately reached
conclusions substantially like Churchill's, as also had, at the least, Byrnes, Leahy,
and Forrestal.

and down that the United States was not going to enter into an alliance with England. I pursued the subject by saying that Dick Casey had indicated that there would be 20 million Hindus starving to death in the next few months. Truman said that Casey had sat "right there in that chair" and told him the same thing. I said furthermore that Casey had told Walter Lippmann that Nehru was going to use the starvation situation to promote revolt in India. He said yes, Casey had told him that also. I said furthermore that Casey had told Walter Lippmann that in his opinion England would be forced out of India within two years. Truman said Casey had not told him that much. I told Truman that the British Empire was going to have so much trouble that it would very probably be beyond our strength to bolster the empire up, and that therefore we ought to devote our attention to bringing about a just relationship between Britain and Russia in their conflicting spheres of interest.

Truman then brought out a map of Europe and the Near East. He indicated that he had tried at Potsdam to get the Rhine and the Danube internationalized, as well as the Dardanelles and the Bosporus, the Suez Canal and the Kiel Canal. He said at Potsdam he had tried to get the Russians to agree not only to this but also to getting out of Manchuria and reserving her warm water port rights at Port Arthur and Darien. I told Truman I thought it very important at the present time, now that there was a change in ambassadors (I spoke very highly of Bedell Smith[1]) to bring in a new set of underlings at the American embassy in Moscow who would be more sympathetic in their dealings with the Russian government. I told the President that the three fundamentals of the Democratic Party program should be based on wise handling of atomic energy, wise relationships with Russia, and wise handling of the full production–full employment program. I told the President about the bad situation in the Senate committee with regard to McMahon's atomic energy bill. I spoke highly about General Eisenhower's attitude on atomic energy. I said to him that no Army attitude is good as long as General Groves is in power. Truman said he was working on the General Groves matter . . .

The . . . story by Marquis Childs saying that the President went over the text of Churchill's Fulton, Missouri, speech before it was delivered is interesting in view of the fact that the President told me specifically that he did not know in advance what Churchill was going to say. Undoubtedly there are some people around the President who

---

[1] General Bedell Smith had been appointed ambassador to the Soviet Union following the resignation of Averell Harriman.

have been urging him to go into a military alliance with Great Britain. Undoubtedly they have been putting out false information. Their information might perhaps have proved to be correct if I had not stepped in and spoke decisively to the President.

MARCH 13, 1946

The only significant event of the day was the speech made by Averell Harriman to the BAC. It was a strictly anti-Russian speech. Harriman made it clear that he was in accord with Winston Churchill and that we should be tough with the Russians, even though by so doing we were running the risk of war. He said the communists in every country in the world were simply stooges for Stalin and that they were out to overthrow our form of government. It was mostly old, old stuff of the kind we have heard for the last 25 years. Harriman said he had great hopes that the Russians were going to come along all right until the time of the Yalta Conference in March of 1945. At that time he became convinced that they would not reform.

Harriman said he spoke only for himself and not for the State Department. Chip Bohlen and Elbridge Durbrow[1] were present at the meeting. Every so often Harriman would stop and turn to them for confirmation. The BAC found it very impressive and were in enthusiastic accord with Harriman. They will now go out over the country and spread the word that we are going to get tough with Russia even though it means war. Harriman made the point, however, that he was sure Stalin did not want war, and that he was going to do everything he could to expand territorially without war. Harriman thinks we are in the same position relative to Russia in 1946 that we were relative to Germany in 1933; that the important thing is to stop Russia before she expands any further.

Hoffman[2] of Studebaker got up after Harriman had completed and said that he thought the talk was perfectly marvelous; that it ought to be given in every town in the United States, and asked Harriman why he didn't go on a speaking tour carrying the banner. Harriman replied, saying that he couldn't consider going on a speaking tour; that if he said what he had said there he would be immediately

[1] Elbridge Durbrow, then chief of the Division of Eastern European Affairs in the State Department, had held several positions in the American embassy in Moscow (1934–37) and was about to return to that embassy as counselor.
[2] Paul G. Hoffman, president of the Studebaker Corporation, a Republican whom Truman later appointed first head of the Economic Cooperation Administration, the agency to administer the Marshall Plan.

subject to attack. He said all the commies in the CIO would be after him.

There was considerable discussion then on how important it was to fight any organization that had any commies in it. It was obvious to me as I listened to Harriman and those in the discussion afterwards, that these businessmen don't have the slightest idea of what is going on in the world or what is going to happen. It was also obvious to me that Harriman in spite of the fact that he has been in Russia for several years, never really found out what the score was. He is a nice fellow whom I like personally but I don't think he understands either Russia or the world situation. He and his kind if they have their way will bring on a war which will result in the United States eventually becoming a dictatorship either to the left or the right.

MARCH 14, 1946

. . . Mrs. Roosevelt . . . then went on to talk about the Russian situation and what she proposes to say tonight.[1] She is going to say plenty but will watch her step with regard to the State Department. She was very much put out with Churchill and feels that Churchill took advantage of Truman in a most terrible way. She said that Roosevelt and Churchill always got along well together because they both liked ships and had many cultural interests in common. She said Roosevelt never had any illusions as to Churchill when peace came. We may be sure that Mrs. Roosevelt will do everything she can to prevent war with Russia.

Bedell Smith is going to be a much better man in Russia than Harriman. He will talk very frankly with the Russians but at the start, at any rate, he won't have that concealed hatred for the Russians which animates Harriman. Smith was born in Indiana, is a Catholic, and took his college work at Rensselaer Polytechnic. He has a very attractive personality. He is going to make quite a little change in the embassy personnel and is taking with him Elbridge Durbrow and G. Frederick Reinhardt.[2]

I cleared with Bedell Smith the letter to Truman which appears

[1] Mrs. Roosevelt, critical of Churchill's Fulton speech, questioned whether the American and British people could be trusted to work successfully for peace without regard to their own national interests. An Anglo-American alliance, she predicted, would motivate "other nations" also to form independent alliances and move the world backward to balance of power politics.

[2] G. Frederick Reinhardt, foreign service officer.

herewith.[1] Smith hopes I can come over to Russia at the right time because he thinks that I can help ease over some particularly difficult situation. I said I would like very much to do that but I thought it was important for us both to think it over very, very carefully before we made a move in this direction . . .

Sidney Hillman wanted me to speak at the American Labor Party Convention on May 22. I told him I didn't think I could do it then but I might be able to do it on May 24. He said the American Labor Party has had an increase in its membership in nearly every county in New York and that the increase has been about 20 percent at a time when the membership in both the Republican and Democratic parties has been going down.

Harold Young was very much disturbed about my speaking before the American Labor Party meeting because there are a number of commies attached to the American Labor Party. Hillman denies that these commies have any significance . . . The word "communist" is used so loosely nowadays that no one can say what the truth is. Anyone who is further left than you are and whom you don't like is a commie. Of course the reverse of it is that anyone who is further to the right than you are and whom you don't like is a fascist.

MARCH 15, 1946

. . . There was considerable comment about Russia having furnished wheat to France. Jimmie Byrnes said that Bidault[2] of France, who is a very great friend of the United States, claimed that the Russian wheat going to France was going there for purely political reasons. Bidault is fighting the communists in France. Bidault told

---

[1] On March 15, 1946, Wallace wrote Truman urging "a new approach" to the Soviet Union "along economic and trade lines." He said that "much of the recent Soviet behavior which has caused us concern has been the result of their dire economic needs and of their disturbed sense of security," their fear of "capitalist encirclement." He believed that the United States could "disabuse the Soviet mind and strengthen the faith of the Soviets in our own sincere devotion to the cause of peace" if the United States could prove "to them that we want to trade with them." He recommended "extended discussions of the background needed for future economic collaboration rather than negotiations related to immediate proposals such as a loan." For a fresh start on those discussions, he advised the President to appoint a new group of Americans to a special mission to Moscow.

[2] Georges Bidault, Christian Democrat, president of the National Council of Resistance during the war and at this time a member of the cabinet of the National Union then governing France, was elected the following June president of the French provisional government.

him that the United States is right in her stand on Spain and that France would not have taken her stand against Spain had it not been for the communist influence in France. Jimmie thinks we should get a lot of wheat to France if need be in order to keep the communists from having too much of an opportunity in the elections which come in June.

At the close of the cabinet meeting I showed the President my March 19 Russian Relief speech.[1] He read every page of it carefully and agreed with it all . . . Also he read the letter with regard to Bedell Smith and said he would transmit that to Bedell Smith so he could use it when he got to Russia.[2]

I told the President that I had talked some with Smith about my eventually going to Russia but said that I didn't want to go to Russia and thought that definitely I should not go unless Smith and the State Department after careful consideration, felt I should go. The President said he thought it might be a good idea if I went to Russia. When he said this I backed off a little further from it.

It seems curious that all of a sudden a great many people, including Jimmie Roosevelt, seem to have reached the conclusion that I could do a lot of good by going to Russia . . .

When the President finished reading my Averell Harriman Russian Relief speech I said to him, "Now if you get into any trouble or embarrassment as a result of this speech don't hesitate to repudiate it in any way you want." The President replied, "Don't worry about that; what you are saying here is good sense."

---

1 Wallace gave the speech at a dinner honoring Averell Harriman. He spoke first of the American debt to the Russian people for their unequaled contribution to victory in the war. He then noted the Russian fear of capitalist encirclement. He next called the thought of war between the United States and the Soviet Union "monstrous and preposterous." There "is a race," Wallace said, "between us as to who will" best serve the interests of mankind, a race between democracy and communism. He interpreted Stalin's speech of February 9 as a challenge to "such a race in furnishing the needs of the common people without war or business crisis." The United States, he said, was willing to take up that challenge, to defeat communism by doing "a better and smoother job of maximum production and optimum distribution." But the race had to be clean, peaceful, and in the service of humanity. He turned then to a plea for better understanding of the Russians and for their better understanding of American policies. He concluded by answering Churchill, by opposing "any ideas of the 'American Century' or the 'Anglo-Saxon Century.' The common people of the world will not tolerate any recrudescence of imperialism even under enlightened Anglo-Saxon atomic bomb auspices. If the English-speaking people have any destiny at all, it is to serve the world not to dominate it."

2 Wallace in a note to Truman said General Smith had read his letter to the President of March 15 and wanted to take a copy of it to Moscow.

MARCH 19, 1946

Johnny Green[1] told a most interesting story of the way in which the American Army treats the German scientists. It seems the British army treats the German scientists best, the French the next best, the Russians the next best, and our Army treats them the worst. It is the result of ignorance and bad organization on our part. The story comes via Professor Roger Adams[2] of Illinois who has been General Clay's scientific adviser.

I took three memoranda from John Green and passed them on to Secretary of War Patterson. The data was amazing, indicating that the Russians had an extraordinary respect for science and were courting the German scientists in every way possible, whereas we have been engaged in slapping the German scientists down. The German scientists would very much like to get back into the Russian zone because they are treated so much better there. However, now they are afraid to go back because they feel that the Russians would retaliate because of the distrust they showed of the Russians in the first instance. It all indicates that we are a very immature nation, poorly organized for dealing either with science or with other peoples. I hope that Bob Patterson is impressed with the documents that I gave him . . .

President Truman, when he came into the luncheon, came over to me at once and congratulated me on the speech I made yesterday.[3] He said he agreed with me entirely. He was referring to the extemporaneous speech I made to the Democratic women and presumably to the Washington *Post* account . . . . When I went out at the close of the luncheon he again referred to it and said he was going to "crib" some from it in his Jackson Day speech Saturday night. He said, as a matter of fact, he had written down something along this line already before he had read what I had said. I said well, there was one thing to bear in mind: that maybe there would be some objections from the South. Sam Hobbs[4] had called me on the phone this morning asking if I had been correctly quoted. Sam did not say anything about

[1] John C. Green, director of the Office of Declassification and Technical Services.
[2] Roger Adams, head of the Chemistry Department at the University of Illinois.
[3] Speaking to the Women's Democratic Club on March 18, Wallace had recommended that both Republican and Democratic organizations impose party discipline on such major questions as the British loan, foreign relations, full employment, and atomic energy. The definition of major issues, he suggested, should be left to the President, Vice President, Speaker of the House, and the majority leaders of both houses, perhaps with some help from party caucuses.
[4] Sam F. Hobbs, since 1935 Democratic congressman from Alabama.

FEPC or poll tax or anything of that sort but I can't help thinking he had it in his mind.

The President then went on to say that there must be some sort of party discipline that would give parties the same sense of responsibility to the electorate that the parliamentary system gives in England.

The only serious subject up for discussion during the luncheon was calling off the atomic bomb trial in the Pacific.[1] Jim Forrestal opened it up and then Jimmie Byrnes and I promptly chimed in. Bob Patterson did not object and the President agreed. The President was very happy to agree because Sam Rayburn had been putting him on the spot with regard to sending a lot of congressmen to witness the test. The President didn't want a lot of Democratic congressmen out witnessing the test when their votes were needed here in Washington. The test would be postponed until next year.

Jimmie Byrnes told an extended story about the great good which he had done to the Supreme Court by getting them together to take a drink. He said neither Murphy nor Black drank but nevertheless being in the presence of others who were drinking had a mellowing influence on them. The great cure for discord in Jimmie's opinion is more free-hearted drinking.

MARCH 21, 1946

. . . Ruben Karlsted[2] told me that the Scandinavian countries had been concerned for some months about the Russians remaining so long in the Danish island of Bornholm. He said they were very happy now that the Russians were pulling out and that they were beginning to wonder when the Americans were going to pull out of Iceland. I told him that I thought the Scandinavians wanted the Americans in Iceland as a protection against Russia. He said, no, that wasn't the case. I said that for my own part, speaking as an individual, I thought it would be better for the peace of the world if the United States could be pulled out of Iceland; that undoubtedly the Russians looked on it as a direct threat against them. I asked him how the Icelanders felt about the presence of our troops there. He said he thought that Iceland felt very much like a sovereign nation and would very much prefer to have the American troops out. I told him that with regard

[1] The Bikini tests, originally scheduled to begin in May, were postponed until July so that a select group of congressmen could conveniently attend them.
[2] Ruben Karlsted of the Associated Press.

to my remarks concerning Iceland I wanted him to understand that I was speaking as a private citizen and not as a member of the United States government . . .

MARCH 22, 1946

At cabinet the only subject up for discussion was whether or not the atomic bomb test should be postponed. Forrestal had brought in Admiral Blandy and read a carefully prepared statement from the Navy strongly in opposition to the postponement of the test. Secretary Byrnes said that from the standpoint of international relations it would be very helpful if the test could be postponed or never held at all.

It appears that the Navy had planned on having an atomic bomb test against 101 vessels with the explosion coming from the air, sometime in May, and a second test with the explosion coming from the surface, or slightly under the surface of the water, sometime in July, and a third test with the explosion coming from deep under the water sometime next January. I raised the question as to whether the third test, which would be the most destructive, should not be held first. It might make the others unnecessary. Admiral Blandy apparently did not want to hold the third test first for fear that he might lose all his ships and not have them for the first and second tests. He also made the point that it was more difficult to set off the atomic bomb charge deep under the water and that in actual practice the attack would more likely come from above the water.

I also made the point that it might not be necessary to hold any tests at all if we could arrange for a really effective inspection service in every nation in the world. It was finally decided to have the first test in July unless something on the foreign front should warrant delay. I said if the Navy had absolute certainty that atomic bombs were not going to be constructed anywhere else on the earth they could go ahead and build ships as they had always built them, without fear of blasting by atomic bombs . . .

During the cabinet meeting there was one other thing discussed besides the atomic bomb test. The President mentioned that there were more lobbyists in Washington now than there had ever been. Bob Hannegan said he knew the way to handle the lobbyists—that was for Secretary Vinson to put out the word that in connection with the Internal Revenue Department he was going to look into the expense accounts of businessmen who were spending more time than they should in Washington. Vinson was very scornful of Hannegan's suggestion. I couldn't help but laugh and laugh as I watched these two gentlemen bat the ball back and forth, Vinson looking more and more like an indignant turkey gobbler . . .

Joe Alsop came in very much disturbed about the speech which I gave Tuesday night up in New York.[1] He claimed my foreign policy was diametrically opposed to that of the President and Jimmie Byrnes. I said to him that the President had read every sentence of my speech in my presence and had said that it was only common sense. Joe was completely floored and said that Truman was a much smaller man than he thought he was; that apparently he doesn't realize that Jimmie Byrnes and I are going in completely opposite directions. He said to me, "I think you are in a completely indefensible position in the cabinet." I said to him, "So you are going to try to write columns to get me out." He said, "No, Henry, I am your true friend." He said, "I agree completely with you on your domestic policy but I think your foreign attitude is altogether wrong." I replied, "I think yours is altogether wrong and that it leads inevitably to war." He came back with the statement that I and the liberals who were going along with me were acting just exactly like Chamberlain and Sir John Simon acted in 1938. I said to him, "So you think that Stalin today is equivalent to Hitler and Russia is equivalent to Germany."

He then took me to task for advocating that the United States Army get out of Iceland. I said the only person I had spoken to along that line was the Scandinavian journalist who had been in to see me the day before, who mentioned to me that the Russians were getting out of the Danish island of Bornholm and the Scandinavian people were beginning to wonder when the United States troops would get out of Iceland. (I didn't tell Joe the following but in the course of the conversation with the journalist I had said to him that I thought the Scandinavian countries wanted us to stay in Iceland so as to be a threat against Russia and he said no, this was not true; that the Scandinavian countries believed in taking care of their own affairs and hoped that the United States troops would get out of Iceland. I replied then that I hoped they would too; that I felt the Russians would inevitably look on the United States troops and airplanes in Iceland as a threat against them.)

I didn't remind Joe of the statement which he made a couple of months or so ago that if he were Russia and saw our troops at air bases like Iceland he would fight at once.

[1] The speech at the dinner for Harriman.

Without going into the full details of Joe's statement, it all boils down to this: that he thinks the element in the State Department which stands for being tough with Russia even though it may mean war is absolutely sound in its position. He thinks I am sabotaging this position; that my sabotaging makes war more likely rather than less likely. I said to Joe, "It seems to me that your approach means that the UNO will never get off the ground." Joe came back with the statement that UNO will never amount to anything if it allows itself to be bluffed at the very start by Russia on the Iranian matter. I said, "I don't believe we have the full truth with regard to Iran." Joe claimed to have the full truth from irreproachable American sources in Iran.

I had the feeling that Joe in effect was a secret agent sent by the get-tough-with-Russia boys in the State Department to come over and sound me out. These boys will move heaven and earth to break the point of view as represented by myself, Senator Pepper, and others. Undoubtedly they have worked successfully on Senator Ball.

Joe was on the verge of hysterics and I couldn't help feeling sorry for him. He thinks the whole world is going to be ruined because we don't get sufficiently tough with Russia. I think it is going to be ruined because of our trying to put Russia in an impossible position by ganging up with Britain against her. I am sure that Joe and the hard-boiled element in the State Department are wrong and Joe is sure that I and the liberals are wrong . . .

MARCH 26, 1946

. . . The meeting in John Snyder's office was for the purpose of seeing if some satisfactory wording for the Vandenberg amendment could not be worked out.[1] Snyder produced a wording which seemed

---

[1] On March 13, 1946, the Senate Committee on Atomic Energy had adopted an amendment, sponsored by Vandenberg, to the McMahon bill. It established a Military Liaison Board to be appointed by the President. The Atomic Energy Commission was to "advise and consult with the board on all atomic energy matters which the board deems to relate to the common defense and security." The board was to have "full authority to acquaint itself with all matters before the commission," and the authority to make recommendations to the commission. The board could also appeal to the President to reverse actions of the commission which it deemed inimical to national security. All in all, the Vandenberg amendment gave the military substantially a veto over decisions of the commission, but only McMahon of the members of the Senate committee opposed it. So did Wallace, who in public warned against delivering the nation into the hands of "military fascism," and so did many atomic scientists. Their protests, which McMahon and others used effectively, stirred up considerable

to me to be satisfactory; it seemed satisfactory to Condon also. In the evening, however, I got in touch with Brien McMahon and found that he did not like it. He said the new wording still gave the military too much power. I put him on the phone to talk to Bob Patterson and both men spent about ten minutes insulting each other over the phone. Bob Patterson is as stiff-necked as McMahon is hot-headed. The truth of the matter is, McMahon confessed, "I have to think of everything of this sort in terms of General Groves." I suggested that he get in touch with General Eisenhower and said I thought that he and Eisenhower between them could surely work out some satisfactory wording. I gave McMahon the description by one of the Time-Life-Fortune men who had sat in on a meeting with General Groves . . . After reading this statement McMahon said, "You know, the first time Groves ever came to see me, when I was made chairman of the Atomic Energy Committee of the Senate, he spent a half hour telling me what a bad person you were and what a bad person Boris Pregel was, and how close you were to each other." He then went on to say, "I would like to get hold of Pregel to find out what he knows about Groves." He went on to say further, "I don't dare to call him on the phone, however, because his wires are tapped. I know that." I told McMahon that I thought Pregel's great sin had been that he contributed too much to the early stages of the atomic bomb work. Moreover, he knew too much about it in the early stages and this reflected so serious on Groves' ego that he couldn't tolerate it.

In our conference with Eisenhower and Patterson in the afternoon, Patterson said that Groves had set up the "compartmentalization" to which the scientists so much objected so as to prevent the agents of any foreign power getting the secret. Of course he meant Russia, although he didn't say so. It was very clear to me that Groves could use the plea of protecting against Russian spies to do anything he wants to. A fellow like Groves, using the Russian phobia as a screen, can, if the military is given the power it desires, go to almost any excess.

General Eisenhower is certainly an unusually likable fellow who wants to do the right thing and get the whole matter cleaned up so that atomic energy can be used for peacetime purposes.

public opposition to the amendment, enough to permit McMahon to move toward a compromise. Eisenhower assisted in that process by revealing his impatience with Groves, and his desire to assure only a reasonable liaison between the commission and the armed services. Early in April Vandenberg, McMahon, and the committee agreed upon language which, as they saw it, achieved Eisenhower's purpose and insured civilian control; see Hewlett and Anderson, *The New World*, pp. 505–513.

APRIL 2, 1946

. . . One of the Department of Justice boys made the point that J. Edgar Hoover listened in on all their conversations. These Justice Department boys are anxious to restore free enterprise to the business world. They have all kinds of evidence of monopoly. The business world generally probably looks on them as a bunch of Reds. As a matter of fact, all they are trying to do is to preserve our system from itself.

APRIL 5, 1946

I got over to the White House at 9:30. Clint Anderson was not there and the President asked me to come in. I took advantage of the opportunity to tell him that the one point I wanted to ask him about particularly in my speech to be given at the Roosevelt dinner on the evening of April 12 had to do with the sentence in which I said that aside from our common language and common literary tradition, we had no more in common with imperialistic England than we had with communistic Russia. The President said that was exactly the way he looked on it and he didn't see any reason in the world why I shouldn't say it. He then gave me a copy of the speech he was going to make the afternoon of April 12.

I also told the President about the atomic energy scientists' fear concerning the secrecy provision which came up a couple of days ago.[1] I said I thought this could be handled by restricting these secrecy restrictions to the military phases only. The President said he agreed and I asked him if I could quote him to that effect. He said, "Yes."

When Anderson came in he said that the reason he had been delayed was because he had been talking with Fitzgerald in London. He said that Fitzgerald, who is traveling with Hoover, reported that the situation in Europe was very much worse than it had been represented and that it was especially bad in Poland. Anderson wanted me to sign with him the letter which he was then submitting to the President. I told him that in view of the fact that it was suggesting

---

[1] The Senate Atomic Energy Committee, increasingly concerned about the Canadian spy case, had rewritten the section of the McMahon bill on dissemination of information. The revised section made no distinction between basic scientific and related technical information. The committee also removed a declaration that free dissemination was to be the cardinal principle of information policy. Instead the new draft stressed restrictions, including the authority of the Secretaries of War and of the Navy to prescribe further safeguards over information about military applications of atomic energy.

raising the price of corn 25 cents a bushel, I would prefer not to. I said that the Hi-Bred Corn Company had sold all its corn for this season and that it would not be advancing its prices anyway. Nevertheless, I said there were bound to be people who would say that I was advocating an advance in the price of corn because of my connection with the Corn Company . . .[1]

MAY 15, 1946

Sprague[2] told me the story of how the manufacture of the sex hormones was controlled by three foreign concerns: (1) a German concern known as Schering, owned by the Alien Property Custodian, (2) a Swiss concern known as LaRoche, and (3) a Swiss concern known as Ciba. Apparently both the male and female sex hormones are made by these three concerns out of the spinal cords of cattle. Sprague, however, has a very unusual Negro chemist by the name of Julian,[3] who has discovered how to make the sex hormones out of the steorols of the soybean. The demand for the sex hormones is so great that there is not a sufficient supply of the spinal cords of cattle. Apparently the demand in recent years has grown by leaps and bounds. From a patent point of view there are two aspects to the situation: (1) The method of making the product, and (2) the product itself. It seems that in England you are allowed to patent the process of making a product but you are not allowed to patent the product finally made. In the United States, however, you are allowed to do both. Dr. Julian has undoubtedly discovered a new way of making the sex hormones. The Schering Corporation, however, claims infringement on the basis of the end product. They have brought suit with regard to the manufacture by the Glidden Company of "Progesteron." The Glidden contention is that "Progesteron" has been manufactured by pregnant women for a million years or so past, and that Schering is not entitled to a patent on it. I told Mr. Sprague I would be glad to meet Dr. Julian sometime and that I would be glad to make arrangements for him to call on Wendell Berge over at the Department of Justice. I said it seemed to me that in all matters of this sort the Department of Commerce should as far as possible throw its influence on the side of abundant, cheap production . . .

1 Away on speaking trips much of the time, Wallace kept no diary during the rest of April and the first two weeks of May 1946.
2 Paul E. Sprague, vice president of the Glidden Company of Cleveland.
3 Percy L. Julian, director of research of the soya products division of the Glidden Company.

MAY 21, 1946

Jim Forrestal started out by saying that he noted Senator Pepper,[1] in reporting on Senator Byrnes' report to the nation Monday night, had said that the "American offensive for peace was started with a broadax." President Truman then interjected to say that a broadax was about the only language the Russians understood . . .

The talk with Walter Lippmann was exceedingly interesting. He said I was the only one in the administration who had displayed the slightest interest in what he had seen on his recent trip to Europe. He thinks the present international negotiations by the State Dept. are being conducted by a bunch of amateurs and that the final result is bound to be very bad. He said Jimmie Byrnes didn't know anything about foreign affairs until a year ago and that Vandenberg and Connally are unbelievably ignorant.

Lippmann says he shares the alarm of the State Department with regard to the Russian behavior but he doesn't see any sense to the get-tough-with-Russia policy unless that policy is exercised in those areas where we can get tough and get away with it. He says we are foolish to think that we can scare Russia with the atomic bomb; that Russia has a perfect answer; that even though she doesn't have any atomic bombs herself she can move at once with her soldiers all the way across western Europe to Antwerp and occupy all the European industrial areas. We would not dare bomb the cities of Europe and kill 100 million people. We couldn't succeed in landing troops on the continent of Europe because we would not have the sympathy of the people of Europe. They don't want to have Europe fought over anymore. Lippmann said that for strategic reasons we ought to insist on Trieste remaining in the hands of Italy but that we are on very weak ground in urging ethnic reasons for the retention by Italy. He pointed out that the South Tyrol was being left in Italian hands although the population was Austrian. He said he was deeply shocked at the exploitation by the Russians of Rumania through a type of oil company in which the Russians held 50 percent of the stock and had management control. He said this device was going to be employed in other of the Balkan states and that it was worse than

---

[1] Pepper had become the most persistent critic within the Senate of Truman's emerging foreign policy. He opposed an Anglo-American alliance, distrusted Byrnes' hard bargaining tactics, advocated working out Soviet-American differences either through the United Nations or at a summit conference, and urged international sharing of basic scientific information about atomic energy; see Thomas G. Patterson, ed., *Cold War Critics* (Chicago, 1971) pp. 114–139.

any type of 19th-century imperialism from the standpoint of exploitation.

Lippmann says that the fundamentally important difference between Russia and the British has to do with the way in which Germany is handled. Russia knows that the British did not really break up the German army. Moreover, they treat the German officers with very great consideration. He confidentially quoted Churchill as having said repeatedly that we could count on 40 German divisions in a fight against Russia. The Russians know this. Lippman mentioned sitting in on a discussion between an American officer and an English officer in which the American officer was taking the point of view that we shouldn't rely on the German troops except for purposes of maintaining the line of supply. The British officer was taking the view that the German troops could be used in fighting the Russians. Lippmann said that Churchill was pushing the point of view that it was important to fight the Russians sometime during the next five years. He said that while he didn't say it in so many words, this was really what he meant in his speech at Fulton, Missouri. He says the Russians naturally know exactly what the British are up to and that accounts for a considerable part of their behavior. He says, however, that the Russians are incredibly bad in their public relations. He thinks we can manage the Russians, be firm with the Russians, and build a peaceful world, but that it will require a lot more skill than the men who are now in charge possess. I asked him what he thought of Dean Acheson. He said he didn't think Dean had so very much on the ball. I showed him the article in the May 20 issue of *Life* magazine by Alsop.[1] He said the thing I should do would be to call in the newspapermen and put out a statement that I had given no interview on Iceland. He said in view of the fact that I had talked on a purely personal basis with the Scandinavian correspondent I could properly say that. He said Alsop was a mouthpiece for a certain clique in the State Department. The only member of the clique he mentioned was Chip Bohlen. He says Chip Bohlen was too young to know what was going on at the time of the last peace conference . . .

---

[1] Joseph and Stewart Alsop, "Tragedy of Liberalism," opened with an attack on Wallace's interview about American bases in Iceland. Pepper had taken the same position as Wallace. They and their supporters, the Alsops argued, had provoked the Icelandic government to frown upon any agreement to provide peacetime bases for United States forces. Such bases, the Alsops believed, were essential as part of American preparedness for resisting the ambitions of the Soviet Union.

MAY 27, 1946

. . . Chester Bowles came in to talk about when he should resign. He definitely doesn't want to hurt the Democratic Party or President Truman. He wants to resign in such a way as to be helpful rather than harmful. He wants to run for senator in Connecticut. I asked him if he had talked the matter over with Brien McMahon. He said he had. I told him I thought he should not resign until and unless OPA legislation had been passed which insured inflation. When he resigned he should tell the country just what it was in for. I asked him to keep me posted as to what he thought I should do and agreed to keep him posted as to what I thought he should do. I told him as far as the present situation was concerned it was a good time for everybody to engage in a little cooling off. Bowles feels about Truman's congressional appearance on Saturday the same way as all the other liberals.[1]

I talked to Bob Hannegan over the phone. He told me he had not attended the special Cabinet Committee meeting on Friday afternoon to discuss legislation. He said he thought the legislation had been drafted by Attorney General Clark and one of his young men, together with Fred Vinson and an attorney by the name of Lesser.[2] He said he did not know himself on Friday that the President was going to propose legislation. He said he himself had advocated the President's going on the air, but going on the air for the purpose of

[1] For several months Truman had been trying to avert a national railway strike. All but two of the railroad unions had agreed to his formula for a wage increase of 18½ cents an hour and various improvements in the rules for arbitration. Two union leaders dissented, Alvanley Johnston of the Brotherhood of Locomotive Engineers and Alexander F. Whitney of the Brotherhood of Railway Trainmen. They called a strike for May 23. On the radio the next day Truman announced that, unless operations resumed at once, he would call in the Army to run the railroads and appear before Congress with a longer-range proposal. On May 25, before a joint session of Congress, he asked for temporary emergency legislation, applicable to national industries designated by the President, to authorize the use of injunctions to prevent any union leader from encouraging members to leave work, to deprive workers who persisted in striking of their seniority rights, to provide penalties against both employers and employees who violated the act, and most extraordinary of all, to empower the President to draft into the armed forces all workers striking against the government. Before Truman had finished making his admittedly drastic proposals, the two dissenting unions had called off the strike. But the President did not withdraw his recommendations, partly because of a pending coal strike. The Congress rejected those recommendations, which drew severe criticism especially from Senators Pepper and Taft, ordinarily antagonists but now linked by their opposition to Truman's extravagant suggestions.
[2] Lawrence S. Lesser.

explaining things to the people. I asked Bob who wrote the President's speech and presidential message. He said the President himself had written a good bit of it but with the help of Clark Clifford and Sam Rosenman. He said Sam Rosenman was against the President doing what he did.

MAY 28, 1946

At the cabinet luncheon the labor situation was the only thing up for discussion. All remarks were quite restrained except the President's comments on Claude Pepper. He has a very deep animus against Pepper. He says Pepper's only motive is to get publicity. He related how when the members of the Truman Committee were at the Bath Shipyards in Maine, at the launching of a destroyer, when Truman was broadcasting to England Pepper tried to take the microphone away from him. He said all that was necessary to get 90 percent of the senators against anything was to have Claude Pepper come out on the floor for it. He says Pepper is purely opportunistic. Truman has very much the same feeling about Downey and Guffey. He calls them both synthetic liberals. He says they both were in touch with the White House a week ago asking for vigorous action on the strikes. When the action came it was so much more vigorous than they expected that they completely right-about-faced. Lew Schwellenbach volunteered that he did not like very much the provision of the President's bill for drafting labor into the Army. I said I felt the same way as Lew did. Jimmie Byrnes and Vinson both said the President should stand pat. I than intervened and said, "Well, if the Senate changes it on him, he doesn't need to feel too badly." Truman grinned and I could see that he wouldn't feel at all badly if the Senate changed. It is obvious, of course, that he won't propose a change, at any rate until after the coal strike is out of the way.

Bob Hannegan mentioned that Bowles was working with both Bill Green and Phil Murray to get them to agree on a no-strike pledge which both men would make to the President. The President said that such a statement would be meaningless; that they had given him such a pledge two weeks after the war ended, again last December, and still again at another time. He said they had not kept their pledge. Schwellenbach intervened to say that they couldn't keep their pledge; that they had no way of controlling their men.

Clint Anderson volunteered that the President's emergency bill would never pass the Senate. There was a lot of comment about the phenomenon of Claude Pepper and Bob Taft sleeping in the same bed. I volunteered the opinion that it was the President's statement about conscripting of profits that put Taft in bed with Pepper. Lew Schwellenbach brought up the story of the refusal of Allis Chalmers to negotiate with labor. He had a hair-raising story in which justice was obviously on the side of labor. He then suggested that the President go on the air this Friday night and make a speech as vigorous against Allis Chalmers . . . as he had made against Whitney and Johnston. The President said, "Well, while I am at it I might as well get everybody mad at me" . . .

While we were waiting for the automobile, Forrestal said to me that he was going to be having dinner tonight with Saltonstall and that he was going to suggest to Saltonstall to use his influence to knock out the provision of the President's emergency bill providing for drafting striking union labor in the Army. Forrestal said he felt the same way as Schwellenbach and I did. He wanted to know how I thought the President would feel about knocking that provision out. I told him my judgment was that the President would really be very happy if it were knocked out but that obviously he couldn't say so. I said my information was based solely on the expression on the President's face when I made my comment during the luncheon.

As I left the luncheon and waved good-by to the President he said, "I want to have a talk with you as soon as this situation is out of the way."

During the luncheon Jimmie Byrnes spent considerable time telling about the conversations he had had with Whitney and Johnston. The reason for his conversations originated in the fact that a year or so ago he and Vinson conducted negotiations with railroad labor. Byrnes made much of the fact that Whitney was the hard fellow to get along with. The President said that the railroad trainmen had not supported him when he ran for senator. I expressed some surprise at this and then Bob Hannegan chimed in and said, "Yes, they supported you, Mr. President." Truman then said, "Well, they didn't come in until the last minute." Schwellenbach said, "Well, there isn't anyone I'd rather have for me in an election than the railroad trainmen. They circulate more and do more to get out the vote than any other group."

Lew Schwellenbach told about a New York friend of his by the name of Murphy, a Democrat, who was sitting in the Racquet Club in New York when the President made his statement to Congress Saturday afternoon. Murphy reported that all the members of the Racquet Club were extravagant in their praise of the President. Murphy then turned upon them and said, "You blankety-blank bastards, you know that not a one of you would vote for him when election time comes!" It was obvious to me that Schwellenbach was very gently trying to tell the President that his new-found support would not be of any value to him but that his new-found enemies in railroad labor would be of great damage to him.

The President made reference to the need for a real draft bill to get manpower for the armed forces, and, looking at Jimmie Byrnes, said, "I know that in your difficult task you are anxious to have a real draft bill passed." This statement, taken in connection with the statement from Buenos Aires in the Tuesday, May 28, New York *Times* about proposed military cooperation between the United States and Argentina against Russia,[1] to me seemed to be very illuminating. Things have reached a very interesting pass when the brother of German Nazis operating in Argentina is looked on as a military co-operator by the United States . . .

Henry Morgenthau phoned to say that on his last radio broadcast Wednesday night he was going to deal with Truman's failure to carry out Roosevelt's policies. He outlined what he was going to say and I told him I thought he was being too harsh. He went into some detail and it was a little difficult to show where he was wrong. I pointed out to Henry, however, that Truman was definitely sold on the Roosevelt policies and wanted to do everything he could to carry them out.

JUNE 6, 1946

At the luncheon at the White House on Thursday, June 6, the President thanked me for the material I had sent over on the Case bill and said he was going to use two paragraphs in his veto message.[2] The

---

[1] The *Times* had reported that General Carlos von der Becke, wartime chief of staff of the Argentine army, was about to leave for Washington. The War Department, the *Times* added, concerned about Soviet-American tensions, was eager to make additional arrangements for hemispheric defense. Further, American Ambassador Messersmith, newly arrived in Argentina, had presented his credentials to the government that Perón dominated. On May 29 the *Times* reported that General Eisenhower and Admiral Nimitz appealed to Congress to permit unprecedented closeness of military and naval cooperation among nations of the Western Hemisphere. To that end, they supported a proposal of the President and the State, War, and Navy Departments to transfer warship and other arms and to standardize military equipment in the Americas.

[2] Truman was about to veto the Case bill, Congress's measure for preventing strikes. As he saw it, the bill had many faults. It placed a five-man board over the Conciliation Service, which he felt had worked effectively since 1913. He considered the bill's terms for mediation punitive. Further, the bill stripped the Secretary of Labor of all responsibility for the mediation board. Most important, Truman much preferred his own proposals to those the bill incorporated.

following excerpts from the veto message are in subtantially the form submitted:

From veto message	*Proposed message submitted by HAW*
At that time I requested temporary legislation to be effective only for a period of six months after the termination of hostilities, and applicable only to those few industries which had been taken over by the Government and in which the President by proclamation declared that an emergency had arisen which affected the entire economy of the country.	Before the Joint Session of the House and Senate I requested the Congress for temporary legislation to be effective only for a period of six months after the declaration by the President or the Congress of the termination of hostilities. I specifically requested that it should be applicable only to those industries in which the President by proclamation declares that an emergency has arisen which affects the entire economy of the United States and it should be effective only in those situations where the President of the United States has taken over the operation of the industry.
In 1943, in the heat of a controversy over a stoppage of war production in the coal mines, the Congress passed the War Labor Disputes Act, more commonly known as the Smith-Connally Act. In his veto message of June 25, 1943, President Roosevelt warned the Congress that the strike-vote provisions of Section 8 of the Smith-Connally Act would not lessen but would promote industrial strife. That prediction was fully borne out by subsequent events. It is my belief that a similar result would follow the approval of this bill.	In 1943, in the heat of a controversy over a stoppage of war production in the coal mines, the Congress passed the War Labor Disputes Act, more commonly known as the Smith-Connally Act. In his veto message of June 25, 1943, President Roosevelt warned the Congress that the Smith-Connally Act would not lessen, but would promote, industrial strife. That prediction was fully borne out by subsequent events. The analogy is well taken in connection with the present bill.
It must be remembered that industrial strife is a symptom of basic economic maladjustments. * * * * A solution of labor-management difficulties therefore is to be found not alone in well considered legislation	Finally, it must always be remembered that industrial strife is a symptom of basic underlying maladjustments. A solution to labor-management difficulties is to be found not only in well considered legislation

dealing directly with industrial relations, but also in a comprehensive
legislative program designed to remove some of the causes of the in-
security felt by many workers and
employers.

dealing directly with industrial relations, but, also, in the comprehensive legislative program which I have
submitted to the Congress designed
to deal with the immediate dangers
of inflation and prevent ultimate
economic collapse.

JUNE 11, 1946

. . . Bob Hannegan went over my St. Louis speech and liked it.[1]
He had no suggestions whatsoever. He told me how deeply appreciative Truman was of the way in which I had stayed by him.

While we were eating at the cabinet luncheon word came in as to
the vote on the Case bill. Truman had not expected the veto to be
upheld in the House. Before the luncheon had taken up I had said to
him, "I assume your veto will be upheld in the Senate, at any rate, and
that the next move will be to tack the Case bill onto your legislation."
He said, "Well, then, I will veto that." In other words, Truman's
enemies have given him a perfect "out."

JULY 17, 1946

Welch Pogue came in to say that tomorrow would be his last day
as Chairman of the Civil Aeronautics Board.[2] He is going to set up a

[1] Wallace spoke on June 14 in St. Louis to a meeting sponsored by the Liberal
Voters League of St. Louis and the National Citizens Political Action Committee. He was there, he said, "fighting for the New Deal" and for progressivism
within the Democratic Party. Third-party advocates should "stop kidding
themselves," for a third party in 1948 would serve only to help the Republicans,
and progressives had no occasion for leaving the Democratic Party. Turning
then to substantive issues, Wallace said:

> We must have job security at an adequate annual wage—a job security that
> will provide an ever-increasing standard of living for all our people . . .
> President Truman has vetoed the Case bill. He vetoed this bill because it
> was a completely unwarranted and unjustifiable attack on the rights of
> labor . . . The butchering of OPA will be as responsible as anything else
> for the industrial strife which we may experience in the coming year . . .
> We need and must have a full implementation by Congress of the Employ-
> ment Act of 1946. We need—and must have—such measures as the extension
> of social security provisions to all American workers; health and medical
> insurance for all; and a minimum wage provision. We need—and must have
> —a real national housing program; and a provision for useful public works,
> including river valley developments and flood control projects. And right
> here in St. Louis, I say that we need a Missouri Valley Authority—and we
> need it now.

[2] James M. Landis had been appointed to succeed Pogue.

private practice of law here in the District of Columbia. He wanted to let me know how much he enjoyed his association with me and how delighted he was that I was reorganizing the Department of Commerce. I told him it was a pretty slow job. He said, "Well, it isn't nearly as difficult a job as reorganizing the Department of State. That is a job which is long overdue." He said they had been having very great difficulty with the Department of State in getting certain aviation routes set up terminating in Russian territory because of the strong anti-Russian feeling in the State Department. He said they especially had difficulty with Stokeley W. Morgan, head of the Aviation Division of the State Department. Mr. Morgan's wife is a White Russian and it could be seen at all times that he was doing his best to prevent any friendly relationship between the United States and Russia. Pogue referred in somewhat the same terms to George P. Baker, Director of the Office of Transport and Communications Policy of the State Department. He did not go into any details with regard to Baker, however. He said the CAB was interested in air routes terminating in Leningrad, Moscow, and Odessa. Also they were interested in a place to land in Siberia on the way to Chungking by the Great Circle Route. The methods followed by the State Department made it impossible to make any progress, however, because the Russians thoroughly distrust the people who are in charge of transportation in the State Department. I asked him if all the members of the CAB felt the same way that he does. He said yes, they all felt much the same way. He referred especially to Oswald Ryan, who is now serving as vice chairman. He doesn't know how Landis will be, who is going in as chairman. He referred especially to a visit which he had with General Clay and General Harper[1] over in Berlin. He said that Clay and Harper were both very seriously disturbed about the way in which the State Department was continually managing things to create the impression of maximum tension between the United States and Russia. He said that he had found it difficult at times to get along with the Russians but on the whole their relationship was excellent. We both agreed that on many subjects the truth is not told in the press and that the only purpose in reading the press is to find out what certain people are up to. Pogue is convinced that we are certainly not being told the truth in the press about Russia—that was based on his observations in Germany. I told him I would write General Clay a friendly letter . . .

[1] General Lucius D. Clay and General Robert W. Harper, one of his staff in the American Occupation Zone in Germany.

JUNE 20, 1946

. . . . The President addressed the BAC dinner Thursday night very briefly. John Snyder[1] was present and the President used John Snyder and myself as his text. He first spoke of me, saying how well he knew me, what great confidence he had in me, how he understood me, and so on and so on—all very complimentary. He said that in certain quarters I was very much misunderstood but that he understood me and knew I was all right. Then he turned to John Snyder and said the same things about John Snyder that he had about me. He said that in certain other quarters John Snyder was very much misunderstood but that he knew John Snyder was all right. He said in the final analysis John Snyder and I both stood for the same things, and that they were the same things that he himself stood for.

On starting the President mentioned that among the folks present at the BAC there was one who had given him credit when he was a haberdasher and to whom he owed quite a bit of money and whom he hoped he had finally gotten paid off. After the meeting was over I walked to the Wardman Park Hotel with Robert Palmer of Cluett, Peabody & Company. He was the man to whom Truman referred. Apparently Truman, after he went bankrupt as a haberdasher, took a long time paying out of his salary what he owed to Cluett, Peabody & Co. This story got abroad among the businessmen and they were all greatly impressed by it. They think Truman is a fine, sincere, earnest, honest man.

JUNE 25, 1946

Felix Belair came in to ask what I thought of Russia now in view of the atomic blast in Pravda on June 24.[2] Knowing how close the New

[1] Truman had appointed Snyder Secretary of the Treasury to succeed Vinson, whom the President had named Chief Justice of the United States.

[2] *Pravda* had condemned the Baruch proposals for controlling atomic weapons as reflecting "an obvious tendency toward world domination," an American intention to consolidate monopoly in the production of bombs, and a threat to the principle of the veto in the United Nations Charter. *Pravda* particularly objected to the idea of a step-by-step movement toward the sharing of information, for during each step the United States could continue to produce and store weapons while other nations could not. However inflammatory *Pravda*'s rhetoric, there was substance to its arguments, as Wallace realized. Baruch's proposals, less generous than those previously formulated by Dean Acheson and David Lilienthal, reflected both congressional hostility to the sharing of atomic information and the administration's growing suspicions of the Soviet Union. In presenting the plan to the General Assembly of the UN on June 14, Baruch had emphasized precisely the points *Pravda* attacked; see Hewlett and Anderson, *The New World*, Ch. 15.

York *Times* is to Mr. Baruch I was rather cautious in my answer and said that in view of the reasonableness of our proposal the Russian action indicated to me that the Russians simply don't trust us. I said that it seemed to me that the most important thing in the world right now was to avoid war with Russia and that I was certain in view of Russia's present reactions that she had some very real and probably very well-founded reasons for not trusting us. Felix wanted to know just what those reasons were and I refused to specify.

Felix went on to say that the United States was awfully cocky about its ability to lick Russia. He said that some little time ago the President had the newspapermen from their boat over on the presidential yacht, the *Williamsburg*, and on that occasion said that the United States could lick Russia. Felix said that the President was very indiscreet in the way he talked to newspapermen off the record. I said to Felix, "Suppose we can lick Russia—what happens then? Moreover, suppose we start dropping atomic bombs on Russian cities—what happens next? Russian troops will immediately occupy all of Europe. Will we then proceed to drop atomic bombs on the cities of France, Belgium, Holland, and others? Are we going to stage another landing on the Normandy beaches? After the war is over is there any guarantee that we ourselves won't go communistic as a result of the unexpected psychological forces let loose?" . . .

JUNE 27, 1946

At the special meeting called by the President to consider whether or not he should veto OPA were present John Steelman, John Snyder, Krug, Chester Bowles, Paul Porter, Charles Ross, Hassett, and a number of men representing the minor agencies dealing with wages and prices. Snyder came out for signing the Taft version of OPA. So also did Krug. I came out for the veto and so also did Charles Ross and Hassett.[1] When the meeting was over I assumed that the President would probably sign the bill. Most of those present either took an in-

[1] The President did veto the bill because of amendments that vitiated its purpose. The Taft amendment stipulated that the OPA permit increases in the prices not only in initial products themselves but also for the benefit of every processor and distributor who handled a product on its way to the ultimate consumer. Wallace and others regarded the cumulative effect of those increases as dangerously inflationary and the task of administering the increases as hopeless. Another group of amendments gave special advantages to certain industries, especially textiles and clothing. A third group, bearing particularly on food products, either removed all authority for controls or transferred authority to the Department of Agriculture or to a decontrol board. In the months following the emasculation of the bill and its veto, prices predictably soared.

between stand or were in favor of signing the bill. Chester Bowles and Paul Porter said that it would be impossible to administer the bill but they didn't come out nearly as strongly for the veto as either myself, Ross, or Hassett. I made the point that there would be almost as much inflation with the mutilated bill as with no bill at all and that therefore we had better meet the issue head on in the hope that under the lash of public opinion Congress would do at least a little something constructive. I said it would be unfortunate for the administration to be in the position of trying to administer the unworkable Taft amendment.

JULY 2, 1946

At the cabinet luncheon the President indicated that Sam Rayburn had gone along very well on the OPA matter but Alben Barkley had not. He said that when he talked with Alben at the Roosevelt memorial services on the Hill he found him very cold.

After I returned to my office from the cabinet luncheon I called up Les Biffle and told him the current situation reminded me a little of the situation between Roosevelt and Barkley at the time of the tax fight. I asked him what he might be able to do to get Barkley into a frame of mind to support the President enthusiastically on the OPA fight. He thought he could do something.

JULY 9, 1946

After the White House luncheon the moving pictures of Bikini were shown. Again and again, from different angles, was portrayed the way in which the explosion had taken place. It looked like the rapid growth of a tremendous, beautiful chrysanthemum. After the showing was over I said to Dean Acheson, "Fifteen or twenty years hence from your farm twenty miles north of the city you will look toward Washington and see these beautiful chrysanthemums arising one after another." Then, more seriously, I said, "Really, you had better get busy on your international atomic energy or something of that sort will come to pass!" . . .

JULY 11, 1946

. . . At the staff meeting Amos Taylor[1] reported on his trip to . . . the West Coast. He said the employment situation was much better

[1] Amos E. Taylor, director of the Bureau of Foreign and Domestic Commerce.

than he had anticipated; that government orders were keeping both the shipyards and the airplane factories more fully employed than had been expected. He referred especially to the Boeing plant in Seattle putting out large numbers of B-29s for the Army. This means to me that the Army is still getting ready to fight Russia.

JULY 16, 1946

At the cabinet luncheon the chief discussion was about Jimmie Byrnes' experiences at the Paris Conference. He dealt particularly with Trieste[1] and his difficulties in keeping Arthur Vandenberg in line. It seems that when the first Trieste proposal was brought out, Mr. Orlando, an Italian eighty-three years old who had had some part in the peace conference after World War I, had come out with a statement about Trieste, "Justice is being murdered." Certain of the Hearst newspapermen were seeing Vandenberg and stirring him up. So Jimmie Byrnes got some of the newspapermen who were more interested in peace than in war with Russia, to go around to see Vandenberg. Among others Jimmie Byrnes listed Joe Alsop as one of those who was strong for peace with Russia. This rather amazed me, knowing what I know of Joe Alsop. It indicated to me quite clearly that Joe Alsop is continuously being used by the State Department.

The particular point that Jimmie Byrnes made about Joe Alsop's presentation to Vandenberg was that Joe Alsop got over to Vandenberg the idea that if there were not some type of internationalization of Trieste it would be only a matter of time until the Russians and Yugoslavs moved in and took Trieste away from Italy anyway. At any rate, Senator Vandenberg came out with a proposal on Trieste which Jimmie Byrnes promptly accepted and then had given out to the press as being prepared jointly with Vandenberg. Vandenberg didn't altogether like getting public credit for it . . .

[1] The Soviet Union supported the Yugoslavian claim to the whole eastern coast of the Adriatic, including Trieste. The United States at first backed Italy's demand for retention of Trieste and the Italian-speaking area around the city. As Wallace's account indicates, Byrnes then retreated to a recommendation creating a Free Territory of Trieste under international administration. While debate over the question continued, Anglo-American forces confronted Yugoslav troops along a line close to the city in the former Italian province of Venezia Giulia. With tensions there mounting, on August 9, 1946, the Yugoslavs forced down, and on August 19 shot down, American transport planes flying over Venezia Giulia. Truman then reinforced the American position. In 1947 a temporary compromise placed the city itself under the administration of the United States and Great Britain with local authorities in charge of municipal functions, while Yugoslavia administered the environs.

Jimmie Byrnes said facetiously that Italy looked on herself not only as one of the nations that had contributed greatly to the victory but also as a nation entitled to reparations from the United States.

Jimmie told with great gusto how he had turned down the pleas of the French, the British, and the Russians for secret conferences. He said that at the first one of their conferences he had gone along with them on the secret thing until he found out that there had been a leak about the American position and when he traced it down he found out that the leak really came through the French Foreign Office. Another leak happened and when he traced it down he found that it came through the British Foreign Office. And then a third leak came and when he traced it down he found it had come out through the Russian Foreign Office. He decided, therefore, that there was nothing to the secrecy business and that he didn't propose to be left out on a limb any longer keeping secrets when the others were leaking. At the next conference Molotov led off with a speech which he had had mimeographed and distributed to the press.

Jimmie said that Tom Connally had failed rapidly during the last three or four months; that the failure was not so obvious in his physical appearance as in his mental alertness. He tells stories very rarely now. Vandenberg, on the other hand, is very alert mentally. Jimmie Byrnes complained that he had to take into conference with him both Vandenberg and Connally, whereas the British, the French and the Russians could take in their experts. It seems that Bevin said to Byrnes, "I'd be in a hell of a fix if I had to take Churchill in with me." Bevin also said to Byrnes, "If you became Secretary of State for fun you would go to hell for pleasure" . . .

JULY 18, 1946

I found Phil Murray eager to see the President call a national stabilization conference. He pointed out that his unions had entered into year-long contracts with the companies at the behest of the President, the President saying that he would do his part in holding the cost of living stable. Due to Congress the President had not been able to keep his part of the bargain; therefore, Philip Murray proposes to write a letter to the President asking for a national stabilization conference. I asked Murray what the CIO was going to do about CIO-PAC. He said they were going to set up a committee under the chairmanship of Jack Kroll of Cincinnati. There are four other members, among whom are David McDonald, secretary of the Steel Workers, George Addes, secretary of the Automobile Workers, and William Pollock, secretary of the Textile Workers. Phil couldn't remember the fourth one. He said the proposal was to have this committee run the CIO-PAC until the election. Jack Kroll as chairman is not taking Sidney Hillman's place. Phil Murray is going away to Atlantic City with his wife for a couple of weeks and after he comes back he will be able to sit down with Claude Pepper, Beanie Baldwin, Henry Morgenthau, and myself to talk over the prospects. I asked him if he would be willing to meet with the President. He said he would . . .

I told Murray that I thought his idea for a national stabilization conference was a good one; that if the President handled it properly it might make the difference between having a Democratic and a Republican Congress. I told Murray I thought he would be doing the President a good turn in calling for such a conference and expressed the hope that he would write the letter to the President in such a way that it would help most toward electing the right kind of a Democratic Congress . . .

I told Truman how important I thought it was to get Phil Murray participating fully in the congressional elections. He agreed and I think will have Murray in sometime tomorrow.

I told Truman that I thought it was important that the Export-Import Bank have more money and that if asking for the larger sum brought in the Russian question at the present time, it might be well to ask for only five or six hundred million dollars. I indicated that there might come a time sometime during the next five or six months when it would be very important to world peace and world trade to be in a position to loan Russia a little money. I indicated that the NAC was now loaning not on a country basis but on a project basis and therefore it seemed to me to be possible to keep the Russian discussion out of the request for additional funds.[1]

I then discussed Russia at some little length. The President said, "We don't have any aggression whatever in our plans against Russia." I then . . . said . . . many important people in Russia felt the United States had designs. They felt this . . . because of the way in which the United States was handling the atomic bomb, because of its air bases all over the world, etc., etc.

The President showed me a dispatch from "Beetle" Smith in which it was pointed out that the Russians were having a very hard time both in White Russia and the Ukraine. There are still 70,000 families

---

[1] The National Advisory Council, with the Secretary of the Treasury as its chairman, had to approve all foreign credits.

without homes, the making of bricks has been going at only 10 percent of the rate planned, and the people have a rather hopeless attitude. Truman said that we could be a great deal of help to Russia if Russia would only let us help her. But she is continuously suspicious of us. I told the President I was going to give to him when I saw him next Tuesday a letter with some comments on the Russian situation. I told him that we were much concerned with Russia because it had a great deal to do with the future volume of world trade. I said I would be pleased to get the President's judgment as to whether I should send a copy of this letter to Jimmie Byrnes. Truman said he had told Stalin at Potsdam that we very much wanted to help Russia in her reconstruction problem.

JULY 23, 1946

I started out my conversation with the President by speaking of the statement by Madame Sun Yat-sen that the Kuomintang was trying to bring about war between the United States and Russia. I said that when I was in China in 1944 I found that there were certain elements in the Kuomintang advocating a policy which could mean nothing but war between the United States and Russia. I told the President that I had spoken flatly to these people saying that we definitely were not going to pursue a policy that might mean war with Russia, no matter how much the Kuomintang might want it.

President Truman said he had never met the Generalissimo but he had met Madame Chiang and he didn't like her. He pulled out a letter from General Marshall dated July 22 in which it appeared that the situation in China was exactly the same as when I was there. The Kuomintang was taking a very hard-boiled, extremist attitude toward the Chinese communists, figuring that they could get the United States to back them up in their hard-boiled attitude. The President said that the Kuomintang was just like any other dictatorship; that you couldn't trust it as far as human rights were concerned.

I then gave the President a copy of my book on Soviet Asia. He said he very much wanted to read it; that he had been hoping I would give him a copy.

I spoke about Roosevelt's very great interest in China and how Roosevelt had been suspicious of the British in the Far East and had worked out an arrangement whereby he hoped to get the British out of Hongkong, and how Roosevelt wanted me to speak to the Generalissimo about this arrangement. I also mentioned how much interested

588 *The Price of Vision*

Roosevelt was in the long frontier between China and Soviet Asia and how he wanted me to observe this area because of the possibility of trouble between China and Russia which might involve the United States.

I then gave the President the letter on Russia[1] . . . saying that this letter would not have the approval of those who believed that war with Russia was inevitable. The President then said very firmly that he was sure that war with Russia was not inevitable. I said that I thought it was just as important to have cordial relations with Russia as with England; that, as a matter of fact, from our own selfish point of view, it might be even more important. I said that we should no more appease England than we should appease Russia. I said that we should stand up very firmly to England as to Russia. Truman said that he agreed wholeheartedly, and that he thought the same applied also to France. I said the British were conducting as much propaganda in the United States as the Russians; that they spent millions of dollars a year on it; that the difference was that the British conducted their propaganda skillfully whereas the Russians were very crude . . .

When I spoke to the President about establishing cordial relations with Russia he said he felt that way and that he was prepared to be very patient with Russia because he felt that Russia during the past 25 years had come a very long distance in a relatively short space of time. He said he hoped it would not be many years until they could be a regular democracy. I said, "Well, it will probably take quite a little time." The President spoke of putting in spare time reading about the peace at Vienna in 1815. Apparently he had been getting his information from Ferrero's last book dealing with the principle of legitimacy as worked out at the Council at Vienna.[2]

At the cabinet luncheon Jimmie Byrnes spent most of the time describing his foreign experiences. He showed no bitterness whatsoever concerning Molotov but it was obvious that he looked on Molotov as his continuous opponent. He had been pressed by the British Ambassador to get the President to come out with a statement deploring the Jewish terrorism in Palestine.[3] He went into considerable detail about

[1] The letter follows this diary entry.
[2] Guglielmo Ferrero, eminent Italian historian and a vocal critic of fascism, had died in 1942. Among his many important books were *The Reconstruction of Europe: Talleyrand and the Congress of Vienna* (English translation, 1941) and *The Principles of Power* (English translation, 1942).
[3] European Jews had migrated to Palestine in increasing numbers during World War II. As their numbers grew along with their bitterness about the German terror, they became more and more dissatisfied with the British Plan of 1939,

the way in which the Russians were expelling the Germans from Austria. President Truman said he thought the Russians had killed eight million Germans in East Prussia.

Secretary Byrnes spoke about how Ben Cohen, Chip Bohlen, and Vishinsky were talking together at one end of the table while he and Molotov, with Pavlov as interpreter, were talking together at the other end. Secretary Byrnes said he didn't know what could be done with these people (the Germans in Austria). Looking down at the other end of the table he heard Vishinsky laugh, pointing his thumb down on the table. Jimmie asked what they were laughing about and it was reported that Vishinsky said, "Put them under." Jimmie Byrnes interpreted this to mean, "Put them under the ground." Jimmie thinks that Vishinsky is a very cruel man. He says, however, that General Zhukov is a very fine man with great strength of character. Unfortunately, General Zhukov has been transferred, he says, and there has been a deliberate effort to minimize his influence. President Truman said it was probably because he had been too friendly with Eisenhower . . .

JULY 23, 1946
HENRY A. WALLACE TO HARRY S. TRUMAN

My dear Mr. President:

I hope you will excuse this long letter. Personally I hate to write long letters, and I hate to receive them.

My only excuse is that this subject is a very important one—probably the most important in the world today. I checked with you about this last Thursday and you suggested after cabinet meeting on Friday that you would like to have my views.

I have been increasingly disturbed about the trend of international affairs since the end of the war, and I am even more troubled by the apparently growing feeling among the American people that another war is coming and the only way that we can head it off is to arm ourselves to the teeth. Yet all of past history indicates that an armaments race does not lead to peace but to war. The months just ahead may well be the crucial period which will decide whether the civilized

---

which provided for an independent Palestine state with a special treaty relationship to Great Britain, and with a government in which both Jews and Arabs shared. By 1946, supported by growing Zionist sentiment among American Jews, the Jews in Palestine were demanding a Jewish state and a Jewish army. Their guerrilla troops and those of the Arabs constantly violated the official but trembling truce.

world will go down in destruction after the five or ten years needed
for several nations to arm themselves with atomic bombs. Therefore
I want to give you my views on how the present trend toward conflict
might be averted.

You may think it strange, in reading further, that I should express so
much concern at this particular time, just after the foreign ministers'
conference at which real progress was made on peace treaties for several eastern European countries and for Italy. Others have expressed a
feeling of increased optimism that still further progress could be made
through continued negotiations on the same basis, even though the
remaining European issues are much more difficult than those on which
a measure of agreement has already been reached. I am fully appreciative of the efforts that have been made and the patience that has been
exercised by our various representatives who have carried on negotiations with the Russians during the last few years. I am conscious of
the aggravations they have put up with and of the apparent incon-
sistencies on the part of Russian representatives. On the other hand, I
feel these very difficulties make it necessary for some of us who, from
the outside, are watching the course of events to voice our opinions.

Incidentally, as Secretary of Commerce I talk to a good many businessmen, and I find them very much concerned over the size of the
federal budget and the burden of the national debt. For the next fiscal
year and for the year immediately ahead by far the largest category
of federal spending is the national defense. For example, the total
recommended federal appropriations for the fiscal year 1947 submitted
to the Congress in the official budget amounted to about $36 billion.
Of the total budget some $13 billion was for the War and Navy De-
partments alone. An additional $5 billion was for war liquidation
activities. Ten billion represented interest on the public debt and veterans' benefits, which are primarily the continuing costs of past wars.
These items total $28 billion, or about 80 percent of the total recom-
mended expenditures.

Clearly, a large reduction in the federal budget would require a cut
in military appropriations. These appropriations are now more than
ten times as great as they were during the thirties. In the 1938 budget
appropriations for national defense were less than a billion dollars,
compared with $13 billion for the present fiscal year. Thus, even
from a purely dollars-and-cents standpoint American business and the
American people have an interest in organizing a peaceful world in
which the completely unproductive expenditures on national defense
could be reduced.

Of course, dollars and cents are not the most important reason why we all want a peaceful world. The fundamental reason is that we do not wish to go through another war—and especially an atomic war, which will undoubtedly be directed primarily against civilian populations and may well mean the end of modern civilization.

Yet are we really concentrating all our efforts on a program to build a lasting peace? There can be no doubt that the American people want and expect that their leaders will work for an enduring peace. But the people must necessarily leave to their leaders the specific ways and means to this objective. I think that at the moment the people feel that the outlook for the elimination of war is dark, that other nations are willfully obstructing American efforts to achieve a permanent peace.

How do American actions since V-J Day appear to other nations? I mean by actions the concrete things like $13 billion for the War and Navy Departments, the Bikini tests of the atomic bomb and continued production of bombs, the plan to arm Latin America with our weapons, production of B-29s and planned production of B-36s, and the effort to secure air bases spread over half the globe from which the other half of the globe can be bombed. I cannot but feel that these actions must make it look to the rest of the world as if we were only paying lip service to peace at the conference table. These facts rather make it appear either (1) that we are preparing ourselves to win the war which we regard as inevitable or (2) that we are trying to build up a predominance of force to intimidate the rest of mankind. How would it look to us if Russia had the atomic bomb and we did not, if Russia had 10,000-mile bombers and air bases within a thousand miles of our coastlines and we did not?

NO LASTING SECURITY IN ARMAMENTS

Some of the military men and self-styled "realists" are saying:

> "What's wrong with trying to build up a predominance of force? The only way to preserve peace is for this country to be so well armed that no one will dare attack us. We know that America will never start a war."

The flaw in this policy is simply that it will not work. In a world of atomic bombs and other revolutionary new weapons, such as radioactive poison gases and biological warfare, a peace maintained by a predominance of forces is no longer possible.

Why is this so? The reasons are clear:

First. Atomic warfare is cheap and easy compared with old-fashioned war. Within a very few years several countries can have atomic bombs and other atomic weapons. Compared with the cost of large armies and the manufacture of old-fashioned weapons, atomic bombs cost very little and require only a relatively small part of a nation's production plant and labor force. *Second.* So far as winning a war is concerned, having more bombs —even many more bombs—than the other fellow is no longer a decisive advantage. If another nation had enough bombs to eliminate all of our principal cities and our heavy industry, it wouldn't help us very much if we had 10 times as many bombs as we needed to do the same to them.

Third. And most important, the very fact that several nations have atomic bombs will inevitably result in a neurotic, fear-ridden, itching-trigger psychology in all the peoples of the world, and because of our wealth and vulnerability we would be among the most seriously affected. Atomic war will not require vast and time-consuming preparations, the mobilization of large armies, the conversion of a large proportion of a country's industrial plants to the manufacture of weapons. In a world armed with atomic weapons, some incident will lead to the use of those weapons.

There is a school of military thinking which recognizes these facts, recognizes that when several nations have atomic bombs, a war which will destroy modern civilization will result and that no nation or combination of nations can win such a war. This school of thought therefore advocates a "preventive war," an attack on Russia *now* before Russia has atomic bombs. This scheme is not only immoral but stupid. If we should attempt to destroy all the principal Russian cities and her heavy industry, we might well succeed. But the immediate countermeasure which such an attack would call forth is the prompt occupation of all continental Europe by the Red Army. Would we be prepared to destroy the cities of all Europe in trying to finish what we had started? This idea is so contrary to all the basic instincts and principles of the American people that any such action would be possible only under a dictatorship at home.

Thus the "predominance of force" idea and the notion of a "defensive attack" are both unworkable. The only solution is the one which you have so wisely advanced and which forms the basis of the Moscow statement on atomic energy. That solution consists of mutual trust and confidence among nations, atomic disarmament, and an effective system of enforcing that disarmament.

INTERNATION CONTROL OF ATOMIC ENERGY

There is, however, a fatal defect in the Moscow statement, in the Acheson report, and in the American plan recently presented to the United Nations Atomic Energy Commission. That defect is the scheme, as it is generally understood, of arriving at international agreements by "easy stages," of requiring other nations to enter into binding commitments not to conduct research into the military uses of atomic energy and to disclose their uranium and thorium resources while the United States retains the right to withhold its technical knowledge of atomic energy until the international control and inspection system is working to our satisfaction. In other words, we are telling the Russians that if they are "good boys" we may eventually turn over our knowledge of atomic energy to them and to the other nations. But there is no objective standard of what will qualify them as being "good" nor any specified time for sharing our knowledge.

Is it any wonder that the Russians did not show any great enthusiasm for our plan? Would we have been enthusiastic if the Russians had a monopoly of atomic energy, and offered to share the information with us at some indefinite time in the future at their discretion if we agreed now not to try to make a bomb and give them information on our secret resources of uranium and thorium? I think we would react as the Russians appear to have done. We would have put up counter-proposal for the record, but our real effort would go into trying to make a bomb so that our bargaining position would be equalized. That is the essence of the Russian position, which is very clearly stated in the *Pravda* article of June 24, 1946.

It is perfectly clear that the "step-by-step" plan in any such one-sided form is not workable. The entire agreement will have to be worked out and wrapped up in a single package. This may involve certain steps or stages, but the timing of such steps must be agreed to in the initial master treaty. Realistically, Russia has two cards which she can use in negotiating with us: (1) our lack of information on the state of her scientific and technical progress on atomic energy and (2) our ignorance of her uranium and thorium resources. These cards are nothing like as powerful as our cards—a stockpile of bombs, manufacturing plants in actual production, B-29s and B-36s, and our bases covering half the globe. Yet we are in effect asking her to reveal her only two cards immediately—telling her that after we have seen her cards we will decide whether we want to continue to play the game.

Insistence on our part that the game must be played our way will only lead to deadlock. The Russians will redouble their efforts to manufacture bombs, and they may also decide to expand their "security zones" in a serious way. Up to now, despite all our outcries against it, their efforts to develop a security zone in eastern Europe and in the Middle East are small change from the point of view of military power as compared with our air bases in Greenland, Okinawa and many other places thousands of miles from our shores. We may feel very self-righteous if we refuse to budge on our plan and the Russians refuse to accept it, but that means only one thing—the atomic armament race is on in deadly earnest.

I am convinced therefore that if we are to achieve our hopes of negotiating a treaty which will result in effective international atomic disarmament we must abandon the impractical form of the "step-by-step" idea which was presented to the United Nations Atomic Energy Commission. We must be prepared to reach an agreement which will commit us to disclosing information and destroying our bombs at a specified time or in terms of specified actions by other countries, rather than at our unfettered discretion. If we are willing to negotiate on this basis, I believe the Russians will also negotiate seriously with a view to reaching an agreement.

There can be, of course, no absolute assurance the Russians will finally agree to a workable plan if we adopt this view. They may prefer to stall until they also have bombs and can negotiate on a more equal basis, not realizing the danger to themselves as well as the rest of the world in a situation in which several nations have atomic bombs. But we must make the effort to head off the atomic bomb race. We have everything to gain by doing so, and do not give up anything by adopting this policy as the fundamental basis for our negotiation. During the transition period toward full-scale international control we retain our technical know-how, and the only existing production plants for fissionable materials and bombs remain within our borders.

The Russian counterproposal itself is an indication that they may be willing to negotiate seriously if we are. In some respects their counterproposal goes even farther than our plan and is in agreement with the basic principles of our plan, which is to make violations of the proposed treaty a *national and international crime* for which individuals can be punished.

It will have been noted that in the preceding discussion I have not mentioned the question of the so-called "veto." I have not done so because the veto issue is completely irrelevant, because the proposal to "abolish the veto," which means something in the general activities of the Security Council, has no meaning with respect to a treaty on atomic energy. If we sign a treaty with other nations, we will all have agreed to do certain things. Until we arrive at such a treaty, we as well as the other major powers will have the power of veto. Once the treaty is ratified, however, the question of the veto becomes meaningless. If any nation violates the treaty provision, any [provision] of permitting inspection of suspected illegal bomb-making activities, what action is there that can be vetoed? As in the case of any other treaty violation, the remaining signatory nations are free to take what action they feel is necessary, including the ultimate step of declaring war.

OTHER PROBLEMS OF AMERICAN-RUSSIAN RELATIONSHIPS

I believe that for the United States and Russia to live together in peace is the most important single problem facing the world today. Many people, in view of the relatively satisfactory outcome of the recent Paris Conference, feel that good progress is being made on the problem of working out relations between the Anglo-Saxon powers and Russia. This feeling seems to me to be resting on superficial appearances more productive of a temporary truce than of final peace. On the whole, as we look beneath the surface in late July of 1946, our actions and those of the western powers in general carry with them the ultimate danger of a third world war—this time an atomic world war. As the strongest single nation, and the nation whose leadership is followed by the entire world with the exception of Russia and a few weak neighboring countries in easten Europe, I believe that we have the opportunity to lead the world to peace.

In general there are two overall points of view which can be taken in approaching the problem of the United States–Russian relations. The first is that it is not possible to get along with the Russians and therefore war is inevitable. The second is that war with Russia would bring catastrophe to all mankind, and therefore we must find a way of living in peace. It is clear that our own welfare as well as that of the entire world requires that we maintain the latter point of view. I am sure that this is also your opinion, and the radio address of the Secretary of State on July 15 clearly indicates that he is prepared to negotiate as long as may be necessary to work out a solution on this basis.

We should try to get an honest answer to the question of what the factors are which cause Russia to distrust us, in addition to the question of what factors lead us to distrust Russia. I am not sure that we have as a nation or an administration found an adequate answer to either question, although we have recognized that both questions are of critical importance.

FACTORS IN AMERICAN DISTRUST OF RUSSIA

Our basic distrust of the Russians, which has been greatly intensified in recent months by the playing up of conflict in the press, stems from differences in political and economic organization. For the first time in our history defeatists among us have raised the fear of another system as a successful rival to democracy and free enterprise in other countries and perhaps even our own. I am convinced that we can meet that challenge as we have in the past by demonstrating that economic abundance can be achieved without sacrificing personal, political, and religious liberties. We cannot meet it as Hitler tried to by an anti-Comintern alliance.

It is perhaps too easy to forget that despite the deep-seated differences in our cultures and intensive anti-Russian propaganda of some twenty-five years' standing, the American people reversed their attitudes during the crisis of war. Today, under the pressure of seemingly insoluble international problems and continuing deadlocks, the tide of American public opinion is again turning against Russia. In this reaction lies one of the dangers to which this letter is addressed.

FACTORS IN RUSSIAN DISTRUST OF THE WESTERN WORLD

I should list the factors which make for Russian distrust of the United States and of the Western world as follows: The first is Russian history, which we must take into account because it is the setting in which Russians see all actions and policies of the rest of the world. Russian history for over a thousand years has been a succession of attempts, often unsuccessful, to resist invasion and conquest—by the Mongols, the Turks, the Swedes, the Germans, and the Poles. The scant thirty years of the existence of the Soviet government has in Russian eyes been a continuation of their historical struggle for national existence. The first four years of the new regime, from 1917 through 1921, were spent in resisting attempts at destruction by the Japanese, British, and French, with some American assistance, and by the several White Russian armies encouraged and financed by the Western powers. Then, in 1941, the Soviet state was almost conquered by the Germans after a period during which the Western European powers had apparently acquiesced in the rearming of Germany in the belief that the Nazis would seek to expand eastward rather than westward. The Russians, therefore, obviously see themselves as fighting for their existence in a hostile world.

Second, it follows that to the Russians all of the defense and security measures of the Western powers seem to have an aggressive intent. Our actions to expand our military security system—such steps as extending the Monroe Doctrine to include the arming of the Western Hemisphere nations, our present monopoly of the atomic bomb, our interest in outlying bases, and our general support of the British Empire —appear to them as going far beyond the requirements of defense. I think we might feel the same if the United States were the only capitalistic country in the world, and the principal socialistic countries were creating a level of armed strength far exceeding anything in their previous history. From the Russian point of view, also, the granting of a loan to Britain and the lack of tangible results on their request to borrow for rehabilitation purposes may be regarded as another evidence of strengthening of an anti-Soviet bloc.

Finally, our resistance to her attempts to obtain warm-water ports and her own security system in the form of "friendly" neighboring states seem, from the Russian point of view, to clinch the case. After twenty-five years of isolation and after having achieved the status of a major power, Russia believes that she is entitled to recognition of her new status. Our interest in establishing democracy in eastern Europe, where democracy by and large has never existed, seems to her an attempt to reestablish the encirclement of unfriendly neighbors which was created after the last war and which might serve as a springboard of still another effort to destroy her.

WHAT SHOULD WE DO

If this analysis is correct, and there is ample evidence to support it, the action to improve the situation is clearly indicated. The fundamental objective of such action should be to allay any reasonable Russian grounds for fear, suspicion, and distrust. We must recognize that the world has changed and that today there can be no "one world" unless the United States and Russia can find some way of living together. For example, most of us are firmly convinced of the soundness of our position when we suggest the internationalization and defortification of the Danube or of the Dardanelles, but we would be horrified and angered by any Russian counterproposal that would involve also the internationalizing and disarming of Suez or Panama. We must recognize that to the Russians these seem to be identical situations.

We should ascertain from a fresh point of view what Russia believes to be essential to her own security as a prerequisite to the writing of the peace and to cooperation in the construction of a world order. We should be prepared to judge her requirements against the background of what we ourselves and the British have insisted upon as essential to our respective security. We should be prepared, even at the expense of risking epithets of appeasement, to agree to reasonable Russian guarantees of security. The progress made during June and July on the Italian and other treaties indicates that we can hope to arrive at understanding and agreement on this aspect of the problem.

We should not pursue further the question of the veto in connection with atomic energy, a question which is irrelevant and should never have been raised. We should be prepared to negotiate a treaty which will establish a definite sequence of events for the establishment of international control and development of atomic energy. This, I believe, is the most important single question, and the one on which the present trend is definitely toward deadlock rather than ultimate agreement.

We should make an effort to counteract the irrational fear of Russia which is being systematically built up in the American people by certain individuals and publications. The slogan that communism and capitalism, regimentation and democracy, cannot continue to exist in the same world is, from a historical point of view, pure propaganda. Several religious doctrines, all claiming to be the only true gospel and salvation, have existed side by side with a reasonable degree of tolerance for centuries. This country was for the first half of its national life a democratic island in a world dominated by absolutist governments.

We should not act as if we too felt that we were threatened in today's world. We are by far the most powerful nation in the world, the only Allied nation which came out of the war without devastation and much stronger than before the war. Any talk on our part about the need for strengthening our defenses further is bound to appear hypocritical to other nations.

THE ROLE OF ECONOMIC RELATIONSHIPS

We should also be prepared to enter into economic discussion without demanding that the Russians agree *in advance* to discussion of a series of what are to them difficult and somewhat unrelated political and economic concessions. Although this is the field in which my Department is most directly concerned, I must say that in my opinion this aspect of the problem is not as critical as some of the others, and certainly is far less important than the question of atomic energy control. But successful negotiation in this field might help considerably to bridge the chasm that separates us. The question of a loan should be approached on economic and commercial grounds and should be disassociated as much as possible from the current misunderstandings which flow from the basic differences between their system and ours. You have already clearly disassociated yourself and the American people from the expressions of anti-Soviet support for the British Loan. If we could have followed up your statement on signing the British Loan Bill with a loan to USSR on a commercial basis and on similar financial terms, I believe that it would have clearly demonstrated that this country is not attempting to use its economic resources in the game of power politics. In the light of the present Export-Import Bank situation, it is now of the greatest importance that we undertake general economic discussions at an early date.

It is of the greatest importance that we should discuss with the Russians in a friendly way their long-range economic problems and the future of our cooperation in matters of trade. The reconstruction program of the USSR and the plans for the full development of the Soviet Union offer tremendous opportunities for American goods and American technicians.

American products, especially machines of all kinds, are well established in the Soviet Union. For example, American equipment, practices, and methods are standard in coal mining, iron and steel, oil, and nonferrous metals.

Nor would this trade be one-sided. Although the Soviet Union has been an excellent credit risk in the past, eventually the goods and services exported from this country must be paid for by the Russians by exports to us and to other countries. Russian products which are either definitely needed or which are noncompetitive in this country are various nonferrous metal ores, furs, linen products, lumber products, vegetable drugs, paper and pulp, and native handicrafts.

I feel that negotiations on the establishment of active trade might well help to clear away the fog of political misunderstanding. Such discussions might well be initiated while we are endeavoring to reach a common ground on security issues, and if conducted in an understanding manner, could only serve to make that problem easier. In the memorandum which I sent to you in March and which I suggested should be given to General Smith to take to Moscow, I made certain suggestions for trade discussions and a trade mission. In preference to proposed discussions in this country I want to renew my original proposal and urge the appointment of a mission to Moscow. Such a mission might have as its objective the drafting of a proposal involving Russian reconstruction and collaboration with Russia in the industrial and economic development of areas in which we have joint interests, such as the Middle East. As I stated at that time, I am prepared to make suggestions for the composition of the mission and some of the specific economic questions to be discussed. The Department of Commerce has already arranged, with the cooperation of the State Department, to send two representatives to Moscow for the months of July and August for preliminary discussions of a much more limited scope. I think it is very significant that most of the more optimistic reports about the possibilities of getting along with the Russians have come from American observers who were businessmen. I have in mind such men as Wendell Willkie, Eric Johnston, and former Ambassador Joe Davies. The Russians seem to be friendly to, and seem to have respect for, capitalist businessmen.

A number of observers have reported that the Soviet leaders are "isolationists" and appear to be lacking a true insight into the principles, motives, and ways of thinking in other nations. We must admit, however, that they pointed out the symptoms and the way to prevent World War II in their promotion of the concept of collective security. And aside from that, it seems to me we should try to do something constructive about their isolationism and ignorance, and I believe the aforementioned trade mission could accomplish much in that direction. I gather, too, that is part of what you have had in mind in inviting Premier Stalin to visit America.

Many of the problems relating to the countries bordering on Russia could more readily be solved once an atmosphere of mutual trust and confidence is established and some form of economic arrangements are worked out with Russia. These problems also might be helped by discussions of an economic nature. Russian economic penetration of the Danube area, for example, might be countered by concrete proposals for economic collaboration in the development of the resources of this area, rather than by insisting that the Russians should cease their unilateral penetration and offering no solution to the present economic chaos there.

SUMMARY

This proposal admittedly calls for a shift in some of our thinking about international matters. It is imperative that we make this shift. We have little time to lose. Our postwar actions have not yet been adjusted to the lessons to be gained from experience of Allied cooperation during the war and the facts of the atomic age.

It is certainly desirable that, as far as possible, we achieve unity on the home front with respect to our international relations; but unity on the basis of building up conflict abroad would prove to be not only unsound but disastrous. I think there is some reason to fear that in our earnest efforts to achieve bipartisan unity in this country we may have given way too much to isolationism masquerading as tough realism in international affairs.

The real test lies in the achievement of international unity. It will be fruitless to continue to seek solutions for the many specific problems that face us in the making of the peace and in the establishment of an enduring international order without first achieving an atmosphere of mutual trust and confidence. The task admittedly is not an easy one. There is no question, as the Secretary of State has indicated, that negotiations with the Rusisans are difficult because of cultural differences, their traditional isolationism, and their insistence on a visible quid pro quo in all agreements. But the task is not an insuperable one if we take into account that to other nations our foreign policy consists not only of the principles that we advocate but of the actions we take. Fundamentally, this comes down to the point discussed earlier in this letter, that even our own security, in the sense that we have known it in the past, cannot be preserved by military means in a world armed with atomic weapons. The only type of security which can be maintained by our own military force is the type described by a military man before the Senate Atomic Energy Committee—a security against invasion after all our cities and perhaps 40 million of our city population have been destroyed by atomic weapons. That is the best that "security" on the basis of armaments has to offer us. It is not the kind of security that our people and the people of the other United Nations are striving for.

I think that progressive leadership along the lines suggested above would represent and best serve the interests of the large majority of our people, would reassert the forward-looking position of the Democratic Party in international affairs, and, finally, would arrest the new trend toward isolationism and a disastrous atomic world war . . .[1]

JULY 24, 1946

The meeting on OPA at the White House was exceedingly interesting. Everybody favored signing the new bill, although everybody had

---

[1] On August 8 Truman acknowledged receipt of the letter but invited no further conversation about its substance. In September Drew Pearson planned to print a copy of the letter which he had obtained from one of his sources of information in the Department of State. Wallace therefore released the letter to the press himself on September 17, 1946.

qualms about the new bill.[1] Paul Porter indicated that under the new bill the cost of living would rise from June 28 to December by 7.22 percent. I whispered to Krug that I thought this was spurious accuracy. Porter said this was based on the assumption of a rollback in agricultural prices to the June 28 level. Anderson said there couldn't be a rollback in prices to the June 28 level. Marriner Eccles said that something had to be done budgetwise to relieve the continuous pressure toward inflation; that you couldn't do everything via the OPA route.

I said that I had come to the meeting fully prepared to recommend that the President sign the bill but after hearing the discussion between Porter and the Secretary of Agriculture, I was beginning to have some reservations. I said that 99 times out of a hundred the best politics was what was best for the people. I said in this case probably what was best for the people was to sign the bill, but I wasn't altogether sure it was the best politics to sign the bill. I said I thought that President Truman should sign the bill expressing considerable misgivings. I also said that the administration of the bill, because of the agricultural situation, was going to be exceedingly difficult—probably even more difficult than Porter himself realized. Porter replied that that was impossible . . .

The President spoke very vigorously in one part of the meeting about the necessity of cutting down on the budget, saying that he had already pruned it about $3 billion. He said the place to cut was in the askings of the Army and Navy. This agreed completely with conversations I had had with him earlier. But within half an hour he was saying that after the last war we had cut our Navy too much; that we had to be careful not to cut our Army and Navy; that if we had not cut our Army and Navy after the last war there would not have been World War II. I was utterly amazed that he could go two different directions within the hour. It reminded me of Tuesday when within the hour he spoke about being patient with Russia to me and then at the cabinet luncheon agreed completely with Jimmie Byrnes in a number of cracks he took against Russia. I suspect there has never been a President who could move two different directions with less time intervening than Truman. He feels completely sincere and earnest at all times and is not disturbed in the slightest by the different directions

[1] On July 25, Truman, in signing the new OPA bill, expressed his reluctance at having to accept so limited a measure. The act placed no controls on commodities, the prices of which began at once to rise. The act also lifted controls from hundreds of lesser items. The ensuing inflation, and the withholding from market of products still under controls, persuaded Truman in November to remove all controls over prices and wages.

in which his mind can go almost simultaneously. I say this realizing that he has always agreed with me on everything.

JULY 26, 1946

TELEPHONE CONVERSATION BETWEEN THE PRESIDENT
AND SECRETARY WALLACE

Secretary asked if the President had seen the front-page story in the New York *Times* today—on Palestine.[1] President said he had not, but that both Mead and Wagner had tried to get to him. He talked with Mead but Wagner wasn't able to make it. The President said the Cabinet Committee is, he thinks, implementing to the letter the report of the British-American Commission. The reports that the President has are excellent and it looks as if we are going to get the 100,000 Jews in there immediately; that is, as fast as they can be absorbed.

Secretary said when this story hit the streets yesterday one of the high Republicans—Secretary gets this indirectly through a Jewish friend (Abe Spanel)—saw a great opportunity to prepare some extensive publicity to break next Monday, and a large part of the attack is going to be on the basis of the British setting up what amounts to a Jewish ghetto. The President said it doesn't do anything of the kind—the Jews get the best part of Palestine as their province. Secretary said the area amounted to probably 30 miles by 50 miles. The President said they are just as wrong as they can be—as soon as the agreement has been reached it will be made public and it sets up an autonomous Jewish province and an autonomous Arab province under the trusteeship of the United Nations. Secretary said then this New York *Times* piece is completely inaccurate. The President said yes, if that is what it says it isn't true at all. Secretary then read a portion of the New York *Times* piece to the President. The President said the only thing "it" controls is foreign relations and excise taxes for the time being until the whole thing gets properly implemented. They

[1] The *Times* had reported from London that the proposed constitution for Palestine would "vest strong powers in a British-controlled central government, leaving very little authority to . . . separate Arab and Zionist provinces." Further, admission to Palestine of 100,000 homeless European Jews, which Truman had recommended, was to be conditional upon acceptance of the constitution. Further still, the Jewish area was to be confined to a narrow coastal strip. The report said that Byrnes' deputy in negotiations over Palestine, Henry F. Grady, was pleased with the proposals, but that leaders of the Jewish Agency for Palestine, who were distressed, had been unsuccessful in their efforts to see him.

will allocate the import quantities to each one of the provinces but from there on every part of the government is entirely independent just like our states—as a matter of fact, it is modeled on our state setup.

Secretary said he is suspicious of the New York *Times* thing—they are playing hand-in-hand with the Republicans. President said it implements the provisions of the American-Palestine Committee. Said he would give the Secretary a copy just as soon as it is ready. The President said he would get hold of Byrnes immediately and see how soon we are going to have a release. Wagner and Mead were champing at the bit to see the President, but the President is happy at the way things are working out. The Jewish setup will be completely autonomous, following exactly the recommendations of the commission.

The President said there is an Arab section of Palestine, which, with the proposed setup of public works, is going to be made livable and retained for the use of the Jews when it is made ready for occupancy —all lower half of the Palestine. Secretary asked if that would make possible the Jordan River Authority, and the President said yes.

Secretary said the Republican drive would be in effect that we are setting up a ghetto. President reiterated that the Jews are getting the best part of Palestine—the only part that can be cultivated and all that section where their *historical background* is.[1] Secretary said he is sure there is poison being brewed in the New York *Times* story. The President said he thinks this is going to be a solution of the thing— he has been in touch with these people every day and has given them explicit instructions and they followed them exactly.

JULY 26, 1946

At the cabinet meeting President Truman first asked for a report from Forrestal on the atomic bomb. Forrestal said there had been too much Hollywood reporting and then said there was really nothing he could add. He then went on to say that MacArthur in Japan and Clay in Germany were doing a marvelous job. Truman kidded Bob Patterson about getting such a compliment from the Navy. Forrestal then went on to say that we had our Marines strung out very thinly all over China along the railroads; that in many places there were only five to fifteen marines; that the Chinese communists could clean them out at any time and that it was a perilous situation and something ought to be done about it. Forrestal then said he didn't think we should get out of China. He said the Russians had lots of propagandists in various parts of China. He said there were more Russian

[1] Wallace considered that remark "an amazing statement."

propagandists carrying on work in Shanghai now than there had ever been before. All this indicates to me rather clearly that the United States is going to make the same mistake with China after this war that we made with Russia after the last war. China eventually will be very much more progressive than the present Kuomintang crowd and these progressives will feel that they have earned their place in the sun as a result of help from Russia and in spite of the opposition of the United States. It will not make for the maximum of trade and good will in China . . .

JULY 29, 1946

. . . Abe Spanel called up all hot and bothered about the Palestine situation, claiming that Taft and Vandenberg had given two hot speeches[1] and urging me to get in touch with the President at once urging the President not to let Jimmie Byrnes give out any statement on Palestine until the whole thing had been carefully considered. I passed the whole matter on to the President, who said he was very grateful. He told me that Jimmie Byrnes and Attlee were not going to give out any statement at the present time. I called up Abe Spanel later and hold him that Truman had received my suggestions in very good spirit. He said this was quite different from the reception that Mead, Wagner, and James McDonald[2] got. To McDonald (who is a very good Catholic) Truman said, "I'm not a New Yorker. All these people are pleading for a special interest. I am an American." Whereupon McDonald became intensely indignant with Truman and Truman backed up some.

JULY 29, 1946

TELEPHONE CONVERSATION BETWEEN THE PRESIDENT
AND SECRETARY WALLACE

The Secretary said he didn't like to bother the President again on the Palestine matter. He thought the President probably knew that

[1] Taft was especially emphatic. "The new British plan," he said, "means not only complete frustration for the Jews of Palestine, but deep despair for the million and one-half surviving Jews of Europe." On the Democratic side, Wagner described the plan as "a deceitful device," while Celler repeated the criticisms implicit in the *Times* report of July 26. Celler also said that Truman's reception of a delegation of nine Representatives had been "disappointing."

[2] James G. McDonald, honorary chairman of the Foreign Policy Association and chairman of the President's Advisory Commission on Political Refugees.

Taft and Vandenberg had broken loose this morning. Said the reason he is calling now is because it is very important that Attlee and Byrnes do not issue a joint statement on it. He also said that the thing is boiling up in Massachusetts in a way he had not expected and that Taft is a specialist in this particular field. The President said, "Yes, I know he is. But Byrnes and Attlee are not going to issue a joint statement." Mr. Wallace said that he can see Rabbi Silver's hand in this; that he had been working with the Republicans. He called the President's attention to the orders issued by a British general in Palestine that there be no fraternization with Jews and no trading in Jewish stores. Finally, I said "I do hope you will avoid getting out any premature statement and that Byrnes is not going to issue a statement."

The President said that he had talked with Byrnes this morning and that no statement will be issued. Thanked the Secretary for calling him.

In these telephone conversations I emphasized the political angle because that is the one angle of Palestine which has a really deep interest for Truman.

JULY 30, 1946

The whole cabinet luncheon was devoted to a discussion of the Palestine problem. President Truman had a sheaf of telegrams about four inches thick from various Jewish people; also a telegram from Jimmie Byrnes. Attlee proposed to make a speech tomorrow in the House of Commons on the Jewish settlement as contained in the New York *Times* of last Friday. Apparently, this New York *Times* report was very accurate.

Dean Acheson and Forrestal were all for the President going ahead. Jimmie Byrnes, sensing the political hotness of the question, had taken a strictly neutral attitude in his telegram. I gave the President the carbon copy of Taft's speech which Oscar Cox had sent over to me. I said the whole matter was loaded with political dynamite; that the Jews expected more than 1500 square miles; that they hoped to be in on a part of the Jordan River Development; that I hoped he would not go ahead on the Attlee proposal without looking into the matter further.

Clinton Anderson developed the thesis that we ought to get Republican cooperation on the plan finally arrived at. Truman finally told Dean Acheson to wire Jimmie Byrnes that we would not go along with Attlee. John Snyder joined Anderson and myself in this attitude.

President Truman expressed himself as being very much "put out" with the Jews. He said that "Jesus Christ couldn't please them when he was here on earth, so how could anyone expect that I would have any luck?" Truman said he had no use for them and didn't care what happened to them. I said, "You must remember that it is easy for them to get into quite a state of mind because nearly all the Jews in this country have relatives in Europe and they know that about 5 million out of the 6 million Jews have been killed and that no other people have suffered in this way." Jim Forrestal had previously undertaken to say that the Poles had suffered more than the Jews. Forrestal brought up the question of the oil in Saudi Arabia and said if another war came along we would need the oil in Saudi Arabia. President Truman said he wanted to handle this problem not from the standpoint of bringing in oil but from the standpoint of what is right.

A map of the area assigned to the Jews in Palestine has the shape of the legs of an "L" upside down. I could easily see, after looking at the map, why Taft should call it a "splintered area" and why the Jews would not want to go along.

President Truman really thinks that the plan worked out by Henry Grady, representing the State Department, and two other men representing War and Navy (as it appeared in the New York *Times* of last Friday) is really fair . . .

AUGUST 2, 1946

At the cabinet meeting there first was a discussion of the proposed World Food Board[1] . . . It was proposed, and everybody agreed to, a statement that had been worked out generally. The statement in effect accepted the principles of Sir John Orr but not the method. It was provided that at the forthcoming Copenhagen FAO Conference a committee should be appointed to look into various methods of obtaining the principles. It seemed to me that Secretary Anderson was rather lukewarm about Sir John Orr's proposal. I spoke very vigorously on behalf of Sir John Orr's proposal and said that while no one

[1] Sir John B. Orr, Director General of the United Nations Food and Agricultural Organization, had proposed the establishment of a World Food Board which would operate to stabilize agricultural commodity prices in world markets, to create a world food reserve for use in case of shortages, and to dispose of surplus farm products on special terms to countries needing them. An interagency committee had recommended cabinet approval in principle of Orr's proposal, which Wallace later accurately described as an international "evernormal granary."

could indicate the time, it was obvious that sooner or later there would be a very marked drop in agricultural prices and it was essential at that time that something embodying the principles of Sir John Orr's proposal should be in operation. It was obvious to me that in the final showdown State Department and Treasury would be fighting on the other side, due to the influence of the grain trade. I must say, however, that Dean Acheson came out flat-footedly and wholeheartedly for the interdepartmental agreement . . . The President wants to be sure there is not an international cartel. Lew Schwellenbach wants to be sure that the nations abroad are not given food cheaper than in the United States.

The discussion then turned to China. The President day before yesterday received a very discouraging letter from General Marshall. Dean Acheson gave a pretty clear-cut summary of the Chinese situation as it actually exists. He indicated very clearly that the United States was in China not to help either side but to conciliate between the two sides. It was especially necessary to be in China while the Japanese soldiers were being gotten out. There was a good and defensible reason for the presence of our troops there during that period. Now that the Japanese soldiers are all out the picture changes to some extent. Dean Acheson still thinks we should maintain our troops there. We have 21,000 Marines there.[1] Jim Forrestal was emphatic that we should maintain our troops there. He made the point very strongly that if we didn't maintain our troops there Russia would come in. The United States, ever since 1898, has stood strongly for the Open Door policy and against any nation's dominating China. We don't want to dominate the Chinese, we merely want a strong democratic government there that really represents the Chinese people. Acheson admits that the present national government does not represent the Chinese people, that it is a dictatorship, and that in process of time it is bound to pass out of the picture. He says that a good many of the Chinese being sent by the national government to govern Manchuria come from the southern part of China and that they have been acting in a very tactless way toward the Manchurian government and toward the Russians who live in Manchuria.

I made the point that it was my observation that the extreme element in the Kuomintang is eager to provoke a war between the United

[1] Acheson considered the presence of the Marines necessary to support General Marshall's efforts to effect a unified national government, including both the Kuomintang and the communists. Like Marshall, he realized how little Chiang Kai-shek was disposed to move toward compromise and an end to civil strife; see Walter Millis, ed., *The Forrestal Diaries* (New York, 1951) p. 90.

States and Russia. Lew Schwellenbach very vigorously said that he didn't think there ought to be any American troops in China. He said this had been his attitude in the '30s when he was in the Senate and it was still his attitude . . .[1]

AUGUST 14, 1946

At the Hannegan party . . . Bartley Crum[2] told me that the inspired story in Wednesday's New York *Times* with regard to Palestine represented the proposal that was agreeable to the Jews. He said that Democratic Congressman Havenner[3] would quite possibly be defeated this fall simply because he voted for the British loan and the Jews felt that the British were not entitled to a loan in view of the way they had acted. Paul Fitzpatrick, Democratic State Chairman for New York, said that Congressman Klein had been burned in effigy by the Jewish brethren because he had been for the British loan. He said the situation was very bad politically. Both Crum and Fitzpatrick said, however, that the President was looked on highly by the Jews because of the fine way in which he had insisted continually on the 100,000 immigrants coming into Palestine . . .

Stuart Symington[4] reported on his trip around the world. He said that all military folks, with the exception of General Clay, preached the doctrine of war with Russia. Clay was the only one who thought we could learn to get along with the Russians. He said that Clay told him that with regard to relations with the Russians in Germany the Americans had the upper hand. We had shot more Russians and put more of them in jail than the Russians had shot Americans and put them in jail. Clark's[5] attitude is much more hard-boiled than that of

---

1 Wallace made no entries in his diary during the periods August 3–11 and 16–26. Most of that time he was on vacation at the farm he had recently purchased in South Salem, New York.

2 Bartley C. Crum, one of the American members of the joint Anglo-American Commission of Inquiry on Palestine, gave strong support to the immediate admission of 100,000 Jews to Palestine, as did the New York *Times*. Increasingly irritated by State Department aides who seemed to him to be frustrating Truman's policy on Palestine, Crum on August 21 attacked the Department, called for the resignation of L. W. Henderson, the chief of the Near Eastern Affairs office, and condemned the British plan for the division of Palestine. When Acheson denied Crum's charges, Crum asked, with predictable futility, for the release of State Department files on Palestine negotiations.

3 Franck R. Havenner, Democratic congressman from San Francisco (1937–41, 1945–51) did win re-election in 1946.

4 Stuart Symington had become Assistant Secretary of War for Air.

5 General Mark W. Clark was then the American member of the Allied Commission for Austria.

Clay. It seems that on one occasion, when Clark had a secret agent on the Russian side of the border, he had received word that this agent was likely to be getting into trouble, so Clark stationed a force of American soldiers with machine guns on buildings, in a typical gangster setup. The Russians moved in to apprehend Clark's secret agent. When Clark overpowered the Russians he found them all in American Military Police uniforms. He sent them over to Konev, the Russian military commander, who immediately had them all shot. According to Symington, their crime had been that they got caught.

Symington said that in talking with Bedell Smith and with Clay he reached the conclusion that Russia definitely did not want war; that she couldn't possibly be ready for war in less than ten years and it would probably take fifteen; that she certainly couldn't be pressed into war until she had the atomic bomb. Symington said, however, that one thing the Russians should realize was that we can be pushed so far and no farther. It all indicates to me that our American military is spoiling for a fight. They don't realize that the Russian slant may be very similar to our own. In other words, the Russians can be pushed only so far and no farther. And so we shall both go on being tough and building up armaments and making sure that the next war and the next depression will be bigger and worse than the last one. Three cheers for the military! They are so helpful to humanity . . .

AUGUST 28, 1946

I had a very interesting lunch with Spruille Braden. He told me that . . . Messersmith, just before he left Mexico, spoke at a luncheon where he dwelt on the forthcoming war with Russia and the necessity of Mexico and the United States fighting against the common enemy. When this got into the press Messersmith tried to beg off by saying that he was speaking off the record. It appears now, however, that he has made the same kind of a speech in Argentina.[1] Braden says the account of the speech appears in today's *Daily Worker*. I have never seen the *Daily Worker* but perhaps I should take a look at it from time to time. Braden says he has no question but that the *Daily Worker's* report is correct in this instance. Braden says that Messer-

[1] While ambassador to Argentina, Braden had openly criticized the suppression of a free press by the Perón government. Declared persona non grata on that account, he was recalled to Washington where in October 1945 he became Assistant Secretary of State for American Republic Affairs. Messersmith, whose conservative views had offended the Mexican government, replaced Braden in Argentina in April 1946.

smith, ever since he got to Argentina, has been pleading continually for reconciliation with Perón. I said, "That sounds just like the doctrine that Pauley is preaching in Brazil." He said yes, Pauley had talked the same thing all around Washington and New York City and in Brazil. I asked Braden how Pauley happened to get into the State Department.[1] He said that Bob Hannegan had gotten him in; that he was supposed to have given $50,000 to the Democratic Party. He said of course he couldn't give $50,000 directly and legally but that he had given it indirectly. I said that I had it indirectly from the War Department that Pauley's record was pretty bad in China. Braden said he had the same story.

Braden is very much against our furnishing arms to all the Latin American countries under the bill which the War Department sponsored in the last Congress. This bill did not pass but will undoubtedly be brought up again in the next Congress. Braden says that with a bill of this sort in effect, middle-class liberalism would have no chance in Latin America. He said he used to think about this when he saw Batista with his tanks parading in the Prado in Havana. I said I thought about it in Peru when I was standing with President Prado in that country looking at the great military parade . . . He went on to say that it is standing practice in Latin America for the fascists and the communists to hook up together the same way as Hitler and Stalin hooked up together for a time in 1939. Each one of them thinks when they get into power they can cut the throat of the other one. Braden says he doesn't look on Russia as the same kind of menace as Germany. He says the Russians are acting the way they are now because they are scared to death. Moreover, he thinks they have no designs for territorial aggression. He says the Army is very strong about furnishing arms to all of Latin America so as to be ready for war with Russia. He says they sold Jimmie Byrnes on this approach. He, himself, is dead against it and refused to testify in Congress on behalf of this project for furnishing arms to Latin America.

Braden says the War Department boys like to go on military missions. He calls them "ribbon hunters." I said, "Well, the Latin American boys themselves like to put on uniforms and come up to the United States."

According to Braden, Messersmith has been trying to protect the Nazis in Argentina in order to arrive at an agreement with Perón . . .

[1] Since 1945 Edwin Pauley had served, with the rank of ambassador, as American representative on the Reparations Commission. In 1947 he became adviser about reparations to the State Department.

Braden says the real Army attitude is, "Let's forget now about Nazism and remember that Russia is our real enemy." Braden quotes Messersmith as saying that we have to be ready for a war with Russia soon. He said when Messersmith was asked what was meant by "soon," he said, "Well, it may be as long as five years." Braden said such talk was worse than nonsense. I said, "Yes, it is criminal."

Braden says he is making a speech in Chicago in the near future where he is going to tell the businessmen that they have got to get in vigorously to bring about more industrialization in Latin America. I told him I was going to tell the American businessmen in Mexico the same thing[1] . . .

SEPTEMBER 12, 1946

At the meeting with the President I went over page by page with him my Madison Square Garden speech to be given on September 12.[2] Again and again he said, "That's right"; "Yes, that is what I believe." He didn't have a single change to suggest. He twice said how deeply he appreciated my courtesy in showing him my speech before I gave it.

The President said that Secretary Byrnes' speech of September 6[3]

[1] On August 29, 1946, Wallace left for Mexico. There he attended the opening session of the Mexican Congress, talked with President Avila Camacho and Secretary of Commerce Gustavo Sorreno, and investigated recent developments in Mexican agriculture. He returned to Washington September 10.

[2] Wallace was to speak that night at Madison Square Garden to a meeting under the joint auspices of the National Citizens Political Action Committee and the Independent Citizens' Committee of the Arts and Sciences. For the text of his speech, see Appendices. Before Wallace gave the address, Truman, at his September 12 press conference, said he had approved "the entire speech, not just one paragraph." He said, too, that he considered the speech to be "exactly in line" with Secretary Byrnes' foreign policy.

[3] At Stuttgart, Germany, on September 6, 1946, Byrnes had made a major foreign policy speech focused upon the problem of Germany and critical of the position of the Soviet Union in the Allied Control Council for Germany. He attacked the Soviet Union for departing from the Potsdam agreements about Germany, particularly for preventing the Allied Control Council from taking steps "to enable the German economy to function as an economic unit." He called for the "obliteration" of zonal lines in German economic life, and for the establishment of a provisional government for all of Germany, a government that "should not be hand-picked by other governments" (a remark addressed against Soviet policy in its zone of occupation, now East Germany). Byrnes opposed permanent assignment of Silesia to Poland, which the Soviet Union was affecting, and opposed, too, in this instance attacking French policy, any controls that would "subject the Ruhr and the Rhineland to the political domination or manipulation of outside powers." The United States, Byrnes concluded, could not relieve Germany from the hardships inflicted upon her as the result of a war her leaders had started, but the United States did not intend to increase

had been cleared with him over the telephone and then it had been sent back to Washington for minor checking. He said also that he thought it must be a pretty good speech because neither the British, the French, nor the Russians nor the Germans liked it.

The President apparently saw no inconsistency between my speech and what Byrnes was doing—if he did he didn't indicate it in any way. He spoke very hopefully about the future, saying that he thought the situation between the United States and Russia was much more peaceful than the newspapers would have us believe. He said the dark cloud on the horizon was the state of Stalin's health; that Stalin was now an old man. He said also it was almost impossible to do business with Molotov . . .

SEPTEMBER 16, 1946
TELEPHONE CONVERSATION

HAW told the President that he wanted him to know that he thought he did the only thing he could have done on Saturday; thought he did exactly the right thing.[1] The President said he appreciated Mr.

---

those hardships: "The American people want to return the government of Germany to the German people. The American people want to help the German people to win their way back to an honorable place among the free and peace-loving nations of the world." To the Russians and the French, and to many of the British, those statements stirred deep anxieties about a renaissance of Germany and of German power in Europe, an alarming prospect in the immediate postwar period in Europe.

[1] Secretary Byrnes and most newspaper analysts interpreted Wallace's September 12 speech as inconsistent with the State Department's stance toward the Soviet Union and potentially embarrassing during Byrnes' pending negotiations at a Paris meeting of the foreign ministers. Truman therefore hastily called a press conference on September 14. "There has been," he said, "a natural misunderstanding regarding the answer I made to a question asked at the press conference on . . . September 12, with reference to the speech of the Secretary of Commerce delivered in New York later that day. The question was asked extemporaneously and my answer did not convey the thought I intended it to convey.

"It was my intention to express the thought that I approved the right of the Secretary of Commerce to deliver the speech. I did not intend to indicate that I approved the speech as constituting a statement of the foreign policy of this country.

"There has been no change in the established foreign policy of our government. There will be no significant change in that policy without discussion and conference among the President, the Secretary of State, and congressional leaders."

That statement, necessary in Truman's view, ended on an honest note, for he was not planning to become less firm with the Soviet Union. His disavowal of what he had said so clearly two days earlier about Wallace's speech, however, seemed even to friendly observers at best an expedient fabrication.

Wallace saying that. Mr. Wallace said he thought this thing . . . is
going to create an immense amount of interest and is going to help get
out the vote. Said he thought the Pres. had given him a good out—that
he stood up for his right to say what he wanted to say, which was a
good out for him (HAW). HAW thinks we ought to get all the enthusiasm we can in our congressional people and he thinks this line
. . . then he said that, in the first place, one reason he made the speech
was that he felt the Republicans were going to attempt to accuse the
Democrats of warmongering, and that now he thinks we have prevented
them from doing this—that we have done something about it early
enough that the line is formed; on the other hand, if we are going to
get the liberal elements, we will have to . . . then the Pres. cut in
saying, "Let's you and I have a session on this to see what we can do
without cutting the ground from under Byrnes. I think it can be done.
I don't want to hurt anyone—either you or Byrnes. Let's get together
when we can sit down for a while undisturbed—luncheon or something." HAW said he had agreed to go to Providence, R.I., on the
24th to make a speech under the NCPAC auspices. HAW said that,
frankly, he thought the Pres. had an out in that this is a democratic
country and that in an election year, in particular, we have to ascertain the will of the people; and in an off-term election, we have to
ascertain it through elected congressmen. HAW said the Democratic
party is somewhat notorious for its differences of opinion. HAW said
that if we are to get the votes necessary to control the Congress,
we have to pick them up in the North, in the progressive area. HAW
said that Jimmie may feel that the ground is being cut out from under
him. The Pres. said he didn't want to do anything that would interfere
with getting those treaties signed before the United Nations meeting
in New York—that things are not in as bad shape as they were.

SEPTEMBER 16, 1946

I talked to Truman on the telephone this morning, saying I thought
he had done the only thing he could do in his statement on Saturday.
He replied that he appreciated deeply my feeling. He said he wanted

---

Wallace on September 16 also issued a statement to the press: "I stand upon my
New York speech. It was interesting to find that both the extreme right and
the extreme left disagreed with the views I expressed. Feeling as I do, however,
that most Americans are concerned about, and willing to work for, peace, I
intend to continue my efforts for a just and lasting peace and I shall, within
the near future, speak on this subject again."

to make a statement that would hurt neither Jimmie Byrnes nor myself. I told him that the object of my speech was not to hurt Jimmie Byrnes.

On Monday afternoon Charles Ross called me saying that he had it from Joe Smart on the Baltimore *Sun* that Drew Pearson had a copy of the letter I had written the President with regard to Russia[1] and that he was going to run it soon. Joe Smart wanted it so he could have an even break with Drew Pearson. I told Charles Ross I would check on it and see what I could find out. I called Harold Young and Harold said that, a month or so ago, right after Drew Pearson came back from abroad, Pearson was at a luncheon at the Mayflower at which . . . some others were present. Pearson said to one of his men, "Did Henry Wallace kick in with that guest column while I was abroad?" The man said, "No," and Pearson then said, "Well, then, suppose we run that letter from Henry Wallace to the President that we got out of the State Department." I passed this back to Charles Ross and Ross said he was not surprised; that the State Department leaked like a sieve.

At four o'clock I went out to see Justice Black. Black said he thought we were headed straight for war with Russia. He said the only trouble with my speech was that it didn't go far enough. He said I ought not to have put in any qualifications. He said he had given a speech on this same subject last summer and that he had gotten a lot of the data from Ben Cohen. In fact, Ben had written quite a lot of the speech. He said Ben had put in many of the qualifications that I had put in but that he, himself, had insisted on striking them out. He said that of course my criticisms of Russia were well founded but you couldn't confuse people by presenting both sides of the case. He said the one thing we had to keep in mind was that the Army and the State Department were carrying us into war with Russia just as fast as they could. I said to him, "You were in the Senate with Truman, weren't you? What was your impression?" Black replied, "Well, he always voted right. He was with us on practically every progressive issue. His heart is in the right place; he is not dishonest. Those who claim that because he was a part of the Pendergast machine he was therefore dishonest are altogether wrong." Then he went on and said the trouble with Truman was that he was a man with no background or understanding. He has no fundamental philosophy and very little knowledge of history. Because of Truman's lack of background Black thought it a tragedy that Truman should be President. He thought Barkley would have been much better. He said the whole trouble

[1] The letter of July 23, 1946; see above.

arose because Roosevelt had been sick. He said he didn't want to minimize Truman's excellent work with the Truman Committee.

After Black had proceeded this far I said, "I asked the question because I wanted light as to how my efforts could best count for peace." I said the cost of war consisted not only in the suffering caused to the young men and their dear ones but also in the inevitable and unexpected types of confusion arising afterwards. I told him I felt warranted in going to almost any lengths if I could use the current situation to help prevent war. Black seemed to think the die was already cast and that it was impossible. Black has a large number of contacts with Army officers and other governmental people who speak to him in confidence. I suspect he knows what he is talking about. I told him that the President thinks there is no danger whatever of war. He said the President can't see it because he doesn't have the background to realize how nations react once a certain channel for events has been created.

I told Black that I thought there was a much greater chance of preventing war than he thought. I said I was sure the people of the United States were peace-minded. Black replied, "But there is no way of getting the facts to the people"—and then went on to talk about the funeral plans for the fliers killed over Yugoslavia, with newsreel cameras present and with the certainty that an atmosphere would be created like the "Remember the Maine" atmosphere created back in 1898. He says that when you touch the emotions of people they don't reason things out, and he then went on to say that Russia has no aggressive designs against the United States and that in effect we would be fighting for King George of Greece and King Peter of Yugoslavia. He said this ironically and I know he didn't mean it in exactly this sense. But he was in dead earnest about the danger. He hated the thought of his sons' getting back into the Army again. He had no advice whatever to give me as to how I should handle myself in meeting with the President. In general he seemed to feel that the President had closed the door to peace when he made his statement last Saturday.

Black said that when he was in the Senate Byrnes was used continually as a compromiser by the White House and his compromises were nearly always not compromises but concessions to the reactionary group in the Senate. He said Byrnes and Vandenberg had long been very close personally and that in his opinion the present foreign policy was not a Democratic foreign policy but was a Republican foreign policy that had been forced on Byrnes by Vandenberg. He said the Republicans were waiting to see the Democratic Party get the country into war and then in 1948 defeat them on the basis of the slogan, "The Democrats got us into war" . . .

SEPTEMBER 17, 1946

At the luncheon at Postmaster General Hannegan's office various people in the executive branch of the government met with the Democratic candidates for Congress from New Jersey, Massachusetts, and Pennsylvania. They were remarkably cordial to me. Many of them said they were with me 100 percent and that the atmosphere in their district was that way. I said I didn't see how people could be for me in view of what they read in the newspapers. They replied that people now knew how to read between the lines.

Father Sheehy said that after his experiences in the recent war he was very strong for peace and he thought my speech would do a service in that direction. Like Justice Black, he thought we were a long way on the road to war and that it would be almost impossible to prevent it. He raised the question as to whether it might not be helpful if sometime during the next six months I went to Moscow. He said he had read all my speech and he agreed with practically all of it.

Clark Eichelberger came in to say that he had read all my speech and agreed with 75 percent of it. He said he thought if I had developed further my ideas with regard to regionalism he might have been able to agree ninety or 100 percent.[1] I talked with him in detail on this point and think I should try to clarify it in my Providence, Rhode Island, speech.[2]

Charles Ross called up to tell me to go ahead and release the Russian letter. I called in the boys and got them to work at once. A little later on he called up to say not to release it. It was too late; the letter was out . . .

SEPTEMBER 18, 1946

Before I called on the President I had received the following information: First, of the 1150 communications received at the Depart-

[1] Wallace later said: "Eichelberger was right, that my September 12 speech did not indicate with sufficient strength how strong I am for one world. My handling of the problem of regionalism gave too much the impression that I stood for a world divided into segments." (Oral History, 3997.)
[2] A speech Wallace soon canceled at Truman's request.

ment, 950 were favorable—almost five to one—and today the ratio was six to one. Second, I had information via Helen Fuller[1] that the whole group around the President had gone in to see him one by one and had advised him that I must stop talking on foreign affairs. They had advised him to be nice to me but to leave no room for any doubt that I must talk no more on this subject. They had advised him that if I refused to quit talking he must fire me.

When I came in Mr. Truman said he had had more sleepless nights than at any time since the Chicago convention. He said Jimmie Byrnes had been giving him hell, that he had wires on the unfavorable reactions caused by my speech in Brazil and Bulgaria. He said Jimmie Byrnes threatened to leave Paris at once and come home unless I stopped talking on foreign affairs. Jimmie had blamed Truman more than he had me. Truman said he himself was really more to blame than I.

I then said, "The public is profoundly interested in peace. My own mail is running five to one in favor of my speech. Peace is going to be an issue in this campaign. The people are afraid that the 'get tough with Russia' policy is leading us to war. You, yourself, as Harry Truman really believed in my speech."

He rejoined, "But Jimmie Byrnes says I am pulling the rug out from under him. I must ask you not to make any more speeches touching on foreign policy. We must present a united front abroad."

I said, "I have the specific problem of what to say at Providence, Rhode Island, on September 24. How would it be if I issued a specific disclaimer saying I was not representing you or the official policy of the administration?" I then read to him the following:

"The people are entitled to be fully informed about our foreign policy, to know the issues, and to take part in the framing of that policy. The success or failure of our foreign policy will mean the difference between life and death for our children and our grandchildren.

"We are fortunate to have a President who believes that foreign affairs *is* the people's affair; who is willing that the people be informed about the momentous issues involved, and about the differences in judgment on how to meet them; and who has enough faith in the workings of democracy not to fear the consequences of free, open, and honest discussion.

"Much of the bitter opposition to the views I have expressed has surprisingly taken the form of openly denouncing me for making our

[1] Helen Fuller of the *New Republic*.

foreign policy a public matter and a matter for public debate. Does this opposition really insist on playing the game of secret diplomacy, of freezing the people out of an opportunity to take part in deciding the momentous issues on which their very lives and the lives of their children will depend? I have enough faith in the workings of democracy, and so has our Democratic President, to believe that a government 'of the people, for the people, and by the people' has no business excluding the people from matters with which they are vitally concerned. I believe there is no more important problem in the world today than the problem of achieving and maintaining peace. I insist on my right to express my views and to encourage other people to think the issues through.

"I do not agree with our present bipartisan, Republican-dominated foreign policy. I am fighting for modification of this policy at this time because I think the Democratic Party, if freed from the entangling Republican alliances, can lead the people of this nation on the road to peace.

"The record clearly shows that the Republican Party can never be expected to find a way of living in one world with Russia and with the other nations of the world. The record shows that the Republicans stand for warmongering against Russia. The record shows that the Republicans have learned nothing from the experience of our two world wars and would inevitably lead us into the Armageddon of the third world war.

"The Democratic party is the only party of hope in international affairs. President Roosevelt wisely led the forging of a bipartisan foreign policy essential to achieving the united front necessary for winning the war and preparing for the peace. Bipartisan agreement on foreign policy is still desirable; but it is much more important to find the path to peace than to preserve bipartisan agreement in foreign affairs. It is much more important that we save the lives of millions of Americans and millions of other peoples and prevent destruction of our civilization than that we keep foreign affairs out of politics.

"The time has come to revert to Democratic leadership in international policy; and if the Republicans cannot agree that it is possible to live in one world with Russia, then I say the time has come to cast them out as partners in our foreign policy.

"It is ridiculous that as a result of my Madison Square Garden speech the impression was given that *I* advocated two worlds instead of one. Because of the paper shortage my New York speech of two weeks ago was not printed in full in the New York papers. As a

620 The Price of Vision

result, it was widely misquoted. I don't have to tell anyone who has followed my views on international affairs that I began talking about one world more than fifteen years ago and that no one, not even Wendell Willkie, who became abhorrent to his Republican colleagues, has been more continuous and ardent in advocacy of the principles and realities of living in one world.

"How can we achieve peace? How can we achieve an enduring peace? And by peace I do not mean the absence of open war. I also mean the avoidance of an armed truce. How can we learn to live in one world?"

Truman would have none of it. I must quit talking on foreign affairs. I then said, "Can you get the State Department to stay out of foreign economic affairs if I stay out of foreign political affairs?" He said I had something there and that he was working on this problem. He said as a result of the war, State had got too far into foreign economic work and that he was going to build up a really strong Department of Commerce and return to the Department the functions really belonging to it. (He doesn't know what he is getting into on this one.)

I told Truman that he was looking at the whole situation in too much of a negative light—that the emotions and interest aroused would help get out the vote and that if he himself would help channel this emotional interest in the right way it would mean the difference between a Democratic and a Republican Congress. He said he thought the Congress was going to go Republican anyway. I said, "Yes, that is probable unless we really arouse the people's interest."

I then told about talking with the Democratic candidates in Bob Hannegan's office and how many of them had volunteered the information that they and their constituents were for my approach.

I said I was eager to get into the campaign, supporting the traditional Democratic anti-imperialistic foreign policy. I had said at Madison Square Garden on September 12 that peace would be the dominant issue in 1946 and 1948. I wanted to talk about the Democratic Party as the party of peace.

I then quoted Justice Black, saying first how Black had said Truman had always voted right. I said Black said we were headed straight for war with Russia as a result of a foreign policy which was not Democratic but Republican—a policy imposed on Byrnes by Vandenberg.

I quoted Father Sheehy as a friend of Byrnes who felt we were headed straight for war. I mentioned that Father Sheehy wanted me to go to Russia and negotiate face to face.

Truman then said he had always liked Stalin and Stalin like him and he thought he could do business face to face but unfortunately Stalin would not come to the United States.

Truman denied there was a "get tough with Russia" policy. He said he would see to it that we did not get into war with Russia. He said he was not an imperialist.

I said, "I know you are not an imperialist, but what about Admiral Halsey's jingoistic statement?" He said he had called Admiral Halsey down. I said, "What about writing FDR's initials on the skies of Greece? That was a most sickening use of FDR's name." He said he had not authorized it. He said he had called down the Commandant of the Veterans of Foreign Wars who was trying to use the Yugoslav incident for warmongering. He showed me the letters. He told me he had worked on Roy Howard to try to tone down his warmongering in the Scripps-Howard press.

He said that as soon as the peace treaties were signed he was prepared to go to Congress and ask a loan for Russia just as he had for Great Britain. I said, "Without political strings attached to it?" He said, "Yes, without political strings but assuming we get matters cleaned up in the next few months as I have reason to hope they will be cleaned up." I said, "Do you think for a moment you can get a loan of this sort through Congress? I don't think you know your Congress. It will take a lot of effort during the next six weeks to elect the kind of Congress that will put through a Russian loan."

He still thought he could put it through. I was too dumbfounded to say anything except I feared his only possibility would be to cancel the Chinese loan in the Export-Import Bank. He said, "Yes, that was a possibility because it looked like we could not let the Chinese have the money."

I said, "What shall I tell the press when I go out? There are a hundred or more hungry wolves out there."

We called in Charles Ross and my first attempt at a draft was as follows:

"The President and the Secretary had a most detailed and friendly discussion and reached the conclusion that the Secretary would make no statements or speeches until the Paris Peace Conference is concluded. At that time, in conformity with the President's statement of last Saturday, he feels free to express himself in such ways as he feels to be wise and in conformity with the peace objective which he feels to be the supreme issue in this campaign and in 1948."

Ross objected to the last sentence. Then we talked for forty minutes about the first sentence. Ross wanted me to get into the campaign on domestic issues. I said I had become a Democrat after World War I on the basis of foreign issues and it would be impossible to campaign without getting into foreign issues. I said the people who believed in a genuine Democratic foreign policy would sooner or later have to have a means of expression and that if the bottling-up process continued the result would be the same as in 1860—the splitting of the Democratic party into two parts. I said the practical thing for Truman was to work with the progressive element during the election months, remembering that he would have to live with the reactionary Southerners after the election was over. I said he could not hope to win the election unless he went way over to the left not merely with the words but with the tune. I told him the people didn't believe he was a progressive. I told of the boos his name received in Madison Square Garden. I said the people just didn't believe him to be as progressive as I knew him to be at heart. He must cut loose before election and tell the people just what he really believes.

Ross urged him to make a speech on foreign policy in late October. I judge he will do it. Probably the speech will come out of the State Department and Truman will think he is being progressive while the country will reach the opposite conclusion.

I put in a bid for sitting down with Truman and Byrnes to talk over the foreign policy. I question whether anything comes of this.

Ross finally agreed to the statement as it appeared in the press,[1] saying to me privately, "There must never be any last word between friends."

The President agreed when I changed the wording to make it appear that the conclusion to make no speeches was my own conclusion and not our joint conclusion.

The President very much wanted me to make speeches on his health program, social security, and on all the other things on which the Republicans had turned him down. I told him there were others who could make that kind of speech better than I. I told him campaigning was hard work, that I had paid my own expenses in 1944 but I had enjoyed it because I could say what I believed. I said it was

---

[1] Wallace read to the press a handwritten statement: "The President and the Secretary of Commerce had a most detailed and friendly discussion, after which the Secretary reached the conclusion that he could make no public statements or speeches until the Foreign Ministers' Conference in Paris is concluded." Wallace also said he expected that conference to end before the congressional elections in November, which implied to the New York *Times* that he expected to speak during the campaign. "With flat emphasis" Wallace told the press that he would not resign from the cabinet.

impossible to make extemporaneous speeches and go through the hardships of a campaign unless you could say what you believed. He said he had made 54 speeches in 1944 and he hoped they had done some good. He is very humble about his own abilities except in the field of "fixing," where he feels he is a past master. He thinks he has the peace with Europe and the peace with Russia all fixed up. I do not share his conviction, but I should certainly give him a chance during the next four weeks.

Charlie Ross raised the question, "What happens next October fifteen or twenty when the conference is over? We are just postponing a decision."

The President said, "We can take that up later. We will have a cabinet meeting on foreign policy and I will give a speech laying down the foreign policy."

I said, "Are the people going to have a chance to know and discuss the issues?"

Ross evidently favored muzzling me after the Peace Conference was over. The President was willing to wait and take a chance.

When I told Truman of Black's praise of his voting record he replied, "Yes, I was a New Dealer before Roosevelt was."

Before Ross came in I told Truman that the reactionaries were conducting a drive against Hannegan and that I hoped he would not let them succeed. He said yes, it was true, but he and Bob were old friends and nothing would come of it.

In the early part of the conversation the threat of forcing a resignation in case I refused to stop talking was definitely in the background of his conversation.

Throughout as always the atmosphere was cordial and direct. We have never had an unkind word. I disagreed with him when he said the Harding disarmament conference in 1922 was the chief cause of World War II. I said with the economic causes for war as they were, the mere fact of our being heavily armed would merely have made the explosion greater when it came.

I am convinced that in the final showdown he is a big Army and a big Navy man, although half the time he may deny it even to himself. He believes in military force because of his experience with the Army in World War I.

I talked at some little length with Truman about the general theory of a united front on the part of the cabinet. I reminded the President of when I talked with the Democratic women about the desirability of a situation under which the party would in a democratic way adopt a platform and then all the members of the party would be obligated to go down the line for that platform. I said that we didn't have that situation at the present time; that there was the greatest diversity of opinion in the Democratic Party and that until we did, by appropriate action on the Hill and through the party machinery, adopt such a system I did not feel bound by this approach, especially when I was urging the point of view which I knew the President himself in his own heart believed in. At various times in the conversation I appealed to the President's own beliefs and he never denied them. His final refuge is the thought that Jimmie's views and mine are really the same and that he doesn't really believe in getting tough with Russia.

I told Truman with Mr. Ross present that it was important in assessing the political future accurately to bear in mind the rather extraordinary demonstration against Truman's name both times I mentioned it in Madison Square Garden. I said of course there probably were a number of commies present at the meeting. The first time I mentioned his name was in the prepared text of the speech and the second time was after I had referred to the Chinese policy and somebody in the crowd had said, "Why doesn't the administration stand for that policy?" I replied, "President Truman has read just what I have stated and it has his approval." They booed vigorously at this.

I said I mentioned this because I thought the progressives of the country did not realize that Truman is as progressive as he really is in his heart. They have a false impression of him and therefore it will be necessary in order for him to get the left-wing vote to demonstrate his attitude very decisively and wholeheartedly.

Truman complained repeatedly of being caught in the center and complained of how much the newspapers had criticized him. I said he was certain to be caught in the center all the time he was President and that he might as well reconcile himself to getting battered from both sides.

Before Ross came in I made the point very strongly with Truman that I was gravely concerned with the probability that we were now taking actions which would lead to Russia's taking reprisals against us twenty or thirty years hence when she would be much stronger than we. I said that with the Russian population increasing at its present rate Russia would have many more men of military age than the United States and Britain combined; that industrially she would be fully as strong as the United States; that her women would fit into a war economy much better than our women; and that her people would be much more willing to put up with hardship. I said he, as a

Midwestern farm boy, would know just what I meant because he knew the contempt which Midwestern farm boys had for city boys. He said yes, he knew exactly what I meant. I said furthermore that 20 or 30 years hence, when the Russians had the atom bomb, they would not have the scruples about dropping it that we would have.

At another point in the discussion I went into great detail with regard to the tom-toms being continually beaten by the daily press against Russia and said that I had no doubt that a good bit of this material came directly or indirectly from three departments of the government. Truman said he himself was not responsible for it in any way. With regard to being tough with Russia he said we couldn't be tough because we didn't have the military equipment to be tough with. We had reconverted our industry and we had only one full division. At another stage in the discussion I referred to Vandenberg as strongly anti-Russian. The President said that wasn't true; that he was quite friendly toward Russia. I said simply that I had heard Vandenberg talk very vigorously along this line and apparently he didn't follow the same tack in the presence of the President. I said Jimmie Byrnes in effect was under the control of Vandenberg. At any rate, Vandenberg had the veto power over him.

I said my one great regret in not being able to speak during the next two weeks was that I wanted to clear up exactly where I stood with regard to one world; that I had believed and spoken about one world long before Wendell Willkie had used the words; that I was strongly for it now. I had not had time in my New York speech to develop in any detail just where regional considerations should enter and where the one-world consideration should come in. I said I also regretted that I didn't have the opportunity to develop in detail an indictment of imperialism and dictatorship wherever it might be found, whether exhibited by the Russians, the Americans, or the British. I told the President considerably about what Lorwin, who had just got back from Russia, had found in Russia, and I don't think he was particularly interested. I mentioned among other things that Mikoyan, the Russian Secretary of Commerce, was one of the 19 men at Baku resisting the British when they were trying to help the Georgians overthrow the Russian government. The British shot 18. Mikoyan was the only one who escaped. I also referred to how Bill Bullitt went to Lenin in February or March of 1919 and worked out a deal under which the Bolsheviks would have only Moscow, Leningrad, and a small territory, and how Churchill turned down Bill Bullitt's proposition and said, "No, we will destroy the Bolsheviks entirely." I said the present-day Russians were quite familiar with all of this and they think we today are playing very much the same game as the British and French did back in 1919, except we don't have as good an opportunity to get away with it. These tactics may not lead to war now for the simple reason that the Russians are so weak, but they will leave scars that can lead to war very readily 20 or 30 years hence if the world situation is bad.

I want to go on record now for the sake of my grandchildren and great-grandchildren as indicating that if there is war with Russia the criminals will be those who beat the tom-toms for war in 1946. There will also be blame attached to those who were so blind they could not see.

I told Truman I was canceling my East-West talk and the Rhode Island talk. I said the East-West talk was dealing with foreign affairs in such a way I was sure the State Department would not disapprove. The President was clearly against my giving the talk so I shall cancel it.

SEPTEMBER 19, 1946

At the Business Advisory Council meeting on Thursday morning, after they had finished up all their other business, Clay Williams[1] brought up a bitterly critical resolution concerning the following two paragraphs of my letter to the President of July 23:

> Incidentally, as Secretary of Commerce I talk to a good many businessmen, and I find them very much concerned over the size of the federal budget, and the burden of the national debt. For the next fiscal year and for the year immediately ahead by far the largest category of federal spending is the national defense. For example, the total recommended federal appropriations for the fiscal year 1947 submitted to the Congress in the official budget amounted to about $36 billion. Of the total budget some $13 billion was for the War and Navy Departments alone. An additional $5 billion was for war liquidation activities. Ten billion represented interest on the public debt and veterans' benefits, which are primarily the continuing costs of past wars. These

[1] Samuel Clay Williams, chairman of the board of directors of the R. J. Reynolds Tobacco Company, former chairman of the National Industrial Recovery Board (1934–35), since 1933 a member and since 1934 chairman of the Business Advisory Council.

items total $28 billion, or about 80 percent of the total recommended expenditures.

Clearly, a large reduction in the federal budget would require a cut in military appropriations. These appropriations are now more than ten times as great as they were during the thirties. In the 1938 budget appropriations for national defense were less than a billion dollars, compared with $13 billion for the present fiscal year. Thus, even from a purely dollars-and-cents standpoint American businessmen and the American people have an interest in organizing a peaceful world in which the completely unproductive expenditures on national defense could be reduced.

He claimed, and apparently several others of the BAC agreed, that the general public will infer my phrase, "a good many businessmen," to refer to them. He said they resented the idea that they wanted the national budget cut at the expense of our preparedness. As a matter of fact, it was very clear in listening to Williams talk that he believes strongly in arming to the hilt in order to fight Russia. A majority of the men in the Business Advisory Council apparently would like to see a war with Russia. They did not put it that bluntly but that was the only conclusion I could reach from their psychological state of mind. It is true, of course, that a good many men in the Council furnished goods to the Army and Navy and their business would be reduced by reduced military appropriations. Williams' resolution was finally not brought to a vote and all the businessmen seemed to feel happy because they had let me know their willingness to be taxed heavily so as to be in position to fight Russia if the need arose.

I made a brief talk indicating that my letter to the President was meant only for the President; that the leak on the letter did not take place in the Department of Commerce but elsewhere; and that I had released the letter only when directed to do so by Charlie Ross; and that the wording which appears herewith was the specific dictation of Charlie Ross:

RELEASE ON RECEIPT   Tuesday, September 17, 1946
In view of the fact that a copy of Secretary Wallace's letter of July 23, 1946, to the President was filched from the files and is in the hands of a newspaper columnist, the Secretary of Commerce is today releasing this copy of the letter:

I said that in view of the fact that this was private personal correspondence between myself and the President and that it had leaked through no fault of myself or the Department of Commerce, it seemed to me that the resolution of Mr. Williams was most unjust. I said, moreover, that not only members of the Council had spoken to me about high taxes but that there were a great many businessmen with whom I had talked who were not members of the Council and that they should not look on themselves as the only men to whom the phrase "businessmen" should be applied. I finally suggested to them a phraseology which seemed to represent the viewpoint of the majority present. They were very happy with the suggested phraseology and afterward many of them came up and shook hands with me, including Clay Williams, expressing a high esteem for me personally even though they might disagree with me on the Russian matter.

I can't help feeling that Clay Williams was put up to his resolution by some of the reactionary southern politicos. On the other hand, Clay himself is probably the force behind a number of the reactionary Southern politicos. I was very happy to have the businessmen say exactly what they thought. It gave me an insight into how powerful and widespread is the desire to be ready to fight Russia.

SEPTEMBER 20, 1946
HENRY A. WALLACE TO HARRY S. TRUMAN

Dear Harry:

As you requested, here is my resignation. I shall continue to fight for peace. I am sure that you approve and will join me in that great endeavor.

Respectfully yours . . .

*   *   *

Truman first requested Wallace's resignation by letter. "The telephone call," Wallace later recalled (Oral History, 5028), which Truman mentioned to the press, came about 9:30 in the morning. It was a short conversation.

"As a matter of fact what Truman did was to write me a letter of a low level and I called him up and said, 'You don't want this thing out.' He agreed. 'No, I'll send a man over to pick it up.' He got over in about five minutes and I gave it to him.

"When I called Truman the conversation was very amicable because he realized he'd been very hot-headed. I suppose Clark Clifford and General Vaughan and the rest of them had talked to him. I don't know just which ones they were.

"I called him at once after I received the letter and he was very happy to take it back. I think it was dated that morning. It was not abusive, but it was on a low level. I don't remember anything about it—it didn't contain profanity—I just remember that it was on a low level and took it back."

At his press conference that day, Truman read the following statement:

> The foreign policy of this country is the most important question confronting us today. Our responsibility for obtaining a just and lasting peace extends not only to the people of this country but to the nations of the world.
>
> The people of the United States may disagree freely and publicly on any question, including that of foreign policy, but the government of the United States must stand as a unit in its relations with the rest of the world.
>
> I have today asked Mr. Wallace to resign from the cabinet. It had become clear that between his views on foreign policy and those of the administration—the latter being shared, I am confident, by the great body of our citizens—there was a fundamental conflict. We could not permit this conflict to jeopardize our position in relation to other countries. I deeply regret the breaking of a long and pleasant official association, but I am sure that Mr. Wallace will be happier in the exercise of his right to present his views as a private citizen. I am confirmed in this belief by a very friendly conversation I had with Mr. Wallace on the telephone this morning.
>
> Our foreign policy as established by the Congress, the President, and the Secretary of State remains in full force and

effect without change. No change in our foreign policy is contemplated. No member of the executive branch of the government will make any public statement as to foreign policy which is in conflict with our established foreign policy. Any public statement on foreign policy shall be cleared with the Department of State. In case of disagreement, the matter will be referred to me.

As I have frequently said, I have complete confidence in Mr. Byrnes . . .

That evening, Wallace broadcast a statement of his own:

My fellow Americans:

Winning the peace is more important than high public office. It is more important than any consideration of party politics.

The success or failure of our foreign policy will mean the difference between life and death for our children and our grandchildren. It will mean the difference between the life or death of our civilization. It may mean the difference between the existence and the extinction of man and of the world. It is therefore of supreme importance, and we should every one of us regard it as a holy duty, to join the fight for winning the peace. I, for my part, firmly believe that there is nothing more important that I can do than work in the cause of peace.

The action taken by the President this morning relieves me of my obligation of last Wednesday. I feel that our present foreign policy does not recognize the basic realities which led to two world wars and which now threatens another war—this time an atomic war. However, I do not wish to abuse the freedom granted me by the President this morning by saying anything tonight which might interfere with the success of the Paris Conference. But I do feel it proper to clear up some points about which there has been widespread misunderstanding of my Madison Square Garden speech.

I don't have to tell anyone who has followed my views on international affairs that I began talking about "one world" more than fifteen years ago. I do not believe in two worlds. I have continuously and wholeheartedly advocated the principle of living in one world. We cannot have peace except in "one world."

I wish to make it clear again that I am against all types of imperialism and aggression, whether they are of Russian, British, or American origin.

Also I wish to emphasize that the "one world" concept must be held steadfastly; and that any regionalism necessary to give practical form to the world economic and political realities must take into account the rights of small nations just as the nations of the Western Hemisphere have done under Franklin Roosevelt's "Good Neighbor" policy.

The success of any policy rests ultimately upon the confidence and the will of the people. There can be no basis for such success unless the people know and understand the issues, unless they are given all the facts and unless they seize the opportunity to take part in the framing of foreign policy through full and open debate.

In this debate, we must respect the rights and interests of other peoples, just as we expect them to respect ours. How we resolve this debate, as I said in my New York speech, will determine not whether we live in "one world" but whether we live at all.

I intend to carry on the fight for peace.

Later Wallace recalled:

I always had in my mind that if I were going to get out of the cabinet I should get out on the peace issue. Ever since Morgenthau and Ickes had left, I figured it was only a question of months until I'd be getting out. I did want to get out on a basis which would help bring about an understanding between the United States and Russia and insure peace. I wanted to dramatize peace.

It wasn't my objective to have the September 12 speech do that. Knowing the number of people in the cabinet and in Congress who felt the importance of having a showdown with Russia instead of any understanding, I felt it was inevitable that sooner or later I would get out on that issue. So if it hadn't been this speech, it would have been another one, I have no doubt.

Truman may have been convinced politically that the cost of breaking with Byrnes was greater than the cost of breaking with me. I think that was probably the way it finally shaped up in his mind. I think he'd lost his personal esteem for

Byrnes at this time, but the combination of Vandenberg, and Byrnes and Connally—two of them senators and one of them a former senator and all three of them known to Truman when he was a senator for many years—was just too much for him. So he swung over to their point of view. He didn't really want to do it but he was forced to do it.

Appendices

The Price of Free World Victory

*Statement by Vice President Wallace,
Chairman of the Board of Economic Warfare*

The Way to Peace

The Price of Free World Victory

(May 8, 1942)

THIS IS A FIGHT between a slave world and a free world. Just as the United States in 1862 could not remain half slave and half free, so in 1942 the world must make its decision for a complete victory one way or the other.

As we begin the final stages of this fight to the death between the free world and the slave world, it is worthwhile to refresh our minds about the march of freedom for the common man. The idea of freedom—the freedom that we in the United States know and love so well—is derived from the Bible, with its extraordinary emphasis on the dignity of the individual. Democracy is the only true political expression of Christianity.

The prophets of the Old Testament were the first to preach social justice. But that which was sensed by the prophets many centuries before Christ was not given complete and powerful political expression until our nation was formed as a Federal Union a century and a half ago. Even then the march of the common people had just begun. Most of them did not yet know how to read and write. There were no public schools to which all children could go. Men and women cannot be really free until they have plenty to eat, and time and ability to read and think and talk things over. Down the years, the people of the United States have moved steadily forward in the practice of democracy. Through universal education, they now can read and write and form opinions of their own. They have learned, and are still learning, the art of production—that is, how to make a living. They have learned, and are still learning, the art of self-government.

If we were to measure freedom by standards of nutrition, education, and self-government, we might rank the United States and certain nations of Western Europe very high. But this would not be fair to other nations where education has become widespread only in the last twenty years. In many nations, a generation ago, nine out of ten of the people could not read or write. Russia, for example, was changed from an illiterate to a literate nation within one generation and, in the process, Russia's appreciation of freedom was enormously enhanced. In

China, the increase during the past thirty years in the ability of the people to read and write has been matched by their increased interest in real liberty.

Everywhere, reading and writing are accompanied by industrial progress, and industrial progress sooner or later inevitably brings a stronger labor movement. From a long-time and fundamental point of view, there are no backward peoples which are lacking in mechanical sense. Russians, Chinese, and the Indians both of India and the Americas all learn to read and write and operate machines just as well as your children and my children. Everywhere the common people are on the march.

When the freedom-loving people march—when the farmers have an opportunity to buy land at reasonable prices and to sell the produce of their land through their own organizations, when workers have the opportunity to form unions and bargain through them collectively, and when the children of all the people have an opportunity to attend schools which teach them truths of the real world in which they live— when these opportunities are open to everyone, then the world moves straight ahead.

But in countries where the ability to read and write has been recently acquired or where the people have had no long experience in governing themselves on the basis of their own thinking, it is easy for demagogues to arise and prostitute the mind of the common man to their own base ends. Such a demagogue may get financial help from some person of wealth who is unaware of what the end result will be. With this backing, the demagogue may dominate the minds of the people, and, from whatever degree of freedom they have, lead them backward into slavery.

The march of freedom of the past 150 years has been a long-drawn-out people's revolution. In this great revolution of the people, there were the American Revolution of 1775, the French Revolution of 1792, the Latin American revolutions of the Bolivian era, the German Revolution of 1848, and the Russian Revolution of 1917. Each spoke for the common man in terms of blood on the battlefield. Some went to excess. But the significant thing is that the people groped their way to the light. More of them learned to think and work together.

The people's revolution aims at peace and not at violence, but if the rights of the common man are attacked, it unleashes the ferocity of a she-bear who has lost a cub. When the Nazi psychologists tell their master Hitler that we in the United States may be able to produce hundreds of thousands of planes, but that we have no will to fight, they are only fooling themselves and him. The truth is that when the rights of the American people are transgressed, as those rights have been transgressed, the American people will fight with a relentless fury which will drive the ancient Teutonic gods back cowering into their caves. The *Götterdämmerung* has come for Odin and his crew.

The people are on the march toward even fuller freedom than the most fortunate peoples of the earth have hitherto enjoyed. No Nazi counterrevolution will stop it. The common man will smoke the Hitler stooges out into the open in the United States, in Latin America, and in India. He will destroy their influence. No Lavals, no Mussolinis will be tolerated in a Free World.

The people, in their millennial and revolutionary march toward manifesting here on earth the dignity that is in every human soul, hold as their credo the Four Freedoms enunciated by President Roosevelt in his message to Congress on January 6, 1941. These Four Freedoms are the very core of the revolution for which the United Nations have taken their stand. We who live in the United States may think there is nothing very revolutionary about freedom of religion, freedom of expression, and freedom from the fear of secret police. But when we begin to think about the significance of freedom from want for the average man, then we know that the revolution of the past 150 years has not been completed, either here in the United States or in any other nation in the world. We know that this revolution cannot stop until freedom from want has actually been attained.

And now, as we move forward toward realizing the Four Freedoms of this people's revolution, I would like to speak about four duties. It is my belief that every freedom, every right, ever privilege has its price, its corresponding duty without which it cannot be enjoyed. The four duties of the people's revolution, as I see them today, are these:

1. The duty to produce to the limit.
2. The duty to transport as rapidly as possible to the field of battle.
3. The duty to fight with all that is in us.
4. The duty to build a peace—just, charitable, and enduring.

The fourth duty is that which inspires the other three.

We failed in our job after World War I. We did not know how to go about building an enduring worldwide peace. We did not have the nerve to follow through and prevent Germany from rearming. We did not insist that she "learn war no more." We did not build a peace treaty on the fundamental doctrine of the people's revolution. We did not strive wholeheartedly to create a world where there could be freedom from want for all the peoples. But by our very errors we learned much, and after this war we shall be in position to utilize our knowledge in building a world which is economically, politically, and, I hope, spiritually sound.

Modern science, which is a by-product and an essential part of the people's revolution, has made it technologically possible to see that all of the people of the world get enough to eat. Half in fun and half seriously, I said the other day to Madame Litvinov: "The object of this war is to make sure that everybody in the world has the privilege of drinking a quart of milk a day." She replied: "Yes, even half a pint." The peace must mean a better standard of living for the common man, not merely in the United States and England, but also in India, Russia, China, and Latin America—not merely in the United Nations, but also in Germany and Italy and Japan.

Some have spoken of the "American Century." I say that the century on which we are entering—the century which will come out of this war—can be and must be the century of the common man. Everywhere the common man must learn to build his own industries with his own hands in a practical fashion. Everywhere the common man must learn to increase his productivity so that he and his children can eventually pay to the world community all that they have received. No nation will have the God-given right to exploit other nations. Older nations will have the privilege to help younger nations get started on the path to industrialization, but there must be neither military nor economic imperialism. The methods of the nineteenth century will not work in the people's century which is now about to begin. India, China, and Latin America have a tremendous stake in the people's century. As their masses learn to read and write, and as they become productive mechanics, their standard of living will double and treble. Modern science, when devoted wholeheartedly to the general welfare, has in it potentialities of which we do not yet dream.

And modern science must be released from German slavery. International cartels that serve American greed and the German will to power must go. Cartels in the peace to come must be subjected to international control for the common man, as well as being under adequate control by the respective home governments. In this way, we can prevent the Germans from again building a war machine while we sleep. With international monopoly pools under control, it will be possible for inventions to serve all the people instead of only the few.

Yes, and when the time of peace comes, the citizen will again have a duty, the supreme duty of sacrificing the lesser interest for the greater interest of the general welfare. Those who write the peace must think of the whole world. There can be no privileged peoples. We ourselves in the United States are no more a master race than the Nazis. And we can not perpetuate economic warfare without planting the seeds of military warfare.

If we really believe that we are fighting for a people's peace, all the rest becomes easy. Production, yes—it will be easy to get production without either strikes or sabotage, production with the wholehearted co-operation between willing arms and keen brains; enthusiasm, zip, energy geared to the tempo of keeping at it everlastingly, day after day. Hitler knows as well as those of us who sit in on the War Production Board meetings that we here in the United States are winning the battle of production.

I need say little about the duty to fight. Some people declare, and Hitler believes, that the American people have grown soft in the last generation. Hitler agents continually preach in South America that we are cowards, unable to use, like the "brave" German soldiers, the weapons of modern war. It is true that American youth hates war with a holy hatred. But because of that fact and because Hitler and the German people stand as the very symbol of war, we shall fight with a tireless enthusiasm until war and the possibility of war have been removed from this planet.

The American people have always had guts and always will have. You know the story of Bomber Pilot Dixon and Radioman Gene Aldrich and Ordnanceman Tony Pastula—the story which Americans will be telling their children for generations to illustrate man's ability to master any fate. These men lived for thirty-four days on the open sea in a rubber life raft, eight feet by four feet, with no food but that which they took from the sea and the air with one pocketknife and a pistol. And yet they lived it through and came at least to the beach of an island they did not know. In spite of their suffering and weakness, they stood like men, with no weapon left to protect themselves, and no shoes on their feet or clothes on their backs, and walked in military file because, they said, "if there were Japs, we didn't want to be crawling."

The American fighting men, and all the fighting men of the United Nations, will need to summon all their courage during the next few months. I am convinced that the summer and fall of 1942 will be a time of supreme crisis for us all.

We must be especially prepared to stifle the fifth columnists in the United States, who will try to sabotage not merely our war-material plants, but even more important, our minds. We must be prepared for the worst kind of fifth-column work in Latin America, much of it operating through the agency of governments with which the United States at present is at peace. When I say this, I recognize that the people, both of Latin America and of the nations supporting the agencies through which the fifth columnists work, are overwhelmingly on the side of the democracies. We must expect the offensive against us on the military, propaganda, and sabotage fronts, both in the United States and in Latin America, to reach its apex some time during the next few months. But in the case of most of us, the events of the next few months, disturbing though they may be, will only increase our will to bring about complete victory in this war of liberation. Prepared in spirit, we cannot be surprised. Psychological terrorism will fall flat. As we nerve ourselves for the supreme effort in this hemisphere, we must not forget the sublime heroism of the oppressed in Europe and Asia, whether it be in the mountains of Yugoslavia, the factories of Czechoslovakia and France, the farms of Poland, Denmark, Holland, and Belgium, among the seamen of Norway, or in the occupied areas of China and the Dutch East Indies. Everywhere the soul of man is letting the tyrant know that slavery of the body does not end resistance.

There can be no half measures. North, South, East, West, and Middle West—the will of the American people is for complete victory.

No compromise with Satan is possible. We shall not rest until all the victims under the Nazi yoke are freed. We shall fight for a complete peace as well as a complete victory.

The people's revolution is on the march, and the devil and all his angels cannot prevail against it. They cannot prevail, for on the side of the people is the Lord.

He giveth power to the faint; to them that have no might He increaseth strength . . . They that wait upon the Lord shall mount up with wings as eagles; they shall run, and not be weary; they shall walk and not be faint.

Strong in the strength of the Lord, we who fight in the people's cause will never stop until that cause is won.

Statement by Vice President Wallace, Chairman of the Board of Economic Warfare

(June 29, 1943)

As Originally Prepared for the Senate Committee on Appropriations

ON JUNE 4, 1943, the Chairman of this Committee discussed the work of the Board on the floor of the Senate. His statement contained certain inaccuracies for which the Senator was not responsible. He was basing his comments on testimony which he said Mr. Jesse Jones had given before the Joint Committee on the Reduction of Non-Essential Federal Expenditures.

I realize that when the distinguished Senator from Tennessee made his remarks on the floor of the Senate he felt he had been correctly informed by the Secretary of Commerce. The actual facts are at variance with the information given the Senator, however, and I feel compelled to state the correct information for the record.

Senator McKellar said on June 4: "No Congressional appropriation has ever been made for the payment of a single person employed in the Board of Economic Warfare. The Senate Appropriations Committee, of which I happen to be temporarily the head, has never appropriated any money for the Board of Economic Warfare."

On May 30, 1942, the President transmitted for the consideration of Congress an estimate of an appropriation for the salaries and expenses of the Board of Economic Warfare for the fiscal year 1943 (Document No. 760, 77th Congress, 2nd Sess.). After hearings before the House Appropriations Committee, during which we gave detailed testimony, that Committee favorably reported HR 7319, which contained an item for salaries and expenses of the Board of Economic Warfare (Report No. 2295, 77th Congress, 2nd Sess.). The bill passed the House on June 30, 1942, and was reported by Senator McKellar, for the Senate Committee on Appropriations, on July 10, 1942. The report suggested changes in some other items in the bill but left unchanged the item for salaries and expenses of the Board of Economic Warfare (Senate Report No. 1542). The bill as passed by the Senate on July 16, 1942, and approved by the President on July 25, 1942, contained an item in the amount of $12,000,000 for salaries and expenses of the Board of Economic Warfare (Public Law No. 678, 77th Congress). Mr. Perkins was not called upon to testify with regard to the item when it was considered by the Senate Committee on Appropriations. However, on October 12, 1942, Mr. Perkins appeared before the subcommittee of the Senate Committee on Appropriations, with Senator McKellar presiding, to explain the need for certain amendments in the appropriation language, primarily to take care of the payment of living and quarters allowances to employees stationed abroad. These amendments were included in an item entitled "Board of Economic Warfare" in Public [Law] No. 763, 77th Congress, approved October 26, 1942.

In the same statement on the floor of the Senate on June 4, 1943, Senator McKellar said: "Mr. Jesse Jones testified a day or two ago before the so-called Economy Committee, that Mr. Milo Perkins absolutely ran the entire establishment of 2620 employees; that his word was law, even over him, Mr. Jesse Jones, and that he had received a directive from Mr. Perkins to furnish the money to pay all these employees."

The Board has never obtained money for administrative purposes from the Reconstruction Finance Corporation, nor has the Board ever directed Mr. Jesse Jones or any Reconstruction Finance Corporation subsidiary to furnish money to pay the salaries of any of the Board's employees or any of its administrative expenses. All such salaries and expenses are paid from funds appropriated by the Congress to the Board of Economic Warfare.

There have been a few occasions where, in connection with the joint operations of the Board of Economic Warfare and the Reconstruction Finance Corporation field staffs in foreign countries, arrangements have been worked out jointly for the payment of certain joint staff expenses by either the Board or the Corporation. In these cases reimbursement by the one agency or the other has been made in accordance with established government procedures.

On June 4, Senator McKellar also said: "The Board of Economic Warfare was not created by the Congress."

The Board of Economic Warfare was established by the President on July 30, 1941, by executive order, as were other war agencies. From time to time additional functions have been transferred to the Board of Economic Warfare by the President pursuant to authority vested in the President by the Congress, particularly by the First War Powers Act of December 18, 1942 (Public Law No. 354, 77th Congress). Congress has appropriated the monies which the Board is using to discharge these responsibilities. Furthermore, Congress has specifically directed in Public Law No. 638, 77th Congress, approved June 30, 1942, that unless the President shall determine otherwise, the Board of Economic Warfare shall administer the Export Control Law.

It is not enough to make these corrections. The false impression which Mr. Jones created before the Byrd Committee is similar to the impression he created in early December before the Senate Banking and Currency Committee. It is time to prevent further harmful misrepresentations of this nature.

On April 13, 1942, the President vested in the Board of Economic Warfare complete control of all public purchase import operations. Mr. Jones has never been willing to accept that fact. He has instead done much to harass the administrative employees of the Board in their single-minded effort to help shorten this war by securing adequate stocks of strategic materials.

The report of the Truman Committee, dated May 6, 1943, has set the proper pattern for dealing with situations of this kind. Two brief paragraphs from that report are of particular relevance:

> Energetic, aggressive men, striving to meet war needs, will tend to clash when their duties bring them into conflict. But destructive, wasteful feuding must be suppressed.
>
> The task of control and guidance is of utmost importance. Clear leadership in strong hands is required. The influence from above must be always toward unity. Where necessary, heads must be knocked together.

The President's Order of April 13, 1942, provided for "clear leadership" in programming the import of strategic materials. As a consequence of Mr. Jones' reluctance to accept that leadership there has been too much "destructive, wasteful feuding." The Board of Economic Warfare has tried for over a year now to do its job in spite of the obstructionist tactics Mr. Jones has employed from time to time.

The Congress showed great foresight, very early, in authorizing government stockpiling of strategic materials by passing legislation and by making funds available for this purpose way back in 1939 and 1940. In June of 1939, the Secretary of the Treasury was empowered to purchase and stockpile strategic materials as directed by the Secretary of War and the Secretary of the Navy. This program was comparatively small. Then in the summer of 1940, the Congress made substantial funds available to the Reconstruction Finance Corporation for carrying out a program for purchasing and stockpiling all critical and strategic materials.

From the summer of 1940 until well past December 7, 1941, the Reconstruction Finance Corporation failed dismally, so far as the import field was concerned, to build the government stockpiles authorized and directed by the Congress nearly eighteen months before Pearl Harbor.

During this period, of course, private purchasing of imports continued on a somewhat increased scale due to better business, and the Reconstruction Finance Corporation entered into various underwriting agreements with some countries under which we agreed to take surpluses if they were not bought privately. This seems to us to have been a timid, business-as-usual procedure; at least it was a "far cry" from the aggressive government stockpiling which the Congress directed and authorized so that this nation might have a margin of security in its imported raw materials inventories.

On December 8, 1942, Mr. Perkins and I testified before the Senate Banking and Currency Committee and gave partial evidence of the delays to our work for which we felt Mr. Jones was responsible. We gave testimony on his failure to meet the Office of Production Management's directive to stockpile industrial diamonds and block mica. We gave evidence on the extent to which he had delayed the foreign rubber program and cited specifically his stalling in the gathering of wild rubber in South America and the planting of rubber plantations in Africa and in the planting of cryptostegia for natural rubber in the Caribbean. We also presented evidence on the months of delay in starting a preclusive buying program in European neutral countries to prevent strategic materials from going to the Axis. These delays took place before Pearl Harbor and extended beyond Pearl Harbor right up to the 13th of April 1942, at which time the President transferred import powers from the Reconstruction Finance Corporation and its subsidiaries to the Board of Economic Warfare.

The evidence which we presented on December 8, 1942, to the Senate Banking and Currency Committee was only partial evidence. It is a matter of public record in Hearings on S. 2900.

I now desire to present additional evidence on government stockpiling—commodity by commodity, for consideration by this Committee, by the entire Congress, and by the public at large.

I want to point out first that all of our administrative work on imports is done under the broad direction of the War Production Board and in some cases under the broad direction of the War Food Administration. I now feel it my duty to get down to specific cases. For reasons of military security, I shall not include figures which might be of value to the enemy. The figures I am able to use, however, have not been previously presented to the Congress . . .

BERYL ORE

Beryl ore has very important military uses, the outstanding one being its use as an alloy with copper.

On December 1, 1941, the Office of Production Management, the forerunner of the War Production Board, recommended the purchase by Reconstruction Finance Corporation of 3000 metric tons of beryl ore.

As of April 13, 1942, the day the President transferred import powers from the Reconstruction Finance Corporation to the Board of Economic Warfare, one 300-ton contract had been made, and no deliveries effected.

As of December 31, 1942, eleven contracts calling for the delivery of 4118 metric tons of ore from four different countries (Argentina, Brazil, India, South Africa) had been made; 640 tons had been delivered. This was done under Board of Economic Warfare directives.

CASTOR SEEDS

The oil extracted from castor seeds is vitally important for war purposes. Among other things, it is used as a hydraulic fluid for jacks and brakes in war machines, as a solvent in paint, and (dehydrated) as a special protective coating for testing airplane motors. No adequate substitute is known.

On November 19, 1941, the Office of Production Management recommended to Reconstruction Finance Corporation the purchase of 178,571 long tons of castor seeds.

As of April 13, 1942, over four months after Pearl Harbor, none had been purchased.

As of December 31, 1942, at the direction of the Board of Economic Warfare, spot purchases totaling 73,799 long tons had been made and long-term contracts had been executed for another 220,000 long tons.

COBALT

Cobalt is vitally important to our military effort, its chief use being in high-speed cutting steels.

On November 17, 1941, Office of Production Management recommended to the Reconstruction Finance Corporation the purchase of ores containing 2500 short tons of cobalt metal.

As of April 13, 1942, contracts had been made by the Metals Reserve Company for the purchase of ores containing only about 159 tons of cobalt metal.

As of December 31, 1942, government contracts for ore purchases from foreign sources totaled about 876 short tons of cobalt metal. Increased private purchases have now put us in a comfortable supply position.

CORUNDUM

Corundum, vitally important for its use as an abrasive for grinding optical glass and telescope lenses, is obtained almost exclusively from South Africa. There is practically none in the United States, although there are some interesting experiments being carried on now, in the southeastern section of the country.

On November 18, 1941, the Office of Production Management recommended to the Reconstruction Finance Corporation the purchase of 6000 long tons of South African corundum. The recommendation was subsequently increased.

As of April 13, 1942, over four months after Pearl Harbor, no purchases had been made.

As of December 31, 1942, there were under contract (one contract; made by Metals Reserve Company in June 1942) 12,000 long tons of South African corundum for delivery during 1943 and 1944. This was done under the Board of Economic Warfare directives.

FATS AND OILS

The fats and oils group includes approximately 25 different products, ranging all the way from sunflower seeds to ouricury nuts and whale oil. These products are critically needed in the war effort for a variety of industrial uses as well as for human consumption.

There is one large group of edible oils, needed for Army, Navy, Lend-Lease, and civilian uses.

Another group, which includes babassu nuts, coconuts, palm kernels, murumuru nuts, tucum nuts, and ouricury nuts, contains a high percentage of lauric acid, from which glycerine—used in the manufacture of explosives—is derived. These products are also used for plasticizers (to reduce brittleness) and in the manufacture of soap and synthetic rubber.

Oiticica oil and linseed oil are used as solvents in paints.

There is no adequate substitute for cashew nut oil, which is used to impregnate and toughen brake linings and for magneto harness coverings.

Neats-foot oil is used in impregnating leather.

Tallow, seal oil, and whale oil are used in soap-making processes, in the course of which glycerine is produced.

Palm oil is essential in the manufacture of tinplate.

Certain marine engines require rapeseed oil as a lubricant.

Sperm oil is used as a special lubricant for airplane engines (allowing the "cold" breaking in of motors), in the rifling of gun barrels, and as a high-pressure smokeless lubricant in Diesel engines.

One would think, in view of the critical military urgency of going out to get these imported raw materials, that Mr. Jones would have moved aggressively to build government stockpiles of these fats and oils, and yet here are the facts:

In October 1941, the Office of Production Management recommended to the Reconstruction Finance Corporation the purchase of approximately 30,000 long tons of various types of fats and oils from foreign sources. In November this total was increased to 208,571 long tons; in January 1942, to 308,571 tons; in February to 317,499 tons. (The total has, since April 13, 1942, been increased much beyond this last figure.)

As of April 13, 1942, the Reconstruction Finance Corporation had purchased (according to the best information we have) only 2200 long tons (rapeseed oil); none had arrived in this country. The purchases were all spot; no development program had been devised. There may be a minor error in this particular figure due to the inadequate commodity accounting records of the Reconstruction Finance Corporation, but we believe the figures to be substantially accurate. For all practical purposes, however, virtually nothing was done by Mr. Jones to build a government stockpile of fats and oils even after Pearl Harbor, when the Japs were conquering the Far East, from which we had been getting tremendous supplies.

The Board of Economic Warfare, shortly after it was given its responsibility in the import field, on April 13, 1942, shifted the financing of the fats and oils program to the Commodity Credit Corporation, but retained general administration of it.

As of December 31, 1942:

(1) 276,622 tons of foreign fats and oils had been bought on a spot purchase basis.

(2) The Board of Economic Warfare had negotiated and the Commodity Credit Corporation had entered into development and long-term purchase contracts calling for the delivery of 500,000 tons. Several additional development contracts beyond this total were subsequently negotiated.

(3) The private import trade, dealing in fats and oils, which was threatened with extinction because of distortions in the world price structure, was organized into the Emergency Group for Foreign Vegetable Oils, Fats and Oil-Bearing Materials, and its services made use of as an integrated part of the program.

(4) Agreements for joint purchasing were made with the British and Canadians, eliminating competitive buying and resulting in a substantial reduction in the prices paid for a number of fats, oils, and oil-bearing materials.

PALM OIL

Since there is no adequate substitute for palm oil, which is used in the manufacture of tinplate, I desire to call special attention to it.

On October 20, 1941, the Office of Production Management recommended to the Reconstruction Finance Corporation the purchase of 30,000 long tons of palm oil.

As of April 13, 1942, none had been purchased.

As of December 31, 1942, purchases (spot) totaled 23,928 long tons. This took place under Board of Economic Warfare directives.

FLAX FIBER

I now want to discuss flax fiber, which is used for parachute webbing and which is also used as industrial sewing thread for high-tension purposes.

On October 27, 1941, the Office of Production Management recommended the purchase by the Reconstruction Finance Corporation of 6500 tons of flax.

As of April 13, 1942, the day the President transferred import powers from the Reconstruction Finance Corporation to the Board of Economic Warfare, no purchases had been made.

As of December 31, 1942, contracts had been made for approximately 8000 tons annually from Canada, Peru, and Egypt under Board of Economic Warfare directives.

JUTE

Jute is another commodity which must be imported from abroad.

On September 5, 1941, the Office of Production Management had directed the purchase of 80,000 long tons of jute, nearly all of which comes from India.

As of April 13, 1942, over four months after Pearl Harbor, the Reconstruction Finance Corporation had done practically nothing to fulfill this important directive, having bought only 1210 long tons, although the situation in India during this period was highly uncertain.

As of December 31, 1942, the Board of Economic Warfare had arranged for the purchase of the full 80,000 long tons, plus another 8000 long tons to cover a supplementary directive. Moreover, most of this jute was shipped from Indian ports by the end of 1942.

The Board of Economic Warfare's insistence on maintaining in Calcutta, India, a special agent, with a full business background in this industry, has been an important factor in the establishment of this performance record.

SISAL

Sisal is a hard fiber needed particularly in the manufacture of binder twine for the harvesting of our grain crops.

As of September 5, 1941, the Office of Production Management had recommended the purchase of 100,000 short tons of sisal (increased to 250,000 tons on March 18, 1942).

As of April 13, 1942, the Reconstruction Finance Corporation had purchased only an approximate 33,600 short tons against this urgent directive.

As of December 31, 1942, the Board of Economic Warfare had negotiated contracts for approximately 310,000 short tons, all to be produced by June 1945, and of which 150,000 tons is expected to be produced by the middle of 1943. By December 31, 1942, some 88,000 tons had been delivered.

We lost many of our fibers sources in the Far East to the Japanese. By December 31, 1942, the Board of Economic Warfare had entered into contracts for the development and purchase of a number of hard fibers in Mexico and Caribbean areas as well as in Africa, as part of a tremendous development program. We are planning to put 70,000 acres in these crops. 40,000 acres have already been planted. During a war we have to fight as vigorously to buy goods as we have to fight in peace time to sell them.

TANTALITE

Tantalite is another strategic material carrying the very highest military priorities. It is used, among other things, for contact points in radio tubes.

In December 1941 there was an exchange of correspondence between the Office of Production Management, the State Department, and the Reconstruction Finance Corporation which made clear the necessity of increasing substantially United States tantalite imports by public purchase. On March 13, 1942, the War Production Board formally recommended the purchase by the Reconstruction Finance Corporation of 1,000,000 pounds.

As of April 13, 1942, over four months after Pearl Harbor, no tantalite had been purchased by the Reconstruction Finance Corporation.

As of December 31, 1942, some 322,000 pounds had been purchased.

This increase has been due in large measure to an aggressive Board of Economic Warfare program of tracing down every possible source of an ore which occurs only in very small and scattered deposits. Most purchases have been in exceedingly small lots.

In order to open up new sources of supply which will permit fulfilling the purchase recommendations we have received from the War Production Board, the Rare Metals Section of the Board of Economic Warfare's Metals and Minerals Division has contacted private producers or government representatives in Australia, Brazil, South Rhodesia, Argentina, French Equatorial Africa, Nigeria, Portuguese East Africa, India, and Uganda.

It is estimated that, very largely as the result of Board of Economic Warfare efforts, 1943 imports into the United States may be 60 percent above 1942 imports and ten times the total world production in 1939. This program is typical of the way in which the Board of Economic Warfare fights for every pound of strategic materials as though a soldier's life depended upon it—which, of course, it does.

ZIRCONIUM

I now desire to discuss zirconium, which is so important in the manufacture of flares, signals, tracer ammunition, and blasting caps.

On September 5, 1941, Office of Production Management recommended to the Reconstruction Finance Corporation the purchase of "reasonable amounts" of zirconium from Brazil.

As of April 13, 1942, the day on which the President transferred import powers from the Reconstruction Finance Corporation to the Board of Economic Warfare, no purchase contracts had been made under the Office of Production Management directive.

As of December 31, 1942, contracts had been made for the purchase from foreign sources of 21,575 short tons of zirconium ores, of which 16,500 short tons were from Brazil. This was done under Board of Economic Warfare directives.

As previously indicated, I have deliberately given figures of the Board of Economic Warfare accomplishments through December 31, 1942, only, for the purposes of military security. The progress in the foreign field for the first six months of 1943 is even more encouraging, considering the difficulties we have faced, than it was during the last six months of 1942. As an overall figure for this committee to bear in mind, I should like to point out that total purchases of imported raw materials subject to Board of Economic Warfare directives will run roughly a billion and one-half dollars for the 1943 fiscal year and slightly over two billion dollars for the fiscal year of 1944. Over two hundred critically needed strategic materials will be included in these public purchase programs. Contracts will be made in over thirty foreign countries.

Mr. Perkins is in position to give this Committee detailed and current information on any imported strategic material in a completely secret and off-the-record discussion if this Committee desires to have such facts placed before it in this manner. He can indicate the figures for the full fiscal year 1943 as well as contemplated figures for the 1944 fiscal year. Under no conditions would we make such current information a matter of public record. We are, however, very anxious to inform this committee as to how such vast sums are being spent. I used the word "spent," but imported strategic materials are, of course, sold by subisidiaries of the Reconstruction Finance Corporation to our war industries. Public purchase is used to assure adequate supplies. Detailed information has already been given the House Committee on Appropriations. We want to give the fullest possible information to the Senate Committee.

Since the 13th of April 1942, when full import powers were transferred from the Reconstruction Finance Corporation to the Board of Economic Warfare, tremendous progress has been made in stepping up the procurement of certain strategic materials, shortages of which could not adequately have been foreseen by the Office of Production Management prior to Pearl Harbor. Outstanding among these is the increased production of balsa wood and mahogany, largely in this Hemisphere. When the full story can be told, it will be one of the most dramatic successes of the war effort. Our country can be proud of having achieved what seemed to be almost impossible on this front.

Although the President, on April 13, 1942, transferred full control over the programming of imported strategic materials from the Reconstruction Finance Corporation to the Board of Economic Warfare, which operates under broad directives received from the War Production Board, Mr. Jones has never fully accepted that authority. He and his personnel down the line have thrown a great many obstacles in the way of our exercise of the powers given us to carry out our wartime assignments. Some of these obstructionist tactics have been minor and annoying and some have been of major consequence in this gigantic job of waging total war. I now desire to inform this Committee and the Congress, and the public at large about some of these delays, which have not yet seen the light of day.

First of all I desire to discuss quinine. Brig. Gen. H. C. Minton has informed us that: "Antimalarial preparations derived from cinchona are, of course, essential to adequate control and treatment of malaria, in conjunction with the accepted synthetic anti-malarials."

Far East cinchona bark contains 7 to 10 percent quinine sulphate; Latin American bark about 2 percent.

On April 14, 1942, General MacArthur wired Washington that two million seeds of a high grade strain had been brought out of the Philippines (on one of the last planes leaving for Australia); adding that they "must be planted *without delay*."

I am sorry to have to inform this committee that Jesse Jones and Will Clayton stalled for months on this program. As I indicated to the Senate Banking and Currency Committee last December, there are times when what we need is more fights and fewer shortages.

Lt. Col. Arthur F. Fischer, who brought those seeds from the Philippines to the United States, came to the Board of Economic Warfare with his proposal—to plant the seeds in Costa Rica—on August 24, 1942. Within three weeks, the Board of Economic Warfare had worked out a detailed plan and submitted it to the other interested agencies. Reconstruction Finance Corporation representatives at first acquiesced in the proposal when it was discussed with them on September 11 and 29. Undersecretary of War Patterson approved it formally on October 7, 1942.

Then, on October 10, the Reconstruction Finance Corporation notified the Board of Economic Warfare that "the matter requires further consideration." Those "considerations" continued for four months. Mr. Jones said that our proposal was postwar planning because of the time it takes for cinchona trees to come to full maturity for profitable stripping. The Fischer trees couldn't be harvested for 2½ years at the earliest; normally, seven years pass before stripping of the bark begins.

During 1941 Mr. Jones may have felt that this would be a short war in which we wouldn't become involved; in any event he did not buy quinine during that period in adequate amounts for government stockpiles; during 1942 he acted as though the war might be over by 1944, if we can take his attitude toward this quinine project as a criterion. A United Press story in the New York *Journal of Commerce* of February 3, 1942, quotes Jesse Jones as follows: "Secretary of Commerce Jesse H. Jones told the House Banking Committee today that he believed the United States will be getting 'all the rubber we need from the Dutch East Indies' by the end of 1943 despite the present Japanese threat to that area." Mr. Jones may be right, but we dare not take chances and base our imports work on any such optimistic estimate.

As a matter of fact, Mr. Jones may have been considering something else. He takes great pride in the profits of the Reconstruction Finance Corporation and some of its subsidiaries, as evidenced by his recent testimony before the Byrd Committee. If the cinchona trees which we have been discussing have to be stripped after 2½ years because of desperate military needs for quinine, they will yield about 10,000 ounces of quinine—and a $125,000 loss to the Reconstruction Finance Corporation. That will mean red ink on the books of the Reconstruction Finance Corporation. I do not like to assign motives, but it is difficult to escape the conclusion that a possible dollar loss held up this production project. Like many things in total war this project may, of course, prove to be an expensive undertaking in terms of dollars. It seems to us to be a wise investment in terms of saving lives, however.

Whatever his reasons may have been, the facts are that Mr. Jones disregarded the constant proddings by the Board of Economic Warfare, and for a while he ignored the fact that I, as Chairman of the Board of Economic Warfare, had personally investigated the matter and recommended immediate action. His "considerations" continued right on through the battle—with malaria and with the Japs—at Guadalcanal.

It was not until late January 1943 that the Reconstruction Finance Corporation finally announced that it would spend some money for this quinine project. For all the full power the President has given the Board of Economic Warfare over imports, we are helpless when Jesse Jones, as our banker, refuses to sign checks in accordance with our directives. Finally, we have won out in all such cases, but the time lost has been precious time which there was no excuse for losing. There have been many other times, of course, when personnel down the line in both the Reconstruction Finance Corporation and the Board of Economic Warfare have found themselves in complete agreement and have moved forward together with speed. The situation is better than it was a while back, and Mr. Perkins emphasized this fact in his recent testimony before the House Appropriations Committee.

Colonel Fischer is now in Costa Rica and the quinine project is under way. Some of his seeds have been germinating in the Department of Agriculture's experimental station in Beltsville and are about to be sent to Costa Rica. The rest will be planted there. It will be 1946 before quinine from the seeds brought out of the Philippines by Colonel Fischer can be put to work fighting malaria in the tropics. Even so, our armed forces may need it desperately by that time if they are still fighting in the malarial regions of the Southwest Pacific. We and the Army would be quite willing to strip a greater part of the young trees at the end of 2½ years if we have to do so to get quinine for our soldiers, even though the Reconstruction Finance Corporation may lose a little money through not waiting seven years to let the trees mature for the most profitable period of stripping.

In fairness to the Reconstruction Finance Corporation I want to report that on a recent development project in Guatemala, where three hundred million cinchona trees for quinine are being planted under Board of Economic Warfare directives, we have thus far had no opposition from the RFC. We had previously won our fight in terms of principle on the Fischer project just described and Mr. Jones has not yet opposed us on the much larger project we have worked out in Guatemala.

The other quinine programs of the Board, such as gathering wild cinchona bark in Latin America, have been pushed aggressively by the Board of Economic Warfare, and Army officers are now surveying this work in the foreign field with members of our staff. Even this work, I am sorry to report, was held up by Mr. Jones in the late summer of 1942, some nine months after Pearl Harbor. I want to submit the following facts:

In February 1943 the Board of Economic Warfare took over the actual import purchase negotiations under Order No. 5, which I signed as chairman of the Board of Economic Warfare. Order No. 5 is a part of our formal budget presentation. These negotiations had previously been handled by the Reconstruction Finance Corporation subsidiaries. The 1942 record of Reconstruction Finance Corporation's purchases of cinchona bark, under Board of Economic Warfare directives, illustrates why the procedures were changed in the interest of shortening this war.

(1) On June 19, 1942, the Board of Economic Warfare gave De-

fense Supplies Corporation a detailed outline of a program for purchasing Latin American cinchona bark from United States importers, and directed that it be put into immediate effect. A checkup five days later revealed that nothing had been done; the Federal Loan Administrator had "objected to the tone of finality" about the letter of June 19. Another week was lost because Mr. Clayton "has apparently mislaid the directive and requests another copy." That's the way the Reconstruction Finance Corporation was handling the cinchona program for quinine three months after we had lost Bataan.

(2) The Reconstruction Finance Corporation waited one month to accept an offer of 25 tons; by that time the particular bark had been sold to Brazil. Another offer for 20 tons was withdrawn—five weeks after it had been made. Those delays meant the loss of 1800 ounces of anti-malarial alkaloids for United States soldiers fighting in the tropics. In three months the Reconstruction Finance Corporation bought just 75 tons of bark. In the following seven weeks a single Board of Economic Warfare agent got firm commitments for 750 tons for immediate shipment, 1500 more for future delivery. By this time, our Imports Office was better organized than in the spring of 1942, and swinging vigorously into action.

(3) The Board of Economic Warfare learned that the Reconstruction Finance Corporation was getting firm offers on cinchona bark but referring them to processors—with whom the importers were then haggling about price while the bark stayed in Colombia and Ecuador. When the Board of Economic Warfare directed the Reconstruction Finance Corporation to accept all firm offers, the Reconstruction Finance Corporation responded by calling two meetings, each after another ten-day delay. Then the Reconstruction Finance Corporation explained its reluctance; it didn't want to take the risk of financial loss involved in dealing with unknown and possibly "irresponsible" suppliers.

The Reconstruction Finance Corporation thus held up the vital quinine program while it objected to the "tone" of our letters, mislaid papers, forgot about offers, and hand-picked its suppliers from the "right kinds of people," instead of making a desperate fight to buy every pound of cinchona bark it could locate from any source whatsoever, regardless of the financial risks involved.

QUARTZ CRYSTALS

I now desire to discuss quartz crystals, the use of which is so utterly important to some of our war industries.

For two years now Brazilian quartz crystal, essential element in airplane, tank, and submarine radio sets, has been in critically short supply.

During 1941 and early 1942, the Reconstruction Finance Corporation agent in Brazil bought 2000 tons of crystals. He was paid a commission of 1½ percent on his gross purchases, and he bought those crystals without checking to see whether they were of the quality needed and paid for. Over 85 percent of them weren't. The government lost between two and six million dollars, and we have heard that United States quartz fabricators began raiding museums to get usable crystals.

Shortly after April 13, 1942, the Reconstruction Finance Corporation replaced this agent although it gave him equally lucrative work in New York. But the situation in Brazil wasn't improved. The Reconstruction Finance Corporation had been burned where it hurt most, by having to take a loss on a hazardous undertaking. The new Reconstruction Finance Corporation agent began eliminating dollar losses the easy way. Not a pound of quartz crystal was purchased by the Metals Reserve Company for six months. The Board of Economic Warfare finally had to send a top official to Rio to get the public purchasing resumed. I feel that Board of Economic Warfare personnel should have fought the delaying tactics of the Reconstruction Finance Corporation more vigorously in this instance.

The Board of Economic Warfare finally insisted upon inspection facilities in Rio so that crystals could be tested before payment and shipment. The Army Signal Corps has been of great assistance to us on this project by supplying 20 trained inspectors and the necessary arc lights, inspection baths, Polaroid screens, etc. The Army, of course, had a critical military stake in this phase of our work and has co-operated readily and effectively.

Reconstruction Finance Corporation policy had been to keep a staff in Rio—and to wait for the business to come in. When the Board of Economic Warfare sent 100 engineers and qualified purchasing agents into the up-country areas where the crystals are mined, Reconstruction Finance Corporation representatives in Brazil at first cooperated in supplying purchase money and contracting authority; then they refused to cooperate—on "instructions from Washington." The Board of Economic Warfare set up a purchasing station at outlying Campo Formosa; then we had to move it back to Bahia—so that Reconstruction Finance Corporation funds could be spent through the bank there.

In April 1943, Board of Economic Warfare representatives in Rio advised that restrictions put upon Metals Reserve Company agents' purchasing authority by Reconstruction Finance Corporation was preventing our meeting market prices in our buying there and that purchases were coming to a halt. The Board of Economic Warfare, therefore, directed the Reconstruction Finance Corporation to relax its restrictions. Reconstruction Finance Corporation refused, stating that we didn't need quartz enough to pay any more for it. Three weeks later, after advice from their own Brazilian representatives, they reconsidered—and changed their instructions. But not in time to head off the Special Representative of the Board of Economic Warfare in Brazil. Fed up with Reconstruction Finance Corporation obstruction to his Brazilian program, he arrived in Washington to report. It took his report, plus a morning which I spent with Jesse Jones and Will Clayton, to break this particular logjam. Throughout the period of these bureaucratic, obstructionist tactics on the part of the Reconstruction Finance Corporation, the need for quartz crystals was critically urgent.

As I previously indicated, the reason Mr. Jones could hold up our quartz crystal and quinine programs is because he signs the checks to pay for the procurement and development of these commodities. To put it differently, he has been able to delay this part of the war effort because of his position as banker for us, notwithstanding the complete delegation of powers over imports which the President gave the Board of Economic Warfare on the 13th of April, 1942, following the failure of the Reconstruction Finance Corporation to build the government stockpiles of strategic materials which Congress authorized and directed in the summer of 1940.

The delays on the two programs just mentioned were major matters. More annoying, because there are more of them, have been the minor delays which have taken place from time to time throughout this past year. I now desire to discuss some of these, more by way of illustration than by way of presenting any completely documented cases:

Since February 1943 the Board of Economic Warfare has been negotiating and drafting all imported materials contracts, getting them executed by the sellers, then sending them to the Reconstruction Finance Corporation subsidiaries for execution. This has been done under Order No. 5, to which I referred earlier. The purpose in establishing these new procedures was to eliminate delay and duplication.

Those purposes have been in large measure accomplished—but only in the face of an exasperating rearguard action by Reconstruction Finance Corporation officials who are still fighting the war with peacetime red tape, corporate technicalities, and with what seems to us to be an unnecessary caution. None of the following obstructionist efforts of the Reconstruction Finance Corporation is major in itself, but the cumulative effect has been maddening to the businessmen with foreign trade background who have left lucrative positions in private industry to work for the Board of Economic Warfare at government salaries for the duration in a patriotic effort to help shorten this war.

The tactics are better illustrated than described. During the past four months, for example, one of the Reconstruction Finance Corporation subsidiaries, Metals Reserve Company:

(1) Took four weeks to execute a group of three metal contracts drafted by the Board of Economic Warfare which the sellers had executed and returned within ten days.

(2) Held a copper contract for five weeks because one letter had been left out of one unimportant word and because two minor clauses "could have been more clearly stated." (The seller had supplied the missing letter and had found no difficulty in understanding the two clauses.)

(3) Wrote three letters to the Board of Economic Warfare complaining because a form recital clause (without legal effect) referred to the Board of Economic Warfare's "direction" that the contract be entered into. (A similar reference to the War Production Board had always been included by the Reconstruction Finance Corporation draftsmen.)

(4) Demanded that a simple five-ton wash sale contract for tantalite be broken up into two contracts—so that Reconstruction Finance Corporation attorneys might draft one of the two. The wash sale technique was used on this small lot in order to provide government ownership while in transit, as it was necessary to ship the goods by air and the Air Transport Command carries only government-owned materials.

(5) Refused to sign a contract with a Nigerian tantalite producer before the producer signed it—even though the alternative meant a three-week delay in getting a new mine into production.

(6) Refused, on a legal technicality, to honor a directive authorizing the "loan *or* rental" of equipment to the Brazilian government —because of information from government representatives in Rio, received subsequent to our directive, that the equipment would be *rented*, and not *loaned*.

(7) Held a Brazilian tantalite contract for four weeks because it

had been entered into without a formal approval required by the Secretary of Commerce.

All this, and I want to emphasize it, is bureaucracy at its worst; it is utterly inexcusable in a nation at war.

We are quite willing to rest our case with the Congress and stand on our record. While I realize that the suggestion which I am about to make is not a matter directly before this Committee, I should like to express a personal judgment.

It seems to me that we could end this wrangling and improve the administrative efficiency so essential to winning this war, if program money were appropriated directly to the Board of Economic Warfare for its purchase and development of *all* imported strategic materials, just as money is now appropriated directly to us for administrative expenses in connection with our imports work. These difficult wartime jobs cannot be tackled effectively, as pointed out so truly in the report of the Truman Committee from which I read in the early part of this statement, without the full power to carry out specific assignments.

The Board of Economic Warfare is a war agency; it is not a part of the permanent machinery of government. We have recruited what we feel to be an extremely competent group of businessmen and technical engineers with foreign trade background to carry out our job of importing strategic materials. Shortly after the war is over, most of these men will be wanting to get back to their peacetime responsibilities.

For the duration, however, I feel that they should be given adequate latitude for a job which is extremely difficult even under the best of conditions. They should be free from this hamstringing bureaucracy and backdoor complaining of Mr. Jones and his employees. It is my hope that this statement has cleared up any misunderstandings which may have been caused by Mr. Jones' appearance before the Byrd Committee.

The Way to Peace*
(September 12, 1946)

FIRST OFF, I want to give my own personal endorsement to the candidates chosen by the Democratic Party and the American Labor Party in New York. James Mead long has been one of the ablest public servants in Washington—a constant, faithful, and intelligent proponent of the New Deal of Franklin Roosevelt. The Senate will miss him—but Albany needs him. He will make a great governor—worthy of the tradition of Smith and Roosevelt and Lehman.

Herbert Lehman knows full well the problems and the opportunities facing the State of New York, the United States, and the United Nations. His great heart and great mind will be increasingly useful when he is a member of the United States Senate.

Victory for Mead and Lehman in November will mean a long stride in the people's progress.

Tonight I want to talk about peace—and how to get peace. Never have the common people of all lands so longed for peace. Yet, never in a time of comparative peace have they feared war so much.[1]

Up till now peace has been negative and unexciting. War has been positive and exciting. Far too often, hatred and fear, intolerance and deceit have had the upper hand over love and confidence, trust and joy. Far too often, the law of nations has been the law of the jungle; and the constructive spiritual forces of the Lord have bowed to the destructive forces of Satan.

During the past year or so, the significance of peace has been increased immeasurably by the atom bomb, guided missiles, and airplanes which soon will travel as fast as sound. Make no mistake about it—another war would hurt the United States many times as much as the last war. We cannot rest in the assurance that we invented the atom bomb—and therefore that this agent of destruction will work best for us. He who trusts in the atom bomb will sooner or later perish by the atom bomb—or something worse.

I say this as one who steadfastly backed preparedness throughout the thirties. We have no use for namby-pamby pacifism. But we must

* In reading, Wallace made several changes in his text. His omissions are indicated by square brackets, his interpolations in notes starting on page 668.

realize that modern inventions have now made peace the most exciting thing in the world—and we should be willing to pay a just price for peace. If modern war can cost us four hundred billion dollars, we should be willing and happy to pay much more for peace. But certainly, the cost of peace is to be measured not in dollars but in the hearts and minds of men.

The price of peace—for us and for every nation in the world—is the price of giving up prejudice, hatred, fear, and ignorance.

Let's get down to cases here at home.

First we have prejudice, hatred, fear, and ignorance of certain races. The recent mass lynching in Georgia was not merely the most unwarranted, brutal act of mob violence in the United States in recent years; it was also an illustration of the kind of prejudice that makes war inevitable.

Hatred breeds hatred. The doctrine of racial superiority produces a desire to get even on the part of its victims. If we are to work for peace in the rest of the world, we here in the United States must eliminate racism from our unions, our business organizations, our educational institutions, and our employment practices. Merit alone must be the measure of man.

Second, in payment for peace, we must give up prejudice, hatred, fear, and ignorance in the economic world. This means working earnestly, day after day, for a larger volume of world trade. It means helping undeveloped areas of the world to industrialize themselves with the help of American technical assistance and loans.

We should welcome the opportunity to help along the most rapid possible industrialization in Latin America, China, India, and the Near East. For as the productivity of these peoples increases, our exports will increase.

We all remember the time, not so long ago, when the high tariff protectionists blindly opposed any aid to the industrialization of Canada. But look at our exports to Canada today. On a per capita basis our Canadian exports are seven times greater than our exports to Mexico.

I supported the British loan of almost four billion dollars because I knew that without this aid in the rehabilitation of its economy, the British government would have been forced to adopt totalitarian trade methods and economic warfare of a sort which would have closed the markets of much of the world to American exports.

For the welfare of the American people and the world it is even more important to invest four billion dollars in the industrialization of undeveloped areas in the so-called backward nations, thereby promoting the long-term stability that comes from an ever-increasing standard of living. This would not only be good politics and good morals. It would be good business.

The United States is the world's great creditor nation. And low tariffs by creditor nations are a part of the price of peace. For when a great creditor demands payment, and at the same time, adopts policies which make it impossible for the debtors to pay in goods—the first result is the intensification of depression over large areas of the world; and the final result is the triumph of demagogues who speak only the language of violence and hate.

Individual Republicans may hold enlightened views—but the Republican Party as a whole is irrevocably committed to tariff and trade policies which can only mean worldwide depression, ruthless economic warfare, and eventual war. And if the Republicans were in power in the United States today, intelligent people all over the world would fear that once more we would be headed straight for boom, bust, and worldwide chaos.

I noticed in the papers recently that Governor Dewey doesn't like my prophecies. I said weeks before the last election—and said it repeatedly—that Franklin Roosevelt would carry thirty-six states and have a popular majority of three million. Of course, Mr. Dewey didn't like that one. I say now—as I have said repeatedly—that Republican foreign economic policies carried into action would mean disaster for the nation and the world. Mr. Dewey won't like that one either.

The Republican Party is the party of economic nationalism and political isolation—and as such is as anachronistic as the dodo and as certain to disappear. The danger is that before it disappears it may enjoy a brief period of power during which it can do irreparable damage to the United States and the cause of world peace.

Governor Dewey has expressed himself as favoring an alliance of mutual defense with Great Britain as the key to our foreign policy. This may sound attractive because we both speak the same language and many of our customs and traditions have the same historical background. Moreover, to the military men, the British Isles are our advanced air base against Europe.

Certainly we like the British people as individuals. But to make Britain the key to our foreign policy would be, in my opinion, the height of folly. We must not let the reactionary leadership of the Republican Party force us into that position. We must not let British balance-of-power manipulations determine whether and when the United States gets into war.

Make no mistake about it—the British imperialistic policy in the Near East alone, combined with Russian retaliation, would lead the United States straight to war unless we have a clearly defined and realistic policy of our own.

Neither of these two great powers wants war now, but the danger is that whatever their intentions may be, their current policies may eventually lead to war. To prevent war and insure our survival in a stable world, it is essential that we look abroad through our own American eyes and not through the eyes of either the British Foreign Office or a pro-British or anti-Russian press.

In this connection, I want one thing clearly understood. I am neither anti-British nor pro-British—neither anti-Russian nor pro-Russian. And just two days ago, when President Truman read these words, he said that they represented the policy of his administration.

I plead for an America vigorously dedicated to peace—just as I plead for opportunities for the next generation throughout the world to enjoy the abundance which now, more than ever before, is the birthright of man.

To achieve lasting peace, we must study in detail just how the Russian character was formed—by invasions of Tartars, Mongols, Germans, Poles, Swedes, and French; by the czarist rule based on ignorance, fear, and force; by the intervention of the British, French, and Americans in Russian affairs from 1919 to 1921; by the geography of the huge Russian land mass situated strategically between Europe and Asia; and by the vitality derived from the rich Russian soil and the strenuous Russian climate. Add to all this the tremendous emotional power which Marxism and Leninism gives to the Russian leaders—and then we can realize that we are reckoning with a force which cannot be handled successfully by a "Get tough with Russia" policy. "Getting tough" never bought anything real and lasting— whether for schoolyard bullies or businessmen or world powers. The tougher we get, the tougher the Russians will get.

Throughout the world there are numerous reactionary elements which had hoped for Axis victory—and now profess great friendship for the United States. Yet, these enemies of yesterday and false friends of today continually try to provoke war between the United States and Russia. They have no real love of the United States. They only long for the day when the United States and Russia will destroy each other.

We must not let our Russian policy be guided or influenced by those inside or outside the United States who want war with Russia. This does not mean appeasement.

We most earnestly want peace with Russia—but we want to be met halfway. We want cooperation. And I believe that we can get cooperation once Russia understands that our primary objective is neither saving the British Empire nor purchasing oil in the Near East with the lives of American soldiers. We cannot allow national oil rivalries to force us into war. All of the nations producing oil, whether inside or outside of their own boundaries, must fulfill the provisions of the United Nations Charter and encourage the development of world petroleum reserves so as to make the maximum amount of oil available to all nations of the world on an equitable peaceful basis—and not on the basis of fighting the next war.

For her part, Russia can retain our respect by cooperating with the United Nations in a spirit of open-minded and flexible give-and-take.

The real peace treaty we now need is between the United States and Russia. On our part, we should recognize that we have no more business in the *political* affairs of eastern Europe than Russia has in the *political* affairs of Latin America, western Europe, and the United States. We may not like what Russia does in eastern Europe. Her type of land reform, industrial expropriation, and suppression of basic liberties offends the great majority of the people of the United States.[2]

But whether we like it or not the Russians will try to socialize their sphere of influence just as we try to democratize our sphere of influence. This applies also to Germany and Japan. We are striving to democratize Japan and our area of control in Germany, while Russia strives to socialize eastern Germany.

As for Germany, we all must recognize that an equitable settlement, based on a unified German nation, is absolutely essential to any lasting European settlement. This means that Russia must be assured that never again can German industry be converted into military might to be used against her—and Britain. Western Europe and the United States must be certain that Russia's German policy will not become a tool of Russian design against western Europe.

The Russians have no more business in stirring up native communists to political activity in western Europe, Latin America, and the United States than we have interfering in the politics of eastern Europe and Russia.[3] We know what Russia is up to in eastern Europe, for example, and Russia knows what we are up to. We cannot permit the door to be closed against our trade in eastern Europe any more than we can in China. But at the same time we have to recognize that the Balkans are closer to Russia than to us—and that Russia cannot permit either England or the United States to dominate the politics of that area.

China is a special case and although she holds the longest frontier in the world with Russia, the interests of world peace demand that China remain free from any sphere of influence, either politically or economically.[4] We insist that the door to trade and economic development opportunities be left wide open in China as in all the world. However, the open door to trade and opportunities for economic development in China are meaningless unless there is a unified and peaceful China—built on the cooperation of the various groups in that country and based on a hands-off policy of the outside powers.

We are still arming to the hilt. Our excessive expenses for military purposes are the chief cause of our unbalanced budget. If taxes are to be lightened we must have the basis of a real peace with Russia —a peace that cannot be broken by extremist propagandists. [We do not want our course determined for us by master minds operating out of London, Moscow, or Nanking.]

Russian ideas of social-economic justice are going to govern nearly a third of the world. Our ideas of free-enterprise democracy will govern much of the rest. The two ideas will endeavor to prove which can deliver the most satisfaction to the common man in their respective areas of political dominance. But by mutual agreement, this competition should be put on a friendly basis [and the Russians should stop conniving against us in certain areas of the world just as we should stop scheming against them in other parts of the world]. Let the results of the two systems speak for themselves.

[Meanwhile, the Russians should stop teaching that their form of communism must, by force if necessary, ultimately triumph over democratic capitalism—while] we should close our ears to those among us who would have us believe that Russian communism and our free enterprise system cannot live, one with another, in a profitable and productive peace.

Under friendly peaceful competition the Russian world and the American world will gradually become more alike. The Russians will be forced to grant more and more of the personal freedoms;[5] and we shall become more and more absorbed with the problems of social-economic justice.

Russia must be convinced that we are not planning for war against her and we must be certain that Russia is not carrying on territorial expansion or world domination through native communists faithfully following every twist and turn in the Moscow party line. But in this competition, we must insist on an open door for trade throughout the world. There will always be an ideological conflict—but that is no reason why diplomats cannot work out a basis for both systems to live safely in the world side by side.

Once the fears of Russia and the United States Senate have been allayed by practical regional political reservations, I am sure that concern over the veto power would be greatly diminished. Then the United Nations would have a really great power in those areas which are truly international and not regional. In the worldwide, as distinguished from the regional, field, the armed might of the United Nations should be so great as to make opposition useless. Only the United Nations should have atomic bombs and its military establishment should give special emphasis to air power. It should have control of the strategically located air bases with which the United States and Britain have encircled the world. And not only should individual nations be prohibited from manufacturing atomic bombs, guided missiles, and military aircraft for bombing purposes, but no nation should be allowed to spend on its military establishment more than perhaps 15 percent of its budget.

Practically and immediately, we must recognize that we are not yet ready for World Federation. Realistically, the most we can hope for now is a safe reduction in military expense and a long period of peace based on mutual trust between the Big Three.

During this period, every effort should be made to develop as rapidly as possible a body of international law based on moral principles and not on the Machiavellian principles of deceit, force, and distrust—which, if continued, will lead the modern world to rapid disintegration.

In brief, as I see it today, the World Order is bankrupt—and the United States, Russia, and England are the receivers. These are the hard facts of power politics on which we have to build a functioning, powerful United Nations and a body of international law. And as we build, we must develop fully the doctrine of the rights of small peoples as contained in the United Nations Charter. This law should ideally apply as much to Indonesians and Greeks as to Bulgarians and Poles—but practically, the application may be delayed until both British and Russians discover the futility of their methods.

In the full development of the rights of small nations, the British and Russians can learn a lesson from the Good Neighbor policy of

Franklin Roosevelt. For under Roosevelt, we in the Western Hemisphere built a workable system of regional internationalism that fully protected the sovereign rights of every nation—a system of multilateral action that immeasurably strengthened the whole of world order.

In the United States an informed public opinion will be all-powerful. Our people are peace-minded. But they often express themselves too late—for events today move much faster than public opinion. The people here, as everywhere in the world, must be convinced that another war is not inevitable. And through mass meetings such as this, and through persistent pamphleteering, the people can be organized for peace—even though a large segment of our press is propagandizing our people for war in the hope of scaring Russia. And we who look on this war-with-Russia talk as criminal foolishness must carry our message direct to the people—even though we may be called communists because we dare to speak out.

I believe that peace—the kind of a peace I have outlined tonight—is the basic issue, both in the congressional campaign this fall and right on through the presidential election in 1948. How we meet this issue will determine whether we live not in "one world" or "two worlds"—but whether we live at all.

NOTES

1. For the first four paragraphs of his written text, Wallace substituted the following remarks: "Mr. Chairman, the gamblers say you people here tonight don't mean business. They say it doesn't mean anything when the Democratic Party, the Liberal Party, the American Labor Party—all three—are behind Jim Mead. They say you're blowing off steam here tonight, and that you won't get out to vote on November fifth.

"With their cold, steely eyes, and their long bankrolls, they say this is just emotion, and that you won't work.

"We'll find out on November fifth whether you really did mean business, whether you really did get out to vote. Because the votes for Jim Mead are there.

"Yes, the Senate will miss Jim Mead. He voted for the New Deal Roosevelt legislation. But Albany needs him to carry on the tradition of Smith and Roosevelt and Lehman.

"Those steely-eyed gamblers look with somewhat more favor on Herbert Lehman, but they don't give him much better than an even chance. Yes, we need Lehman, with his grasp on New York problems, his grasp on United States problems, his grasp on United Nations problems. We need his great heart; we need his great mind. We need him as a member of the United States Senate.

"Above all, we need the victory of both men, because New York in 1946 is so important for the nation in 1948; and a victory for Mead and Lehman may make all the difference between a world which, on the one hand, would mean imperialism and war, and on the other hand would mean peace and productivity for the Common Man.

"Tonight, above everything else, I want to talk about peace—and how to get peace. Never have the common people of all lands so longed for peace. And yet, never in a time of comparative peace have the common people so greatly feared war."

2. Here the audience hissed. Wallace then said:

"Yes, I'm talking about people outside of New York City when I talk about that, and I think I know about people outside of New York City. Any Gallup poll will reveal it—we might as well face the facts."

3. Here Wallace interpolated the following two paragraphs and went on slightly to alter his text:

"Now, when I say that, I realize that the danger of war is much less from communism than it is from imperialism, whether it be of the United States or England—or from fascism, the remnants of fascism, which may be in Spain or Argentina.

"Let's get this straight, regardless of what Mr. Taft or Mr. Dewey may say, if we can overcome the imperialistic urge in the Western world, I'm convinced there'll be no war.

"We know what Russia is up to in eastern Europe, for example, and Russia knows what we are up to. But we cannot permit the door to be closed against our trade in eastern Europe any more than we can in China. I'm Secretary of Commerce, and I'm interested in trade. And I want the biggest market we can get. I want China, I want eastern Europe, as places where we can trade. But, at the same time, we have to recognize that the Balkans are closer to Russia than to us, and that Russia cannot permit either England or the United States to dominate the politics of that area."

4. Again hissing, and Wallace interpolated, with further hissing where ellipses occur:

"And I know of my own positive knowledge that that was in Roosevelt's heart and mind, most specifically in the spring of 1944—because I talked it over with him in detail" . . .

"Mr. Truman read that particular sentence, and he approved it" . . .

"All right—you've already passed a good resolution on this, and I understand you're forwarding it. That's enough."

5. More hissing, and Wallace interpolated four sentences:

"You don't like the word 'forced'? I say that in the process of time they will find it profitable enough and opportune to grant more and more of the personal freedoms. Put it any way you want. That's the course of history just the same."

Index

Index

Rubber, *contd.*
ian, 74, 110; and postwar planning, 82, 85; and Jones, 82, 187–88, 191, 195, 245; and Weizmann, 188–89; and Haiti, 260–61; and Baruch, 278–79
Rural Electrification Administration, 81
Russell, Donald S., 469
Russell, Richard B., 254, 553
Russia, *see* Soviet Union
Russian Military Mission, 109
Ryan, Bishop James H., 379
Ryan, Oswald, 580

Sabath, Adolph J., 224
Sachs, Alexander, 499–500
Salazar, Antonio, 262
Saltonstall, Leverett, 542, 576
Saudi Arabia, 254, 255, 256, 300; and oil, 607
Scandinavia, 271, 565, 567
Schacht, Hjalmar, 467
Schindler, Alfred, 435, 465, 487
Schlesinger, Arthur, Jr., 66n
Schriber, Walter R., 270
Schwellenbach, Lewis B., 437, 455, 462, 466, 468, 475, 497, 576; and labor-industry relationships, 478–79, 526, 540; and sharing of atomic secrets, 484, 492; and wage-price policy, 494; and nuclear policy, 516; and government intervention in strikes, 518–19, 530–31; and steel controversy, 555; and railway strike legislation, 575–77; and proposed World Food Board, 608; opposes stationing of U.S. troops in China, 609
Selective Service, 477. *See also* Manpower
Semenov, Major General Ilya S., 335, 340
Senate, 252–54; Agricultural Committee, 116, 117; Banking and Currency Committee, 155–56, 187; B²H² Resolution, 247–48, 253; Foreign Relations Committee, 257, 332, 421, 424–25; and Barkley, 302–3; Committee on Atomic Energy, 525, 530, 534, 552, 570n
Service, John S., 314n, 520
Sevareid, Eric, 167
Shapley, Harlow, 493, 498, 502
Shaw, G. Howland, 312
Sheehy, Father Maurice S., 379–80, 617, 620
Shelly, Jack, 402–3
Sheng, Madame, 349

Sheng Shih-tsai, 347, 349
Sherwood, Robert, 237
Shiel, Bishop Bernard J., 375
Shipping, 117–18, 120; postwar, 114, 415
Shirer, William L., 71–72
Short, J. H., 224
Shotwell, James T., 514
Shulgen, Colonel, 218
Siberia, 14, 35, 85, 107, 125, 177, 256–57; Wallace visit to, 234, 309, 311, 312, 315, 329, 332n, 335–47; future importance of, 310; mineral deposits, 316, 339; Wallace's Russian companions in, 335n; development, 337, 340; industrialization of, 344–45; Wallace describes to Chiang Kai-shek, 349; Wallace discusses with FDR, 363
Sikorski, General Wladyslaw, 152–53
Silver, Rabbi Abba Hillel, 313, 606
Smart, Joe, 615
Smathers, William H., 131, 380
Smith, Alfred E., 11, 165, 333, 407
Smith, Mrs. Alfred E., 165
Smith, Colonel Cyrus R., 105–6
Smith, Edwin S., 499
Smith, Ellison D., 282
Smith, Gerald K., 225
Smith, H. Alexander, 494
Smith, Harold D., 42, 57–58, 64–65, 68–69, 73, 426; and BEW-State Department struggle, 75, 78; and atom bomb, 92n, 498n; and postwar domestic problems, 133–34; and postwar occupation policy, 136, 137; and FDR's abolition of BEW, 226–27; and planning function of government, 252; and postwar unemployment, 372–73; and Bush proposal, 438, 441–42; and patent policy, 439n, 441; and Rayburn, 458; and reconversion planning, 459; and cabinet economic committee, 491; Wallace praises, 546
Smith, Horace H., 348
Smith, Howard W., 224
Smith, Major General Walter Bedell, 463, 559, 561–62, 563, 599, 610; report on Russian reconstruction program, 586–87
Smith-Connally Act, 267, 274n
Snow, Edgar P., 328
Snyder, John W., 39, 485, 487, 491, 498, 516, 540, 581; and wage policy, 493, 494, 553; and May-Johnson bill, 507, 509; and steel controversy, 555; and